Bus

THE BACKYARD BUILDER'S
BOOK OF OUTDOOR BUILDING PROJECTS

by the editors of *Rodale's Practical Homeowner*™ magazine

Rodale Press, Emmaus, Pennsylvania

We at Rodale Press have tried to make this book as accurate and correct as possible. Plans, illustrations, photographs, and text have been carefully researched by our in-house staff. However, due to the variability of all local conditions, construction materials, personal skills, etc., Rodale Press assumes no responsibility for any injuries suffered or damages or other losses incurred that result from material presented herein. All instructions and plans should be carefully studied and clearly understood before beginning any construction.

Printed in the United States of America on recycled paper containing a high percentage of de-inked fiber.

Library of Congress Cataloging-in-Publication Data

The Backyard builder's book of outdoor building projects.

Includes index.
1. Garden structures — Design and construction.
2. Building. I. Rodale's practical homeowner.
II. Title: Outdoor building projects.
TH4961.B34 1987   624   87-4696
ISBN 0-87857-696-7   hardcover

2 4 6 8 10 9 7 5 3   hardcover

Project Director: Al Gutierrez
Writer: George Campbell
Senior Editor: Ray Wolf
Copy Editor: Dianne Talmage
Art Director: Tim White
Illustrators: Eric Olson
               Ron Chamberlain
               Robert Swensen
               Dennis Sommer
Editorial Assistants: Cheryl Clark
               Dianne Imdieke
Photography: Media Management Group
Cover Design: Jerry O'Brien
Woodworkers: Floyd Jones
               Jerry Krie
               Richard Tolzman
Produced By: Media Management Group, Cannon Falls, Minnesota 55009
Other Credits: See credits beginning page 494

Table Of Contents

I. Outdoor Building Techniques

Materials selection, tool use, wood selection, joints and fastening techniques,

II. Barbecue Centers

III. Children's Projects

IV. Decks

V. Fences

VI. Furniture Projects

VII. Gazebos

VIII. Hot Tub Installations

IX. Lawn and Garden Projects

X. Outbuildings

XI. Projects for Bird Lovers

Note: Most of the projects found in this book have an accompanying materials list. These lists should be taken only as guides to help you determine what a given project entails, rather than used as precise shopping lists. The actual sizes and quantities of materials that you need to purchase may vary according to what materials you already have on hand, what is available in your area, and how much waste occurs in the construction process. Therefore, we strongly recommend that before you purchase materials for a given project, you read the step-by-step instructions for that project carefully and calculate for yourself what you will need to buy.

A couple of the larger projects are not provided with a materials list because of the fact that they must be adapted to an existing structure or site.

In a few cases, minor design and dimensional differences can be found between the photos and the text and drawings for a project. These differences are intended either to show a variety of possible design variations or to suggest what we consider an improvement in the design followed in construction of the original project.

I.

Outdoor Building Techniques

OUTDOOR BUILDING TECHNIQUES

HOW TO BEGIN

For today's homeowner, living space does not end with the walls of the house. During the spring and summer months, families everywhere move to the great outdoors. Everything takes on a special flavor when done outside, whether it be dining, entertaining, or playing games with the kids.

The handyman in your family can add style and comfort to outdoor living by building projects that fit your lifestyle and needs. Supplying those designs, and helping you build them, is the purpose of this book.

Projects designed to fit into every corner of your outdoor living space are included here. You will find projects for every type of outdoor activity, all of which are designed to enhance your outdoor spaces and to show off your skills.

As you page through the book, individual projects will seem perfect for your yard, deck or patio. We have included a wide range of styles for each type of project. One is bound to be right for your outdoor needs.

Before starting on a project, it is important to assess your woodworking skills and workshop equipment. Complete step-by-step instructions accompany each project, so read these to determine whether that project can be built with your tools and knowledge of woodworking.

Do not be afraid, though, to take on a challenging project. By building some of the more difficult designs, you will stretch and expand your woodworking skills. And when a particular project does mean buying a new tool or two, remember that you are also upgrading your shop equipment.

Each of the projects includes detailed diagrams, photos of critical construction steps, and step-by-step instructions to help you. Tools needed for a project can be found by reading the instructions. Wherever possible, we suggest the alternative tools and techniques that can be used for a particular job.

A shopping list of materials is also included for the majority of projects. This will help you choose materials when you go to your lumberyard or home center.

The diagrams shown with each project are designed to make construction as simple as possible. All of the dimensions you'll need are shown in the diagrams, along with information about fasteners and other hardware.

If a project calls for parts with curved profiles, a grid diagram is included to make layout easy. To use these, simply draw a grid of squares, sized as stated in the diagram, on a sheet of hardboard, such as Mason-

1

TOOLS AND TECHNIQUES

1. Keep your handsaw sharp and stand as shown in the photo to help keep the cut square and true. Sight along the saw to cut the line.

2. Commercial sanding blocks are the best choice for hand sanding. Attachment of the abrasive paper varies among sanding block manufacturers.

ite. Transfer the design to the hardboard and cut this out with a saber saw. Then use it as a pattern to lay out the parts.

Use the plans as they are, or customize the projects to suit your specific needs. The designs in this book are only suggestions. Change dimensions; choose different materials; use a different finish. The final choice is up to you.

TOOLS AND TECHNIQUES

The projects in this book, wherever possible, can be built with basic shop tools. Most of the time, these will be tools you already own and know how to use. Occasionally, however, a particular project will call for a tool that is not in your shop.

You may be able to use a different tool or technique to build the project. Otherwise, consider purchasing the tool you need. It will certainly be useful for many other projects in the future.

Hand tools: While most of the projects are designed to be built with

3. Whether you are hand sanding or working with a power sander, always sand in the direction of the wood grain to avoid hard-to-remove sanding scratches.

power tools, there are a few hand tools that are essential to many woodworking operations.

Every shop should have a high-quality crosscut handsaw with 8 to 12 teeth per inch. Do not try to save money on this tool; buy the best saw available. Keep it sharp and protect it from rust and corrosion. Sharpening handsaws is a specialized skill. Professional sharpening is expensive, but it's well worth the money.

A hacksaw is also an essential tool. Once again, avoid cheap and flimsy saw frames, and buy only high-quality steel blades. For most purposes, blades with 20 to 24 teeth per inch are perfect.

An assortment of wood chisels, again of high quality, is an important addition to any shop. Store these in a protected drawer or case to protect their edges. Several of the projects in this book have stopped dadoes, which must be finished by hand with a chisel.

Every project has to be fastened together. You will need a standard 16-oz. claw hammer and a good assortment of screwdrivers. Always choose a screwdriver that fits a particular screw perfectly to avoid damage to the screw heads and the wood. A basic ratchet and socket set will cover other fastening needs.

Practically every project requires sanding. Much of the sanding can be done with power sanders, but a hand-held sanding block is needed when sanding in tight areas. Commercial sanding blocks are inexpensive and much easier to use than the traditional block of wood wrapped with abrasive paper. When buying abrasive paper, choose garnet paper for most projects. It cuts well and outlasts less expensive paper.

POWER TOOLS:

While hand tools, properly used, can perform almost all woodworking operations, the majority of today's woodworkers use power tools for most jobs. Many of the projects in this book can be built faster and easier by using portable and stationary power tools. Both types will be discussed in two separate sections.

Portable power tools: The saber saw is a tool that belongs in every shop. With the appropriate blades, it can cut almost any material. Straight cuts and intricate profiles are possible. Many projects included in this book call for curved profiles to be cut with a saber saw.

When choosing blades for your saber saw, stick with high-quality blades. Expect to pay about $1 per blade. Cheap blades are no bargain.

Since you will use this tool primarily to cut curves, here is a tip to help you: guide the saw slowly and keep the blade centered in the notch in the saw's foot plate. This helps keep the blade vertical in the kerf.

For other cutting operations, a circular saw is needed. Any of the major brands of saws will serve you well, but avoid buying the least expensive models. They often have too little power for good cuts.

A selection of blades should include a combination blade, a rip blade, and a plywood-cutting blade with at least 80 teeth. Consider buying carbide-tipped blades. While they are more expensive, they stay sharp almost indefinitely, insuring accurate and smooth cutting.

Before using a circular saw, or any other power tool, read the owner's manual and follow all safety precautions.

Straight cuts with your circular saw will be easier and more accurate if you use a guide. The rip guide furnished with your saw will help with narrow cuts, but for cutting plywood, a clamp-on guide is an essential accessory. Use either a commercial guide, or a length of aluminum channel molding, clamped to the workpiece with C-clamps.

An electric drill, along with an assortment of accessories, can perform

POWER HAND TOOLS

1. *Use a saber saw to make many of the curved cuts used in this book's projects. The edge-guide accessory helps you cut straight lines.*

2. *Straight cuts with a circular saw are easy when you use a clamp-on guide. Use either a commercially available guide or fashion your own.*

3. *An assortment of bits will allow you to use your electric drill for many purposes. A portable drill guide can help you bore straight and true holes.*

4. *For straight cuts with your router, an edge-guide attachment helps keep you on the track. Purchase this accessory where you bought your router.*

5. *Keep a firm grip on your belt sander at all times. If it gets away from you, it will certainly mar the project and may cause an injury.*

6. *To make several curved parts identical, clamp them together after cutting and use a belt sander to even them up. Avoid cutting too deeply.*

more jobs around the shop than almost any other tool. Choose a ⅜-in. variable-speed drill for maximum versatility.

For boring holes, a variety of bit styles is available. Projects in this book call for twist drills, spade bits for large-diameter holes, and pilot bits for various screw sizes. When buying pilot bits, choose bits with built-in countersinks. Always buy high-quality drill bits made by reputable companies.

Other accessories for your electric drill can expand its capabilities. A portable drill guide will help keep holes aligned, while a doweling jig is essential for the dowel joints used in several projects in this book.

Adding a router to your collection of portable power tools will make many new operations possible. Equipped with the proper bits and accessories, it will let you form rabbets and grooves, decorate surfaces, and make profiles on wood edges.

Choose a router with a motor of at least ¾ horsepower. Anything less will not handle some materials and operations. Follow the manufacturer's safety instructions carefully, and always wear eye protection when using a router.

Start with a basic bit assortment and add other bits as you need them. Carbide bits are more expensive, but will outlast steel bits many times over. An edge-guide attachment is a useful accessory for your router, and you'll find that it's needed for several of the projects included in this book.

Preparing surfaces for finishes is a time-consuming, but critical, job. Power sanders can ease the load. There are two basic types: belt sanders and pad-type sanders.

Choose the belt sander when you need to remove wood to level table tops and other large areas. A belt sander makes short work of heavy sanding jobs. On the other hand, it can also quickly mar a surface, so take some time to practice using this tool.

For maximum versatility choose a sander that uses a 3-in.-wide belt. When buying belts, select open-coat belts, and save by buying packages of several belts. Be careful to observe the correct mounting direction printed on each belt.

Pad-type sanders are ideal for finish sanding. Fine-grit paper, cut from standard sheets, does an excellent job of finish preparation.

Most pad-type sanders can be shifted from orbital to straight-line sanding. In the orbital mode the paper moves in a small circular pattern, which leaves slight marks on the wood but removes material faster. In the straight-line mode, the movement is in one direction, which is ideal for fine work. As with all sanding, work in the direction of the wood grain.

Stationary power tools: While portable power tools are an essential part of your equipment, stationary power tools are the foundation of high-quality woodworking.

Since these tools require a relatively large investment of money, choosing the right tools for your needs is important. A good stationary tool will last a lifetime, so think twice before purchasing a cheap or poorly made tool.

It is not necessary, either, to buy top-of-the-line power tools. These are designed for the professional woodworker, not for the weekend

STATIONARY POWER TOOLS

1. Whenever you use any stationary tool, like this table saw, observe all the safety precautions and never disable the tool's safety features.

2. Wobble-type dado blades are extremely useful accessories for your saw. When using them, however, work carefully and wear eye protection.

3. Sawing thin strips from a piece of wood is an ideal job for the band saw. Use a short fence, as shown here, to help guide the cut.

craftsman. Look for modestly priced power tools made by major manufacturers. This will guarantee quality at a reasonable price.

A power saw is the foundation of your woodworking equipment and should be your first investment in stationary tools. You have two basic choices: table saws and radial arm saws. Each has advantages for specific types of operations.

Table saws are the traditional choice. Ideal for ripping operations, a table saw can also crosscut, miter, bevel, and form dadoes and grooves. With a shaper attachment, it can form intricate profiles on the edges of wood. However, every operation on the table saw involves moving the workpiece into the blade, and this makes crosscutting of long workpieces awkward.

The radial arm saw, on the other hand, works differently. For crosscutting, the workpiece remains stationary, while the blade is pulled through the wood. Only on rip-type operations does the workpiece move into the blade. Additionally, a

radial arm saw can be equipped with accessories that allow it to perform operations not possible with a table saw.

The nature of a radial arm saw, however, means that careful attention must be paid to the tool's alignment. Periodic adjustments are required, and the saw is not as well suited to ripping operations as the table saw.

Both tools are good. The choice is up to you. If you mostly do crosscutting operations, choose the radial arm saw. For frequent ripping, the table saw is a better choice.

Whichever you choose, you will need blades. A basic assortment should include a combination-type blade, a rip blade, a plywood blade, and a wobble-type dado blade. Carbide-tipped blades, while more expensive, are a worthwhile investment. They stay sharp up to 50 times longer. In fact, if you are a typical weekend woodworker, you may never have to sharpen carbide blades.

As with all power tools, read the owner's manual carefully, and follow all safety precautions to the letter. Never disable a safety feature on a power saw. They are there to keep your fingers attached to your hands.

A band saw is not an essential tool in the average shop. It is, however, an extremely useful addition to any shop. With it you can cut intricate profiles in wood of almost any thickness. It is also ideal for re-sawing lumber into thin strips, such as those used in the lamp projects in this book.

For boring accurate holes in any material, a drill press is a real help. While a portable drill guide, used carefully, can be substituted for a drill press for some operations, a drill press is the only tool that will bore absolutely perfect holes.

Lightweight, bench-type drill presses, however, are scarcely worth the money. To get the most out of a drill press, choose a high-quality bench-type or floor-type drill press with a $\frac{1}{2}$-in. chuck and at least an 8-in. throat depth.

FINISHING TOOLS

Every project made of wood in this book needs to be finished to protect it from the weather. The tools you choose for applying finishes can make a real difference in the final appearance of any project.

Most finishes can be applied with hand tools—brushes, pads, and rollers. When choosing finish-applica-

WOODWORKING TIPS

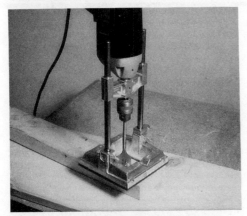

1. Use a portable drill guide and a spade bit to bore accurate, large-diameter holes. Back up the workpiece with scrap to prevent splintering.

2. When using any power tool, protect your eyes with proper safety gear. Full-face masks, such as the one shown here, provide maximum safety and visibility.

tion tools, avoid cheap, poorly made products. Cheap brushes, for example, always shed hairs, spoiling your carefully built project. Buy high-quality tools only.

Choose the correct tools for your project's finish. If you are applying varnish, use a varnish brush. Similarly, when applying enamel, use a brush designed for enamel. When you're done with the brushes or other finishing tools, clean them carefully and store them properly.

Some projects are best finished with spray equipment. This is especially true for projects with complicated surfaces.

Either airless or compressor-driven spray guns can be used to apply finishes ranging from wood sealers and varnishes to latex enamel.

Unless you already own a compressor, your best spray-painting investment is in airless equipment. They apply all types of finishes well, and with less overspray. Choose a self-contained, high-quality airless sprayer for most applications.

If you own a compressor, an air-driven sprayer is a good alternative, especially for thin-bodied finishes. This type of sprayer is less well suited, however, for heavy materials, such as latex-based enamels.

Whichever type you choose, always use a respirator when spraying any finish. The type with two filter canisters is ideal. Simple paper masks do not protect you from potentially toxic fumes.

TOOL SAFETY

Almost every woodworking operation involves a potential risk of injury. You can minimize the risk by taking basic safety precautions.

First, become familiar with the safety requirements of each tool you own. The owner's manual for every tool contains a chapter on safety. Read the section, and keep it in mind whenever you use the tool.

Second, never disable a safety feature on a power tool. Plug power tools into the correct outlets, and use guards and anti-kickback features religiously. Always stay out of

HOW TO SELECT LUMBER

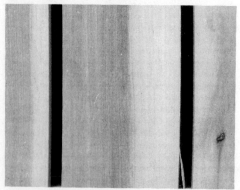

1. Avoid using garden-grade redwood, with its light-colored sapwood, in outdoor projects. Choose all-heart grades, which are more weather resistant.

2. When you select plywood for use outdoors, look at the grade stamp to be certain that you have an exterior grade, made with waterproof glue.

the line of cut when operating table and radial arm saws. Wear eye protection when using any power tool. Full-face masks provide the best protection and the most visibility.

The most important piece of safety equipment, however, is your brain. Before performing any operation, analyze what you want to do. Work slowly and patiently, and assess each operation to make sure you are taking every precaution to avoid injury.

HOW TO SELECT LUMBER

Outdoor projects make special demands on wood. Rainy weather, combined with sunlight, can destroy most woods in an amazingly short time. Protective finishes help, but the best way to assure long project life is to select the best wood for each project.

Projects in this book call for several species of lumber. Each variety has advantages and disadvantages for outdoor use. Here is a brief guide.

Redwood: In many ways, redwood is the premium wood for outdoor projects. It is attractive, easy to work with, and very weather resistant. On the minus side, it is relatively expensive and soft.

Redwood is available in two basic grades: all-heart and garden grade. Only the heartwood has the weather-resistant qualities needed for outdoor projects, so select all-heart material. For most uses, construction heart grade is the best choice.

A penetrating wood sealer is the best finish for redwood projects. Other clear finishes tend to blister and peel when used outdoors.

Pine and fir: These two softwoods, while less weather resistant than redwood, are suitable for use outdoors when properly finished and maintained. They also have the advantage of being relatively inexpensive.

Both woods are available in a wide variety of grades. The clear grade, free of knots, is an expensive choice. For most projects, grade no. 1 or 2

3. Cupping is one of the most common wood defects you will encounter. Pass up lumber with this flaw, since it will likely spoil your project.

4. To spot warping in lumber, sight down the edge of the board. Any deviation from a straight line means trouble and wasted money.

will work well. Their tight knots can add interest to project surfaces.

When constructing with pine and fir, finish with paint or apply a stain and varnish. Varnished wood will eventually blister, but will remain attractive for years.

Oak and other hardwoods: Hardwoods are used in a few of this book's projects. With the exception of oak and teak, most hardwoods do not fare well outdoors. In addition, they are more difficult to work with, less readily available, and expensive.

Their chief advantages are strength and beauty, combined with good weather resistance. Oak can take considerable abuse, while teak is the premium wood for projects exposed to water.

Finish these materials with stain and varnish, or with clear wood sealer. Both finishes show off the attractive grain of the wood, and also help prevent the sun's rays from fading it.

Plywood: Just a few projects shown on the following pages call for the use of plywood. This material is inexpensive, is ideal for covering large surfaces, and also resists warping.

Choose plywood made with waterproof glue. This grade is identified with an X on the grade stamp. The grade marked ACX is best for most uses. One face is unblemished, while the other is less attractive.

The best finish for plywood is latex enamel, although plywood can be finished with clear finishes.

SHOPPING FOR LUMBER

Once you have selected the type of lumber to be used in a project, shop at a lumberyard that will let you hand-select your materials. This allows you to find the most attractive materials and cuts down on waste.

Choose kiln-dried materials when dimensional stability is important. Some grades of lumber, however, will only be available green or air-dried. Avoid green lumber, as it will shrink and warp as it dries.

When choosing any lumber, watch for defects in the material.

JOINT AND FASTENERS

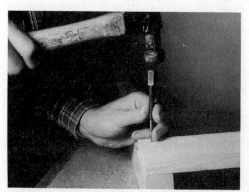

1. Bore pilot holes for nails when working near the end of a part and when nailing hardwoods. Use a bit slightly smaller than the nail's shank.

2. Set finishing nails below the surface of the wood with the proper size of nail set. This helps avoid unsightly hammer marks on your project.

Cupping, a common defect, is easily detected. Lay a straightedge across the width of a board and look for gaps.

Bowing, another common defect, can be spotted by sighting down the length of one edge. If the board is twisted, skip that piece. While sighting the edge, you can also spot crooked or kinked lumber, which also should be avoided.

If you are choosing any grade less than clear in softwoods, the material will have knots. While these are often acceptable, be certain that all knots are tight in the wood.

A good overall rule to follow is to look at the lumber and imagine it in your project. If it doesn't seem right, select a better grade.

Do not be afraid to substitute different types of wood for the ones specified in this book. If you decide to use another material, however, avoid substituting a weaker wood than the one in the materials list.

JOINTS AND FASTENERS

Every woodworking project involves joining wood components together. The strength and appearance of the project depend on the types of joints used and the way they are fastened.

The designs in this book use several jointing and fastening methods. Each has been selected to suit that particular project.

Butt joints: Butt joints, as the name implies, are formed by butting two pieces of wood together. A butt joint is the simplest joint to make, but it is also the weakest. Used properly, however, it is suitable for many applications.

Aside from a lack of strength, a butt joint also exposes the end grain of one of the components. End grain is weaker and less attractive than edge or face grain.

Simplicity is the butt joint's best feature. If the wood is cut square, making the joint fit is simple. To make good butt joints, be certain that your saw is set up properly.

Butt joints are commonly joined with glue and nails, screws, or dow-

3. *Use the correct size of combination screw pilot bit to bore countersunk pilot holes for screws. A depth stop on the bit prevents drilling through the wood.*

4. *You can conceal screw heads by countersinking the screw head below the surface of the wood and installing a wood screw hole plug.*

els. All of these methods are used in this book's projects.

Rabbet joints: A number of projects utilize the rabbet joint and its close relative, the dado joint. These are formed by making a recess in one component that is sized to accept the mating part.

These joints are stronger than butt joints, allowing more surface area for glue. They also expose less end grain, improving the appearance of the joint.

Use a dado blade on your table or radial arm saw to form these joints. Wobble-type dado blades are the easiest to use and can be adjusted to cut a wide variety of widths. For best results, be certain that your saw is set up accurately.

If you have several identical rabbets or dadoes to cut, make a simple jig to help you. On a radial arm saw, clamp a block of wood to the fence to help you position each board. Clamp a similar block to the table of a table saw to align the workpiece.

You can also use a straight bit in your router to form these joints. Clamp a guide to the workpiece to align the tool, and cut the joint in several deepening passes for smooth results.

Some projects require a stopped rabbet or dado. Form these with either technique, but stop the cut just short of the end of the joint. Finish the end of the rabbet or dado with a sharp wood chisel.

Rabbet and dado joints are usually fastened with glue and screws or nails.

Miter joints: Miter joints, commonly seen in picture frames, are relatively weak. Their chief advantage is that they hide end grain completely.

To make successful miter joints, the angles of the joints must be perfect. Whether you make these joints with a stationary saw or a miter box, test the tool's adjustment before cutting the actual joint. Make a sample joint, then use a square to check it.

Miter joints are fastened with a combination of glue and nails, screws, or dowels. Before tightening the final assembly, use a square to check for proper alignment.

Lap joints: Whenever two parts cross each other, lap joints are commonly used to make the final assembly only as thick as one of the components. Since lap joints have exceptional strength, they are often used in furniture frames.

To form a lap joint, both components are notched. The notches are typically half the thickness of the wood so that when interlocked, the surface of the joint is flush.

Use a dado blade on your stationary saw to form lap joints. Adjust the depth of cut carefully.

When angled lap joints are called for, measure carefully and check the adjustment of your saw for best results. Fasten lap joints with glue and screws or nails.

FASTENING METHODS

The final strength of any joint depends on the strength of the fasteners used to secure the joint. The projects in this book use a number of fastening methods, each designed to suit that particular project.

Glue: Except for when joints have

to be disassembled, glue is the most common and important fastener. Other fasteners mainly hold the joint together until the glue sets.

It is important to use waterproof glue on projects that will be exposed to the weather. Ordinary carpenter's glue will eventually dissolve under the constant attack of moisture.

Two types of waterproof glue are most commonly used today: resorcinol and epoxy. Each has advantages as well as disadvantages.

Resorcinol glue is a resin-based compound, supplied in a two-part form. For best results, mix only what you need right away, since the glue has a limited working life after being mixed.

Epoxy glue, also a two-part product, is mixed before use. Its working time is even more limited than resorcinol glue. That rapid setting time is both an advantage and a drawback. The glue sets up quickly, but at the same time it must be used quickly.

Both glues are useful, but resorcinol glue is the one specified for most of these projects. Many brands are available and all function equally well.

Glued joints that are not secured with other fasteners must be clamped together until the adhesive sets up. A wide variety of clamps are available, each suited for a different clamping operation. You will not go wrong by buying a few 18-in. bar clamps and several pipe-type clamps.

When clamping wood components together, always use clamp pads or scraps of wood between the clamp's jaws and the project to prevent damage.

Nails: Nails, in a wide range of types and sizes, are one of the most commonly used fasteners. Many of the following projects call for their use. Each project specifies the nail best suited for the job.

When working on outdoor projects, use corrosion-resistant nails. Hot-dipped galvanized, aluminum, and stainless steel nails are three types that will not spoil your project with unsightly rust stains.

Where appearance is important, use finishing nails. Drive these down so that the heads are just above the surface of the wood, then set them below the surface with a nail set.

When driving nails near the ends of boards, drill pilot holes to prevent splitting the wood. Use the same technique when nailing in hardwoods. Choose a pilot bit that is slightly smaller than the shank of the nail.

Screws: When maximum strength is needed in a wood joint, use wood screws. These apply a powerful clamping force to any joint. Additionally, they allow disassembly of the joint when needed.

As with nails, corrosion-resistance is important. Ordinary plated screws soon rust under typical outdoor conditions, so use brass or stainless steel screws.

Where appearance is important, choose flathead screws that can be countersunk flush with the wood's surface. You can even countersink them below the surface and fill the opening with wood filler or a screw hole plug.

Before driving any screw, bore a pilot hole in the wood. This hole must accommodate both the screw threads and the shank of the screw.

Combination screw pilot bits not only drill properly sized pilot holes, but can also countersink the hole flush with the surface or below the surface. Many styles of pilot bits are available, but choose a type that has an adjustable depth stop. The added precision will help you create better-looking projects.

Dowels: Several of the projects in this book call for glued and doweled joints. This technique allows the fasteners to be completely invisible and is commonly used in frame joints.

Wooden dowel pins are available in a wide variety of sizes. The size of dowel pin needed for each of these outdoor projects is specified in the materials list. Choose dowel pins with straight or spiral flutes, which allow air to escape from the joint as it is assembled.

Dowel pin holes in wood parts must be accurately located or the joint will not line up. Doweling jigs are available to help you with this job. Since many styles of jigs are sold, all of which are useful, read and follow the owner's manual for best results.

Bore holes for dowel pins $\frac{1}{8}$ in. deeper than half the length of the dowel pin. This allows a small space for air and excess glue.

Assemble doweled joints with glue on both the wood surfaces and the dowels. Draw the joint together with clamps, then leave the clamps in place until the glue sets firmly.

FINISHING PREPARATION

Any project you build for outdoor use needs some sort of finish to pro-

tect it from the wind, sun, and rain. While redwood can be left unfinished, in time it often darkens to an unattractive color.

Proper preparation of the project before finishing is just as important as the choice of finish. If preparation and finishing are done carefullly, your projects will look as good years later as they did when they came out of your shop.

Sanding: Preparation for finishing always involves sanding. Careful sanding leaves a smooth surface that is ideal for any finish.

Much of the sanding on most projects can be done with power sanders. Belt sanders are useful for leveling surfaces and for removing tool marks. Be careful, however, to prevent marring the wood when using this tool.

Pad-type sanders are ideal for finish sanding. Use finer abrasive paper on these tools, and set the tool to sand in a straight line, if possible. Always sand in the direction of the grain to avoid marring the project.

In some cases, you will have to resort to hand sanding, especially to finish tight corners. Use a sanding block rather than your hands to hold the abrasive paper.

There is a bewildering variety of abrasive papers available for the woodworker ranging from simple sandpaper to garnet paper and cloth-backed emery paper. Choosing the best abrasive material can be confusing.

For most woodworking operations, garnet paper is the best choice. Use 80-grit paper for rough sanding, and work down to 220-grit paper to finish. Coarser grades will spoil outdoor projects, while abrasives finer than 220-grit are finer than necessary for outdoor work.

Use 60-grit and 80-grit belts on your belt sander for leveling and the preliminary sanding. These grit sizes will remove material quickly, so be careful to keep fingers well away.

FINISHES

When choosing a finish for your outdoor project, consult the project directions first. Finishes suggested in this book are designed to work best for each project. If you decide to change the finish specified, follow the guidelines given below.

Stain and varnish: Varnish is a traditional finish for many outdoor projects. While it protects the wood from moisture, varnish has the annoying property of blistering and peeling after a few years of exposure.

Polyurethane varnishes are available that include an ingredient to block some of the sun's ultraviolet rays. These will last somewhat longer, so check the product label for this important ingredient.

You may wish to stain projects before varnishing. Use an oil-based stain in the color of your choice for best results. Follow the instructions on the can carefully for an even finish.

Wood sealer: Simple wood sealers are a better choice of finish for most outdoor projects. They penetrate the wood, sealing it against moisture, but leave no surface film that can blister or peel.

Check the label on these products to make sure that they contain no toxic pesticides or fungicides. These

FINISHING PROJECTS

When you spray any finish, protect yourself from toxic fumes and pigments with a proper respirator. Simple paper masks are not enough.

dangerous chemicals have no place in any yard.

Paint: Some projects, especially those made of pine or fir, are best finished by painting. Painted projects hold up well outdoors and add color to your deck or patio decor.

Before painting raw wood, apply a coat of enamel primer. This seals the wood and makes an ideal undercoat.

Use either latex-based or oil-based enamels to finish your projects. Latex-based materials last well, and clean-up is easy. Small projects can be finished with spray cans of enamel.

Apply finishes according to the instructions provided by the manufacturer. Use only high-quality application tools for best results.

Most outdoor projects require little maintenance. Since they are designed to withstand the extremes of the weather, you can clean up most projects by simply washing them. After a few years, varnished projects may have to be refinished.

II.

Barbecue Centers

This barbecue cart offers plenty of storage and work space for all your outdoor cooking needs.

BARBECUE CENTER

Barbecues and outdoor dining usually mean going in and out of the house several times to get supplies. You can save steps and enhance your outdoor enjoyment by building this rolling work center. From its cutting board and plastic laminated work surface to the spacious cabinet, it is designed to make cooking outdoors a pleasure.

Both of the work surfaces are removable for easy cleaning, while the casters allow you to roll the cart quickly to any area of your deck or patio.

Start by building the cabinet. Make the panels of glued-up tongue-and-groove siding. You can use redwood, cedar, or fir, depending on your preference and the availability of lumber in your area. Typically, this siding has a V-groove on one side and is flat on the other. Build the cabinet with either side facing out.

Assemble the panels with waterproof resorcinol glue. Apply a thin film of the glue to the tongue side of each joint, then assemble the panel and clamp it with bar clamps. Apply clamps to both sides of the panel to minimize warping, but do not overtighten the clamps. As always, use wooden cauls between the clamps and the panels.

Make each panel slightly oversized at this stage to simplify construction. Once the glue has dried, trim the panels to the dimensions shown in the diagram. Use a combination planer-type blade to produce a smooth edge.

Rip the sides of the panels equally to reach the desired width, then trim both ends of the panels. Cut half the excess material from one end, then cut the panels to length on the other end.

Begin assembly with the bottom panel. The flat side of this panel must face up to provide a gluing surface for the plastic laminate. Draw pencil lines $3/4$ in. in from all edges of the panel.

Cut 1X1 cleats to fit inside the lines, as shown in the diagram. Attach these to the panel with resorcinol glue and 3d galvanized finishing nails. Rip a $1/4$-in.-thick strip of $3/4$-in. redwood and cut it to fit inside the cleats. This will be the door stop as shown in Detail 1 of the diagram. You will need more of these later, so cut additional strips at this time.

Now, cut a piece of plastic laminate to fit inside the cleats and the stop strip. Measure accurately for a close fit. Apply contact cement to the laminate and the wood. Allow the cement to dry, then apply the laminate. Use firm pressure to complete the bond.

As you did on the base, attach 1X1 cleats to the inside of the cabinet's top with nails and glue. Assemble all of the panels, securing the joints with 3d galvanized finishing nails and resorcinol glue. Drive the nails from the inside of the cabinet. Attach the 1X4 door frame members in the same way. Check the assembly for squareness as you work.

Next, form the $1/4$-in. X $1 3/4$-in. rab-

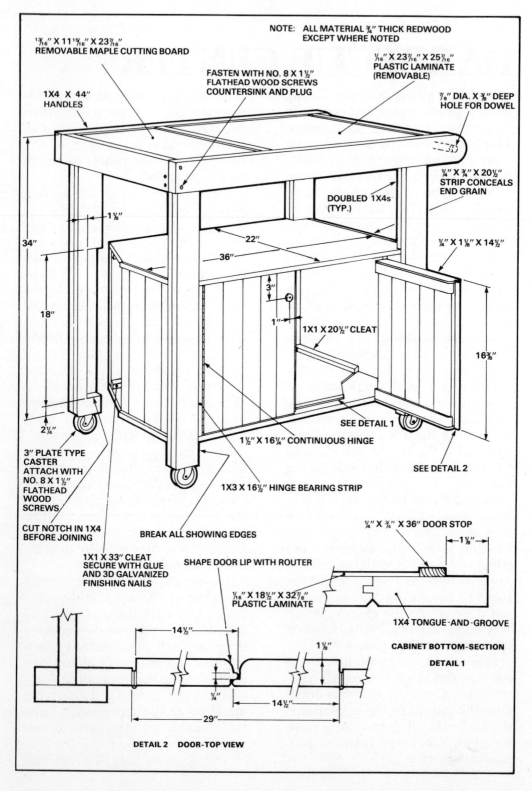

NOTE: ALL MATERIAL ¾" THICK REDWOOD
EXCEPT WHERE NOTED

¹³⁄₁₆" X 11¹⁵⁄₁₆" X 23⁷⁄₁₆"
REMOVABLE MAPLE CUTTING BOARD

FASTEN WITH NO. 8 X 1½"
FLATHEAD WOOD SCREWS
COUNTERSINK AND PLUG

¹⁄₁₆" X 23⁷⁄₁₆" X 25⁷⁄₁₆"
PLASTIC LAMINATE
(REMOVABLE)

1X4 X 44"
HANDLES

⅞" DIA. X ⅜" DEEP
HOLE FOR DOWEL

¼" X ¾" X 20½"
STRIP CONCEALS
END GRAIN

1⅛"

DOUBLED 1X4s
(TYP.)

¼" X 1⅛" X 14½"

34"

22"

36"

3"

18"

1"

1X1 X 20½" CLEAT

16⅜"

2¼"

SEE DETAIL 1

3" PLATE TYPE
CASTER
ATTACH WITH
NO. 8 X 1½"
FLATHEAD
WOOD
SCREWS

1½" X 16¼" CONTINUOUS HINGE

SEE DETAIL 2

CUT NOTCH IN 1X4
BEFORE JOINING

1X3 X 16½" HINGE BEARING STRIP

BREAK ALL SHOWING EDGES

1X1 X 33" CLEAT
SECURE WITH GLUE
AND 3D GALVANIZED
FINISHING NAILS

SHAPE DOOR LIP WITH ROUTER

¼" X ¾" X 36" DOOR STOP

1⅛"

¹⁄₁₆" X 18½" X 32⁷⁄₈"
PLASTIC LAMINATE

1X4 TONGUE-AND-GROOVE

CABINET BOTTOM-SECTION

DETAIL 1

14½"

1⅛"

¼"

14½"

29"

DETAIL 2   DOOR-TOP VIEW

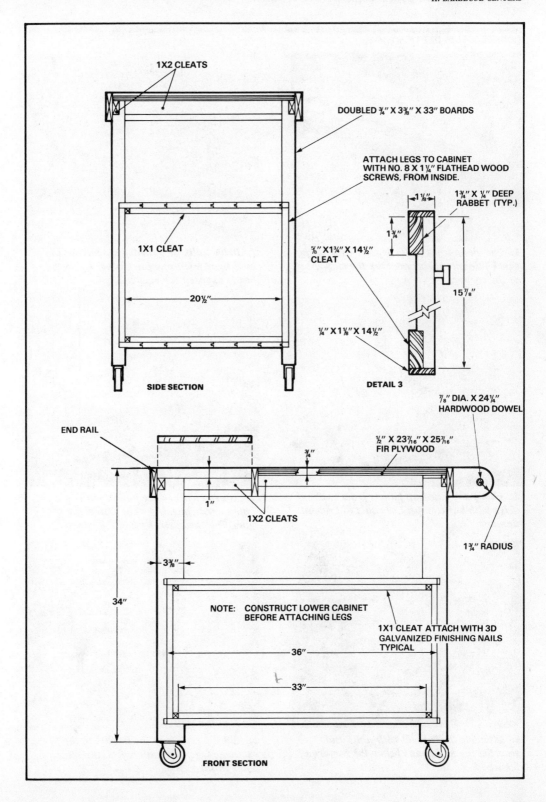

1X2 CLEATS

DOUBLED ¾" X 3⅜" X 33" BOARDS

ATTACH LEGS TO CABINET WITH NO. 8 X 1 ¼" FLATHEAD WOOD SCREWS, FROM INSIDE.

1 ¾" X ¼" DEEP RABBET (TYP.)

1 ⅛"

1 ¾"

15⅞"

⁵⁄₁₆" X1¾" X 14½" CLEAT

¼" X 1⅛" X 14½"

1X1 CLEAT

20½"

SIDE SECTION

DETAIL 3

⅞" DIA. X 24¼" HARDWOOD DOWEL

END RAIL

½" X 23⁷⁄₁₆" X 25⁷⁄₁₆" FIR PLYWOOD

¾"

1"

1X2 CLEATS

1¾" RADIUS

3⅜"

34"

NOTE: CONSTRUCT LOWER CABINET BEFORE ATTACHING LEGS

1X1 CLEAT ATTACH WITH 3D GALVANIZED FINISHING NAILS TYPICAL

36"

33"

FRONT SECTION

CONSTRUCTION DETAILS

1. Cut the notches in the legs by raising the saw blade into the wood. Stop the cuts short of the corners.

2. Drive nails into the leg assemblies to hold their positions for gluing. Leave the heads exposed for removal.

3. Clamp the glued-up panels from both sides with bar clamps. Use cauls to prevent damage.

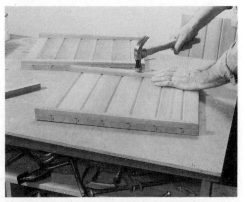

4. Attach cleats to the panels with 3d galvanized finishing nails and resorcinol glue. The cleats strengthen the panels.

5. Assemble the cabinet with nails and glue. Set the nail heads below the surface of the wood.

6. Add the rails and the handle to the cabinet's legs. The handle fits into blind holes in the rails.

bets on the doors as shown in the diagram.

Cut cleats to fit the rabbets, and round one end to the profile shown in Detail 2. Attach the cleats with nails and glue. Add the top and bottom $\frac{1}{4}$-in. X $1\frac{1}{8}$-in. strips to the cleats, gluing them in place.

Next, form the door lip profiles. Use a cabinet door lip router bit, with pilot, on your router. Several styles of bits are available. Hang the doors with continuous hinges, and add knobs to suit your taste.

To make the legs, cut 1X4s to length. Cut notches in the inside half of each leg pair. Measure accurately for a good fit. Make the long cuts on your table saw by raising the blade slowly through the wood, then continuing the cut. Mark the ends of the cut with masking tape.

After making the longer cut, use your miter gauge to cut part of the crosscuts, then finish the corners with a handsaw. Glue the leg halves together, clamping them securely. If your measurements were accurate,

the legs should form two sets of identical parts.

Fit the notched legs around the cabinet and then secure the assembly with no. 8 X $1\frac{1}{4}$-in. flathead wood screws, driven from inside. Glue $\frac{1}{4}$-in. X $\frac{3}{4}$-in. strips to the exposed end grain on the cabinet.

Cut the handles to length, rounding one end as shown in the diagram. Using a Forstner bit, bore $\frac{7}{8}$-in.-dia. X $\frac{3}{8}$-in.-deep holes for the handle. Attach the rails and the handle to the legs, driving the screws from the inside. Be sure to install the rails so that the top is 1 in. above the legs.

Now, add the end rails and the divider, securing these parts with screws and glue. Bore counterbored screw holes to accept wood screw hole plugs. Cut 1X2 cleats and install them in the positions shown in the diagram. As you did before, use screws and glue. Install 3-in.-dia. plate-mounted casters on the bottoms of the legs with no. 8 X $1\frac{1}{2}$-in. flathead wood screws.

Cut a maple cutting board to fit the smaller opening. Sand the cut edges, then apply cutting board oil to protect the wood.

Cut a piece of $\frac{1}{2}$-in. exterior plywood to fit the other opening. Attach plastic laminate to the top of the board with contact cement. Use an oversized piece of laminate. After gluing, trim away the excess with a laminate-trimming bit in your router.

Sand the completed project thoroughly, working down to 220-grit garnet paper for a smooth finish. Apply clear wood sealer or satin-finish polyurethane varnish to the cart to seal the wood against spills.

Design and photos courtesy of The Family Handyman, 1999 Shepard Rd., St. Paul, MN 55116.

MATERIALS LIST

Item	Quantity
1X4 tongue-and-groove siding	124 ft.
1X4 lumber	40 ft.
1X6 lumber	8 ft.
1X2 lumber	11 ft.
1X1 lumber	16 ft.
$\frac{1}{2}$" exterior plywood	$\frac{1}{4}$ sheet
Maple cutting board	to suit
$\frac{1}{16}$" plastic laminate	2 ft. X 6 ft.
$\frac{7}{8}$" hardwood dowel	36"
$\frac{3}{8}$" wood screw hole plugs	16
$1\frac{1}{2}$" X 18" continuous hinges	2
No. 8 X $1\frac{1}{4}$" flathead wood screws	as needed
No. 8 X $1\frac{1}{2}$" flathead wood screws	16
3d galvanized finishing nails	as needed
3" plate-mounted casters	4
Resorcinol glue	as needed
Contact cement	1 small can
Finishing materials	as needed

Open or closed, this rolling beverage cart is an attractive way to bring your favorite beverages outdoors.

BEVERAGE CART

Outdoor entertaining on hot summer days means serving up large quantities of refreshing beverages. Build this rolling beverage cart and you will have the perfect portable bar.

Built of all-heart redwood, its attractive appearance will complement your outdoor decor. The lid folds back, revealing a large work space with room for bottled drinks in a well.

Open the door to gain access to a large storage area, with glass holders and shelves for snacks. Even the doors offer storage space for bottles and stemware. A key-operated lock in the doors keeps children out.

Begin building the cart by making the front, back and two side panels from tongue-and-groove redwood lumber. You can use ready-made 1X6 tongue-and-groove siding or create your own stock from 1X6 clear all-heart redwood boards.

Use a shaper head on your table saw or radial arm saw to mill the tongue-and-groove joints on the edges of the raw stock. If the edges of your lumber are slightly rounded, trim them on your saw to prepare them for milling.

If you have a shaper, forming the joints is even easier. You can also make the joints with your router and a set of tongue-and-groove bits.

Whether you use ready-made material or create your own stock, glue up the top, side, door, and back panels. Make each panel oversized, in both length and width, to simplify the job.

Apply waterproof resorcinol glue to the joints, then assemble the panels. Clamp each panel with bar clamps, applying clamps to both sides to minimize warping. Use wood cauls between the clamps and the panel to keep from marring the wood.

Once the glued joints have dried completely, trim the panels to the dimensions shown in the diagram on page 27. Cut equal amounts from each side of the panel, then trim both ends to reach the final dimensions. Use a combination planer-type blade on your table saw or radial arm saw for a smooth finish.

Remove any excess glue from the panels and give them a smooth finish with a cabinet scraper (see the step-by-step photographs on pages 28 and 29). Finish up by sanding each panel.

Next, cut a piece of $3/4$-in. exterior plywood to form the bottom of the cabinet. The dimensions provided in the diagram are typical, but measure your components accurately to get the exact dimension.

Attach a slightly oversized piece of plastic laminate to the cabinet base. Apply contact cement to both surfaces, then allow it to dry. Line up the parts, then lower the laminate onto the plywood. Apply firm pressure to the top of the laminate to complete the bond.

Insert a laminate-trimming bit in your router and remove the excess plastic, making it flush with the edge of the plywood.

Now, cut a $22\frac{1}{2}$-in. X $34\frac{1}{2}$-in. plywood panel for the top work surface of the cart. Lay out the $3\frac{3}{4}$-in. X 23-in. notch for the bottle well on the rear edge of the panel.

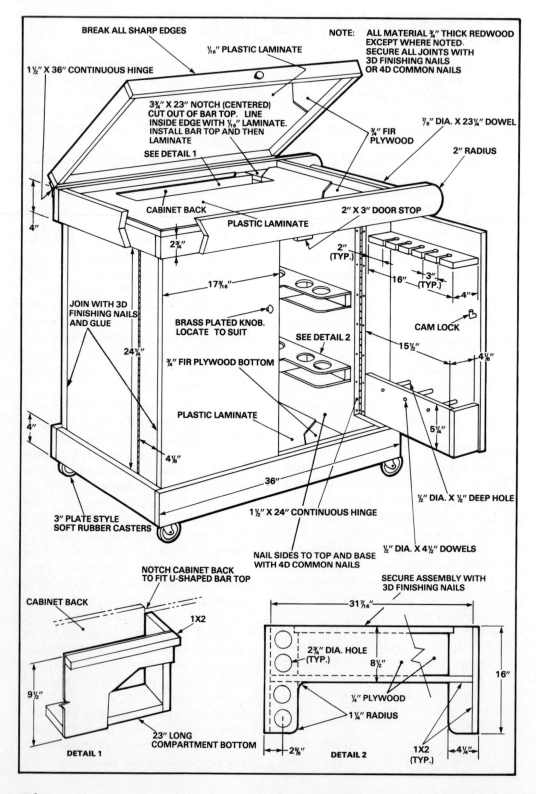

BREAK ALL SHARP EDGES

1/16" PLASTIC LAMINATE

NOTE: ALL MATERIAL 3/4" THICK REDWOOD
EXCEPT WHERE NOTED.
SECURE ALL JOINTS WITH
3D FINISHING NAILS
OR 4D COMMON NAILS

1 1/2" X 36" CONTINUOUS HINGE

3 3/4" X 23" NOTCH (CENTERED)
CUT OUT OF BAR TOP. LINE
INSIDE EDGE WITH 1/16" LAMINATE.
INSTALL BAR TOP AND THEN
LAMINATE

SEE DETAIL 1

7/8" DIA. X 23 1/4" DOWEL

3/4" FIR
PLYWOOD

2" RADIUS

CABINET BACK

PLASTIC LAMINATE

2" X 3" DOOR STOP

4"

2 3/4"

2"
(TYP.)

16"

3"
(TYP.)

4"

JOIN WITH 3D
FINISHING NAILS
AND GLUE

17 3/16"

BRASS PLATED KNOB.
LOCATE TO SUIT

SEE DETAIL 2

CAM LOCK

24 1/4"

15 1/2"

4 1/8"

3/4" FIR PLYWOOD BOTTOM

PLASTIC LAMINATE

5 1/4"

4"

4 1/8"

36"

3" PLATE STYLE
SOFT RUBBER CASTERS

1 1/2" X 24" CONTINUOUS HINGE

1/2" DIA. X 1/2" DEEP HOLE

NAIL SIDES TO TOP AND BASE
WITH 4D COMMON NAILS

1/2" DIA. X 4 1/2" DOWELS

NOTCH CABINET BACK
TO FIT U-SHAPED BAR TOP

SECURE ASSEMBLY WITH
3D FINISHING NAILS

CABINET BACK

1X2

31 7/16"

2 3/4" DIA. HOLE
(TYP.)

8 1/2"

16"

9 1/2"

1/4" PLYWOOD

1 1/4" RADIUS

23" LONG
COMPARTMENT BOTTOM

DETAIL 1

2 5/8"

DETAIL 2

1X2
(TYP.)

4 1/4"

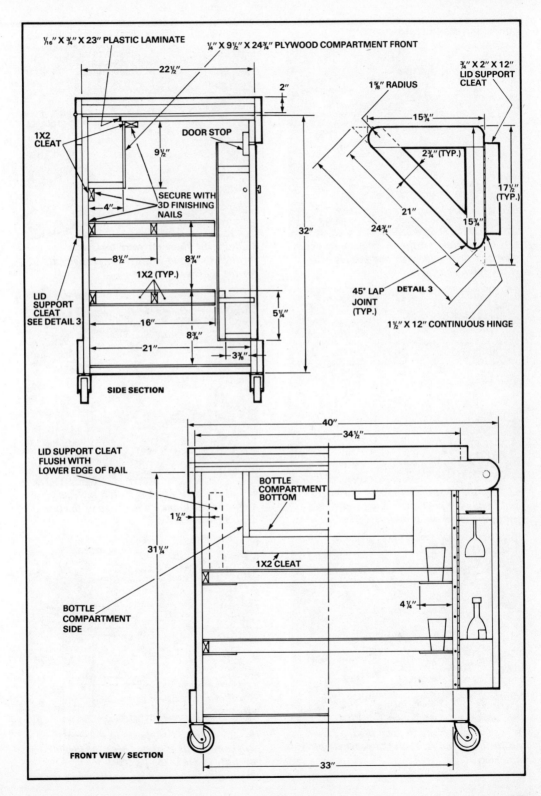

¹⁄₁₆″ X ¾″ X 23″ PLASTIC LAMINATE

¼″ X 9½″ X 24¾″ PLYWOOD COMPARTMENT FRONT

¾″ X 2″ X 12″ LID SUPPORT CLEAT

22½″

2″

1⁵⁄₈″ RADIUS

1X2 CLEAT

DOOR STOP

9½″

15¾″

2¾″ (TYP.)

17½″ (TYP.)

SECURE WITH 3D FINISHING NAILS

4″

21″

32″

24¾″

15¾″

8½″

8¾″

1X2 (TYP.)

LID SUPPORT CLEAT SEE DETAIL 3

16″

5¼″

45° LAP JOINT (TYP.)

DETAIL 3

8¾″

21″

3³⁄₈″

1½″ X 12″ CONTINUOUS HINGE

SIDE SECTION

40″

34½″

LID SUPPORT CLEAT FLUSH WITH LOWER EDGE OF RAIL

BOTTLE COMPARTMENT BOTTOM

1½″

31¼″

1X2 CLEAT

BOTTLE COMPARTMENT SIDE

4¼″

FRONT VIEW / SECTION

33″

CONSTRUCTION DETAILS

1. *Use a cabinet scraper to remove excess glue and to give the redwood panels a glass-smooth surface.*

2. *Raise the blade on your table saw through the wood to start the plunge cuts for the notches.*

5. *Trim the plastic laminate on the edges and inside the notch with a laminate-trimming bit in your router.*

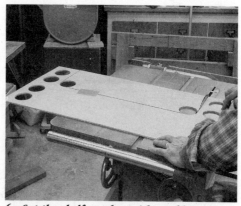

6. *Cut the shelf notches with a table saw. Align the cut to match the edge of the pre-drilled corner holes.*

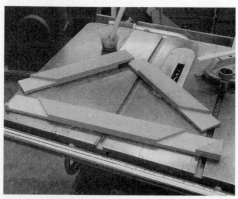

9. *Use a dado blade to form the lap joints on the lid supports. Trim the supports after assembly.*

10. *Attach the lid supports to the cleats with continuous hinges. Check the height carefully to make the lid level.*

3. *After gluing plastic laminate to the edges of the notch, use a file to trim it flush with the surface.*

4. *Assemble the cabinet with 4d common nails and glue. Check the squareness as you work.*

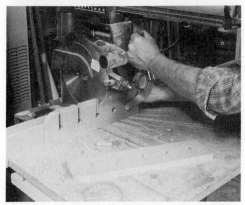

7. *Cut slots for the stemware racks on your radial arm saw after drilling the end holes. Use the tool's safety guards.*

8. *Check the door's fit carefully before attaching the continuous hinges to the side of the cabinet.*

Make two crosscuts to form the edges of the notch. Do not cut clear to the corner. Now, set the rip fence on your table saw to cut the long side of the notch. Retract the saw blade below the table and position the workpiece over the blade.

Raise the blade slowly into the plywood, as shown in the photo, then move the panel over the blade to cut the line. Once again, stop the cut short of the corner. Finish the notch with a handsaw.

Attach three strips of plastic lam-inate to the edges of the notch. Use contact cement as you did before. Trim these strips flush with the sur-face of the plywood with a mill bas-tard file.

Now, glue laminate to the top of the panel, using the same technique you did for the bottom panel. Once the plastic is in place, trim the edges and the inside of the notch with your router.

Form the 4$\frac{1}{8}$-in. X 24$\frac{1}{4}$-in. notches in the side panels, where the doors will be hinged. Cut the notches the same way you did for the top. Do not laminate the edges of these notches.

Before assembling the cabinet, cut notches in the back panel to accommodate the top (see Detail 1 of the diagram). Use a band saw or a saber saw for this job.

Cut the sides and bottom of the bottle well from 4-in.-wide redwood stock, ripped from 1X6 material. Cut the front panel of the well from a piece of ¼-in. plywood. Attach the well to the back panel with a 1X2 cleat and 3d finishing nails. Add the front panel and the 1X2 upper cleat. Be sure to allow for the thickness of the top panel.

Assemble the cabinet components, securing the joints with glue and 4d common nails. The nail heads will be hidden by trim boards. As you work, use a framing square to check the assembly for squareness.

Next, cut two ¼-in. plywood shelf components to the size shown in De-tail 2. Lay out the recess and the tumbler holes on the panels. Use a compass and a square to help with the layout.

Bore the tumbler holes with a hole saw on your drill press. Use a backup board to prevent splintering the plywood. Bore additional 2½-in.-dia. holes at the corners of the recess.

Cut away the waste from the recess on your table saw, making the cuts at a precise tangent to the holes. Raise the saw blade through the plywood to cut the back of the opening. Finish the shelves by cutting a 1¼-in. radius at the front corners of the recess.

Cut two additional pieces of plywood to form the lower shelf panels. Cut these to match the sides of the upper plywood shelves.

Now make the H-shaped brace assemblies from 1X2 redwood stock. Nail the lower panels to the braces with 3d finishing nails. Cut the back cleats to length, and attach them to the back cabinet panel with glue and nails to locate the shelves.

Insert the brace assemblies, lining them up carefully with the cleats. Make certain they are level, then attach the braces to the cabinet's sides with glue and 3d finishing nails. Once they are in position, add the plywood shelves and glue them in place.

Next, rip 4-in.-wide stock from 1X6 redwood, and cut the trim boards and the handle rails to the sizes indicated in the diagram. Round one end of the rails to a 2-in. radius, then bore blind holes for the handle with a Forstner bit on your drill press.

Attach the trim and the dowel handle to the cabinet assembly with

MATERIALS LIST

Item	Quantity
1X6 clear all-heart redwood	140 ft.
1X4 clear all-heart redwood	30 ft.
1X2 redwood	20 ft.
¾" exterior plywood	¾ sheet
¼" exterior plywood	½ sheet
½" dowel	36"
¾" dowel	36"
¹⁄₁₆" X 24" X 36" white plastic laminate	3
1½" X 36" continuous hinge	1
1½" X 24" continuous hinge	2
1½" X 18" continuous hinge	2
3" plate-type casters	4
4d common nails	as needed
3d finishing nails	as needed
Cabinet knobs	3
Key-operated cam lock	1
Contact cement	1 small can
Resorcinol glue	as needed
Satin finish polyurethane varnish	1 qt.

3d finishing nails and glue. Set all exposed nail heads below the surface of the wood, then fill the holes with redwood-colored wood filler.

Make the doors next. Rip redwood lumber to the widths shown in the diagram. Attach the door edges and the bottle rack components to the door panels with 3d finishing nails and glue.

Bore $\frac{1}{2}$-in.-dia. holes for the dowel separators with a long bit on your drill press. Do not bore completely through the door panel. Use a depth stop on the bit to make the holes $\frac{1}{2}$ in. deep. Insert the dowels, gluing them in place.

Now, cut the stemware rack boards to size. Lay out the positions for the slots on the workpieces. Bore $\frac{3}{4}$-in.-dia. holes at the ends of each slot. Cut the $\frac{1}{2}$-in.-wide slots on your radial arm saw as shown in the photo. Attach the glass racks to the doors with glue and nails.

Hang the doors with continuous hinges, checking their alignment carefully. Fasten the hinges to the doors first, then align the door and mark the sides to show the position of the hinges. Add brass knobs and a cam lock to complete the door assemblies.

Make the lid next. Rip 2-in. stock for the sides of the lid, then cut the glued stock to the lengths shown in the diagram. Assemble the sides with glue and 3d finishing nails. Check the frame carefully for squareness and make sure it matches the trim on the cabinet.

Next, attach plastic laminate to the underside of the glued-up lid panel. Use contact cement as you did for the other panels. Trim the edges with your router, then insert the top in the frame. Secure the top with 3d finishing nails and glue. Make the top panel flush with the top of the frame. Align the lid carefully, then attach it to the trim with a continuous hinge.

Cut the components for the lid support brackets from $2\frac{3}{4}$-in.-wide stock. Lay the components together as they will be when assembled. Mark the intersections on all components to lay out the half-lap joints.

Cut the notches for the joints with multiple passes of a dado blade. Make certain that the depth of cut is exactly half the thickness of the stock.

Assemble the triangular supports, fastening the half-lap joints with glue and 3d finishing nails. Once the glue has dried, lay out and cut the rounded ends of the supports as shown in the diagram.

Cut the 2-in. X 12-in. lid support cleats, then attach the cleats to the back of the cabinet with glue and nails. Fasten the supports to the cleats with continuous hinges. Check the height of the supports carefully to allow the lid to be level when opened.

Add the casters to the base, then sand the entire project thoroughly. Work down to 220-grit garnet paper for a smooth finish, and use both hand- and power-sanding techniques to produce a good surface. Always sand in the direction of the wood grain. Break all sharp edges slightly as you sand.

Finish the project with two coats of satin-finish polyurethane varnish, sanding lightly between coats. Mask the laminated surfaces to keep the varnish off the plastic.

Design and photos courtesy of The Family Handyman, 1999 Shepard Rd., St. Paul, MN 55116.

DECK WITH FIREPIT

There are few social activities more enjoyable than sitting around a blazing fire, sharing friendly conversation. Most people experience that warm, friendly atmosphere only on camping trips, but there is no reason not to have the same pleasant feeling right in your own backyard.

The main feature of this deck is its central firepit, just waiting for you and a bag of marshmallows. Four benches provide comfortable seating at the perfect distance from the fire, while the herringbone pattern of the deck dresses up your yard.

Of course, you will want to use the deck even when a fire is not needed. A slatted wooden cover that fits neatly over the firepit serves as a handy table to hold refreshments while you enjoy relaxing on the deck.

Start building the project by excavating a 10-ft. X 10-ft. area in your yard. Dig down 3½ in. and level the bottom of the cavity carefully. Use a 10-ft.-long, straight 2X4 and a carpenter's level to help you make the grade as even as possible.

Check the squareness of the excavation by measuring the diagonals. When the measurements are equal, the site is perfectly square. Make adjustments as needed. Careful preparation of the site at this point will make the remaining construction jobs much simpler.

Before building the wooden part of the project, construct the firepit. Locate the center of the excavation by connecting the diagonal lines across the corners. Lay out a 36-in. square around this center, with the sides parallel to the sides of the excavation.

The firepit is made of 4-in. X 16-in. solid concrete blocks, laid directly on the earth. Mortar is used to bind the blocks together.

Start building the firepit by mixing a batch of commercial mortar mix in a wheelbarrow or a mortar boat. Add just enough water to the mix to make the mortar the consistency of heavy mashed potatoes. You will need three bags of mortar mix for the project.

Lay one block at a corner of the firepit square, then apply mortar to the end of the adjoining block with a bricklayer's trowel. Position the new block in a perfect line with the first. Aim for a $3/8$-in.-wide mortar joint.

Continue adding blocks until you have completed the first course of the masonry. At this point, check the structure for squareness, and make certain that the sides are even and the top of the first course is level. Make any necessary adjustments to the square of blocks before proceeding.

Apply a layer of mortar to the top of the first course of blocks, then place the next course, following the same procedure you did before. Alternate the direction of the corner blocks to stagger the joints and to tie the structure together.

As you work, keep the blocks carefully aligned. Make minor adjustments by tapping the blocks with the wooden handle of your trowel. As you finish each course of blocks, remove any excess mortar with the trowel. Check the course for evenness and a level top before proceeding.

Give the mortar joints a concave finish with a bricklayer's striking tool. If you do not have this tool, you can finish the joints with any round object that's about $1/2$ in. in diameter. A piece of $1/2$-in. copper tubing, bent slightly, works well.

Continue adding courses to the firepit in the same way until you complete four courses of blocks. Stagger the corner blocks for each course and carefully align the blocks for the best appearance.

Before the mortar has set completely, clean the exposed faces of the blocks with a stiff brush and a bucket of water to remove any mortar stains. Be careful not to scrub away the finished mortar joints.

Once the mortar has set up, attach the wood trim to the firepit. Cut 2X6 lumber with mitered ends to fit the outside of the pit. Measure each side of the structure to allow for slight construction variations.

Bore $1/4$-in. mounting holes in the wood, 6 in. from each end. Position the sides 3 in. down from the top of the firepit and mark through the pre-drilled holes to locate the hole positions on the blocks.

Use a long $5/16$-in. masonry bit to drill through the blocks. Work slowly and keep the bit level as you drill. Once the holes are finished, mount the trim boards to the blocks using $1/4$-in. X 6-in. carriage bolts with nuts and washers. The $5/16$-in.-dia. holes in the blocks will help you make minor adjustments for a perfect fit.

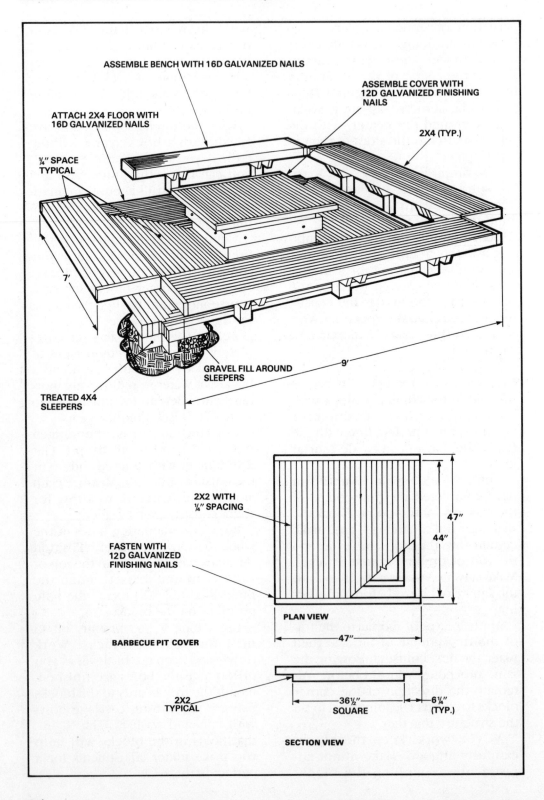

ASSEMBLE BENCH WITH 16D GALVANIZED NAILS

ASSEMBLE COVER WITH
12D GALVANIZED FINISHING
NAILS

ATTACH 2X4 FLOOR WITH
16D GALVANIZED NAILS

2X4 (TYP.)

¼" SPACE
TYPICAL

7'

GRAVEL FILL AROUND
SLEEPERS

9'

TREATED 4X4
SLEEPERS

2X2 WITH
¼" SPACING

47"

44"

FASTEN WITH
12D GALVANIZED
FINISHING NAILS

PLAN VIEW

47"

BARBECUE PIT COVER

2X2
TYPICAL

36½"
SQUARE

6¼"
(TYP.)

SECTION VIEW

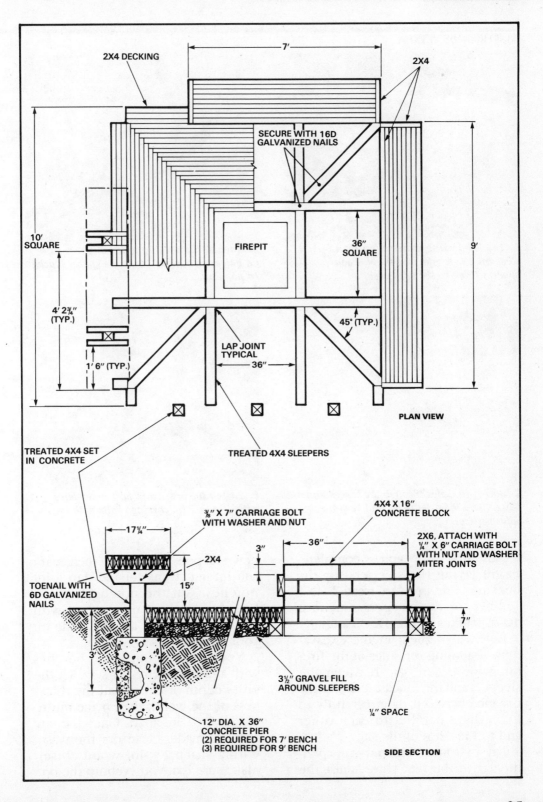

2X4 DECKING

7'

2X4

SECURE WITH 16D
GALVANIZED NAILS

10'
SQUARE

FIREPIT

36"
SQUARE

9'

4' 2¾"
(TYP.)

45° (TYP.)

LAP JOINT
TYPICAL

1' 6" (TYP.)

36"

PLAN VIEW

TREATED 4X4 SET
IN CONCRETE

TREATED 4X4 SLEEPERS

⅜" X 7" CARRIAGE BOLT
WITH WASHER AND NUT

4X4 X 16"
CONCRETE BLOCK

17¼"

3"

36"

2X6, ATTACH WITH
¼" X 6" CARRIAGE BOLT
WITH NUT AND WASHER
MITER JOINTS

2X4

15"

TOENAIL WITH
6D GALVANIZED
NAILS

7"

3'

3½" GRAVEL FILL
AROUND SLEEPERS

¼" SPACE

12" DIA. X 36"
CONCRETE PIER
(2) REQUIRED FOR 7' BENCH
(3) REQUIRED FOR 9' BENCH

SIDE SECTION

35

CONSTRUCTION DETAILS

1. *Lay the decking material on the 4X4 sleepers. Use scraps of ¼-in. plywood spacers to make the gaps even.*

2. *Toenail the decking to the sleepers with 6d galvanized nails. Leave the spacer blocks in position.*

5. *Bore ⅜-in. holes through the braces and posts. Use a long-shank bit and keep the holes vertical.*

6. *Fasten the brace and post assemblies with ⅜-in. X 7-in. carriage bolts with nuts and washers.*

Now that the firepit is complete, begin laying the sleepers for the decking. Use pressure-treated 4X4 lumber for the sleepers. Cut four 10-ft. lengths of the 4X4 material.

Lay two of them in the excavation, straddling the sides of the firepit, with a ¼-in. gap between the sleepers and the blocks. Measure the distance between them carefully to keep them parallel to each other and to the sides of the site.

Lay two more sleepers, perpendicular to the first pair. Adjust the new sleepers accurately, then mark the intersections for half-lap joint notches. Cut the notches exactly half the depth of the lumber with multiple passes of a dado blade on your radial arm saw.

You can also cut these notches with a portable circular saw. Set the saw's depth of cut to half the thickness of the wood, then make multiple kerfs ¼ in. apart. Once the saw cuts are made, clean out the waste with a sharp 1½-in. wood chisel. Make sure that you even up the bot-

3. *Secure the corners of the decking with two 16d galvanized nails. Drill pilot holes to prevent splitting.*

4. *Lay the decking in a herringbone pattern for an attractive appearance. Cut each board to fit.*

7. *Use wood shims to equally space the bench's 2X4 slats. Attach the bench top with 16d galvanized nails.*

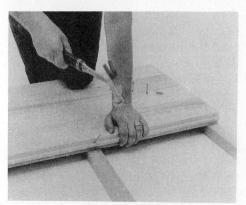

8. *Form the firepit cover with 2X2s, or use tongue-and-groove material as shown here. Never place the cover over warm coals.*

tom of the cut as well.

Now, lay the notched 4X4 sleepers in the excavation, interlocking the notches. Fasten the joints with 16d galvanized nails.

Measure the corners of the structure for the diagonal sleepers. To allow for slight variations, measure each corner separately.

Cut 4X4 stock to fit, making two 45 degree cuts as shown in the diagram to form points on the ends of the sleepers. Lay these in the excavation, one at a time, and toenail

MATERIALS LIST

Item	Quantity
4X4 pressure-treated lumber	100 ft.
2X4 lumber	900 ft.
2X6 lumber	16 ft.
2X2 lumber	130 ft.
4" X 16" concrete blocks	40
Medium gravel	1 cu. yd.
Mortar mix	3 bags
Concrete mix	10 bags
¼" X 6" carriage bolts with nuts and washers	8
⅜" X 7" carriage bolts with nuts and washers	20
12d galvanized finishing nails	as needed
6d, 16d galvanized nails	as needed

them to the existing sleepers with 16d galvanized nails. Keep the tops of the sleepers even, and drill pilot holes for the nails to simplify construction.

Next, level the sleepers carefully, using a carpenter's level and a straight 2X4 on edge. Spend as much time as you need to do this job. Adjust the level of the sleepers by removing or adding soil. With each adjustment, compact the soil by jumping on the sleeper. You may feel a bit silly, but this step will compact the soil under the sleeper, preventing it from settling later.

The evenness of the entire deck depends on the stability and evenness of the sleepers. Level them in all directions and keep working until you are satisfied.

Once the sleepers are as level as possible, fill the excavation with medium-sized gravel, right up to the top of the sleepers. Finish off the gravel surface with a long 2X4 on edge, striking off the gravel flush with the top of the 4X4 lumber.

Place gravel inside the firepit as well. A 6-in.-deep layer should be just right to position the firewood at a suitable height.

Now, begin installing the deck boards. Choose straight and unwarped stock for the decking. You can use any variety of wood you want for this project, as long as you keep durability in mind.

Start by cutting two pieces of the decking stock to match the width of the firepit, plus the gaps between the sleepers and the blocks. Lay these, on edge, alongside the firepit. Measure and cut two more pieces to fit. Butt joints are used, so allow for the width of the two deck boards you already cut.

Fasten the butt joints with 16d galvanized nails, then align the square carefully with the firepit. When you are satisfied, toenail the 2X4 stock to the sleepers.

Continue adding deck boards. Use scraps of ¼-in. plywood as spacers to separate the boards accurately. Create the herringbone pattern by aligning all the butt joints in the same way.

When toenailing the decking to the sleepers, position a piece of the ¼-in. plywood scrap at each of the nailing points. This will help keep the decking aligned properly.

Allow plenty of time to complete the decking. Measure accurately, allowing for the ¼-in. spacing, and add one square of decking before cutting the boards for the next square. A little extra care taken in the deck installation will pay off in a better-looking finished project.

Once all the decking is installed, begin building the seats. Measure along the sides of the deck to locate the positions of the seat posts. Follow the dimensions given in the diagram carefully, locating the open corner of the deck to suit your particular location.

Dig 12-in.-dia. X 36-in.-deep holes for the posts. Extend the holes under the deck area, as shown in the diagram.

Now, build the seat tops. Cut ten 2X4 seat slats for each seat. Two of the seats are 7 ft. long, while the other two are 9 ft. long. Cut the slats 3 in. shorter than that dimension to allow for the end boards.

Working on a level surface, nail the end boards for each seat to the slats with 16d galvanized nails. Space the slats with pieces of ¼-in. plywood, as you did for the decking.

To help keep the slats aligned and to prevent the wood from splitting, drill pilot holes for the nails, especially for those near the ends.

Cut seat braces, two for each post, as shown in the diagram. Bevel the ends on your radial arm saw or table saw. To help keep each piece the same length, clamp a stop block to your saw's fence or table.

Cut the 4X4 pressure-treated posts to the length shown in the diagram, then attach the braces to the posts. Use a framing square to position the braces at the top of the posts, then nail them into place temporarily. Use double-headed nails, or leave the nail heads slightly above the wood's surface for easy removal.

Bore two $\frac{3}{8}$-in.-dia. holes through both braces and the post for the mounting bolts. You will need a long-shanked bit for this job. Position the holes diagonally, as shown in the diagram, and make the holes as vertical as possible.

Assemble the structure using $\frac{3}{8}$-in. X 7-in. carriage bolts with nuts and washers. After tightening the nuts securely, remove the temporary nails from the braces.

Attach the posts and braces to the undersides of the bench tops by toenailing the braces to the slats. Use 6d galvanized nails and drill pilot holes for accurate assembly. Measure the spacing of the posts to match the holes you dug earlier.

Now, place the bench assemblies in the holes. Adjust the height of each bench to make it level in both directions. As you can see in the diagram, the benches touch at the corners.

Once you are satisfied with the bench installation, toenail the posts to the decking to hold the position. Check once again to make sure that the bench tops are level in both directions.

Pour concrete into the holes, filling them to within 6 in. of the surface of the deck and the surrounding grade. You will need one 1-cu.-ft. bag of concrete mix for each post. Once the concrete sets, backfill the rest of the hole with soil and replant the scars to match the surrounding landscaping.

Next, build the lid for the firepit. Cut two 47-in.-long 2X2s to form the ends of the lid and twenty-seven 2X2 slats 44 in. long.

As you did for the seats, nail the end boards to the slats, spacing the slats $\frac{1}{4}$ in. apart with the aid of plywood scraps. Nail with 12d galvanized finishing nails for a clean appearance and drill pilot holes for the nails when working near the ends of the structure.

Measure the outside of the firepit, then build a square of 2X2 stock to fit outside. Make the square $\frac{1}{2}$ in. larger than the firepit measurements for an easy fit.

Turn the lid upside-down and center the smaller square on it. Nail it in place with 12d galvanized finishing nails driven into every third slat.

Before using your completed deck, go over it carefully, sanding off any rough or splintery areas. Apply two coats of clear wood sealer to the wood to help prevent weather damage. Allow the first coat to dry overnight. If you choose, you could also apply exterior stain to the deck to match your home's exterior or to suit your taste.

Project and photos courtesy of Western Wood Products Association, Yeon Building, Portland, OR 97204.

OAK BARBECUE CART

When outdoor dining is on the program for a spring or summer evening, a well-designed serving cart helps the evening roll smoothly. This solid oak cart is the ideal addition to your barbecue equipment.

Start construction by making the top and the middle shelf. Rip ³/₄-in.-thick oak stock 2¹/₈ in. wide, then cut the material to a length of 28 in. You will need 36 of these pieces.

Joint both edges of all the components, removing a minimum of material. To keep the width of the parts the same, make the same number of passes on the jointer for each workpiece. If you don't have a jointer, cut the parts to width on a table saw equipped with a planer-type blade.

Now, joint the faces of 28 of the boards to prepare them for gluing. Apply carpenter's glue to the faces and assemble the cart's top. Use bar clamps to hold the assembly while the glue dries.

Assemble the shelf as well, this time applying the glue to the edges of the remaining components. Clamp the shelf, using bar clamps on both sides of the assembly.

After the glue has dried, level the top and the shelf with a belt sander, starting with an 80-grit belt. Work down to 220-grit. Trim the shelf to its final width.

Rip the remaining oak stock to the dimensions shown in the diagram. Use a combination planer blade on your table or radial arm saw for a smooth edge finish.

Cut the upper skirt and handle components to length and cut the rounded ends of the handles with a saber or band saw. Bore 1-in.-dia. holes for the dowel handle, then assemble the upper skirt and handle unit with no. 8 X 1¹/₄-in. flathead wood screws and carpenter's glue. Bore counterbored pilot holes for the screws to allow for wood screw hole plugs.

Next, bore the pilot holes for the screws that will attach the skirt to the top of the cart. Use a Forstner bit to counterbore these holes 1 in. deep. Attach the skirt to the top with no. 12 X 2¹/₂-in. flathead wood screws and glue. Measure carefully for proper alignment.

Use a dado blade on your table or radial arm saw to form the ³/₄-in. X ¹/₈-in. dadoes in the legs of the cart for the shelves.

Cut the bottom skirt components to length, then form ³/₈-in. X ³/₄-in.-deep stopped rabbets in these components, as shown in the diagram. End the rabbets short of their stopping points, then finish them with a chisel. Assemble the skirt as you did before, counterboring the screw holes for wood plugs.

Before final assembly of the cart, round over all exposed edges of the parts with a ¹/₄-in. rounding-over bit, with pilot, in your router. Sand all parts thoroughly, working down to 220-grit paper for the best finish.

Now, assemble the cart, using

CONSTRUCTION DETAILS

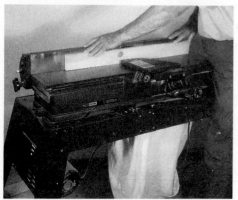

1. Prepare the edges of the shelf boards for gluing on the jointer. Work in the grain direction to prevent damage.

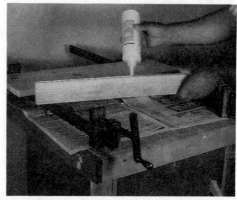

2. Edge-glue the shelf with carpenter's glue, clamping the assembly with bar clamps until the glue has dried.

3. Glue up the top, face-to-face, in the same way. Apply a thin, even coat of carpenter's glue to each face.

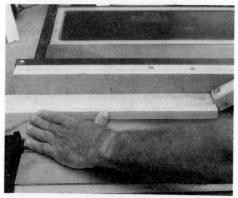

4. Use a dado blade on your saw to form the lower skirt's stopped rabbets. Check the stock's thickness before setting the blade.

5. Finish the stopped rabbets in the lower skirt with a sharp chisel, after forming the rest of the rabbet.

6. Use a Forstner bit to counterbore the mounting holes in the upper skirt rails. Bore the holes 1 in. deep.

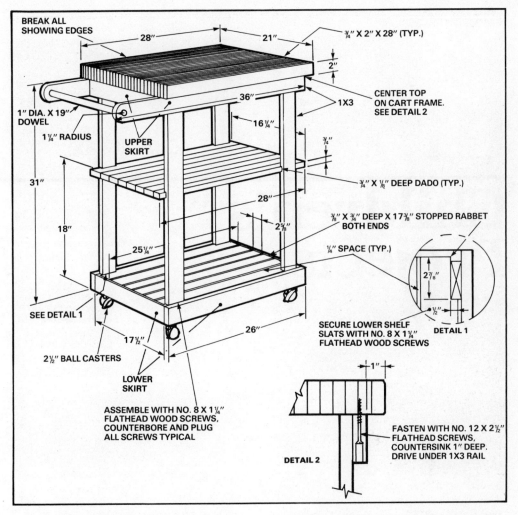

BREAK ALL SHOWING EDGES

28"

21"

¾" X 2" X 28" (TYP.)

2"

CENTER TOP ON CART FRAME. SEE DETAIL 2

36"

1X3

1" DIA. X 19" DOWEL

1¼" RADIUS

UPPER SKIRT

16¼"

¾"

¾" X ⅛" DEEP DADO (TYP.)

31"

18"

28"

2⅝"

⅜" X ¾" DEEP X 17⅞" STOPPED RABBET BOTH ENDS

¼" SPACE (TYP.)

25¼"

2⅞"

SEE DETAIL 1

26"

SECURE LOWER SHELF SLATS WITH NO. 8 X 1¼" FLATHEAD WOOD SCREWS

½"

DETAIL 1

17½"

2½" BALL CASTERS

LOWER SKIRT

ASSEMBLE WITH NO. 8 X 1¼" FLATHEAD WOOD SCREWS, COUNTERBORE AND PLUG ALL SCREWS TYPICAL

1"

FASTEN WITH NO. 12 X 2½" FLATHEAD SCREWS, COUNTERSINK 1" DEEP. DRIVE UNDER 1X3 RAIL

DETAIL 2

glue and no. 8 X 1¼-in. flathead screws on the joints. Check the assembly for squareness as you go. Add the wood screw hole plugs, gluing them in place. Leave the plugs slightly proud of the surface, then sand them flush after the glue dries. Space the bottom shelf components ¼ in. apart.

Turn the cart upside-down and bore holes in the legs for the caster sockets. Drive the sockets in place, then insert the caster stems.

Finish the cart with two coats of exterior polyurethane varnish, sand-ing lightly between coats with 400-grit garnet paper. If you would like a dark oak finish, apply stain before varnishing.

MATERIALS LIST

Item	Quantity
1X3 oak lumber	90 ft.
1" dia. dowel	19"
¾" oak screw hole plugs	36
No. 8 X 1¼" flathead wood screws	48
No. 12 X 2½" flathead wood screws	12
2½" ball casters	4
Carpenter's glue	as needed
Exterior polyurethane varnish	1 qt.

III.

Children's Projects

BIKE RACK

If your children's bicycles seem to turn up in all the wrong places, this outdoor bike rack is the perfect project. Designed for sturdiness and ease of use, it could be the solution to a real problem, and your children will be the envy of all their friends.

Built entirely of pressure-treated lumber, the rack is designed to resist the harshest weather, while its light weight makes it easy to move to new locations. Triangular braces reinforce the rack, so it will stand up to any abuse your children dish out.

Start construction by building the rack unit. Cut five 24-in.-long pieces of 2X2 pressure-treated lumber for the uprights, and two 19½-in.-long pieces for the top and bottom.

It is important that the vertical members be exactly the same length. Clamp a stop block on your radial arm saw's fence to make each part identical. If you use a table saw, clamp a block to the edge of the table. Line up the workpiece with the block, then use the miter gauge to hold that position for the cut.

You may find that 2X2 pressure-treated lumber is not available in your area. If this is the case, buy 2X4 material and rip it to the correct width.

Since lumber widths vary somewhat, measure your 2X4 stock and mark the center. Set your saw's fence so that the saw kerf splits the line exactly. Work with stock at least 48 in. long and be sure to observe the safety precautions provided with your saw.

Assemble the rack with no. 10 X 3-in. flathead wood screws. Drill pilot holes for the screws with a combination pilot bit and countersink. Countersink the pilot holes so that the screw head will be below the surface of the wood.

For added strength, use waterproof resorcinol glue on the joints. Apply a thin layer of the glue to both parts, allowing a little to squeeze out when the joint is tightened.

Space the vertical members of the rack 3 in. apart. Before final tightening of the screws, check the assembly for squareness with a framing square. Correct any errors, then tighten the screws securely. Fill the countersunk areas over the screw holes with waterproof wood filler. Leave the wood filler a little above the wood's surface to allow for sanding.

Once the glue and wood filler dry, sand the assembly thoroughly with a belt sander. Start with an 80-grit belt to level the rack and remove saw marks, then finish up with a fine belt to prepare the rack for painting. Spend a little extra time on the end grain of the top crossbar.

Next, cut a 20-in. square of ½-in. exterior plywood. Choose plywood with two good sides for this project to insure clean-looking results. Draw a diagonal line, dividing the plywood square in half, then cut the two triangular braces with a plywood blade on your circular saw. Guide the saw with a board clamped to the plywood.

Sand the edges of the plywood to smooth any minor splintering. Now, on a perfectly flat surface, attach the plywood supports to the rack. Both

CONSTRUCTION DETAILS

1. *Cut a 20-in. square of ½-in. plywood in half diagonally to make the triangular braces. Use a plywood blade.*

2. *Clamp a stop block on the fence of your saw when cutting the rack components to make all parts identical.*

3. *Use a pad sander to sand the rack assembly. Start with a medium-grit sandpaper to level the surface.*

4. *Assemble the rack on a flat surface to keep the structure square. Use resorcinol glue on all joints.*

the supports and the rack should touch the surface. Use no. 10 X 1¾-in. flathead screws, spaced 3 in. apart. As you did before, countersink the pilot holes below the surface of the wood and use resorcinol glue.

Install the top screw on each side first, then add the bottom screw after making certain that the rack assembly is vertical. Add the remaining screws to finish this step of construction, then fill the countersunk screw holes with wood filler.

Finally, cut the 30-in.-long legs of the rack and attach them to the outside of the plywood supports. Center the legs on the plywood sides so

that they extend equally from both ends. Follow the same fastening procedures as you did before.

Once the rack is assembled, give the entire unit a good sanding. Pay special attention to the end grain of both the lumber and the plywood. Start with 80-grit paper and work down to 120-grit. When sanding the plywood, it is especially important to sand with the grain of the wood for a good finish.

Finish the project with three coats of high-quality latex exterior enamel. Allow each coat to dry thoroughly before applying the next coat. If you have airless spray equipment, use it to get a perfect finish.

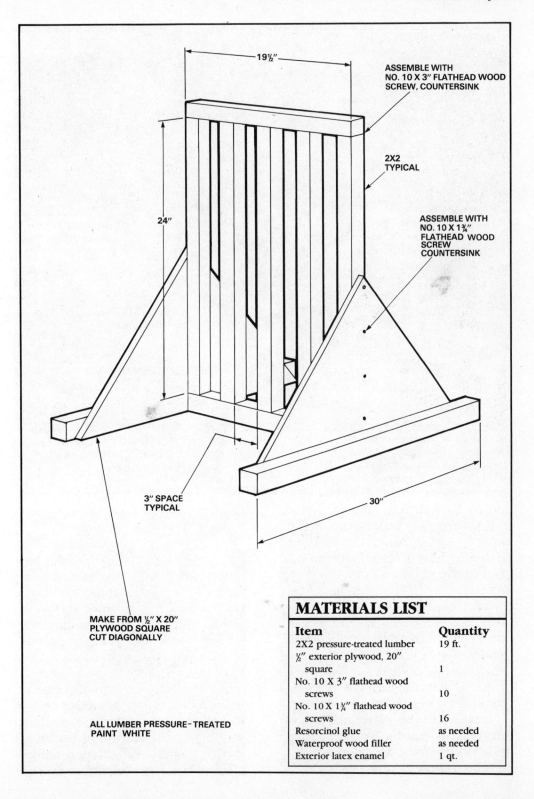

19½"

ASSEMBLE WITH
NO. 10 X 3" FLATHEAD WOOD
SCREW, COUNTERSINK

2X2
TYPICAL

ASSEMBLE WITH
NO. 10 X 1¾"
FLATHEAD WOOD
SCREW
COUNTERSINK

24"

30"

3" SPACE
TYPICAL

MAKE FROM ½" X 20"
PLYWOOD SQUARE
CUT DIAGONALLY

ALL LUMBER PRESSURE-TREATED
PAINT WHITE

MATERIALS LIST

Item	Quantity
2X2 pressure-treated lumber	19 ft.
½" exterior plywood, 20" square	1
No. 10 X 3" flathead wood screws	10
No. 10 X 1¾" flathead wood screws	16
Resorcinol glue	as needed
Waterproof wood filler	as needed
Exterior latex enamel	1 qt.

49

CHILDREN'S LAWN FURNITURE

The world is an oversized place for children. They have to climb up to use almost all furniture, and outdoor furniture is no exception. If there are children in your family, why not build this three-piece set of lawn furniture?

The sling chair, chaise, and table are sized to fit children age six to ten. All-hardwood construction and replaceable slings guarantee that the furniture will last for years.

Begin construction of all three pieces by ripping $\frac{3}{4}$-in.-thick birch lumber to a width of $1\frac{3}{4}$ in. All major components are this wide.

Begin construction of the sling chair by cutting the $1\frac{3}{4}$-in. stock to the lengths shown in the diagram. Lay out the locations of the notches in the components, measuring carefully for accuracy.

Set up a dado blade on your radial

Each of the three pieces of children's outdoor furniture is scaled for kids age six to ten. From lower left to lower right are the lounge, chair and table. Solid hardwood construction and replaceable slings insure sturdiness and long life.

arm saw and cut the notches with multiple passes. Check your setup on scrap material before working on the chair materials.

Next, lay out and bore the holes for the dowel frame member as shown in the diagram. Cut the bevels on the lower ends of the legs with your radial arm saw, and then form the rounded notches in the lower ends of the back braces.

Use a saber saw to cut the rounded profiles shown in the diagram. Then lay out and bore the $\frac{3}{8}$-in. pivot holes using a drill press or a drill guide.

Assemble the components using waterproof resorcinol glue and no. 8 X $1\frac{1}{2}$-in. brass flathead wood screws. Bore pilot holes for the screws. Do not glue the crossbars that hold the canvas sling.

Insert the $\frac{3}{4}$-in.-dia. dowel brace in position, and then drill $\frac{1}{4}$-in.-dia. holes for the locking pins.

Use a $\frac{1}{4}$-in.-radius rounding-over bit, with pilot, in your router to round off all exposed edges of the the chair. Sand the completed frames carefully, working down to 150-grit garnet paper.

Apply a coat of enamel primer to the frames, followed by two coats of exterior enamel. Spraying the finish will give you the best results.

Lay out the pattern of the sling on colorful, heavyweight canvas. Cut the canvas, then double-stitch the hems and seams. Any upholstery shop will do this job for a nominal fee.

CONSTRUCTION DETAILS

1. When cutting notches in frame members, clamp matching pieces together. Cut notches at the same time.

2. Both the slat table and the sling chair have dowel stretchers held in place with glued dowel pins.

5. Leave the sling braces unglued to allow them to be slipped through the loops of the canvas sling.

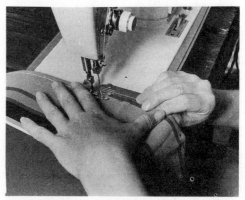

6. Use heavy-duty thread to stitch the side hems of the slings. A ball-point needle does the best job.

9. Clamp stop blocks to the fence of your radial arm saw to make identical cuts on all the table slats.

10. Measure carefully before cutting the notches on the table's top brace. Use a sharp dado blade.

3. *Round over the edges on each frame member with a ¼-in.-radius rounding-over bit. A router table helps.*

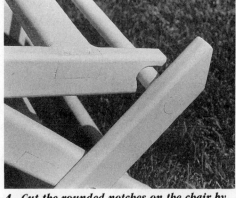

4. *Cut the rounded notches on the chair by boring ¾-in. holes, then cut away the waste with a saber saw.*

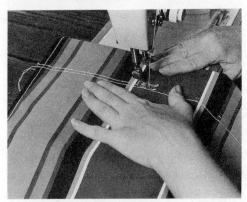

7. *Double-stitch the loops on both ends of the slings. The added strength will help make the slings last.*

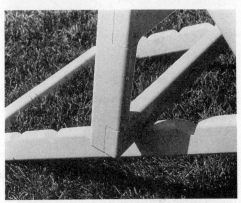

8. *Cut the notches for the chaise's back brace after making a trial assembly of the chaise. Each notch is different.*

11. *Attach ¾-in. spring clips, normally used as broom holders, to the underside of the table top.*

12. *The clips snap securely over the dowel braces on the table frame. To fold the table, just snap off the top.*

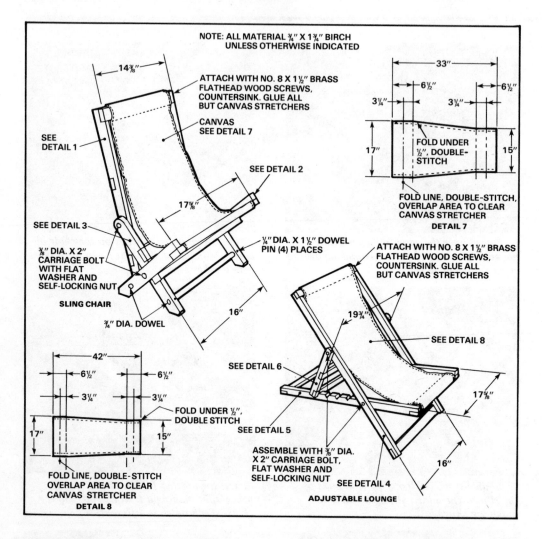

NOTE: ALL MATERIAL ¾" X 1¾" BIRCH
UNLESS OTHERWISE INDICATED

14⅜"

ATTACH WITH NO. 8 X 1½" BRASS
FLATHEAD WOOD SCREWS,
COUNTERSINK. GLUE ALL
BUT CANVAS STRETCHERS

CANVAS
SEE DETAIL 7

SEE
DETAIL 1

SEE DETAIL 2

17⅝"

SEE DETAIL 3

¾" DIA. X 2"
CARRIAGE BOLT
WITH FLAT
WASHER AND
SELF-LOCKING NUT

¼" DIA. X 1½" DOWEL
PIN (4) PLACES

SLING CHAIR

¾" DIA. DOWEL

16"

33"

6½"   6½"

3¼"   3¼"

17"   FOLD UNDER   15"
½", DOUBLE-
STITCH

FOLD LINE, DOUBLE-STITCH,
OVERLAP AREA TO CLEAR
CANVAS STRETCHER
DETAIL 7

ATTACH WITH NO. 8 X 1½" BRASS
FLATHEAD WOOD SCREWS,
COUNTERSINK. GLUE ALL
BUT CANVAS STRETCHERS

19¾"

SEE DETAIL 8

42"

6½"   6½"

3¼"   3¼"

FOLD UNDER ½",
DOUBLE STITCH

17"   15"

SEE DETAIL 6

SEE DETAIL 5

FOLD LINE, DOUBLE-STITCH
OVERLAP AREA TO CLEAR
CANVAS STRETCHER
DETAIL 8

17⅝"

ASSEMBLE WITH ⅜" DIA.
X 2" CARRIAGE BOLT,
FLAT WASHER AND
SELF-LOCKING NUT   SEE DETAIL 4

16"

ADJUSTABLE LOUNGE

Assemble the completed frames using ⅜-in. X 2-in. carriage bolts and self-locking nuts. Use washers under the nuts and between the frames.

Remove the braces that fit through the sling, slide them in place, and reattach the braces to the frame.

The construction steps for the chaise are identical, with one exception. After all the frames are constructed, but before painting, make a trial assembly of the complete unit.

Hold the back support in the positions of the notches, and mark the notches using a straightedge to establish the correct angles.

Disassemble the chaise and cut the notches with a saber saw or a band saw, then complete the chaise as you did the chair.

To build the table frames, follow the same basic procedures you used for the chair and the chaise.

To build the table top, cut the components, lay out the notches on one slat, and then use multiple

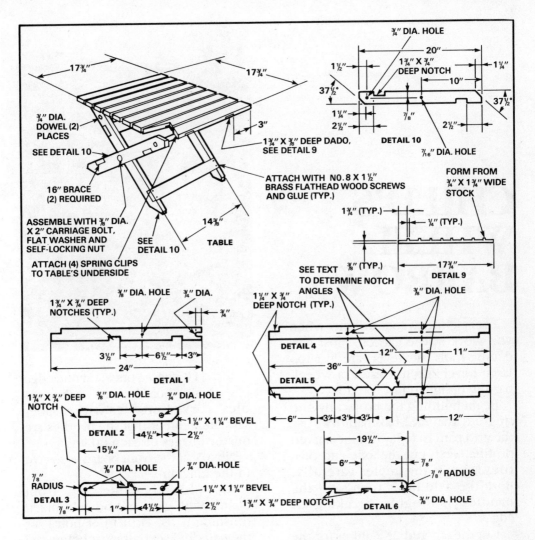

passes of a dado blade to form the notches. Since you will be cutting several identical slats, clamp stop blocks to the saw's fence to help make the notches uniform.

Cut the multiple notches in the braces with the dado blade as well. Lay these out carefully. Assemble the table top with no. 6 X ⅝-in. brass flathead wood screws after drilling countersunk pilot holes. Attach spring clips to the underside of the table top to mate with the dowels in the frame.

MATERIALS LIST

Item	Quantity
1X8 birch lumber	32 ft.
¼"-dia. birch dowel	6 ft.
¼" X 1½" dowel pins	as needed
44"-wide heavy canvas	1½ yds.
¾" spring clips	4
⅜" X 2" carriage bolts with flat washers and self-locking nuts	10
No. 8 X 1½" brass flathead wood screws	as needed
No. 6 X ⅝" brass flathead wood screws	as needed
Resorcinol glue	as needed
Enamel primer and exterior enamel	as needed

CHILD'S WHEEL-BARROW

Every child wants to help when you work in the garden. Most gardening tools, however, are just too large for children. Here is a wheelbarrow designed just for kids.

Begin building the project by cutting out the 2X2 oak handles. Use the grid pattern to lay out the curved profile. Next, cut the axle end profile. Lay out the angles carefully. Bore the axle hole, then sand the handles thoroughly, breaking all edges.

Cut the tapered 2X2 shims for the bed of the wheelbarrow, then attach the shims to the handles with resorcinol glue and no. 8 X 1½-in. brass flathead wood screws.

Install the wheel as shown in the diagram, then center the 15-in.-long floor boards over the handles and attach them with 4d galvanized finishing nails and resorcinol glue. Bore pilot holes for the nails, and set the nails below the surface of the wood.

Lay out the 5 degree angle on the floor boards, then cut with a circular saw set at a 10 degree bevel.

Rip a 10 degree bevel on one edge of each side board, then cut the handles' curved profiles with a saber saw. Remember that the handles are mirror images of each other.

Next, cut the front board as shown in the diagram.

Assemble the side and front boards with glue and 6d galvanized finishing nails. Drill pilot holes for the nails and set them just below the surface.

Attach the box to the floor of the wheelbarrow with nails and glue, then sand the completed wooden assembly after removing the wheel. Finish the wheelbarrow with clear wood sealer.

While the finish is drying, make the legs from ⅛-in. X 1-in. mild steel flat bar. Drill ¼-in. mounting holes in the legs, then finish them with black spray enamel. After they are dry, attach them to the handles with ¼-in. X 1-in. lag screws.

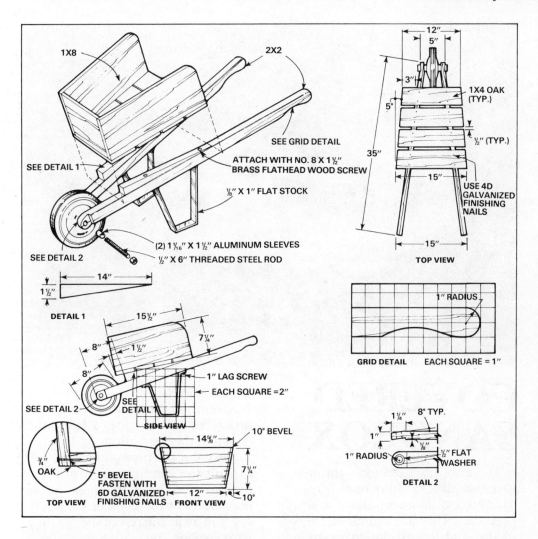

1X8

2X2

SEE GRID DETAIL

ATTACH WITH NO. 8 X 1½"
BRASS FLATHEAD WOOD SCREW

SEE DETAIL 1

⅛" X 1" FLAT STOCK

SEE DETAIL 2

(2) 1 ¹⁄₁₆" X 1 ½" ALUMINUM SLEEVES
½" X 6" THREADED STEEL ROD

1X4 OAK
(TYP.)

12"
5"
3"
5"
35"
15"
15"

USE 4D
GALVANIZED
FINISHING
NAILS

½" (TYP.)

TOP VIEW

14"
1½"

DETAIL 1

1" RADIUS

GRID DETAIL   EACH SQUARE = 1"

15½"
8"
1½"
7¼"
8"

1" LAG SCREW

EACH SQUARE =2"

SEE DETAIL 2

SEE
DETAIL 1

SIDE VIEW

¾"
OAK

5° BEVEL
FASTEN WITH
6D GALVANIZED
FINISHING NAILS

TOP VIEW

14⅝"
10° BEVEL
7¼"
12"
10°

FRONT VIEW

1¼"
1"
8° TYP.
⅛"
½" FLAT
WASHER

1" RADIUS

DETAIL 2

CONSTRUCTION DETAILS

*1. Bend the legs, as shown in the diagram,
in a vise. Be sure to make both legs
identical. Paint the legs black.*

MATERIALS LIST

Item	Quantity
1X8 oak	4 ft.
1X4 oak	5 ft.
2X2 oak	7 ft.
8"-dia. wheel	1
⅛" X 1" steel flat bar	6 ft.
1¹⁄₁₆" X 1½" aluminum sleeves	2
½" X 6" threaded rod with (2) washers and (2) nuts	1
¼" X 1" lag screws	4
No. 8 X 1½" brass wood screws	4
4d, 6d galv. finishing nails	as needed
Clear wood sealer and black spray enamel	as needed

COVERED SANDBOX

There is no question: children love to play in sandboxes. Open sandboxes, however, have a few problems. They are natural catchers of dirt and leaves, not to mention even more unpleasant things. This covered sandbox solves the problems.

Start construction by cutting the frame components to the lengths indicated in the diagram. Assemble with waterproof resorcinol glue and 16d galvanized finishing nails. Square the assembly by measuring the diagonals and adjusting until they are equal.

Next, cut out the 2X6 rails. Miter the corners as shown in the diagram. Drill ⅜-in.-dia. holes, 1⅝ in. deep, for the dowels.

Assemble the rails with waterproof resorcinol glue. Clamp the rails together and allow to dry.

Next, cut the plywood for the lid. Lay out the handle as shown in the diagram. Use a 1½-in. spade bit to bore holes at the ends of the opening. Cut away the rest of the opening with a saber saw.

Glue and nail the lid to the 2X2 cleats using 3d galvanized finishing nails.

Attach the rails to the sandbox with 12d galvanized finishing nails and glue.

Sand the assembled project well, and apply a coat of redwood stain, followed by two coats of wood sealer.

Once the sandbox is in position, put a 2-in. layer of gravel in the bottom, followed by a 6-in. layer of clean sand.

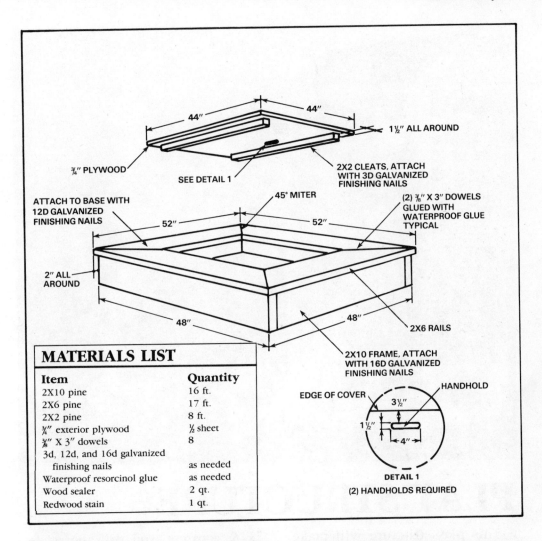

44"   44"

1½" ALL AROUND

¾" PLYWOOD

SEE DETAIL 1

2X2 CLEATS, ATTACH WITH 3D GALVANIZED FINISHING NAILS

ATTACH TO BASE WITH 12D GALVANIZED FINISHING NAILS

45° MITER

(2) ⅜" X 3" DOWELS GLUED WITH WATERPROOF GLUE TYPICAL

52"   52"

2" ALL AROUND

48"   48"

2X6 RAILS

2X10 FRAME, ATTACH WITH 16D GALVANIZED FINISHING NAILS

MATERIALS LIST

Item	Quantity
2X10 pine	16 ft.
2X6 pine	17 ft.
2X2 pine	8 ft.
¾" exterior plywood	½ sheet
⅜" X 3" dowels	8
3d, 12d, and 16d galvanized finishing nails	as needed
Waterproof resorcinol glue	as needed
Wood sealer	2 qt.
Redwood stain	1 qt.

EDGE OF COVER   HANDHOLD

3½"

1½"

4"

DETAIL 1

(2) HANDHOLDS REQUIRED

CONSTRUCTION DETAILS

1. Attach the rail components together with waterproof glue and dowels.

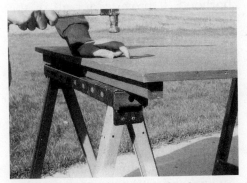

2. Attach the plywood top to the cleats with nails and waterproof resorcinol glue.

PLAY STRUCTURE

This play structure will make your children the envy of the neighborhood. It provides for all of the activities children enjoy the most. They can climb up into the building using a ladder, and a slide adds to the fun when they are ready to leave. The building can be a fort, a treehouse, or anything else their active minds can imagine.

Below the playhouse itself, a sandbox, covered when not in use, is an ideal spot for building castles. Swings and a trapeze provide additional possibilities for creative play.

As a parent, you will appreciate the pull-up ladder, which allows you to control access to the upper level. This safety feature will help keep younger children on the ground and out of danger when you're not there to supervise.

Start building the structure by laying out the positions of the posts on a level site in your yard. Drive stakes at the locations, using the dimensions shown in the diagram. Set all of the stakes at the same height above the ground, checking them with a level.

Now, run a string line around the perimeter of the layout and check it for squareness by measuring the diagonals. When the measurements are equal, the layout is correct. Make any necessary adjustments to the layout before proceeding.

Once you are satisfied with the layout, dig 12-in.-dia. X 36-in.-deep holes at each post location. Use a clam-shell posthole digger, and center the holes around the stake positions.

Fill the holes with concrete. Mix bagged concrete mix in a wheelbarrow. Mix the dry ingredients well, then add just enough water to reach a stiff consistency.

When the holes are filled, smooth the piers to make the tops flat and level. Allow the concrete to cure for several days before continuing.

Next, install galvanized steel post brackets. Place the brackets on the piers, then check the layout once more for squareness and the correct dimensions. Nail the brackets to the concrete with specially-hardened concrete nails. When working with hardened nails, wear eye protection.

Cut two 4X4 posts for the outer beam support. Cut a third 4X4 to form the beam. Assemble the beam and posts with $\frac{3}{8}$-in. X 4-in. lag screws. Using a 1-in.-dia. bit, counterbore the pilot holes 1 in. deep to locate the screw heads below the surface of the wood.

After the beam is attached, cut 1-in. dowel plugs to fill the holes, then glue them in place with resorcinol glue. Next, cut two diagonal braces from 4X4 stock. Miter the ends of the braces at a 45 degree angle. Attach the diagonal braces using 16d galvanized nails.

Position the post and beam assembly in the post brackets and secure it with 8d joist hanger nails. Check the assembly with a level to make it perfectly vertical in both directions.

Prepare the 11-ft.-long main posts next. Measure 6 ft. from the bottom of each post and lay out the double notches for the beams, as shown in Detail 5. Make 1-in.-deep X 3½-in.-wide notches on two sides of the post. Check the orientation of the notches carefully; they should match the individual post positions.

Form the notches with multiple passes on your radial arm saw. Make saw kerfs every ¼ in., then remove the waste with a sharp chisel. Take care to make the notches match on all of the posts.

Erect the posts on the concrete piers. Nail temporary angled braces in place to hold the posts vertical while you continue with construction. Fasten the posts to the brackets with 8d joist hanger nails, as you did before. Be extra cautious from this point on. Unsupervised children may attempt to move the posts when playing. This is dangerous. Check the bracing to make sure that the structure is safe to walk on. Allow a full day to errect and brace the structure securely.

Now, cut the 4X4 beams to length. Form notches in two of the beams to allow them to fit together as shown in Detail 5. Install the beams in the notches, fastening them with $\frac{3}{8}$-in. X 4-in. lag screws and washers. Counterbore the pilot holes ½ in. deep.

As you build, check the posts and beams frequently with a level to keep the assembly true. Once the beams are in place, cut and install

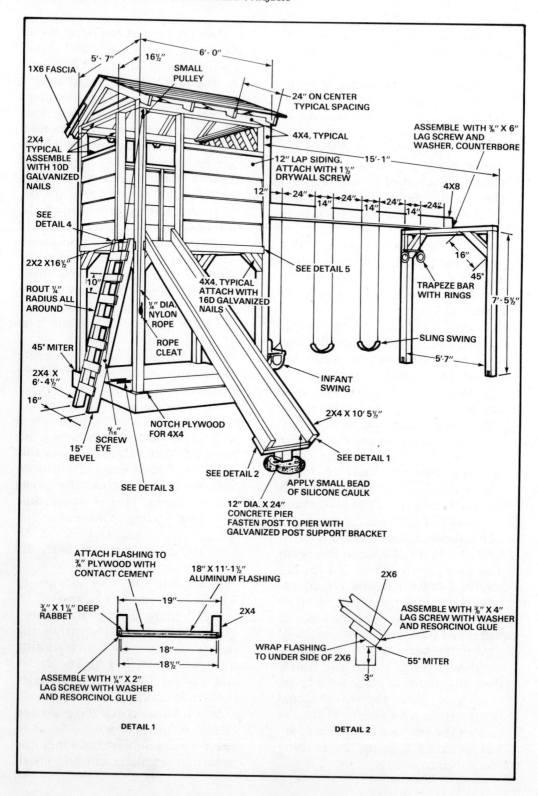

1X6 FASCIA

2X4 TYPICAL ASSEMBLE WITH 10D GALVANIZED NAILS

SEE DETAIL 4

2X2 X16½"

ROUT ¼" RADIUS ALL AROUND

45° MITER

2X4 X 6'-4½"

16"

15° BEVEL

⁵⁄₁₆" SCREW EYE

SEE DETAIL 3

SEE DETAIL 2

NOTCH PLYWOOD FOR 4X4

5'-7"   16½"   6'-0"

SMALL PULLEY

24" ON CENTER TYPICAL SPACING

4X4, TYPICAL

12" LAP SIDING, ATTACH WITH 1½" DRYWALL SCREW

12"   24"   14"   24"   14"   24"   14"   24"

15'-1"

4X8

ASSEMBLE WITH ⅜" X 6" LAG SCREW AND WASHER, COUNTERBORE

SEE DETAIL 5

¼" DIA. NYLON ROPE

ROPE CLEAT

4X4, TYPICAL ATTACH WITH 16D GALVANIZED NAILS

16"

TRAPEZE BAR WITH RINGS

45°

SLING SWING

5'-7"

7'-5½"

INFANT SWING

2X4 X 10' 5½"

SEE DETAIL 1

APPLY SMALL BEAD OF SILICONE CAULK

12" DIA. X 24" CONCRETE PIER FASTEN POST TO PIER WITH GALVANIZED POST SUPPORT BRACKET

ATTACH FLASHING TO ¾" PLYWOOD WITH CONTACT CEMENT

18" X 11'-1½" ALUMINUM FLASHING

¾" X 1¼" DEEP RABBET

19"

2X4

18"

18½"

ASSEMBLE WITH ¼" X 2" LAG SCREW WITH WASHER AND RESORCINOL GLUE

DETAIL 1

2X6

ASSEMBLE WITH ⅜" X 4" LAG SCREW WITH WASHER AND RESORCINOL GLUE

WRAP FLASHING TO UNDER SIDE OF 2X6

55° MITER

3"

DETAIL 2

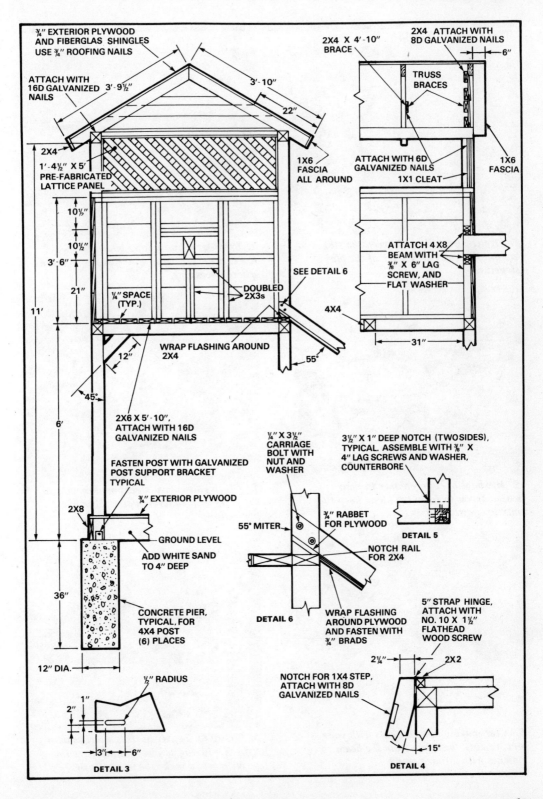

¾" EXTERIOR PLYWOOD
AND FIBERGLAS SHINGLES
USE ¾" ROOFING NAILS

ATTACH WITH
16D GALVANIZED
NAILS

3'-9½"

3'-10"

22"

2X4 X 4'-10"
BRACE

2X4 ATTACH WITH
8D GALVANIZED NAILS

6"

TRUSS
BRACES

2X4

1'-4½" X 5'
PRE-FABRICATED
LATTICE PANEL

1X6
FASCIA
ALL AROUND

ATTACH WITH 6D
GALVANIZED NAILS

1X6
FASCIA

1X1 CLEAT

10½"

10½"

3'-6"

DOUBLED
2X3s

SEE DETAIL 6

ATTATCH 4 X8
BEAM WITH
⅜" X 6" LAG
SCREW, AND
FLAT WASHER

21"

¼" SPACE
(TYP.)

11'

WRAP FLASHING AROUND
2X4

4X4

31"

12"

55°

45°

2X6 X 5'-10",
ATTACH WITH 16D
GALVANIZED NAILS

6'

¼" X 3½"
CARRIAGE
BOLT WITH
NUT AND
WASHER

3½" X 1" DEEP NOTCH (TWO SIDES),
TYPICAL. ASSEMBLE WITH ⅜" X
4" LAG SCREWS AND WASHER,
COUNTERBORE

FASTEN POST WITH GALVANIZED
POST SUPPORT BRACKET
TYPICAL

¾" EXTERIOR PLYWOOD

2X8

GROUND LEVEL

ADD WHITE SAND
TO 4" DEEP

55° MITER

¾" RABBET
FOR PLYWOOD

NOTCH RAIL
FOR 2X4

DETAIL 5

5" STRAP HINGE,
ATTACH WITH
NO. 10 X 1½"
FLATHEAD
WOOD SCREW

36"

CONCRETE PIER,
TYPICAL, FOR
4X4 POST
(6) PLACES

DETAIL 6

WRAP FLASHING
AROUND PLYWOOD
AND FASTEN WITH
¾" BRADS

2¼"

2X2

12" DIA.

½" RADIUS

1"

2"

3"

6"

DETAIL 3

NOTCH FOR 1X4 STEP,
ATTACH WITH 8D
GALVANIZED NAILS

15°

DETAIL 4

63

CONSTRUCTION DETAILS

1. Stretch string lines between the stakes to lay out the outer perimeter of the play structure.

2. Use a level and a long board to check the evenness of your site. Make corrections where necessary.

3. Mix bags of concrete mix in your wheelbarrow to form the piers. Keep the mixture fairly stiff.

4. Attach galvanized steel post brackets to the piers with concrete nails. Wear eye protection.

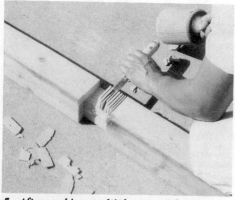

5. After making multiple cuts with your saw, remove the waste from the beam notches with a sharp chisel.

6. Secure the beams in their notches with ⅜-in. X 4-in. lag screws. Counterbore the screw holes to make the heads flush.

the 4X4 diagonal braces. Nail the braces in position with 16d galvanized nails.

Place a temporary floor of planks on the beams to make a safe work surface. Secure the planks with double-headed nails. Cut two 4X4 beams to fit the top of the posts. Take these up and fasten them to the posts with lag screws.

Cut 2X4 joists to fit between the upper beams on both ends of the

building. Nail them in place with 10d galvanized nails. Add the two door frame members, nailing them to the joists and to the floor beams.

Frame in the window openings next with 2X4s. Measure carefully to locate all of the components at the same height. Secure the parts with 10d galvanized nails, toenailing where necessary.

Add 2X3 framing to the openings, making the inside edge of the frame members flush with the inside of the other components. This allows for installation of the lap siding.

Pay special attention to the framing on the end of the building, facing the outer beam support. Measure accurately to make the swing support beam level. Space the 2X3 vertical members 24 in. on center, nailing them in place with 10d galvanized nails.

Cut a 4X8 beam 15 ft., 1 in. long. Position it, with help, on the outer support and the framing. Secure the beam with $3/8$-in. X 6-in. lag screws on both ends. Check the top of the beam with a level, and make any needed adjustments to the support framing.

Now, cut the 2X6 floor boards to the length shown in the diagram. Lay these in place, spacing them $1/4$ in. apart. Notch the floor boards to fit around the framing materials, then nail them to the beams with 16d galvanized nails.

Build the roof trusses next. Lay out the peak angle on one end of each rafter with a protractor. Cut the rafter with your circular saw, following the marked line carefully. Cut the other end square to make the rafter fit the dimensions given in the diagram.

MATERIALS LIST

Item	Quantity
4X8 lumber	16 ft.
4X4 lumber	96 ft.
2X8 lumber	25 ft.
2X6 lumber	650 ft.
2X4 lumber	120 ft.
2X3 lumber	70 ft.
2X2 lumber	2 ft.
1X6 lumber	38 ft.
1X4 lumber	10 ft.
1X1 lumber	36 ft.
¾″ exterior plywood	3 sheets
12″ Waferwood lap siding	80 ft.
Pre-fabricated redwood lattice	18″ X 60″
Fiberglas shingles	2 bundles
Roof felt	¼ roll
6d, 8d, 10d, 12d, 16d galvanized nails	as needed
4X4 galvanized post brackets	7
8d joist hanger nails	as needed
¾″ roofing nails	as needed
¾″ X 6″ lag screws, flat washers	6
¾″ X 4″ lag screws, flat washers	20
½″ X 2″ lag screws, flat washers	36
¼″ X 3½″ carriage bolts, flat washers, and nuts	4 each
No. 12 X 3½″ flathead wood screws	as needed
No. 10 X 1½″ flathead wood screws	12
1½″ drywall screws	as needed
5″ strap hinges	2
⁵⁄₁₆″ screw eye	1
Pulley and cleat bracket	1 each
¼″-dia. nylon rope	25 ft.
Resorcinol glue, contact cement	as needed
16-gauge X 18″ aluminum	12 ft.
100-lb. concrete bags	7
Silicone caulk	1 tube
Latex house paint	as needed

CONSTRUCTION DETAILS

7. The beams for the platform fit together with interlocking notches. Measure carefully for a tight fit.

8. Build the wall framing with 2X3 stock to allow for the siding. Space the studs 24-in. on center.

9. Cut the rabbets on the sides of the slide with two, intersecting cuts on your table saw.

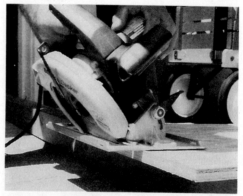

10. Cut a 45-degree bevel on the end of the slide's bottom with your circular saw. Keep the cut straight.

11. Cement the slide's sheet metal with contact cement. Carefully follow the manufacturer's application tips.

12. Cut the notches on the ladder rails with a dado blade. For accuracy cut both rails at once.

Cut the 2X4 cross braces next. Use a framing square to help you position the cross-brace stock on a pair of rafters, as shown in the photograph. When the alignment is correct, mark the brace and cut it with your circular saw. Use this brace as a pattern to lay out the remaining three braces.

Assemble one truss, securing the joints with 10d galvanized nails. Check the alignment of the parts with a framing square as you work. Once this truss is complete, assemble the other three on top of the first truss to help make them identical.

Take one truss to the top of the structure, and place it in position on one end. Center it over the beams, then mark the locations and angles for the notches. Use a straightedge to help draw the notch lines.

With the truss back on the ground, cut the notches with your saber saw. Follow the lines carefully. Once you have cut the notches on the first truss, use them as patterns for the other three.

Secure the trusses to the beams with 16d galvanized nails. Toenail the trusses to the beam from both sides, checking the assembly to keep it vertical. Space the trusses 24 in. on center.

Once all four trusses are in place, cut 3/4-in. plywood sheathing to fit. Allow the plywood to overhang the ends of the playhouse by 6 in. Nail the sheathing in place with 8d galvanized nails spaced 4 in. apart.

Complete the roof by applying roof felt and Fiberglas shingles according to the manufacturer's directions. Use 3/4-in. roofing nails to keep the nail points from penetrating the roofing.

Finish the exterior of the playhouse with 12-in.-wide Waferwood lap siding. Attach the siding to the 2X3 framing with 1½-in. drywall screws. Use a good ladder, positioned properly, when installing the siding. Also, install the fascia.

Finally, cut a 16½-in. X 60-in. rectangle of pre-fabricated lattice panel to fit the opening at one end of the building. Install this, holding it in place on both sides with a frame of 1X1 material.

You can finish the interior of the building with any type of material you choose. If you like, leave the inside unfinished, allowing the framing to show.

Build the ladder unit next. Cut two rails, beveling the ends at the angles shown in the diagram. Place the rails together, then measure 10 in. up from the bottom and mark this position. Continue marking the rung positions, spacing them 10 in. apart. Measure down 3½ in. from each previous mark to complete the layout.

Cut notches for the rungs, 3/4 in. deep, between your layout lines. Use a dado blade in your radial arm saw to form the notches. Make multiple passes with the blade. For maximum accuracy, clamp the rails together and form both sets of notches at once.

Cut the rungs from 1X4 stock and assemble the stair unit with 8d galvanized nails. Check the assembly with a framing square as you work. Once all of the rungs are in place, add a 14½-in.-long 2X2 filler to the top of the deck (see Detail 4 of the diagram).

Use a ¼-in.-radius rounding-over bit, with pilot, in your router to

CONSTRUCTION DETAILS

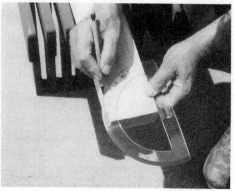

13. Lay out the angles on the ends of the ladder and slide rails with a protractor. Make sure both sides match.

14. Check the alignment of the truss brace with a framing square. Accuracy is critical here.

15. Toenail the trusses in place from both sides with 16d galvanized nails. Keep the trusses vertical.

16. Install the structure's plywood roof and 1X6 fascia. Make sure your ladder is well secured.

17. Apply roof felt and install the Fiberglas roofing. Use the lines on the felt to align the shingles.

18. Attach the ladder to the floor of the structure with 5-in. strap hinges and no. 10 X 1½-in. flathead wood screws.

round off all the edges of the ladder. This step helps prevent splinters from forming.

Lean the completed ladder against the doorway, with its top flush with the flooring material. Secure the ladder in place with two 5-in. strap hinges and no. 10 X 1½-in. flathead wood screws.

Attach the pulley, screw eye, and cleat as shown in the diagram. Position the cleat bracket high enough to prevent small children from reaching it. Add the ¼-in.-dia. nylon rope and check to make sure the ladder swings freely.

Build the slide next. Cut the side rails to the length shown in the diagram. Cut the upper ends at a 55 degree angle. Form the rabbets for the plywood floor of the slide by making two intersecting cuts in the rails on your table saw. Set up the saw accurately to form the rabbets at the correct dimension.

Now, cut the plywood floor and the aluminum flashing material to the sizes shown in the diagram. Attach the flashing to the plywood with contact cement. Coat both surfaces with cement, then allow them to dry. Carefully position one edge of the flashing, then lower it onto the prepared plywood. Allow the flashing to extend past both ends of the plywood. Apply firm pressure to the flashing to form a tight bond.

Attach the rails to the slide with ¼-in. X 2-in. lag screws, flat washers, and resorcinol glue. Space the screws 4 in. apart for maximum strength. Next, add the 2X6 bottom brace to the unit. Secure it to the rails with ⅜-in. X 4-in. lag screws. Counterbore the pilot holes to make them flush with the wood's surface.

Wrap the aluminum flashing around the slide's top and bottom and secure with brads. Add the short 4X4 block to the 2X6 that will support the bottom end of the slide (slide support). Now, round over the edges of the rails with your router and sand the wood smooth.

Place the slide temporarily in position and determine the slide support location. Remove the slide. Dig the pier hole and pour the concrete. Install a 4X4 galvanized post bracket and secure the slide support.

Attach the slide to the opening in the building using ¼-in. X 3½-in. carriage bolts with nuts and washers where it contacts the 2X4 framing. Secure the slide to the slide support with lag screws. In both cases, counterbore the pilot holes to set the screw heads below the surface.

Build the sandbox as the last step in construction. Cut 2X8 lumber with mitered corners to form the outer frame of the box. Fasten them to the posts with 16d galvanized nails. Cut two pieces of ¾-in. plywood to form the lid of the sandbox. Notch the plywood to fit around the posts, then cut hand openings in the lid halves as shown in the diagram.

Once construction is complete, inspect the entire unit thoroughly. Sand any rough surfaces, and round over all sharp edges and corners. Once you are satisfied, paint the unit with high-quality latex house paint in the color of your choice.

Finish up by installing heavy-duty screw eyes to hold the chains for the swings. Add a 4-in. layer of clean, white sand to the sandbox, and you are ready to turn the play structure over to your children.

PONY SWING

Every child loves horses and swings. Combine the two by building this glider swing and watch your children's eyes light up.

Start by laying out the profile of the head on graph paper. Copy the design shown in the diagram, then use carbon paper to trace it onto oak stock. Cut out the pattern with a band saw.

If you can find an oak board 12 in. wide, you can make the head out of a single piece. Otherwise, edge-glue narrower boards to make the head.

Cut the remaining components to the sizes shown in the diagram, then round all edges with a $\frac{1}{4}$-in.-radius bit, with pilot, in your router.

Lay out the dowel holes in the components, then bore these with a spade or Forstner bit. Use a drill press for accuracy and a backup board to prevent splintering.

Bore the $\frac{5}{16}$-in.-dia. holes in the dowels on your drill press as well. Use a V-block (V-groove cut into block) to help align the holes.

Assemble the glider, beginning with the head. Attach the head with no. 10 X 3-in. brass flathead wood screws and resorcinol glue. Bore countersunk pilot holes with a combination bit.

Assemble the dowel joints next. Secure each dowel with $\frac{1}{4}$-in. dowel pins and glue, as shown in the diagram. At the pivot points, use flat washers between the wood parts for smooth action.

Attach each seat to the completed swing with glue and three no. 10 X 2-in. brass flathead wood screws.

Sand the completed horse thoroughly, then finish with either clear wood sealer or polyurethane varnish.

Screw a large screw eye into a suitable beam or tree limb, then hang the glider with $\frac{1}{4}$-in. nylon rope. Use washers between the knots and the dowel.

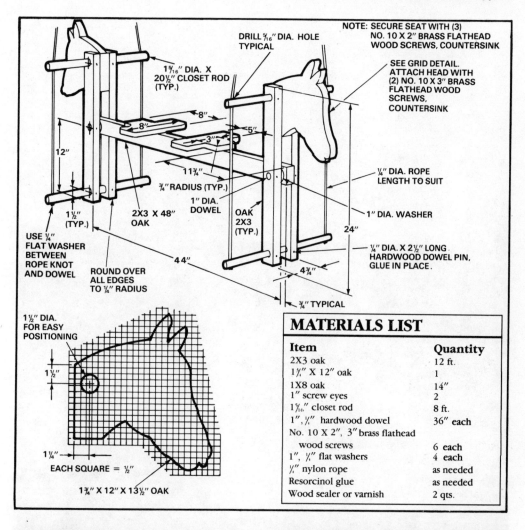

DRILL ⁵⁄₁₆" DIA. HOLE TYPICAL

NOTE: SECURE SEAT WITH (3) NO. 10 X 2" BRASS FLATHEAD WOOD SCREWS, COUNTERSINK

SEE GRID DETAIL. ATTACH HEAD WITH (2) NO. 10 X 3" BRASS FLATHEAD WOOD SCREWS, COUNTERSINK

1⁵⁄₁₆" DIA. X 20½" CLOSET ROD (TYP.)

8"

8"

5"

3"

12"

11¾"

¾" RADIUS (TYP.)

1" DIA. DOWEL

OAK 2X3 (TYP.)

¼" DIA. ROPE LENGTH TO SUIT

2X3 X 48" OAK

1½" (TYP.)

USE ¼" FLAT WASHER BETWEEN ROPE KNOT AND DOWEL

ROUND OVER ALL EDGES TO ¼" RADIUS

44"

24"

1" DIA. WASHER

¼" DIA. X 2½" LONG HARDWOOD DOWEL PIN, GLUE IN PLACE.

4¾"

¾" TYPICAL

1½" DIA. FOR EASY POSITIONING

1½"

1¼"

EACH SQUARE = ½"

1¾" X 12" X 13½" OAK

MATERIALS LIST

Item	Quantity
2X3 oak	12 ft.
1¾" X 12" oak	1
1X8 oak	14"
1" screw eyes	2
1⁵⁄₁₆" closet rod	8 ft.
1", ¼" hardwood dowel	36" each
No. 10 X 2", 3" brass flathead wood screws	6 each
1", ¼" flat washers	4 each
¼" nylon rope	as needed
Resorcinol glue	as needed
Wood sealer or varnish	2 qts.

CONSTRUCTION DETAILS

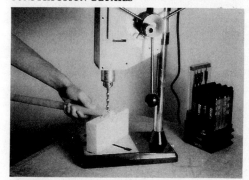

1. Drill ⁵⁄₁₆-in. holes for the glider's rope on your drill press. Use a V-block to help align the holes.

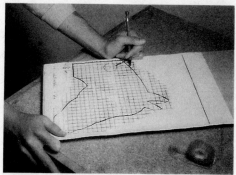

2. Draw the horse pattern on ½-in. graph paper, then transfer the pattern to the wood with carbon paper.

71

SHADED SANDBOX

Every toddler needs a sandbox to play in. Children's imaginations can create ships and forts out of the sand, and they can spend hours pretending to be almost anything at all.

This sandbox is sure to become the envy of all the children in your neighborhood. Covered to provide shelter from the sun, its sturdy construction and pleasing lines will make it a favorite play area. The high sides help keep sand inside, while the seats along the sides of the box are designed to be just the right height for small children.

Build the project using any wood you choose. Avoid pressure-treated lumber, however. The chemicals used to preserve the wood are toxic, and children love to chew on things. Redwood, with its high resistance to decay, is an excellent choice for this project. Pine or fir can be used as an alternative.

Start building the sandbox by cutting the 2X10 base components to the lengths shown in the diagram. Lay out the angled lines on the end boards, following the dimensions provided. Mark the end points of the angles, then draw pencil lines to guide your saw.

Cut the angles with a circular saw. If you choose, clamp a guide to the boards to help keep the cut straight. You can also cut the angles on a radial arm saw or table saw. Use an adjustable bevel to match the marked angle, then transfer the angle to the saw.

Assemble the sides and ends of the base with no. 10 X 2½-in. flathead wood screws. For maximum corrosion resistance, choose brass screws. Bore pilot holes for the screws with a combination pilot bit and countersink to make the screw heads flush with the surface of the wood.

For an even cleaner appearance, you can counterbore the holes ⅜ in. deep to accommodate wood screw hole plugs. Glue the plugs in place with waterproof resorcinol glue, leaving the plugs standing slightly above the surface of the wood.

As you assemble the base, check it for squareness with a framing square. As an alternative, measure the diagonals of the base. If they are equal, the assembly is perfectly square. Make any necessary adjustments before tightening the screws.

Prepare the seat boards by cutting a 1-in.-radius on the outside corners. Use a circle template to lay out the curves, then cut these profiles with a saber saw, taking care to keep the blade vertical in the cut.

Attach the seats to the base with no. 10 X 2½-in. screws, following the same procedure you used before. Notice that the inner edge of the seats are flush with the inside of the sides. This establishes the small overhang shown in the diagram. Space the screws 6 in. apart.

Next, begin building the curved

roof of the sandbox. Cut two 45-in.-long pieces of 2X6 lumber to form the sides of the roof. Mark the center on the edge of one workpiece to help you lay out the curved profile.

Make a simple bar compass from a 10-ft. length of 1X2. Near one end, drive a nail through the board to serve as a pivot point. Measure 9 ft. from the nail, then drill a hole to accept a pencil. Both the nail and the pencil should be located on the center line of the 1X2 stock.

Place one of the roof sides on a flat surface such as a driveway or patio, then place a piece of scrap lumber the same thickness as the side about 9 ft. away. Drive the nail in the compass lightly into this pivot block. The bar must be able to move freely.

Position the pencil end of the compass so it just touches the outside of the center line on the roof's side. Adjust the pivot block to make the compass bar perpendicular to the workpiece. Use a framing square to check the adjustment.

Now, have a helper hold the pivot block stationary while you mark the arc on the 2X6 stock. Be careful not to shift the workpiece as you mark the profile. Check your layout by measuring the marked width on both ends of the part; they should be equal.

Once the outline is correct, cut the arc with a coarse blade in your saber saw. Cut slowly, and keep the blade vertical in the cut by avoiding side pressure on the saw. Small amounts of unevenness can be removed later, but aim for a smooth, accurate curve.

Use this cut part as a template to lay out the second side of the roof. Cut the second piece, then clamp

the two together and even up the profiles with a belt sander. Use a coarse belt to level the parts, then finish up with a medium-grit belt. Be careful not to remove too much material at the ends of the roof's sides.

Form a 15 degree bevel on one edge of two 32-in.-long 1X4s to form the ends of the roof. The short side of the cut boards should be 3 in. wide after ripping. Use a bench plane for this job, and work carefully to maintain the proper angle.

Assemble the roof frame with countersunk screws, as you did before. Check the assembly for squareness, then use a medium-grit belt on your belt sander to even up the beveled ends to match the arc of the sides.

Cut a 32-in. X 50-in. piece of ¼-in. exterior grade plywood to form the roof of the sandbox. Nail one end of the plywood sheet to the end of the roof frame with 6d galvanized siding nails. The edge should be flush with the outside of the frame. Align the plywood carefully so the sides will be flush when the roof is nailed down.

Working from the nailed end, start bending the plywood to match

MATERIALS LIST

Item	Quantity
2X10 lumber	24 ft.
2X6 lumber	8 ft.
2X4 lumber	19 ft.
1X4 lumber	6 ft.
1X2 lumber	10 ft.
¼" X 48" X 50" exterior grade plywood	1
No. 10 X 2½" flathead wood screws	60
No. 8 X 2" flathead wood screws	8
6d galvanized siding nails	as needed
Exterior latex enamel	as needed
Sand	6½ cu. ft.

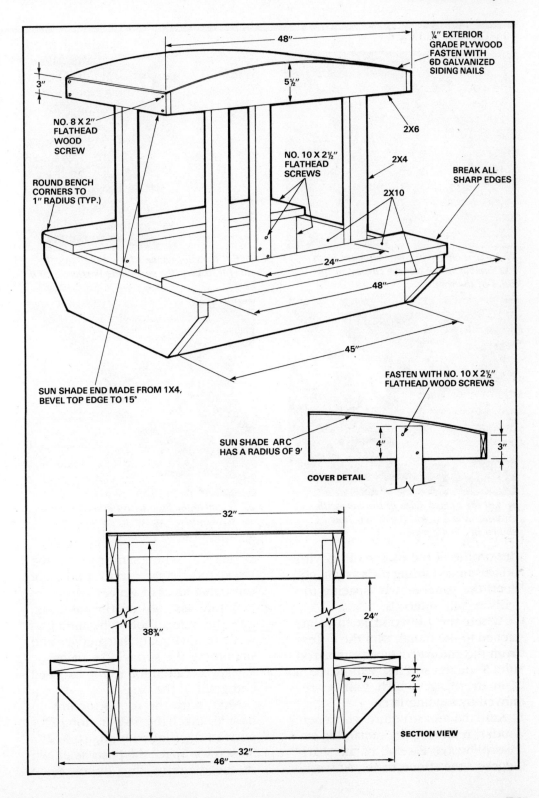

48"

3"

¼" EXTERIOR
GRADE PLYWOOD
FASTEN WITH
6D GALVANIZED
SIDING NAILS

5½"

2X6

NO. 8 X 2"
FLATHEAD
WOOD
SCREW

NO. 10 X 2½"
FLATHEAD
SCREWS

2X4

BREAK ALL
SHARP EDGES

ROUND BENCH
CORNERS TO
1" RADIUS (TYP.)

2X10

24"

48"

45"

SUN SHADE END MADE FROM 1X4,
BEVEL TOP EDGE TO 15°

FASTEN WITH NO. 10 X 2½"
FLATHEAD WOOD SCREWS

SUN SHADE ARC
HAS A RADIUS OF 9'

4"

3"

COVER DETAIL

32"

24"

38¾"

7"

2"

SECTION VIEW

32"

46"

75

CONSTRUCTION DETAILS

1. Make a temporary bar compass from 1X2 lumber to lay out the curves on the sides of the roof.

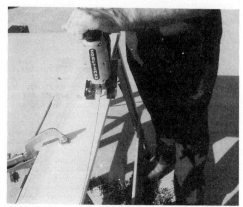

2. Cut the roof curve with a saber saw. Be careful to keep the saw blade vertical in the kerf.

5. Cut the angled sides of the base with a circular saw. Lay out the dimensions as shown in the diagram.

6. Assemble the base with flathead wood screws. Countersink the screw holes to make the assembly flush.

the profile of the roof, nailing with 6d galvanized siding nails as you go. Bend the panel slowly, spacing the nails at 3-in. intervals.

When the plywood is fully attached to the frame, trim the excess from the end with a saber saw tilted at 15 degrees. This will leave a ⅛-in overhang, which will be removed by sanding later.

Sand the roof structure with a belt sander, removing the remaining excess plywood. Ease all of the sharp edges of the structure as you work.

Be careful when sanding the plywood roof; it is easy to sand right through a layer of veneer.

Before assembling the sandbox, give the base a thorough sanding as well, removing all sharp edges and smoothing the surface for painting. Pay special attention to the exposed end grain of the base.

Next, with the roof structure on its side, attach the 38¾-in.-long 2X4 posts to the roof with no. 10 X 2½-in. screws. Space the posts as shown in the diagram, and check them

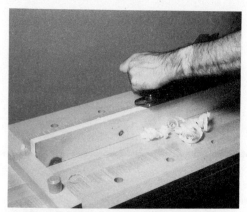

3. *Using a bench plane, cut a 15 degree bevel on the ends of the roof frame to match the roof's curve.*

4. *Secure the top to the rails with screws or nails. Slowly bend the plywood over the frame, nailing as you go.*

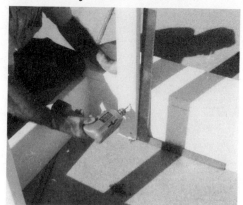

7. *Attach the posts to the base frame in the same way. Check carefully to keep the posts vertical.*

8. *The roof of the sandbox is attached to the posts with screws as well. Notice the spacing at the top of the posts.*

carefully with a framing square.

Once all four posts are attached to the roof, insert the posts into the base of the project and fasten with screws as you did before. Center the posts along the sides of the sandbox, and make them flush with the bottom of the base. Check again for squareness.

Set the completed assembly up on blocks temporarily for finishing. Do any touch-up sanding that's needed, then apply at least two coats of exterior latex enamel to the project.

You can paint the sandbox in any color scheme you choose. Be sure to coat the bottom edges of the base to protect them from water damage.

After the paint has dried thoroughly, move the sandbox to its final location in your yard. Fill it with clean sand, leaving a 2-in. space at the top to minimize spilling. Clean, white sand is available at most lumber yards and home centers, either in bags or in bulk. You will need about 6½ cu. ft. to fill the box to the required depth.

IV.

Decks

BI-LEVEL DECK

If you would like to build a deck that is different, this two-tiered deck could be the answer. Designed with a rugged, contemporary appearance, its angular upper level breaks away from the typical rectangular deck design to create a new look for your outdoor entertaining.

The upper deck is supported by beams that extend to an existing structure, such as your house. If you like, you can support the free end of the upper level with piers and posts, allowing you to place the deck away from any other buildings.

The angle and position of the upper deck can vary according to your taste. Use the diagram as a guideline, but keep in mind that you will have to adapt the deck to your yard. For this reason, a materials list is not provided. If you make the deck larger, you'll need additional joists and piers.

When selecting lumber for this project, choose only straight, sound materials with tight knots. Inspect the 4X8 beams especially carefully, since they form the framework for the deck. If these components are not straight, the appearance of the entire deck will suffer. Western cedar is the best choice for this project.

Start construction by choosing a level site for the deck, near your home or another structure. Next, locate the positions of the concrete support piers, as shown in the diagram. Space the piers on 24-in. centers. Drive a stake in the center of each pier position, then check the layout for squareness by measuring the diagonals from the outer piers.

Dig oversized holes at these locations, centered on the stake positions, then set pre-fabricated 8-in.-dia. X 30-in.-long piers in the holes. The tops of the piers should extend slightly above the grade.

Use a long, straight 2X8 and a level to help adjust the heights of the individual piers to make the structure perfectly level. Add earth to the holes, or dig them deeper, as required. Once all the piers are set, backfill the holes and compact the earth around the concrete. For good measure, check them for level once more. The final level of the deck depends on the care you take at this stage.

If commercial piers are not available, you can pour your own using bagged concrete mix. Dig 8-in.-dia. pier holes 30 in. deep. Build up an earthen dam around the holes to allow you to make the top of the pier higher than the surrounding grade.

If you cast your own piers, level their tops carefully while the concrete is still wet. You can simplify this job by leveling the earth dams before pouring the concrete. Insert a $\frac{1}{2}$-in. X 10-in. J-bolt in the wet concrete to anchor the post brackets shown in the diagram. Allow the concrete to cure at least one week before continuing construction.

Cut three 2X8 joists 161 in. long. Bevel the lower corners of each joist at a 45 degree angle, as shown in Detail 1. Measure $1\frac{1}{2}$ in. from the corner of the joist to locate the ends of the bevel. Use your radial arm saw or a portable circular saw to form the bevels.

Attach 4X4 post brackets to the piers, then position the joists. If you have cast your own piers, bore 1-in.-dia. holes in the joists to allow clearance for the ends of the anchor bolts. Align the joists carefully, making sure that the ends of the joists fall in a straight line and that the joists are parallel. Take your time with this job.

Once you are satisfied with the alignment, place short, 1-in.-thick spacer blocks between the joists and the brackets. Center the joists by placing blocks on both sides. Secure the joists with 10d galvanized nails, driven in from both sides.

Next, using a sharp wood chisel, cut a shallow notch at the upper end of each joist to accommodate inverted joist hangers. The top of the metal hanger should be flush with, or slightly below, the top of the joist.

Position the joist hangers, then secure them with 8d joist hanger nails. These nails are made of hardened steel and provide the strength needed to support the deck. They are available at most lumberyards and home centers.

Cut two 10-ft.-long 4X8 frame members. Cut the ends with 45 de-

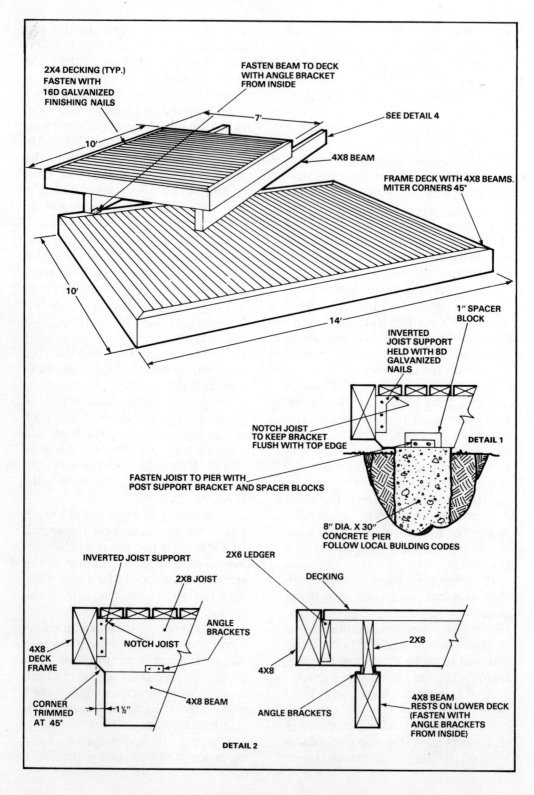

2X4 DECKING (TYP.) FASTEN WITH 16D GALVANIZED FINISHING NAILS

FASTEN BEAM TO DECK WITH ANGLE BRACKET FROM INSIDE

SEE DETAIL 4

7'

10'

4X8 BEAM

FRAME DECK WITH 4X8 BEAMS. MITER CORNERS 45°

10'

14'

1" SPACER BLOCK

INVERTED JOIST SUPPORT HELD WITH 8D GALVANIZED NAILS

NOTCH JOIST TO KEEP BRACKET FLUSH WITH TOP EDGE

DETAIL 1

FASTEN JOIST TO PIER WITH POST SUPPORT BRACKET AND SPACER BLOCKS

8" DIA. X 30" CONCRETE PIER FOLLOW LOCAL BUILDING CODES

INVERTED JOIST SUPPORT

2X8 JOIST

2X6 LEDGER

DECKING

ANGLE BRACKETS

4X8 DECK FRAME

NOTCH JOIST

2X8

4X8

CORNER TRIMMED AT 45°

1½"

4X8 BEAM

ANGLE BRACKETS

4X8 BEAM RESTS ON LOWER DECK (FASTEN WITH ANGLE BRACKETS FROM INSIDE)

DETAIL 2

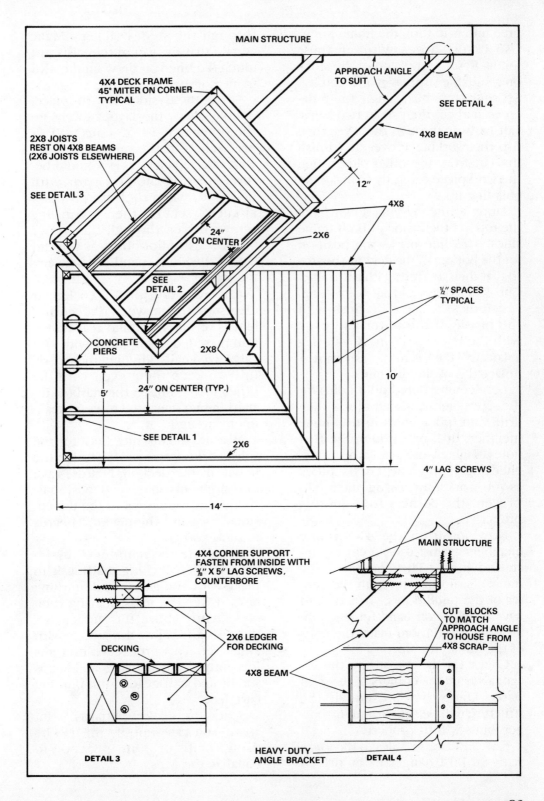

MAIN STRUCTURE

4X4 DECK FRAME
45° MITER ON CORNER
TYPICAL

APPROACH ANGLE
TO SUIT

SEE DETAIL 4

4X8 BEAM

2X8 JOISTS
REST ON 4X8 BEAMS
(2X6 JOISTS ELSEWHERE)

SEE DETAIL 3

12"

4X8

24"
ON CENTER

2X6

SEE
DETAIL 2

½" SPACES
TYPICAL

CONCRETE
PIERS

2X8

10'

24" ON CENTER (TYP.)

5'

SEE DETAIL 1

2X6

14'

4" LAG SCREWS

MAIN STRUCTURE

4X4 CORNER SUPPORT.
FASTEN FROM INSIDE WITH
⅜" X 5" LAG SCREWS,
COUNTERBORE

CUT BLOCKS
TO MATCH
APPROACH ANGLE
TO HOUSE FROM
4X8 SCRAP

DECKING

2X6 LEDGER
FOR DECKING

4X8 BEAM

HEAVY-DUTY
ANGLE BRACKET

DETAIL 3

DETAIL 4

gree miters to form the frame joints. Use a radial arm saw to cut these joints. Rest the free end of the stock on a suitable support while cutting. Set your saw's blade angle to 45 degrees, and cut the part in two steps. Cut halfway through the 4X8, then flip the workpiece over and finish the cut from the other side. Align the workpiece carefully to make the cuts line up.

Draw a line, 1½ in. down from the top, on the inside of both frame sides. This line marks the position for the bottom of the decking boards so that they are flush with the frame. Cut 4X4 corner blocks 6 in. long. Fasten these to the 4X8, flush with the inside of the miter and even with the line. Use ⅜-in. X 5-in. lag

Locate the screws as shown in Detail 3 of the diagram.

Bore counterbored pilot holes for the screws in the corner block, then drill ¼-in. pilot holes in the frame member, drilling through the first holes. Tighten the screws securely, checking the alignment of the block as you work. Any misalignment will prevent the corners from joining properly.

Now, position the 4X8 frame members against the previously installed joists. The center of the frame should line up with the center of the middle joist. It is best to have a helper on hand for this job. Measure carefully to make the ends of the frame line up.

Check this by measuring the diagonals from the corners of the 4X8 parts. Once they are equal, the structure will be square and the corner joints will fit properly.

Fasten the frame sides to the joists with 8d joist hanger nails, driven

through the steel brackets. Make certain that the top of the joists just touch the line you drew on the 4X8 frame component.

Once these sides are in place, double check the layout to ensure the other two 14-ft. sides will fit precisely. Cut the remaining sides with mitered corners as you did before. Position the new parts with help and, when they are properly aligned, secure them with lag screws driven through the corner blocks. Drill pilot holes, as you did before, avoiding conflicts between the screws.

Cut two additional 2X6 ledger cleats to fit between the corner blocks on the front and rear frame. Nail these ledgers in place with 16d galvanized nails, aligning them carefully to keep them even with the other joists. Space the nails 6 in. apart in two staggered rows for maximum strength.

Measure the distance between the sides of the frame to determine the length of the decking boards. Take measurements in several positions. If you find variations in the dimensions, measure the decking boards to fit as you go.

Complete the main deck by installing 2X4 decking, nailing it in place with 16d galvanized finishing nails. Drive the nails, leaving each one slightly above the surface. Set the nails just below the surface with a nail set. This procedure prevents unsightly hammer marks and keeps sun-heated nail heads from burning bare feet.

Space the decking boards ½ in. apart. You can simplify this job by using scraps of ½-in. plywood to equalize the gaps.

Once the main deck is finished, begin building the angled upper level. Start by positioning a 4X8 beam at an angle of your choice. It should cross the main deck at approximately the point shown in the diagram. Extend the beam to touch the wall of the main structure and prop the free end in position to make the beam level.

Use a board as a straightedge to mark a line on the beam parallel with the wall. Measure the angle of the line with a protractor, then cut the end of the beam at that angle with your radial arm saw, following the same procedure you did when cutting the 4X8 frames. Cut one end of the second support beam to match.

Reposition the two beams on the deck. They should be 48 in. apart from center to center, and the free ends should touch the wall of the building. Prop the ends up so the beams are parallel and level, then use a long, straight board and a framing square to mark the end of the beams. The shorter beam should rest fully on the outer frame of the main deck.

Remove the beams and cut them to their finished lengths on your radial arm saw. Once they are cut, place them back on the deck in their final positions, once again propping up the free ends to make them level. Fasten the ends of the beams to the deck with heavy-duty angle brackets and lag screws.

Cut four triangular blocks 7¼ in. long to match the approach angle of the beams to the main structure. Rip the blocks from scrap 4X8 stock and pre-drill fastener holes. Use these blocks with angle brackets and lag

screws to secure the beams.

If you choose, you can also support the free end of the upper deck with concrete piers and posts, eliminating the beams that extend to the building. If you choose this method, use post brackets to secure the posts to the 4X8 beams, and adjust the post height carefully to make the deck level.

Cut two 2X8 joists 113 in. long. Place these on edge on the centers of the beams. Align their ends carefully, then fasten them to the beams with angle brackets and lag screws. Position the angle brackets 12 in. apart on both sides of the joists.

As you did on the main deck, notch the upper ends of the joists for inverted joist hanger brackets and install the brackets on the joists with 8d joist hanger nails.

Cut the 4X8 end frame members with mitered joints and attach the corner blocks. Position the frame's ends, aligning them carefully, then secure them to the joists. Be sure to allow a 1½ in. space for the decking.

Add the sides to the frame, then install the remaining center joist and the 2X6 ledgers. Finish the upper deck by laying the 2X4 decking in the same way you did on the main deck.

Once both decks are complete, check them carefully for splinters and rough spots. Touch these up with your belt sander and a 120-grit belt. Round off all sharp edges to prevent injuries. Finish the project with two coats of clear, non-toxic wood sealer and preservative, or use semi-transparent stain in the color of your choice.

Design and photo courtesy of Western Wood Products Association, 1500 Yeon Building, Portland, OR 97204.

CONCRETE COVER-UP

If your home has a concrete patio that is cracked or in poor condition, why not cover it up with an attractive and durable redwood deck? Since the existing patio will serve as the foundation for the new deck, you will save a great deal of money and labor.

All materials used in the deck should be of construction heart grade redwood. This material is extremely weather resistant, as well as attractive in an outdoor setting. Use only hot-dipped galvanized nails to

You can convert an unsightly concrete slab like this into an attractive redwood deck.

assemble the deck; this will prevent unsightly rust stains later.

This design for a patio cover-up was installed on an existing two-level slab. If the concrete area of your home is only on one level, you may want to build this cover-up without the raised area.

If you would like to have the look of a bi-level deck on a flat slab, simply attach 2X8 or 2X10 redwood risers to the 2X4 sleepers you nail to the slab. Set these risers next to each 2X4 and nail into place. Similarly, on the outside edge of the raised area, attach a riser to the ends of the lower sleepers.

The apron on the outer perimeter of the new deck extends beyond the original slab. Its straight-line decking forms a pleasing border for the angled decking of the main area, and also increases the area of the deck.

Prepare the perimeter area by digging a trench about 1 ft. deep and as wide as the border area. Fill this trench with gravel to provide good drainage for both the main deck and the border. Also install pre-formed concrete piers, which can be bought at masonry suppliers.

Sweep the concrete slab clean, then lay 2X4 sleepers flat on the slab, 24 in. apart. Where the slab is cracked or has low spots, use pieces of wood shingles as shims to fill the gaps.

Check the overall level of the sleepers by laying a long, straight board across several sleepers. Use shims to bring all the sleepers up to the same level. Take your time on this phase of the project. Careful leveling will make a world of difference in the finished appearance of the deck.

Now, fasten the sleepers in place with concrete nails driven by an explosive-type nail gun. This tool can be rented at any equipment rental store. For safety's sake, read the instructions that come with the tool before using it. Always make sure that the loaded gun is pressed firmly against the wood before striking the firing pin. Be sure to also wear safety glasses or a face shield when using this tool. Nail every 12 inches.

Begin laying the 2X6 decking in place. Choose an angle that looks pleasing in your setting and lay several decking boards in place before nailing. Allow ½-in. spaces between the decking boards for good drainage.

Any joints should be directly over a sleeper, but avoid placing two joints side by side. Allow the decking to overhang the edge of the slab. You will trim the boards later.

Attach the decking to the sleepers with 12d galvanized nails, drilling pilot holes in the decking when you nail near the end of a board. This helps to prevent splitting.

CONSTRUCTION DETAILS

1. Attach 1X6 sleepers to the slab with concrete nails and an explosive-type nail gun.

2. A separate frame is used for the border area. Attach this to the slab with concrete nails.

3. Lay several decking boards in place before nailing. Stagger the joints over the sleepers.

When all the decking is laid, use a chalk line to mark the perimeter of the deck area. Trim with a circular saw, taking your time to make the cut as accurate as possible. Set the saw's depth of cut to just cut through the decking material, and cut to the outside of the line to avoid unsightly gaps between the main deck and the perimeter.

Next, using the diagram as a guide, build the frames for the border decking. Use 16d galvanized nails to assemble the frames. As shown in the photograph, the braces in the corners are cut at a 45 degree angle. Cross braces are spaced on 24-in. centers.

Position the framework around the perimeter of the deck, shimming the frame at the proper height on the concrete piers. Attach the frame to the slab with concrete nails as you did before.

Apply 2X6 decking to the frame, measuring each piece carefully to form the mitered joints in the corners. Lay all the decking in place before nailing.

Finally, complete construction by nailing 2X8 fascia boards to the perimeter of the border, making it flush with the top of the decking. Simple butt joints are used in the corners.

Use a belt sander to remove any rough or splintery areas on the deck, then apply two coats of a wood sealer, such as Thompson's Water Seal. Allow 24 hours between coats.

Design and photos courtesy of the California Redwood Association, 591 Redwood Highway, Suite 3100, Mill Valley, CA 94941.

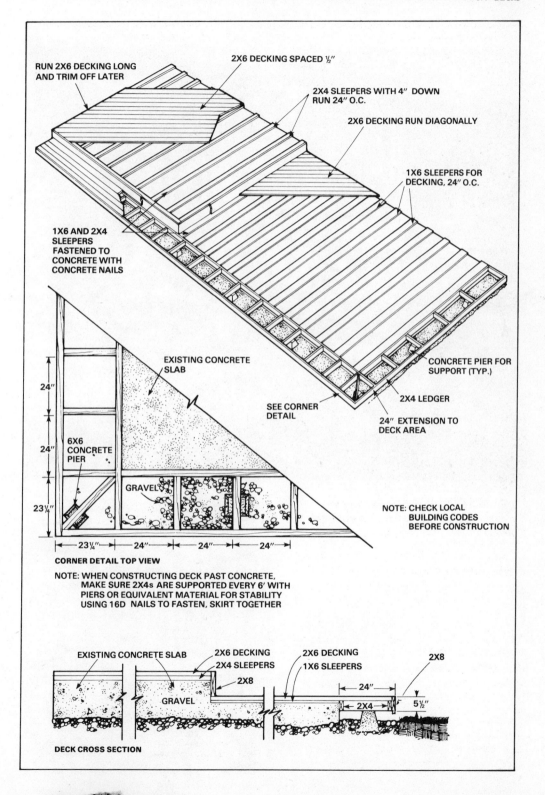

RUN 2X6 DECKING LONG AND TRIM OFF LATER

2X6 DECKING SPACED ½"

2X4 SLEEPERS WITH 4" DOWN RUN 24" O.C.

2X6 DECKING RUN DIAGONALLY

1X6 SLEEPERS FOR DECKING, 24" O.C.

1X6 AND 2X4 SLEEPERS FASTENED TO CONCRETE WITH CONCRETE NAILS

EXISTING CONCRETE SLAB

CONCRETE PIER FOR SUPPORT (TYP.)

2X4 LEDGER

SEE CORNER DETAIL

24" EXTENSION TO DECK AREA

6X6 CONCRETE PIER

24"

24"

23¼"

GRAVEL

NOTE: CHECK LOCAL BUILDING CODES BEFORE CONSTRUCTION

23¼" 24" 24" 24"

CORNER DETAIL TOP VIEW

NOTE: WHEN CONSTRUCTING DECK PAST CONCRETE, MAKE SURE 2X4s ARE SUPPORTED EVERY 6' WITH PIERS OR EQUIVALENT MATERIAL FOR STABILITY USING 16D NAILS TO FASTEN, SKIRT TOGETHER

EXISTING CONCRETE SLAB

2X6 DECKING
2X4 SLEEPERS

2X6 DECKING
1X6 SLEEPERS

2X8

2X8

GRAVEL

24"

2X4

5½"

DECK CROSS SECTION

This attached deck is constructed from cedar and features perimeter seating (right photo).

DECK WITH BENCHES

This deck, designed to fit against your home, makes an ideal outdoor entertainment area. Built-in benches provide plenty of seating for your family and guests, while its 144 sq. ft. of space is large enough for most deck activities.

Working from the basic design shown here, you can customize the deck to fit your personal needs. You can make it free-standing or increase its size. Simply change the overall dimensions and add additional concrete piers for support. Add backs to the seats, if you choose, following the detail diagram. Backs should be added if the deck is higher than 24 in. above the ground or if you have small children.

Choose materials carefully for this deck. You can use any of a number of softwoods for its construction, but select straight materials from your lumberyard for easy building. Use pressure-treated lumber for the framework of the deck to protect it against the weather.

For the longest-lasting deck, use cedar or all-heart redwood for the decking, seats, and trim. If you choose a less weather-resistant material, finish the deck with clear wood sealer and preservative. For your family's safety, select a sealer that is non-toxic when dry.

Start building the deck by locating the positions of the concrete piers that support the front posts. Center these piers 12 ft. apart and 12 ft. from the building. Once all four pier locations have been marked, check the layout for squareness by measuring the diagonals. When the diagonal measurements are equal, the layout is square.

Dig 12-in.-dia. X 36-in.-deep holes for the piers. Fill these with concrete mix. You will need at least two 1-cu.-ft. bags for each hole. When the hole is filled, smooth the concrete to a flat, level surface. Sink a ½-in. X 10-in. J-bolt into the concrete, leaving 1 in. protruding from the top. Measure the layout once again, making any adjustments to keep it square and properly dimensioned.

While the concrete is curing, locate the studs in the wall of your house. You can do this with a commercial stud locator, or by inspecting the siding for nailing points. Mark the positions of each stud.

Cut a 2X8 to a length of 11 ft., 7½ inches. Position the 2X8 against the wall as it will be when the deck is built, and transfer the stud locations to this board.

Drill ½-in.-dia. holes for the lag screws along the center line of the board, then reposition it against the wall at the height of the deck. Allow 1¼-in. for the decking. Prop the 2X8 in position and use a level to adjust it carefully.

Now, using a ⅜-in.-dia. bit, bore through the pre-drilled holes into the wall studs of your house. Fasten the beam to the wall with ½-in. X 3½-in. lag screws, spacing the 2X8

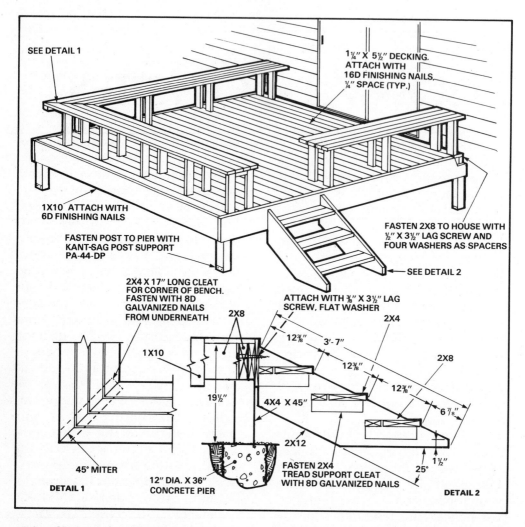

SEE DETAIL 1

1¼" X 5½" DECKING. ATTACH WITH 16D FINISHING NAILS. ¼" SPACE (TYP.)

1X10 ATTACH WITH 6D FINISHING NAILS

FASTEN POST TO PIER WITH KANT-SAG POST SUPPORT PA-44-DP

FASTEN 2X8 TO HOUSE WITH ½" X 3½" LAG SCREW AND FOUR WASHERS AS SPACERS

SEE DETAIL 2

2X4 X 17" LONG CLEAT FOR CORNER OF BENCH. FASTEN WITH 8D GALVANIZED NAILS FROM UNDERNEATH

ATTACH WITH ⅜" X 3½" LAG SCREW, FLAT WASHER

2X8

2X4

1X10

12¾₆"   3'-7"

12¾₆"

2X8

19½"

4X4 X 45"

12¾₆"

6⅞"

2X12

45° MITER

FASTEN 2X4 TREAD SUPPORT CLEAT WITH 8D GALVANIZED NAILS

1½"

25°

DETAIL 1

12" DIA. X 36" CONCRETE PIER

DETAIL 2

away from the wall with four flat washers between the beam and the wall. Tighten the screws securely.

Install steel post supports on each concrete pier. Use the type specified in the materials list or a suitable substitute.

Measure the distance from the bottom of the ledger, which you just attached to the house, to the top of the piers. Cut 4X4 posts to the measured length. Bore 1-in.-dia. holes in the bottom of each post to slip over the anchor bolts. Insert the posts in the steel brackets and secure them

with joist nails. Check each post with a level to make it perfectly vertical.

Cut the front posts to the lengths needed to make the deck level. Check the posts with a long, straight board and a level to make the deck even.

Cut two pieces of 2X8 stock, making them 11 ft., 7½-in. long. Nail these together to form the front beam for the deck. Set these upright on the 4X4 posts at the front of the deck. Position them flush with the front of the post.

MATERIALS LIST

Item	Quantity
4X4 redwood	8 ft.
2X12 redwood	8 ft.
2X8 redwood	180 ft.
1¼″ X 5½″ redwood	300 ft.
2X4 redwood	180 ft.
1X10 redwood	36 ft.
4X4 steel post brackets, Kant-sag PA-44-DP or equivalent	4
2X8 steel joist hangers, Kant-sag JR-SSS or equivalent	16
4d joist hanger nails	as needed
½″ X 10″ J-bolts with nuts and washers	4
½″ X 3½″ lag screws	18
½″ flat washers	94
¼″ X 3½″ lag screws	4
No. 8 X 1¼″ flathead wood screws	48
16d galvanized common nails	as needed
6d, 8d, 10d, 12d, 16d galv. finishing nails	as needed
Concrete mix, 1 cu. ft. bags	10
Wood sealer or stain	1 gal.

Measure the distance between the rear of the ledger and the front of the beam, and cut two 2X8 joists to this length. Nail these joists to the ends of the ledger and beam with 16d galvanized common nails. Drill pilot holes for the nails to prevent splitting the wood.

Check the assembly once more to make sure that it's square and level, then toenail the joists and beams to the posts with 12d galvanized nails.

Mark the locations for the joists, 16 in. on center on both the front beam and the ledger. Measure the distance between the beam and ledger, then cut eight 2X8 joists to that length. It is a good idea to measure each joist individually to allow for slight variations in the overall dimensions.

Install the joists with joist hanger brackets designed for 2X8 lumber. Use the brackets specified in the materials list or a suitable substitute. Nail the brackets to the wood with special joist hanger nails. They are especially hardened for added strength and are usually available wherever the brackets are sold.

Make the bench supports next. Cut two 23½-in.-long 2X4 posts for each support. You will need 24 of these for the layout shown in the diagram. Cut an additional twelve pieces of 2X4, measuring 13¾-in. long, for the horizontal support member.

Position one set of the supports together as they will be when assembled. Mark the intersections on all three components to lay out the half-lap joints.

Form the notches for the joints with a dado blade on your radial arm saw. Set the blade's width of cut to ¾ in. and the depth of cut to exactly half the thickness of your stock. For accuracy and speed, clamp a stop block to the saw's fence to help locate the end of the notches.

Cut each notch with multiple passes of the dado blade, finishing the cut with the end of the component against the stop block. Cut one set of parts, then check the assembly. Adjust the depth of cut, if necessary, for a perfect fit of the joints.

Once the parts are cut, fasten each joint with four no. 8 X 1¼-in. flathead wood screws. Bore countersunk pilot holes for the screws with a combination pilot bit and countersink to make the screw heads flush with the surface.

The seven bench supports that will be installed on the deck's sides must be notched, as shown in the diagram on page 94, to fit the joists. Cut these notches with a handsaw or your saber saw.

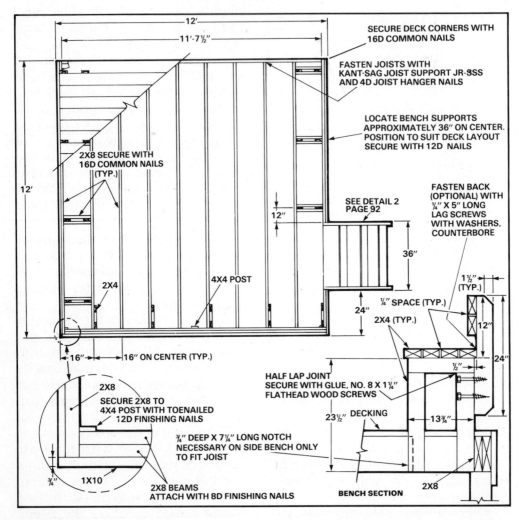

SECURE DECK CORNERS WITH 16D COMMON NAILS

FASTEN JOISTS WITH KANT-SAG JOIST SUPPORT JR-3SS AND 4D JOIST HANGER NAILS

LOCATE BENCH SUPPORTS APPROXIMATELY 36" ON CENTER. POSITION TO SUIT DECK LAYOUT SECURE WITH 12D NAILS

2X8 SECURE WITH 16D COMMON NAILS (TYP.)

SEE DETAIL 2 PAGE 92

FASTEN BACK (OPTIONAL) WITH ¼" X 5" LONG LAG SCREWS WITH WASHERS, COUNTERBORE

2X4

4X4 POST

¼" SPACE (TYP.)

2X4 (TYP.)

1½" (TYP.)

16"   16" ON CENTER (TYP.)

2X8

SECURE 2X8 TO 4X4 POST WITH TOENAILED 12D FINISHING NAILS

HALF LAP JOINT SECURE WITH GLUE, NO. 8 X 1¼" FLATHEAD WOOD SCREWS

¾" DEEP X 7¼" LONG NOTCH NECESSARY ON SIDE BENCH ONLY TO FIT JOIST

23½" DECKING

13¾"

1X10

2X8 BEAMS ATTACH WITH 8D FINISHING NAILS

2X8

BENCH SECTION

Install the bench supports at the front of the deck in the positions shown in the diagram. Position the legs flush with the bottom of the joists, and nail the supports in place with 12d galvanized nails.

Locate the positions of the supports along the sides of the deck. Space the supports evenly along the side, approximately 36 in. on center. Use the positions shown in the diagram as a guide.

Cut 2X8 blocks to straddle the legs of the supports. Nail one of these blocks alongside the position

of each support, with 16d galvanized common nails driven through the frame members. Add the bench support, nailing it to the block, then add the second block and nail it in place as well. Check the bench supports with a level as you work.

At this point, you can begin installing the 1¼-in. X 5½-in. decking. Use 12-ft.-long decking boards. They will overhang the structure slightly, allowing you to trim them flush later. Start laying the deck at the rear. Where the decking contacts a bench support assembly, measure carefully and cut notches to clear the supports. Cut the notches with a saber saw.

Nail the decking to the joists with 16d galvanized finishing nails. Drive each nail, leaving it slightly above the surface, then set it below the surface of the wood with a nail set. This step will help prevent unsightly hammer marks in your deck. Space the deck boards $\frac{1}{4}$ in. apart. The last deck board will overhang the front beam slightly.

Once all of the decking is laid, snap chalk lines on the top of the deck to mark the trimming lines. Measure accurately to make these lines match the outside of the frame.

Install a combination blade on your portable circular saw, then set the saw's depth of cut to just clear the underside of the decking. Trim the decking, following the lines carefully. When you are finished, the outside of the decking should be flush with the frame.

Complete the basic deck structure by nailing 1X10 fascia boards to the frame and decking. Attach the fascia with 6d galvanized finishing nails. Set the nails below the surface of the wood as you did before.

Now, cut 2X4 seat boards to match the length of the side bench. Nail these in place with 12d galvanized finishing nails, following the techniques described earlier. Space the boards $\frac{1}{4}$ in. apart. Use scraps of $\frac{1}{4}$-in. plywood to help make the spaces even.

Next, cut a 12-ft. length of 2X4 stock to form the outer seat board at the front of the deck. Cut one end at a 45 degree angle to form the miter joint at the corner. Nail this board in place on the front of the seat supports, allowing for a $\frac{1}{2}$-in. overhang.

Keep it perfectly parallel with the front of the deck.

Once this board is in place, cut the matching board for the side bench. Measure accurately from the wall of the house to the end of the 45 degree miter for a perfect fit.

Follow the same procedure for the remaining three seat boards for the bench. Again, use scraps of $\frac{1}{4}$-in. plywood to control the spacing.

Once all of the boards are secured, cut a 17-in. length of 2X4 stock to form the corner cleat. At one end, cut two 45 degree angles to form a point. Attach this cleat to the underside of the bench top with 8d galvanized nails. Drive the nails from the underside after drilling pilot holes in the cleat. If necessary, have a helper hold a block of wood on top of the bench to help with the nailing.

If you wish, you can add backs to any of the benches. Cut a 24-in.-long piece of 2X4 stock for each bench support. Bevel the outside corners at a 45 degree angle, then cut the $\frac{1}{2}$-in.-deep notch shown in the diagram.

Bore $\frac{1}{4}$-in.-dia. pilot holes in the bench support's rear leg. Counterbore these holes $\frac{1}{2}$ in. deep with a $\frac{3}{4}$-in.-dia. bit. Position the back support against the leg and bore $\frac{3}{16}$-in.-dia. pilot holes. Secure the assembly using $\frac{1}{4}$-in. X 5-in. lag screws with washers. Check the back support to make sure that it's vertical before tightening the screws.

Attach two 2X4 back boards to the supports with 12d galvanized finishing nails, setting the nails below the surface of the wood. Space the back boards $\frac{1}{4}$ in. apart as you did before.

Build the stair unit next. Cut two

CONSTRUCTION DETAILS

1. *Attach a 2X8 ledger to the side of the building with lag screws. Allow for the decking when setting the height.*

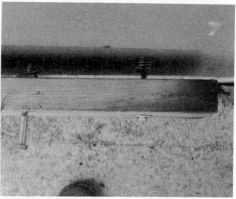

2. *When attaching the ledger, space it away from the building with four flat washers behind the ledger.*

5. *When installing the decking, mark the deck boards for notches where they interfere with the bench supports.*

6. *Attach the seat slats to the supports with finishing nails. Use ¼-in. plywood scraps to space the slats.*

2X12 boards for the stringers. Cut one end of each board at a 65 degree angle to fit against the deck fascia. Cut the other end of the board at a 25 degree angle to rest flat on the ground. Finish the sides by cutting 1½-in.-wide flats, perpendicular to the angled cuts, at the end that will rest flat on the ground.

Lay out the angled cuts with a protractor, then use your portable circular saw to make the cuts. Use a combination blade for a smooth finish, and clamp a guide to the boards

to help keep the cuts straight.

Cut six 2X4 cleats for the stair treads, then nail them to the stringers at the positions indicated in the diagram. Use 8d galvanized nails. Make certain the two sides match accurately.

Cut 2X8 and 2X4 stock 36 in. long for the stair treads. Nail these to the cleats with 12d galvanized finishing nails. Check the assembly with a framing square as you work.

Once the stair unit is finished, position it against the side of the deck,

3. *Nail the deck framing together with 16d galvanized common nails. Keep the structure level as you work.*

4. *The decking is supported by 2X8 joists, spaced 16 in. on center. Measure these parts accurately.*

7. *Cut the miter joint for the benches on your radial arm saw. Measure accurately for a good fit.*

8. *Lay out the positions of the stair cleats accurately. Check to make sure that both sides are identical.*

placing it 24 in. from the front. Secure it in position temporarily with 8d nails driven into the stairs' stringers, through the fascia.

Attach the stairs permanently with $\frac{3}{8}$-in. X $3\frac{1}{2}$-in. lag screws. Drive the screws from inside the deck, through the deck's frame. Drill appropriate pilot holes for the screws.

Give the completed deck a thorough inspection. Use a belt sander with a 120-grit belt to sand any rough or splintered areas. Round off any sharp edges, especially on the benches, with the sander.

Apply two coats of clear wood sealer and preservative to the deck. A paint roller is an excellent tool for this job. Allow the first coat of sealer to dry 24 hours before applying the second coat.

As an alternative finish, apply two coats of semi-transparent exterior stain to the deck. If you used a wood other than redwood for the project, stain will make the deck more attractive and help protect it against weather damage.

FAMILY-SIZED DECK

If you are planning to build a deck for your yard and you need one big enough for serious entertaining, this one offers over 325 sq. ft. of space. Its angled side adds interest, while a wide rail at the top makes a perfect spot for guests to place their refreshments.

The dimensions shown in the diagram for this deck are typical. Naturally, you will have to customize the deck to fit your yard. For this reason, a materials list is not provided. You can simplify construction by eliminating the angled side. Add more benches if you desire. Use your creativity and the basic design to make a deck that fits your needs.

The deck can be made of any available softwood, such as fir or redwood. Choose pressure-treated lumber for the joists and sleepers for maximum rot-resistance. The visible portions of the deck should be made of no. 1 or better grade lumber. Whatever lumber you choose, select straight material with tight knots.

Begin construction by digging holes for the concrete piers that support the deck. Follow the dimensions shown in the diagram to lay out the pier locations on a level building site.

Dig oversized holes for the piers, then cut 36-in.-long sections of 12-in.-dia. Sonotubes or other column forms. Place these in the holes, then use a long, straight 2X4 to bridge across the tops of the forms. Use a level to help you adjust the tubes to make the deck perfectly level. The tops of the piers should be approximately 4 in. above the grade. Pack earth around the forms to hold them in position.

If your site is not level, make the tops of the piers extend more or less above the grade, as necessary. The minimum height is 2 inches.

Once the forms are level, fill them with concrete. Use a board to strike off the top of the concrete even with the top of the forms. After the concrete has set, you can either remove the paper forms or leave them in place. In either case, backfill the hole with well-compacted earth.

The position and the size of the piers are typical of deck construction, but check with your local building department to make certain the layout meets your local building codes.

Once the concrete has cured for a week or so, begin constructing the deck. Start by building the sleepers. Cut 2X12 pressure-treated lumber to the lengths shown in the diagram. You will need three lengths for each sleeper.

Stack the 2X12 sleeper components together and bore $\frac{3}{8}$-in.-dia. holes through the stack for the bolts that fasten the assembly. Space the bolt holes 12 in. apart. Be careful to keep the stack aligned as you work.

Counterbore both sides of the

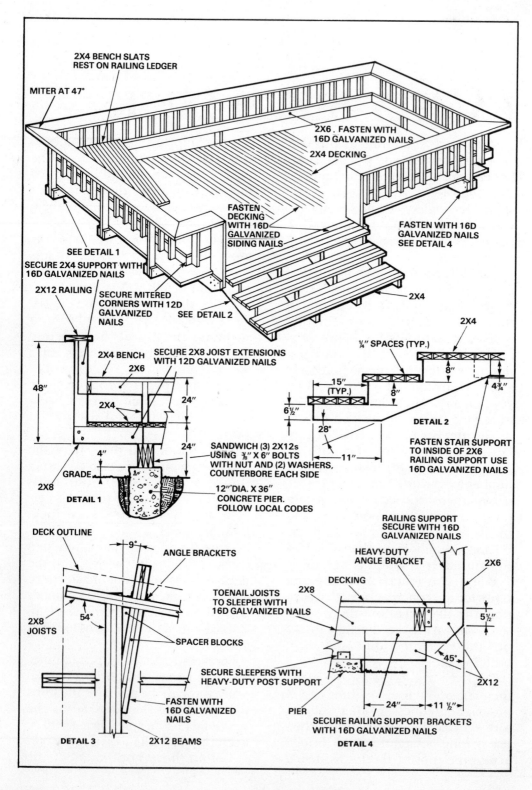

2X4 BENCH SLATS
REST ON RAILING LEDGER

MITER AT 47°

2X6 . FASTEN WITH
16D GALVANIZED NAILS

2X4 DECKING

FASTEN
DECKING
WITH 16D
GALVANIZED
SIDING NAILS

FASTEN WITH 16D
GALVANIZED NAILS
SEE DETAIL 4

SEE DETAIL 1

SECURE 2X4 SUPPORT WITH
16D GALVANIZED NAILS

2X12 RAILING

SECURE MITERED
CORNERS WITH 12D
GALVANIZED
NAILS

SEE DETAIL 2

2X4

2X4 BENCH

2X6

2X4

SECURE 2X8 JOIST EXTENSIONS
WITH 12D GALVANIZED NAILS

48"

24"

24"

4"

GRADE

2X8

DETAIL 1

SANDWICH (3) 2X12s
USING ⅜" X 6" BOLTS
WITH NUT AND (2) WASHERS,
COUNTERBORE EACH SIDE

12"DIA. X 36"
CONCRETE PIER.
FOLLOW LOCAL CODES

¼" SPACES (TYP.)

2X4

8"

15"
(TYP.)

8"

6½"

28°

11"

4¾"

DETAIL 2

FASTEN STAIR SUPPORT
TO INSIDE OF 2X6
RAILING SUPPORT USE
16D GALVANIZED NAILS

RAILING SUPPORT
SECURE WITH 16D
GALVANIZED NAILS

HEAVY-DUTY
ANGLE BRACKET

DECK OUTLINE

9°

ANGLE BRACKETS

DECKING

2X6

2X8

TOENAIL JOISTS
TO SLEEPER WITH
16D GALVANIZED NAILS

5½"

2X8
JOISTS

54°

SPACER BLOCKS

SECURE SLEEPERS WITH
HEAVY-DUTY POST SUPPORT

45°

2X12

FASTEN WITH
16D GALVANIZED
NAILS

PIER

24"

11½"

DETAIL 3

2X12 BEAMS

SECURE RAILING SUPPORT BRACKETS
WITH 16D GALVANIZED NAILS

DETAIL 4

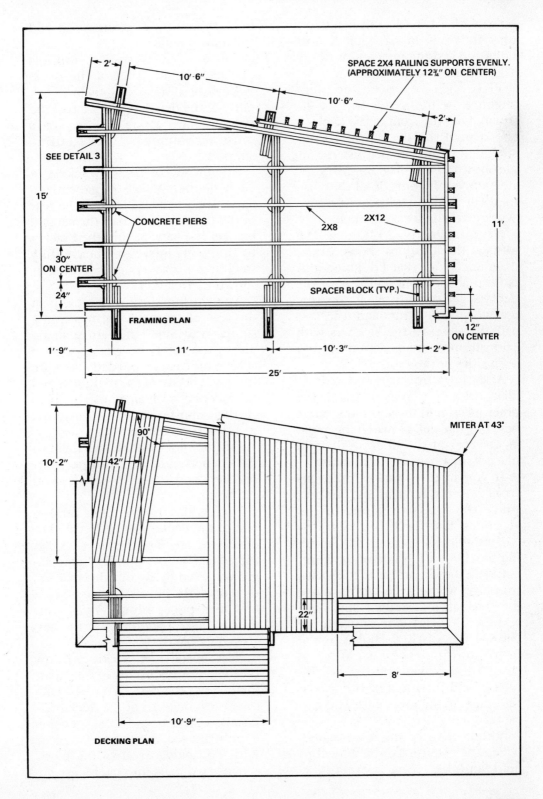

SPACE 2X4 RAILING SUPPORTS EVENLY.
(APPROXIMATELY 12¾" ON CENTER)

2'

10'-6"

10'-6"

2'

SEE DETAIL 3

15'

CONCRETE PIERS

2X8

2X12

11'

30"
ON CENTER

24"

SPACER BLOCK (TYP.)

FRAMING PLAN

12"
ON CENTER

1'-9"

11'

10'-3"

2'

25'

MITER AT 43°

90°

10'-2"

42"

22"

8'

10'-9"

DECKING PLAN

holes with a 1-in.-dia. bit to a depth of ½-in. Now, insert ⅜-in. X 6-in. bolts and add the nuts and washers. Tighten the assembly well.

Place the sleepers on the piers, aligning the front ends so they are square with the front of the deck. At the rear of the deck, use a long, straight 2X8 joist to establish the angle shown in the diagram. Mark the sleepers on the outside of the joist, then cut them off with a chain saw. Work carefully for a clean cut.

Next, install the 25-ft.-long 2X8 joists at the locations shown in the diagram. Notice that a doubled joist is used at the front and rear of the deck. Space the joist 30 in. on center, except at the front and rear. Toenail the joists to the sleepers with 16d galvanized nails driven in from both sides of the joists.

After installing the rear pair of joists, trim their ends to match the other joists. Add the short joist, after beveling one end to match the angle at the rear of the deck. Nail it in place with 12d galvanized nails.

If you need to make the joists from shorter lengths of lumber, place the joints over one of the sleepers. Reinforce the joints by nailing two 12-in.-long 2X8 splicing blocks on each side of the joint.

Check the alignment of the joists, trimming where necessary to make the ends fall in a straight line. Now add the 2X8 joist extensions to the ends of the joists, as shown in the detail drawing. These should just reach the sleepers and extend 5½ in. beyond the ends of the joists. Nail them to the joists with 12d galvanized nails.

Add the 2X6 railing supports between the extensions. Use a level to help you make these supports ver-

tical. Secure the supports with 16d galvanized nails.

Cut six 2X12 railing support brackets for the front of the deck. Follow the dimensions given in Detail 4 of the diagram. Notice that the two brackets alongside the stairs must accommodate 2X12 railing supports.

Attach one of these brackets to each sleeper with 16d galvanized nails. Add a spacer block to the rear of the bracket, then nail the second bracket in place. Secure the bracket to the front joist with heavy-duty steel angle brackets and screws, as shown in Detail 4.

The railing support brackets at the rear of the deck are made in a similar way. Since they are at an angle to the sleepers, wedge-shaped spacer blocks are needed. Measure the angle between the rear joists and the sleepers with an adjustable bevel, then transfer it to 2X6 material to lay out the blocks.

Cut the blocks, then nail them to the sleepers. Add the railing support brackets and spacer blocks as you did before.

Notice that the bracket on one end of the deck must be beveled to match the angle of the sleepers. Set the adjustable bevel at the same angle you used to lay out the spacers, then mark the bevels on one bracket and the spacer block. Take your time to make a good fit. Cut the bevels with a handsaw.

Now, install the decking. Allow the decking boards to extend past the edge of the deck. You will trim the excess once all of the decking is installed. Space the 2X4 decking ½ in. apart. Nail the material in place with 16d galvanized siding nails, driving two nails into each joist.

Once all of the decking is in position, snap a chalk line at the front and rear of the deck to mark it for trimming. Set the depth of cut on your circular saw to just cut through the decking, then carefully trim the excess overhang. The edge of the deck should line up with the 2X6 railing supports.

Install the railing supports between the brackets, nailing them in place with 16d galvanized nails driven from both sides. Use a level to help you make them perfectly vertical.

Cut two 2X12 supports 48 in. long to fit beside the stairs. Bevel one end at a 45 degree angle to form the joint with the railing. Install these supports, making certain that the lower side of the bevel lines up with the tops of the other railing supports. Notch the decking as needed.

Cut 2X6 stock to form the lower railing. Miter the corners, and nail the railing to the supports with 16d galvanized nails. The top of the rail should be 24 in. from the decking. Fasten the mitered corners with 12d galvanized nails. Drill pilot holes for the nails to prevent splitting.

Now, install the 2X4 railing supports, nailing them to the 2X6 rail with 16d galvanized nails. Cut the 2X4 material to match the height of the 2X6 supports. Space these parts 12 in. on center along the sides and front of the deck. At the rear of the deck, space them evenly, approximately 12¾ in. on center.

Add the 2X12 railing to the top of the supports. Cut 45 degree miters at the corners, as shown in the diagram. Install galvanized corner brackets on the underside of the miter joints to secure the assembly.

Add benches to the deck, as desired. Make simple supports for the benches with 2X4 posts and 2X6 rails. Nail the 2X4 bench tops to the railing and to the supports.

To make the angled bench, cut the 2X4 top components to match the angles of the deck, as shown in the diagram. When nailing near the ends of the material, drill pilot holes to prevent splitting.

Constructing the stairs is the final phase of this project. If you choose to build the kind shown in the diagram, first cut four stair stringers from 2X12 material. Follow the dimensions given in the diagram carefully. Lay out and cut one of the stringers, then use it as a pattern to mark the other three.

Nail the two outer stringers to the inside of the railing supports with 16d galvanized nails. Keep the stringer perpendicular to the deck. Nail the 2X4 decking onto the stringers to form the top step, which should be even with the deck's top.

Now, insert the remaining stringers, spacing them evenly. Make certain they are parallel to the outer stringers. Nail them into position, nailing through the already-installed decking. Add the remaining decking, spacing it ¼ in. apart.

Once construction is complete, give the deck a careful inspection. Sand any rough or splintered areas and round off all sharp edges.

To preserve the deck from weather damage, apply two coats of clear wood sealer and preservative. Use a sealer that is non-toxic when dry. If you choose, you could also finish the deck with a transparent oil-based stain and sealer.

Design and photos courtesy of Western Wood Products Association, Yeon Building, Portland, OR 97204.

GARAGE-TOP DECK

If you use the roof of your garage as a deck area, and the surface is anything other than wood, you are probably less than satisfied.

Converting the area to a wood deck is a home improvement well worth the cost. Entertaining outdoors will be more attractive and comfortable, while the overall appearance of your home will be much improved.

The design shown here is an excellent way to add a deck over your garage. It is designed to be easy to build, but it's also very attractive.

Naturally, your application will be different from the one shown in the photographs. You will need to adapt the design to your own home. Start by drawing a sketch that shows the dimensions of the garage area you plan to convert. Draw the overall dimensions of the deck, including any overhang you want to include.

With these sketches in hand, you can plan a materials list. For the best weather resistance, use construction heart grade redwood for all components of the deck. Redwood not only resists water damage, but its color also adds beauty to any home.

When you are working on a roof, it is important to be constantly aware that you are high above the ground. It is easy to get lost in what you are doing, creating a potentially hazardous situation.

Two safety rules can help prevent problems: (1.) Never turn your back

DECK DETAILS

Construction heart grade redwood is used throughout the deck for beauty and durability.

Space the 2X6 decking ½ in. apart for both proper drainage and safety.

on the edge of the roof. Face the outside, especially when working near the edge.(2.) Never step backward when working on any roof, no matter how far from the edge you are. It is too easy to trip over a tool or lumber and take a dangerous fall.

Before any construction begins, the existing roof needs to be thoroughly weatherproofed. If you neglect this step, you are likely to face expensive repair bills in the future. For a typical roof, the ideal treatment is a good coat of hot tar roofing under the new deck conversion. Leave this job for the pros, and tell the roofer what you are planning to do.

Test the finished job by running a garden sprinkler on the roof for at least two hours. Check for leaks carefully. Once the deck is in place, leaks will be extremely difficult to repair.

After the roof is properly sealed, attach the brackets that support the new deck's beams. These brackets are available in a variety of configurations to match different applica-

tions. Do not confuse these brackets with the thin metal brackets used for framing applications. Brackets used to support the deck beams should be made of steel at least ¼ in. thick, with welded joints.

Since your particular situation will not be identical to the one shown in the photographs, you will have to choose the appropriate brackets at your lumberyard or home center. Be certain that the brackets are aligned exactly with the rafters under the existing garage roof. Attach them with lag screws long enough to reach well into the substructure, and seal them to the roof with plenty of asphalt roof cement to prevent leaks.

Once the brackets are in place, cut the 2X12 beams to the lengths required for your application and, with help, position the beams in place in the brackets. Bore ½-in. holes through the beams for the bolts used to secure them to the brackets.

If you choose to extend the deck area more than 2 ft. beyond the roof-

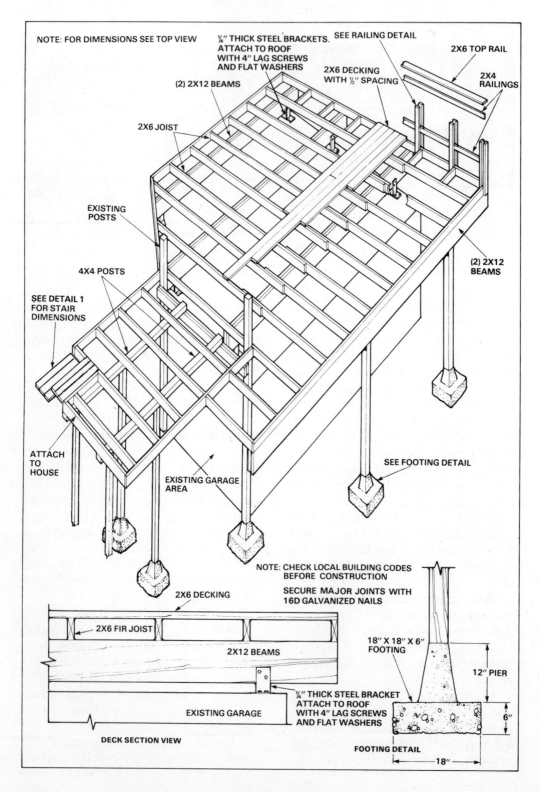

NOTE: FOR DIMENSIONS SEE TOP VIEW

¼" THICK STEEL BRACKETS. ATTACH TO ROOF WITH 4" LAG SCREWS AND FLAT WASHERS

SEE RAILING DETAIL

2X6 TOP RAIL

2X6 DECKING WITH ½" SPACING

2X4 RAILINGS

(2) 2X12 BEAMS

2X6 JOIST

EXISTING POSTS

4X4 POSTS

(2) 2X12 BEAMS

SEE DETAIL 1 FOR STAIR DIMENSIONS

ATTACH TO HOUSE

SEE FOOTING DETAIL

EXISTING GARAGE AREA

NOTE: CHECK LOCAL BUILDING CODES BEFORE CONSTRUCTION

SECURE MAJOR JOINTS WITH 16D GALVANIZED NAILS

2X6 DECKING

2X6 FIR JOIST

2X12 BEAMS

18" X 18" X 6" FOOTING

12" PIER

¼" THICK STEEL BRACKET ATTACH TO ROOF WITH 4" LAG SCREWS AND FLAT WASHERS

EXISTING GARAGE

6"

DECK SECTION VIEW

FOOTING DETAIL

18"

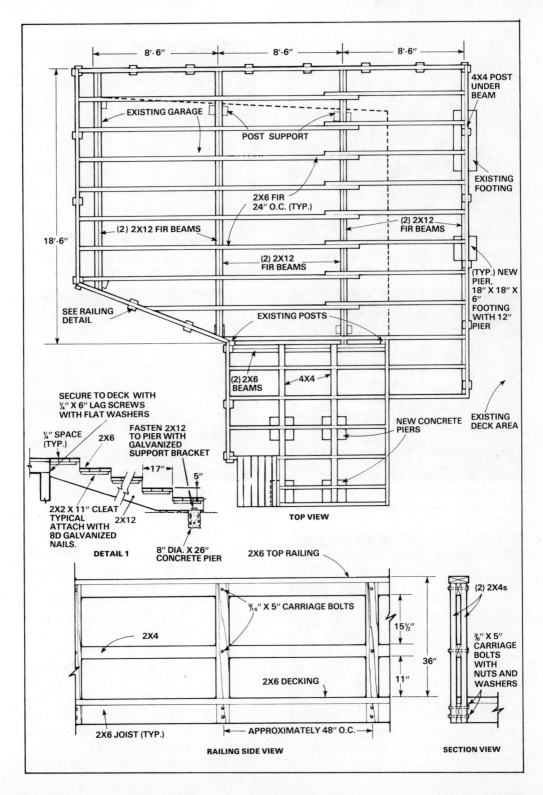

8'-6"   8'-6"   8'-6"

4X4 POST
UNDER
BEAM

EXISTING GARAGE

POST SUPPORT

EXISTING
FOOTING

2X6 FIR
24" O.C. (TYP.)

(2) 2X12 FIR BEAMS

(2) 2X12
FIR BEAMS

(2) 2X12
FIR BEAMS

18'-6"

(TYP.) NEW
PIER,
18" X 18" X
6"
FOOTING
WITH 12"
PIER

SEE RAILING
DETAIL

EXISTING POSTS

(2) 2X6
BEAMS

4X4

NEW CONCRETE
PIERS

EXISTING
DECK AREA

SECURE TO DECK WITH
¼" X 6" LAG SCREWS
WITH FLAT WASHERS

FASTEN 2X12
TO PIER WITH
GALVANIZED
SUPPORT BRACKET

¼" SPACE
(TYP.)   2X6

17"   5"

2X2 X 11" CLEAT
TYPICAL
ATTACH WITH
8D GALVANIZED
NAILS.

2X12

DETAIL 1

8" DIA. X 26"
CONCRETE PIER

TOP VIEW

2X6 TOP RAILING

(2) 2X4s

⁵⁄₁₆" X 5" CARRIAGE BOLTS

2X4

15½"

⅜" X 5"
CARRIAGE
BOLTS
WITH
NUTS AND
WASHERS

36"

2X6 DECKING

11"

2X6 JOIST (TYP.)

APPROXIMATELY 48" O.C.

RAILING SIDE VIEW

SECTION VIEW

CONSTRUCTION DETAILS

1. Call in professional roofers to prepare your existing roof for the new deck.

2. Use heavy steel brackets to support the deck's beams. Seal them well to the roof.

3. Toenail joists to the beams. Trim, then add the fascia boards. Note the overlaps.

4. Your application may include angled decking sections as well as pre-existing posts.

5. Apply the decking, notching around posts. Stagger any joints in the decking material.

line, you will need to install 4X4 support posts and another beam. Use concrete piers to support the posts, or set them in concrete, at least 3 ft. in the ground. Again, your particular situation will require different solutions. Posts used to support an overhang should be on 8-ft. centers.

Next, cut and install 2X6 deck joists on 24-in. centers. Toenail these in place with 16d galvanized nails. You may find this job easier if you drill pilot holes for the nails.

Once all the joists are in place, measure the end joists and mark their finished length. Snap a chalk line to mark the ends of the remaining joists, and trim them with a circular saw to even them for the fascia boards.

Install the 2X6 fascia boards on the perimeter of the deck area. You will need two helpers to do this job safely. Work on stepladders of an appropriate height. Position the fascia boards, and trim the joists where necessary. Nail the fascia in place with 16d galvanized nails.

The next step is to install the railing posts. Each post is made of two 2X4s, which straddle the fascia boards. Use $\frac{3}{8}$-in. X 5-in. carriage bolts with nuts and washers to attach the posts to the fascia boards. Use a 2X4 spacer block to evenly space the posts. Clamp the post in position before drilling the bolt holes. Check the posts to make certain they are vertical before drilling, as well.

Once the posts are in place, begin installing the 2X6 redwood decking lumber. Start at the center of the deck, measuring from both sides to locate the decking in perfect alignment.

Allow the decking material to overhang the fascia slightly. Any excess will be trimmed later. Space the decking to allow a $\frac{1}{2}$-in. gap between the boards. Use 16d galvanized nails to attach the decking to the joists.

Drill pilot holes for the nails when you nail near the ends of the decking. This will prevent any possible splitting of the decking lumber.

Notch the decking, as needed, where the decking material butts against a railing post. Careful measurements here will make for a tight fit.

Once all the decking is in place, use a chalk line to mark the edge of the deck. Cut off excess material with a circular saw, following the line closely. Near the railing posts, finish the trimming with a handsaw.

Add the 2X4 intermediate rails to the posts as shown in the diagram. To simplify alignment of the rails, clamp them in place at each end before drilling. Bolt the railings in place with carriage bolts, as you did previously.

This is the time to add any built-in benches, such as the ones shown in the photographs. The framework for the benches should be made of 2X4 redwood, with 2X6 material used on the seats. Legs can be of 2X4 stock. Add an additional rail between the posts for back support.

Finally, add the 2X6 cap to the railing. Notice that the cap has mitered corners. Measure carefully to insure a perfect fit. Nail the cap to the posts with 16d galvanized finishing nails. Set each nail just below the surface with a nail set.

Inspect the completed deck thoroughly, looking for splintery areas. Sand these well with a belt sander. Sand the railings and any benches especially well, since these are the areas that people will come into contact with most often.

Finish the deck with at least two coats of a wood sealer, such as Thompson's Water Seal, which can be applied with an airless sprayer or a paint roller. Allow 24 hours between coats.

Design and photos courtesy of the California Redwood Association, 591 Redwood Highway, Suite 3100, Mill Valley, CA 94941.

V.

Fences

COVERED GATE

The entry gate to your yard gives visitors their first impression of your home. This covered gate will add charm to any fence, and is guaranteed to make your guests smile.

Designed in 1927 for a house on the California coast, it has withstood the test of time. Build it for your own yard, and it will be welcoming guests into your home for years to come.

Choose all-heart redwood lumber for the gate for weather resistance, and fasten all joints with brass or stainless steel screws.

Begin construction by cutting the 4X4 posts to their finished 106-in. length. On the top of each post, form a 1½-in. X 3½-in. notch for the spreaders. Cut the notches with multiple passes of a circular saw. Space the cuts ¼ in. apart, then clean out the waste with a chisel.

Next, locate the post positions and dig postholes, 12 in. in dia. and 36 in. deep. Drop the posts into the holes and fill with concrete. Before the concrete sets, use a level to help you make the posts vertical. Check on two adjacent sides of each post.

While the concrete is setting up, build the gate. Start with the diamond-shaped insert. Cut 1X4 stock, 24 in. long, with 45 degree miters. Use a doweling jig to bore ⅜-in.-dia. matching dowel pin holes, 1⅝ in. deep. Assemble the diamond with dowel pins and resorcinol glue. Clamp the insert with pipe or bar clamps and set aside to dry.

The stiles and rails are made by sandwiching three layers of ¾-in. material. Cut the stiles and rails, paying careful attention to their various widths and lengths. Also, cut the angles on the tops of the stiles. Now, lay out the four pieces forming the middle sandwich. Place the diamond-shaped insert on top, and mark the top and bottom rails for cutting. Then cut these marked areas with a saber saw.

Now, assemble the sandwiched gate along with the diamond insert using no. 10 x 2-in. brass flathead wood screws and glue. Countersink the screw heads flush with the surface of the wood.

Rip 2-in.-wide strips from 1X6 stock to form the slats for the gate. Cut these 31 in. long, then attach them to the diamond-shaped insert with 4d galvanized finishing nails. Space the strips 1 in. apart.

Next, build the rafters for the gate's cover. Cut 45 degree bevels on each end of the outer sections, and a 75 degree miter on the inner end. The middle section has two 75 degree miters. Fasten the components together with dowel pins and resorcinol glue.

Cut two 2X4 spreaders, 12 in. long, and fasten them to the posts with no. 10 X 3-in. flathead wood screws and glue. Attach the rafter assemblies to these spreaders, making certain that they are centered and even with each other.

Next, cut 23 strips of 1X2 stock, 21 in. long, for the slatted roof. Nail these to the top of the rafters with 4d galvanized finishing nails, spacing the slats evenly, about 1 in. apart.

Hang the gate between the posts with decorative T-hinges. Position the gate flush with the posts on the

CONSTRUCTION DETAILS

1. *Notch the center section of the gate to hold the diamond-shaped insert, then sandwich the stiles and rails.*

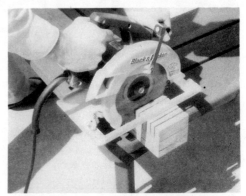

2. *Notch the 4X4 post for the spreaders with several passes of a circular saw. Remove the waste with a chisel.*

3. *Cut the 75 degree miters on the rafters using a power miter saw, table saw, or radial arm saw.*

4. *Assemble the rafters with dowel pins and glue. Use a doweling jig to bore the dowel pin holes $1\frac{5}{8}$ in. deep.*

hinge side and $1\frac{1}{2}$ in. above the surface of the ground. Add a matching gate latch to the hinge side of the opening, and the project is complete.

You can leave the gate unfinished to weather naturally or apply clear wood sealer and preservative. Another option is to paint the gate to match your home or the color of your fence. If you paint it, use high-quality exterior latex enamel for a long life.

Design courtesy of Virginia Culbert.

MATERIALS LIST

Item	Quantity
4X4 redwood	20 ft.
2X4 redwood	14 ft.
1X6 redwood	30 ft.
1X4 redwood	42 ft.
1X2 redwood	48 ft.
⅜" X 3" dowel pins	32
No. 10 X 3" flathead wood screws	36
No. 10 X 2" brass flathead wood screws	24
4d galvanized finishing nails	1 lb.
T-hinges	2
Latch, to suit	1
Concrete mix	2 bags
Resorcinol glue	as needed
Finish	as needed

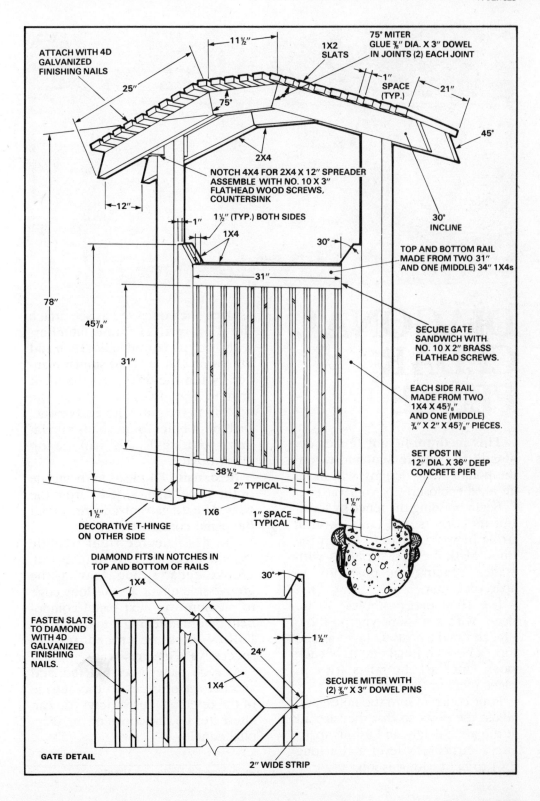

ATTACH WITH 4D GALVANIZED FINISHING NAILS

25"

75°

11½"

1X2 SLATS

75° MITER GLUE ⅜" DIA. X 3" DOWEL IN JOINTS (2) EACH JOINT

1" SPACE (TYP.)

21"

45°

2X4

NOTCH 4X4 FOR 2X4 X 12" SPREADER ASSEMBLE WITH NO. 10 X 3" FLATHEAD WOOD SCREWS, COUNTERSINK

12"

30° INCLINE

1" 1½" (TYP.) BOTH SIDES

1X4

30°

TOP AND BOTTOM RAIL MADE FROM TWO 31" AND ONE (MIDDLE) 34" 1X4s

31"

78"

45⅞"

31"

SECURE GATE SANDWICH WITH NO. 10 X 2" BRASS FLATHEAD SCREWS.

EACH SIDE RAIL MADE FROM TWO 1X4 X 45⅞" AND ONE (MIDDLE) ¾" X 2" X 45⅞" PIECES.

38½"

2" TYPICAL

1X6

1" SPACE TYPICAL

1½"

SET POST IN 12" DIA. X 36" DEEP CONCRETE PIER

1½"

DECORATIVE T-HINGE ON OTHER SIDE

DIAMOND FITS IN NOTCHES IN TOP AND BOTTOM OF RAILS

1X4

30°

FASTEN SLATS TO DIAMOND WITH 4D GALVANIZED FINISHING NAILS.

1½"

24"

1X4

SECURE MITER WITH (2) ⅜" X 3" DOWEL PINS

GATE DETAIL

2" WIDE STRIP

DIAGONAL CEDAR FENCE

This medium-height fence, designed to complement most contemporary home designs, will make an ideal enclosure for your yard.

Begin building the fence by locating its corners and ends. Stretch string between stakes to set up the lines. Mark the post locations with stakes, spacing the posts 96 in. apart on center.

Dig 10-in.-dia. postholes, 36 in. deep, with a scissors-type posthole digger. Cut the posts 92 in. long, and form a beveled finial on top of each post. Once all the posts are cut, place them in the holes.

Pour concrete into the holes, and adjust the posts so that they are all at the same height and 96 in. apart. Use a carpenter's level and a long 2X4 to help with this job.

Once the concrete has set, attach the 2X4 vertical frame members with 16d galvanized nails. Then add the lower 2X4 rails in a similar manner. Notch the 2X6 top rails to fit around the 4X4 posts. Cut the notches in the rails with a saber saw. Drill pilot holes for the nails to minimize splitting. Finally, nail the top rails in place.

Next, nail 1X1 cleats to the inside of the panel frames, ⅝ in. from the edge. Use 4d galvanized nails for all the panel construction.

Cut a 45 degree right triangle from a piece of 1X8 tongue-and-groove cedar siding, leaving the groove side uncut. Use its long edge to measure the next panel component before fastening it to the cleats. Follow the same procedure with successive segments.

As each panel is completed, add another set of cleats to the outside of the opening. For variety, you can alternate the directions of the diagonal panels.

Design courtesy of John Heystee, Morro Bay, CA.

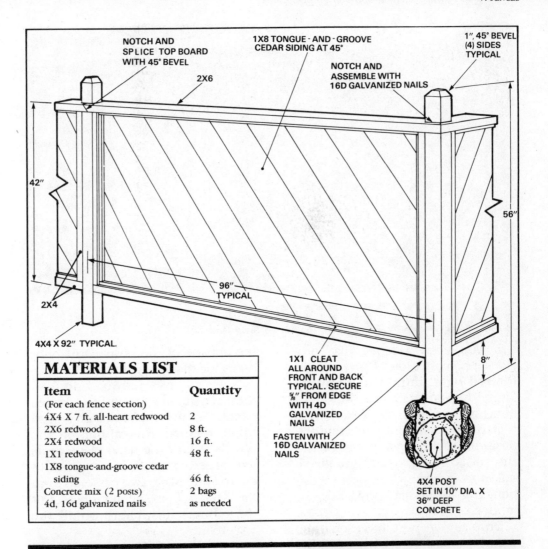

NOTCH AND
SPLICE TOP BOARD
WITH 45° BEVEL

1X8 TONGUE - AND - GROOVE
CEDAR SIDING AT 45°

1", 45° BEVEL
(4) SIDES
TYPICAL

2X6

NOTCH AND
ASSEMBLE WITH
16D GALVANIZED NAILS

42"

56"

2X4

96"
TYPICAL

8"

4X4 X 92" TYPICAL.

1X1 CLEAT
ALL AROUND
FRONT AND BACK
TYPICAL. SECURE
⅝" FROM EDGE
WITH 4D
GALVANIZED
NAILS

FASTEN WITH
16D GALVANIZED
NAILS

4X4 POST
SET IN 10" DIA. X
36" DEEP
CONCRETE

MATERIALS LIST

Item	Quantity
(For each fence section)	
4X4 X 7 ft. all-heart redwood	2
2X6 redwood	8 ft.
2X4 redwood	16 ft.
1X1 redwood	48 ft.
1X8 tongue-and-groove cedar siding	46 ft.
Concrete mix (2 posts)	2 bags
4d, 16d galvanized nails	as needed

CONSTRUCTION DETAILS

1. Cut the beveled tops of the posts with your radial arm saw. Set the depth of cut to suit.

2. If you choose, you can make your own tongue-and-groove cedar siding by using a shaper head on your saw.

117

LATTICE FENCE

If you need a fence that provides a combination of privacy and filtered light, build this redwood lattice fence. Its elegant look will improve the appearance of any yard.

Start construction by locating the positions of the fence posts. Center the posts 48 in. apart and drive stakes to indicate each post's position. Dig 10-in.-dia. postholes, 36 in. deep.

Drop an 8-ft. post into each hole, then fill the holes with concrete mix. You will need 1½ bags of concrete mix for each hole.

Adjust the height of the posts, using a long 2X4 and a level to help make all the posts the same height. At the same time adjust the posts to be perfectly vertical. Use temporary braces to hold them in postion. Run a string line along the top and bottom of the posts to make certain they are aligned properly.

Once the concrete has set, cut 2X4 rails to fit between the posts. Toenail these in place, flush with the outside of the posts. Drill pilot holes for the 16d galvanized nails.

Now, cut 1X3 redwood stock to form the frames around the lattice panels. Set up your saw with a dado blade to form the rabbets in the boards. Adjust the dado blade to its widest setting and set the depth of cut to ½ in. Make two passes to form the ⅞-in. X ½-in.-deep rabbets. Cut the rabbets full length on all the 1X3 frames.

If your fence turns a corner, miter the edges of two 1X4 corner caps, then rabbet them as you did before. See Detail 1 in the diagram for the correct pattern.

Next, cut pre-fabricated lattice panels to fit your fence. Each panel should overlap the posts and rails 1⅜ in., except at corner posts, where they overlap 1⅝ in. Attach the bottom and one vertical 1X3 frame with 8d galvanized nails. Install the lattice and then secure the remaining frames. The lattice panel is not nailed. Follow this procedure

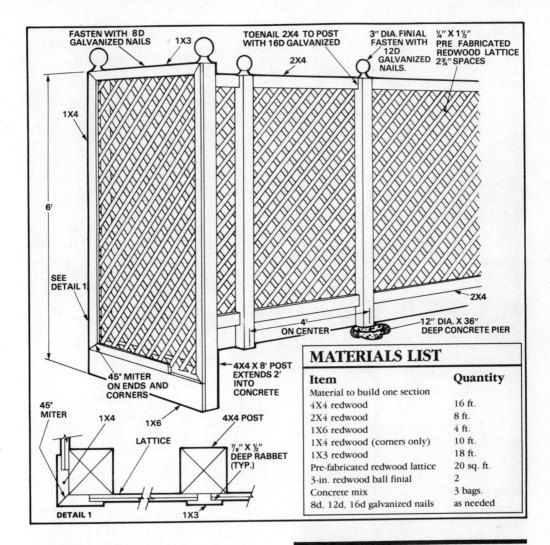

FASTEN WITH 8D GALVANIZED NAILS

1X3

TOENAIL 2X4 TO POST WITH 16D GALVANIZED

2X4

3″ DIA. FINIAL FASTEN WITH 12D GALVANIZED NAILS.

¼″ X 1½″ PRE FABRICATED REDWOOD LATTICE 2¾″ SPACES

1X4

6′

SEE DETAIL 1

2X4

4′ ON CENTER

12″ DIA. X 36″ DEEP CONCRETE PIER

45° MITER ON ENDS AND CORNERS

4X4 X 8′ POST EXTENDS 2′ INTO CONCRETE

45° MITER

1X4

1X6

4X4 POST

LATTICE

⅞″ X ½″ DEEP RABBET (TYP.)

DETAIL 1

1X3

MATERIALS LIST

Item	Quantity
Material to build one section	
4X4 redwood	16 ft.
2X4 redwood	8 ft.
1X6 redwood	4 ft.
1X4 redwood (corners only)	10 ft.
1X3 redwood	18 ft.
Pre-fabricated redwood lattice	20 sq. ft.
3-in. redwood ball finial	2
Concrete mix	3 bags.
8d, 12d, 16d galvanized nails	as needed

for the remaining lattice panel installations.

Add the 1X6 bottom trim boards, nailing them with 8d galvanized nails. Adjust the width of these boards to suit the grade. Finally, nail 3-in. finials to the tops of the posts with 12d galvanized nails. Drill pilot holes for the nails to prevent splitting.

You can leave the fence unfinished to weather naturally, or apply two coats of wood sealer. Use a spray gun to speed application.

CONSTRUCTION DETAIL

1. Dig 10-in. dia. post holes, 36 in. deep. Keep the holes centered around the stake locations.

LATTICE-TOPPED FENCE

If a medium-height fence is what your yard needs to be complete, this redwood fence with a lattice top might be just the answer. Designed to screen a front yard, it is the perfect combination of solid panels and open lattice work.

Choose redwood lumber for the fence to provide a combination of beauty and weather resistance. Once the fence is built, you can let it weather naturally or finish it with wood sealer and preservative. Paint is another possible finish.

Start construction by locating the post positions along the fence line. Space the centers of the posts 8 ft. apart. At each post location, dig a 10-in.-dia. hole 36 in. deep. Local building codes may differ, so check them before building the fence.

Place the posts in the holes and fill with concrete. A 100-lb. bag of cement mix is required for each post. Before the concrete sets, adjust the posts to be perfectly vertical and equal in height using a carpenter's level.

Add temporary braces, if necessary, to hold the posts in place while the concrete sets up. To brace the posts properly, use two braces on each post, attached to adjacent sides. Notice in the diagram that the posts extend only 30 in. into the holes.

Check the height of the posts with a long 2X4 and a level, and stretch a string along the outside of the fence line to make sure the posts are aligned correctly. The more time you spend in aligning the posts, the better the finished fence will look.

To give yourself plenty of time, set only two posts at a time, proceeding when these are perfect. Allow at least one or two days for the concrete to set well before continuing to build the rest of the fence.

After the posts are set, install the lower 2X4 rails, which should be 4½ in. above the grade. Toenail them in place with 12d galvanized nails. Drill pilot holes for the nails to simplify construction and to prevent splitting. Use a level to help align the rails.

The top rails have a ¾-in. X ¾-in. groove on the bottom to accommodate the fence panels. Form this groove with a ¾-in straight bit in your router. Use an edge guide attachment to keep the groove properly aligned. Make several passes, deepening the cut with each pass until the correct depth is reached.

You can also form the grooves in the rails with a dado blade on your table saw or radial arm saw. Be sure to follow the correct anti-kickback steps.

Attach these grooved rails to the posts. Measure carefully to locate

CONSTRUCTION DETAILS

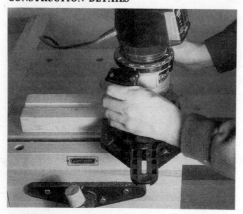

1. Plow a ¾-in. X ¾-in. groove in the top rails with a straight bit in your router. Make several deepening passes.

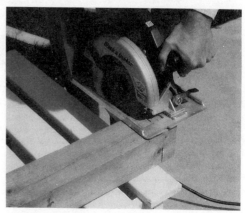

2. To cut the tops of the posts square, make two passes with your circular saw: one on the top and one on the bottom.

them exactly parallel with the lower rails. This will insure a proper fit for the panel components.

Now, on one side of the rails and posts, nail 1X1 strips to form cleats for the panel. Use 6d galvanized nails, and locate the cleats ⅝ in. from the edge of the post and rail material to center the panel.

Cut 1X6 redwood stock to fit between the rails with the upper end in the groove. Install the panel components, one by one, until you reach the last slat in each opening. Rip this slat to the appropriate width.

Add the remaining 1X1 cleats to the other side of the posts and rails to complete the lower panels.

Next, attach the 2X6 cap to the top of the posts with 16d galvanized nails. To prevent splitting, drill pilot holes for the nails. Center the joints over the posts, and equalize the overhang of the cap material.

As you did before, nail a frame of 1X1 material to one side of the opening to serve as a frame for the redwood lattice.

Cut redwood lath with 45 degree miters to fit the opening. Space the lath 2¾ in. apart with a spacer block cut from scrap. Except for two pieces at each end of the lattice panel, all the pieces are the same length, which simplifies the cutting. Nail the lath to the 1X1 frame with 4d galvanized nails.

If you choose, you can substitute pre-fab lattice with handmade lattice panels. If you do, measure the material carefully before cutting.

Once the lattice panels are in place, add the 1X1 frame strips to the opposite side to complete the fence.

MATERIALS LIST

Item	Quantity
For each 8-ft. section:	
4X4 X 86½″ redwood	2
2X6 redwood	8 ft.
2X4 redwood	16 ft.
1X6 redwood	54 ft.
1X1 redwood	48 ft.
1½″ redwood lath	30 ft.
Concrete mix, 100-lb. bags	2
4d, 6d, 12d, 16d galv. nails	as needed
Paint or clear wood sealer and preservative	to suit

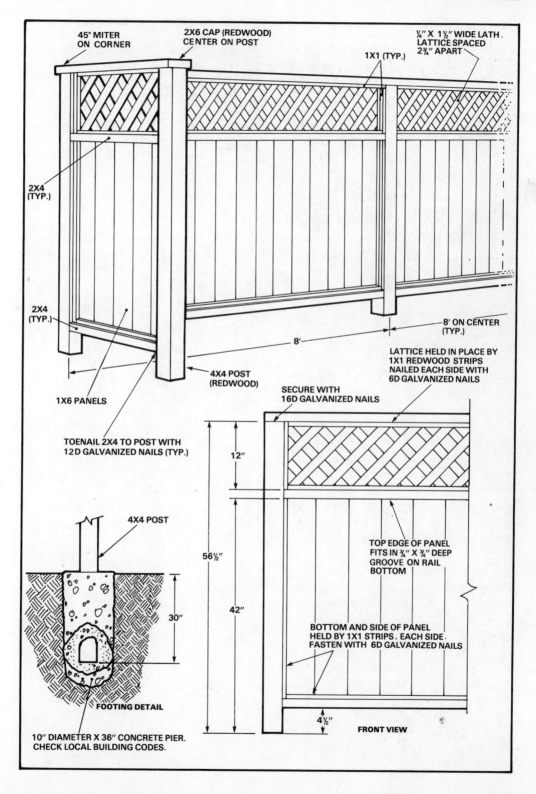

45° MITER ON CORNER

2X6 CAP (REDWOOD) CENTER ON POST

¼" X 1½" WIDE LATH . LATTICE SPACED 2¾" APART

1X1 (TYP.)

2X4 (TYP.)

2X4 (TYP.)

4X4 POST (REDWOOD)

1X6 PANELS

8'

8' ON CENTER (TYP.)

TOENAIL 2X4 TO POST WITH 12D GALVANIZED NAILS (TYP.)

LATTICE HELD IN PLACE BY 1X1 REDWOOD STRIPS NAILED EACH SIDE WITH 6D GALVANIZED NAILS

SECURE WITH 16D GALVANIZED NAILS

TOP EDGE OF PANEL FITS IN ¾" X ¾" DEEP GROOVE ON RAIL BOTTOM

BOTTOM AND SIDE OF PANEL HELD BY 1X1 STRIPS . EACH SIDE . FASTEN WITH 6D GALVANIZED NAILS

12"

56½"

42"

4½"

FRONT VIEW

4X4 POST

30"

FOOTING DETAIL

10" DIAMETER X 36" CONCRETE PIER . CHECK LOCAL BUILDING CODES.

SADDLEBACK FENCE

If a low fence is what your yard needs, it would be hard to find a more attractive one than this. Its gentle curves and finials will blend with any home to present an attractive appearance to passersby.

To make your fence last for years, choose redwood lumber for all the fence components. Posts should be cut from pressure-treated 4X4 redwood to prevent them from rotting where they contact the ground.

Start construction by locating the post positions along the fence line. Space the centers of the posts 8 ft. apart. At each post location, dig a 12-in.-dia. hole 36 in. deep.

Place the posts in the holes and fill with concrete. One 100-lb. bag of concrete mix should be enough for each post. Before the concrete sets, use a carpenter's level to adjust the posts so that they're perfectly vertical. If necessary, add temporary braces to hold the posts in place while the concrete sets up.

Check the height of the posts with a long 2X4 and a level, and stretch a string to make sure that the posts are aligned correctly. For best results, set only two posts at a time, proceeding when these are perfect. Allow at least one day for the concrete to set before building the rest of the fence.

Cut the 2X4 fence rails to fit between the posts, and toenail them in place with 10d galvanized finishing nails. Drill pilot holes for the nails to simplify the job. As you work, check the rails with a carpenter's level.

Next, add the 1X6 base boards to the bottom of the fence, nailing them to the posts with 6d galvanized finishing nails. The joints between the boards should meet at the center of a post. Once again, check the boards with a carpenter's level to make them even.

Now, take seven of the 1X4 picket boards and lay them on a flat surface, such as a driveway or patio. Space the pickets according to the dimensions shown in the diagram.

Drive a nail near one end of a 12-ft.-long piece of 1X2 lumber, to use as a pivot, and drill a hole for a pencil 110 in. from the nail. Line up this improvised compass to make the shortest board 24 in. long, then mark the remaining boards to form the correct curve.

Cut the pickets to the marked profiles with a saber saw, then use this set as a template to mark all the pickets you need. The pickets that are nailed to the posts should be cut square at the top. Keep this set of pattern templates separate and use them on the last section of the fence.

Attach the pickets to the rails with 6d galvanized nails, spacing them accurately. Notice that the gap decreases to 2½ in. at each post.

Form the finials from three pieces of 1X6 X 5½-in. stock. Surface glue the pieces, then set your table saw to cut a 45 degree bevel. Adjust the depth of cut to form bevels half the thickness of the wood. Since you will be working with small workpieces, be especially careful.

Fasten the finials to the posts with 12d galvanized finishing nails. To

CONSTRUCTION DETAILS

1. *Cut the bevels on the finial stock on your table or radial arm saw. Set the blade to cut a 45 degree bevel.*

2. *Space seven slats on a level surface and use an improvised compass to lay out the 110-in. radius.*

3. *Cut the slats with a saber saw, following the lines carefully. The slats that attach to the posts are cut square.*

4. *Use the pre-cut slats as templates to lay out the remaining slats for each section of the fence.*

prevent splitting, drill pilot holes for these nails. Finally, finish the corners of the fence with trianglar filler strips ripped from ³/₄-in. stock, as shown in the diagram.

Once the fence-building is completed, paint your fence with high-quality exterior latex house paint in the color of your choice. If you want a natural appearance, apply clear wood sealer.

MATERIALS LIST

Item	Quantity
For each fence section:	
4X4 X 78″ pressure-treated redwood	2
2X4 redwood	16 ft.
1X6 redwood	11 ft.
1X4 redwood	40 ft.
Concrete mix, 100-lb. bags	2
6d, 10d, 12d galvanized finishing nails	as needed
Resorcinol glue	as needed
Paint or clear wood sealer	as needed

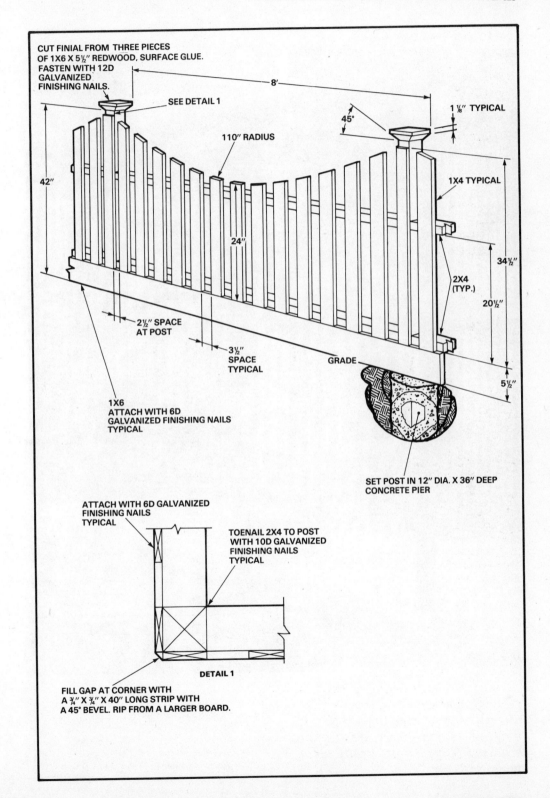

CUT FINIAL FROM THREE PIECES
OF 1X6 X 5½" REDWOOD, SURFACE GLUE.
FASTEN WITH 12D
GALVANIZED
FINISHING NAILS.

SEE DETAIL 1

8'

1 ⅛" TYPICAL

45°

110" RADIUS

42"

1X4 TYPICAL

24"

34½"

2X4
(TYP.)

20½"

2½" SPACE
AT POST

3½"
SPACE
TYPICAL

GRADE

5½"

1X6
ATTACH WITH 6D
GALVANIZED FINISHING NAILS
TYPICAL

SET POST IN 12" DIA. X 36" DEEP
CONCRETE PIER

ATTACH WITH 6D GALVANIZED
FINISHING NAILS
TYPICAL

TOENAIL 2X4 TO POST
WITH 10D GALVANIZED
FINISHING NAILS
TYPICAL

DETAIL 1

FILL GAP AT CORNER WITH
A ¾" X ¾" X 40" LONG STRIP WITH
A 45° BEVEL. RIP FROM A LARGER BOARD.

TRELLIS FENCE

This redwood trellis-style fence is the perfect solution for any home needing a privacy screen. The overhanging trellis makes it possible to dress up your home with hanging plants.

The slat design of this fence is designed to provide both privacy and filtered light, while a built-in bench adds comfortable seating or a spot for container plants.

This design is flexible enough to be used either as a fence or as a protective screen for deck or patio areas. You can easily alter the width of the trellis to suit any application.

Start construction by locating the post positions along the outer fence line. Space the centers of the posts 8 ft. apart. At each post location, dig a 12-in.-dia. hole 36 in. deep. Check your local building codes to make sure that these post foundations are correct for your area. Notice that the posts extend only 30 in. below the grade.

Locate a second line of posts for the trellis supports. Place these in line with the outer fence posts, with the posts 48 in. apart from center to center. If you wish, you can alter this distance to fit a particular application, up to a maximum of 8 ft.

Place the posts in the holes and fill with concrete. One 100-lb. bag of concrete mix should be enough for each post. Before the concrete sets, adjust the posts to be perfectly vertical using a carpenter's level. Add temporary braces, if necessary, to hold the posts in place while the concrete sets up.

Check the height of the posts with a long 2X4 and a level, and stretch a string to make sure that the posts are aligned correctly. To give yourself plenty of time, set only two posts at a time, proceeding when these are aligned perfectly. Allow at least one day for the concrete to set before continuing to build the fence.

Once the concrete has set, attach the 2X6 joists to the posts. Center the joints on a post and fasten the joists with 16d galvanized nails. Once again, check the posts with a level to make sure they are vertical. At the ends of the fence, let the joists overhang the posts 12 in.

Add the 2X4 rails between the posts, toenailing them in place with 12d galvanized nails. Drill pilot holes for the nails to simplify construction. Locate the lower rail 12 in. above the grade. The upper rail should be 60 in. high. Use a level to help you position these rails.

Next, cut the 2X2 slats to 75-in. lengths. Nail the first slat in each

CONSTRUCTION DETAILS

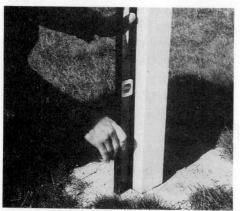

1. Use a carpenter's level to check the post. To make sure it's absolutely vertical, check it from two sides.

2. Toenail the rails to the posts. Use a level to make sure the rails are level and are 12-in. above grade.

section into position, observing the dimensions shown in the diagram. Locate the bottom of the slat 3 in. above the grade. Use 12d galvanized nails and check the slat with a level to make it vertical.

Continue adding slats, spacing them 1½ in. apart. Use a spare slat as a spacer block to make the gaps even. One nail is sufficient at each rail. Follow the same procedure to attach the slats to the roof of the trellis. Align the roof slats with the face slats for a clean appearance.

Cut the roof slats long enough to allow for a 6-in. overhang. If you use the dimensions given in the diagram, the slats will be 63½ in. long. If you alter the dimensions, be sure to allow for the overhang.

Locate the position of any benches you wish to add. Dig an 18-in.-deep hole for the outer leg of each bench, then construct the leg as shown in the diagram. You can make the bench any width you choose by cutting the cross brace to a multiple of 3 inches.

Nail the bench slats to the cross-

piece, spacing them, as you did before, with a scrap of the slat material. Now, interlace the bench slats with the slats in the fence. Drop the leg into the pre-dug hole and fill with concrete.

Before the concrete sets up, use a level to make the bench top even. Nail the bench slats to the adjacent fence slats with 8d galvanized nails. Drill pilot holes for the nails to minimize splitting. Although the bench in the diagram is shown on the outside of the fence, it could be located on the inside as well.

Leave the fence unfinished if you would like it to weather naturally, or apply two coats of wood sealer and preservative to keep it looking fresh for years.

MATERIALS LIST	
Item	**Quantity**
For each 8-ft. section:	
4X4 X 10-ft. redwood	4
2X6 redwood	32 ft.
2X4 redwood	16 ft.
2X2 redwood	360 ft.
Concrete mix, 100-lb. bags	4
8d, 12d, 16d galvanized nails	as needed

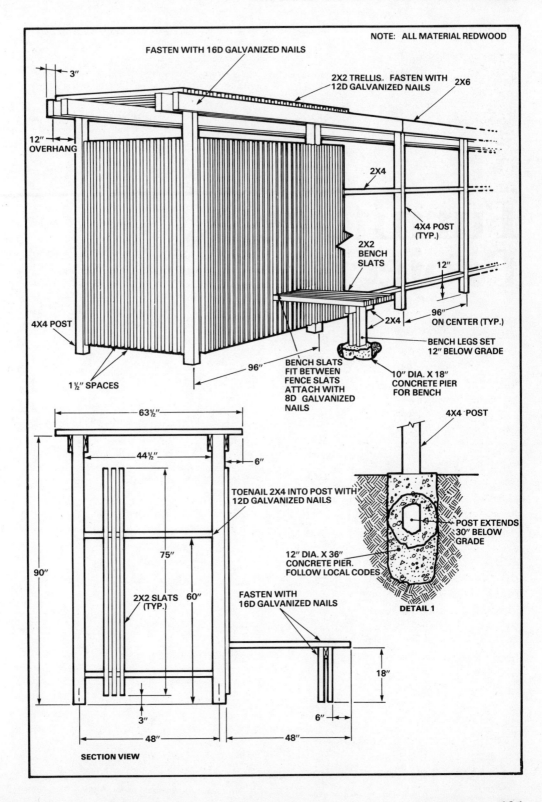

NOTE: ALL MATERIAL REDWOOD

FASTEN WITH 16D GALVANIZED NAILS

2X2 TRELLIS. FASTEN WITH
12D GALVANIZED NAILS

2X6

3"

12"
OVERHANG

2X4

4X4 POST
(TYP.)

12"

2X2
BENCH
SLATS

96"
ON CENTER (TYP.)

4X4 POST

2X4

BENCH LEGS SET
12" BELOW GRADE

1½" SPACES

96"

BENCH SLATS
FIT BETWEEN
FENCE SLATS
ATTACH WITH
8D GALVANIZED
NAILS

10" DIA. X 18"
CONCRETE PIER
FOR BENCH

63½"

4X4 POST

44½"

6"

TOENAIL 2X4 INTO POST WITH
12D GALVANIZED NAILS

POST EXTENDS
30" BELOW
GRADE

75"

90"

2X2 SLATS
(TYP.)

60"

FASTEN WITH
16D GALVANIZED NAILS

12" DIA. X 36"
CONCRETE PIER.
FOLLOW LOCAL CODES

DETAIL 1

18"

3"

6"

48"

48"

SECTION VIEW

131

VI.

Furniture Projects

This Adirondack furniture makes casual get togethers a pleasure. Notice that the Adirondack's back is supported at the arm and base.

ADIRONDACK FURNITURE

One of the most popular styles of outdoor furniture comes from the Adirondack Mountain resorts of New York. For comfort and rugged good looks, it is hard to beat these simple designs.

Construction of the chair and the love seat follows the same basic steps. The only difference between the two is the width.

Begin by laying out the rear leg (Detail 3) on a piece of 1X12 pine. If you build both the chair and the love seat, you will need four of these components. After cutting the first, use it as a pattern for the rest.

Next, lay out and cut the front legs, then assemble the pairs of components with no. 8 X 1¼-in. flathead wood screws and waterproof resorcinol glue. Drill pilot holes, counterbored for wood screw hole plugs, with a combination pilot bit.

Lay out the back support pattern (Detail 2). First draw the pattern on a piece of hardbord with a grid of ½-in. squares. Transfer the pattern to the hardboard, then cut this out to use as a pattern for the other parts.

Attach the support to the inside of the leg assembly with screws and glue, counterboring for wood plugs as you did before.

Cut the remaining components to the sizes shown in the diagram. No-tice that the second lowest back cleat and the front seat boards are cut with a 9 degree bevel.

Cut all the back boards 36 in. long. The radius on the back of the furniture will be formed after assembly.

Round over the edges of the parts indicated in the diagram with a ⅜-in.-radius rounding-over bit, with pilot, in your router.

Now, assemble the cleats to the back with 3d galvanized finishing nails and resorcinol glue. Align the components carefully, maintaining a ½-in. gap between the slats. Nail the cleats to the back slats from the rear. Set the nails below the surface of the wood, then fill the gaps with wood filler.

After making the assembly, use a bar compass to lay out the 25-in. radius on the top of the back. At the edges of the back, add a ¾-in. radius to smooth the curve. Cut the back profile with a fine-toothed blade in your saber saw. Work carefully to prevent the blade from creeping away from a vertical cut.

Begin the final assembly by nailing the seat slats to the legs with 8d galvanized finishing nails. Use glue on the joints as well.

Add the leg braces and the front 1X6 skirt, checking the assembly for squareness as you go, then fasten the

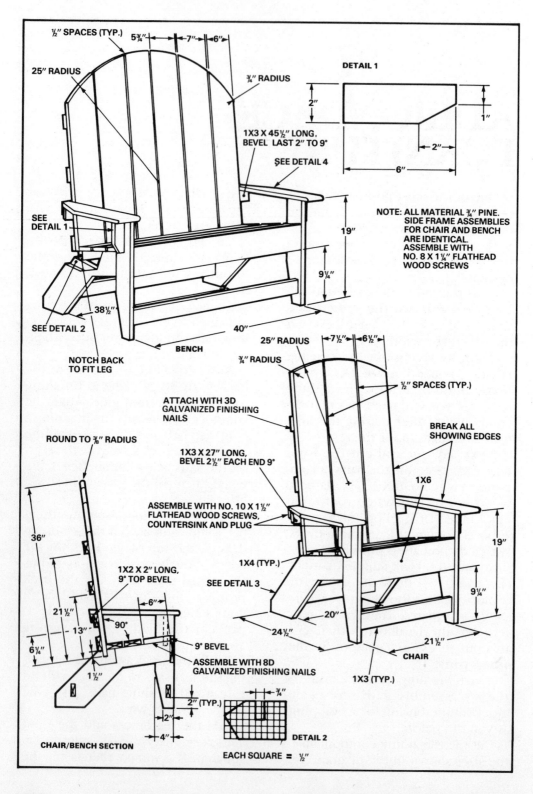

½" SPACES (TYP.)

5¾"   7"   6"

25" RADIUS

¾" RADIUS

DETAIL 1

2"

1"

2"

6"

1X3 X 45½" LONG, BEVEL LAST 2" TO 9°

SEE DETAIL 4

SEE DETAIL 1

19"

9¼"

NOTE: ALL MATERIAL ¾" PINE. SIDE FRAME ASSEMBLIES FOR CHAIR AND BENCH ARE IDENTICAL. ASSEMBLE WITH NO. 8 X 1¼" FLATHEAD WOOD SCREWS

38½"

SEE DETAIL 2

40"

BENCH

NOTCH BACK TO FIT LEG

25" RADIUS

¾" RADIUS

7½"   6½"

½" SPACES (TYP.)

ATTACH WITH 3D GALVANIZED FINISHING NAILS

BREAK ALL SHOWING EDGES

ROUND TO ⅜" RADIUS

1X3 X 27" LONG, BEVEL 2½" EACH END 9°

1X6

36"

ASSEMBLE WITH NO. 10 X 1½" FLATHEAD WOOD SCREWS, COUNTERSINK AND PLUG

19"

1X4 (TYP.)

1X2 X 2" LONG, 9° TOP BEVEL

SEE DETAIL 3

9¼"

6"

21½"

90°

20"

13"

24½"

6¼"

9° BEVEL

21½"

1½"

ASSEMBLE WITH 8D GALVANIZED FINISHING NAILS

CHAIR

1X3 (TYP.)

2" (TYP.)

2"

¾"

4"

CHAIR/BENCH SECTION

DETAIL 2

EACH SQUARE = ½"

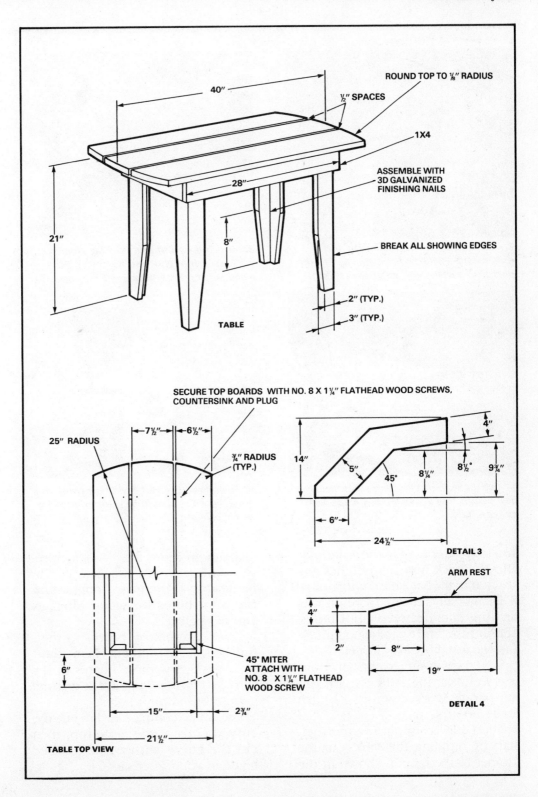

ROUND TOP TO ⅛″ RADIUS

½″ SPACES

40″

1X4

ASSEMBLE WITH
3D GALVANIZED
FINISHING NAILS

28″

BREAK ALL SHOWING EDGES

21″

8″

2″ (TYP.)

3″ (TYP.)

TABLE

SECURE TOP BOARDS WITH NO. 8 X 1¼″ FLATHEAD WOOD SCREWS,
COUNTERSINK AND PLUG

7½″   6½″

25″ RADIUS

¾″ RADIUS
(TYP.)

14″

5″

45°

8¼″

8½°

4″

9¾″

6″

24½″

DETAIL 3

ARM REST

4″

2″

8″

19″

DETAIL 4

6″

45° MITER
ATTACH WITH
NO. 8 X 1¼″ FLATHEAD
WOOD SCREW

15″   2¾″

21½″

TABLE TOP VIEW

137

CONSTRUCTION DETAILS

1. *Lay out the rear leg, following the dimensions shown in the diagram. Cut the part with a saber saw. Refer to diagram.*

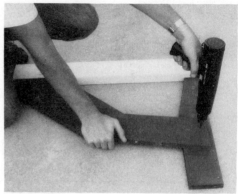

2. *Attach the front and rear leg components with resorcinol glue and no. 8 X 1¼ in. wood screws. Keep the assembly square.*

5. *Cut the back curve with a saber saw. For best results, use a fine-toothed blade and cut carefully.*

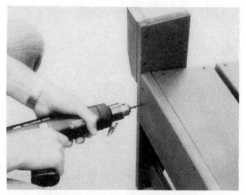

6. *Install the 1X6 rail inside the front legs. All screw holes should be counterbored for screw hole plugs.*

arm to the front leg in the same way. Slip the back into the notches and fasten it to the back cleat with no. 10 X 1½-in. flathead wood screws, after drilling counterbored pilot holes. Add the arm braces and wood plugs, and the assembly is complete.

Sand the completed chair and love seat well, starting with 80-grit garnet paper. Work down to 120-grit for a smooth surface.

The table is simple to construct. Start by building the skirt. Cut the lumber to the lengths shown in the diagram and join the parts with re-sorcinol glue and no. 8 X 1¼-in. flathead wood screws. Counterbore the pilot holes for wood plugs as you did before.

Next, rip the top boards to their finished widths and cut them all 40 in. long. Screw these boards to the skirt assembly, once again drilling counterbored pilot holes.

Use a bar compass to lay out the curved ends of the table top, then cut the curve with a fine-toothed blade in your saber saw.

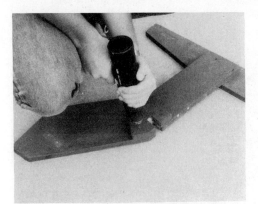

3. Attach the back brace (Detail 2) to the inside of the leg set with resorcinol glue and no. 8 X 1¼ in. flathead wood screws.

4. Lay out the profile of the back with a bar compass. At the ends of the curve, add a ¾-in. radius.

7. Screw the back of the arm to the cleat with no. 10 X 1½-in. flathead wood screws. The cleat is beveled to match the arm's angle.

8. Install table's legs inside the skirt. Use no. 8 X 1¼-in. flathead wood screws from inside the leg after drilling pilot holes.

Cut out the leg components, first mitering the edges as shown in the diagram. Assemble the legs with glue and screws, following the same procedure you did before. Once the glue has dried, assemble the project, screwing the legs to the table skirt from inside.

Sand the table as you did the other pieces, then apply a coat of enamel primer to the furniture. Follow this with two coats of semi-gloss exterior latex enamel in the color of your choice.

MATERIALS LIST

Item	Quantity
1X12 pine or fir	10 ft.
1X8 pine or fir	42 ft.
1X6 pine or fir	20 ft.
1X4 pine or fir	40 ft.
1X3 pine or fir	30 ft.
¾″ wood screw hole plugs	as needed
3d, 8d galv. finishing nails	2 lbs.
No. 8 X 1¼″ flathead wood screws	as needed
No. 10 X 1½″ flathead wood screws	as needed
Resorcinol glue	as needed
Enamel primer	2 qts.
Semi-gloss exterior latex enamel	2 qts.

BEACH CHAIR

Whether you are at the beach or just relaxing in your own yard, it is hard to beat the traditional wood and canvas adjustable chair. Our version, made of oak, is designed for comfort and built to last for years.

Start the project by ripping 2-in.-wide strips from 1-in.-thick oak stock. Use a combination planer blade for a smooth finish. Cut the resulting strips to the lengths shown in the diagram.

Next, form the rounded profiles at the ends of the components with a saber saw. Clamp the pieces together and smooth the ends with a belt sander.

Break the edges of all components with a 45 degree beveling bit, with pilot, in your router. If you have a router table, the job will be easier.

Now, lay out all of the holes and

counterbores as shown in the diagram and form these on a drill press. Use a backup board when drilling through the material.

Lay out the notches on the rear legs with an adjustable bevel and cut them carefully with a fine-toothed blade in your saber saw.

Sand the individual components well, then apply a finish. Sprayed lacquer, such as Deft, makes an ideal finish for this project.

While the finish is drying, make the sling seat of medium-weight canvas. Hem the edges first, then form the looped ends, double-stitching all seams. The finished sling should measure $19\frac{3}{4}$ in. X 50 in.

Assemble the chair as shown in the diagram. Drill countersunk pilot holes for the screws that secure the dowels. When tightening the pivot bolts, allow for free movement of the joints. Finally, attach the beveled stop with no. 10 X $1\frac{1}{2}$-in. brass flathead wood screws.

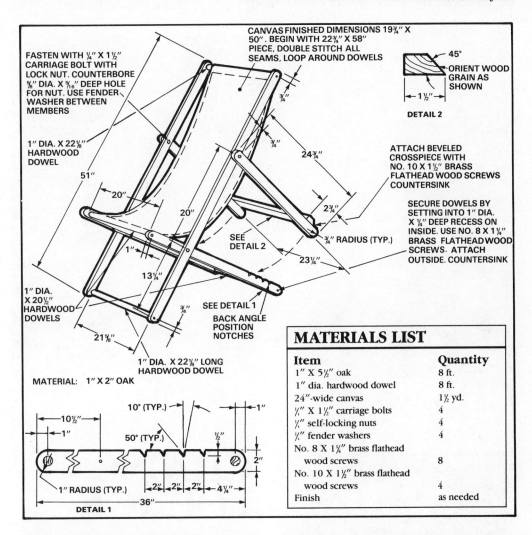

FASTEN WITH ¼" X 1½" CARRIAGE BOLT WITH LOCK NUT. COUNTERBORE ⅝" DIA. X ⁵⁄₁₆" DEEP HOLE FOR NUT. USE FENDER WASHER BETWEEN MEMBERS

1" DIA. X 22⅛" HARDWOOD DOWEL

51"

20"

20"

1" DIA. X 20½" HARDWOOD DOWELS

21⅝"

13¼"

1"

¾"

SEE DETAIL 2

SEE DETAIL 1

BACK ANGLE POSITION NOTCHES

1" DIA. X 22⅛" LONG HARDWOOD DOWEL

MATERIAL: 1" X 2" OAK

CANVAS FINISHED DIMENSIONS 19¾" X 50". BEGIN WITH 22¾" X 58" PIECE, DOUBLE STITCH ALL SEAMS, LOOP AROUND DOWELS

¾"

¾"

24¾"

2¾"

¾" RADIUS (TYP.)

23¼"

45°
ORIENT WOOD GRAIN AS SHOWN
1½"
DETAIL 2

ATTACH BEVELED CROSSPIECE WITH NO. 10 X 1½" BRASS FLATHEAD WOOD SCREWS COUNTERSINK

SECURE DOWELS BY SETTING INTO 1" DIA. X ¼" DEEP RECESS ON INSIDE. USE NO. 8 X 1¼" BRASS FLATHEAD WOOD SCREWS. ATTACH OUTSIDE. COUNTERSINK

DETAIL 1

10½"
1"
50° (TYP.)
10° (TYP.)
1"
½"
2"
1" RADIUS (TYP.)
2" 2" 2" 4¼"
36"

MATERIALS LIST

Item	Quantity
1" X 5½" oak	8 ft.
1" dia. hardwood dowel	8 ft.
24"-wide canvas	1½ yd.
¼" X 1½" carriage bolts	4
¼" self-locking nuts	4
¼" fender washers	4
No. 8 X 1¼" brass flathead wood screws	8
No. 10 X 1½" brass flathead wood screws	4
Finish	as needed

CONSTRUCTION DETAILS

1. Break the edges of all components with a 45 degree beveling bit, with pilot, in your router.

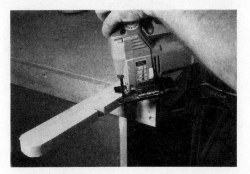

2. Cut the stop notches in the rear legs with a saber saw. Lay out these notches carefully for proper action.

CHAISE LOUNGE

Every patio or deck needs a chaise lounge. Here is one you can build yourself. Constructed of pine lumber, its back can be adjusted to four different angles for comfortable relaxation.

The chaise can be finished with paint or varnish, and may be used as is or with commercial chaise lounge pads for even more comfort. The pine construction makes the chaise light enough for easy portability.

Begin building the project by forming the legs. After cutting the 4X4 stock to length, use a dado

This pine chaise lounge features a four-position backrest, and can be fitted with commercially available lounge pads for added comfort.

blade on your table or radial arm saw to cut the mortises for the frame of the chaise. Make multiple passes of the blade to form these wide mortises.

Once the mortises are cut, lay out the tapered sections on each leg and cut these on a band saw. Keep in mind that the legs on each side of the chaise are mirror images of one another. Always be aware of the location of the outside corner of each leg when laying out the tapers.

Next, cut the frame components to length and assemble the basic frame of the project. Attach the frame parts to the legs with no. 8 X 1½-in. flathead wood screws and waterproof resorcinol glue. Drill a counterbored pilot hole for each screw to make room for wood screw hole plugs. Use a combination pilot bit/counterbore to form these pilot holes.

Now, cut the notched side rails to the profiles shown in the diagram (Detail 2). Form the notches by boring ¾-in.-dia. holes, then cut away the waste with a saber or band saw. Cut the rounded profiles with a saber saw. Lay out these parts carefully for best results.

Cut the back rails (detail 3) and pivoting support components (detail 1) as shown in the diagram. Locate and bore holes for the dowels. Notice the notch in the back rails that allows the pivoting support to fold up completely. Careful measurement is critical here for smooth back movement. Clamp identical parts together and even them up with a belt sander.

Attach the pivoting supports to the rails with carriage bolts. Use washers between the components and under the nuts. Tighten the nuts, but only enough to secure the components. The supports must be able to pivot freely.

Insert the dowels into the back rails and supports, then into the notched side rails. Observe the measurements shown in the diagram for proper positioning, then glue and nail the dowels to the rails and pivoting supports. Drill pilot holes for the 6d galvanized finishing nails. Do not glue the dowels into the side rails, they must be free to pivot.

Once this subassembly is complete, insert it into the frame of the chaise, after applying resorcinol glue to the outsides of the notched supports. Align the parts carefully, then clamp them temporarily in place. Attach the supports to the frame with no. 8 X 1¼-in. flathead wood screws, again using a combination bit to drill countersunk pilot holes.

Cut the seat and back slats to length, then install them on the frame and back rails with resorcinol glue and 4d galvanized finishing nails. Set the nails below the surface of the wood. Space the slats 1 in. apart, using a 1-in.-thick piece of wood as a spacer to keep the gaps equal. Hide the nail holes with wood filler.

Notice the shorter slat used at the joint between the seat and the back. This slat allows the back to pivot properly.

Round over all exposed edges of the project with a ⅜-in.-radius rounding-over bit, with pilot, in your router to prevent sharp edges from digging into tender skin. These rounded edges also improve the appearance of the project.

Sand the completed chaise thoroughly, starting with 80-grit paper.

CONSTRUCTION DETAILS

1. Take special care when laying out the support. Accuracy here will pay off in smooth back action.

2. Cut the leg mortises with a dado blade on your radial arm saw or table saw. Make multiple passes at the same depth.

3. Assemble the frame to the legs with waterproof resorcinol glue and screws. Counterbore for screw hole plugs.

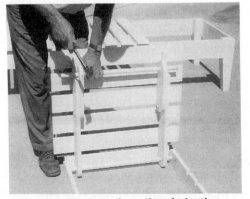

4. Attach dowels to the rail and pivoting supports with glue and 6d galvanized finishing nails. Bore pilot holes.

Work down to 120-grit paper in stages, and use a combination of power sanders and a hand-sanding block. Pay special attention to exposed end grain when sanding to insure a smooth finish.

Once the project is sanded, finish it with a coat of exterior enamel primer, followed by two coats of exterior latex enamel. You can also finish the project with stain and satin-finish polyurethane varnish. The latter finish, however, may be prone to blistering in direct sunlight.

5. Attach the completed back assembly to the inside of the frame with glue and flathead wood screws.

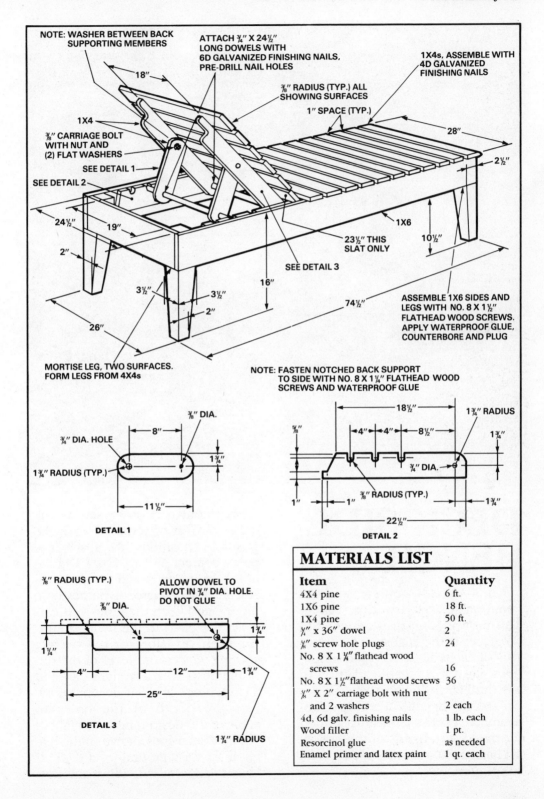

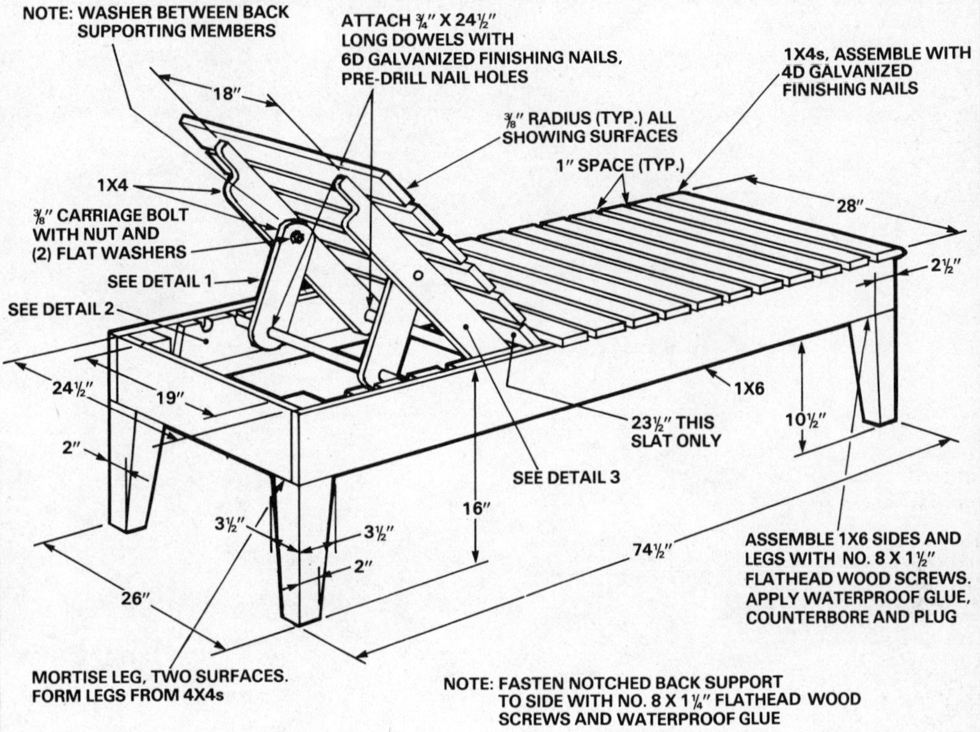
NOTE: WASHER BETWEEN BACK SUPPORTING MEMBERS
ATTACH ¾" X 24½" LONG DOWELS WITH 6D GALVANIZED FINISHING NAILS, PRE-DRILL NAIL HOLES
1X4s, ASSEMBLE WITH 4D GALVANIZED FINISHING NAILS
18"
⅜" RADIUS (TYP.) ALL SHOWING SURFACES
1" SPACE (TYP.)
28"
1X4
⅜" CARRIAGE BOLT WITH NUT AND (2) FLAT WASHERS
SEE DETAIL 1
SEE DETAIL 2
2½"
24½"
19"
1X6
10½"
23½" THIS SLAT ONLY
2"
SEE DETAIL 3
16"
3½"
3½"
2"
74½"
26"
ASSEMBLE 1X6 SIDES AND LEGS WITH NO. 8 X 1½" FLATHEAD WOOD SCREWS. APPLY WATERPROOF GLUE, COUNTERBORE AND PLUG
MORTISE LEG, TWO SURFACES. FORM LEGS FROM 4X4s
NOTE: FASTEN NOTCHED BACK SUPPORT TO SIDE WITH NO. 8 X 1¼" FLATHEAD WOOD SCREWS AND WATERPROOF GLUE

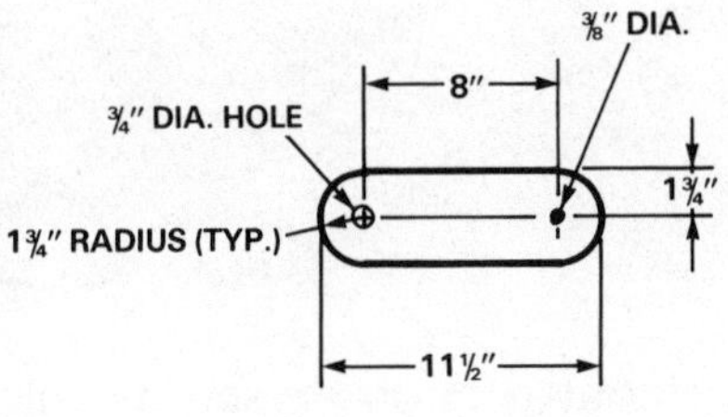
⅜" DIA.
8"
¾" DIA. HOLE
1¾"
1¾" RADIUS (TYP.)
11½"

DETAIL 1

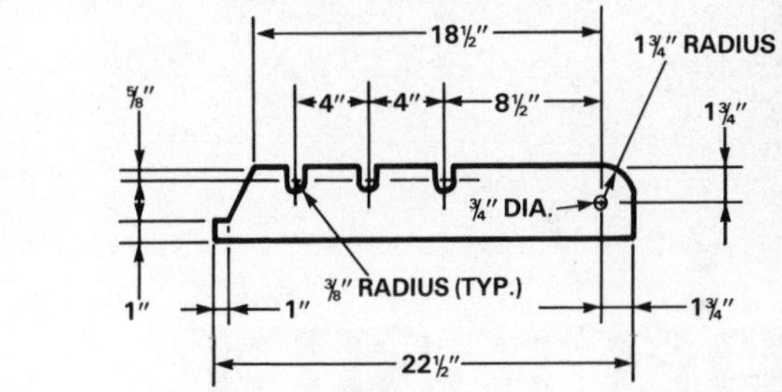
18½"
1¾" RADIUS
⅝"
4"
4"
8½"
1¾"
¾" DIA.
⅜" RADIUS (TYP.)
1"
1"
1¾"
22½"

DETAIL 2

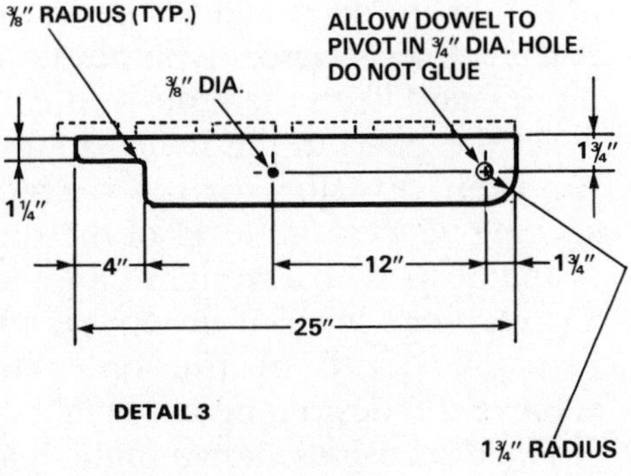
⅜" RADIUS (TYP.)
ALLOW DOWEL TO PIVOT IN ¾" DIA. HOLE. DO NOT GLUE
⅜" DIA.
1¾"
1¼"
4"
12"
1¾"
25"
1¾" RADIUS

DETAIL 3

MATERIALS LIST

Item	Quantity
4X4 pine	6 ft.
1X6 pine	18 ft.
1X4 pine	50 ft.
¾" x 36" dowel	2
¾" screw hole plugs	24
No. 8 X 1¼" flathead wood screws	16
No. 8 X 1½" flathead wood screws	36
⅜" X 2" carriage bolt with nut and 2 washers	2 each
4d, 6d galv. finishing nails	1 lb. each
Wood filler	1 pt.
Resorcinol glue	as needed
Enamel primer and latex paint	1 qt. each

DECK-SIDE BENCH

No deck is complete without comfortable and attractive seating. This redwood bench is designed to be placed at the edge of any deck or patio area. Its slatted top and simple lines make it a suitable addition to any outdoor decorating scheme.

For long life and an attractive appearance, choose all-heart redwood for the exposed parts of the bench. All-heart redwood is also less prone to splintering.

Start construction by setting the 4X4 posts in concrete. Locate the posthole positions to space the post's centers 35½ in. apart. Dig the holes 24 in. deep and 10 in. in diameter. Use a scissors-type posthole digger, and keep the holes vertical.

Set the posts in the holes, adjusting their position for the correct spacing. Check the level of the top of the posts with a straight 2X4 and a carpenter's level. If necessary, adjust the depth of the holes to achieve the desired bench height.

The dimensions shown in the diagram are for a ground-level deck. If your deck is raised, adjust the post height to make the top of the bench 16 in. above the deck.

If you are building a new deck, this bench can also be positioned inside the deck area. Simply locate the bench so that its posts are adjacent to the floor joists. When applying the decking, cut it to fit around the posts.

Mix the concrete and pour it into the holes, filling them to just above the level of the grade. Round off the top of the concrete so that water drains away from the posts. Check your posts for spacing and use a level to make them vertical. Allow the concrete to set, checking the posts' alignment once more before the concrete hardens.

Now, build the frame for the bench. Cut two 12½-in. pieces of 2X6 redwood, and mark the bevels as shown in the diagram. Use the posts and the rails of the bench to guide you in laying out the bevels. Start the bevels on the bottom of the braces to line up with the post edges. The other end should match the side rails.

Cut the profile of the end brace on your band saw. If you don't have a band saw, you can also use a circular saw, a table saw, or a radial arm saw.

Cut the two side rails, 42 in. long, from all-heart 2X4 stock. Attach them to the end braces with no. 12 X 3-in. flathead wood screws and waterproof resorcinol glue. Drill countersunk pilot holes with a combination pilot bit and countersink. Use two screws at each joint.

Add a 2X4 brace to the center of the frame, attaching it with glue and countersunk screws. Be certain that the brace is flush with the top of the frame. Sand the frame with your belt

sander, paying special attention to the exposed end grain.

Next, position the frame on the posts. Adjust its position so that the posts are flush with the top of the frame. Check to make sure that the frame is level, then clamp it into position. Bore ¼-in.-dia. holes through the end braces and the posts with a spade bit in your drill.

Attach the frame permanently to the posts with ¼-in. X 5½-in. carriage bolts. Insert the bolts, tapping them home with a hammer, then add flat washers and nuts.

Build the slatted bench top next. Cut nine 2X2 slats 45 in. long, and two end pieces 15½ in. long. Use a stop block on your saw to make certain that all the parts are identical.

Begin assembling the bench top by attaching the end pieces to the outer slats. Use resorcinol glue and 16d galvanized finishing nails. Drill pilot holes for the nails to prevent splitting, and set the nails below the surface of the wood with a nail set. For a clean final finish, fill the nail holes with redwood-colored waterproof wood filler.

Add the remaining slats, spacing them evenly, about ¼ in. apart. Nail and glue these slats as you did before. If necessary, twist each slat slightly to align it with the end pieces. Minor unevenness will be removed in the next step.

Once the glue has dried, sand the top of the bench with a belt sander to even it up. Start with an 80-grit belt, working down to a 150-grit belt for the final finish. While you are sanding, ease the edges of the bench top to a ¼-in. radius.

Attach the top to the frame of the bench with 16d galvanized finishing nails. As you did before, set the

CONSTRUCTION DETAILS

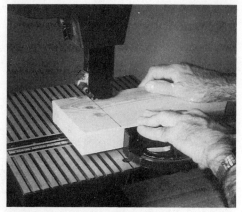

1. *Cut the profiles of the end braces with a band saw. Lay these braces out as described in the text.*

2. *Assemble the frame with flathead wood screws and resorcinol glue. Countersink the screw heads flush with the surface.*

3. *Space the slats ¼ in. apart as you assemble the bench top. Drill pilot holes for the 16d galvanized finishing nails.*

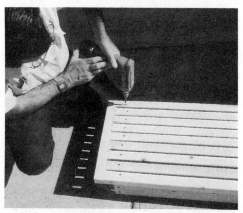

4. *Attach the bench top to the frame with 16d galvanized finishing nails or wood screws. Set the fasteners below the wood's surface.*

nails below the surface of the wood with a nail set and fill the holes with redwood-colored filler. To avoid marring the soft redwood, leave the nail heads slightly above the surface when hammering.

Once the bench is assembled, apply two or more coats of clear wood sealer. Allow each coat to dry overnight before adding another coat of sealer.

Design courtesy of Joy Kelly.

MATERIALS LIST

Item	Quantity
4X4 redwood	7 ft.
2X6 redwood	30″
2X4 redwood	9 ft.
2X2 redwood	39 ft.
No. 12 X 3″ flathead wood screws	12
¼″ X 5½″ carriage bolts with nuts and washers	4
16d galvanized finishing nails	as needed
Resorcinol glue	as needed
Concrete mix	1 bag
Clear wood sealer	as needed

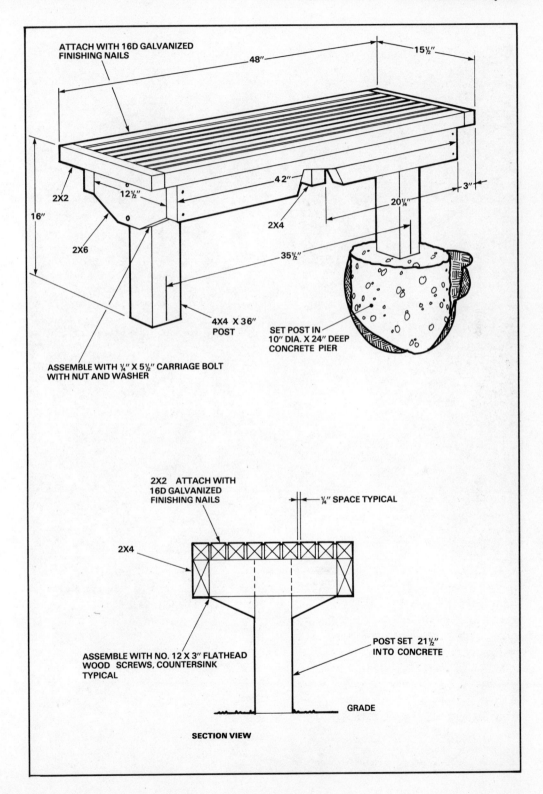

ATTACH WITH 16D GALVANIZED
FINISHING NAILS

48"

15½"

2X2

12½"

16"

2X6

42"

2X4

20¼"

3"

35½"

4X4 X 36"
POST

SET POST IN
10" DIA. X 24" DEEP
CONCRETE PIER

ASSEMBLE WITH ¼" X 5½" CARRIAGE BOLT
WITH NUT AND WASHER

2X2   ATTACH WITH
16D GALVANIZED
FINISHING NAILS

¼" SPACE TYPICAL

2X4

ASSEMBLE WITH NO. 12 X 3" FLATHEAD
WOOD SCREWS, COUNTERSINK
TYPICAL

POST SET 21½"
INTO CONCRETE

GRADE

SECTION VIEW

FOLDING STOOL

Folding stools like this one are popular for outdoor use. Not only are they easy to build, but when they are not in use they fold up easily for storage. They are also ideal for camping and picnic trips.

This folding stool is a slightly larger version of the typical folding seat. It also features invisible Roto-Hinges for a clean appearance. Solid oak construction is used in this project for strength, and all screw heads are hidden with wood screw hole plugs.

Begin building the stool by cutting 1X3 oak lumber to the lengths shown in the diagram. If 1X3 oak stock is not available in your area, purchase wider boards and rip them to the correct width on your table saw or radial arm saw. Use a combination planer-type blade for a smooth finish on the cut edges.

Use a circle template to lay out the 1/2-in.-radius corners on the legs. Cut these corners with a saber saw or band saw. You can also round the corners on a stationary belt sander.

After rounding the corners, ease the edges of all the stool's components with a belt sander. Work carefully to avoid removing too much material. Before assembling the components, sand them thoroughly. Start with 80-grit garnet paper and work down to 120-grit.

Locate and mark the exact center of the inside of each leg component.

Bore 1/2-in.-dia. holes 9/16 in. deep with a Forstner-type bit or another type of bit that leaves a flat-bottomed hole. For accuracy, use a portable drill guide or a drill press to make the holes square with the wood's surface.

Use a depth stop on your bit, or set the depth gauge on your drill press to make the holes exactly 9/16 in. deep.

Next, apply a thin layer of glue to one side of each Roto-Hinge and insert it into the hole in one leg component. Add the other leg in the same way. Be certain that the hinges seat fully.

Add the braces to the legs, securing them with no. 8 X 1 1/2-in. flathead wood screws. Bore counterbored pilot holes for the screws with a combination pilot bit and counterbore. The counterbore should be 3/8 in. deep to accommodate the wood screw hole plugs.

Make a trial assembly of the stool's frame, checking the stool for squareness as you go. Once assembly is complete, apply the finish of your choice to the frame. A good choice of finish is stain followed by two coats of satin-finish polyurethane varnish.

While the finish is drying, make the canvas seat for your stool. Cut medium-weight canvas to the dimensions shown in the diagram. After cutting the corner notches, fold

CONSTRUCTION DETAILS

1. Lay out the corners of the legs with a circle template. Use the 1-in.-dia. circle on the template.

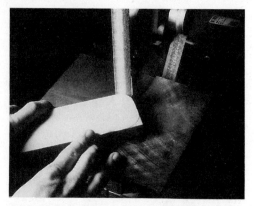

2. Round the edges of the wood parts on a stationary sander. Work carefully for a smooth curve.

3. Glue the Roto-Hinges into the pre-drilled holes in the legs. Be sure the hinges seat fully.

4. Slip the canvas seat over the upper braces of the frame, then secure the braces with flathead wood screws.

the sides in and double-stitch with heavy-duty thread on a sewing machine.

Next, fold the ends of the sling on the lines shown in the diagram. Fold again to make a loop, then double-stitch as you did before.

Canvas is a difficult material for the average home sewing machine. Work at a slow speed and use a ball-point needle for best results. If you do not have a sewing machine, any upholstery shop can make up the seat.

Remove the top bars of the stool and insert them into the loops of the seat fabric, then reattach them to the legs. Do not glue this joint, as you may need to replace the seat sometime in the future.

Glue the ⅜-in. wood screw hole plugs in the counterbored pilot holes. Allow them to protrude slightly above the surface of the wood, then sand them flush once the glue dries. Touch up the plugs with the finish you used on the frame of the stool.

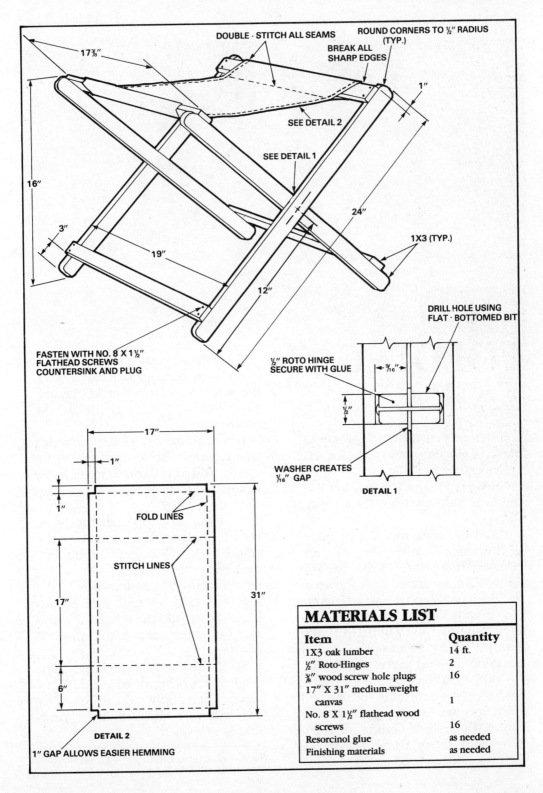

DOUBLE - STITCH ALL SEAMS

ROUND CORNERS TO ½" RADIUS (TYP.)

BREAK ALL SHARP EDGES

17⅜"

1"

SEE DETAIL 2

SEE DETAIL 1

16"

24"

3"

1X3 (TYP.)

19"

12"

DRILL HOLE USING FLAT - BOTTOMED BIT

FASTEN WITH NO. 8 X 1½" FLATHEAD SCREWS COUNTERSINK AND PLUG

½" ROTO HINGE SECURE WITH GLUE

⁹⁄₁₆"

½"

WASHER CREATES ¹⁄₁₆" GAP

DETAIL 1

17"

1"

1"

FOLD LINES

STITCH LINES

17"

31"

6"

DETAIL 2

1" GAP ALLOWS EASIER HEMMING

MATERIALS LIST

Item	Quantity
1X3 oak lumber	14 ft.
½" Roto-Hinges	2
⅜" wood screw hole plugs	16
17" X 31" medium-weight canvas	1
No. 8 X 1½" flathead wood screws	16
Resorcinol glue	as needed
Finishing materials	as needed

FOLDING TABLE

Whether you use this fold-up table as a garden work center or as a serving table, its design will complement your outdoor living. After use, the table folds up neatly for compact storage.

Build the table top first by edge-gluing pine lumber. Prepare the edges with a jointer. Make the top larger than the dimensions shown in the diagram, then trim to size later.

Use carpenter's glue, and clamp the assembly with multiple bar clamps. Clamp from both sides of the panel to help prevent warping.

Cut the leg components to length, then form the grooves in the legs and stretchers with a straight bit in your router. Use an edge guide for accuracy. Square up the ends of the grooves with a wood chisel.

Cut the stretcher tenons with a dado blade on your radial arm or table saw. Take care to make the tenons line up perfectly with the grooves.

Glue the slats in place on one leg of each pair, spacing them ½ in. apart. Add the stretcher, then the other leg. Clamp these assemblies until dry.

Trim the table top to size and sand it with a belt sander. Round over the edges with a ¼-in.-radius rounding-over bit in your router.

Attach the leg assemblies to the top with cut-to-length continuous hinges, then add the folding leg supports, making certain that they do not bind.

Sand the completed table thoroughly, working down to 220-grit paper. Then apply stain, followed by two coats of satin-finish polyurethane varnish.

Reprinted with permission from Katie and Gene Hamilton and Steve Wolgemuth in conjunction with Popular Mechanics.

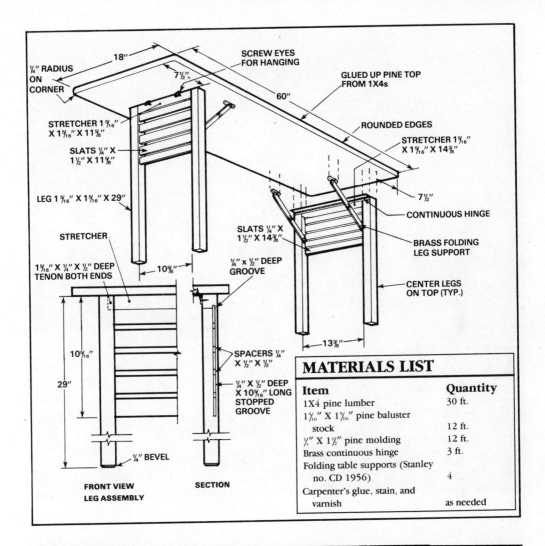

SCREW EYES FOR HANGING

18"

¼" RADIUS ON CORNER

7½"

GLUED UP PINE TOP FROM 1X4s

60"

STRETCHER 1⁵⁄₁₆" X 1⁵⁄₁₆" X 11⅝"

ROUNDED EDGES

STRETCHER 1⁵⁄₁₆" X 1⁵⁄₁₆" X 14⅜"

SLATS ¼" X 1½" X 11⅝"

LEG 1⁵⁄₁₆" X 1⁵⁄₁₆" X 29"

SLATS ¼" X 1½" X 14⅜"

7½"

CONTINUOUS HINGE

STRETCHER

BRASS FOLDING LEG SUPPORT

1⁵⁄₁₆" X ¼" X ½" DEEP TENON BOTH ENDS

10⁵⁄₈"

¼" X ½" DEEP GROOVE

CENTER LEGS ON TOP (TYP.)

13⅜"

10⁵⁄₁₆"

SPACERS ¼" X ½" X ½"

29"

¼" X ½" DEEP X 10⁷⁄₁₆" LONG STOPPED GROOVE

¼" BEVEL

FRONT VIEW LEG ASSEMBLY

SECTION

MATERIALS LIST

Item	Quantity
1X4 pine lumber	30 ft.
1⁵⁄₁₆" X 1⁵⁄₁₆" pine baluster stock	12 ft.
¼" X 1½" pine molding	12 ft.
Brass continuous hinge	3 ft.
Folding table supports (Stanley no. CD 1956)	4
Carpenter's glue, stain, and varnish	as needed

CONSTRUCTION DETAILS

1. Glue the slats and stretcher to one leg, then add the other leg. Square up the assembly and clamp.

2. After attaching the legs with continuous hinges, mount the folding leg supports as shown.

FOLDING TABLE/BENCH

No matter how large your deck or patio, there never seems to be enough space for everything. One of the chief offenders is the typical outdoor table. It takes up a large area, and when outdoor dining is not on the schedule, it just gets in the way.

Here is a perfect solution for that problem. This outdoor table, when not in use, folds up to make two comfortable benches that can be moved to a convenient location. When it is time for outdoor meals, the benches can be converted back to a table in just a minute or two.

When you use the project as a table, a pair of wood braces joins the two halves to make a solid structure. Eyebolts, with wing nuts, make it simple to change the configuration of the project from a table to benches and back again.

You can build the project from any wood you choose. For maximum weather resistance, however, choose redwood lumber for the bench/table unit. If you choose another material, be sure to treat the wood with a non-toxic clear wood sealer and preservative. This will help make it last in the outdoors for many years.

Whatever type of wood you select, pick the materials by hand at your local lumberyard or home center. Choose stock that is straight, sound, and without any loose knots or other serious flaws. If your lumberyard does not allow hand-picking of materials, choose no. 1 or better lumber, or check with a different lumberyard.

Begin construction by cutting the legs from 2X4 stock. As indicated in the diagram on page *159*, cut the ends of the legs to form a 5 degree bevel. The bevels should be parallel. Use a power miter box or your table saw or radial arm saw for this job. Measure the parts accurately.

Next, lay out the notches in the rear legs for the horizontal braces. Follow the dimensions shown in the diagram, and make certain that the notches are identical on all of the legs. Aim for a tight fit when the braces are installed.

After laying out these notches, cut them with a saber saw. Cut carefully and keep the blade of the saw vertical at all times. To do this, avoid any side pressure on the saw as you cut, and keep the blade centered in the notch in the saw's shoe.

To simplify cutting the back of the notch, drill $3/8$-in.-dia. holes in the corners of the notch. Finish up any flaws with a sharp wood chisel. Try the fit with one of the braces and make any necessary adjustments.

As an alternative, form the notches with a dado blade on your table saw or radial arm saw. Make multiple passes at a $3/4$-in. depth of cut, then increase the depth to $1\frac{1}{2}$ in. and complete the notches.

Cut the notches on all four legs at one depth setting before changing the setup. If you choose, clamp all four legs together and form all the notches at once. This will insure that the notches are identical.

Measure down $3\frac{7}{8}$ in. from the top of each rear leg, then drill a $5/16$-in.-dia. hole in the center of the leg for the pivot bolt. Follow this with another $5/16$-in. hole for the positioning bolt. Locate this hole 2 in. above the first, and 1 in. from the front of the leg.

Cut the 2X4 side braces next, following the dimensions shown in the diagram. To assemble the legs, lay the front and rear parts on a flat surface. Butt the bottom bevel of the legs against a straight 2X4 to line them up correctly. Space the legs to match the length of the brace.

Position the brace flush with the top of the front leg, then measure from the 2X4 block to make the brace level. Once the parts are properly aligned, bore $\frac{5}{16}$-in.-dia. bolt holes through both parts in the pattern shown in the diagram.

Before assembling any of the components of the project, sand the individual parts thoroughly. Use a combination of power and hand sanding, starting with 120-grit abrasive and finishing with 220-grit for a smooth surface. Round over sharp edges as you go.

Assemble the leg sets using $\frac{5}{16}$-in. X 3½-in. hex bolts, with nuts and washers, tightening the nuts securely. Once one leg set is assembled, you can use it as a pattern to help build the other three. They must be identical.

Add the rear horizontal braces next, attaching them in their notches with no. 12 X 3-in. flathead wood screws. Bore pilot holes with a combination pilot bit and countersink to make the screw heads flush. For maximum weather resistance, choose brass screws for this project.

Now, cut four 16-in.-long pieces of 2X8 stock to form the tilting table supports. Lay out the profile of the support, as shown in the diagram, on one of the workpieces. Measure accurately, and use a protractor to mark the 30 degree angles.

Cut the part with your saber saw, once again taking care to keep the blade vertical while cutting. Use a blade designed for cutting thick lumber. You could also cut the part on a band saw, if one is available.

Use this first support as a pattern to lay out the other three. Cut the rest of the supports, then clamp all four together and even up the profiles with a belt sander.

Bore the $\frac{5}{16}$-in. pivot hole in each support, followed by the hole used to attach the brace that joins the two tables. Control splintering by using a backup board. Measure the parts carefully to make all of the hole positions identical. If possible, bore the holes with a drill press or a portable drill guide for accuracy.

Now, attach the table supports to the rear legs with $\frac{5}{16}$-in. X 3½-in. hex bolts through the pivot holes. Use a washer and a nylon-insert, self-locking nut to secure the assembly. This type of nut will hold the adjustment needed to allow easy folding of the pivoting support.

Place the assembled table frames back-to-back on a level surface, such as your deck or patio. Line up the frames so that the pivoting supports are touching. Adjust the supports to be perfectly even with each other. Use a long carpenter's level to help you adjust the supports.

Once you have the supports correctly aligned, tighten the nut on the pivot bolt to hold them in position. Bore through the supports with a $\frac{5}{16}$-in.-dia. bit. Drill from in-

MATERIALS LIST

Item	Quantity
Material for two benches (one table)	
2X8 lumber	64"
2X6 lumber	50 ft.
2X4 lumber	35 ft.
No. 12 X 3" flathead wood screws	48
$\frac{5}{16}$" X 3½" hex bolts	20
$\frac{5}{16}$" X 3½" eyebolts	8
$\frac{5}{16}$" flat washers	28
$\frac{5}{16}$" wing nuts	8
$\frac{5}{16}$" nuts	16
$\frac{5}{16}$" nylon-insert, self-locking nuts	4
Stain and clear wood sealer	2 qts.

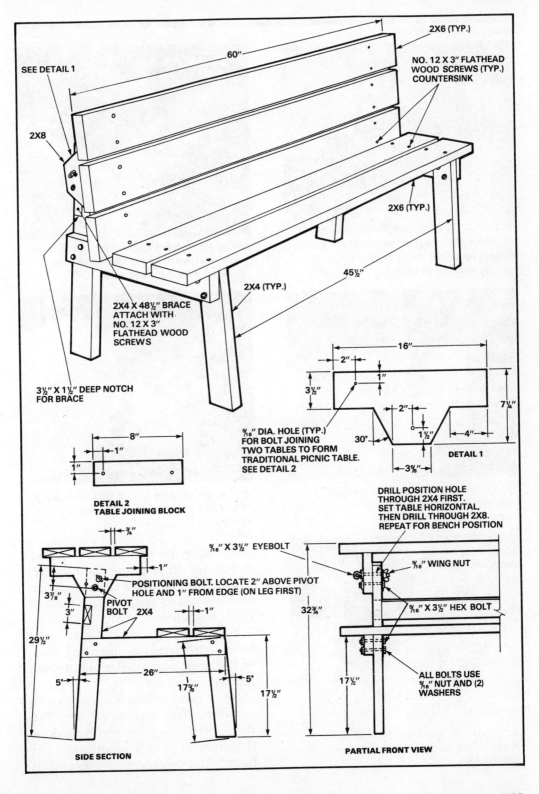

SEE DETAIL 1

2X6 (TYP.)

60"

NO. 12 X 3" FLATHEAD
WOOD SCREWS (TYP.)
COUNTERSINK

2X8

2X6 (TYP.)

2X4 (TYP.)

45½"

2X4 X 48½" BRACE
ATTACH WITH
NO. 12 X 3"
FLATHEAD WOOD
SCREWS

3½" X 1½" DEEP NOTCH
FOR BRACE

16"

2"

1"

3½"

7¼"

2"

1½"

30°

3⅝"

4"

DETAIL 1

5/16" DIA. HOLE (TYP.)
FOR BOLT JOINING
TWO TABLES TO FORM
TRADITIONAL PICNIC TABLE.
SEE DETAIL 2

8"

1"

1"

DETAIL 2
TABLE JOINING BLOCK

DRILL POSITION HOLE
THROUGH 2X4 FIRST.
SET TABLE HORIZONTAL,
THEN DRILL THROUGH 2X8.
REPEAT FOR BENCH POSITION

5/16" X 3½" EYEBOLT

5/16" WING NUT

¾"

1"

POSITIONING BOLT. LOCATE 2" ABOVE PIVOT
HOLE AND 1" FROM EDGE (ON LEG FIRST)

32¾"

5/16" X 3½" HEX BOLT

3⅞"

PIVOT
BOLT

3"

2X4

1"

29½"

26"

5°

5°

17⅝"

17½"

17½"

17½"

ALL BOLTS USE
5/16" NUT AND (2)
WASHERS

SIDE SECTION

PARTIAL FRONT VIEW

159

CONSTRUCTION DETAILS

1. *Use a power miter saw to cut the 5 degree bevels on the ends of the legs. All parts should be identical.*

2. *Cut the notches in the rear legs to fit the horizontal brace. Use a saber saw, then finish up with a wood chisel.*

3. *Lay out the profile of the pivoting support with a protractor and a straightedge.*

4. *Cut the support to size with your saber saw. Cut carefully to keep the blade vertical.*

5. *To simplify finishing, sand all of the parts before assembly. Round over all sharp edges.*

side, using the pre-drilled positioning holes in the legs as a guide. Check the alignment of the supports as you work to make certain none of them has shifted.

Install the $5/16$-in. X $3\frac{1}{2}$-in. eyebolts, with washers and wing nuts, in the positioning holes and tighten the wing nuts securely.

Next, cut the seat and back components. You will need ten 2X6 parts, 60 in. long. As you have done throughout this project, sand the boards thoroughly before assembly.

Pay special attention to the end grain of the wood, and round off any sharp edges or corners as you sand. Sand only in the direction of the wood's grain.

Position the outer seat board on the frame. The front of the board should be flush with the horizontal brace. Equalize the amount of overhang on each end of the frame.

Attach the seat board to the side braces with two no. 12 X 3-in. flathead wood screws. Position the screws 1½ in. from each edge of the board. Use a combination pilot bit and countersink to bore pilot holes for the screws. Countersink the screw heads well below the surface of the seat to keep sun-heated screw heads away from you and your guests.

If you would like to hide the screw heads completely, counterbore the pilot holes ⅜ in. deep for ½-in. wood screw hole plugs. After driving the screws, install the plugs with waterproof resorcinol glue. Leave the plugs standing slightly proud of the surface, then sand them flush once the glue dries.

Install the second seat board, spacing it 1 in. from the first. Be careful to make the ends of the seat line up perfectly.

Follow a similar procedure to attach the boards to the pivoting support. Install the center board first. Mark the center of the supports and the center of the underside of the board. Position it carefully, then screw it to the support as you did before.

Add the outer parts, spacing them ¾ in. from the center board. Use ¾-in.-thick scrap to help you position them accurately.

Once the three top boards are attached, loosen the nut on the pivot bolt slightly, then remove the positioning bolts. Fold the table's top down into the position it will assume to form the back of the bench. You can adjust the back angle to suit your own taste.

When you have established the desired back angle, bore through the positioning hole in the rear leg, as you did earlier. Install the positioning bolt in this new location to hold the seat back in position.

Cut two 8-in.-long 2X4 table joining blocks. Bore ⁵⁄₁₆-in.-dia. holes, 1 in. down from the top of the blocks and 1 in. in from each end. Use a drill press or a portable drill guide for maximum precision.

To use the blocks, fold the bench back up into the table-top position. Place the two tables back-to-back, then join them with the blocks using ⁵⁄₁₆-in. X 3½-in. eyebolts with washers and wing nuts. Changing from bench to table and vice versa should only take a minute or two.

Once the two bench/table units are assembled, adjust the nylon-insert, self-locking nuts to allow the pivoting supports to move easily.

Finish the project by sanding any areas that need a little touch-up. If you built the unit of redwood, protect the wood from weather damage and spills by applying two coats of clear wood sealer. Be sure that the sealer you use contains no toxic ingredients when dry. Thompson's Water Seal is a good choice.

If you used any other variety of wood, you can either finish it with wood sealer alone, or stain the wood in the color of your choice before sealing it.

Design and lead photograph courtesy of Shopsmith, Inc., 6640 Poe Ave., Dayton, OH 45414.

FOLDING TRAY

Build one or more of these handy folding tables and you will be ready for casual outdoor dining or unexpected guests. When not in use, the tables fold up neatly for easy storage.

The pivoting joints on this project use Roto-Hinges, a product that allows joints to pivot without any exposed hardware. See the Credits section of this book beginning on page 494.

Start construction of the table by cutting all of the components to the sizes shown in the diagram.

The center pair of top slats are rabbeted. Form these $\frac{1}{8}$-in. X $\frac{1}{2}$-in.-deep rabbets with a $\frac{1}{8}$-in. rabbeting bit, with pilot, in your router.

Measure carefully to locate the pivot points on the legs and rails. Bore the holes for the Roto-Hinges on a drill press, using a Forstner bit. The holes are $\frac{1}{2}$ in. in dia. and $\frac{9}{16}$ in. deep. Use a depth stop to prevent boring through the wood.

Begin assembly by joining the leg pairs. Apply yellow carpenter's glue

to the holes, then insert the Roto-Hinges. Press the parts together until the Roto-Hinges seat completely.

Next, bore countersunk pilot holes through the inner rails, at the bottom of the holes for the Roto-Hinges. Attach the dowel to these rails with no. 8 X 1-in. flathead wood screws.

Next, install the Roto-Hinges in the rails and the legs of the table as you did before. Attach the leg braces, nailing them to the legs with 4d galvanized finishing nails.

Add the top slats, nailing them in place as well. Notice that three of the slats are fastened to the outer rails, while the other three are nailed to the inner rails. This allows the table to fold when you lift up on the top.

Sand the table thoroughly, starting with 120-grit garnet paper and working down to 220-grit paper. Apply two or more coats of semi-gloss polyurethane varnish, sanding lightly between coats.

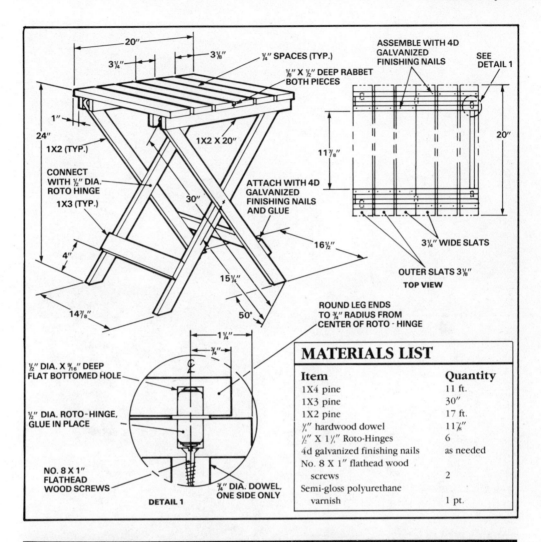

20"
3¹⁄₈"
3¹⁄₄"
¹⁄₄" SPACES (TYP.)
¹⁄₈" X ¹⁄₂" DEEP RABBET BOTH PIECES
ASSEMBLE WITH 4D GALVANIZED FINISHING NAILS
SEE DETAIL 1
1"
24"
1X2 (TYP.)
1X2 X 20"
20"
CONNECT WITH ¹⁄₂" DIA. ROTO HINGE
1X3 (TYP.)
ATTACH WITH 4D GALVANIZED FINISHING NAILS AND GLUE
11⁷⁄₈"
30"
4"
15¹⁄₄"
16¹⁄₂"
3¹⁄₄" WIDE SLATS
14⁷⁄₈"
50°
OUTER SLATS 3¹⁄₈"
TOP VIEW
ROUND LEG ENDS TO ³⁄₄" RADIUS FROM CENTER OF ROTO · HINGE

1¹⁄₄"
³⁄₄"
¹⁄₂" DIA. X ⁹⁄₁₆" DEEP FLAT BOTTOMED HOLE
¹⁄₂" DIA. ROTO-HINGE, GLUE IN PLACE
NO. 8 X 1" FLATHEAD WOOD SCREWS
³⁄₄" DIA. DOWEL, ONE SIDE ONLY
DETAIL 1

MATERIALS LIST

Item	Quantity
1X4 pine	11 ft.
1X3 pine	30"
1X2 pine	17 ft.
³⁄₄" hardwood dowel	11⁷⁄₈"
¹⁄₂" X 1¹⁄₄" Roto-Hinges	6
4d galvanized finishing nails	as needed
No. 8 X 1" flathead wood screws	2
Semi-gloss polyurethane varnish	1 pt.

CONSTRUCTION DETAILS

1. To unfold the table, grasp one half of the top in each hand and pull up. The legs will scissor for folding.

2. Install the Roto-Hinges by pressing them into the holes after applying yellow carpenter's glue.

163

GATELEG TABLE

Warm spring and summer evenings make outdoor dining an attractive idea. This gateleg table will add a touch of elegance to your deck or patio. It is based on a traditional Early American design, updated and modified for outdoor use.

Designed to seat four when open, it quickly folds into a compact package for easy storage. The table can also be used against a wall with just one leaf unfolded. All-heart redwood gives it a warm look that will blend with any outdoor setting.

After cutting all the components to the rough sizes shown in the diagram, lay out the table top components on a flat surface. Mark the centers of the top slats, then draw lines to locate the positions of the battens and cleats. Use a $\frac{1}{2}$-in.-thick piece of scrap to space the slats $\frac{1}{2}$ in. apart.

Secure the battens to the slats with resorcinol glue and no. 8 X 1$\frac{1}{4}$-in. flathead brass wood screws. Drill countersunk pilot holes for the screws using a combination pilot bit and countersink. Check the adjustment of the bit to prevent drilling through the wood.

Screw the cleats to the center board next, then attach the leaves to the center cleats with strap hinges as shown in the photo. Use a depth stop on the drill bit when boring pilot holes to prevent drilling through the wood. Check the alignment and spacing of the leaves before attaching them.

Place the completed top assembly, face-up, on sawhorses, and lay out the 42-in.-dia. circular profile. Use a bar compass, or make a simple compass with brads, 21 in. apart, in a piece of thin scrap.

Cut out the circle with a fine-toothed blade in your saber saw. Work slowly and keep the blade centered in the saw's base slot to prevent the blade from creeping off a vertical line.

Round over the top edge of the table top with a $\frac{1}{4}$-in. rounding-over bit, with pilot, in your router. Round over the bottom edge, carefully, by resting the router's base on the edge of the table top. Be especially careful when rounding over near the gaps in the table top. It is easy to let the tool slip into the gaps, marring the top.

Add the stop blocks to the leaves. Make these parts from scrap, forming the rabbets with a router or dado blade. Form the rabbets on a long piece of stock, then cut the parts off. This helps avoid working too close to the tool's blade.

Next, begin building the base. Cut the notches in the lower stretcher as shown in the diagram, then attach both stretchers to their leg cleats using no. 8 X 1$\frac{1}{4}$-in. flathead brass wood screws and resorcinol glue. Attach the braces to the legs, along with the stretcher and cleat assemblies, to complete the base. Using a framing square, check squareness carefully as you work.

Round over the edges of the base,

CONSTRUCTION DETAILS

1. Stop blocks are used on each leaf to make a pad for the gateleg assemblies. Position these carefully.

2. Use self-locking, nylon-insert nuts to secure the pivot bolts. Tighten these just enough to allow easy movement.

as you did for the table top, avoiding the notches and the top ends of the legs.

Form notches for the lap joints in the components of the gateleg assemblies. Use multiple passes with a dado blade on your table or radial arm saw. Measure carefully for a perfect fit. You can help yourself make identical parts by clamping the parts together and making the notches with one pass of the dado blade.

Before assembling the legs, drill the pivot holes as shown in the diagram. Use a portable drill guide to make the holes line up correctly.

Assemble the legs using flathead brass wood screws and resorcinol glue, then round over the edges with a router.

Place each gateleg into the base, with the longer leg resting in the notches of the lower stretcher. Mark the positions of the pivot holes, then drill through with a 5/16-in. bit. Use a backup board to prevent splintering.

Install the carriage bolts with washers and self-locking, nylon-insert nuts. Tighten the nuts to provide

easy swinging action of the legs without excess play.

Before final assembly, sand the table components thoroughly, starting with 120-grit garnet paper and working down to 220-grit paper. Use a straight-line power sander or a hand-sanding block, and always sand with the grain. This is especially important with a soft wood like redwood.

Attach the table top to the base assembly, using standard chair leg braces to add additional stability. The screws provided with the braces are too long, so substitute no. 10 X 5/8-in. flathead brass wood screws.

Finally, apply two coats of a clear wood sealer, such as Thompson's Water Seal. Allow 24 hours between coats, and sand lightly for best results.

If you are tempted to apply varnish to this project, think twice. Redwood, when exposed to sunlight, undergoes a chemical change that will break the bond between the wood and the varnish. This causes blistering.

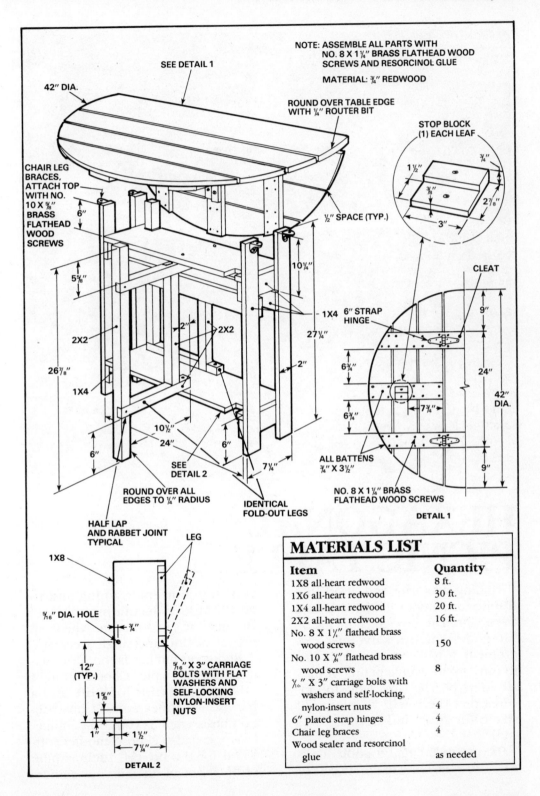

NOTE: ASSEMBLE ALL PARTS WITH
NO. 8 X 1¼" BRASS FLATHEAD WOOD
SCREWS AND RESORCINOL GLUE

MATERIAL: ¾" REDWOOD

42" DIA.

SEE DETAIL 1

ROUND OVER TABLE EDGE
WITH ¼" ROUTER BIT

STOP BLOCK
(1) EACH LEAF

1½"   ¾"

⅜"   2⅞"

3"

CHAIR LEG
BRACES,
ATTACH TOP
WITH NO.
10 X ⅝"
BRASS
FLATHEAD
WOOD
SCREWS

6"

½" SPACE (TYP.)

CLEAT

5⅞"

10¼"

9"

1X4   6" STRAP
HINGE

2X2

2"   2X2

27¼"

24"

6¾"

26⅞"

7¾"

42"
DIA.

1X4

2"

6¾"

10½"

24"   6"

6"

7¼"

SEE
DETAIL 2

ROUND OVER ALL
EDGES TO ¼" RADIUS

IDENTICAL
FOLD-OUT LEGS

ALL BATTENS
¾" X 3½"

9"

NO. 8 X 1¼" BRASS
FLATHEAD WOOD SCREWS

DETAIL 1

HALF LAP
AND RABBET JOINT
TYPICAL

LEG

1X8

⁵⁄₁₆" DIA. HOLE

¾"

12"
(TYP.)

1⅝"

1"   1½"

7¼"

⁵⁄₁₆" X 3" CARRIAGE
BOLTS WITH FLAT
WASHERS AND
SELF-LOCKING
NYLON-INSERT
NUTS

DETAIL 2

MATERIALS LIST

Item	Quantity
1X8 all-heart redwood	8 ft.
1X6 all-heart redwood	30 ft.
1X4 all-heart redwood	20 ft.
2X2 all-heart redwood	16 ft.
No. 8 X 1¼" flathead brass wood screws	150
No. 10 X ⅝" flathead brass wood screws	8
⁵⁄₁₆" X 3" carriage bolts with washers and self-locking, nylon-insert nuts	4
6" plated strap hinges	4
Chair leg braces	4
Wood sealer and resorcinol glue	as needed

HEXAGONAL PICNIC TABLE

Finding adequate and affordable seating for outdoor dining is always a problem. This hexagonal picnic table is designed to solve just that problem. It will seat six people easily, and up to twelve people if they are friendly. The large table top insures that there will be plenty of space for food and beverages as well.

The table's rugged good looks will also contribute to the success of your outdoor entertaining and to your outdoor decorating scheme. Designed to last a lifetime, the project can be built in a single weekend.

Redwood lumber is the ideal material for the table. Choose straight all-heart stock for long life and a handsome appearance. Construction heart grade is your best choice.

You can also choose another softwood for the project, such as pine or fir. If one of these is your choice, finish the table with wood sealer and preservative after applying an oil-based stain. Whichever type of lumber you choose, hand-select the materials at the lumberyard.

Begin construction of the project by cutting the legs. Select straight-grained 2X4 lumber without knots for these components. Any flaws in the wood will reduce the strength of the table, shortening its life. Other components are less critical.

Set your radial arm saw or table saw to cut a 30 degree miter. Measure the stock carefully, then cut all six legs. Notice that the miters on the legs are parallel. Once the legs are cut, stack them up and check their lengths. All of the legs must be identical for the table to rest evenly on your deck or patio.

Lay out the positions of the seat and top braces on the legs. Follow the dimensions shown in Detail 3 of the diagram on page 170, and measure carefully. Using a protractor or an adjustable bevel gauge, draw pencil lines on one side of each leg. Accuracy is important in this layout, since the alignment of the parts depends on the guidelines.

Now, cut one 2X4 seat brace 96 in. long, and a top brace 66 in. long. Bevel the ends of the braces at a 45 degree angle, as shown in the diagram (p. 171). Notice that the bevel on the top brace is different from that on the seat brace. Start the bevel 1½ in. from the top of the top brace to accommodate the supports.

Take the braces and legs to a flat surface for assembly. Place the bottom of the legs against a straight 2X4 to align them at the correct angle. Adjust the leg positions to make the distance between the outer cor-

ner of the legs exactly 79 inches. Make certain that the bottom edge of each leg fits flat against the 2X4, and check the leg angle with a protractor.

Now, mark the centers of both braces and lay the braces on top of the legs. Adjust the braces' positions to center them. Use the guidelines you drew on the legs to help you locate the braces accurately. At each stage, check the alignment of all the parts to make certain that the components have not shifted.

Take your time with this stage of construction. Once the main brace and leg assembly is complete, you will use it to help set up the remaining assemblies. Any errors will be compounded, preventing the table from resting evenly on your deck or patio.

Once you are satisfied with the alignment, bore $5/16$-in.-dia. pilot holes and fasten the parts together with $5/16$-in. X $3½$-in. carriage bolts. Tighten the nuts securely, then lay the assembly flat on the work surface.

Next, cut the remaining braces. Cut four seat braces and four top braces. Each of the parts should be half the length of the full-length parts. Form the outer bevels on these shorter braces as you did before.

Reset the blade on your table or radial arm saw to cut a 60 degree bevel. Cut a single bevel on each of the braces, $7/16$ in. from the inner end. On two of each type of brace, cut a second bevel to form a point. Cut the second bevel $1¼$ in. back from the first. See Detail 2 in the diagram for the layout of these bevels.

Once all of the parts are cut,

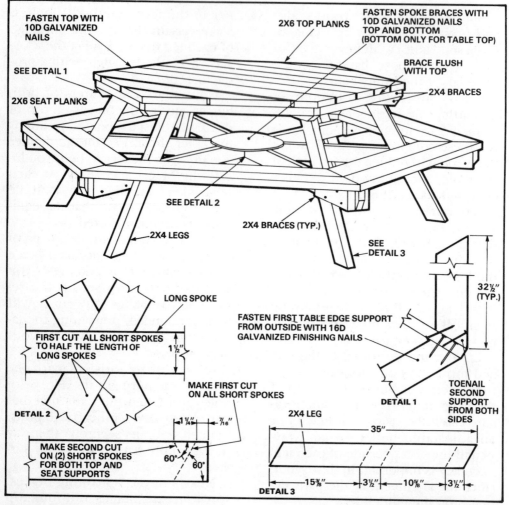

FASTEN TOP WITH 10D GALVANIZED NAILS

2X6 TOP PLANKS

FASTEN SPOKE BRACES WITH 10D GALVANIZED NAILS TOP AND BOTTOM (BOTTOM ONLY FOR TABLE TOP)

SEE DETAIL 1

BRACE FLUSH WITH TOP

2X6 SEAT PLANKS

2X4 BRACES

SEE DETAIL 2

2X4 LEGS

2X4 BRACES (TYP.)

SEE DETAIL 3

32½" (TYP.)

LONG SPOKE

FIRST CUT ALL SHORT SPOKES TO HALF THE LENGTH OF LONG SPOKES

1½"

FASTEN FIRST TABLE EDGE SUPPORT FROM OUTSIDE WITH 16D GALVANIZED FINISHING NAILS

MAKE FIRST CUT ON ALL SHORT SPOKES

DETAIL 2

TOENAIL SECOND SUPPORT FROM BOTH SIDES

DETAIL 1

MAKE SECOND CUT ON (2) SHORT SPOKES FOR BOTH TOP AND SEAT SUPPORTS

1¼" 7/16"

60° 60°

2X4 LEG

35"

15⅜" 3½" 10⅝" 3½"

DETAIL 3

check them against each other. As before, all of the matching parts must be identical if the table's com-

MATERIALS LIST

Item	Quantity
2X6 lumber	120 ft.
2X4 lumber	80 ft.
¾" X 12" X 36" exterior plywood	1
7/16" X 3½" carriage bolts with nuts and washers	24
No. 12 X 3½" flathead wood screws	48
16d galvanized finishing nails	as needed
10d galvanized nails	as needed
Stain and wood sealer	as needed

ponents are to fit together properly.

Take the leg and brace components to the work area you used before. Lay one leg and two braces on top of the previously built leg and brace assembly. Align each leg and brace set to match the main assembly. Check the alignment with a carpenter's square or a straightedge.

Pay special attention to the direction of the inner bevels on the braces. Refer to the diagram to be certain the assembly will fit together properly. Once each leg and brace assembly is aligned, bore pilot holes

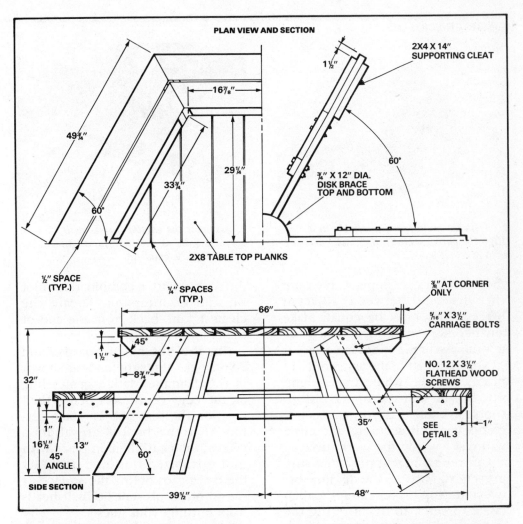

PLAN VIEW AND SECTION

2X4 X 14" SUPPORTING CLEAT

1½"

16⅞"

49¾"

29¼"

60°

¾" X 12" DIA. DISK BRACE TOP AND BOTTOM

33¾"

60°

2X8 TABLE TOP PLANKS

½" SPACE (TYP.)

¼" SPACES (TYP.)

⅜" AT CORNER ONLY

66"

45°

⁵⁄₁₆" X 3½" CARRIAGE BOLTS

1½"

8¾"

32"

NO. 12 X 3½" FLATHEAD WOOD SCREWS

1"

16½"

13"

45° ANGLE

60°

35"

SEE DETAIL 3

1"

SIDE SECTION

39½"

48"

and fasten the parts with carriage bolts, with nuts and washers, as you did before.

Once all of the assemblies are complete, cut three 12-in.-dia. disks of ¾-in. exterior plywood. Lay these out with a bar compass, and cut them with a band saw or a saber saw. Mark the center of each disk. Sand the circumference of the disks smooth.

Turn the main leg and brace assembly upside-down on your work surface, propping it up with the legs vertical. Center one of the disks on the underside of the top brace, then nail it to the brace with 10d galvanized nails. Nail another disk to the center of the seat brace.

Now, one at a time, add the remaining assemblies. Make certain that they are centered and that they line up with the opposite assembly before nailing the disks to the braces. Use an adjustable bevel gauge to check the angles between the braces as you work.

Drive only one nail into each brace, leaving its head protruding for possible removal. When all of

CONSTRUCTION DETAILS

1. Build the main frame assembly first. Align the parts carefully, then assemble with carriage bolts.

2. Assemble the partial frames with carriage bolts as well. Careful alignment is essential for a good fit.

the assemblies are in place, measure the distance between adjacent braces. They must be equal. Make any necessary adjustments, then fasten the assemblies permanently.

Now, with all of the assemblies in place, turn the whole frame right-side-up and add the upper disk to the seat braces. If your measurements were all accurate, the table will rest level on the work surface.

Cut the table's upper edge supports next. Measure the distance between the top braces carefully, then cut 2X4 stock to fit, mitering the ends at a 30 degree angle.

Install the supports with 16d galvanized finishing nails. Start by nailing through the brace into one support, then drive nails from both directions to secure the adjacent support. Detail 1 of the diagram shows this assembly procedure. Drill pilot holes for the nails.

Cut twelve seat support cleats 14 in. long from 2X4 stock. Fasten these to both sides of the seat braces, as shown in the diagram, with no. 12 X 3½-in. flathead wood screws. Countersink pilot holes for

the screws with a combination pilot bit and countersink. Locate the cleats 1½ in. back from the end of the brace.

Cut the outer seat boards from 2X6 stock. Miter the ends as shown in the diagram. Mark a center line on the edge of the seat brace, then position the seat boards. Make certain that the boards are aligned evenly, then nail them in place with 16d galvanized finishing nails. Set the nail heads below the surface of the wood to prevent hot nail heads from burning your guests.

Measure the ½-in. gap on the center line, then measure between the center lines to determine the length of the second row of seat boards. Cut the six inner boards, then nail them in place after positioning them accurately.

Now, begin building the table top. Cut a top plank and place it at the center of the table top (refer to the diagram). Make sure the overhangs are equal. Nail this plank in place with 16d galvanized finishing nails, setting the nail heads below the surface as you did for the seats.

3. *Plywood disks attach the spokes together and brace the table. Nail them in place with 10d galvanized nails.*

4. *Nail 2X4 top supports between the braces. Nail through the brace for one support, then from both sides.*

Add planks to the table top, spacing them ¼ in. apart. Cut the planks longer than necessary. You will trim them flush once all of the planks are attached. Note that the planks overhang 1 in. only at the corners; otherwise they are flush with the table edge supports.

After you have nailed all of the planks to the braces and support rails, locate the center point of the first plank you laid. Mark this point lightly, then measure out to the side edge support from the table's center. Draw lines across the planks at these points to locate the outer edges of the table. Use a framing square to make the lines perpendicular to the plank.

Also, mark the center of the center plank on each end. Now, measure 16⅞ in. from the center of these points to locate the ends of the sides of the table. Use a straightedge to lay out the top's sides. Once all of the lines are drawn, check the dimensions of the table's sides. Each side should be 33¾ in. long.

When you are satisfied with the layout, cut the table to its finished shape with a circular saw. Clamp a straight board to the table top to guide the cuts accurately. Use a combination planer-type blade for a smooth finish. The top should overhang the frame by 1 inch.

Now, sand the table thoroughly. Start with a belt sander and an 80-grit belt to even up the table top and seats. Sand only in the direction of the wood grain. Round over all sharp edges and corners to a ¼-in. radius as you work.

Finish the sanding with a combination of power and hand sanding, working down to 220-grit abrasive for a smooth finish. Pay special attention to exposed end grain.

If you built the table of redwood, apply at least two coats of clear wood sealer and preservative. Allow each coat to dry for 24 hours before applying the next one.

If you chose another softwood, stain the wood with an oil-based stain in the color of your choice. Follow the stain with wood sealer and preservative.

Design and photos courtesy of Shopsmith, Inc., 6640 Poe Ave., Dayton, OH 45414.

NESTING TABLES

This table, with its nesting seats, is the perfect project for the small deck or patio. It provides plenty of room for four, but takes up very little space when the seats are pushed in under the table.

An attractive diamond design on the top of the table and the seats combines with sled-based frames to give the set a contemporary feeling that will blend in with any outdoor decorating scheme.

Choose redwood lumber for this project to provide good weather resistance and an attractive appearance. You can use clear material or lumber with tight knots for a more rustic look. The project can also be built of any other lumber, but redwood is the best choice for durability and ease of maintenance.

Begin construction by making the base frames for the table and seats. Construction is identical for both; however, the table frame is made out of 2X4 stock while the seat requires 1X4s.

Cut to length the base components, following the dimensions shown in the diagram. Measure accurately for an even base. Lay out the cross-lap notches in the rails of the frames. The depth of the notches should be exactly half the width of the rail material. Since lumber varies in width, measure the stock accurately.

Once the notches have been marked, cut them with a dado blade on your radial arm saw. For accuracy, clamp stop blocks to your saw's fence to locate the notches on the joint fits correctly.

As an alternative, you can cut the notches with another type of saw. Cut multiple kerfs to the depth of the notch, then remove the waste with a sharp chisel.

Mark the frame components to indicate matching joints, then bore mating dowel pin holes in the components with a doweling jig. Make each ⅜-in.-dia. hole 1⅝ in. deep to allow space for excess glue. Use two dowels in each joint, spacing them 2 in. apart.

Lay out the ½-in.-radius corners on the lower rails of the frames and cut these profiles with a saber saw, then sand the corners smooth.

Now, assemble one of the rectangular frames for each seat and the table. Glue the dowel pins into the rails, then apply a thin coat of waterproof resorcinol glue to the joint and to the protruding dowel pins. Drive the joints together with a hammer and wood block. Clamp the assemblies with bar clamps until the glue has set.

Interlock the cross-lap joints of the rails, then add the remaining components, driving them together as you did before. Clamp these joints, then set the assemblies aside to dry. Continue this process until all five frames are assembled.

Once the glue has dried thoroughly, sand the bases. Start with 80-grit abrasive on a belt sander to level the joints. Begin by sanding the vertical components, working across the joint to even up the wood. Switch to the horizontal parts to remove scratches and to finish the job. Be careful not to let the sander drift onto the parts already finished.

Continue with a 120-grit belt, following the same sanding pattern.

Finish up with 220-grit abrasive paper on a sanding pad or a straight-line finishing sander for a perfect surface. Take your time with the sanding to produce a fine finish.

Add 1X1 X 22-in. cleats to the top of the table and chair bases. Secure the two cleats to the top edge of each base leg. Miter where the 1X1s join the table's hub.

Now, begin building the table and seat tops. For both, cut a 7¼-in.-square piece of 1X8 redwood to form the center of the top. Measure carefully to make the boards perfectly square. Center these boards accurately on the base frames, then attach them to the base with 6d galvanized finishing nails. Set the nails below the surface of the wood with a nail set.

Cut the 1X6 parts for the outer square of the seat tops. Each component is 18½ in. long with 45 degree miters on the corners. Use a radial arm saw to cut the miters. To make all of the parts identical, clamp stop blocks to the saw's fence.

As you did before, use a doweling jig to bore mating ⅜-in. dowel pin holes in the components. Space the holes 3 in. apart and be careful not to locate them too near the edges of the boards. As you did before, bore

MATERIALS LIST

Item	Quantity
2X4 redwood	19 ft.
1X8 redwood	24 ft.
1X6 redwood	8 ft.
1X1 for cleat	15 ft.
1X4 (4 chairs)	45 ft.
¼″ X 3″ fluted dowel pins	144
6d galvanized finishing nails	as needed
No. 8 X 1¼″ flathead screws	as needed
Resorcinol glue	as needed
Redwood filler	as needed
Finishing materials	as needed

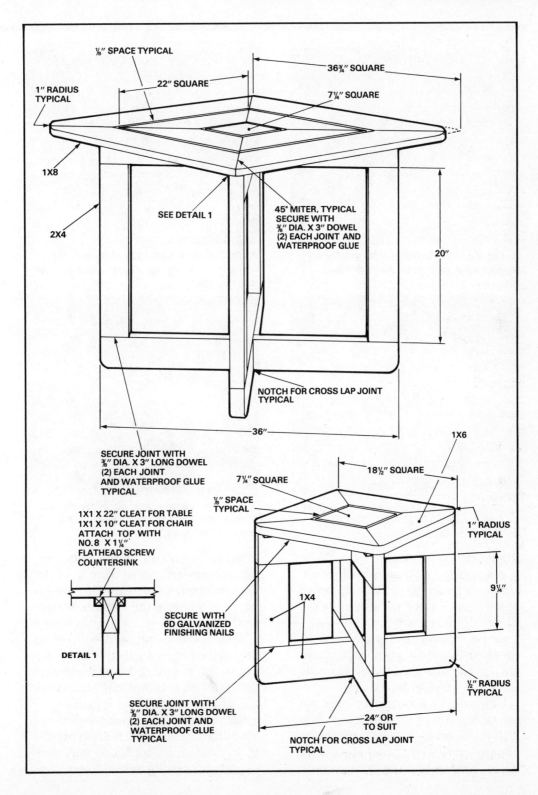

⅛" SPACE TYPICAL

22" SQUARE

36¾" SQUARE

7¼" SQUARE

1" RADIUS TYPICAL

1X8

2X4

SEE DETAIL 1

45° MITER, TYPICAL
SECURE WITH
⅜" DIA. X 3" DOWEL
(2) EACH JOINT AND
WATERPROOF GLUE

20"

NOTCH FOR CROSS LAP JOINT
TYPICAL

36"

SECURE JOINT WITH
⅜" DIA. X 3" LONG DOWEL
(2) EACH JOINT
AND WATERPROOF GLUE
TYPICAL

1X1 X 22" CLEAT FOR TABLE
1X1 X 10" CLEAT FOR CHAIR
ATTACH TOP WITH
NO. 8 X 1¼"
FLATHEAD SCREW
COUNTERSINK

DETAIL 1

1X6

18½" SQUARE

7¼" SQUARE

⅛" SPACE
TYPICAL

1" RADIUS
TYPICAL

9¼"

1X4

SECURE WITH
6D GALVANIZED
FINISHING NAILS

½" RADIUS
TYPICAL

SECURE JOINT WITH
⅜" DIA. X 3" LONG DOWEL
(2) EACH JOINT AND
WATERPROOF GLUE
TYPICAL

NOTCH FOR CROSS LAP JOINT
TYPICAL

24" OR
TO SUIT

177

CONSTRUCTION DETAILS

1. Cut the interlocking notches for the leg joints with a dado blade on your radial arm saw.

2. Drill mating dowel pin holes with the aid of a doweling jig. Measure carefully for a perfect fit.

5. Assemble the rectangles with dowel pins and glue. Careful alignment of the dowel holes is important.

6. Cut the square center panel for the tops from a piece of 1X8 stock. Measure the panels accurately.

the holes 1⅝ in. deep.

Assemble the squares with resorcinol glue and ⅜-in. X 3-in. fluted dowel pins. Clamp the assembly until dry, then lay out the 1-in.-radius corners. Cut these with a finetoothed blade in your saber saw. Guide the saw carefully, keeping the blade vertical in the cut.

Make the two center squares for the table's top in the same way. Use 1X8 redwood for these squares. The components of the inner square are 22 in. long, while the outer square

is made of 36¾-in. parts. As before, the corners are cut to form a 45 degree mitered joint. Cut 1-in.-radius corners on only the outside square of the table top.

Attach the completed squares to the bases with 6d galvanized finishing nails, as you did before, setting the nail heads below the surface to allow for wood filler. Equalize the spaces between the components before nailing. The spaces are typically ⅛ in. wide, although this may vary slightly according to the dimensions

3. Drive the doweled joints together with a hammer. Use a backup block to prevent scarring the wood.

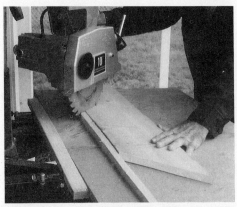

4. Cut the miters for the table and seat tops with a radial arm saw. Use a combination blade for a smooth finish.

7. With a saber saw, round the corners of the tops to a 1-in. radius. Use a fine-toothed blade.

8. Sand the tops with a pad-type sander. Follow the grain direction of the components carefully.

of your lumber.

Fill the nail holes with waterproof wood filler that matches the redwood. If redwood filler is not available, make your own using resorcinol glue and redwood sawdust from sanding. Allow the filler to dry completely before sanding the tops.

Now, sand the table and seat tops well with a pad-type sander. Start with 120-grit garnet paper and work down to 220-grit for a smooth finish. To avoid unsightly scratches, sand in the direction of grain. Be

especially careful when sanding near the mitered joints. Sand the rounded corners of the tops, then round the sharp edges of the tops slightly with the pad sander.

Finish the project with at least two coats of clear wood sealer and preservative or use two coats of satin-finish polyurethane varnish. If you use sealer, be certain it contains no toxic materials. Thompson's Water Seal is ideal. Allow each coat of either finish to dry for 24 hours before applying the second coat.

OAK FOLDING CHAIR

You can never have too many folding chairs, especially for outdoor entertaining. This attractive oak and canvas chair is so easy to build that you might want to make several.

Begin construction by cutting all of the components to the sizes shown in the diagram. Lay out and cut the beveled ends of the frame sides. Be careful to make matching pieces identical. Locate the positions of the pivot holes in the frame sides, and then use a drill press to bore the holes.

Before assembling the chair, sand the individual parts thoroughly. Start with 80-grit paper and work down to 150-grit paper. Break all sharp edges slightly.

Next, attach the seat slats to the frame. Use no. 8 X 1½-in. brass flathead wood screws and resorcinol glue for the assembly. Bore pilot holes for the screws with a combination pilot bit and countersink.

Attach the top brace to the back frame, then put the two frames together. Insert the dowel pivot rod, gluing it to the outer frame only. If the rod is a tight fit in the inner pair of holes, ream the holes out slightly.

Set the chair up on a level surface and adjust it until the legs sit evenly. Position the remaining braces, which serve as stops, then clamp them securely. Screw and glue these braces as you did the others.

Apply a coat of a stain of your choice to the completed assembly, then follow that with two coats of satin-finish polyurethane varnish.

Cut the canvas back to the size shown in the diagram and stitch up the side hems. Use a ball-point needle and heavy-duty thread. Fold the ends of the canvas, as shown, and double-stitch the seams for strength.

Attach the canvas to the frame with no. 8 X 1-in. stainless steel panhead sheet metal screws with flat washers. Drill pilot holes for the screws.

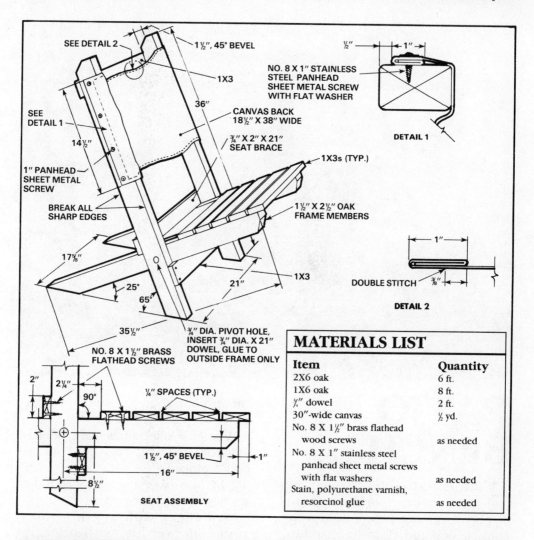

SEE DETAIL 2

1½", 45° BEVEL

1X3

NO. 8 X 1" STAINLESS STEEL PANHEAD SHEET METAL SCREW WITH FLAT WASHER

½" 1"

DETAIL 1

36"

SEE DETAIL 1

CANVAS BACK 18½" X 38" WIDE

14½"

¾" X 2" X 21" SEAT BRACE

1X3s (TYP.)

1" PANHEAD SHEET METAL SCREW

BREAK ALL SHARP EDGES

1½" X 2½" OAK FRAME MEMBERS

17⅝"

1X3

1"

25°

21"

DOUBLE STITCH ⅜"

65°

DETAIL 2

35½"

¾" DIA. PIVOT HOLE, INSERT ¾" DIA. X 21" DOWEL, GLUE TO OUTSIDE FRAME ONLY

NO. 8 X 1½" BRASS FLATHEAD SCREWS

2" 2¼"

90°

¼" SPACES (TYP.)

1½", 45° BEVEL

1"

16"

8½"

SEAT ASSEMBLY

MATERIALS LIST

Item	Quantity
2X6 oak	6 ft.
1X6 oak	8 ft.
¾" dowel	2 ft.
30"-wide canvas	½ yd.
No. 8 X 1½" brass flathead wood screws	as needed
No. 8 X 1" stainless steel panhead sheet metal screws with flat washers	as needed
Stain, polyurethane varnish, resorcinol glue	as needed

CONSTRUCTION DETAILS

1. *Install the bottom stop brace after setting the chair up to make certain that it is properly located.*

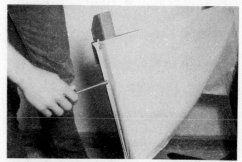

2. *Use stainless steel panhead sheet metal screws with flat washers to secure the canvas to the chair's frame.*

PATIO BENCH

Whether you use this bench for patio or deck seating or as a stand to display container plants, its sturdy construction and clean lines add to your outdoor decor.

Construction is simple; cut lap joints on the end frames for strength and good looks. Begin by cutting the components for the support frames to the sizes shown in the diagram. Measure carefully when laying out the half-laps on the ends of each part. Use a wobble-type dado blade on your radial arm saw to cut the joints, being careful to make the cuts exactly half of the wood's thickness.

If you do not have a radial arm saw, cut these joints with a straight bit in your router. Clamp an edge guide in place for accuracy.

Assemble the frames using 6d galvanized finishing nails and waterproof glue. Better yet, use no. 8 X 1¼-in. brass wood screws. Once the frames are dry, round over all exposed edges with a ¼-in.-radius rounding-over bit, with pilot, in your router.

Next, cut the braces and nail them in place with 10d galvanized finishing nails, after rounding off their edges as you did on the frames.

Add the seat slats, spacing them with a 9/16-in.-thick block of wood. Attach the slats with 6d galvanized finishing nails, set just below the surface.

Round off the edges of the seat slats as you did the frames, then sand and apply two coats of exterior sealer.

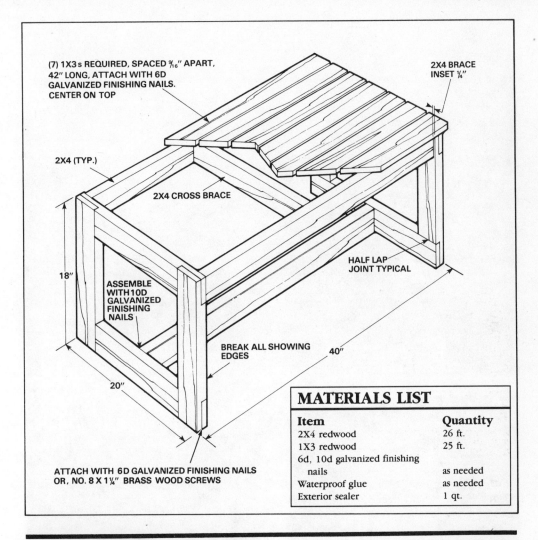

(7) 1X3 s REQUIRED, SPACED ⁹⁄₁₆″ APART, 42″ LONG, ATTACH WITH 6D GALVANIZED FINISHING NAILS. CENTER ON TOP

2X4 BRACE INSET ¼″

2X4 (TYP.)

2X4 CROSS BRACE

HALF LAP JOINT TYPICAL

18″

ASSEMBLE WITH 10D GALVANIZED FINISHING NAILS

BREAK ALL SHOWING EDGES

40″

20″

ATTACH WITH 6D GALVANIZED FINISHING NAILS OR, NO. 8 X 1¼″ BRASS WOOD SCREWS

MATERIALS LIST

Item	Quantity
2X4 redwood	26 ft.
1X3 redwood	25 ft.
6d, 10d galvanized finishing nails	as needed
Waterproof glue	as needed
Exterior sealer	1 qt.

CONSTRUCTION DETAILS

1. Cut the half lap joints with a dado blade on your radial arm saw.

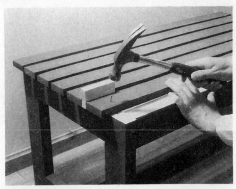

2. Use a block as a spacer to position the seat slats at a uniform distance apart.

PATIO DINING SET

You can add a touch of Pennsylvania Dutch design to your outdoor dining by building this three-piece furniture set. Built entirely of all-heart redwood, the set seats six and is designed to last a lifetime.

Start construction by cutting all of the components to the lengths shown in the diagram. Use a planer-type blade on your saw for smooth edges.

Next, form the dadoes in the table top components and the bench side parts with multiple passes of a dado blade. The dadoes on most of the parts are the same distance from the ends of the boards, so make guideline marks on your saw's fence or table to speed up the job.

Assemble the table top first, starting with the two outside boards. Fasten these to the cleats with resorcinol glue and no. 10 X 1¼-in. brass flathead wood screws. Bore countersunk holes with a combination pilot bit and countersink.

Add the center board, equalizing the gaps between the boards. Round the corners of the table top with a saber saw. Use a compass to lay out the 2-in.-radius profiles.

Make the table leg assemblies in the same way. After assembly, lay out the curved profiles with a bar compass and cut with a saber saw. If you do not have a bar compass, make a temporary compass using brads and a strip of thin scrap stock.

With the table top upside-down on sawhorses, prop the leg assemblies in place, then add the upper braces. Drill and counterbore the fastener holes as shown in the diagram, then attach them to the top with lag screws and resorcinol glue. After drilling counterbored pilot holes, screw the leg assemblies to the braces as well.

Add the lower brace. Measure carefully before boring the counterbored pilot holes to insure proper alignment.

To bore the counterbored holes used in this project, start by boring ⅞-in.-dia. holes to the depths shown in the diagram. Follow up with a ⁵⁄₁₆-in.-dia. shank clearance hole and a ³⁄₁₆-in. pilot hole for the screw threads. Adjust the depth of these holes to match the application.

Round over the edges of the table top and legs with a ¼-in.-radius rounding-over bit, with pilot, in your router. Finish off inaccessible edges with a medium-cut flat file.

Assemble the bench sides as you did the table top, attaching the cleats with screws and glue. Keep the spacing between the boards even.

On one of the bench sides, lay out the pattern shown in the diagram. Use a bar compass as you did on the table legs. Cut the pattern out with your saber saw, then use this bench side as a pattern to mark the others.

Smooth the curved sections with a drum sander in your drill, then round over the edges as you did previously.

CONSTRUCTION DETAILS

1. Bore countersunk screw holes, then attach cleats in their dadoes with screws and resorcinol glue.

2. Cut out the curved profiles on the project with a saber saw. Work slowly for smooth results.

Now, measure carefully and draw light pencil lines to locate the positions of the 2X2 cleats on the bench sides. Attach the cleats to the sides with no. 10 X 2½-in. brass flathead screws, after boring countersunk pilot holes.

Round over the edges of the seat and back boards with your router, then attach them to the cleats with glue and no. 8 X 2-in. brass flathead wood screws. Countersink the screw heads.

Cut the notches in the seat braces as shown in the diagram, then install them under the center line of each seat board. Attach the braces to the cleats with lag screws, then screw the seats to the braces, countersinking the screw holes.

Sand the completed project thoroughly, working down from 80-grit garnet paper to 120-grit paper. Use a straight-line sander and work with the wood grain.

Finish the project with two coats of clear wood sealer, such as Thompson's Water Seal.

3. Attach the notched seat braces with lag screws into the cleats. Screw the seat boards to the braces.

Reprinted with permission from The Family Handyman, Webb Publishing Co., 1999 Shepard Rd., St. Paul, MN 55116.

MATERIALS LIST

Item	Quantity
2X12 redwood	20 ft.
2X8 redwood	50 ft.
2X6 redwood	5 ft.
2X4 redwood	30 ft.
2X2 redwood	10 ft.
1X8 redwood	50 ft.
1X4 redwood	30 ft.
⅜" X 3" lag screws	10
⅜" X 4" lag screws	12
No. 10 X 2½" brass flathead wood screws	32
No. 10 X 1¼" brass flathead wood screws	175
No. 8 X 2" brass flathead wood screws	60
Wood sealer and resorcinol glue	as needed

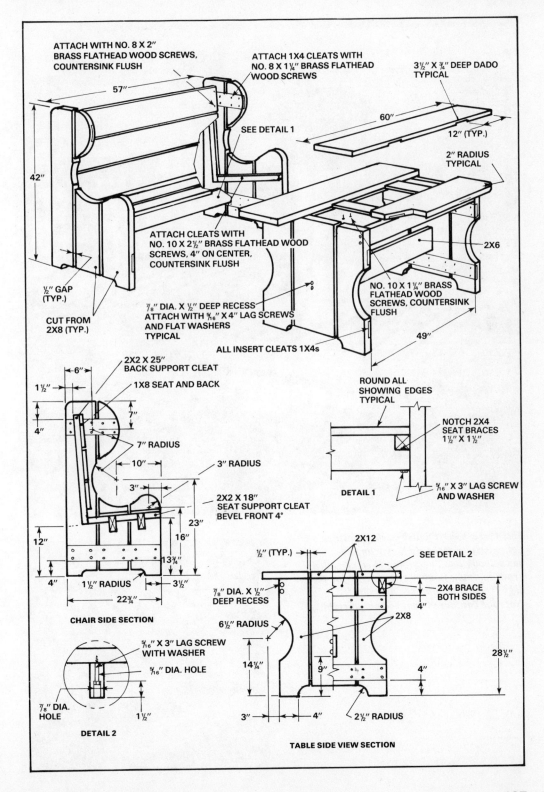

ATTACH WITH NO. 8 X 2"
BRASS FLATHEAD WOOD SCREWS,
COUNTERSINK FLUSH

ATTACH 1X4 CLEATS WITH
NO. 8 X 1¼" BRASS FLATHEAD
WOOD SCREWS

3½" X ¾" DEEP DADO
TYPICAL

57"

60"

12" (TYP.)

SEE DETAIL 1

42"

2" RADIUS
TYPICAL

ATTACH CLEATS WITH
NO. 10 X 2½" BRASS FLATHEAD WOOD
SCREWS, 4" ON CENTER,
COUNTERSINK FLUSH

2X6

½" GAP
(TYP.)

NO. 10 X 1¼" BRASS
FLATHEAD WOOD
SCREWS, COUNTERSINK
FLUSH

CUT FROM
2X8 (TYP.)

⅞" DIA. X ½" DEEP RECESS
ATTACH WITH ⁵⁄₁₆" X 4" LAG SCREWS
AND FLAT WASHERS
TYPICAL

49"

ALL INSERT CLEATS 1X4s

2X2 X 25"
BACK SUPPORT CLEAT

6"

1X8 SEAT AND BACK

1½"

ROUND ALL
SHOWING EDGES
TYPICAL

4"

7"

NOTCH 2X4
SEAT BRACES
1½" X 1½"

7" RADIUS

10"

3" RADIUS

3"

DETAIL 1

⁵⁄₁₆" X 3" LAG SCREW
AND WASHER

2X2 X 18"
SEAT SUPPORT CLEAT
BEVEL FRONT 4°

23"

16"

12"

13¾"

2X12

SEE DETAIL 2

½" (TYP.)

2X4 BRACE
BOTH SIDES

4"

1½" RADIUS

3½"

⅞" DIA. X ½"
DEEP RECESS

4"

22¾"

2X8

CHAIR SIDE SECTION

6½" RADIUS

⁵⁄₁₆" X 3" LAG SCREW
WITH WASHER

14¼"

9"

28½"

⁵⁄₁₆" DIA. HOLE

4"

⅞" DIA.
HOLE

1½"

3"

4"

2½" RADIUS

DETAIL 2

TABLE SIDE VIEW SECTION

This three-piece English-style furniture set is easy to make and easy on the pocketbook too. Everything is constructed from common lumber sizes except for the legs (read story and see diagram). Note the contoured seat bottom at right.

PATIO FURNITURE SET

A coordinated set of furniture for the patio or deck will help tie your outdoor decor together. This set, made up of a bench, chair, and table, is designed to add comfort and beauty to your yard.

Construction procedures are identical for the bench and chair, so begin construction by cutting all the components to the sizes shown in the diagram.

The legs for all three pieces are a full 2 in. thick. Plane 3-in.-thick stock to reach this finished size. If you do not have a planer, most lumberyards will do this job for a modest fee.

Notice the profiles of the back legs of the bench and chair. Lay these out on 2X4 stock and cut with a band saw or a saber saw. After cutting all four, clamp them together and even them up with a belt sander.

Form the $\frac{3}{4}$-in. X $\frac{3}{4}$-in. grooves on the back rails with a dado blade and your radial arm saw or table saw. Notice that the grooves in the lower rails are 8 degrees from vertical. Glue the slats in place with waterproof resorcinol glue, spacing them as shown in the diagram. Be careful to keep the assembly square. Clamp securely with pipe-type clamps and allow them to dry completely.

Once the glue has dried, attach the rear legs. Measure carefully, and then use a doweling jig to bore $\frac{3}{8}$-in.-dia. holes, $1\frac{5}{8}$ in. deep., for the dowels. Join the legs to the frame with $\frac{3}{8}$-in. X $2\frac{1}{2}$-in. dowels and waterproof resorcinol glue.

Next, enlarge the pattern for the seat sides and braces by drawing a grid of 1-in. squares on a piece of hardboard. Cut this out with a band saw or a saber saw, and use it as a pattern to lay out the parts.

Cut the sides and braces with a band saw or a saber saw. After cutting, clamp the pieces together and use a belt sander with a coarse-grit belt to equalize the profiles of the components.

Assemble the seat frames, doweling the joints as you did before. Clamp and set aside to dry.

Add the front legs and the lower braces to the rear assembly, again joining with glue and dowels. Cut out the armrests and attach them with screws and dowels as shown in the diagram.

Use waterproof resorcinol glue on all joints and clamp securely until the glue has dried completely.

Insert the seat frame, attaching it with glue and no. 12 X 4-in. flathead wood screws. Use a combination pilot bit and countersink to drill pilot holes. Place the screw heads just below the surface and fill the space with waterproof wood filler.

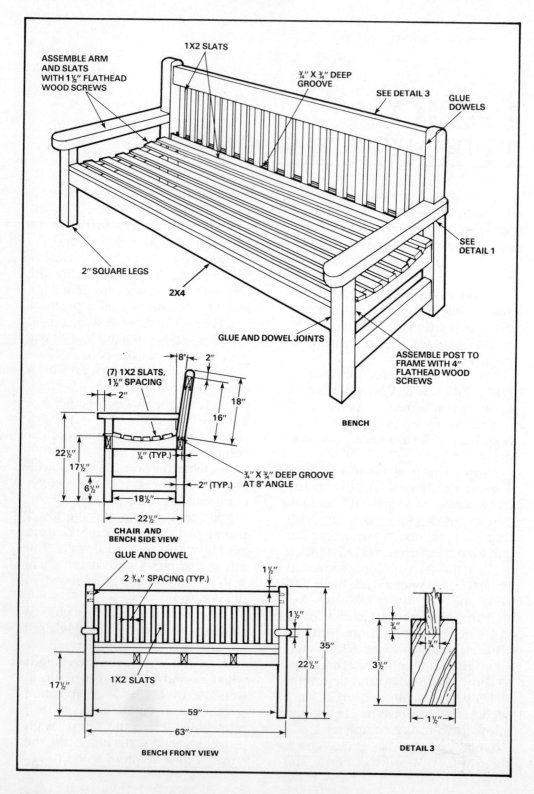

ASSEMBLE ARM
AND SLATS
WITH 1½" FLATHEAD
WOOD SCREWS

1X2 SLATS

¾" X ¾" DEEP
GROOVE

SEE DETAIL 3

GLUE
DOWELS

SEE
DETAIL 1

2" SQUARE LEGS

2X4

GLUE AND DOWEL JOINTS

ASSEMBLE POST TO
FRAME WITH 4"
FLATHEAD WOOD
SCREWS

BENCH

(7) 1X2 SLATS,
1½" SPACING

8°

2"

18"

16"

2"

22½"

17½"

6½"

¼" (TYP.)

2" (TYP.)

¾" X ¾" DEEP GROOVE
AT 8° ANGLE

18½"

22½"

CHAIR AND
BENCH SIDE VIEW

GLUE AND DOWEL

2 ⁷⁄₁₆" SPACING (TYP.)

1½"

1½"

35"

22½"

17½"

1X2 SLATS

59"

63"

BENCH FRONT VIEW

¾"

¾"

3½"

1½"

DETAIL 3

190

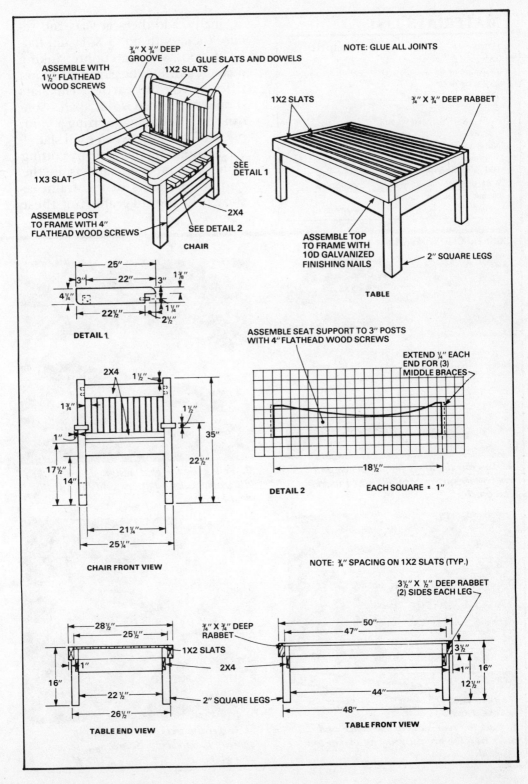

NOTE: GLUE ALL JOINTS

CHAIR

ASSEMBLE WITH 1½" FLATHEAD WOOD SCREWS

¾" X ¾" DEEP GROOVE

1X2 SLATS

GLUE SLATS AND DOWELS

1X3 SLAT

SEE DETAIL 1

ASSEMBLE POST TO FRAME WITH 4" FLATHEAD WOOD SCREWS

SEE DETAIL 2

2X4

TABLE

1X2 SLATS

¾" X ¾" DEEP RABBET

ASSEMBLE TOP TO FRAME WITH 10D GALVANIZED FINISHING NAILS

2" SQUARE LEGS

DETAIL 1

25"
3"   22"   3"
1 ⅜"
4¼"
22½"
1¼"
2½"

DETAIL 2

ASSEMBLE SEAT SUPPORT TO 3" POSTS WITH 4" FLATHEAD WOOD SCREWS

EXTEND ¼" EACH END FOR (3) MIDDLE BRACES

18½"

EACH SQUARE = 1"

CHAIR FRONT VIEW

2X4
1½"
1¾"
1½"
1"
35"
22½"
17½"
14"
21¼"
25¼"

NOTE: ¾" SPACING ON 1X2 SLATS (TYP.)

TABLE END VIEW

28½"
25½"
¾" X ¾" DEEP RABBET
1X2 SLATS
1"
2X4
16"
22½"
2" SQUARE LEGS
26½"

TABLE FRONT VIEW

3½" X ½" DEEP RABBET (2) SIDES EACH LEG

50"
47"
3½"
16"
1"
12½"
44"
48"

191

MATERIALS LIST

Item	Quantity
2X6 pine or fir	10 ft.
2X4 pine or fir	90 ft.
2X2 pine or fir	16 ft.
1X2 pine or fir	80 ft.
⅜″ X 2½″ dowels	70
No. 12 X 4″ flathead wood screws	1 lb.
No. 8 X 1½″ flathead wood screws	1 lb.
10d galvanized finishing nails	as needed
Waterproof resorcinol glue	as needed
Enamel primer and latex enamel	1 qt. each

Finally, add the seat slats and secure them with no. 8 X 1½-in. flathead wood screws, countersinking them and filling the gaps with wood filler as you did earlier. The slats should be spaced ¾ in. apart. Control the spacing by inserting a ¾-in. piece of wood between each slat.

Start building the table by cutting ¾-in. X ¾-in.-deep rabbets in the end components of the frame as shown in the diagram. Cut these

CONSTRUCTION DETAILS

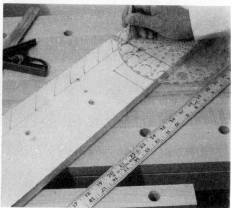

1. Lay out the arms for the bench and chair, measuring carefully when marking the notch.

2. Following the grid design shown in the diagram, make a pattern and lay out the seat braces.

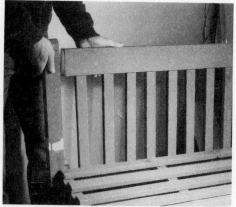

5. Glue the rear slats of the bench and chair into the pre-cut grooves. Clamp the assembly.

6. Insert the slats for the table top, spacing them evenly. Attach with screws and glue.

with a dado blade set ¾ in. wide. For safety's sake, cut the rabbets in the raw stock before cutting the parts to length. Assemble the frame with glue and dowels.

Install the slats in the table frame, securing them with glue and no. 8 X 1½-in. screws. Space the slats evenly.

Install the leg braces with screws and glue; then set the top in place. Nail the top to the legs with 10d galvanized finishing nails, setting the

nails below the surface. Fill the holes with waterproof wood filler.

Sand all three projects thoroughly, starting with 80-grit garnet paper and working down to 150-grit paper.

To finish the furniture, apply a coat of enamel primer, followed by two coats of semi-gloss latex enamel. Sand lightly between coats to level the paint surface. Spray painting will simplify the job.

3. Lay out the pattern of the rear legs following the dimensions shown in the diagram.

4. Before cutting, plane 3-in.-thick stock to 2 in. for the legs of both the bench and chair.

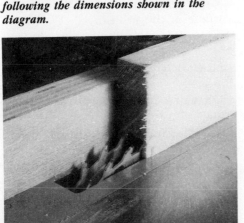

7. Cut the groove in the lower back braces at an angle by setting the dado blade at 8 degrees.

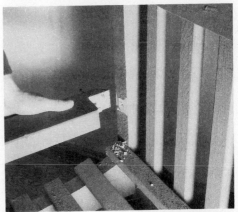

8. Attach the arms to the side frames with one dowel and flathead wood screw. Refer to the diagram.

PATIO TABLE

When outdoor entertaining is on the schedule, this easy-to-build table is a surefire project. You can easily build it in one day, and entertain with it the next.

Start building the table by making the plywood table top. Since the table is 48-in. square, you need to make just one crosscut on a sheet of ¾-in. exterior grade plywood.

Set the plywood, good face down, on a pair of sawhorses and clamp a cutting guide in place to guide your circular saw. Use a plywood blade to minimize splintering.

Next, measure the ¾-in. half-round molding and cut the miters using a miter box or a radial arm saw. Nail these molding segments to the edges of the top with 4d galvanized finishing nails, spaced 2-in. apart. Set the nails just below the surface of the molding.

Cut the components for the table's base to the sizes shown in the diagram; then assemble the base with 10d galvanized finishing nails. Check the squareness of the assembly as you go. To prevent splitting, drill pilot holes for the nails.

Sand both the base and the top before attaching the top with 10d finishing nails. Measure carefully to be certain the top is centered on the base.

Once assembled, the table is ready to be finished with any high-quality redwood stain or exterior enamel paint.

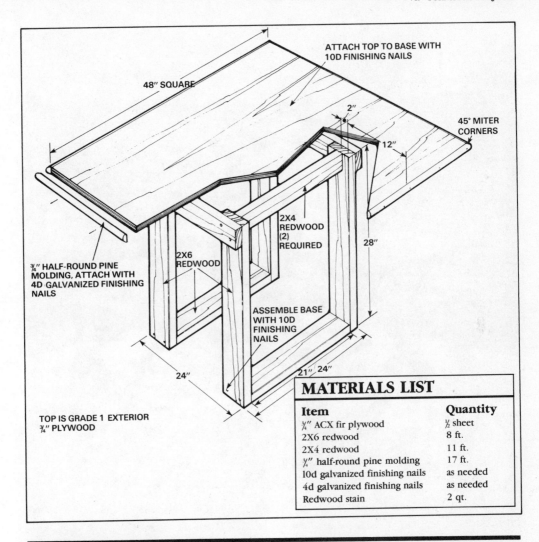

ATTACH TOP TO BASE WITH
10D FINISHING NAILS

48" SQUARE

2"

45° MITER
CORNERS

12"

2X4
REDWOOD
(2)
REQUIRED

28"

2X6
REDWOOD

¾" HALF-ROUND PINE
MOLDING, ATTACH WITH
4D GALVANIZED FINISHING
NAILS

ASSEMBLE BASE
WITH 10D
FINISHING
NAILS

24"

21" 24"

TOP IS GRADE 1 EXTERIOR
¾" PLYWOOD

MATERIALS LIST

Item	Quantity
¾" ACX fir plywood	½ sheet
2X6 redwood	8 ft.
2X4 redwood	11 ft.
¾" half-round pine molding	17 ft.
10d galvanized finishing nails	as needed
4d galvanized finishing nails	as needed
Redwood stain	2 qt.

CONSTRUCTION DETAILS

1. Assemble the solid lumber base with 10d galvanized finishing nails. Set the nails just below the surface with a nail set.

2. For a smooth cut on the table top, cut with the good side down, and use a plywood cutting blade and an edge guide.

195

*Fasten the braces with lag screws.
Counterbore the pilot holes to set the
heads below the surface.*

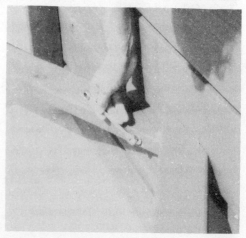

PICNIC TABLE AND BENCH

Simplicity of both design and construction are two of the best features of this traditional picnic table and bench. Built of redwood, this set is designed to last for years.

Start by building the leg assemblies for the table and benches. Cut the legs to the lengths shown in the diagram.

Next, lay each pair of legs together, making certain that they cross in the middle. Establish the correct leg angles by measuring scissor width and using a straightedge to check alignment. Also, mark the lap joints for cutting.

Cut the leg angles for each leg pair and then cut the lap joints.

After boring $1/4$-in.-dia. holes through the center of each pair of legs, join them using $1/4$-in. X 2-in. carriage bolts with nuts and washers.

Cut the cleats for the table and bench tops as shown in the diagram, again noting the provided angles. Attach the pre-cut boards to the cleats with 10d aluminum nails. Space the boards $1/2$ in. apart. Use a $1/2$-in.-thick board as a spacer.

Add the legs to the top assembly using two $1/4$-in. X $3 1/2$-in. carriage bolts with nuts and washers for each joint. This job is simpler to do if the table is upside-down on a pair of sawhorses.

Next, cut the diagonal braces to the lengths and angles shown in the diagram. Secure these with $1/4$-in. X 3-in. lag screws at each end. Bore $3/16$-in. pilot holes at an angle to match that of the braces; then counterbore with a $5/8$-in.-dia. bit to keep the screw heads below the surface.

Notice that the braces are staggered, with one on each side of the leg bolts.

Finish the project by sanding thoroughly. Start with 80-grit paper and work down to 150-grit. Use a belt sander for the rough sanding, and finish up with a straight-line sander or a sanding block.

Finally, apply two coats of wood sealer, such as Thompson's Water Seal, to help protect the project from the weather.

CONSTRUCTION DETAILS

1. *Cross the leg pairs, using a straightedge to line up the ends, and mark the lap joints.*

2. *Cut the legs at the correct angles on your radial arm or table saw. The legs must be equal.*

3. *Fasten the legs together with carriage bolts using a washer and hex nut.*

4. *Attach the top boards to the cleats with 10d aluminum nails to prevent corrosion.*

5. *Use carriage bolts to attach the table top to the legs. Tighten the nuts securely.*

MATERIALS LIST

Item	Quantity
2X6 redwood	24 ft.
2X8 redwood	55 ft.
¼" X 2" carriage bolts with nuts and washers	6
¼" X 3½" carriage bolts with nuts and washers	24
¼" X 3" lag screws with washers	12
10d aluminum nails	as needed
Wood sealer	3 qt.

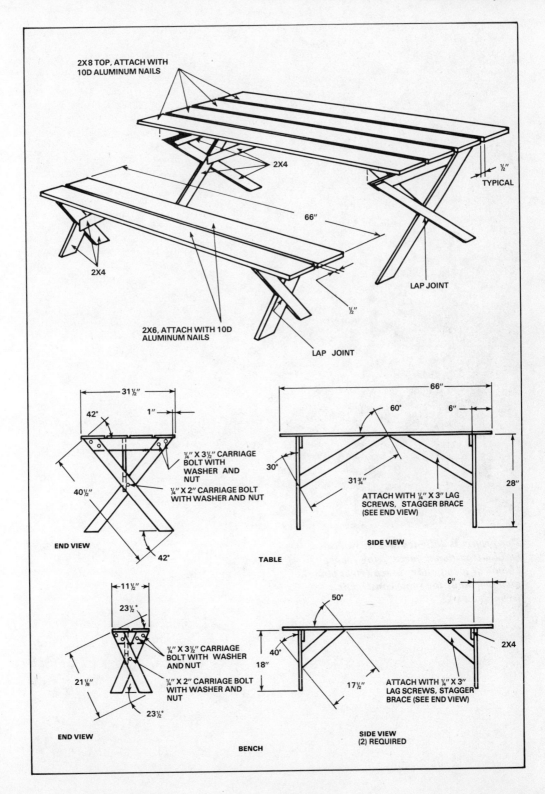

2X8 TOP, ATTACH WITH
10D ALUMINUM NAILS

2X4

½″
TYPICAL

66″

2X4

LAP JOINT

½″

2X6, ATTACH WITH 10D
ALUMINUM NAILS

½″

LAP JOINT

END VIEW

31½″

42°

1″

40½″

42°

¼″ X 3½″ CARRIAGE
BOLT WITH
WASHER AND
NUT

¼″ X 2″ CARRIAGE BOLT
WITH WASHER AND NUT

SIDE VIEW

66″

60°

6″

30°

31¾″

28″

ATTACH WITH ¼″ X 3″ LAG
SCREWS, STAGGER BRACE
(SEE END VIEW)

TABLE

END VIEW

11½″

23½°

23½°

21¹⁄₈″

¼″ X 3½″ CARRIAGE
BOLT WITH WASHER
AND NUT

¼″ X 2″ CARRIAGE BOLT
WITH WASHER AND
NUT

SIDE VIEW
(2) REQUIRED

6″

50°

40°

18″

17½″

2X4

ATTACH WITH ¼″ X 3″
LAG SCREWS, STAGGER
BRACE (SEE END VIEW)

BENCH

199

This project is designed so that you can build a traditional porch swing (above photo) or a stationary bench (right photo) using virtually the same construction techniques.

PORCH SWING/BENCH

For sheer relaxation, it is hard to beat the traditional porch swing. The gentle movement seems to drive away all the cares of the day and bring back pleasant memories of lazy summer evenings.

Here is a porch swing plan with a different twist: It can also be built as a stationary bench, with just minor variations made during construction. If you have room on your porch, why not build both units?

Construction of the two projects is identical, except that the bench requires two more components on the side frames to allow it to sit on the floor rather than hang from the rafters. Solid oak is used for the entire project.

Begin construction by ripping oak stock for the backrest supports. Follow this operation by ripping the back and lower seat supports. Use a planer-type blade for a smooth finish. Cut the components to the lengths and widths shown in the diagram.

Now enlarge the pattern for the seat supports onto a grid of 1-in. squares on heavy paper or cardboard. Cut the pattern out, and use it as template to trace the design onto the pre-cut parts. Cut the patterns on a band saw, following the lines closely. Clamp the two seat supports together and even their profiles with a medium-grit belt on your belt sander.

Next, form the notches for the half-lap joints between the two parts with a dado blade on your radial arm saw. Set the saw's arm to cut the 12 degree angle (see Detail 4 of the diagram on page 203). Clamp a stop block to the saw's fence to make the parts identical.

Make several passes, leaving the notches about $\frac{1}{32}$ in. short of the finished dimension. Use a chisel to pare off the remaining material, checking the fit of the joint frequently until it is perfect. Take your time on this job; the finished appearance of the project depends on your accuracy here.

Assemble the joints with waterproof resorcinol glue, clamping them securely until the glue has dried. Once the glue has set up, bore four $\frac{3}{8}$-in.-dia. dowel holes and glue in dowel pins to reinforce the joints. Do not drill through the outside showing surface.

Next, rip 2-in. wide backrest rails and rear seat rails from the $1\frac{3}{4}$-in. oak stock. Rip the front seat rail 3 in. wide. Cut the parts to the lengths shown in the diagram, taking care to make the parts identical.

The joints between the rails and the frame are doweled and glued. Make a jig for boring the dowel holes from a scrap of the $1\frac{3}{4}$-in. oak. Use a drill press to bore four $\frac{3}{8}$-in.-dia. guide holes in the block, then nail plywood ears to two sides of the jig to help locate it on the parts. Space the dowel holes $\frac{1}{2}$ in. apart.

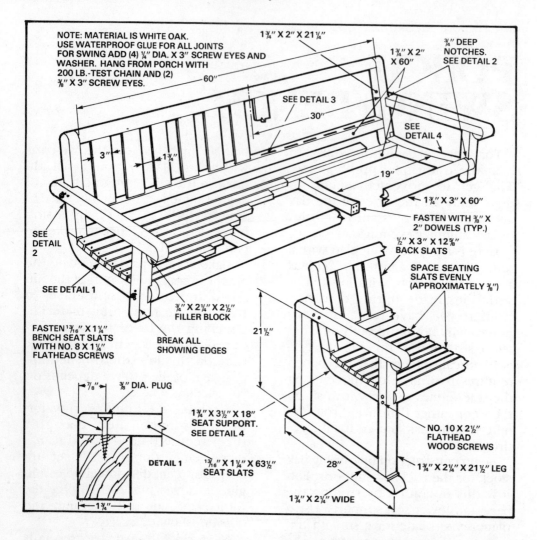

NOTE: MATERIAL IS WHITE OAK. USE WATERPROOF GLUE FOR ALL JOINTS FOR SWING ADD (4) ¼" DIA. X 3" SCREW EYES AND WASHER. HANG FROM PORCH WITH 200 LB.-TEST CHAIN AND (2) ⅜" X 3" SCREW EYES.

1¾" X 2" X 21¼"

¾" DEEP NOTCHES. SEE DETAIL 2

1¾" X 2" X 60"

60"

SEE DETAIL 3

30"

SEE DETAIL 4

3"

1¾"

19"

1¾" X 3" X 60"

FASTEN WITH ⅜" X 2" DOWELS (TYP.)

½" X 3" X 12⅝" BACK SLATS

SEE DETAIL 2

SPACE SEATING SLATS EVENLY (APPROXIMATELY ⅜")

SEE DETAIL 1

¾" X 2¼" X 2½" FILLER BLOCK

FASTEN 1¾" X 1¼" BENCH SEAT SLATS WITH NO. 8 X 1¼" FLATHEAD SCREWS

BREAK ALL SHOWING EDGES

21½"

⅞"   ⅜" DIA. PLUG

1¾" X 3½" X 18" SEAT SUPPORT. SEE DETAIL 4

DETAIL 1

1¾⁄₁₆" X 1¼" X 63½" SEAT SLATS

28"

1¾"

1¾" X 2¼" WIDE

NO. 10 X 2½" FLATHEAD WOOD SCREWS

1¾" X 2¼" X 21½" LEG

Clamp the jig to the rails and bore dowel pin holes 1⅛ in. deep in the ends of the rails. Transfer the hole locations to the frames with dowel center locaters, and drill the frames for the pins on your drill press. Once again, make the holes 1⅛ in. deep to allow excess glue to escape. Cut twelve 3-in.-wide slats, 12⅝ in. long, from ½-in.-thick oak stock.

Next, use a ½-in. straight bit in your router to form the mortises for the back slats. Clamp a guide block to your router to center the mortises on the parts. Lay out the mortise locations on the rails, then cut them ½ in. deep. Make the mortises ⅛ in. longer than the width of the slats to allow for expansion.

Cut the seat stretchers to length, then trace the curve of the seat's side onto them and cut the profiles on your band saw. Use the doweling jig you made to bore dowel pin holes in the stretchers, then transfer and drill matching holes on the front and rear seat rails. Align the

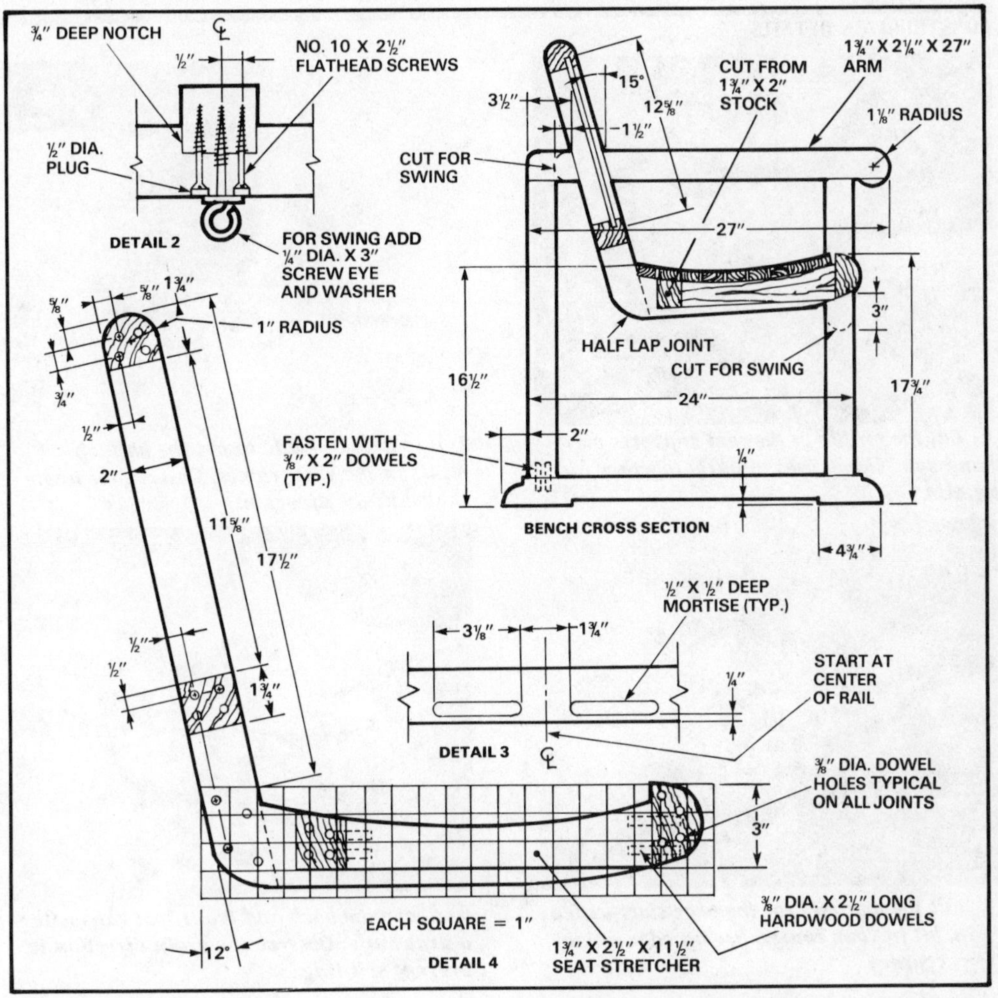
3/4" DEEP NOTCH
1/2"
NO. 10 X 2 1/2" FLATHEAD SCREWS
1/2" DIA. PLUG
DETAIL 2
FOR SWING ADD 1/4" DIA. X 3" SCREW EYE AND WASHER
CUT FOR SWING
3 1/2"
15°
12 5/8"
1 1/2"
CUT FROM 1 3/4" X 2" STOCK
1 3/4" X 2 1/4" X 27" ARM
1 1/8" RADIUS
27"
3"
HALF LAP JOINT
CUT FOR SWING
16 1/2"
24"
17 3/4"
2"
FASTEN WITH 3/8" X 2" DOWELS (TYP.)
1/4"
BENCH CROSS SECTION
4 3/4"
5/8"
1 3/4"
1" RADIUS
3/4"
1/2"
2"
11 5/8"
17 1/2"
1/2" X 1/2" DEEP MORTISE (TYP.)
3 1/8"
1 3/4"
START AT CENTER OF RAIL
DETAIL 3
3/8" DIA. DOWEL HOLES TYPICAL ON ALL JOINTS
3"
3/8" DIA. X 2 1/2" LONG HARDWOOD DOWELS
EACH SQUARE = 1"
12°
DETAIL 4
1 3/4" X 2 1/2" X 11 1/2" SEAT STRETCHER

parts carefully to keep the seat frame square.

Assemble all the components without glue to check the fit. When you are satisfied, make the final assembly with resorcinol glue and 3/8-in. fluted dowel pins. Clamp all of the joints with bar or pipe clamps until the glue has dried completely.

Do not glue the back slats in place; leave them loose to expand and contract with the weather. If necessary, round the edges slightly for an easy fit into the mortises.

MATERIALS LIST

Item	Quantity
1¾" oak	17 bd. ft.
13/16" oak	10 bd. ft.
½" X 3" oak	13 ft.
3/8" X 2" fluted dowel pins	80
3/8" X 1½" fluted dowel pins	8
3/8" oak screw hole plugs	44
No. 10 X 2½" flathead wood screws	8
No. 8 X 1¼" flathead wood screws	36
¼" X 3" screw eyes with washers (swing)	4
3/8" X 3" screw eyes (swing)	2
200 lb.-test chain (swing)	32 ft.
Waterproof resorcinol glue	as needed
Polyurethane varnish	as needed

CONSTRUCTION DETAILS

1. Cut the profile of the seat supports on a band saw. Clamp the cut parts together for sanding.

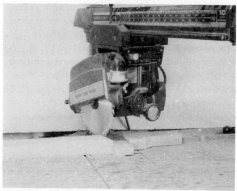

2. Use a dado blade to cut the half-lap joints in the seat frames. Observe the angle shown in the diagram.

5. Cut the mortises for the back slats with a ½-in. bit in your router. Use an edge guide for accuracy.

6. Shape the back and front seat rails with a drawknife. Observe the grain direction to prevent splitting.

Next, build the leg frame assembly for the bench or the arm assembly for the swing. Cut the parts to the sizes shown in the diagram, then dowel and glue them together as you did before. Clamp them securely while the glue dries.

Once the glue has dried on the seat assembly, attach the seat slats to the frame and stretchers. Drill counterbored pilot holes for the screws to allow for the wood screw hole plugs. The counterbores should be ³⁄₈ in. in dia. and ³⁄₈-in. deep. Glue in the plugs, leaving them

standing slightly above the surface. You will sand them flush later.

Shape the upper back rail and the front seat rail with a drawknife, as shown in the photo. Make a cardboard template to help you keep the profiles even. Finish the curves with a belt sander.

Next, clamp the leg or the arm assembly to the seat, adjusting it to make the seat comfortable. Make sure that both end frames line up. Use the dimensions in the diagram as a starting point.

Mark the intersections with a pen-

3. *Cut the joints slightly shallow, then finish the notches with a chisel. Check the fit frequently.*

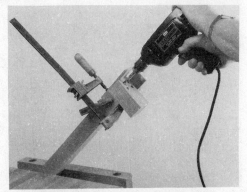

4. *Make a jig of scrap to help align the dowel pin holes in the rails. Mark the mating holes with center locators.*

7. *Smooth the rails with a belt sander. Rough them out across the grain, then finish sanding with the grain.*

8. *Use your router to make the notches for the seat assembly. Make several deepening passes.*

cil, then unclamp the assembly and cut the notches for the seat in the side frames. Use a router with a 3/4-in. straight bit, and make several deepening passes to cut the notches 3/4 in. deep.

Assemble the frames to the seat, fastening the joints with glue and no. 10 X 2½-in. flathead screws. Counterbore for screw hole plugs, as you did on the seat slats. For the swing, add ¼-in. X 3-in. screw eyes with washers for the chain. Bore 3/16-in. pilot holes for the screw eyes.

Sand the completed project thor-

oughly, starting with 80-grit abrasive and finishing up with 220-grit. Do both hand and power sanding, always sanding with the grain of the wood.

Finish your bench or swing with at least two coats of polyurethane varnish, sanding lightly between coats. Hang the swing from your porch rafters with chain tested to at least 200 lbs. Use 3/8-in. X 3-in. screw eyes in the rafters. Adjust the length of the chain to suit your taste.

Design and photos courtesy of Dennis Watson and The Family Handyman.

REDWOOD COFFEE TABLE

A low table is an essential ingredient for successful outdoor entertaining. This one, built of solid redwood, is designed to fit into any outdoor decorating scheme. Its simple lines blend perfectly with both traditional and modern patio furniture.

Begin by cutting the table's legs. Rip a 45 degree bevel on one edge of 1X4 redwood stock. Form the bevel on either your table or radial arm saw, and use a combination planer-type blade for a smooth surface. For safety's sake, work with long lengths of material to avoid kickbacks. Six-foot lengths are perfect and will make two complete leg sets.

To make the leg halves, cut the beveled material to a finished length of 17 1/4 in. Next, cut 1X1 redwood stock into 15-in. lengths to form the cleats that hold the legs together. Assemble each leg with resorcinol glue and no. 8 X 1 1/4-in. flathead wood screws. Drive the screws from inside after boring countersunk pilot holes with a combination pilot bit.

Now, cut the 1X4 components for the table's top frame. The end pieces are 26 1/2 in. long, while the side components are 40 1/2 in. long. Once again, use a planer-type blade on your saw for a smooth finish on the end grain.

Fasten one side board to two of the leg assemblies, driving no. 8 X 1 1/4-in. flathead wood screws from inside the legs. Use resorcinol glue on these joints as well. Notice that the top of the legs should be 3/4 in. down from the top of the frame to accommodate the table's top slats. The end of the side piece should be precisely flush with the corner of the leg.

Assemble the other side in the same way, then add the end frame pieces. If the side pieces were installed properly, the end joints should be tight. Work on a flat surface with the assembly upside-down. Apply glue to the frame joints as well as the leg joint.

Measure the space between the sides of the frame, then cut 1X3 supports to fit. Install these with glue and screws. Counterbore the pilot holes with a 3/8-in. bit to accept wood screw hole plugs. Glue the plugs in place, leaving them slightly proud of the surface of the wood. The excess will be removed when you sand.

Add two more cleats to the ends of the frame, cutting them to fit between the legs. Fasten these cleats with glue and screws driven from inside.

Next, cut the 1X4 table slats to length. Measure the inside of the frame carefully to insure a close fit, and cut all of the slats to exactly the same length.

Lay the slats on the cleats, spacing them approximately 1/16-in. apart. Drive 4d galvanized finishing nails through the slats and into the cleats. To avoid marring the redwood,

CONSTRUCTION DETAILS

1. *Attach the 1X1 cleat to one half of the leg assembly with no. 8 X 1¼-in. flathead screws and glue, then add the second half.*

2. *Either attach the legs to the corners of the top frame or assemble the frame by itself (shown).*

3. *Add the 1X3 cleats to the frame with no. 8 X 1¼-in. flathead wood screws. Drill pilot holes to prevent wood splitting.*

4. *As an alternative to nailing the top, secure with no. 8 X 1¼-in. flathead wood screws, countersunk. Drill pilot holes first.*

leave the nails slightly above the surface, then set them just below the top of the table with a nail set. Fill the holes with redwood-colored wood filler.

Once the table is completely assembled, sand it thoroughly. Use a combination of power and hand sanding to level the top and smooth all exposed surfaces. Start with 100-grit paper and work down to 220-grit for a glass-smooth surface. Pay special attention to the exposed end grain of the frame.

Finish the table with either clear wood sealer, such as Thompson's Water Seal, or two or more coats of satin-finish polyurethane varnish. Sand the table lightly between coats with 400-grit emery paper.

MATERIALS LIST

Item	Quantity
1X4 redwood	48 ft.
1X3 redwood	8 ft.
1X1 redwood	5 ft.
No. 8 X 1¼" flathead wood screws	36
⅜" wood screw hole plugs	8
4d galvanized finishing nails	as needed
Resorcinol glue	as needed
Wood sealer or varnish	as needed

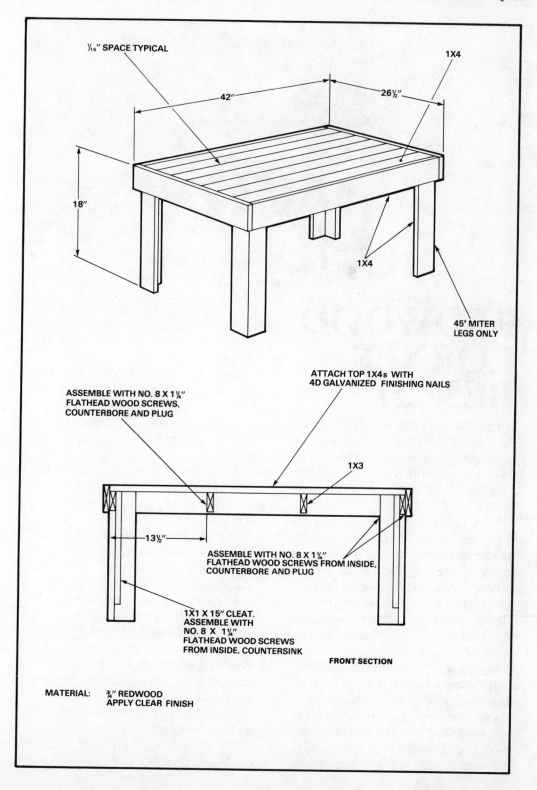

⅟₁₆" SPACE TYPICAL

1X4

42"

26½"

18"

1X4

45° MITER
LEGS ONLY

ATTACH TOP 1X4s WITH
4D GALVANIZED FINISHING NAILS

ASSEMBLE WITH NO. 8 X 1¼"
FLATHEAD WOOD SCREWS,
COUNTERBORE AND PLUG

1X3

13½"

ASSEMBLE WITH NO. 8 X 1¼"
FLATHEAD WOOD SCREWS FROM INSIDE,
COUNTERBORE AND PLUG

1X1 X 15" CLEAT.
ASSEMBLE WITH
NO. 8 X 1¼"
FLATHEAD WOOD SCREWS
FROM INSIDE, COUNTERSINK

FRONT SECTION

MATERIAL: ¾" REDWOOD
APPLY CLEAR FINISH

REDWOOD CORNER BENCH

This bench will help you make the most of a corner on your deck or patio. Built of redwood for good looks and durability, it will provide comfortable seating for you and your guests.

Start construction by cutting all the components to the sizes shown in the diagram. Cut a 45 degree miter on one end of each seat board.

Next, cut the corner cleat to length. Use a dado blade on your table or radial arm saw to form the 1½-in. X ¼-in.-deep groove in the part.

Cut the cleat to the profile shown in the diagram, then cut the 2-in. radius with a saber saw or band saw.

Lay out and cut the remaining rounded ends on the seat boards, then assemble the bench top. With the top upside-down, screw the cleats to the top with no. 10 X 2½-in. brass flathead wood screws. Drill countersunk pilot holes for the screws.

Next, screw the legs to the 2X2 cleats, following the same technique. Once the legs are in place, turn the assembly right-side-up and position the corner legs in the groove.

Bore counterbored pilot holes through the top of the bench into the legs. Drive no. 12 X 4-in. brass flathead wood screws into the legs, using two screws for each leg. Add the screw hole plugs, gluing them in place with waterproof resorcinol glue.

Once the glue has dried, sand the completed bench thoroughly, working down from 120-grit paper to 220-grit. If you use a power sander, work carefully in the direction of the grain to avoid marring the soft redwood.

Finish the bench with two coats of a clear wood sealer, such as Thompson's Water Seal. Allow 24 hours of drying time between coats.

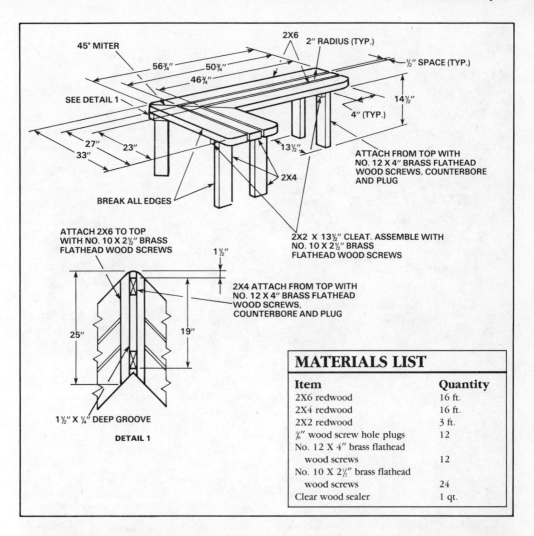

2X6

2" RADIUS (TYP.)

45° MITER

½" SPACE (TYP.)

56¾"   50¾"

46¾"

14½"

SEE DETAIL 1

4" (TYP.)

27"   23"

33"

13½"

2X4

ATTACH FROM TOP WITH
NO. 12 X 4" BRASS FLATHEAD
WOOD SCREWS, COUNTERBORE
AND PLUG

BREAK ALL EDGES

ATTACH 2X6 TO TOP
WITH NO. 10 X 2½" BRASS
FLATHEAD WOOD SCREWS

2X2 X 13½" CLEAT. ASSEMBLE WITH
NO. 10 X 2½" BRASS
FLATHEAD WOOD SCREWS

1½"

2X4 ATTACH FROM TOP WITH
NO. 12 X 4" BRASS FLATHEAD
WOOD SCREWS,
COUNTERBORE AND PLUG

25"   19"

1½" X ¼" DEEP GROOVE

DETAIL 1

MATERIALS LIST

Item	Quantity
2X6 redwood	16 ft.
2X4 redwood	16 ft.
2X2 redwood	3 ft.
¼" wood screw hole plugs	12
No. 12 X 4" brass flathead wood screws	12
No. 10 X 2½" brass flathead wood screws	24
Clear wood sealer	1 qt.

CONSTRUCTION DETAILS

1. Secure all cleats to the bench top with no. 10 X 2½-in. brass flathead wood screws. A portable drill speeds the process.

2. Drive no. 12 X 4-in. screws into all the legs from the top. Counterbore the pilot hole to accept wood screw hole plugs.

This ensemble features a contoured seat and back for comfortable relaxing and entertaining.

REDWOOD FURNITURE SET

Redwood is the ideal material for many outdoor projects. Its weather resistance and attractive color make it a natural complement to any setting. A simple finish of clear wood sealer is all that redwood needs.

This three-piece set of patio furniture is designed to take advantage of those qualities. The chair and love seat have comfortably curved seats, while the matching table is just the right size for entertaining. Contemporary frames make this furniture fit into almost any outdoor decorating scheme.

Both the chair and the love seat are built using the same techniques. The only difference between the two is the width.

Begin both by building the side frames. You can save time by making both sets of frames at once. Cut the 2X4 components to the lengths shown in the diagram, taking care to make matching parts identical.

Use a doweling jig to bore $\frac{3}{8}$-in.-dia. holes, $1\frac{5}{8}$ in. deep, for the dowels that will join the components. Assemble the frames with dowels and waterproof resorcinol glue, clamping them securely with bar clamps until dry. Use clamp pads to avoid marring the wood.

Once the frames are dry, form the rounded corners. Mark the radius on each corner, then use a belt sander to remove the waste. Work carefully to avoid over-cutting.

Cut the components of the L-shaped seat sides to length, and then mark the areas of the lap joints as shown in the diagram. Use multiple passes of a dado blade in your radial arm saw to form the lap joints. Measure carefully to make the joints exactly half the thickness of the wood.

Now, enlarge the patterns for the curved seat profiles. Draw a grid pattern on hardboard, then transfer the design shown in the diagram. Cut this out, then use the hardboard pattern to apply the design to the assembled seat sides. Cut the sides carefully with your saber saw. You have to cut notches for the bench's center L-shaped assembly where it joins the cross braces.

Attach the L-shaped sides to the cross braces with no. 10 X 2-in. wood screws and glue. Secure this assembly to the chair sides using waterproof glue and $\frac{3}{8}$-in. X $3\frac{1}{2}$-in. carriage bolts with nuts and washers.

Next, cut the remaining cross braces to length and attach to the sides. Drill counterbored pilot holes for the screws to allow for wood screw hole plugs. Use a combination screw pilot bit. Also, use resorcinol glue with the screws to make a strong, waterproof joint. After assembly, add the screw hole plugs, gluing them in place. Leave the plugs slightly above the wood's surface. You can level them later when you sand.

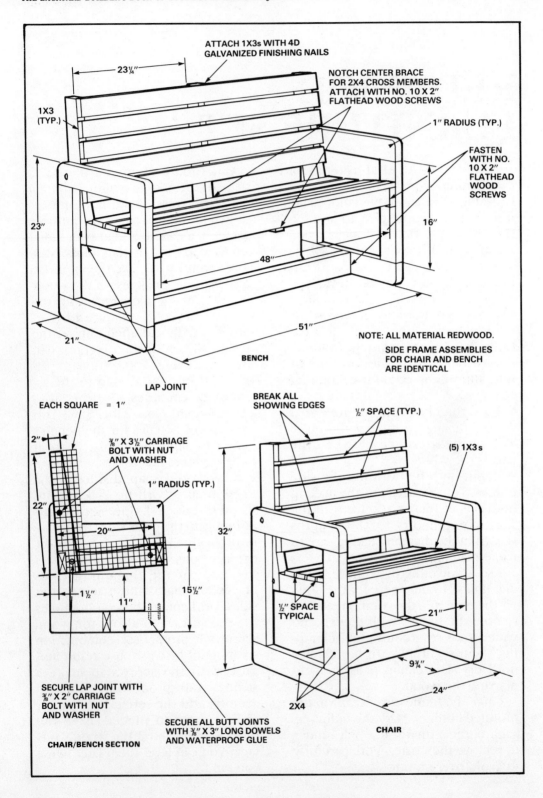

ATTACH 1X3s WITH 4D
GALVANIZED FINISHING NAILS

23¼"

NOTCH CENTER BRACE
FOR 2X4 CROSS MEMBERS.
ATTACH WITH NO. 10 X 2"
FLATHEAD WOOD SCREWS

1X3
(TYP.)

1" RADIUS (TYP.)

FASTEN
WITH NO.
10 X 2"
FLATHEAD
WOOD
SCREWS

23"

16"

48"

21"

51"

LAP JOINT

BENCH

NOTE: ALL MATERIAL REDWOOD.

SIDE FRAME ASSEMBLIES
FOR CHAIR AND BENCH
ARE IDENTICAL

EACH SQUARE = 1"

2"

⅜" X 3½" CARRIAGE
BOLT WITH NUT
AND WASHER

1" RADIUS (TYP.)

22"

20"

1½"

11"

15½"

BREAK ALL
SHOWING EDGES

½" SPACE (TYP.)

(5) 1X3 s

32"

½" SPACE
TYPICAL

21"

9¾"

2X4

24"

SECURE LAP JOINT WITH
⅜" X 2" CARRIAGE
BOLT WITH NUT
AND WASHER

SECURE ALL BUTT JOINTS
WITH ⅜" X 3" LONG DOWELS
AND WATERPROOF GLUE

CHAIR/BENCH SECTION

CHAIR

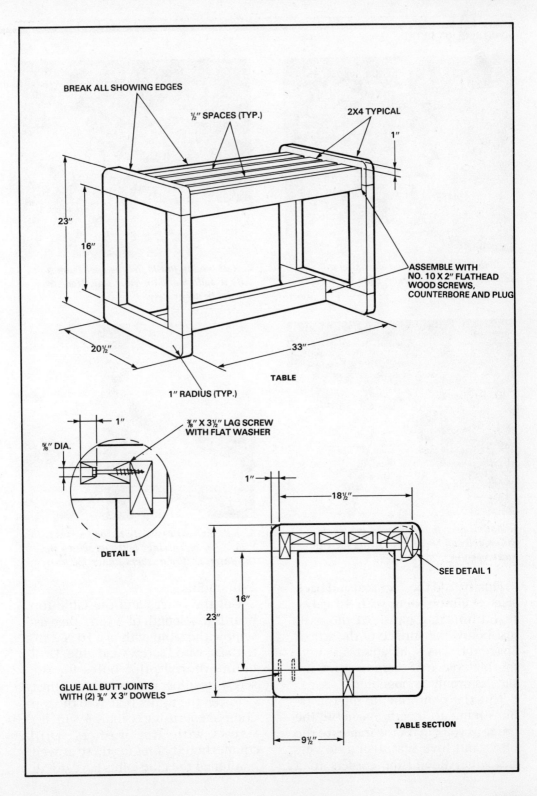

BREAK ALL SHOWING EDGES

½" SPACES (TYP.)

2X4 TYPICAL

1"

23"

16"

ASSEMBLE WITH
NO. 10 X 2" FLATHEAD
WOOD SCREWS,
COUNTERBORE AND PLUG

20½"

33"

TABLE

1" RADIUS (TYP.)

1"

⅜" X 3½" LAG SCREW
WITH FLAT WASHER

⅝" DIA.

DETAIL 1

1"

18½"

SEE DETAIL 1

16"

23"

GLUE ALL BUTT JOINTS
WITH (2) ⅜" X 3" DOWELS

TABLE SECTION

9½"

215

CONSTRUCTION DETAILS

1. *Drill holes for the dowels, using a doweling jig for accuracy. Note the correct depths.*

2. *Cut the lap joints for the seat frames with a dado blade on your saw. Measure the depth accurately.*

5. *Round over the corners of the frames with a belt sander after drawing the 1-in.-radius profiles.*

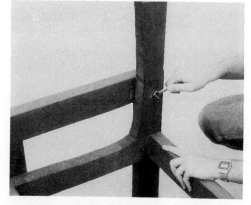

6. *Bolt the seat assembly to the frames with ⅜-in. X 3½-in. carriage bolts, as shown in the diagram. Use washers under the nuts.*

Finally, add the 1X3 seat and back slats, securing them with 4d galvanized finishing nails. Set the nails just below the surface of the wood. Space the slats ½ in. apart. Use a ½-in.-thick piece of scrap to space the slats as evenly as possible.

Cut the components for the table's frame to length. Assemble the frame as you did for the frames of the chair and love seat, using dowels and glue. Round the corners to a 1-in. radius.

Cut the braces and the table top boards to a length of 33 in., then assemble the table with no. 10 X 2-in. flathead wood screws and glue. Drill counterbored pilot holes for the screws to allow for screw hole plugs.

Fasten the upper braces to the top components using ⅜-in. X 3½-in. lag screws with flat washers. Drill counterbored holes for these as well.

After all the glue joints have dried,

3. *Use the grid pattern shown in the diagram to make a pattern for the seat side profiles.*

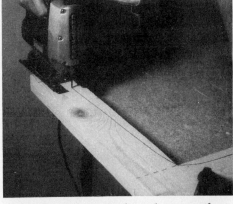

4. *Cut the pattern you have drawn on the seat sides with a fine-toothed blade in your saber saw.*

7. *Secure the lower braces with no. 10 X 2-in. flathead wood screws, counterbored. Then cover the holes with wood plugs.*

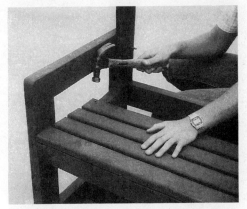

8. *Attach the slats to the frames with 4d galvanized finishing nails. Set the nails below the surface.*

sand all three projects well. Start with 80-grit garnet paper and work down to 150-grit paper. Pay special attention to exposed end grain.

Finish the projects with two coats of wood sealer, such as Thompson's Water Seal, allowing 24 hours between coats. If you choose, you can also use polyurethane varnish, but after a few years the finish will blister and have to be removed before refinishing.

MATERIALS LIST

Item	Quantity
2X4 redwood	110 ft.
1X3 redwood	90 ft.
⅜" X 3" dowels	132
⅜" X 2" carriage bolts	4
⅜" X 3½" carriage bolts	8
⅜" nuts and washers	12 each
No. 10 X 2" flathead wood screws	36
⅜" X 3½" lag screws with flat washers	8
⅜" wood screw hole plugs	36
4d galvanized finishing nails	2 lbs.
Resorcinol glue	as needed
Clear wood sealer	3 qts.

REDWOOD GARDEN TABLE

This redwood table for your garden is just the right height to go with folding outdoor chairs. It is the perfect outdoor table, whether you use it for casual dining or as a work table.

Very lightweight, it is easy to move from place to place, while its solid redwood construction and mitered legs make it an attractive and useful addition to your outdoor furniture collection.

Start building the project by making the legs. Rip a 45 degree bevel along one edge of 1X4 redwood stock. Work with pieces 48 in. long for safety's sake. Each piece will make one finished leg. Rip the material with a combination planer-type blade for a smooth finish.

As always when you rip wood on your saw, be sure to stand out of the line of cut, and use your saw's safety features. Use a push stick when nearing the end of the cut to keep your hands away from the blade.

Cut the stock into 23¼-in. lengths to form the leg halves. It is important that all the pieces be identical. To insure this, clamp a stop block to the fence on your radial arm saw to help you position the workpieces. If you use a table saw, a block clamped to the table's edge will serve the same purpose.

Next, cut four 1X1 cleats 22 in. long. These will brace the leg joints. Now, assemble the legs with resorcinol glue and no. 10 X 1¼-in. flathead wood screws. Start by attaching a 1X1 brace to one leg half.

Align the edge of the brace with the inside edge of the pre-cut miter. Drill pilot holes for the screws, then fasten the brace securely, spacing the screws 4 in. apart.

Apply glue to the mitered joint and the brace, and add the second leg half. If the brace was properly installed, the mitered joint will close perfectly. Stagger the screw positions for maximum strength. Once all four legs are assembled, set them aside to dry.

Build the table's top next. Make a frame of 1X3 redwood lumber, as shown in the diagram. It is not necessary to screw this frame together; simply glue the butt joints. Clamp the assembly until the glue is completely dry.

Now, cut twelve 1X3 slats, 32¾ in. long, for the table's top. Working from the frame's side, attach the frame to the slats with countersunk screws and glue. Space the slats evenly on the frame. Notice in the diagram that the slats bridge the joints in the frame. This helps strengthen the assembly.

With the table top still upside-down, measure the inside of the frame for the 1X2 skirt. Cut 1X2 redwood to fit flush with the inside of the frame, as shown in the diagram. Make the skirt joints bridge the joints in the top frame to further strengthen the structure.

Attach the skirt to the frame with flathead wood screws you used before. This time, however, drill counterbored pilot holes to locate

CONSTRUCTION DETAILS

1. *Rip a 45 degree miter on one edge of 1X4 stock to form the material for the legs. Observe proper safety precautions.*

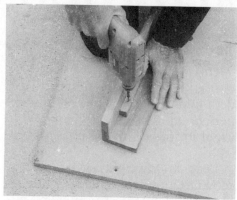

2. *Join the leg halves with a 1X1 cleat. Drive screws through the cleat, into the leg, and use resorcinol glue.*

3. *Drive screws through the table's top frame, into the slats. Countersink the screw holes flush.*

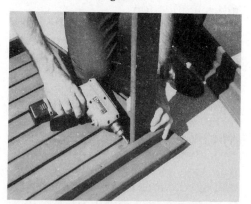

4. *Attach the legs to the 1X2 skirt with screws and glue. All screws are hidden from view in this project.*

the screw heads below the surface of the wood. The ⅜-in.-dia. counterbores should be ¾ in. deep. As you did before, use resorcinol glue on the joints.

Finally, add the legs to the assembly. Attach them to the skirt from the inside, using screws and glue. Drive two screws through each leg half. All screw heads in this project will be hidden from view.

Sand the completed project thoroughly using both hand- and power-sanding techniques. Work in the di-

rection of the wood grain and finish the sanding with 220-grit garnet paper. Pay special attention to any exposed end grain for a clean appearance. While sanding, break all the edges of the table's top to a ⅛-in. radius.

Finish the project with two coats of clear wood sealer, such as Thompson's Water Seal. Allow 24 hours for the first coat to dry, and sand lightly with 400-grit garnet paper before applying the second coat.

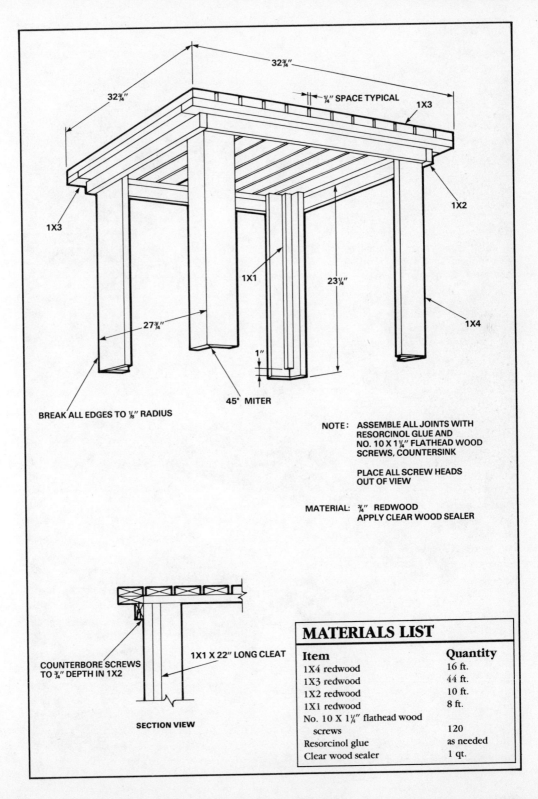

32¾"

32¾"

¼" SPACE TYPICAL

1X3

1X3

1X2

1X1

23¼"

27¾"

1X4

1"

45° MITER

BREAK ALL EDGES TO ⅛" RADIUS

NOTE: ASSEMBLE ALL JOINTS WITH
RESORCINOL GLUE AND
NO. 10 X 1¼" FLATHEAD WOOD
SCREWS, COUNTERSINK

PLACE ALL SCREW HEADS
OUT OF VIEW

MATERIAL: ¾" REDWOOD
APPLY CLEAR WOOD SEALER

COUNTERBORE SCREWS
TO ¾" DEPTH IN 1X2

1X1 X 22" LONG CLEAT

SECTION VIEW

MATERIALS LIST

Item	Quantity
1X4 redwood	16 ft.
1X3 redwood	44 ft.
1X2 redwood	10 ft.
1X1 redwood	8 ft.
No. 10 X 1¼" flathead wood screws	120
Resorcinol glue	as needed
Clear wood sealer	1 qt.

ROLLING PATIO SEATS

The more flexible your outdoor seating arrangements are, the more options you have when you are entertaining. Ideally, you should be able to move your patio furniture easily from place to place to adapt to any situation.

These comfortable padded seats are mounted on easy-rolling casters to make arranging your seating as easy as possible. In addition, two or more of the seats can be connected together with a simple spline joint.

Before beginning construction of the seats, choose or make the 24-in.-square cushions for the project. These cushions are a standard size, available at many department stores, but you can make your own if you choose.

Measure the dimensions of the cushions and, if they are not exactly 24 in. square, adjust the dimensions given in the diagram.

Cut 1X6 stock to the lengths shown in the diagram. You can use any type of wood for this project.

Before assembling the base of the seat, cut dovetailed grooves in one of the short sides of each seat frame. Use a ½-in. dovetail bit in your router, and set the depth of cut to ½ in. Feed the router slowly into the cut.

Use a guide clamped to the workpiece to help you keep the groove straight, and stop the cut to make the groove 4½ in. long. Measure the locations of the grooves accurately to make the seats fit together perfectly.

Now, assemble the 1X6 frame for the seat. Bore counterbored pilot holes for the no. 8 X 1¼-in. flathead wood screws to allow for wood screw hole plugs. Use a combination pilot and counterboring bit for this job. Assemble the frame with screws and resorcinol glue.

Add the 2X2 corner supports to the inside corners of the assembled frame. Fasten them from the inside with countersunk no. 10 X 2-in. flathead wood screws and resorcinol glue. Drive screws into both sides of the frame.

Add the ¾-in.-square cleats to the frame, as shown in the diagram, securing them with no. 8 X 1¼-in. flathead wood screws and glue. Once again, countersink the screw heads flush with the surface of the wood.

Cut a ¾-in. exterior plywood panel to fit inside the frame, and secure it to the cleats with screws and glue.

Now, install 2-in. casters to the bottom of the 2X2 braces with roundhead wood screws. You can use wheel or ball-type casters for this project.

Glue wood screw hole plugs into the counterbores on the outside of the frame. Allow the plugs to protrude slightly above the surface of the wood.

Now, sand the completed base thoroughly, starting with 80-grit garnet paper. Work down to 120-grit paper for a smooth finish. While

CONSTRUCTION DETAILS

1. Before beginning construction, measure the cushions. Make adjustments in the dimensions if necessary.

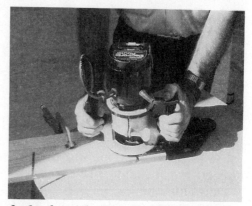

2. Cut dovetail grooves in one side of each bench with a router and a ½-in. dovetail cutter.

3. Cut the oak spline with four passes on your table saw. Keep safety in mind when performing this operation.

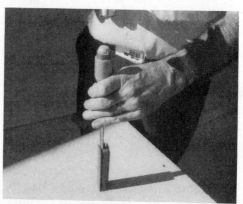

4. After the spline cuts are made, remove the waste with a sharp chisel. The spline should fit loosely.

sanding, soften the edges of the dovetail grooves.

Finish the base with a clear wood finish, or paint it to suit your taste. In either case, give the base two coats of finish for added durability.

Make the splines that join the seats together, using ¾-in. oak stock that's just over 1 in. wide. Set up your table saw to cut an angle which matches that of your router bit.

Work with long pieces of stock for safety, and follow all the safety precautions needed for working with small stock. It is best to use a jig designed for cutting tenons.

Make four cuts, as shown in the photograph, then remove the waste with a chisel. Be sure to align the wood grain as shown in the diagram. The spline should fit loosely in the grooves.

Cut the spline material to 4-in. lengths, then sand each spline smooth, relieving the edges for a good fit. To join two seats together, simply roll them next to each other, then drop the splines in place.

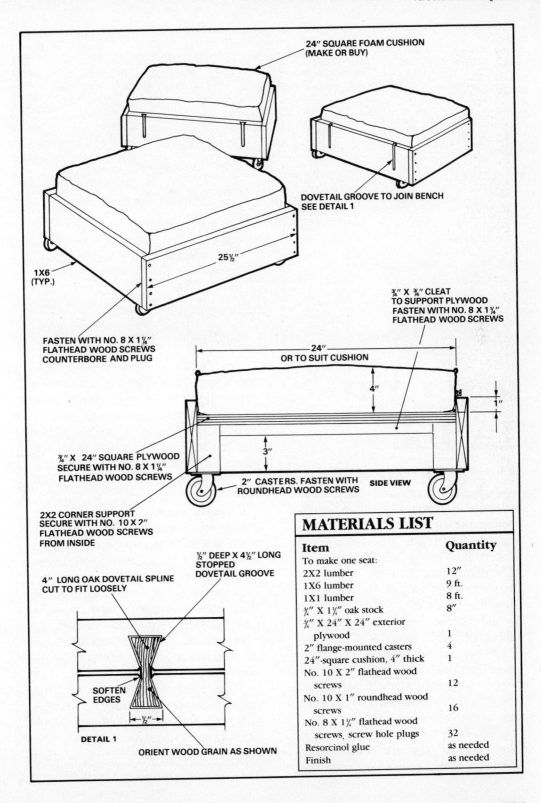

24" SQUARE FOAM CUSHION
(MAKE OR BUY)

DOVETAIL GROOVE TO JOIN BENCH
SEE DETAIL 1

25½"

1X6
(TYP.)

¾" X ¾" CLEAT
TO SUPPORT PLYWOOD
FASTEN WITH NO. 8 X 1¼"
FLATHEAD WOOD SCREWS

FASTEN WITH NO. 8 X 1¼"
FLATHEAD WOOD SCREWS
COUNTERBORE AND PLUG

24"
OR TO SUIT CUSHION

4"

1"

3"

¾" X 24" SQUARE PLYWOOD
SECURE WITH NO. 8 X 1¼"
FLATHEAD WOOD SCREWS

2" CASTERS. FASTEN WITH
ROUNDHEAD WOOD SCREWS

SIDE VIEW

2X2 CORNER SUPPORT
SECURE WITH NO. 10 X 2"
FLATHEAD WOOD SCREWS
FROM INSIDE

½" DEEP X 4½" LONG
STOPPED
DOVETAIL GROOVE

4" LONG OAK DOVETAIL SPLINE
CUT TO FIT LOOSELY

SOFTEN
EDGES

½"

DETAIL 1

ORIENT WOOD GRAIN AS SHOWN

MATERIALS LIST

Item	Quantity
To make one seat:	
2X2 lumber	12"
1X6 lumber	9 ft.
1X1 lumber	8 ft.
¾" X 1¼" oak stock	8"
¾" X 24" X 24" exterior plywood	1
2" flange-mounted casters	4
24"-square cushion, 4" thick	1
No. 10 X 2" flathead wood screws	12
No. 10 X 1" roundhead wood screws	16
No. 8 X 1¼" flathead wood screws, screw hole plugs	32
Resorcinol glue	as needed
Finish	as needed

ROLL-UP TABLE

Space to store outdoor furniture is always at a premium. This table helps solve that problem by simply rolling up into a small package for in-house storage. It's also a great item to take along on a picnic.

Start building the table by cutting the parts to the lengths shown in the diagram. Be careful to cut the slats for the table top so that their lengths match exactly.

Lay the oversized sheet of canvas on a flat work surface and smooth it out, tacking the edges if necessary. Glue the individual slats to the canvas, using yellow carpenter's glue.

Use a scrap of the slat material to establish the 1/4-in. gap between the slats, and work carefully to keep the top square. Once all the slats are in place, lay a sheet of plywood over the assembly and add weights.

While the top is drying, assemble the leg sets. Attach the legs to the supports with hinges, then add the folding leg brackets. Notice the offsets on the legs.

Trim the canvas on the underside of the table top to its finished size with a sharp utility knife and a straightedge, then carefully drill the holes in the top and the supports.

Sand the completed assemblies, then apply stain and two coats of satin-finish polyurethane varnish.

Attach the leg assemblies to the table top with 1 1/2-in. carriage bolts with washers and wing nuts.

To roll the table, simply fold up the legs, loosen the wing nuts, then swing the leg assemblies around to line up with the slats.

Reprinted with permission from Katie and Gene Hamilton and Steve Wolgemuth in conjunction with Popular Mechanics.

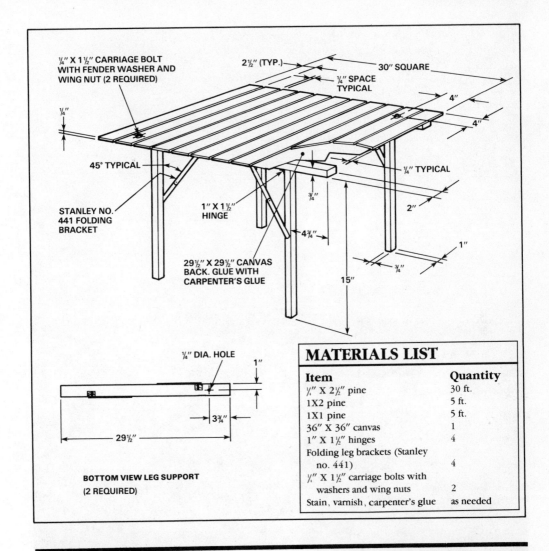

¼″ X 1½″ CARRIAGE BOLT
WITH FENDER WASHER AND
WING NUT (2 REQUIRED)

2½″ (TYP.)

30″ SQUARE

¼″ SPACE
TYPICAL

4″

4″

¼″

45° TYPICAL

¼″ TYPICAL

STANLEY NO.
441 FOLDING
BRACKET

1″ X 1½″
HINGE

2″

¾″

4¾″

1″

15″

¾″

29½″ X 29½″ CANVAS
BACK. GLUE WITH
CARPENTER'S GLUE

¼″ DIA. HOLE

1″

3¾″

29½″

BOTTOM VIEW LEG SUPPORT
(2 REQUIRED)

MATERIALS LIST

Item	Quantity
½″ X 2½″ pine	30 ft.
1X2 pine	5 ft.
1X1 pine	5 ft.
36″ X 36″ canvas	1
1″ X 1½″ hinges	4
Folding leg brackets (Stanley no. 441)	4
½″ X 1½″ carriage bolts with washers and wing nuts	2
Stain, varnish, carpenter's glue	as needed

CONSTRUCTION DETAILS

1. *Glue the slats to the canvas backing with carpenter's glue. Use spacers to establish the correct spacing.*

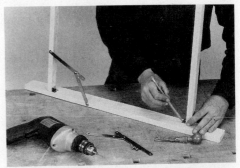

2. *Attach the legs to the supports with hinges and folding brackets. The legs are offset to allow folding.*

227

ROUND PICNIC TABLE

For outdoor dining, nothing matches the traditional round redwood table. Here is one for you to build, complete with matching benches.

Start by building the round table top. Cut the braces with 45 degree bevels on each end. Add the top boards, nailing them in place to the braces and cleats with 12d aluminum nails. Drill pilot holes in the top boards for these nails.

Next, use a pair of trammel points attached to a yardstick to lay out the circular profile of the top. Cut the circle with a saber saw. Use a long blade and cut slowly to keep the saw blade from creeping.

The next step is to cut the legs for the table. Set your radial arm saw, or the miter gauge on your table saw, to form the leg angles.

Now, place each pair of legs together so that they cross exactly at the center. Use a straightedge at the bottom to establish the correct angle, and then mark the overlapping sections on the legs.

Use a wobble-type dado blade on your radial arm saw to form the lap joints of the legs. Set the saw's arm at the correct cutting angle. Be sure to cut exactly halfway through the leg.

Glue the leg pairs together with waterproof resorcinol glue, clamping them securely until dry.

Now, with the table top upside-down on a pair of sawhorses, position the legs against the vertical braces. Bore holes for the 1/4-in. X 3½-in. carriage bolts; then add the bolts, washers, and nuts and tighten securely.

Finally, cut the cross brace and install it between the legs with 1/4-in. X 3½-in. lag screws. Drill a 3/16-in. pilot hole and use a washer under the screw head.

The benches are similar in construction. To cut the profile of the bench tops, lay out a grid of 2-in. squares on a sheet of hardboard. Transfer the pattern shown on the diagram to the hardboard and then cut with a saber saw. Use this template to lay out the four benches.

As you did for the table top, attach the seat boards to the pre-cut cleats with aluminum nails; then trace the pattern and cut the bench tops with your saber saw.

The legs are formed in the same way as those on the table, but notice that different angles are used.

Once the table and benches are assembled, round over the edges with a 1/4-in.-radius rounding-over bit, with pilot, in your router.

Sand the assemblies thoroughly and apply two coats of wood sealer, such as Thompson's Water Seal.

CONSTRUCTION DETAILS

1. *Draw the table top's design with trammel points attached to a yardstick. Draw over the arc several times.*

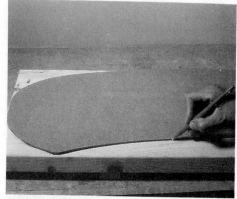

2. *The bench tops are laid out using a hardboard template. A grid pattern helps lay out the template.*

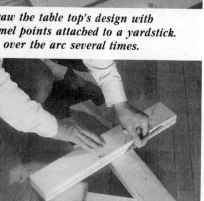

3. *The lap joints for the legs are easily laid out by crossing the legs, then marking the laps.*

4. *Form the leg lap joints on a radial arm saw using a wobble-type dado blade set for a ¾-in. depth.*

5. *Use a saber saw to cut the profiles of the bench tops. Cut slowly for best results.*

MATERIALS LIST

Item	Quantity
2X6 redwood	36 ft.
2X4 redwood	120 ft.
⅛″ X 14″ X 36″ hardboard	1
¼″ X 3½″ carriage bolts with nuts and washers	24
¼″ X 3½″ lag screws with washers	10
12d aluminum nails	as needed
Wood sealer	1 gal.

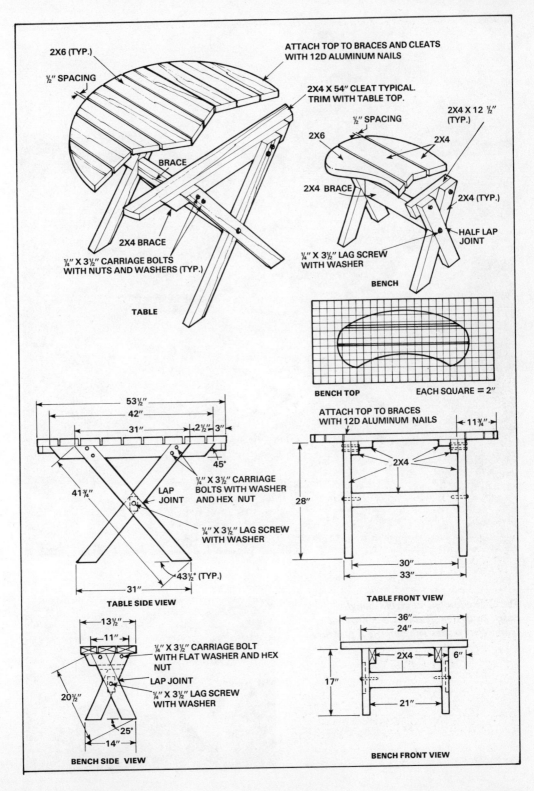

2X6 (TYP.)

½" SPACING

ATTACH TOP TO BRACES AND CLEATS
WITH 12D ALUMINUM NAILS

2X4 X 54" CLEAT TYPICAL.
TRIM WITH TABLE TOP.

2X4 X 12 ½"
(TYP.)

½" SPACING

2X6

2X4

BRACE

2X4 BRACE

2X4 (TYP.)

HALF LAP
JOINT

2X4 BRACE

¼" X 3½" CARRIAGE BOLTS
WITH NUTS AND WASHERS (TYP.)

¼" X 3½" LAG SCREW
WITH WASHER

TABLE

BENCH

BENCH TOP   EACH SQUARE = 2"

53½"

42"

31"

2½" 3"

45°

¼" X 3½" CARRIAGE
BOLTS WITH WASHER
AND HEX NUT

41¾"

LAP
JOINT

¼" X 3½" LAG SCREW
WITH WASHER

43½° (TYP.)

31"

TABLE SIDE VIEW

ATTACH TOP TO BRACES
WITH 12D ALUMINUM NAILS

11¾"

2X4

28"

30"

33"

TABLE FRONT VIEW

13½"

11"

¼" X 3½" CARRIAGE BOLT
WITH FLAT WASHER AND HEX
NUT

LAP JOINT

¼" X 3½" LAG SCREW
WITH WASHER

20½"

25°

14"

BENCH SIDE VIEW

36"

24"

2X4

6"

17"

21"

BENCH FRONT VIEW

231

The chaise lounge, at right, though rustic in design, features a contoured frame that makes sun bathing a pleasure.

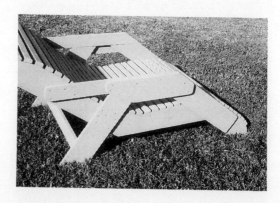

RUSTIC FURNITURE

Here is an outdoor furniture set with a rustic feeling. The lounge, chair, and table are built of pine with oak slats. The set is designed with both comfort and good appearance in mind.

Start construction of the chair and lounge by laying out a grid of 2-in. squares on heavy paper or cardboard. Carefully transfer the design of the profiles to the grid, then cut the paper or cardboard patterns with a sharp utility knife.

Cut separate components apart along the lines shown in the grid pattern. Use these patterns to transfer the designs to your pine lumber. Position the patterns, then trace around them with a pencil.

Use a saber saw or a band saw to cut the components along the lines. It is a good idea to cut the matching parts, then clamp the pairs together and even them up with a medium-grit belt on your belt sander. This will make both parts identical.

Next, cut the remaining frame components for the chair and lounge to the dimensions and angles shown in the diagram. Measure the parts carefully for a good fit on all components.

On a flat work surface, lay one set of the parts cut from the grid pattern together as they will be in the finished project. Lay the leg and brace components on top of these.

When you are satisfied with the fit, bore countersunk pilot holes for the no. 10 X 1¼-in. flathead wood screws used to assemble the frames.

Remove the upper components and apply a coat of waterproof resorcinol glue to the joints. Reassemble the side, this time driving the screws to secure the joints while the glue dries.

Follow the same procedure with the other side frame of each piece of furniture. Take care to make both sides identical. Once the glue has dried, sand the components well with a combination of hand and power sanding. Start with 120-grit abrasive and work down to 220-grit for a smooth final finish.

Add the remaining side braces to the assemblies. Match the profiles of the arm and leg assemblies by tracing around them to mark the braces.

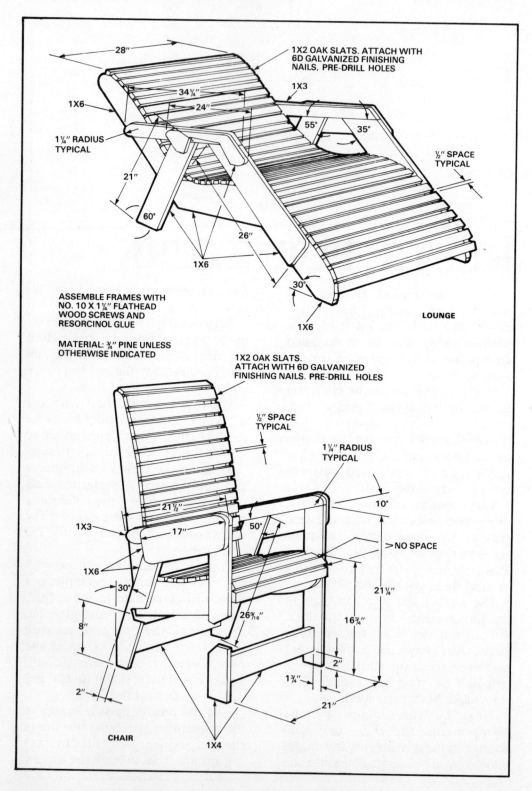

28"

1X2 OAK SLATS. ATTACH WITH
6D GALVANIZED FINISHING
NAILS, PRE-DRILL HOLES

34¼"

1X3

24"

1X6

55°

35°

1¼" RADIUS
TYPICAL

½" SPACE
TYPICAL

21"

60°

26"

1X6

30°

ASSEMBLE FRAMES WITH
NO. 10 X 1¼" FLATHEAD
WOOD SCREWS AND
RESORCINOL GLUE

1X6

LOUNGE

MATERIAL: ¾" PINE UNLESS
OTHERWISE INDICATED

1X2 OAK SLATS.
ATTACH WITH 6D GALVANIZED
FINISHING NAILS. PRE-DRILL HOLES

½" SPACE
TYPICAL

1¼" RADIUS
TYPICAL

10°

21½"

1X3

17"

50°

NO SPACE

1X6

30°

21¼"

8"

16¾"

26⁹⁄₁₆"

2"

2"

1¾"

CHAIR

21"

1X4

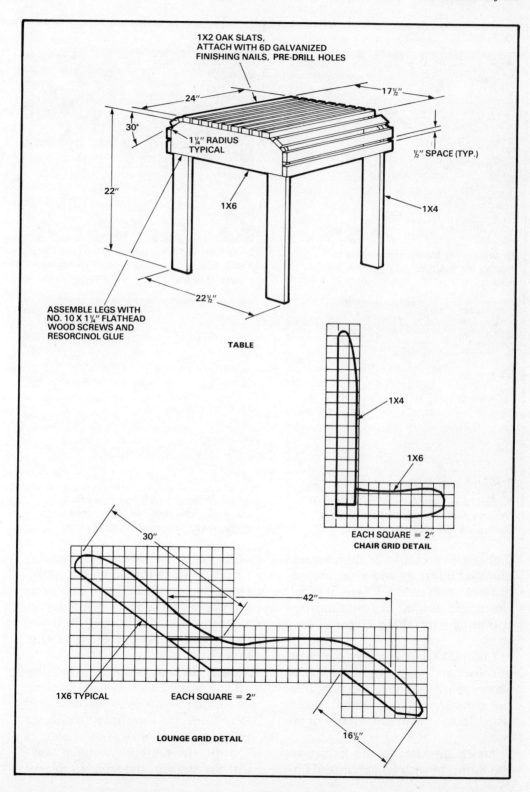

1X2 OAK SLATS,
ATTACH WITH 6D GALVANIZED
FINISHING NAILS, PRE-DRILL HOLES

24"

17½"

30°

1¼" RADIUS
TYPICAL

½" SPACE (TYP.)

22"

1X6

1X4

22½"

ASSEMBLE LEGS WITH
NO. 10 X 1¼" FLATHEAD
WOOD SCREWS AND
RESORCINOL GLUE

TABLE

1X4

1X6

EACH SQUARE = 2"
CHAIR GRID DETAIL

30"

42"

1X6 TYPICAL

EACH SQUARE = 2"

16½"

LOUNGE GRID DETAIL

235

CONSTRUCTION DETAILS

1. Lay out the frame components by tracing the enlarged grid pattern onto the pine stock.

2. Cut out the parts with a saber saw. Use a fine-toothed blade for a smooth finish that is easy to sand.

5. Just as you did for the chair, transfer the grid patterns to ¾-in. pine stock. Darken the silhouette as shown.

6. Attach the lounge's legs and armrest, using glue and flathead wood screws. Again, make sure everything is aligned.

Cut the braces to fit, then attach them with screws and glue, as you did before. Even up the edges of all the frame assemblies by sanding, rounding over sharp edges as you work.

Cut the 1X2 oak slats for the chair and lounge, observing the lengths shown in the diagram. To insure that the parts are equal in length, use a stop block on your saw's fence or table.

Attach the slats to the frames of the furniture with 6d galvanized fin-

ishing nails. To prevent splitting the wood, drill pilot holes for nails. Space the slats ½ in. apart except at the curve on the front of the chair, where no space is needed. Add the lower braces to the chair at this time.

Sand the slats smooth, rounding off any sharp edges. Finish the chair and lounge with clear wood sealer, satin-finish polyurethane varnish, or paint in the color of your choice.

Build the table in a similar way. Cut the sides of the table to the di-

3. *Carefully lay out the chair's leg and arm components. Alignment at this stage is critical.*

4. *Secure the armrest with flathead wood screws to strengthen the joint and to provide a wider area for comfort.*

7. *Add the legs to the side assembly with glue and flathead wood screws. After assembly, sand the side carefully.*

8. *Attach the oak slats to the frame of the lounge and chair with 6d galvanized finishing nails.*

mensions shown in the diagram. Cut the four legs next, matching the curves on the sides carefully.

Assemble the legs and sides in pairs, fastening the joints, as you did before, with glue and countersunk screws. Sand the assemblies to even them up and to provide a smooth surface for finishing.

As you did before, cut the oak slats to their finished length, then attach them to the sides of the table with 6d galvanized finishing nails.

Sand the completed table, once

again rounding off the sharp edges of the slats. Apply a finish to match the chair and lounge.

MATERIALS LIST	
Item	**Quantity**
1X6 pine	36 ft.
1X4 pine	24 ft.
1X3 pine	10 ft.
1X2 oak	140 ft.
No. 10 X 1¼″ flathead wood screws	120
6d galvanized finishing nails	as needed
Resorcinol glue	as needed
Finish	1 gal.

SHADED LOVE SEAT

For those romantic summer evenings on the deck or patio, try this shaded love seat. Its canvas shade is paired with the soft texture of redwood to make a perfect combination. It uses cushions you can buy wherever outdoor furniture is sold.

Start building the love seat by cutting the redwood 2X4s to the lengths shown in the diagram. If you want to change the width of the project to accommodate a particular set of cushions, cut the cross braces to the lengths you choose.

Use a saber saw to cut the rounded profile of the hood members. Next, lay out the lap joints on the back and hood components. Cut these with multiple passes of a dado blade, setting the angle of the cut at 15 degrees. The depth of cut should be exactly half the wood's thickness. Assemble the joints with waterproof resorcinol glue.

Cut the hood braces next. Set your saw's arm or miter gauge to 45 degrees for one end and 60 degrees for the other. Attach the braces to the hood assembly with 1/4-in. X 2-in. lag screws. Drill 3/16-in. pilot holes, counterbored to set the screw heads below the surface.

Bore 1-in.-dia. X 1 1/8-in.-deep holes in the arm members and the lower side brace for the side dowel slats.

Use a doweling jig to bore mating 3/8-in. X 1 5/8-in. holes in the frame components for the dowel pins. The extra 1/8 in. allows excess glue and air to escape.

Assemble the side frames using dowels and resorcinol glue. Clamp the assemblies well with bar or pipe-type clamps. Use scraps of wood between the clamps and the soft redwood to prevent damage.

Next, form the rabbets in the cross members to accommodate the seat and back slats. Use a straight bit in your router, along with an edge guide, or form the rabbets with a dado blade.

Use a doweling jig as you did before to bore mating dowel pin holes in the cross members and the side frames. The holes in the side frames are 1 1/8 in. deep, while those in the cross members are 2 1/8 in. deep.

Bore 1 1/2-in.-dia. holes for the closet rod stock. Use a spade bit, and back up the wood with scrap to prevent splintering.

Assemble the bench with dowels or screws and glue, clamping each joint. Add the 1X3 seat and back slats, attaching them with glue and 3d galvanized finishing nails. Set the nail heads just below the surface.

Once the glue has dried, sand the completed bench thoroughly. Start with 80-grit garnet paper, and work down to 150-grit. Break all sharp edges as you sand.

Apply two coats of clear wood sealer, such as Thompson's Water Seal, to weatherproof the project. Allow 24 hours between coats, and sand lightly before applying the second coat.

Finally, cut out the canvas for the hood. See the diagram for details. Double-stitch all seams, then attach the canvas with decorative tacks.

CONSTRUCTION DETAILS

1. Use a dado blade to cut the lap joints on the hood assembly. See the diagram for the correct angles.

2. Cut the rabbets on the cross braces with a straight bit in your router. Use an edge guide for best results.

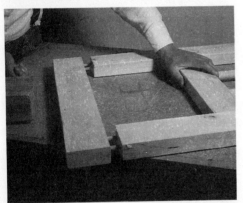

3. When assembling the sides, install the bottom piece last. Use dowels and waterproof glue for all joints.

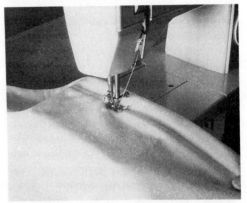

4. Double-stitch all the seams in the canvas hood. Use a ball-point needle and heavy-duty thread.

MATERIALS LIST

Item	Quantity
2X4 redwood	48 ft.
1X3 redwood	18 ft.
1"-dia. dowel	4 ft.
1½"-dia. closet rod	8 ft.
44"-wide canvas	3 yds.
⅜" X 3" dowel	as needed
¼" X 2" lag screws	4
3d galvanized finishing nails	½ lb.
1" decorative brass tacks	10
No. 10 X 2½" flathead wood screws	as needed
Resorcinol glue, wood sealer	as needed

5. Install the sides of the love seat with flathead wood screws and resorcinol glue. Make sure you also install the canvas.

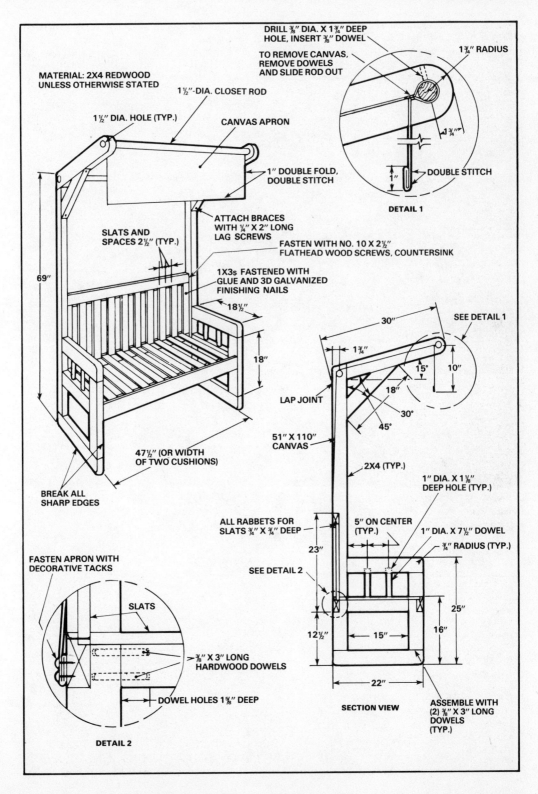

DRILL ⅜" DIA. X 1¾" DEEP
HOLE, INSERT ⅜" DOWEL

TO REMOVE CANVAS,
REMOVE DOWELS
AND SLIDE ROD OUT

1¾" RADIUS

DOUBLE STITCH

1"

DETAIL 1

MATERIAL: 2X4 REDWOOD
UNLESS OTHERWISE STATED

1½"-DIA. CLOSET ROD

1½" DIA. HOLE (TYP.)

CANVAS APRON

1" DOUBLE FOLD,
DOUBLE STITCH

ATTACH BRACES
WITH ¼" X 2" LONG
LAG SCREWS

FASTEN WITH NO. 10 X 2½"
FLATHEAD WOOD SCREWS, COUNTERSINK

SLATS AND
SPACES 2½" (TYP.)

1X3s FASTENED WITH
GLUE AND 3D GALVANIZED
FINISHING NAILS

69"

18½"

18"

30"

SEE DETAIL 1

1¾"

15°

10°

18"

LAP JOINT

30°

45°

51" X 110"
CANVAS

2X4 (TYP.)

1" DIA. X 1⅛"
DEEP HOLE (TYP.)

1" DIA. X 7½" DOWEL

¾" RADIUS (TYP.)

47½" (OR WIDTH
OF TWO CUSHIONS)

BREAK ALL
SHARP EDGES

ALL RABBETS FOR
SLATS ¾" X ¾" DEEP

5" ON CENTER
(TYP.)

23"

SEE DETAIL 2

25"

12½"

16"

15"

FASTEN APRON WITH
DECORATIVE TACKS

SLATS

⅜" X 3" LONG
HARDWOOD DOWELS

DOWEL HOLES 1⅝" DEEP

22"

SECTION VIEW

ASSEMBLE WITH
(2) ⅜" X 3" LONG
DOWELS
(TYP.)

DETAIL 2

SHADED SWING

Sitting in an outdoor swing is a wonderful way to pass a warm summer afternoon or evening. This free-standing swing, with its shaded sides and top, is ideal for those lazy days.

It fits perfectly on any deck or patio, and is ideal for homes without a porch. Designed to last for years, the swing will seat two comfortably.

Take care in selecting the materials for the swing. All lumber should be straight and knot-free, especially the 2X4 material used for the legs and the 2X8 for the beam. Hand-select these parts, if possible, at your lumberyard or home center. You can use any type of lumber you choose, but for long life in harsh weather conditions, select redwood.

Start construction by cutting the lower ends of the legs to the 66 degree angle shown in the diagram. Set the arm of your radial arm saw to the correct angle, then cut one end of each of the 2X4 legs.

You can also cut these angles with a portable circular saw. Use an adjustable protractor guide or a straight piece of 1X4 clamped to the workpiece to help make the angles identical on all four legs.

Now, measure the legs and mark the 76½-in. dimension on each leg. Use a protractor to lay out the 24 degree angle at the tops of the legs. Cut these angles with your portable saw. For the greatest accuracy, clamp a straight board to the legs to help guide your saw. Stack the legs to check their lengths. Trim the legs where necessary to make them identical.

Lay out the notches in the legs to hold the swing support beam. Each notch should be ¾-in. X 5½-in. The sides of the notches should parallel the 24 degree bevel you already cut. Take your time with this layout to make the beam fit tightly.

Cut the notches with a saber saw. Use a blade designed to cut 1½-in.-thick material, and work slowly to make the notches perfectly square. Avoid side pressure as you cut to keep the blade vertical in the wood. Once the notches are cut, place each pair of legs together and check the fit with a scrap of 2X6.

Set the legs aside for the time being, and begin construction of the lattice panels. Set your radial arm saw to cut the 75 degree angles on the lower crosspieces and one end of each side of the side vertical frames. Cut both lower crosspieces to length and cut one end of the vertical side pieces.

To save time and to help make the parts identical, make all of the cuts at one angle before changing your setup. These parts can also be cut with a portable saw. As you did before, use a guide to keep the cuts straight and at the correct angle.

Now, reset the saw to cut the 60 degree angles on the remaining parts forming the side of the frames. Cut

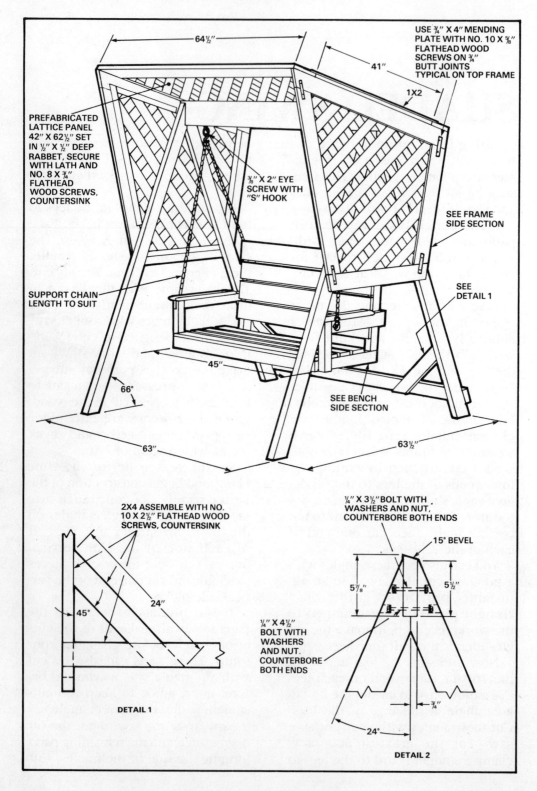

64½"

USE ¾" X 4" MENDING
PLATE WITH NO. 10 X ⅝"
FLATHEAD WOOD
SCREWS ON ¾"
BUTT JOINTS
TYPICAL ON TOP FRAME

41"

1X2

PREFABRICATED
LATTICE PANEL
42" X 62½" SET
IN ½" X ½" DEEP
RABBET, SECURE
WITH LATH AND
NO. 8 X ¾"
FLATHEAD
WOOD SCREWS,
COUNTERSINK

¾" X 2" EYE
SCREW WITH
"S" HOOK

SEE FRAME
SIDE SECTION

SUPPORT CHAIN
LENGTH TO SUIT

SEE
DETAIL 1

45"

66°

SEE BENCH
SIDE SECTION

63"

63½"

2X4 ASSEMBLE WITH NO.
10 X 2½" FLATHEAD WOOD
SCREWS, COUNTERSINK

¼" X 3½" BOLT WITH
WASHERS AND NUT,
COUNTERBORE BOTH ENDS

15° BEVEL

5⅞"

5½"

24"

45°

¼" X 4½"
BOLT WITH
WASHERS
AND NUT,
COUNTERBORE
BOTH ENDS

¾"

DETAIL 1

24°

DETAIL 2

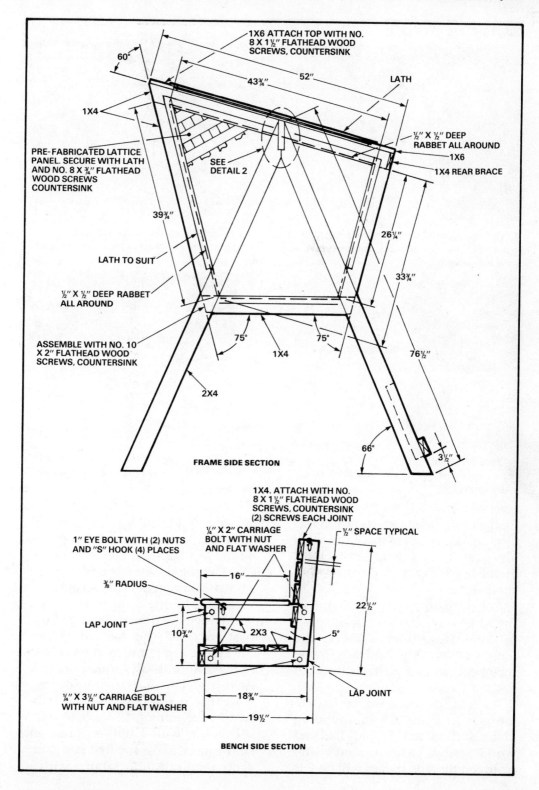

60°

1X6 ATTACH TOP WITH NO. 8 X 1½" FLATHEAD WOOD SCREWS, COUNTERSINK

43¾"

52"

LATH

1X4

½" X ½" DEEP RABBET ALL AROUND

1X6

1X4 REAR BRACE

PRE-FABRICATED LATTICE PANEL. SECURE WITH LATH AND NO. 8 X ¾" FLATHEAD WOOD SCREWS COUNTERSINK

SEE DETAIL 2

39¾"

26¼"

33¾"

LATH TO SUIT

½" X ½" DEEP RABBET ALL AROUND

ASSEMBLE WITH NO. 10 X 2" FLATHEAD WOOD SCREWS, COUNTERSINK

75°

75°

1X4

76½"

2X4

66°

3½"

FRAME SIDE SECTION

1X4. ATTACH WITH NO. 8 X 1½" FLATHEAD WOOD SCREWS, COUNTERSINK (2) SCREWS EACH JOINT

1" EYE BOLT WITH (2) NUTS AND "S" HOOK (4) PLACES

¼" X 2" CARRIAGE BOLT WITH NUT AND FLAT WASHER

½" SPACE TYPICAL

⅜" RADIUS

16"

22½"

LAP JOINT

10¾"

2X3

5°

¼" X 3½" CARRIAGE BOLT WITH NUT AND FLAT WASHER

18¾"

LAP JOINT

19½"

BENCH SIDE SECTION

CONSTRUCTION DETAILS

1. *Cut the angle at the top of each leg with a portable circular saw. Lay out the angle with a protractor.*

2. *Lay out the angles of the side frame carefully. The two frames must be identical for a good fit.*

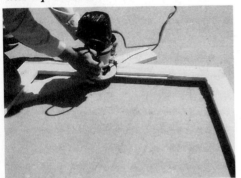

3. *Rout the rabbet on the inside of the frame with a rabbeting bit, with pilot, in your router.*

4. *Install the pre-fab lattice in the rabbets, then secure it by screwing lath strips to the frame.*

each part to the length shown in the diagram. Take care to make the parts identical. Check them by stacking matching parts and trimming as needed.

Cut the parts for the top frame in the same way, this time making all of the angles square. Observe the length of the front and rear frame members carefully to make the final assembly correct.

Assemble the frames, securing the joints with ³⁄₄-in. X 4-in. mending plates and no. 10 X ⁵⁄₈-in. flathead wood screws. The top mending plates on the side frames will be left

in place, while the lower plates will be removed later. Install the plates on the top frame so they will be located on the upper side of the frame after it is fastened to the swing.

Assemble one side frame, then build the second frame on top of the first to keep the two identical. Check the top frame as you build it to make sure it stays square. Check each corner with a framing square.

Next, cut the ¹⁄₂-in. X ¹⁄₂-in. rabbets in the frames. Use a ¹⁄₂-in. rabbeting bit, with a built-in pilot, in your router. Make the first cut ¹⁄₄ in. deep, then finish the rabbets with a second cut that's ½ in. deep.

Make the cuts at a feed rate that cuts easily and smoothly. If the rate of feed is too slow, the pilot will burn the wood and cause an uneven rabbet. Feed the router into the wood so the bit rotates into the stock. If you move the router in the other direction, the wood is likely to splinter.

Finish the corners of the rabbet with a sharp wood chisel. Observe the angles of the sides carefully to make the rabbet's corners parallel with the sides. Push the edge of the chisel into the wood at each side of the rabbet, then cut the chip out to finish the corner. Repeat this process until the corner is the same depth as the rest of the rabbet.

Cut pre-fab lattice panels to fit inside the rabbets on each frame. Expand the lattice until the intersections are at a 90 degree angle. Orient the panels to place the lattice strips at a 45 degree angle.

Lay out the lattice panels carefully for a good fit. Place one of the frames on the lattice, then draw around the inside of the opening. Draw the cut lines ½ in. outside the first set of lines. Use a plywood blade on your saw to reduce splintering. Use your circular saw with a clamp-on guide to help keep the cuts straight.

Lay one pair of legs on a flat surface, positioning them as they will be in their final form. Use a long 2X4 at the base of the legs to help you establish the correct angle. Lay one of the side frames on the legs, positioning it carefully. The outside corners of the lower frame joints should be flush with the outside of the legs. Measure from the 2X4 to make the bottom of the frame parallel with the base of the legs.

Mark the frame with light pencil lines where it crosses the legs. Remove the frame, then cut the lath strips that secure the lattice. Cut the side and bottom lath strips to fit inside the lines you just drew. You can cut the strips with square ends, as shown in the diagram, or cut them to match the angles of the frame and legs for a neater appearance.

Secure the lattice panels in the rabbets by screwing the lath strips to the frames with no. 8 X ¾-in. flathead wood screws. Drill countersunk pilot holes for the screws with a combination pilot bit and countersink. Space the screws 4 in. apart. Center the strips over the inside edge of the rabbet.

Lay one completed side panel on the pair of legs you already aligned. Remove the lower mending plates

MATERIALS LIST

Item	Quantity
2X6 lumber	6 ft.
2X4 lumber	30 ft.
2X3 lumber	18 ft.
1X6 lumber	18 ft.
1X4 hardwood lumber	62 ft.
Pre-fab redwood lattice	40 sq. ft.
Lath	to suit
¼" nuts, flat washers	12 each
¼" X 3½" bolts	4
¼" X 3½" carriage bolts	4
¼" X 2" carriage bolts	4
⅜" X 4" eyebolt, nut, (2) flat washers	4
⅜" X 2" screw eyes	2
200-lb.-test steel chain	24 ft.
S-hooks	6
No. 10 X 2½" flathead wood screws	12
No. 10 X 2" flathead wood screws	24
No. 10 X ⅞" flathead wood screws	32
No. 8 X 1½" flathead wood screws	60
No. 8 X ¾" flathead wood screws	100
¾" X 4" steel mending plates	12

CONSTRUCTION DETAILS

5. *Assemble the seat's side frames with carriage bolts, nuts and washers. Notice the two lap joints.*

6. *Screw the seat and back slats to the seat frames. Countersink the screw heads flush with the slats.*

7. *Attach the side panel frames to the legs. Assemble the sides, stacking the assemblies to make them identical.*

8. *Attach the support chain to the eyes with S-hooks. Adjust the length of the chains for maximum comfort.*

before positioning the panel. Align the panel carefully, then attach it to the legs with no. 10 X 2-in. flathead wood screws. Use two screws through each frame part for maximum strength. Countersink the screw heads flush as you did before.

To make both sides of the swing's frame identical, assemble the second leg and panel on top of the first. Align the parts accurately, then attach the panel as you did before.

To form the beam at the top of the swing frame, rip a 15 degree bevel on one edge of a length of 2X8 lumber. Set up your saw to cut the part

to the $5\frac{7}{8}$-in. maximum width shown in the diagram. Use a combination planer-type blade for a smooth finish. Rip the beam from stock that is longer than the final dimension to minimize any damage at the end of the cut. Use a roller support to hold the beam as it leaves the saw.

Cut the beam to its finished 63-in. length, then cut the lower cross brace to match. Insert the beam in the notches at the top of the legs, then bore $\frac{1}{4}$-in.-dia. holes through the legs and the beams. Locate the holes in the relative positions

248

shown in Detail 2 of the diagram.

Counterbore both ends of the holes with a 3/4-in. bit, then insert 1/4-in. X 4 1/2-in. bolts through the holes. Notice that the lower counterbores are deeper. Add the nuts and washers and tighten securely. Check the assembly with a framing square as you work.

Add the lower cross brace, attaching it with no. 10 X 2 1/2-in. flathead screws, countersunk flush. Finish the frame by cutting the two angled braces. Cut the ends of these braces at 45 degree angles. Attach them to the legs and brace with the same size screws. Fasten the joint between the two braces first, then attach the brace to the leg. Again, check the structure for squareness as you work.

Install the 1X4 rear brace at the back of the side panels. Finally, add the top lattice panel, securing it with no. 8 X 1 1/2-in. flathead wood screws. Drive the screws into the side frames and the rear brace.

Build the seat next. Cut the side frame components to the dimensions shown in the diagram. Cut the 5 degree angles for the backrest and seat supports with a table saw.

Now, lay out the lap joint notches. Lay the parts together and mark the notch positions on all the parts. Be sure to observe the correct angles.

Cut the notches with a dado blade on your saw. Make the notches exactly half the thickness of the wood. Cut the 90 degree notches first, then reset the angle of cut to form the angled notches. Form each notch with multiple passes of your dado blade, increasing the depth of cut to reach the final depth.

Assemble the frames with 1/4-in. X 2-in. carriage bolts. Drill through the joints, then insert the bolts with the heads inside the frame. Add nuts and washers and tighten securely.

Cut eight 1X4 seat and back slats 45 in. long. Attach these to the sides with no. 8 X 1 1/2-in. flathead wood screws, countersinking the screw heads. Use two screws at each joint, spacing them 2 1/2 in. apart. Space the slats 1/2-in. apart. Use a framing square to help keep the seat square as you install the slats.

Add the front brace to the seat, then form a 3/8-in. radius on the edges of the armrests with your router and a rounding-over bit. Install the arms with screws, as you did the slats.

Complete the seat by installing the eyebolts in the locations shown in the diagram. Use nuts and washers on both sides of the wood to position the eyes outside the armrests.

Sand the completed frame and seat thoroughly, starting with 80-grit abrasive paper. Work down to 220-grit for a smooth finish. Round off any exposed sharp edges slightly as you sand. Pay special attention to the end grain of the wood.

To protect the swing from weather damage, apply two coats of clear wood sealer or exterior latex enamel in the color of your choice. If you paint the swing, use an airless sprayer to help apply a smooth finish.

Once the paint is dry, install two 3/8-in. X 2-in. screw eyes in the beam. Drill 5/32-in.-dia. pilot holes, 1 1/2-in. deep, for the eyes. Hang the seat with S-hooks and 200-lb.-test chain. Adjust the length of the chains to hang the seat at an angle that feels comfortable. Finally, close the S-hooks with large pliers.

SLATTED BENCH

Every deck or patio needs plenty of seating. This slatted redwood bench is an ideal way to provide a comfortable and attractive spot for you and your guests to sit.

Start construction by cutting the bench slats to the length shown in the diagram. Next, set your saw to cut a 10 degree angle, and then cut the legs.

Clamp the seat components together and round over the edges with a ⅜-in.-radius rounding-over bit, with pilot, in your router. After rounding, sand the bench top thoroughly.

Now, clamp one pair of legs to a slat. Carefully adjust the angle of the legs to exactly 80 degrees. Once the angles are correct, drill ¹⁄₁₆-in. holes through the parts to locate the positions of the threaded rods.

Use these pre-drilled parts as patterns to mark the remaining components. Transfer the hole locations by tapping a small nail through the holes.

Bore ⁵⁄₁₆-in. holes through all the bench parts on a drill press, using a backup board to prevent splintering. Counterbore the holes on the outside slats, as shown in the diagram.

Next, assemble the bench with glue, and pass the ⁵⁄₁₆-in. threaded rod through the holes. Install nuts and washers on the rods and tighten lightly.

Turn the bench upright and adjust the legs to the proper alignment. Clamp cleats to the legs to hold the position, then tighten the nuts.

Nail the cleats to the legs with 6d galvanized finishing nails to complete the assembly. Set the nails just below the surface of the wood.

Sand the completed bench as necessary, then apply two coats of clear wood sealer, allowing the first coat to dry overnight.

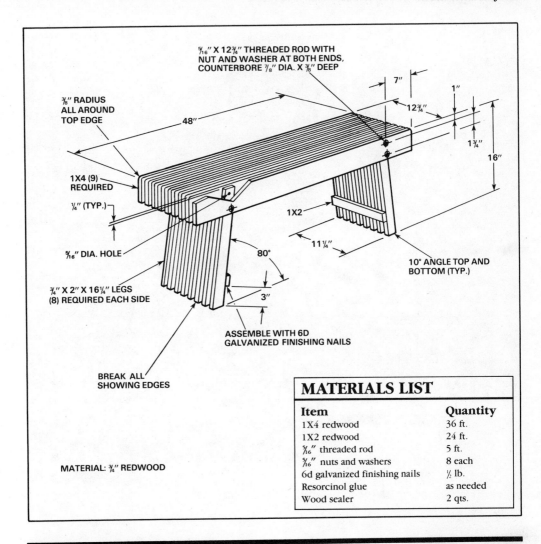

⅝" X 12¾" THREADED ROD WITH
NUT AND WASHER AT BOTH ENDS,
COUNTERBORE ⅞" DIA. X ⅜" DEEP

⅜" RADIUS
ALL AROUND
TOP EDGE

48"

7"

12¾"

1"

1¾"

16"

1X4 (9)
REQUIRED

¼" (TYP.)

1X2

⅝" DIA. HOLE

80°

10° ANGLE TOP AND
BOTTOM (TYP.)

11¼"

¾" X 2" X 16¼" LEGS
(8) REQUIRED EACH SIDE

3"

ASSEMBLE WITH 6D
GALVANIZED FINISHING NAILS

BREAK ALL
SHOWING EDGES

MATERIAL: ¾" REDWOOD

MATERIALS LIST

Item	Quantity
1X4 redwood	36 ft.
1X2 redwood	24 ft.
⁵⁄₁₆" threaded rod	5 ft.
⁵⁄₁₆" nuts and washers	8 each
6d galvanized finishing nails	½ lb.
Resorcinol glue	as needed
Wood sealer	2 qts.

CONSTRUCTION DETAILS

1. Drill ¹⁄₁₆-in. pilot holes in one slat and leg assembly. Drive a small nail through these holes to mark matching parts.

2. Assemble the bench with threaded rod, nuts and washers, and glue. Clamp the leg cleats in place to hold the alignment.

Stack the seats by positioning the second seat over the first, with the legs facing in opposite directions.

STACKING SEATS

If your deck or patio is small, finding space for seating can be a real problem. You can solve this space problem in several ways, but these stacking seats are one of the best.

Built entirely of redwood and redwood plywood, their three-legged design makes it possible to stack them up neatly when not in use. In addition, their light weight makes them easy to move around to suit any occasion.

Begin construction by building the seat frames. First decide how many seats you want to build, then cut all of the components at the same time.

Cut four redwood 1X4 frame components for each seat. Set your table saw's bevel angle to 45 degrees, then make the first mitered cut. Clamp a stop block on your saw's table to help you position each piece so they will all be the same length.

Working with long stock, turn the board over when cutting each successive part, using the beveled end left from the last cut as one end of the next part.

Assemble the four sides of each seat frame with resorcinol glue and 4d galvanized finishing nails. Drill pilot holes for the nails to simplify construction and to help prevent splitting. As you assemble the frames, check them with a try square to keep the corners square.

Next, install four 1X1 cleats on the inside of the frames. Position these exactly ½ in. from the top of the frame. Fasten the cleats with glue and no. 10 X 1¼-in. flathead

wood screws. Use a combination pilot bit and countersink to bore pilot holes for the screws. Measure accurately for a smooth seat.

Measure the inside opening of the frame carefully to determine the exact size for the seat's top. The dimensions shown in the diagram represent a typical seat, but the dimensions of your actual seat may vary slightly. An accurate fit will greatly improve the final appearance of your project.

Cut the plywood inserts on your table saw, using a plywood blade for a smooth finish. Set the saw's rip fence carefully to make the finished part fit the frame perfectly. Work with the good side of the plywood up to minimize splintering.

Install the plywood top with glue and no. 8 X 1-in. flathead wood screws. Drive the screws through the cleats, into the plywood. Use a combination pilot bit and countersink to make the pilot holes, as you did before.

Once the seat and frame are assembled, sand the unit thoroughly, starting with 120-grit garnet paper. Work down to 220-grit paper for a smooth final finish. Sand with a pad-type power sander, always sanding with the grain.

Now, make the legs by cutting 1X4 redwood stock to the length indicated in the diagram. Notice the 45 degree bevel at the top of each leg.

On two leg pairs cut 45 degree bevels along each long edge.

To simplify the job, cut all of the pieces slightly longer than the final dimension, with the saw blade set

CONSTRUCTION DETAILS

1. Cut the mitered edges of the legs at a 45 degree angle on your table saw. Use a combination planer blade.

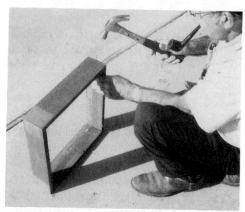

2. Assemble the table frame with resorcinol glue and 4d galvanized finishing nails. Predrill all nail holes to prevent splitting.

3. Screw the 1X1 cleats to the inside of the frame. Measure the gap at the top of the cleats acccurately.

4. Attach the redwood top from below with flathead wood screws and glue. Bore pilot holes with a combination bit.

vertically. Change the bevel angle to 45 degrees, then make the final cut on all of the parts.

Attach the legs to the seat frame in the positions shown in the diagram. Use no. 10 X 1¼-in. flathead wood screws and resorcinol glue, driving the screws from the inside of the seat into the legs. As you did before, drill countersunk pilot holes to make the screw heads flush with the wood's surface.

Position the legs carefully and

check them for squareness with a try square before driving the screws. The top of the beveled end of each leg should be even with the top of the frame.

Sand the legs as you did the frame, and touch up any flaws in the rest of the project. Apply two coats of clear wood sealer, such as Thompson's Water Seal, to protect the wood from weathering. Allow 24 hours for the first coat to dry before applying the second coat.

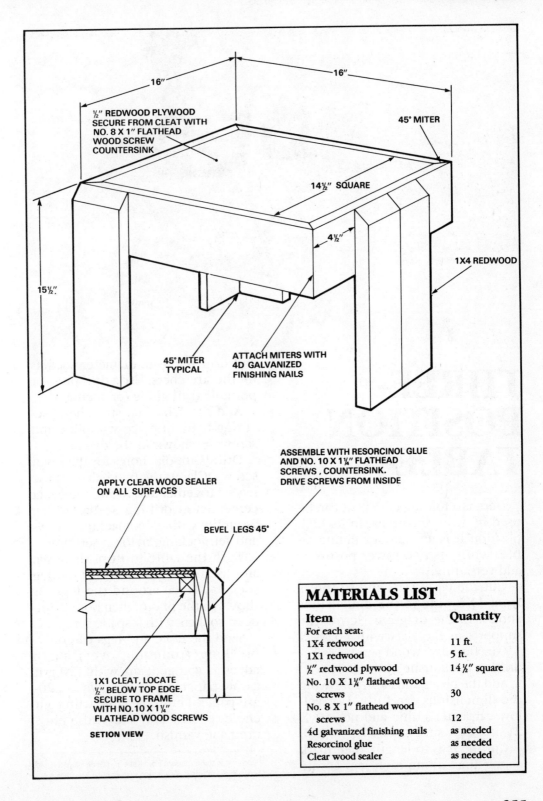

16"

16"

½" REDWOOD PLYWOOD
SECURE FROM CLEAT WITH
NO. 8 X 1" FLATHEAD
WOOD SCREW
COUNTERSINK

45° MITER

14½" SQUARE

4½"

1X4 REDWOOD

15½".

45° MITER
TYPICAL

ATTACH MITERS WITH
4D GALVANIZED
FINISHING NAILS

ASSEMBLE WITH RESORCINOL GLUE
AND NO. 10 X 1¼" FLATHEAD
SCREWS , COUNTERSINK.
DRIVE SCREWS FROM INSIDE

APPLY CLEAR WOOD SEALER
ON ALL SURFACES

BEVEL LEGS 45°

1X1 CLEAT, LOCATE
½" BELOW TOP EDGE,
SECURE TO FRAME
WITH NO.10 X 1¼"
FLATHEAD WOOD SCREWS

SETION VIEW

MATERIALS LIST

Item	Quantity
For each seat:	
1X4 redwood	11 ft.
1X1 redwood	5 ft.
½" redwood plywood	14½" square
No. 10 X 1¼" flathead wood screws	30
No. 8 X 1" flathead wood screws	12
4d galvanized finishing nails	as needed
Resorcinol glue	as needed
Clear wood sealer	as needed

THREE-POSITION TABLE

Here is a folding table that can be used in many situations. In its high position it is an outdoor dining table, while its two lower positions add versatility.

Cut the table slats and supports from 1X6 pine to the dimensions shown in the diagram. Screw the supports to the slats with no. 8 X 1¼-in. flathead wood screws, after drilling countersunk pilot holes.

Add the cleats and caps, following the dimensions carefully. Use yellow carpenter's glue and no. 10 X 2¾-in. screws for assembly.

Cut the legs to length, then mark center lines along each leg. Locate and drill the 1-in.-diameter sockets for the stretchers. Use a drill press or portable drill guide for accuracy.

Add the 1-in.-dia. stretchers, securing them in place with glue and screws as shown in the diagram.

Drill ¼-in.-dia. holes for the pivot screws. Clamp the two halves of the leg set together and locate the exact center before drilling. Secure the leg assembly with ¼-in. machine screws and self-locking, nylon-insert nuts.

Turn the table top upside-down and locate the positions for the leg sockets. Trace around the legs, as shown in the photo, then bore ¼-in.-deep sockets with a spade bit.

Sand the table and legs carefully, breaking (rounding over) sharp edges as you go. Start with 120-grit garnet paper and work down to 220-grit paper. Finish the table with your choice of stain and satin-finish polyurethane varnish.

Reprinted with permission from Katie and Gene Hamilton and Steve Wolgemuth in conjunction with Popular Mechanics.

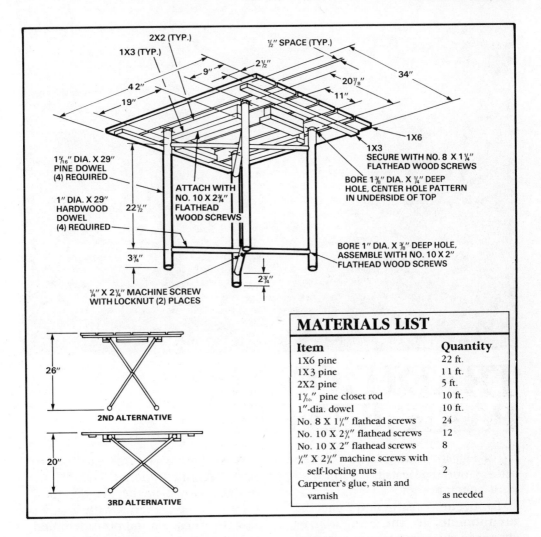

2X2 (TYP.)

1X3 (TYP.)

½" SPACE (TYP.)

2½"

9"

4 2"

19"

20⅞"

34"

11"

1X6

1X3
SECURE WITH NO. 8 X 1¼"
FLATHEAD WOOD SCREWS

1⅝" DIA. X 29"
PINE DOWEL
(4) REQUIRED

BORE 1⅜" DIA. X ¼" DEEP
HOLE, CENTER HOLE PATTERN
IN UNDERSIDE OF TOP

1" DIA. X 29"
HARDWOOD
DOWEL
(4) REQUIRED

22½"

ATTACH WITH
NO. 10 X 2¾"
FLATHEAD
WOOD SCREWS

BORE 1" DIA. X ⅜" DEEP HOLE,
ASSEMBLE WITH NO. 10 X 2"
FLATHEAD WOOD SCREWS

3¾"

2¾"

¼" X 2¼" MACHINE SCREW
WITH LOCKNUT (2) PLACES

26"

2ND ALTERNATIVE

20"

3RD ALTERNATIVE

MATERIALS LIST

Item	Quantity
1X6 pine	22 ft.
1X3 pine	11 ft.
2X2 pine	5 ft.
1⅝" pine closet rod	10 ft.
1"-dia. dowel	10 ft.
No. 8 X 1¼" flathead screws	24
No. 10 X 2¾" flathead screws	12
No. 10 X 2" flathead screws	8
¼" X 2¼" machine screws with self-locking nuts	2
Carpenter's glue, stain and varnish	as needed

CONSTRUCTION DETAILS

1. Clamp the leg stretchers together, measure, then drill the pivot holes. Accuracy counts here.

2. Position the legs so that all the overhangs are equal, then trace around each leg for the socket holes.

TRADITIONAL PARK BENCH

For elegant seating in an outdoor setting, nothing beats the traditional park bench design.

To begin construction, cut the components to the rough sizes shown in the diagram.

On a flat surface, lay out the frame parts as shown in the Grid Detail. Mark the locations of the lap joints directly on the boards. Use an adjustable bevel gauge to transfer the angles of the lap joints to your radial arm saw. Then cut the joints by making multiple passes with a dado blade.

Assemble the rough frames using waterproof resorcinol glue and no. 8 X 1¼-in. brass flathead wood screws. Drill pilot holes for the screws.

Next, lay out a 1-in. grid pattern on a sheet of hardboard. Transfer the designs shown in the diagram, and then cut the patterns with a saber saw. Lay these on the pre-assembled frames and trace around them. Use a saber saw with a long blade to cut the profiles.

Add the braces to the frames, securing them with ¼-in. X 3½-in. lag screws and flat washers.

Drill countersunk pilot holes and attach the slats with no. 8 X 2½-in. brass flathead wood screws.

Sand the completed bench, starting with 80-grit garnet paper and finishing with 150-grit paper. Apply a coat of exterior enamel primer, followed by two coats of semi-gloss latex enamel.

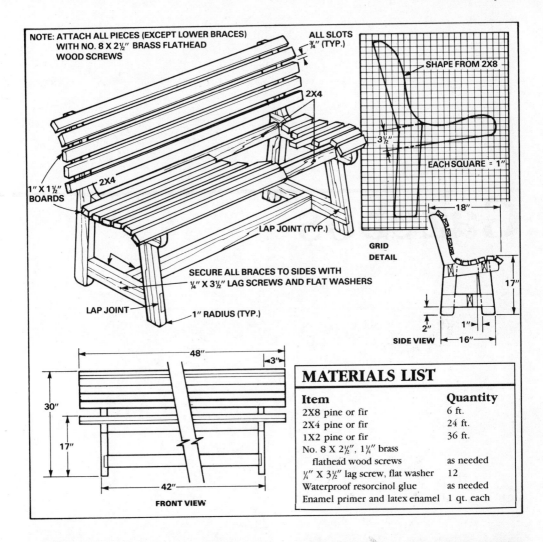

NOTE: ATTACH ALL PIECES (EXCEPT LOWER BRACES) WITH NO. 8 X 2½" BRASS FLATHEAD WOOD SCREWS

ALL SLOTS ¾" (TYP.)

2X4

SHAPE FROM 2X8

3½"

EACH SQUARE = 1"

1" X 1½" BOARDS

2X4

LAP JOINT (TYP.)

GRID DETAIL

18"

SECURE ALL BRACES TO SIDES WITH ¼" X 3½" LAG SCREWS AND FLAT WASHERS

17"

LAP JOINT

1" RADIUS (TYP.)

2"   1"

SIDE VIEW   16"

48"   3"

30"

17"

42"

FRONT VIEW

MATERIALS LIST

Item	Quantity
2X8 pine or fir	6 ft.
2X4 pine or fir	24 ft.
1X2 pine or fir	36 ft.
No. 8 X 2½", 1¼" brass flathead wood screws	as needed
¼" X 3½" lag screw, flat washer	12
Waterproof resorcinol glue	as needed
Enamel primer and latex enamel	1 qt. each

CONSTRUCTION DETAILS

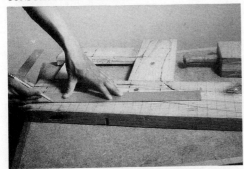

1. Use the grid patterns to lay out the curved profiles directly on the assembled frame or on bardboard (as a template).

2. Cut out the seat and back designs of the frame assemblies with a long blade on your saber saw.

VII.

Gazebos

*A contemporary feeling of airiness and
light are some of the special features of this
redwood gazebo.*

ANGULAR GAZEBO

If your outdoor decor is contemporary, this redwood gazebo will fit right in. Designed for comfortable entertaining, its roofline makes it appear ready to take flight.

A trellis-style roof filters the sunlight to make the interior of the gazebo a pleasant spot even in the heat of summer. Pre-fab lattice panels fill in the open sides to render a feeling of privacy and intimacy. You can choose to close in both sides or just one.

The redwood lumber chosen for this gazebo gives it its good looks and weather resistance. Use construction heart grade for the joists and decking to help guard against rot. The rest of the structure can be made of construction common grade for economy.

After leveling a site in your yard for the gazebo, lay out a 12-ft. square area. Drive stakes at the corners of the square to mark the corners of the gazebo. Locate the stakes accurately, and measure the diagonals to check the squareness of your layout. If the diagonals are equal, the layout is perfectly square.

At the front corner of the site, drive in two more stakes, 8 ft. from the adjacent corners. This will locate the angled entrance to the gazebo.

At each stake location, dig a hole for the concrete piers that will support the deck. Make each hole 12 in. in dia. and 36 in. deep. Fill the holes with concrete, and then center $\frac{1}{2}$-in. X 12-in. J-bolts in the wet concrete. Allow the bolts to extend 5 in. above the concrete for all but the front post, and check with a square to make certain that they are perfectly vertical. Allow the bolt for the front post to extend $1\frac{1}{2}$ inches.

Once the concrete has cured, build the perimeter frame of the deck. Cut two 12-ft.-long pieces of 2X6 construction heart redwood for the long sides of the frame. Cut the remaining side components 8 ft. long, with 45 degree miters on one end of each piece.

Now, assemble the components with 16d galvanized nails, three at each joint. Drill pilot holes for the nails to help prevent splitting the redwood lumber. Square up the assembly, then cut the remaining 2X6 for the front, mitering both ends. Nail this component in place, once again drilling pilot holes.

Bore $\frac{1}{2}$-in. holes through the frame members for the anchor bolts. Counterbore 1-in.-deep holes on the top of the frame with a 1-in.-dia. bit to form a recess for the nuts. With help, set the perimeter frame on the piers, with the J-bolts extending into the pre-drilled holes. Attach the frame to the piers with nuts and washers.

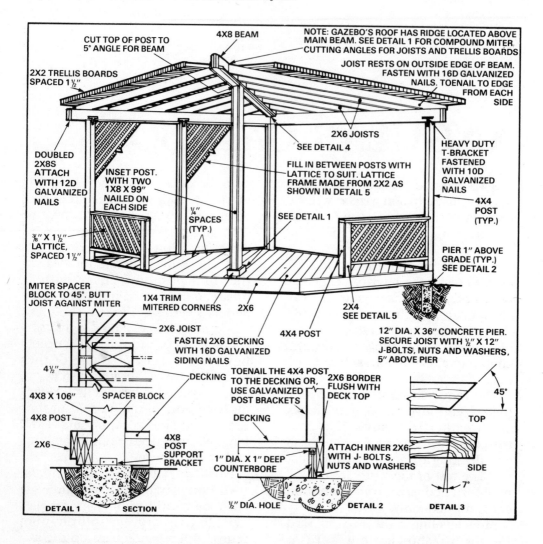

CUT TOP OF POST TO 5° ANGLE FOR BEAM

4X8 BEAM

NOTE: GAZEBO'S ROOF HAS RIDGE LOCATED ABOVE MAIN BEAM. SEE DETAIL 1 FOR COMPOUND MITER, CUTTING ANGLES FOR JOISTS AND TRELLIS BOARDS

2X2 TRELLIS BOARDS SPACED 1½"

JOIST RESTS ON OUTSIDE EDGE OF BEAM. FASTEN WITH 16D GALVANIZED NAILS. TOENAIL TO EDGE FROM EACH SIDE

2X6 JOISTS

DOUBLED 2X8S ATTACH WITH 12D GALVANIZED NAILS

INSET POST. ATTACH WITH TWO 1X8 X 99" NAILED ON EACH SIDE

SEE DETAIL 4

FILL IN BETWEEN POSTS WITH LATTICE TO SUIT. LATTICE FRAME MADE FROM 2X2 AS SHOWN IN DETAIL 5

HEAVY DUTY T-BRACKET FASTENED WITH 10D GALVANIZED NAILS

4X4 POST (TYP.)

¼" SPACES (TYP.)

SEE DETAIL 1

⅜" X 1½" LATTICE, SPACED 1½"

PIER 1" ABOVE GRADE (TYP.) SEE DETAIL 2

MITER SPACER BLOCK TO 45°. BUTT JOIST AGAINST MITER

1X4 TRIM MITERED CORNERS

2X6

2X4 SEE DETAIL 5

2X6 JOIST

4X4 POST

12" DIA. X 36" CONCRETE PIER. SECURE JOIST WITH ½" X 12" J-BOLTS, NUTS AND WASHERS, 5" ABOVE PIER

FASTEN 2X6 DECKING WITH 16D GALVANIZED SIDING NAILS

4½"

DECKING

TOENAIL THE 4X4 POST TO THE DECKING OR, USE GALVANIZED POST BRACKETS

2X6 BORDER FLUSH WITH DECK TOP

45°

TOP

4X8 X 106"

SPACER BLOCK

DECKING

4X8 POST

2X6

4X8 POST SUPPORT BRACKET

1" DIA. X 1" DEEP COUNTERBORE

ATTACH INNER 2X6 WITH J-BOLTS, NUTS AND WASHERS

SIDE

7°

½" DIA. HOLE

DETAIL 1   SECTION

DETAIL 2

DETAIL 3

Add the 2X6 floor joists, spacing them 24 in. on center. Use only very straight lumber for the joists to insure a level floor. Measure the distance between the frame components carefully and cut the joists to fit closely. Cut 45 degree miters where the joists meet the angled frame. Measure these joists especially carefully. Fasten the joints with 16d galvanized nails, once again drilling pilot holes.

Install the 2X6 decking next, spacing the deck boards ½ in. apart.

The decking is installed at a 45 degree angle. Check the angle of the first board carefully to set up the correct alignment. Allow each board to overhang the frame an inch or two.

Attach the decking with 16d galvanized siding nails, using two nails at each joint. Remember, for easy removal later, you need only tack the two boards over the inset pier. Once again, drill pilot holes for the nails, especially near the ends of the boards. For an even appearance,

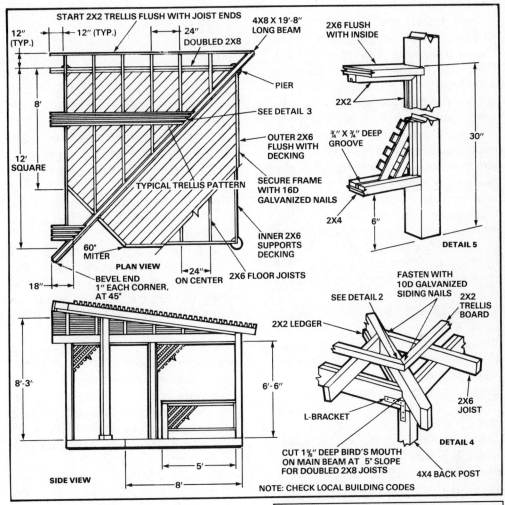

START 2X2 TRELLIS FLUSH WITH JOIST ENDS

4X8 X 19'-8" LONG BEAM

2X6 FLUSH WITH INSIDE

12" (TYP.)

12" (TYP.)

24" DOUBLED 2X8

8'

PIER

SEE DETAIL 3

12' SQUARE

OUTER 2X6 FLUSH WITH DECKING

2X2

¾" X ¾" DEEP GROOVE

30"

TYPICAL TRELLIS PATTERN

SECURE FRAME WITH 16D GALVANIZED NAILS

2X4

6"

60° MITER

INNER 2X6 SUPPORTS DECKING

DETAIL 5

PLAN VIEW

18"

BEVEL END 1" EACH CORNER, AT 45°

24" ON CENTER

2X6 FLOOR JOISTS

FASTEN WITH 10D GALVANIZED SIDING NAILS

2X2 TRELLIS BOARD

SEE DETAIL 2

2X2 LEDGER

8'-3"

6'-6"

2X6 JOIST

L-BRACKET

SIDE VIEW

5'

8'

CUT 1⅝" DEEP BIRD'S MOUTH ON MAIN BEAM AT 5° SLOPE FOR DOUBLED 2X8 JOISTS

DETAIL 4

4X4 BACK POST

NOTE: CHECK LOCAL BUILDING CODES

space the nails at each joint 1 in. in from the board's edge.

Trim the overhang carefully with a circular saw. Snap chalk lines along the line of cut to insure accuracy, and set the saw's depth of cut to just clear the bottom of the decking. Use a combination-type planer blade in your saw for a clean finish on the edge of the deck. For even greater accuracy, clamp a long, straight board on the edge of the decking as a saw guide. Attach a 2X6 border all around the deck, flush

MATERIALS LIST

Item	Quantity
4X8 redwood	28 ft.
4X4 redwood	32 ft.
2X8 redwood	48 ft.
2X6 construction heart redwood	120 ft.
2X6 redwood	420 ft.
2X4 redwood	18 ft.
2X2 redwood	700 ft.
1X8 redwood	17 ft.
1X4 redwood	2 ft.
Pre-fab lattice	120 sq. ft.
6" galvanized L-brackets	2
8" galvanized T-brackets	6
½" X 12" J-bolt, nut, washer	4
10d, 12d, 16d galvanized nails	as needed
4X8 post support bracket	1
100-lb. concrete	4 bags
Preservative, wood sealer	as needed

with the deck's top.

Now install the 4X8 inset post. Cut the 5 degree angles at the top of the 106-in. long 4X8 post and the 99-in. long 1X8 boards. Nail the 1X8 boards to each side of the post. Secure the post as shown in the diagram, holding it in a vertical position with temporary braces. Make each brace about 6 ft. long and position it about 45 degrees from the vertical. Brace the post in two directions.

Next, notch the 2X6 decking planks you removed earlier to accommodate the 4X8 post. Nail the decking in place and add the 1X4 trim at the base of the post, mitering the corners.

Install the 4X4 perimeter posts next. Toenail them to the deck or use galvanized post brackets. Position the post in the center of one side, as shown in the diagram. If you decide to close in both sides, add another center post to the open side.

As you did with the other posts, nail temporary angled braces to the post and the deck frame to hold it vertical during construction.

Nail 2X8 stock together to form the 13-ft. side beams. Use 12d galvanized nails, in pairs and spaced 8 in. apart, for this assembly. Once the beams are assembled, cut a 45 degree miter on one end of each beam for the rear joint. You will have to cut this miter with two passes of either your circular saw or stationary saw.

Raise these doubled 2X8 beams and nail them to the posts with 16d galvanized nails. Nail the mitered joint as well. Reinforce the joints with 8-in. heavy-duty galvanized T-brackets. Choose brackets made of

steel at least $3/16$-in. thick for this application.

Cut a 20-ft.-long 4X8 to a finished length of 19 ft., 8 in. If you have difficulty obtaining a 4X8 beam this long, you can build one up of 2X8 material as you did for the side beams. Using the diagram as a guide, cut two 45 degree bevels on each end of the beam to form a point.

With help, carefully raise the beam and place it on top of the side posts and the center beam. Mark the beam for the bird's mouth, as shown in Detail 4.

When working on the roof line of the gazebo, stand on a stepladder at least 10 ft. high. Avoid standing on a step too close to the top, and make certain that the ladder is stable before proceeding.

Take the beam down again and cut the notch carefully with a handsaw, making several parallel cuts, then remove the waste with a chisel. When the notch is finished, replace the beam, nailing it in place with 16d galvanized nails. Reinforce the joints with L-brackets.

Nail 2X2 ledgers to the lower edges of the beam with 16d galvanized nails. Cut a 45 degree miter on the rear of each ledger to fit the rear of the structure. These ledgers will support the roof joists.

Next, set up your table or radial arm saw to cut the compound miters for the inside ends of the roof joists. Set the saw to cut a 45 degree bevel, then set the arm of your radial arm saw or the miter gauge on your table saw to cut the 5 degree miter.

Cut the rear joists first, and check the setup by putting the joist into position. Make any necessary adjustments, and then check it for fit again. Once the setting is correct, leave the saw set to cut both the joists and the lattice roof.

Cut one end of each joist, raise them into position, and then mark and cut the correct overall length. Use a circular saw to cut the joists to length. This will allow you to leave the stationary saw set for the compound miter.

Space the joists 24 in. on center. Toenail each joist to the center and side beams with 16d galvanized nails. Once again, keep safety in mind as you work on the roof. Whenever you move your ladder, make certain that it is stable before climbing it again to work on the gazebo. Do not be tempted to overreach; reposition the ladder frequently.

Once the beams and joists are in place, you can remove the temporary bracing from the posts. The structure will now stand securely.

Top off the structure with 2X2 trellis boards. As you did for the joists, cut the inner angle (see Detail 2), then position the pieces individually to determine their final length. After measuring one piece, cut the matching slat to the same length.

Use a length of the trellis material as a spacer block to equalize the 1½-in. trellis spacing. Fasten the 2X2 trellis components with 10d galvanized siding nails. Allow plenty of time for this roofing operation.

Use a dado blade on your table or radial arm saw to form ¾-in. grooves in 2X2 redwood stock for the lattice frames, as shown in Detail 5. Notice that a similar groove must be made in 2X4 stock for the lower rails of the handrail panels.

When forming the grooves in the stock, work with long pieces of the material for safety's sake.

These grooves can also be formed by using a router with an edge guide and a ¾-in. straight bit. Make several passes with the router, increasing the depth of cut about ⅛ in. with each pass.

Install the 4X4 rail posts at the front of the gazebo, and then add the top railings, locating them flush with the inside of the post. Attach the 2X2 frame members and the pre-fab lattice material.

To cut the lattice material, first expand it so that the lattice strips are at right angles to each other. Measure the panel, then cut with a plywood blade in your circular saw. Be sure to allow for the depth of the grooves in the frame members.

Notice that the upper corners of the 2X2 handrail frames are mitered. Add the 2X4 outer trim boards to the handrail posts.

Install the lattice panels at the side of the gazebo in the same way, framing the lattice with the grooved 2X2 components. You may find it simpler to build the entire frame and lattice panels, then install the completed assemblies in the openings.

You can leave the gazebo unfinished and allow it to weather naturally, or apply clear wood sealer and preservative to maintain the color of the redwood for a year or two. Be sure to use non-toxic finishing materials.

Airless spray equipment is the easiest way to apply a finish to your gazebo. Be sure to wear eye protection and use a canister-type respirator to avoid inhaling fumes.

Design and photos courtesy of the California Redwood Association, 591 Redwood Highway, Suite 3100, Mill Valley, CA 94941.

LATTICE GAZEBO

For a touch of elegance in your garden, it is hard to beat the traditional gazebo. This redwood gazebo features lattice panels to provide a sense of intimacy, and a cedar shake roof so that you can use it even on rainy days.

Designed to fit in any location in your yard, it is the perfect spot for family gatherings and outdoor parties.

The above-ground portions of the

gazebo are built of construction common grade redwood for economy and an attractive appearance. Choose construction heart grade redwood, however, for the decking, skirt, and floor joists. These come in contact with moisture, and the heartwood will be very rot-resistant.

Start by building the base of the structure. Cut the eight 2X8 redwood skirt components to the lengths shown in the diagram. Miter

A combination of clear openings and lattice panels makes this redwood gazebo an intimate gathering place for family and friends.

both ends of each board at a 22½ degree angle on your table or radial arm saw. This will insure a perfect octagonal base for your gazebo. It is a good idea to check the adjustment of your saw before cutting the actual components. Cut eight lengths of 2X4 scrap, using the angle you have set for the miters. Assemble these test pieces. If a perfect octagon is not formed, adjust the saw's angle slightly and recheck.

If a stationary saw is not available, set the shoe on your circular saw to cut a 22½ degree bevel. Clamp a cutting guide to the 2X8 skirt stock, then cut.

Assemble the skirt on a flat surface with 16d galvanized finishing nails, three per joint. Drill pilot holes, slightly smaller than the diameter of the nails, to help avoid splitting the wood. Pilot holes are always a good idea when nailing near the edge of redwood lumber

Install the 2X8 joists next. Start with one full-length joist across the width of the base. Cut two intersecting, 67½ degree bevels on each end of the joist to match the angles of the skirt. Set the saw's depth of cut to just reach the center of the stock. Nail the joist in place with 16d galvanized finishing nails, after drilling pilot holes as you did before.

Add two 75-in. sections of the joist material, perpendicular to the first joist. Measure the first joist carefully and locate its exact center. Cut a double bevel on one end just as you did for the full-length joist. Nail the joists to the first joist with 16d galvanized nails, toenailing where necessary. Check the assembly with a framing square before nailing.

Finally, add the remaining four joist sections. Cut a double bevel at both ends of these intermediate joist members. Cut one end with the saw set at 67½ degrees, then reset the saw to 22½ degrees for the other end. You can save time by cutting one end of each joist at the first setting before changing your setup. Measure each joist individually to allow for variations in the base.

Before adding the decking, prepare a level site in your yard for the gazebo. To prevent the growth of unsightly weeds on the site, cover the area with heavy plastic sheeting. Then add gravel to enhance the landscape.

With the help of a friend, move the base onto the site, positioning it in its final orientation. Drive small stakes at the corners of the gazebo to locate the positions for the concrete

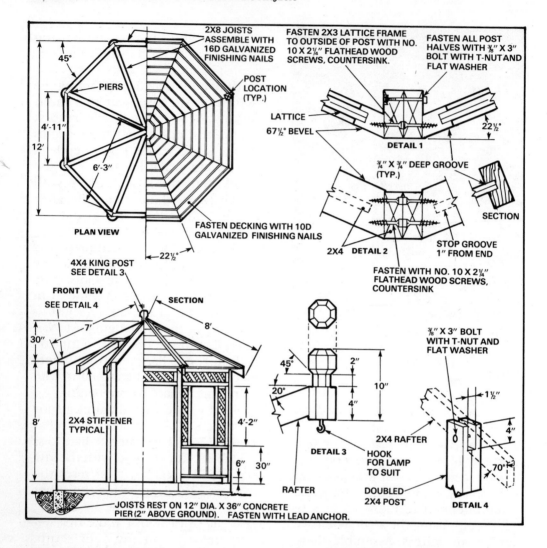

PLAN VIEW

2X8 JOISTS ASSEMBLE WITH 16D GALVANIZED FINISHING NAILS

PIERS

45°

4'-11"

12'

6'-3"

22½°

POST LOCATION (TYP.)

FASTEN 2X3 LATTICE FRAME TO OUTSIDE OF POST WITH NO. 10 X 2¼" FLATHEAD WOOD SCREWS, COUNTERSINK.

FASTEN ALL POST HALVES WITH ⅜" X 3" BOLT WITH T-NUT AND FLAT WASHER

LATTICE

67½° BEVEL

DETAIL 1

22½°

¾" X ¾" DEEP GROOVE (TYP.)

SECTION

2X4   **DETAIL 2**

STOP GROOVE 1" FROM END

FASTEN DECKING WITH 10D GALVANIZED FINISHING NAILS

FASTEN WITH NO. 10 X 2¼" FLATHEAD WOOD SCREWS, COUNTERSINK

4X4 KING POST SEE DETAIL 3

FRONT VIEW

SEE DETAIL 4

7'

8'

30"

8'

2X4 STIFFENER TYPICAL

4'-2"

6"   30"

45°

20°

2"

10"

4"

DETAIL 3

HOOK FOR LAMP TO SUIT

RAFTER

DOUBLED 2X4 POST

⅜" X 3" BOLT WITH T-NUT AND FLAT WASHER

1½"

4"

70°

2X4 RAFTER

DETAIL 4

JOISTS REST ON 12" DIA. X 36" CONCRETE PIER (2" ABOVE GROUND). FASTEN WITH LEAD ANCHOR.

piers. Mark the center of the structure as well.

Remove the base assembly and dig holes for the piers. The piers should be centered under the frame at each corner and at the center. Allow each pier to stand about 2 in. above ground level. Now, use a long, straight 2X4 and a carpenter's level to level each perimeter pier with the center pier. To insure accuracy, double-check the level of adjacent piers as well. Take your time with this job, since the final

level of the gazebo's floor depends on your thoroughness during this step.

Once the final leveling is complete, bore ½-in.-dia. holes in the piers with a carbide-tipped masonry bit to accommodate lead screw anchors. Install the anchors in the holes. These will be used with lag screws to secure the gazebo to the piers.

Reposition the assembled base on the piers, then drill counterbored holes for the lag screws into the top

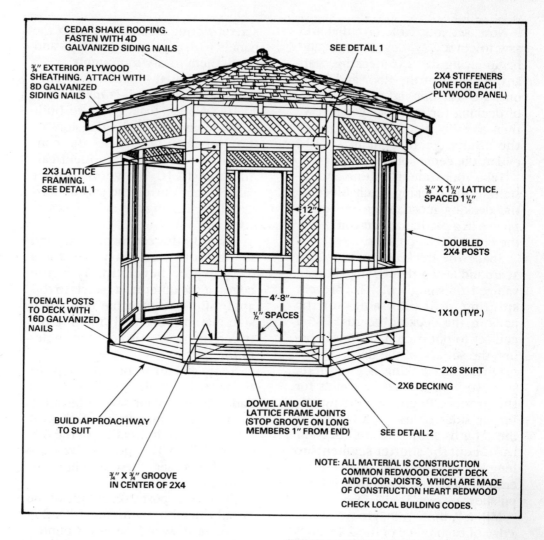

CEDAR SHAKE ROOFING. FASTEN WITH 4D GALVANIZED SIDING NAILS

¾″ EXTERIOR PLYWOOD SHEATHING. ATTACH WITH 8D GALVANIZED SIDING NAILS

2X3 LATTICE FRAMING. SEE DETAIL 1

TOENAIL POSTS TO DECK WITH 16D GALVANIZED NAILS

BUILD APPROACHWAY TO SUIT

¾″ X ¾″ GROOVE IN CENTER OF 2X4

SEE DETAIL 1

2X4 STIFFENERS (ONE FOR EACH PLYWOOD PANEL)

⅜″ X 1½″ LATTICE, SPACED 1½″

DOUBLED 2X4 POSTS

1X10 (TYP.)

2X8 SKIRT

2X6 DECKING

DOWEL AND GLUE LATTICE FRAME JOINTS (STOP GROOVE ON LONG MEMBERS 1″ FROM END)

SEE DETAIL 2

12″

4′-8″

½″ SPACES

NOTE: ALL MATERIAL IS CONSTRUCTION COMMON REDWOOD EXCEPT DECK AND FLOOR JOISTS, WHICH ARE MADE OF CONSTRUCTION HEART REDWOOD

CHECK LOCAL BUILDING CODES.

of the 2X8 base. These holes must align with the lead anchors. Use flat washers under the heads of the lag screws and tighten securely.

MATERIALS LIST

Item	Quantity
4X4 redwood	2 ft.
2X8 redwood	52 ft.
2X6 redwood	250 ft.
2X4 redwood	500 ft.
1X10 redwood	110 ft.
Pre-fab redwood lattice	144 sq. ft.
¾″ exterior plywood	3 sheets
Cedar shakes	1½ squares

Item	Quantity
⅜″ X 3″ bolts with flat washers and T-nuts	32
No. 10 X 2¼″ flathead wood screws	100
Concrete piers	9
Cedar shake nails	10 lb.
⅜″ X 2½″ dowel pins	as needed
10d, 16d galvanized finishing nails	5 lb. each
4d, 8d galvanized siding nails	as needed
6″ lag screws, anchors and flat washers	8 each
Resorcinol glue	as needed
Caulking compound	1 tube
Clear wood sealer and preservative	as needed

Now, set your table or radial arm saw to cut a 22½ degree angle and begin laying the 2X6 decking. Start at the center of the floor and work outward. Lay out and cut one piece of decking for each octagonal row, then use this piece as a pattern for the others. Each segment should end at the center of a joist.

Take your time in cutting and installing the decking. Each piece of the decking must match the other pieces in a particular octagon. Make the central octagon solid.

Space the decking boards ¼ in. apart and fasten them with 10d galvanized finishing nails. To prevent splitting, drill pilot holes for the nails in the decking boards. Use a nail set to put each nail slightly below the surface of the deck.

Once the decking is complete, start work on the lattice panels for the gazebo. Begin by cutting the longer sides of each 2X3 frame to the lengths shown in the diagram. Do not cut the shorter segments to length at this time. The grooving operation would be dangerous if done on short pieces.

Mill a ¾-in. X ¾-in. groove in one edge of each piece of the 2X3 stock to form the panel frames. Use a dado blade on your stationary saw to form the grooves. After the grooves are formed, cut the components to the lengths shown in the diagram.

Now, use a doweling guide to bore mating dowel pin holes in the frame components. Bore the holes 1⅜ in. deep to allow space for excess glue. Cut the pre-fab lattice material to the correct size for each panel. Use ⅜-in. X 2½-in. dowel pins and resorcinol glue to assemble the individual panels, adding lattice

screen during assembly. Clamp the panels with pipe or bar clamps and allow them to dry thoroughly.

Follow similar procedures to construct the solid panels made from 1X10s. Notice that these are built with the grooves in the flat sides of the 2X4 rails. Otherwise, the construction techniques are identical. Add the 1X10 redwood lumber panels later, during the gazebo's assembly, trimming the end pieces as needed.

Once the framed panels are dry, set up your stationary saw for a 67½ degree bevel rip. Trim the edges of the outermost panels to this angle. Be sure to make their final size match the actual opening between the posts. Also cut the angles in the rails.

Next, make the perimeter posts from two 8-ft.-long 2X4s. Use a dado blade in your saw to form the ¾-in. X 4-in. rabbets on each post half, as shown in Detail 4 of the diagram. When the post halves are bolted together, these notches will hold the rafters.

Attach one post to each side of the panel assemblies with no. 10 X 2¼-in. flathead wood screws. Countersink the pilot holes for the screws to set the screw heads just below the surface of the post half. Assemble all eight panel and post sections before proceeding further.

Position a pair of post and panel assemblies on the base of the gazebo, and join the posts with three ⅜-in. X 3-in. bolts, washers, and T-nuts. Clamp the halves together, then bore ⅜-in.-dia. holes for the bolts. Drive the T-nuts home, then install the bolts.

After the first pair of assemblies

are joined, add the remaining segments one at a time. Bolt the post halves together as you did before. Move the segments slightly to equalize the octagonal shape. Once all eight panel assemblies are in place, toenail the posts to the base with 16d galvanized finishing nails at the corners of the structure.

Now, make the king post from a length of redwood 4X4. Start with a piece at least 2 ft. long. Set your saw to rip a 45 degree bevel and rip off the edges of the post. Measure carefully to provide equal widths on all sides of the octagonal profile.

Form the finial at one end of this octagonal stock. Set up a dado blade on your saw and make multiple passes to form the 2-in.-wide notches. Set the dado blade to cut $\frac{1}{2}$ in. deep and cut the notch on each of the post's eight sides.

After all eight are cut, replace the dado blade with a combination blade and set the blade angle to 45 degrees. Set the depth of cut to just meet the bottom of the notch, then form the beveled ball at the top of the king post.

Finally, finish the king post by cutting it to its final 10-in. length. Add the screw hook to its bottom if desired, as shown in Detail 3.

Cut eight rafters next. Each is 96 in. long and is cut with 20 degree angles on each end. Nail two opposing rafters to the king post. Drill pilot holes for the nails and use 16d galvanized finishing nails, setting the nails below the surface of the wood.

With help, raise the assembly into position. Center the king post by equalizing the overhang of the rafters. Bore a $\frac{3}{8}$-in.-dia. hole through the perimeter post and the rafter, then bolt the two together as shown in Detail 4 of the diagram. Use a washer under the bolt head.

Add the remaining rafters, nailing them to the king post and bolting them to the perimeter posts as you did before.

Measure and cut $\frac{3}{4}$-in. exterior plywood sheathing panels to fit the roof segments. Measure each segment separately to allow for slight variations. Add the central stiffeners, then nail the sheathing to the rafters with 8d galvanized siding nails. Due to the compound angle formed by the rafters, the sheathing will not lie flush. Place your nails to enter the rafter near its edge.

Finish construction by applying cedar shakes to the roof. Shingle each segment, trimming the shingles near the edges to fit. Use 4d galvanized siding nails and allow a $3\frac{1}{2}$- in. to 4-in. exposure to the weather for the shingles. Take your time when shingling the roof to make a clean-looking pattern.

Once all the panels are shingled, cap each corner. Apply a layer of shingles to one side, then overlap with a layer on the other side. Where the roof meets the king post, caulk the joint with latex caulking compound.

Protect the completed gazebo with two or more coats of clear wood sealer and preservative, such as Thompson's Water Seal. This material is best applied with an airless sprayer. Be sure to wear safety glasses and a canister-type respirator. Allow 24 hours between coats.

Design and photos, courtesy of the California Redwood Association, 591 Redwood Highway, Suite 3100, Mill Valley, CA 94941.

TRADITIONAL GAZEBO

This octagonal gazebo will give your yard an elegant look, reminiscent of the Victorian period. It makes an ideal spot for outdoor entertaining. The lattice roof allows sunlight to filter into the gazebo, making it feel cooler on hot summer days. Comfortable seats line the inside of the structure.

Allow several weekends for construction, taking your time at each stage.

Choose straight lumber with tight knots for the gazebo. Hand-select your materials at the lumberyard if possible. If you plan to paint the gazebo white, as in the photograph, use fir lumber. If you prefer to leave the gazebo natural, select cedar or redwood lumber.

Begin construction by choosing a level site for the gazebo. Decide on the orientation of the structure, then lay out a 101-in. square on the site. Drive stakes at the corners of the square.

Check the square by measuring the diagonals of the layout. They should be equal to make the square perfect. Move the stakes, if necessary, to adjust the dimensions until the layout is correct.

Once you are satisfied, stretch string around the perimeter of the square. Wrap the string twice around each stake as you go, stretching it tightly.

From each corner post, measure 29½ in. along each side. Drive stakes in each of these locations. Once all of the stakes are in position, you have established the octagonal form of the gazebo.

The stakes mark the positions of the outer corners of the 6X6 posts. Locate the positions of the joist support posts, as shown in the diagram, and drive stakes at each position. Space these posts 32 in. on center.

At each of the stake locations, dig a 12-in.-dia. X 36-in.-deep hole for the concrete piers shown in the diagram. Remember that the stakes mark the outside of the posts, so offset the holes to center the posts on the piers.

Once the holes are dug, fill them with concrete. You can mix the concrete from bags of concrete mix or use pre-mixed concrete available in trailers at your local lumberyard or home center. You will need 30 cu. ft. of concrete, or just over 1 cu. yd.

Make the surface of the wet concrete flat, then insert ½-in. X 12-in. J-bolts in the concrete. Locate these bolts carefully to center them under the post positions. Leave 1 in. of the bolts protruding above the surface of the concrete to allow for brackets, nuts, and washers. Allow the concrete to dry for at least a week.

After the concrete has cured, you can begin to build the gazebo itself. Starting at one perimeter pier, use a long, straight 2X4 and a level to check the height of the other piers. Use a helper on one end of the 2X4 to raise that end to make the board level. Be sure to take notes on the distance the board must be raised to make it level. You will need these dimensions to cut the posts to make their tops level.

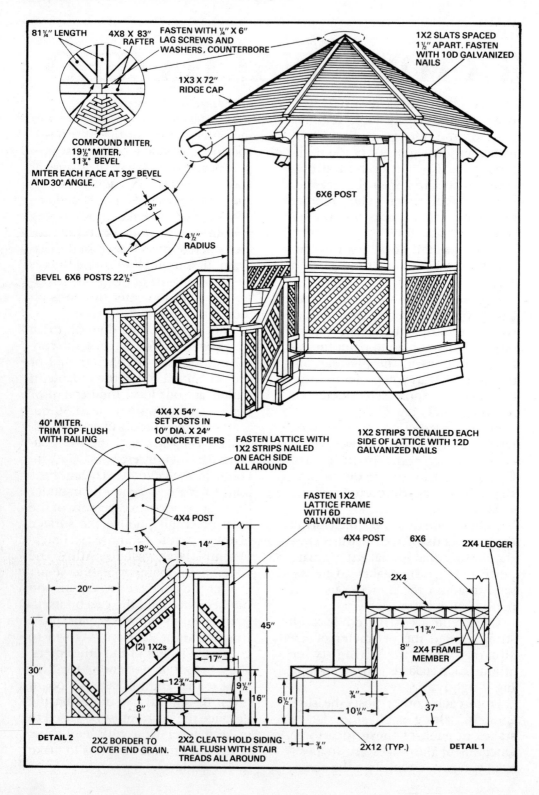

81¼" LENGTH

4X8 X 83" RAFTER

FASTEN WITH ¼" X 6" LAG SCREWS AND WASHERS, COUNTERBORE

1X3 X 72" RIDGE CAP

1X2 SLATS SPACED 1½" APART. FASTEN WITH 10D GALVANIZED NAILS

COMPOUND MITER, 19½° MITER, 11¾° BEVEL

MITER EACH FACE AT 39° BEVEL AND 30° ANGLE,

6X6 POST

3"

4½" RADIUS

BEVEL 6X6 POSTS 22½°

40° MITER. TRIM TOP FLUSH WITH RAILING

4X4 X 54" SET POSTS IN 10" DIA. X 24" CONCRETE PIERS

FASTEN LATTICE WITH 1X2 STRIPS NAILED ON EACH SIDE ALL AROUND

1X2 STRIPS TOENAILED EACH SIDE OF LATTICE WITH 12D GALVANIZED NAILS

4X4 POST

FASTEN 1X2 LATTICE FRAME WITH 6D GALVANIZED NAILS

4X4 POST

6X6

2X4 LEDGER

2X4

18"

14"

20"

45"

(2) 1X2s

17"

2X4 FRAME MEMBER

11¾"

8"

30"

12¾"

9½"

16"

6½"

¾"

10¼"

DETAIL 2

2X2 BORDER TO COVER END GRAIN.

8"

2X2 CLEATS HOLD SIDING. NAIL FLUSH WITH STAIR TREADS ALL AROUND

¾"

2X12 (TYP.)

37°

DETAIL 1

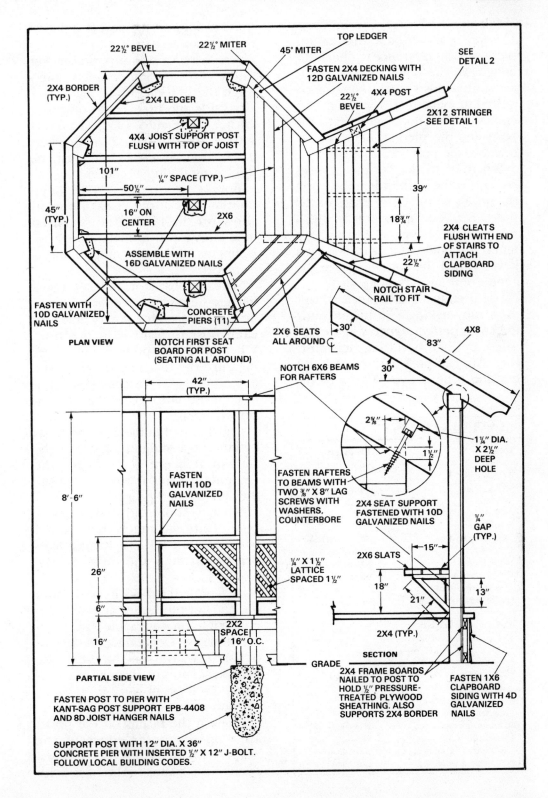

22½° BEVEL
22½° MITER
45° MITER
TOP LEDGER
SEE DETAIL 2

FASTEN 2X4 DECKING WITH 12D GALVANIZED NAILS

2X4 BORDER (TYP.)
2X4 LEDGER
22½° BEVEL
4X4 POST
2X12 STRINGER SEE DETAIL 1

4X4 JOIST SUPPORT POST FLUSH WITH TOP OF JOIST

101"
¼" SPACE (TYP.)
50½"
45" (TYP.)
16" ON CENTER
2X6
39"
18¾"
22½'

2X4 CLEATS FLUSH WITH END OF STAIRS TO ATTACH CLAPBOARD SIDING

ASSEMBLE WITH 16D GALVANIZED NAILS

NOTCH STAIR RAIL TO FIT

FASTEN WITH 10D GALVANIZED NAILS

CONCRETE PIERS (11)

NOTCH FIRST SEAT BOARD FOR POST (SEATING ALL AROUND)

2X6 SEATS ALL AROUND C̸L

30°

83"
4X8
30°

PLAN VIEW

NOTCH 6X6 BEAMS FOR RAFTERS

42" (TYP.)

2⅝"
1½"
1¼" DIA. X 2½" DEEP HOLE

FASTEN WITH 10D GALVANIZED NAILS

FASTEN RAFTERS TO BEAMS WITH TWO ⅜" X 8" LAG SCREWS WITH WASHERS, COUNTERBORE

2X4 SEAT SUPPORT FASTENED WITH 10D GALVANIZED NAILS

¼" GAP (TYP.)

8'-6"

¼" X 1½" LATTICE SPACED 1½"

2X6 SLATS
15"

26"

18"
21"
13"

6"

16"

2X2 SPACE 16" O.C.

GRADE

SECTION

2X4 (TYP.)

2X4 FRAME BOARDS NAILED TO POST TO HOLD ½" PRESSURE-TREATED PLYWOOD SHEATHING. ALSO SUPPORTS 2X4 BORDER

FASTEN 1X6 CLAPBOARD SIDING WITH 4D GALVANIZED NAILS

PARTIAL SIDE VIEW

FASTEN POST TO PIER WITH KANT-SAG POST SUPPORT EPB-4408 AND 8D JOIST HANGER NAILS

SUPPORT POST WITH 12" DIA. X 36" CONCRETE PIER WITH INSERTED ½" X 12" J-BOLT. FOLLOW LOCAL BUILDING CODES.

Cut one 6X6 post 102 in. long. This key post will be located on the pier used as a reference to check the heights of the other piers. Cut the remaining posts to the lengths required to make their tops level. Accuracy is important here. Mark the posts and the piers to help you remember the post locations.

When all of the perimeter posts are cut to the correct lengths, form the bevels on the outer edges of the posts. Set your table saw to rip a 22½ degree bevel. Adjust the rip fence and blade height to cut each bevel so that the cut emerges at the center of the post's side.

Use a scrap of 6X6 stock to test the setup, making adjustments until the cut is perfect. Once you are satisfied, cut one bevel on each post, then flip the post end-for-end and cut the other bevel. Use a roller

stand to support the post as it leaves the saw.

Attach a 6X6 post support bracket to the J-bolt at each perimeter pier. Align the brackets by laying a 2X4 alongside the brackets at opposite corners. The sides of the brackets should line up. Secure the brackets in position with nuts and washers, tightening the nuts securely.

Bore a 1½-in.-dia. X 1-in.-deep hole in the bottom of each post to allow for the J-bolt. The oversized hole allows you to make minor adjustments before fastening the posts in place.

Set each post in its bracket. Use a level to help you make the post vertical, and attach temporary braces to each post to hold it in position. When all of the posts are in place, measure the distance between the outer points of adjacent posts. Adjust the posts to make that dimension 42 inches.

Check the alignment of the posts by holding a straightedge across the flats of adjacent posts. When the straightedge lies flat on the posts, they are aligned properly.

When you are satisfied with the post positions, attach them to the brackets with 8d joist hanger nails driven through the holes in the brackets.

Next, cut the 6X6 beams. Miter the ends of the beams at a 22½ degree angle on your table saw or radial arm saw. Depending on the size of your saw, you may have to make two passes to cut through the material. Each beam is 42-in. long on the outer edge.

Position the beams on the posts, aligning the outer edges of the beams with the bevels on the posts. Toenail the beams to the posts with

MATERIALS LIST	
Item	**Quantity**
4X8 lumber	60 ft.
6X6 lumber	77 ft.
4X4 lumber	24 ft.
2X6 lumber	41 ft.
2X12 lumber	6 ft.
2X4 lumber	500 ft.
2X2 lumber	30 ft.
1X3 lumber	50 ft.
1X2 lumber	320 ft.
1X6 clapboard siding	96 ft.
½" pressure treated lumber	1¼ sheets
Pre-fab redwood lattice	72 sq. ft.
Concrete	30 cu. ft.
6X6 steel post brackets	8
4X4 steel post brackets	5
½" X 12" J-bolts with nuts and washers	11
¾" X 8" lag screws with washers	16
¼" X 6" lag screws with washers	16
8d joist hanger nails	as needed
4d, 6d, 10d, 12d, 16d galvanized finishing nails	as needed
Paint or clear wood sealer	as needed

12d galvanized finishing nails, setting the nail heads below the surface of the wood. Drill pilot holes for the nails to make the job easier. Once all of the beams are in place, remove the temporary braces.

Measure the distance between the key post and an adjacent post, then cut a 2X4 ledger to fit between the two posts. Use the same setup on your saw that you used to cut the beams.

Locate the top of the ledger 16 in. above the grade on the key post. Use a level to adjust the ledger, then toenail it in place with 12d galvanized nails. Again, drill pilot holes for the nails.

Continue adding ledgers around the structure, measuring each one individually for a close fit. Use a level to adjust each ledger.

Next, attach steel post brackets to the remaining piers located in the gazebo's center. Align their sides to be parallel with the floor joists, as shown in the diagram. Secure the brackets with nuts and washers.

Cut three 4X4 posts 18 in. long, then drill a 1-in.-dia. X 1-in.-deep hole in the bottom of each post, as you did for the main posts. Nail the posts temporarily to the brackets.

Now, cut 2X6 joists to fit the structure, beveling the ends at 45 degrees where necessary. Position the joists alongside the posts, then toenail the joists to the ledgers with 10d galvanized nails.

Once the joists are secure, mark the 4X4 posts to be flush with the tops of the joists. Remove the posts and cut them to the correct lengths after marking them to indicate their positions.

Replace the posts, this time nailing them through the brackets with joist hanger nails. Attach the joists to the posts with 16d galvanized nails.

Install the 2X4 decking next. Cut each decking board to fit the structure, making the ends flush with the outside of the 2X4 ledger. Measure the decking carefully, notching it around the posts. Space the decking boards ¼ in. apart. Use scraps of ¼-in. plywood to help control the spacing.

Nail the decking to the joists and ledgers with 12d galvanized finishing nails. Drive the nails, leaving the nail heads above the surface of the decking, then set them below the surface of the wood with a nail set.

Once the decking is in place, cut 2X4 stock to fit the outer perimeter of the posts. Install one row of these frame boards flush with the bottom of the decking. Install the other row at the grade line.

Now, add 2X2 studs between the 2X4 ledgers, toenailing them in place with 10d galvanized nails. Space the studs 16 in. on center.

Cut 2X4 stock to form the border around the deck area. Measure these parts carefully for a good fit, mitering the corners as you did before. Nail the border to the upper ring of 2X4 ledgers with 16d galvanized finishing nails set below the surface of the wood.

Now, cut ½-in. pressure-treated plywood to fit the framework you just installed. Nail this sheathing to the frame on seven sides of the gazebo, leaving the front side open.

Finally, complete the lower part of the gazebo by fitting 1X6 clapboard siding to the unit. Bevel the ends of the siding at the same 22½ degree angle used for the other components. Starting from the grade, nail the siding to the framework with 4d galvanized nails. Work carefully to keep the siding level and matched at the corners.

Now, form the rafter notches at the corners of the beams. Use an adjustable bevel set at 30 degrees to help you guide a handsaw as you make multiple cuts in the beams. Remove the waste with a chisel.

Cut two 83-in. rafters from 4X8 stock. Leave one end square, and cut the other at a 30 degree angle as shown in the diagram. Lay out the profile of the rafter end, then cut the curve with a saber saw. Use a blade designed to cut 4-in.-thick stock. Work slowly to keep the blade vertical in the wood. Better yet, rent a more powerful saber saw or use a band saw.

Working on a flat surface, join the peak ends of the rafter pair with two 1/4-in. X 6-in. lag screws. Counterbore the pilot holes to place the screw heads below the surface of the wood. Nail a temporary brace across the rafters to hold the angle.

Erect the rafters on the beams, using a helper to hold the structure while you attach the unit to the beams. Adjust the position of the rafters to center the peak over the gazebo.

Bore pilot holes for the 3/8-in. X 8-in. lag screws that attach the rafters to the beams. Counterbore these holes 2 1/4 in. deep with a 1 1/4-in.-dia. bit, then drive the screws into the beams and tighten them securely.

Now, form another pair of rafters, this time cutting 4X8 stock to 81 1/4-in. lengths. Place these perpendicular to the first pair, screwing them to the other rafters and to the beams as you did before.

Cut the remaining four rafters with compound miters on the top ends. Cut the 30 degree angle first, then bevel the cut edges at 39 degrees to form the points. Attach these rafters as you did the others.

Once the rafters are secured, begin attaching the lattice roof. Cut the lattice strips with compound miters on each end. Set your radial arm saw to cut a 19 1/2 degree miter and an 11 3/4 degree bevel. Start 10 in. from the lower edge of the roof, measuring carefully to determine the length of the first course of strips.

Cut eight 1X2 strips to length, then nail them in place with 10d galvanized nails. Place the nails near the edges of the rafters. After the first course is in place, use a scrap of 1X2 to establish the spacing between courses and measure for the next course. Continue this process until the roof is complete. A helper will make this job go much more quickly.

Cut 1X3 cap boards 72 in. long and nail them to the lattice, as shown in the diagram, to complete the roof. Use 10d galvanized nails driven through the center of the cap boards.

Build the lattice panels next. Cut the upper and lower 2X4 rails with 22 1/2 degree miters on the ends to fit between the posts. Toenail these in place with 10d galvanized finishing nails. Drill pilot holes for the nails and set the nail heads below the surface of the wood.

Cut pre-fab lattice panels to fit inside the rails and posts. Expand the lattice to make the strips square with each other, then cut the panels with your circular saw. Nail 1X2 strips to the posts and rails on both sides of the lattice to secure it.

Build seat supports next, following the dimensions shown in the diagram. Notice that the supports that fit the entrance of the gazebo must be installed at a 22½ degree angle, so bevel the components as necessary. Attach the supports to the posts with 10d galvanized nails.

Once all of the supports are in place, install the 2X6 seat boards, notching them to fit around the posts. Cut the ends of the seat boards at a 22½ degree angle to form the mitered joints. Position the joints over the center of each support.

Build the stair unit next. Cut three 2X12 stringers to the dimensions shown in the diagram. Lay one stringer out carefully, then cut it with your saber saw. Use this stringer as a pattern to lay out the remaining two.

Position the stringers against the 2X4 frame members at the locations shown in the diagram. Toenail the stringers to the 2X4 with 12d galvanized nails. The top of the stringers should be flush with the bottom edge of the decking.

Cut the 2X4 steps with 22½ degree angles on the ends to match the width of the entrance. Nail this step to the stringers. Position the remaining steps ¼ in. apart, then mark them to match the angle of the first step board. Cut the remaining steps, then nail them in place as well.

Now, cut two 4X4 posts and attach these to the lower step as shown in the diagram. Toenail the posts to the steps with 12d galvanized finishing nails, setting the nail heads below the surface.

Cut 2X4 handrails, notching one end of each rail to fit between the gazebo's posts. Toenail the rails to the post, then nail the other end to the top of the stair post. Add the lower rails, cutting them to fit.

Locate the positions of the outer posts, maintaining the 22½ degree angle of the railing. Dig 10-in.-dia. X 24-in.-deep holes at the post positions. Place 54-in.-long 4X4 posts in the holes, adjusting them to make the tops level, 30 in. above the grade. Align the posts with the existing rail.

Pour concrete into the holes and use a level to make the posts vertical. Allow the concrete to set, then add the handrails and lower rails as shown in the diagram. Cut the middle pair of rails with 40 degree bevels. Trim the middle handrail flush with the top rail.

Once the railings are in position, add 1X2 strips and pre-fab lattice panels as you did before. Finish the stairs by installing clapboard siding and 2X2 trim as shown in the diagram.

Once construction is complete, inspect the gazebo carefully, looking for sharp edges and rough surfaces. Sand these smooth with a pad sander. Round off all exposed sharp corners to a slight radius as you sand.

If you paint the gazebo, apply two or more coats of high-quality latex house paint. Use airless spray equipment for ease of application.

If you chose redwood lumber for the gazebo and wish to keep the original color of the wood, apply two coats of clear wood sealer and preservative. Allow the first coat to dry 24 hours before applying the second coat.

TRELLIS GAZEBO

Your outdoor entertaining will be enhanced by building this gazebo. Whether you are dining or just gathering together with family and friends, the mood will be light and airy, with a feeling of intimacy.

A trellis-style roof lets sunlight filter into the covered area, and the open structure allows cool breezes to flow through the gazebo.

You can build this gazebo on an existing concrete patio slab, or pour a new pad specifically for the project. It could also be installed directly onto an existing wood deck.

To install the gazebo on an existing slab, locate the post positions exactly. Measure the diagonals of the post positions to make the structure perfectly square. If the diagonal measurements are not equal, make adjustments in the post positions. At the center of each post position, bore a ½-in.-dia hole in the concrete with a carbide-tipped masonry bit in your electric drill or hammer-drill. Place a lag screw shield in each hole.

Attach 4X4 steel post brackets to the slab with lag screws driven into the shields. These brackets are available at hardware stores and home centers. Use the heavy-duty variety for this project. Notice that the posts are set at 45 degrees, with a side facing the center of the slab.

To make a new slab, level an area about 12 ft. square. Build a 10½-ft. square form of all-heart redwood 2X6 lumber. Nail the joints with 16d galvanized nails for weather resistance. Position the form on the site, digging shallow trenches to locate the top of the form 3½ in. above the grade. The form will remain in place, making an attractive border for the slab.

Check the squareness of the form before proceeding. Measure the diagonals in both directions. When they are equal, the form is square.

Level the form carefully using a long, straight 2X4 and a carpenter's level. For drainage, you may want to slope the slab slightly. If you do, make certain that the slope is even by checking the bubble on your level. Checked in the other direction, however, the forms should be level.

Cut points on 24 2X2 stakes, 18 in. long, and drive the stakes 2 ft. apart on the outside of the form. The tops of the stakes should be just below the top of the form lumber to allow for easy finishing of the concrete. Avoid forcing the form inward, and do not nail the stakes to the form. This makes them easy to remove later.

Locate the positions of the posts on the inside of the form. Measure from the corners of the form and stretch string between nails to locate the post centers. Mark the points at which the strings cross to locate the post positions. As you did with the form, check to make sure that your post positions are at the corners of a perfect square.

At each post position, dig a hole to form a foundation for the post.

To reinforce the concrete and help prevent cracking, lay in 6-6-10-10 concrete reinforcing steel mesh. Position the wire to lie in the middle of the slab, propping it up where necessary with small stones.

Add 1X3 dividers in the pattern shown in the diagram, or create your own pattern. Toenail the dividers to the form, and prop them up with small stones to match the height of the perimeter form. Use all-heart redwood for these dividers to prevent water damage.

You will need approximately 1¾ cubic yards of concrete for a 12-ft. X 12-ft. slab. The job will be easier if you know of a nearby home center that offers pre-mixed concrete in trailers. Otherwise you can mix the concrete yourself, or order it from a ready-mix concrete firm.

Pour the concrete into your prepared form, spreading it evenly. If necessary, press the wire mesh down into the wet concrete. Screed the concrete with a 12-ft.-long 2X4 to level the surface. You will need another person to help you with this job. Work the 2X4 back and forth

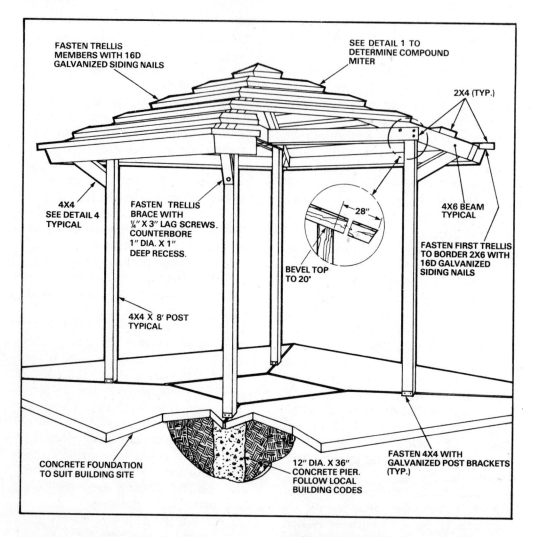

FASTEN TRELLIS MEMBERS WITH 16D GALVANIZED SIDING NAILS

SEE DETAIL 1 TO DETERMINE COMPOUND MITER

2X4 (TYP.)

4X4 SEE DETAIL 4 TYPICAL

FASTEN TRELLIS BRACE WITH ¼" X 3" LAG SCREWS. COUNTERBORE 1" DIA. X 1" DEEP RECESS.

28"

BEVEL TOP TO 20°

4X6 BEAM TYPICAL

FASTEN FIRST TRELLIS TO BORDER 2X6 WITH 16D GALVANIZED SIDING NAILS

4X4 X 8' POST TYPICAL

CONCRETE FOUNDATION TO SUIT BUILDING SITE

12" DIA. X 36" CONCRETE PIER. FOLLOW LOCAL BUILDING CODES

FASTEN 4X4 WITH GALVANIZED POST BRACKETS (TYP.)

across the form, moving from one end of the slab to the other. Add concrete to any low spots you see. It will take two or three passes to level the concrete and make it even with the top of the form.

Allow the concrete to set slightly, then finish the surface with a wooden float. You can simplify this job by bridging the new slab with a 2X12 set on concrete blocks. If you place this bridge across the center of the slab, you will be able to reach every part of the concrete.

MATERIALS LIST

Item	Quantity
4X6 redwood	32 ft.
4X4 redwood	40 ft.
2X6 redwood	84 ft.
2X4 redwood	200 ft.
1X3 redwood	36 ft.
4X4 galvanized post brackets	4
6" galvanized corner brackets	4
6-6-10-10 concrete reinforcing mesh	144 sq. ft.
½" X 10" J-bolts with nuts	4
¼" X 2½" lag screws	36
¼" X 3" lag screws	8
¼" X 2½" carriage bolts	8
6d, 16d galvanized siding nails	as needed
Wood sealer and preservative	as needed

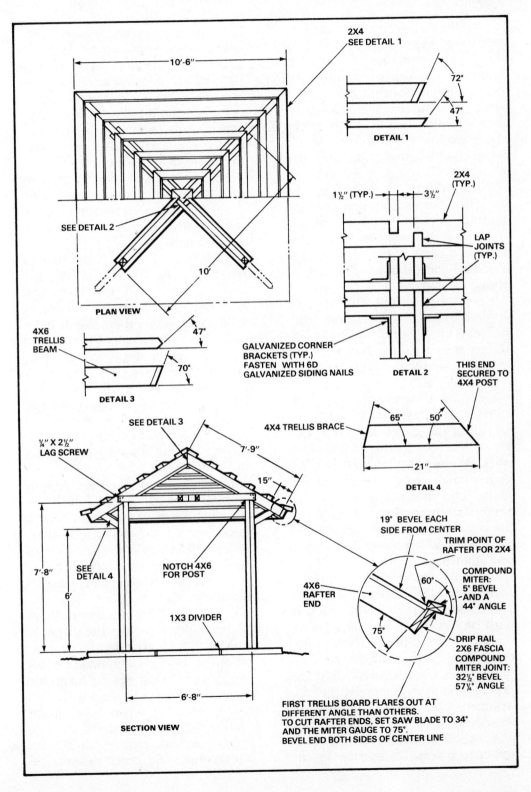

2X4
SEE DETAIL 1

72°
47°

DETAIL 1

← 10'-6" →

SEE DETAIL 2

10'

PLAN VIEW

2X4
(TYP.)

1½" (TYP.) → ← 3½"

LAP
JOINTS
(TYP.)

4X6
TRELLIS
BEAM

47°

70°

DETAIL 3

GALVANIZED CORNER
BRACKETS (TYP.)
FASTEN WITH 6D
GALVANIZED SIDING NAILS

DETAIL 2

THIS END
SECURED TO
4X4 POST

65°   50°

4X4 TRELLIS BRACE

← 21" →

DETAIL 4

SEE DETAIL 3

¼" X 2½"
LAG SCREW

7'-9"

15"

7'-8"

6'

SEE
DETAIL 4

NOTCH 4X6
FOR POST

1X3 DIVIDER

← 6'-8" →

SECTION VIEW

19° BEVEL EACH
SIDE FROM CENTER

TRIM POINT OF
RAFTER FOR 2X4

4X6
RAFTER
END

60°

COMPOUND
MITER:
5° BEVEL
AND A
44° ANGLE

75°

DRIP RAIL
2X6 FASCIA
COMPOUND
MITER JOINT:
32½° BEVEL
57¼° ANGLE

FIRST TRELLIS BOARD FLARES OUT AT
DIFFERENT ANGLE THAN OTHERS.
TO CUT RAFTER ENDS, SET SAW BLADE TO 34°
AND THE MITER GAUGE TO 75°.
BEVEL END BOTH SIDES OF CENTER LINE

The finish left by the float provides a non-skid surface, ideal for this type of structure. If you wish, however, you can smooth the surface even more with a steel trowel after the concrete sets semi-hard. Another finishing option is to sweep the partially set concrete with a broom, which makes an attractive pattern.

Before the concrete sets up, locate the post positions precisely and insert ½-in. X 10-in. J-bolts. As you did before, measure the diagonals to achieve a perfect square. Leave the threaded portion of the J-bolts 1 in. above the surface.

Keep the new concrete damp for several days so that it will cure without cracking. Spray the new slab lightly with a garden hose or, even better, cover the new concrete with a sheet of plastic.

Once the concrete has cured, remove the outer stakes and begin building the gazebo. Attach 4X4 steel brackets to the J-bolts with nuts. Position the brackets at a 45 degree angle, as shown in the diagram. Later on you will need to turn them slightly to align them. If you are building on an existing slab, attach the brackets with lag screws and shields.

Cut a 20 degree angle at the top of each post and install the 4X4 posts, fastening them to the brackets with lag screws. To provide a recess for the J-bolts and nuts, bore 1-in.-dia. holes, 1½ in. deep, in the ends of the posts. Use a level to adjust the posts as you install them. Further adjustments can be made during construction.

Next, cut four redwood 2X4s for the cross braces. Lay out the 1½-in.

X 1¾-in. intersecting notches in the brace components, as shown in Detail 2. Cut the notches with multiple passes on your table or radial arm saw. Check your saw's depth of cut carefully; the notches should be exactly half the width of the lumber. Use a sharp chisel to remove the waste from the notches.

Assemble the brace structure by interlocking the notches. Add corner brackets to strengthen the assembly, attaching them with 6d galvanized nails.

Tack stop blocks of scrap lumber to the posts, lightly nailing the blocks 2 in. from the top. These will hold the braces in place temporarily while you fasten them. With help, raise the braces into position. Adjust them to center the brace structure between the posts.

If necessary, turn the posts slightly to their proper orientation. Bore pilot holes and fasten the braces to the posts with ¼-in. X 2½-in. lag screws. Use washers under the screw heads.

Now, cut the 4X6 rafters. Start by ripping two 19 degree bevels on the upper surface of each rafter. If you have a tablesaw, you will require an outfeed roller stand or table. Set your saw's depth of cut to make the bevels intersect at the center of the rafter.

Cut the profiles of the rafter ends to the angles shown in the diagram. Cut the 70 degree angle on the ends first, then set the blade's bevel angle to 47 degrees to form the outer double bevel shown in Detail 3. To save setup time, make each cut on all four rafters.

Assemble one pair of rafters with a temporary 2X4 brace to keep the rafters stationary. With help, position the rafter pair on the top of the angled posts, with the peak in the center. Make sure these are centered before adding the remaining rafters.

Secure the rafters to the 2X4 cross braces with $\frac{1}{4}$-in. X $2\frac{1}{2}$-in. lag screws and flat washers. Now, raise another rafter, nailing where the first pair peak with 16d nails.

Finally, add the last rafter, again nailing at the peak's joint with 16d nails. Also secure the rafters to the 2X4 cross braces with $\frac{1}{4}$-in. X $2\frac{1}{2}$-in. lag screws and flat washers.

Lay out and cut the posts' angled braces to the dimensions provided. Once again, make matching cuts on each brace before changing your setup. Fasten these braces to the posts and rafters with $\frac{1}{4}$-in. X 3-in. lag screws. Using a 1-in. spade bit, counterbore the pilot holes 1 in. deep.

Rip a 60 degree bevel on the top edge of the 2X6 stock to be used for the fascia boards. Cut the fascia to length and cut the joints at a $32\frac{1}{2}$ degree bevel and $57\frac{1}{4}$ degree angle. Attach the fascia to the rafters with 16d galvanized nails.

Now, add the drip rail. Cut the 2X4 stock to length, mitering the corners to a 5 degree bevel and 44 degree angle.

Complete the shelter by adding the 2X4 trellis boards to the roof. Start by tacking one board in position. Use an adjustable bevel to mark both angles of the compound miters needed for the joints. Check the angles with a protractor, then transfer them to your table or radial arm saw.

Check your setup by making the cap. Cut four pieces of 2X4 stock to form a closed square, as shown in the diagram. Once all four pieces are cut, test them on the gazebo itself. It should fit squarely against the bevels on the rafters. If there are gaps, make minor changes in your setup and try again.

This test avoids wasting valuable lumber while you get the cutting angles exactly right. Once the cap fits properly, you can make the remaining components without changing your settings.

Working on an open-roof structure like this gazebo is potentially dangerous. For safety's sake, use a 10-ft. or taller stepladder. Stand on an intermediate rung, and avoid overreaching. Rather than lean out to drive a nail or fit a section of the roof, climb down and reposition the ladder.

Starting at the lower edge of the roof, cut the trellis members and attach them to the rafters with 16d galvanized siding nails. It is a good idea to measure each board separately to allow for slight variations in the structure. Bore pilot holes for the nails to prevent splitting. Move up the roof, spacing the trellis boards 15 in. apart. Add the cap at the top, and construction is complete.

Finish the shelter by applying two coats of a clear, non-toxic wood sealer and preservative, such as Thompson's Water Seal. This finish is best applied with an airless sprayer. Be sure to wear safety glasses and a canister-type respirator.

Design and photos courtesy of the California Redwood Association, 591 Redwood Highway, Suite 3100, Mill Valley, CA 94941.

VIII.

Hot Tub
Installations

REDWOOD TUB INSTALLATION

Installing a hot tub or spa in your yard is an investment in both your home's value and in your family's entertainment and pleasure. Relaxing in the hot water, with masses of bubbles swirling around you, is a sure way to ease the day's pressures.

This tub installation is designed around a 66-in.-dia. redwood and fiberglass spa. As shown in the photo, the deck fits close to the ground, next to a house, on a slab foundation. Our plans are adjusted to suit a home with a raised foundation.

Every aspect of the design can be customized to fit your particular application. You can increase the size of the deck area or adjust the height of the deck to match your home. Expand the fence on the edge of the deck, if you choose, surrounding the entire deck. If you need additional privacy, increase the height of the fence.

Plan the project carefully, and allow three or four weekends for construction.

Before beginning any spa installation, check with your local building authority for necessary permits. You may also need to adapt the plans to fit your local building codes. Some areas require you to place more support posts or to use deeper foundations. Take the plans in this book along for reference.

Begin building the project by laying out the deck area. Locate the corners and drive stakes to mark their positions. Check the layout by measuring the diagonals between the stakes. When the diagonals are equal, the deck is square.

Now, determine the final position of the spa itself within the area of the deck. Since a tub full of hot water can weigh more than a ton, plan for additional posts near the tub. Use the diagram as a guide to help you lay out the post positions. Be sure to include posts beside each joist, directly under the tub.

If you expand the length of the deck area, add additional posts to support the joists midway along their length. Space the posts to accommodate the joists, which are placed 16 in. on center. Be sure to include the stair support posts at one end or side of the deck, as shown in the diagram on page 293.

Once all the post positions are marked with stakes, dig 12-in.-dia. X 36-in.-deep postholes. Cut 4X4 pressure-treated posts to the length needed to make your deck the correct height for your house. Position the posts in the holes. Allow a 5-in. gap between the bottom of each post and the bottom of the hole. Prop the posts in position with temporary braces.

Now, check the heights of the posts with a long, straight 2X6 and a level. All of the posts must be at the same height. Also check to make sure that the posts line up with each other. The design shown here calls for 42-in.-long posts.

Fill the postholes with concrete mix. One bag should be enough for each hole. Check the posts once again for the correct height and to make sure they are vertical. Allow the concrete to set for a week or more before building the deck.

Next, install the 2X8 redwood perimeter frame members as shown in the diagram. Position these members 1½ in. above the tops of the posts to make the decking flush. Draw lines on the inside of the 2X8 frames to indicate the correct position for the joists.

Attach the framework to the posts with 16d galvanized nails. Add a second row of 2X8 redwood frame members on the back, where the fence is located. Another option is to add this second row all around after you have added the stairs. You will have to nail a 2X4 cleat onto the stair sides and then nail the lower border. Select attractive material, since this portion will be exposed.

Mark the 2X6 joist positions on the frame, then attach heavy-duty galvanized joist hanger brackets to the end boards. Observe the correct height, as marked on the frame ends. Use 8d joist hanger nails. These are hardened nails specially designed for this purpose. When us-

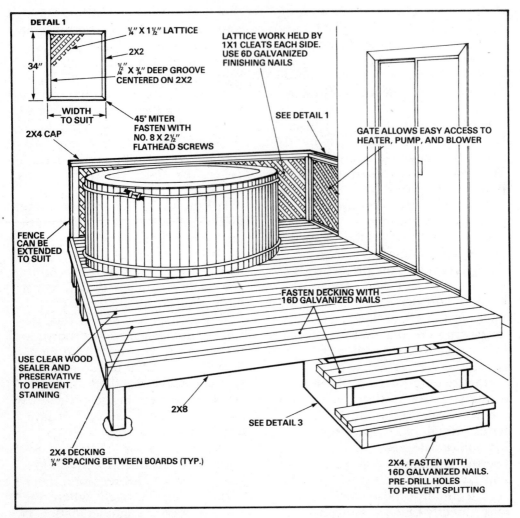

DETAIL 1

¼" X 1½" LATTICE

2X2

½" X ¾" DEEP GROOVE CENTERED ON 2X2

34"

WIDTH TO SUIT

2X4 CAP

45° MITER FASTEN WITH NO. 8 X 2½" FLATHEAD SCREWS

LATTICE WORK HELD BY 1X1 CLEATS EACH SIDE. USE 6D GALVANIZED FINISHING NAILS

SEE DETAIL 1

GATE ALLOWS EASY ACCESS TO HEATER, PUMP, AND BLOWER

FENCE CAN BE EXTENDED TO SUIT

USE CLEAR WOOD SEALER AND PRESERVATIVE TO PREVENT STAINING

2X8

FASTEN DECKING WITH 16D GALVANIZED NAILS

SEE DETAIL 3

2X4 DECKING ¼" SPACING BETWEEN BOARDS (TYP.)

2X4, FASTEN WITH 16D GALVANIZED NAILS. PRE-DRILL HOLES TO PREVENT SPLITTING

ing hardened nails, wear eye protection.

Cut 2X6 joists to fit inside the frame, and set them in the hanger brackets. Nail them in place with joist hanger nails. Where appropriate, nail the joists to the posts with 16d galvanized nails. Check the tops of the joists to make sure they are level before proceeding.

Decide on a convenient location for the heater, filter, and pump units that you purchased with your spa. These should be raised on a concrete pad or a wooden platform. If

you can, locate the pad out of sight but as close to the spa as possible.

If you choose a concrete pad, build a form of 2X4 lumber that's the size of the pad. Place the form on the site, then dig a perimeter footing on the inside of the form. Make this footing at least 12 in. wide and 12 in. deep.

Drive stakes around the form to secure it in position, then fill with concrete. Allow the concrete to cure for one week before installing the pump and other accessories. Install the heater and pump with lag

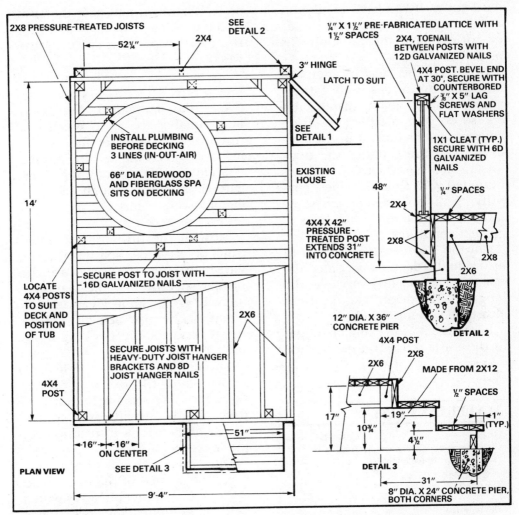

2X8 PRESSURE-TREATED JOISTS

SEE DETAIL 2

52¼"

2X4

3" HINGE

LATCH TO SUIT

¼" X 1½" PRE-FABRICATED LATTICE WITH 1½" SPACES

2X4, TOENAIL BETWEEN POSTS WITH 12D GALVANIZED NAILS

4X4 POST. BEVEL END AT 30°, SECURE WITH COUNTERBORED ⅜" X 5" LAG SCREWS AND FLAT WASHERS

SEE DETAIL 1

INSTALL PLUMBING BEFORE DECKING 3 LINES (IN-OUT-AIR)

66" DIA. REDWOOD AND FIBERGLASS SPA SITS ON DECKING

EXISTING HOUSE

1X1 CLEAT (TYP.) SECURE WITH 6D GALVANIZED NAILS

48"

¼" SPACES

2X4

2X8

2X8

2X6

4X4 X 42" PRESSURE-TREATED POST EXTENDS 31" INTO CONCRETE

12" DIA. X 36" CONCRETE PIER

DETAIL 2

14'

LOCATE 4X4 POSTS TO SUIT DECK AND POSITION OF TUB

SECURE POST TO JOIST WITH 16D GALVANIZED NAILS

2X6

SECURE JOISTS WITH HEAVY-DUTY JOIST HANGER BRACKETS AND 8D JOIST HANGER NAILS

4X4 POST

2X6

2X8

4X4 POST

MADE FROM 2X12

½" SPACES

17"

19"

1" (TYP.)

10¾"

4½"

16" 16"
ON CENTER

SEE DETAIL 3

51"

DETAIL 3

8" DIA. X 24" CONCRETE PIER, BOTH CORNERS

31"

PLAN VIEW

9'-4"

screws and shields.

If you would rather install the heater and the other support units on a wooden platform, build a 2X8 frame of pressure-treated lumber. Fasten the corners with 16d galvanized nails. Place the frame in its final position, and mark locations for postholes at the corners.

Dig 12-in. X 24-in. postholes, then install 28-in.-long 4X4 posts. Place the frame around the posts, then nail the frame to the posts with 16d galvanized nails. Locate the tops of the posts flush with the frame or just below its top. Fill the postholes with concrete and allow it to set. Check the top of the frame with a level and make any necessary adjustments.

Finish the pad by installing one or more joists and 2X4 decking. Attach the heater and other accessories to the platform with lag screws.

Install the pump, filter, and heater units on their pad, and run gas and electrical lines to them. Never hook your lines directly to the main gas line yourself. Contact your gas company. Be sure to follow local codes. If you have any doubts about your ability to connect the accessories, have the job done by professionals.

Now, plan the exact location and orientation of the spa itself. Plumbing layouts vary among manufacturers, so do your planning based on your particular unit. Run the necessary plumbing under the deck joists. Most spa installations are plumbed with flexible pipes, simplifying the job considerably. Be sure to label the individual lines to prevent confusion.

Cut the 2X4 decking material to fit inside the deck frame. Since the exact dimensions may vary over the length of the deck, take frequent measurements for a good fit.

Install the 2X4 decking, nailing it to the joists with 16d galvanized

nails. When you nail near the ends of the decking, drill pilot holes for the nails to prevent splitting the wood.

Space the deck boards ¼ in. apart. Use scraps of ¼-in. plywood between the individual boards to help equalize the gaps. When you reach the locations for the plumbing lines, notch the decking or bore holes to provide room for the pipes. Extend the pipes through the decking, allowing plenty of extra length for easy installation.

Most of the plumbing connections on a typical spa installation will be glued. Be sure to use the primer specified by the manufacturer. Keep the joints clean and use plenty of the pipe cement. Repairing leaks after the decking is installed is difficult.

The connections at the heater, pump, and filter are typically threaded. Use sealant liberally to prevent leaks. In all cases, follow the manufacturer's instructions to the letter.

Once the decking is in place, inspect the surface of the deck. Sand any rough or splintered areas with a belt sander. Protect the deck surface from water damage by applying two coats of clear wood sealer and preservative, such as Thompson's Water Seal.

Sealing the deck is an important step. When you use your spa, water is bound to spill onto the deck. Since spas must be chlorinated, the color of the redwood will soon bleach out if left unprotected.

Now, with help, position the spa itself on the top of the deck. Adjust its position to make plumbing attachments simple and neat. Follow the directions provided by the man-

MATERIALS LIST

Item	Quantity
4X4 pressure-treated lumber	40 ft.
2X12 pressure-treated lumber	5 ft.
2X8 redwood	100 ft.
2X6 redwood	120 ft.
2X4 redwood	500 ft.
2X2 redwood	as needed for gate
1X1 redwood	as needed for fence
Pre-fabricated redwood lattice	as needed for fence panels
Concrete mix	1 cu. yd.
2X6 steel joist hangers	12
No. 8 X 2½-in. flathead wood screws	8
¼" X 5" lag screws with flat washers	6
8d joist hanger nails	as needed
6d, 12d, 16d galvanized nails	as needed
3" hinges	2
Free-standing spa with accessories	1
Plumbing materials	as needed
Clear wood sealer and preservative	as needed

ufacturer to connect the plumbing lines to the spa. Once again, secure the plumbing joints carefully to prevent leaks. There is no need to fasten the spa to the deck. Its weight will keep it in place.

Make the stair assembly next. Form the stair stringers by ripping a 2X12 to a width of 10¾ in. If you have altered the height of the deck, adjust the dimensions to suit your application.

You can also make the stairs wider than the width given in the diagram. Simply add another 2X12 support in the middle of the stair unit.

Dig holes for the concrete piers that will support the end of the stairs, and fill them with concrete mix. Finish the concrete flush with the level of the surrounding grade. Once the concrete dries, nail the 2X12 stair stringers to the 4X4 posts as shown in the diagram. Add a 2X4 spreader to the front of the stair frame to keep the sides parallel.

Now attach the decking for the stair treads with 16d galvanized nails. Use the dimensions given in the diagram. If you have changed the width of the stairs, cut the tread material to allow a 3-in. overhang on both sides. Finish the end of the deck with 2X8 trim boards.

Complete the project by building the fencing. Cut 2X4 and 4X4 fence posts 48 in. long. Bevel one end of each post at a 30 degree angle. Attach the posts to the deck frame, spacing the posts evenly. Use ⅜-in. X 5-in. lag screws and flat washers. Drill counterbored pilot holes to set the screw heads below the surface of the wood.

Install the 2X4 top. Then attach the bottom rails between the posts, toenailing them with 12d galvanized nails. Now, nail 1X1 cleats to one side of the fence frame. Cut prefabricated redwood lattice to fit the opening and secure it with another frame of 1X1 cleats. Fasten the cleats with 6d galvanized nails.

If you choose, extend the fence shown here around two or three sides of the deck. If you need more privacy, cut longer 4X4 posts. For best results, use an intermediate rail between the posts, making two separate lattice panels.

If your deck extends past your home near one end, make a gate to provide easy access to the accessory units. Cut a frame of 2X2 stock, mitering the corners. In the center of each frame component, plow a ½-in. X ¾-in. groove with a dado blade in your table saw or radial arm saw.

For safety's sake, make sure that children cannot access the hot tub when adults are not present. If you do not have a fenced-in yard, extend the wooden fence all around the deck. Add another gate by the steps. You should also extend the deck fence if you have small children. Because of the deck's height, a fall would be dangerous.

Cut a panel of pre-fabricated lattice, then assemble the gate. Fasten the corners with no. 8 X 2½-in. flathead wood screws. Hang the gate with 3-in. hinges on the fence post, then install a suitable latch. You can make the gate swing in or out, depending on your particular needs.

Finally, fill the spa and check the plumbing connection for leaks. Once everything is in order, fire up the spa heater. You will be ready to ease your tired muscles in just a few hours.

Design courtesy of California Cooperage and Maryann Losik.

SPA INSTALLATION

If you would like to install a spa in your yard but want something different from the usual wooden deck, this spa installation might be just the answer. The elegant spa is flush with the ground, surrounded by carefully laid brickwork, and capped off by a lattice arbor.

You can duplicate this installation or adapt it to your own yard by changing the dimensions to suit your taste. The photos on pages 300 and 301 illustrate the spa installation techniques needed to build a project above or below ground.

Before beginning to install the spa, check with your local building authorities for any necessary permits. Depending on your local building codes, you may have to make slight changes in the installation procedures.

For safety, you should have your yard or the structure fenced to prevent small children from accidentally falling into the spa and perhaps drowning. You must fence in the back to brace the structure.

Start construction by laying out the overall site for your project. Choose a level area, then locate the corners of the brick patio. Drive stakes in the corners, then run a string line around the perimeter. Check the layout for squareness by measuring the diagonals. When they are equal, the layout is perfectly square.

Locate the positions for the posts that support the arbor. At each location, dig a 12-in.-square X 36-in.-deep hole for the concrete pier. Fill the holes with concrete and finish them flush with the grade. Insert a $\frac{1}{2}$-in. X 12-in. J-bolt at the center of each pier. Allow the end of the bolt to protrude $1\frac{1}{2}$ in. from the concrete.

Once the concrete has set, excavate the entire site within the string lines to a 6-in. depth. Cut the sides of the excavation square, making the bottom as flat as possible.

Now, excavate a hole for the spa unit. Dig the hole larger than necessary to allow for easy adjustments to the spa. At the same time, dig a trench to a convenient location for the heater, pump, and other accessories.

Locate the pump, heater, filter, and any other appliances on a concrete or wooden pad. Run wiring and gas lines to the accessories, following local codes. If you feel at all unsure about wiring and plumbing jobs, hire a professional to install these units. All wiring must be properly grounded through ground fault interrupters to prevent electrical shock. Do not hook any gas lines to a main source yourself; this must be done by a professional. Call the gas company.

Now, set the spa near the excavation and attach the flexible pipes supplied with the installation materials. Follow the manufacturer's installation instructions to the letter to prevent leaks. In most cases, the pipes are attached with cemented slip joints. Use the proper primer and cement, and keep the joints clean. Allow for the extra distance the pipe must run after the spa is set in place.

Lower the plumbed spa into the hole, routing the pipes in the trench you dug earlier. Prop the spa up on two sides with boards to make it level. The underside of the lip should be even with the grade outside of the patio excavation. Spend as much time as necessary to get the spa exactly right.

Once you are satisfied, partially fill the spa with water to prevent it from floating out during the backfill process. Check its height once again, and check for plumbing leaks.

The base of the spa must rest on a firmly packed bed of sand. Make this by partially backfilling the hole with a mixture of sand and water. Use enough of this mixture to fill the hole at least 12 in. above the base of the spa. Allow the water to drain into the soil completely, then add more of the sand and water mixture to fill low spots. Allow at least two days for the water to drain before continuing.

Finish filling the excavation by using the earth that you removed when you dug the pit. Pack the earth well as you backfill to prevent sags in the brick patio. Remove the temporary props from the tub's rim.

Once the spa is in place, prepare a sand bed for the brickwork. Using clean sand, fill the excavation to a 3-in. depth. Pack the sand with a water-filled roller. You can rent this tool from your local equipment rental outlet. Check the level of the bed with a long 2X4 and add sand wherever it is needed.

Take your time in preparing the bed. It must be level, smooth, and firmly packed to make the patio even. Extend the bed to allow the brickwork to fit under the rim of the spa. Make sure that the excavation

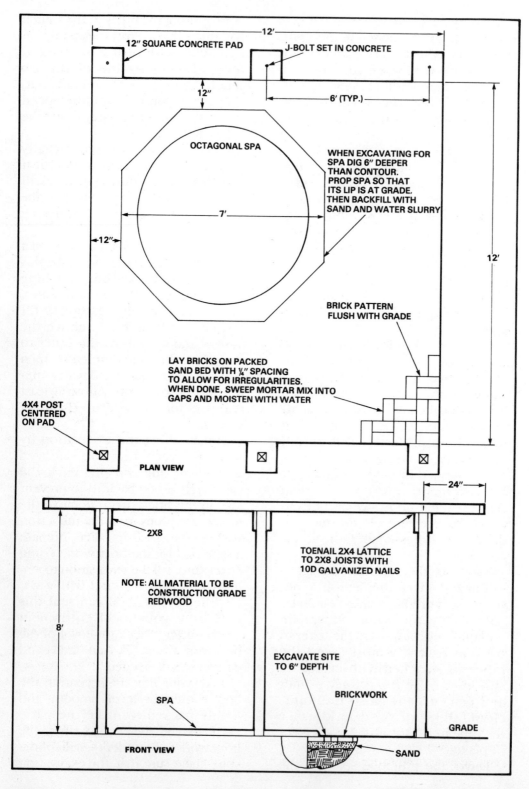

12'

12" SQUARE CONCRETE PAD

J-BOLT SET IN CONCRETE

12"

6' (TYP.)

OCTAGONAL SPA

WHEN EXCAVATING FOR
SPA DIG 6" DEEPER
THAN CONTOUR.
PROP SPA SO THAT
ITS LIP IS AT GRADE.
THEN BACKFILL WITH
SAND AND WATER SLURRY

7'

12"

12

BRICK PATTERN
FLUSH WITH GRADE

LAY BRICKS ON PACKED
SAND BED WITH ¼" SPACING
TO ALLOW FOR IRREGULARITIES.
WHEN DONE, SWEEP MORTAR MIX INTO
GAPS AND MOISTEN WITH WATER

4X4 POST
CENTERED
ON PAD

PLAN VIEW

24"

2X8

TOENAIL 2X4 LATTICE
TO 2X8 JOISTS WITH
10D GALVANIZED NAILS

NOTE: ALL MATERIAL TO BE
CONSTRUCTION GRADE
REDWOOD

8'

EXCAVATE SITE
TO 6" DEPTH

SPA

BRICKWORK

GRADE

FRONT VIEW

SAND

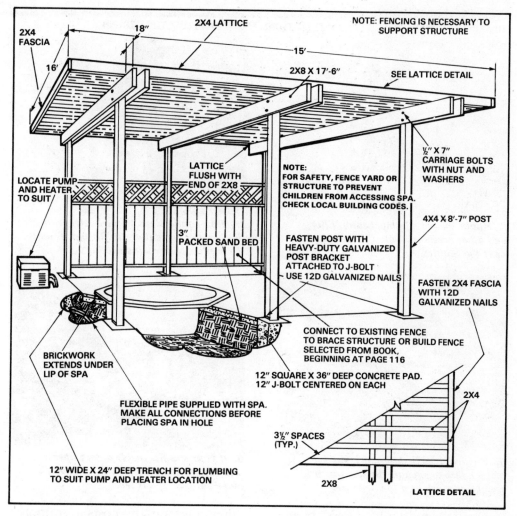

2X4
FASCIA

18"

2X4 LATTICE

16'

NOTE: FENCING IS NECESSARY TO
SUPPORT STRUCTURE

15'

2X8 X 17'-6"

SEE LATTICE DETAIL

LATTICE
FLUSH WITH
END OF 2X8

LOCATE PUMP
AND HEATER
TO SUIT

NOTE:
FOR SAFETY, FENCE YARD OR
STRUCTURE TO PREVENT
CHILDREN FROM ACCESSING SPA.
CHECK LOCAL BUILDING CODES.

½" X 7"
CARRIAGE BOLTS
WITH NUT AND
WASHERS

3"
PACKED SAND BED

FASTEN POST WITH
HEAVY-DUTY GALVANIZED
POST BRACKET
ATTACHED TO J-BOLT
USE 12D GALVANIZED NAILS

4X4 X 8'-7" POST

FASTEN 2X4 FASCIA
WITH 12D
GALVANIZED NAILS

BRICKWORK
EXTENDS UNDER
LIP OF SPA

CONNECT TO EXISTING FENCE
TO BRACE STRUCTURE OR BUILD FENCE
SELECTED FROM BOOK,
BEGINNING AT PAGE 116

12" SQUARE X 36" DEEP CONCRETE PAD.
12" J-BOLT CENTERED ON EACH

2X4

FLEXIBLE PIPE SUPPLIED WITH SPA.
MAKE ALL CONNECTIONS BEFORE
PLACING SPA IN HOLE

3½" SPACES
(TYP.)

12" WIDE X 24" DEEP TRENCH FOR PLUMBING
TO SUIT PUMP AND HEATER LOCATION

2X8

LATTICE DETAIL

is filled with 3 in. of sand.

Once the bed is finished, begin laying the bricks. One possible pattern is shown in the diagram, but you can lay the bricks in any pattern you choose.

Space the bricks ¼ in. apart to allow for irregularities. Use a bricklayer's hammer to trim the bricks as needed where they fit under the spa's rim. As you work, level the top of each brick with the adjacent one.

Once all of the bricks are laid, check the surface to make sure it is even. Sweep dry mortar mix into the gaps with a push broom. Fill the gaps to within ¼ in. of the tops of the bricks. When the gaps are filled, sweep the bricks thoroughly to remove all excess mortar.

Now, use a sprinkler with a very fine spray to wet the mortar. Water the area gently to avoid washing the dry mix out of the gaps. Wet the material thoroughly and evenly, but do not allow any standing water to accumulate.

Let the wet mortar cure for a few days, lightly sprinkling the area occasionally to prevent cracking.

CONSTRUCTION DETAILS FOR SPA INSTALLATIONS ABOVE OR BELOW THE GROUND

1. Mount the spa's pump, heater, filter, and other accessories on a protected pad near the utilities.

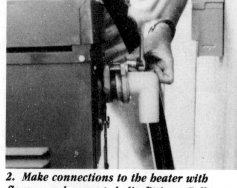

2. Make connections to the heater with flanges and cemented slip fittings. Follow the manufacturer's instructions.

5. For deck-type installations, build a sturdy deck to support the spa, which weighs as much as a ton or more.

6. If your spa fits inside a deck opening, size the opening carefully for a good fit. Make sure the spa is level.

Once the mortar has cured, begin building the arbor. Attach 4X4 galvanized post brackets to the J-bolts on the concrete pads with nuts and washers. Align the brackets carefully before tightening the nuts.

Cut six 4X4 posts 103 in. long. Bore 1-in.-dia. X 2-in.-deep holes in the bottom of each post to accommodate the J-bolt and nut. Place the posts in the brackets, propping them vertically with temporary braces, then attach them to the brackets with 12d galvanized nails.

Cut the 2X8 joists to the length specified in the diagram. Nail temporary cleats to the posts to support the joists in position while you work on them. Use double-headed nails for easy removal.

With help, put the joists in position, nailing them temporarily in place as you did the cleats. Now, bore through the joists and posts with a long ½-in.-dia. bit. Install ½-in. X 7-in. carriage bolts and secure the joists with nuts and flat washers.

Cut 2X4 lattice strips 15 ft. long, and begin laying the lattice roof. Start at the front of the arbor and place the first 2X4 strip 18 in. from the ends of the joists. Equalize the

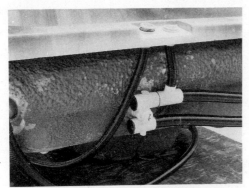

3. *Flexible pipe fits into slip fittings already attached to the spa. Use proper priming and cementing procedures.*

4. *Prime fittings with the correct primer, then apply a liberal coat of cement before assembly.*

7. *Prop the spa up to allow for decking or other finishing materials. Remove the props after supporting the base.*

overhang on both sides.

Toenail the lattice boards in position with 10d galvanized nails. Place a second 2X4 on its side to locate the position of the next board. Continue this process until all of the boards are in place. Make certain that the ends of the 2X4 strips line up. Place the last board flush with the rear of the arbor.

Add the 2X4 fascia boards to the ends of the lattice, attaching them with 12d galvanized nails.

Give the structure several coats of wood sealer and preservative.

Finally, clean the spa thoroughly,

removing any construction debris or sand before using it. Refill the spa with fresh water, and bring it up to the temperature you prefer.

Unlike aboveground spa installations, this spa must be kept full of water at all times. This is especially true during rainy weather or in areas with a high water table. An empty spa will float right out of the ground when the surrounding soil becomes saturated.

Design courtesy of California Cooperage and Rodney Lee.

MATERIALS LIST

Item	Quantity
Fiberglass spa with accessories	1
Plumbing and wiring materials	as needed
4X4 lumber	54 ft.
2X8 lumber	108 ft.
2X4 lumber	600 ft.
4" X 8" bricks	575
Clean sand	2 cu. yds.
Concrete mix	¾ cu. yds.
Mortar mix	6 bags
½" X 12" J-bolts, nuts and flat washers	6
4X4 galvanized post brackets	6
½" X 7" carriage bolts, nuts and two flat washers	12
10d, 12d galvanized nails	as needed
Clear wood sealer and preservative	to suit

IX.

Lawn and Garden Projects

A-FRAME PLANT STAND

This easy-to-build, two-level plant stand is ideal for your collection of potted plants. Painted in the color of your choice, it will be the highlight of your outdoor decor.

Begin construction by making the angled legs. Use a protractor to lay out the angles shown in the diagram. Mark the 18½ degree angles, then mark the third angle at a right angle to the top bevel.

Cut the leg with your saber saw or stationary saw. Use this first leg as a pattern to mark the other three.

Next, build the base of the stand. Cut two 18-in. and two 22½-in. lengths of 1X4 pine. Assemble these

to form the frame. Fasten the joints with no. 8 X 1¼-in. flathead wood screws and resorcinol glue. Drill countersunk pilot holes with a combination pilot bit for the screws. Use the same method to fasten all the joints in this project.

Add the top pieces of the base, spacing them evenly, about ⅝ in. apart. Before continuing, sand the base thoroughly, working down to 150-grit garnet paper.

Now, attach the legs to the base as shown in the diagram. Attach the 6-in.-long cleats to the top of the legs, flush with the top edge. Finally, add the two boards that make up the top shelf, driving screws into the cleats.

Sand the completed assembly well, starting with 100-grit garnet paper and working down to 150-grit. Finish the plant stand with two coats of high-quality exterior latex enamel in the color of your choice.

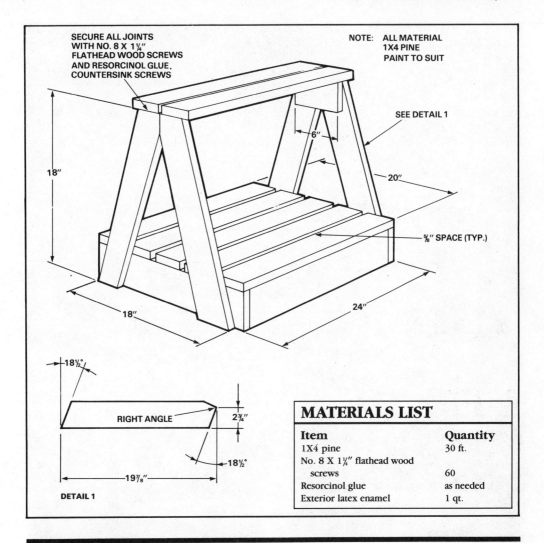

SECURE ALL JOINTS
WITH NO. 8 X 1¼"
FLATHEAD WOOD SCREWS
AND RESORCINOL GLUE,
COUNTERSINK SCREWS

NOTE: ALL MATERIAL
1X4 PINE
PAINT TO SUIT

SEE DETAIL 1

6"

18"

20"

18"

24"

⅝" SPACE (TYP.)

18½°

RIGHT ANGLE

2¾"

18½°

19⅞"

DETAIL 1

MATERIALS LIST

Item	Quantity
1X4 pine	30 ft.
No. 8 X 1¼" flathead wood screws	60
Resorcinol glue	as needed
Exterior latex enamel	1 qt.

CONSTRUCTION DETAILS

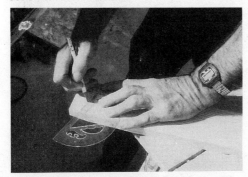

1. *Lay out the beveled ends of the legs with a protractor. After cutting one leg, use it as a pattern for the others.*

2. *Attach the legs to the base with flathead wood screws. Drill countersunk pilot holes with a combination bit.*

305

ARBOR ENTRYWAY

The entrance to your home makes a lasting impression on visitors. This entryway and arbor is designed to make that impression a favorable one. It provides filtered shade, a bench for outdoor seating, and space to display some of your favorite plants.

The arbor connects to your home, and can be modified easily to suit your particular application. Three posts are used to support the roof, leaving the area under the arbor unobstructed. The fourth side is supported by a ledger attached to your house.

If you decide to paint the arbor, you can build it of fir lumber. Choose redwood if you want to leave it in a natural finish.

Begin construction by locating the positions of the corner posts.

Check the layout to make sure it is square, then dig holes at the post locations for the pre-cast concrete piers. The tops of the piers should be approximately 2 in. above the grade. Use a long, straight 2X6 and a level to make the tops of the piers even.

Backfill the holes and compact the earth around the piers well. Attach 4X4 post brackets to the bolt installed on the pre-cast pier. Then cut 84 in.-long 4X4 posts and secure them to the brackets with 12d galvanized nails. Nail temporary angled braces to the posts.

Next, cut two 2X6 bench supports. Nail the supports in place with 16d galvanized nails. Check them with a level as you work. Once they are secured, cut the 2X12 seat and nail it to the supports. Use 16d

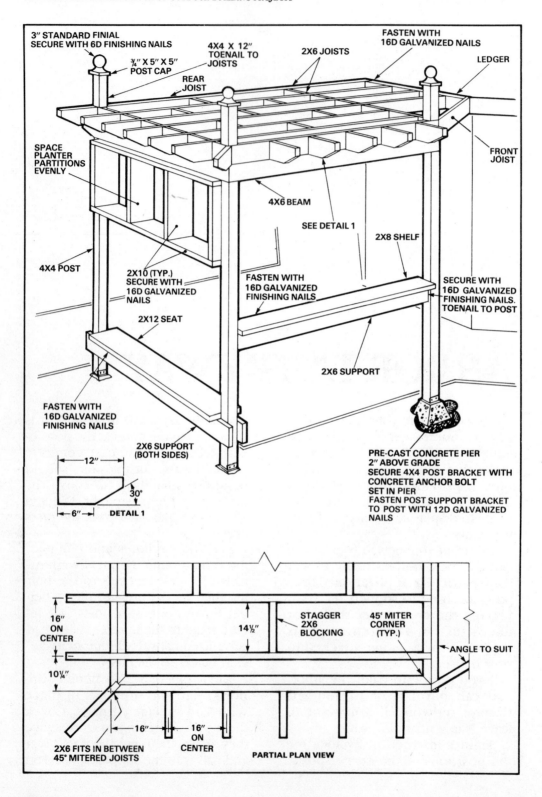

3" STANDARD FINIAL
SECURE WITH 6D FINISHING NAILS

¾" X 5" X 5"
POST CAP

REAR
JOIST

4X4 X 12"
TOENAIL TO
JOISTS

2X6 JOISTS

FASTEN WITH
16D GALVANIZED NAILS

LEDGER

SPACE
PLANTER
PARTITIONS
EVENLY

4X6 BEAM

SEE DETAIL 1

FRONT
JOIST

2X8 SHELF

4X4 POST

2X10 (TYP.)
SECURE WITH
16D GALVANIZED
NAILS

FASTEN WITH
16D GALVANIZED
FINISHING NAILS

SECURE WITH
16D GALVANIZED
FINISHING NAILS.
TOENAIL TO POST

2X12 SEAT

2X6 SUPPORT

FASTEN WITH
16D GALVANIZED
FINISHING NAILS

2X6 SUPPORT
(BOTH SIDES)

12"

6"

30°

DETAIL 1

PRE-CAST CONCRETE PIER
2" ABOVE GRADE
SECURE 4X4 POST BRACKET WITH
CONCRETE ANCHOR BOLT
SET IN PIER
FASTEN POST SUPPORT BRACKET
TO POST WITH 12D GALVANIZED
NAILS

16"
ON
CENTER

14½"

STAGGER
2X6
BLOCKING

45° MITER
CORNER
(TYP.)

ANGLE TO SUIT

10¼"

16"

16"
ON
CENTER

2X6 FITS IN BETWEEN
45° MITERED JOISTS

PARTIAL PLAN VIEW

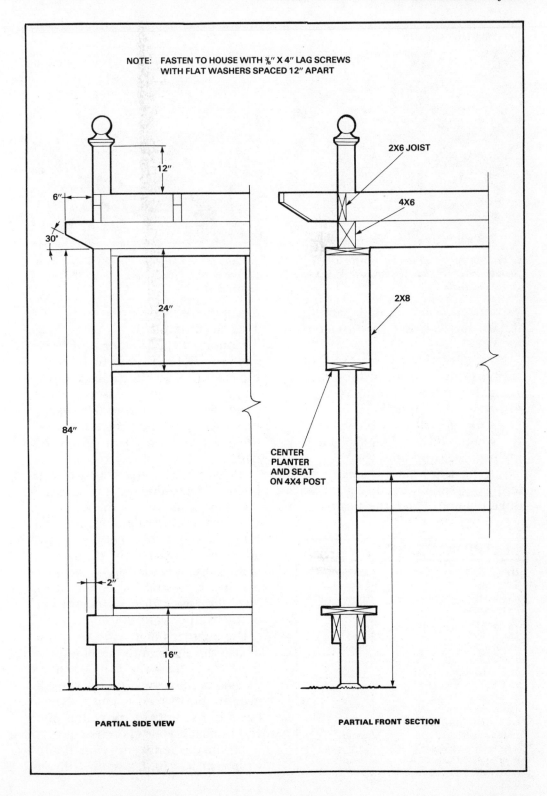

NOTE: FASTEN TO HOUSE WITH ⅜″ X 4″ LAG SCREWS
WITH FLAT WASHERS SPACED 12″ APART

2X6 JOIST

4X6

2X8

12″

6″

30°

24″

84″

CENTER
PLANTER
AND SEAT
ON 4X4 POST

2″

16″

PARTIAL SIDE VIEW

PARTIAL FRONT SECTION

CONSTRUCTION DETAILS

1. *Cut the miters on the joists with a portable circular saw. Set the base shoe to a 45-degree angle.*

2. *Lay the long joist on the 4X6 beams with the outer edges flush. Secure with 16d galvanized nails.*

galvanized finishing nails, setting the nail heads below the surface of the wood.

Now, cut and install the 2X6 shelf support on the front of the arbor. Toenail it into place with 16d galvanized finishing nails. Drill pilot holes for the nails to avoid splitting the wood. Add the 2X8 shelf, nailing it to the support.

Cut the 4X6 beams to length, mitering one end of each beam at a 45 degree angle. Place the beams on top of the posts, securing them with 16d galvanized nails.

Construct the planter unit next. Cut two 2X10 parts to fit between the posts, then cut the ends and partitions 21 in. long. Assemble the plant display shelf with 16d galvanized nails. Position the shelf unit, then secure it with 16d galvanized nails.

Measure from the wall of your home to determine the length of the 2X6 joist at the rear of the arbor. Allow for the overhang. On the overhang end of the joist, cut the 30 degree bevel shown in the diagram.

Place the joist on top of the 4X6 rear beam, flush with its end, then level the joist and mark its position on the wall of your house.

Use another length of 2X6 to establish the angle of the front joist to the house. Mark the wall to show the end of the ledger, then set an adjustable bevel to this angle. Now, cut the 2X6 ledger, beveling one end to match your chosen angle.

Fasten the ledger to your home with ⅜-in. X 4-in. lag screws driven

MATERIALS LIST

Item	Quantity
4X6 lumber	14 ft.
4X4 lumber	24 ft.
2X12 lumber	7 ft.
2X10 lumber	22 ft.
2X8 lumber	7 ft.
2X6 lumber	100 ft.
1X6 lumber	2 ft.
3″ wood finials	3
⅜″ X 4″ lag screws with flat washers	4
4X4 post brackets	3
6d, 16d galvanized finishing nails	as needed
12d, 16d galvanized nails	as needed
Pre-cast concrete piers	3
Paint or clear sealer	as needed

3. Nail the false joist ends to the outer joist with 16d galvanized nails. Space them 16-in. on center.

4. Install the angled trim between the 2X6 components. Miter the 2X6 parts at 45-degrees to fit.

into the house studs. Counterbore the pilot holes to position the screw heads below the surface of the ledger.

Secure the rear joist, nailing it to the ledger and the beam with 16d galvanized nails. Cut three additional joists 1½ in. shorter than the first. Install these, 16 in. on center, tonailing them to the beam and the ledger.

Next, cut the 2X6 angled connector. Bevel the ends to match the angle you chose earlier. Rest one end on the post, then nail the other end to the ledger with 16d galvanized nails. Cut a 2X6 to fit between the connector at the beam's end and the closest joist; nail it into place.

Once this part is in place, cut the angled corner joist, cutting the 30 degree angle as you did on the other joists. Position it on the corner post at a 45 degree angle, then measure for the front joist. Bevel both ends of this joist to match the angles of the connector and the false corner joist.

Cut the remaining false joist ends and nail them to the front joist. Start

at the corner away from the house, and space these trim pieces 16 in. on center.

Cut the remaining two joists to length, matching their ends with the other joists. Nail these to the posts and to the 2X6 cross brace.

Add the blocking at the front and rear of the arbor, nailing them in place with 16d galvanized nails. Measure each piece for a close fit. Add the staggered blocking between the joists as well.

Cut three 12-in.-long 4X4 trim posts. On top of each of these, attach a 5-in. X 5-in. pad of ¾-in. stock and a 3-in. finial with 6d finishing nails. Nail the posts to the corners of the arbor with 12d galvanized nails.

Sand the completed arbor to remove rough areas. Round off any sharp corners as you sand. Paint the arbor in the color of your choice, using high-quality house paint. If you built the arbor of redwood and want a natural finish, give the structure two coats of clear wood sealer and preservative.

BUNNY PLANTER

Rabbits and garden plants are not normally a good combination. The rabbits on this whimsical planter, however, will never eat your plants or multiply to fill your yard.

Copy the designs shown in the diagram onto ½-in. graph paper. Cut two 8-in. X 10-in. pieces of ¾-in. exterior plywood. Transfer the designs to one piece of the plywood with carbon paper.

Copy one rabbit pattern and six tulips, spacing them evenly around the plywood surface. Next, tack the two pieces of plywood together and cut out the patterns on your band saw.

Now, cut the five parts for the planter box itself. Use pressure-treated lumber to protect the planter from water damage.

Bore six ½-in. drainage holes in the base of the planter box with a spade bit. Use a backup board to minimize splintering. Next, bore the ¼-in.-dia. X ½-in.-deep holes for the tulip stems. Space these randomly, as shown in the diagram.

Assemble the planter box with 6d galvanized finishing nails and resorcinol glue. Sand the assembled planter thoroughly.

Before adding the rabbits and the flowers, paint the individual components with spray enamel. Paint the planter box and the flower stems green and the rabbits gray. Paint the tulip heads, in groups of three, blue, red, yellow, and orange.

Once the paint has dried, attach the bunnies to the box with 3d galvanized finishing nails and glue. Nail from inside the box. Glue the flower heads to the stems, then glue the stems into the pre-drilled holes in the base. Mix the colors of the flowers in an attractive pattern.

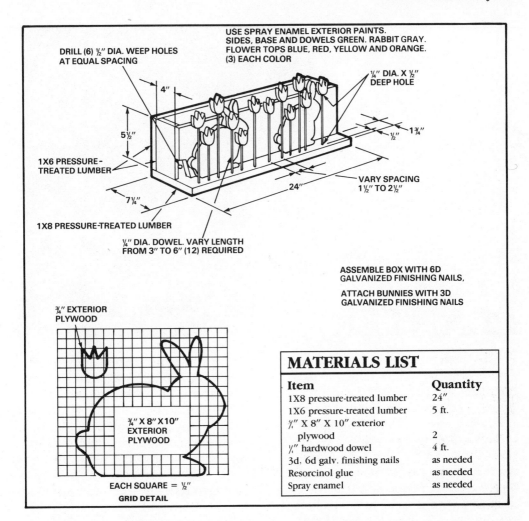

DRILL (6) ½" DIA. WEEP HOLES AT EQUAL SPACING

USE SPRAY ENAMEL EXTERIOR PAINTS. SIDES, BASE AND DOWELS GREEN. RABBIT GRAY. FLOWER TOPS BLUE, RED, YELLOW AND ORANGE. (3) EACH COLOR

¼" DIA. X ½" DEEP HOLE

4"

5½"

1¾"

½"

1X6 PRESSURE-TREATED LUMBER

VARY SPACING 1½" TO 2½"

24"

7¼"

1X8 PRESSURE-TREATED LUMBER

¼" DIA. DOWEL. VARY LENGTH FROM 3" TO 6" (12) REQUIRED

ASSEMBLE BOX WITH 6D GALVANIZED FINISHING NAILS,

ATTACH BUNNIES WITH 3D GALVANIZED FINISHING NAILS

¾" EXTERIOR PLYWOOD

¾" X 8" X10" EXTERIOR PLYWOOD

EACH SQUARE = ½"

GRID DETAIL

MATERIALS LIST

Item	Quantity
1X8 pressure-treated lumber	24"
1X6 pressure-treated lumber	5 ft.
¾" X 8" X 10" exterior plywood	2
¼" hardwood dowel	4 ft.
3d, 6d galv. finishing nails	as needed
Resorcinol glue	as needed
Spray enamel	as needed

CONSTRUCTION DETAILS

1. Copy the bunny and tulip designs onto graph paper. Then transfer the design to the wood with carbon paper.

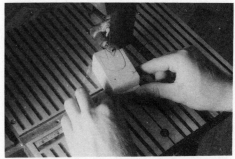

2. Cut the patterns with your band saw. Tack the parts together to cut two patterns at one time.

CEDAR PLANTER

This attractive cedar planter, designed with large box joints, makes an attractive display for any medium-sized plant specimen. The cedar construction insures a long life.

Start building by cutting 2X8 cedar stock, 16 in. long. You will need eight pieces. Next, lay out the 3⅝-in. X 1½-in. notches. Cut these carefully with a saber saw. For best results, use a fine-toothed blade.

Make a trial assembly of the box and mark the positions of each part as it relates to the adjacent components.

Use a drill press to bore ⅜-in.-dia. holes in the notches. Lay out the positions of the holes carefully. Make ¾-in. X ½-in. deep counterbores as shown in the diagram.

If the sides do not align properly use a doweling jig to bore mating dowel pin holes in each pair of the upper and lower boards. Bore ⅜-in.-dia. holes, ⅞ in. deep, for the dowel pins.

Assemble the upper and lower halves of the planter separately with resorcinol glue, then join the two halves with glue.

Insert the threaded rods in the holes, and add washers and nuts to each end. Tighten the assembly securely with a socket wrench, keeping the rods below the surface of the wood at both ends.

Build a frame of 2X2 material for the base of the planter. Cut the ¾-in. exterior plywood bottom and attach it to the frame with 6d galvanized nails. Bore ½-in. dia. weep holes, spacing evenly.

Insert the base in the box, allowing it to extend ⅜ in. from the bottom. Nail the base frame to the sides with 8d galvanized nails.

Sand the completed project well, then apply two coats of a clear wood finish. You can use either clear sealer or polyurethane varnish.

Design by Jeff Milstein. Photos courtesy of Western Wood Products Association, Yeon Building, Portland, OR 97204.

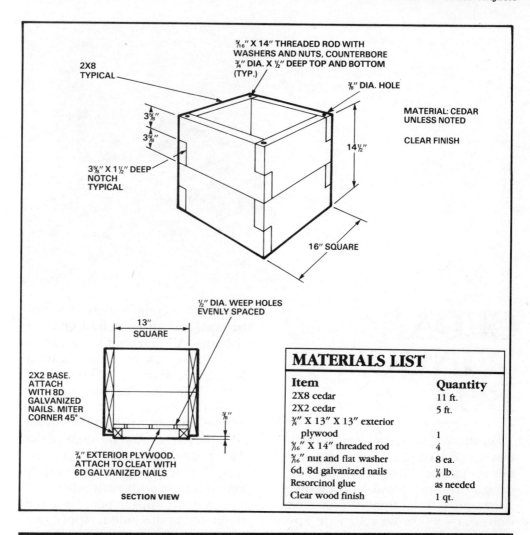

2X8
TYPICAL

⁵⁄₁₆″ X 14″ THREADED ROD WITH
WASHERS AND NUTS, COUNTERBORE
¾″ DIA. X ½″ DEEP TOP AND BOTTOM
(TYP.)

⅜″ DIA. HOLE

MATERIAL: CEDAR
UNLESS NOTED

CLEAR FINISH

3⅝″

3⅝″

14½″

3⅝″ X 1½″ DEEP
NOTCH
TYPICAL

16″ SQUARE

13″
SQUARE

½″ DIA. WEEP HOLES
EVENLY SPACED

2X2 BASE.
ATTACH
WITH 8D
GALVANIZED
NAILS. MITER
CORNER 45°

¾″

¾″ EXTERIOR PLYWOOD.
ATTACH TO CLEAT WITH
6D GALVANIZED NAILS

SECTION VIEW

MATERIALS LIST

Item	Quantity
2X8 cedar	11 ft.
2X2 cedar	5 ft.
¾″ X 13″ X 13″ exterior plywood	1
⁵⁄₁₆″ X 14″ threaded rod	4
⁵⁄₁₆″ nut and flat washer	8 ea.
6d, 8d galvanized nails	¼ lb.
Resorcinol glue	as needed
Clear wood finish	1 qt.

CONSTRUCTION DETAILS

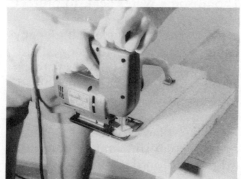

1. Cut the notches in the planter's sides carefully with a fine-toothed blade in your saber saw.

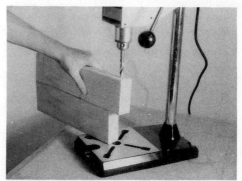

2. Drill the holes for the threaded rods on a drill press. Counterbore where indicated in the diagram.

315

CEDAR WINDOW BOX

Window boxes are a traditional way to add life and color to your home. This one, built of cedar for weather resistance and an attractive appearance, is designed to mount under any window. Its rustic appearance is designed to complement any home.

Measure the width of the window you choose, then cut the front and rear of the box to match the measurement. The bottom board of the box is $1\frac{1}{2}$ in. shorter than the front board. Cut the rest of the 1X8 components to the dimensions shown in the diagram.

Cut the 1X1 cleats to fit your dimensions, then install the cleats on the front and rear boards with no. 8 X $1\frac{1}{4}$-in. brass flathead wood screws. Drill countersunk pilot holes with a combination pilot bit. Use waterproof resorcinol glue on all joints. All screws should be located on the inside of the box for a clean appearance.

Bore $\frac{1}{4}$-in.-dia. drainage holes in the bottom of the planter, then fasten the bottom to the cleats with glue and screws. Add the ends of the planter, driving screws through the cleats. Locate the screws so that they don't interfere with each other.

For a rustic appearance, leave the rough cedar unsanded. Apply two coats of clear wood sealer, such as Thompson's Water Seal, to protect the wood from water damage.

Attach the window box under any window sill. If you have wood siding, use no. 10 X 2-in. brass flathead wood screws. For other types of siding, use an appropriate fastening technique.

Fill the planter box with a high-quality planting mix, and add brightly colored annual flowers. If the box is located in a kitchen window, you may want to plant a miniature herb garden.

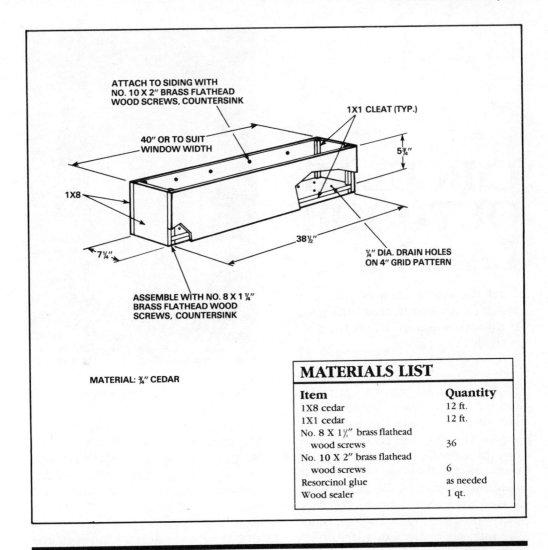

ATTACH TO SIDING WITH
NO. 10 X 2″ BRASS FLATHEAD
WOOD SCREWS, COUNTERSINK

1X1 CLEAT (TYP.)

40″ OR TO SUIT
WINDOW WIDTH

5¾″

1X8

38½″

7¼″

¼″ DIA. DRAIN HOLES
ON 4″ GRID PATTERN

ASSEMBLE WITH NO. 8 X 1¼″
BRASS FLATHEAD WOOD
SCREWS, COUNTERSINK

MATERIAL: ¾″ CEDAR

MATERIALS LIST

Item	Quantity
1X8 cedar	12 ft.
1X1 cedar	12 ft.
No. 8 X 1¼″ brass flathead wood screws	36
No. 10 X 2″ brass flathead wood screws	6
Resorcinol glue	as needed
Wood sealer	1 qt.

CONSTRUCTION DETAILS

1. Bore drainage holes in the bottom board. Bore ¼-in.-dia. holes, 4 in. on center, and use a backup board.

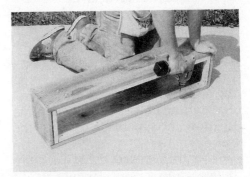

2. Attach the cleats with resorcinol glue and brass flathead wood screws. Use a pilot bit to countersink pilot holes.

CIRCULAR OUTDOOR LAMP

Candle lamps are a popular and attractive way to light up the great outdoors when you entertain on your deck or patio.

This round, slatted lamp combines simplicity with an attractive look. Best of all, you can probably make the lamp from scrap materials left over from other projects.

Start building the lamp by laying out the circular components. Use a compass to draw the circular dimensions shown in the diagram.

Cut the outer diameter of each part with a sharp, fine-toothed blade in your saber saw. Cut carefully to keep the blade vertical in the saw kerf. Saber saw blades tend to creep when cutting curves, so avoid putting any sideways pressure on the saw.

Next, cut out the inner circle on the upper component. Drill a $5/16$-in.-dia. starting hole just inside the line to allow the saw blade to enter the cut.

Form the recess in the lower component with a $1/4$-in. straight bit in your router. Guide the router slowly for best results.

Now, cut the sixteen $1/16$-in. X 1-in. wooden strips that make up the body of the lamp. Starting with 1-in.-thick wood stock, rip successive strips off one edge. Use a band saw or a table saw for this operation. Lay out radial lines on the circular parts to space the strips equally. Draw four lines, crossing each other at 90 degrees and 45 degrees, on both upper and lower pieces.

Attach the strips to the circles with $3/4$-in. brass brads and glue, always working from one side of the lamp to the other. When the eight strips are attached, space the other eight evenly.

Finish the project with two coats of wood sealer and add a candle in a glass holder. For safety's sake use only a tall glassed candle that is as high as the project and make sure that flammables are kept well away from the lit candle.

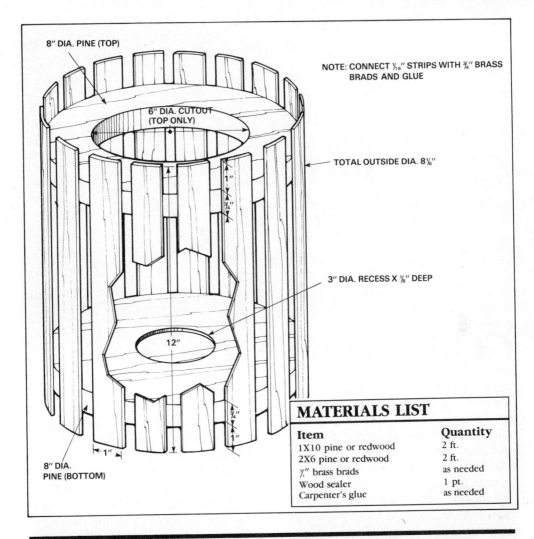

8" DIA. PINE (TOP)

NOTE: CONNECT ⅟₁₆" STRIPS WITH ¾" BRASS BRADS AND GLUE

6" DIA. CUTOUT (TOP ONLY)

TOTAL OUTSIDE DIA. 8⅛"

1"

¾"

3" DIA. RECESS X ⅛" DEEP

12"

¾"

1"

← 1" →

8" DIA. PINE (BOTTOM)

MATERIALS LIST

Item	Quantity
1X10 pine or redwood	2 ft.
2X6 pine or redwood	2 ft.
¾" brass brads	as needed
Wood sealer	1 pt.
Carpenter's glue	as needed

CONSTRUCTION DETAILS

1. Rout the recess for the candle holder with a straight bit in your router.

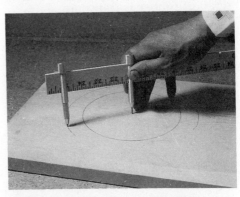

2. Use a beam compass to draw the circular profiles of the lamp's frame.

CORDWOOD RACK

Proper firewood storage is an important part of getting the most for your heating dollar. Besides keeping your valuable wood off the ground, this rack also provides easy access to the fuel.

Select pressure-treated lumber for the rack to protect it from insect and water damage. Since most firewood contains insect pests, using the right type of lumber is important.

Cut all the wood components to the sizes shown in the diagram. Cut the 30 degree bevels on the upper ends of the 2X4 braces, but do not cut the lower angles at this time.

Form $1\frac{1}{2}$-in. X $5\frac{1}{2}$-in. notches in the inner posts. Make multiple cuts with your table or radial arm saw, then remove the waste with a sharp chisel. Check the size of the notches before assembling the rack.

Install the crosspieces in the notches with 16d galvanized nails, then add the outer posts and the 2X4 rails. Use 12d galvanized nails when nailing through the thickness of two boards. Check the assembly for squareness as you go.

Add the 2X4 lower post segments and the lower cross braces, nailing them securely in place. Notice that the edge of the 2X4 is flush with the inside of the post.

Clamp one angled brace in position, then mark the lower angles. Cut this brace, and use it as a pattern to lay out the remaining three braces. Nail the braces in position with 12d galvanized nails to complete the project.

Place the rack in a sheltered area, at least 8 ft. from your home. This helps to keep insects in the firewood away from your house. Use concrete stepping stones or piers under the legs if you place the rack on soft ground.

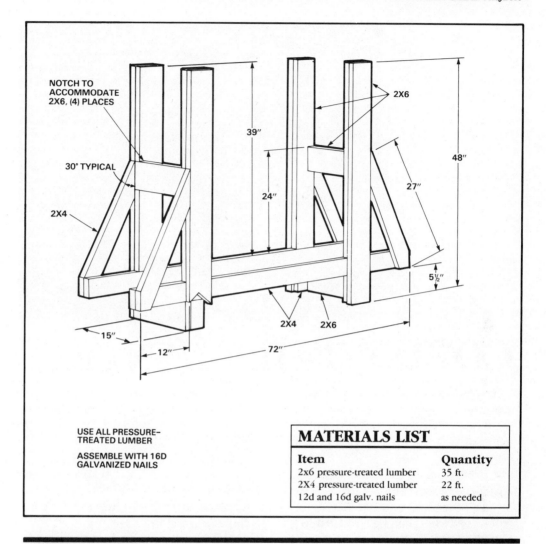

NOTCH TO ACCOMMODATE 2X6, (4) PLACES

30° TYPICAL

2X4

2X6

39″

48″

24″

27″

5½″

15″

12″

72″

2X4   2X6

USE ALL PRESSURE-TREATED LUMBER

ASSEMBLE WITH 16D GALVANIZED NAILS

MATERIALS LIST

Item	Quantity
2x6 pressure-treated lumber	35 ft.
2X4 pressure-treated lumber	22 ft.
12d and 16d galv. nails	as needed

CONSTRUCTION DETAILS

1. Nail the notched 2X6 posts to the outer post with 12d galvanized nails. Check the notch for size before assembly.

2. Clamp one angled brace to the frame, then mark the lower angles. Use this brace as a pattern.

COTTONTAIL PLANTER

This slightly whimsical planter will add a light touch to your patio. Its white plywood rabbits seem intent on devouring any plants you choose.

Construction of the project is straightforward. Start with a 5-ft. length of straight and flat 1X8 cedar stock (redwood can be substituted). Cut the base of the planter first.

Next, attach a dado blade to your table or radial arm saw. Set the blade to cut a ¾-in.-wide rabbet, then set the blade angle to 14½ degrees. Form a ¾-in. X ¼-in.-deep rabbet along one edge of the stock. Notice that the rabbet should be deepest on the outer edge.

Replace the dado blade with a combination planer-type blade, and set up your saw to cut a compound miter at a 14½ degree angle, 43½ degree bevel.

Cut the sides of the planter, mak-ing the first cut from one edge of the stock, and the second from the opposite edge. Take care to make all the sides identical.

Bore four, evenly spaced, ½-in.-dia. weep holes in the base of the planter. Assemble the box with waterproof resorcinol glue and 4d galvanized finishing nails.

Now, enlarge the bunny pattern onto ½-in. grid paper. Transfer the design to ¼-in. exterior plywood with carbon paper and cut out the rabbits. Use a band saw, jigsaw, or saber saw, cutting relief lines where necessary. Form the bunny's tail opening with a ¾-in.-dia. drill.

Before attaching the patterns to the planter box, paint the rabbits white with exterior enamel. Spray paint will do the job best. Fasten the patterns to the box, as shown in the diagram, with resorcinol glue and ¾-in. brass brads.

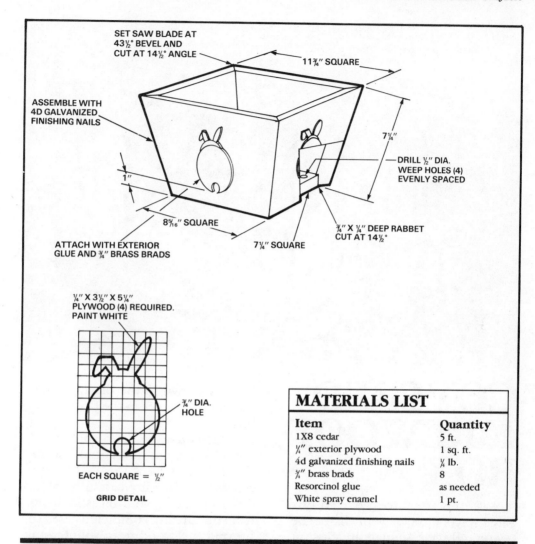

SET SAW BLADE AT
43½° BEVEL AND
CUT AT 14½° ANGLE

11¾" SQUARE

ASSEMBLE WITH
4D GALVANIZED
FINISHING NAILS

7¼"

1"

DRILL ½" DIA.
WEEP HOLES (4)
EVENLY SPACED

8⁵⁄₁₆" SQUARE

7¼" SQUARE

¾" X ¼" DEEP RABBET
CUT AT 14½°

ATTACH WITH EXTERIOR
GLUE AND ¾" BRASS BRADS

¼" X 3½" X 5¼"
PLYWOOD (4) REQUIRED.
PAINT WHITE

¾" DIA.
HOLE

EACH SQUARE = ½"

GRID DETAIL

MATERIALS LIST

Item	Quantity
1X8 cedar	5 ft.
¼" exterior plywood	1 sq. ft.
4d galvanized finishing nails	¼ lb.
¾" brass brads	8
Resorcinol glue	as needed
White spray enamel	1 pt.

CONSTRUCTION DETAILS

1. Form an angled rabbet on one side of the stock before cutting the sides. The rabbet is deepest on the outside edge.

2. Cut the compound miters on your saw. Make one cut from one side of the board and the next from the other side.

COVERED FIREWOOD BOX

With this attractive, covered box for firewood near your barbecue center, all the essentials are close at hand, protected from spring and summer rains. The T1-11 siding that covers the exterior of the project is both attractive and weather resistant.

Start by building the base assembly. Cut the 2X4 frame components and nail them together with 10d galvanized finishing nails. To prevent splitting, drill pilot holes before nailing. Add the ¾-in. plywood floor, spacing the 6d nails 2 in. apart.

Next, cut the 2X2 braces to the lengths shown in the diagram. Nail the bottom braces to the floor of the box.

Set the blade on your table saw to cut a 45 degree bevel, and cut the mitered corners of the T1-11 exterior siding. Measure carefully for an exact fit, taking your measurements from the already-completed base. To prevent the wood from splintering, use a plywood blade on your saw.

Nail the remaining braces in place, and then complete the assembly of the lower section of the box. Check for squareness as you go.

Build the lid next, starting with the frame, then adding the top and sides. Once again, measure accurately before cutting the mitered corners.

Attach the lid to the box with two 2-in. brass hinges as shown in the diagram; then finish up the project with two coats of wood sealer.

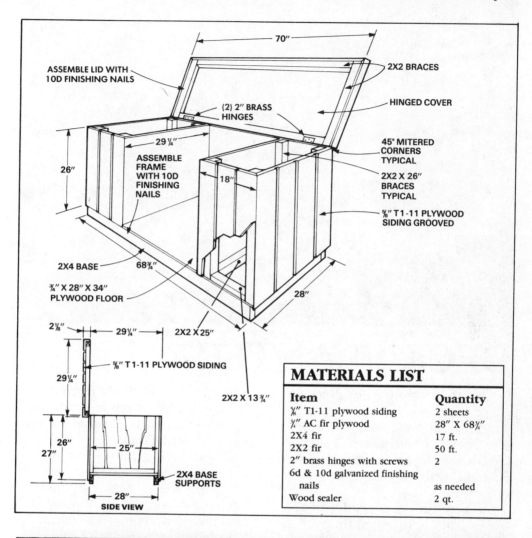

ASSEMBLE LID WITH
10D FINISHING NAILS

70"

2X2 BRACES

HINGED COVER

(2) 2" BRASS
HINGES

29¼"

45° MITERED
CORNERS
TYPICAL

26"

ASSEMBLE
FRAME
WITH 10D
FINISHING
NAILS

18"

2X2 X 26"
BRACES
TYPICAL

⅝" T1-11 PLYWOOD
SIDING GROOVED

2X4 BASE

68¾"

¾" X 28" X 34"
PLYWOOD FLOOR

28"

2⅛"

29¼"

2X2 X 25"

29¼"

⅝" T1-11 PLYWOOD SIDING

2X2 X 13¾"

26"

25"

27"

2X4 BASE
SUPPORTS

28"

SIDE VIEW

MATERIALS LIST	
Item	**Quantity**
⅝" T1-11 plywood siding	2 sheets
¾" AC fir plywood	28" X 68¾"
2X4 fir	17 ft.
2X2 fir	50 ft.
2" brass hinges with screws	2
6d & 10d galvanized finishing nails	as needed
Wood sealer	2 qt.

CONSTRUCTION DETAILS

1. Miter the corners of the T1-11 siding on your table saw. Measure carefully, and use a fine-toothed plywood blade.

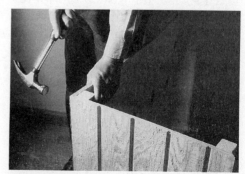

2. As you assemble the plywood sides to the base assembly, be sure to check as you go to keep the unit square.

DECK PLANTER

Colorful ceramic tiles dress up these large planter boxes, giving your deck or patio an added touch of elegance. Construction is similar for both of the boxes shown in the diagram. Only the dimensions and other details vary.

Start by cutting the sides of the boxes from $1/2$-in. pressure-treated plywood. Cut the 2X2 corner braces and assemble the basic box with resorcinol glue and 4d galvanized nails.

Next, cut the floor of the box to size. Use $3/4$-in. pressure-treated plywood, and drill evenly spaced 1-in.-dia. weep holes in the floor.

Make the side trim components next. For the larger box, form $3/4$-in. X $3/4$-in. grooves in the stock with a dado blade or a router.

Miter the corners of the side trim with your circular saw and a T-square guide. You can make your own guide; just check it carefully for squareness. Attach the trim with 4d galvanized nails and glue, nailing from inside the box.

Cut the top trim with a home-made miter guide and your circular saw. Make the guide by cutting a 45 degree angle on a piece of plywood. Nail the plywood to a 1X1 cleat.

Fasten the top trim with glue and 16d galvanized finishing nails. Give the assembly two coats of clear wood sealer before adding the tiles.

To attach the $2 7/8$-in. square ceramic tiles, apply a coat of tile adhesive with a toothed trowel. Locate the tiles 3 in. on center. Once the adhesive has set, fill the gaps with silicone grouting compound to finish the job.

Before adding planting mix and your favorite plants, place a 2-in. layer of coarse gravel in the bottom of the planter for good drainage.

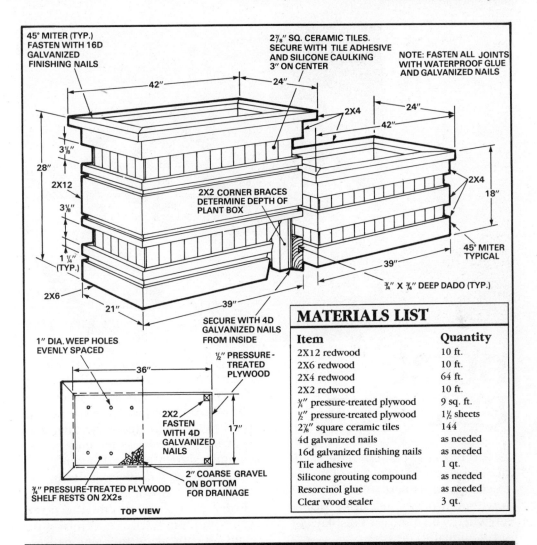

45° MITER (TYP.)
FASTEN WITH 16D
GALVANIZED
FINISHING NAILS

2⅞" SQ. CERAMIC TILES.
SECURE WITH TILE ADHESIVE
AND SILICONE CAULKING
3" ON CENTER

NOTE: FASTEN ALL JOINTS
WITH WATERPROOF GLUE
AND GALVANIZED NAILS

42"

24"

2X4

24"

42"

3⅛"

28"

2X12

3⅛"

1¼"
(TYP.)

2X4

18"

2X2 CORNER BRACES
DETERMINE DEPTH OF
PLANT BOX

45° MITER
TYPICAL

2X6

21"

39"

39"

¾" X ¾" DEEP DADO (TYP.)

SECURE WITH 4D
GALVANIZED NAILS
FROM INSIDE

1" DIA. WEEP HOLES
EVENLY SPACED

36"

½" PRESSURE-
TREATED
PLYWOOD

2X2
FASTEN
WITH 4D
GALVANIZED
NAILS

17"

¾" PRESSURE-TREATED PLYWOOD
SHELF RESTS ON 2X2s

2" COARSE GRAVEL
ON BOTTOM
FOR DRAINAGE

TOP VIEW

MATERIALS LIST

Item	Quantity
2X12 redwood	10 ft.
2X6 redwood	10 ft.
2X4 redwood	64 ft.
2X2 redwood	10 ft.
¾" pressure-treated plywood	9 sq. ft.
½" pressure-treated plywood	1½ sheets
2⅞" square ceramic tiles	144
4d galvanized nails	as needed
16d galvanized finishing nails	as needed
Tile adhesive	1 qt.
Silicone grouting compound	as needed
Resorcinol glue	as needed
Clear wood sealer	3 qt.

CONSTRUCTION DETAILS

*1. Cut the miters on the side trim with
your circular saw and a simple T-square
guide made of scrap.*

*2. Using a circular saw and a homemade
guide, miter the top rail. Check the angle of
the guide with a combination square.*

DUCK PLANTER

This redwood planter in the shape of a duck will add a touch of humor to your garden. Best suited for shallow-rooted plants, it can be placed anywhere you choose to display colorful annuals.

To begin building, copy the duck pattern onto graph paper. Transfer the design with carbon paper onto a 17-in.-long piece of 1X10 redwood.

Attach this piece of redwood to an identical piece using 3d galvanized finishing nails. Place the nails outside of the duck's profile.

Cut out both ducks at once with a band saw or saber saw. Make relief cuts wherever sharp corners or tight curves require them. Once the ducks are cut, clamp them together and sand the edges smooth.

Cut the remaining components from a piece of redwood 1X6. Set your table or radial arm saw to cut a 45 degree bevel and cut the angled end piece first. Reset the saw, and cut the base and other end to the lengths shown in the diagram.

Bore four ½-in.-deep holes in the base with a spade bit, spacing the holes evenly. Assemble the three components with resorcinol glue and 6d galvanized finishing nails.

Add the duck profiles, attaching them with no. 8 X 1½-in. flathead wood screws and resorcinol glue. Bore countersunk pilot holes with a combination pilot bit. To make certain the positions of the ducks match, mark the location of the front end of the planter on both ducks.

Finish the completed planter with your choice of exterior finish. You can use clear wood sealer, or paint the ducks with exterior enamel to match the colors of a real duck.

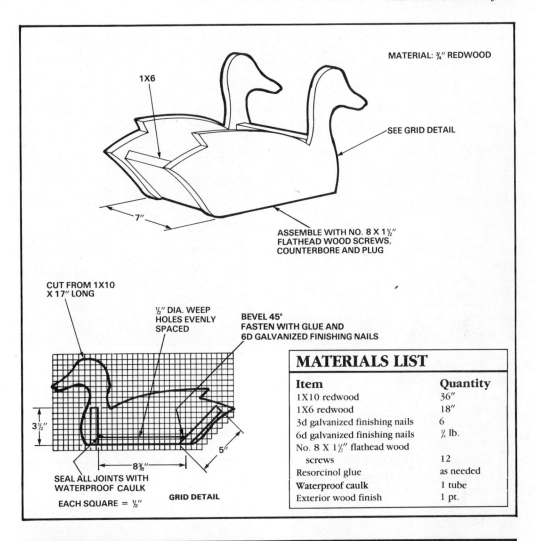

MATERIAL: ¾" REDWOOD

1X6

SEE GRID DETAIL

7"

ASSEMBLE WITH NO. 8 X 1½"
FLATHEAD WOOD SCREWS,
COUNTERBORE AND PLUG

CUT FROM 1X10
X 17" LONG

½" DIA. WEEP
HOLES EVENLY
SPACED

BEVEL 45°
FASTEN WITH GLUE AND
6D GALVANIZED FINISHING NAILS

3½"

8⅜"

5"

SEAL ALL JOINTS WITH
WATERPROOF CAULK

EACH SQUARE = ½"

GRID DETAIL

MATERIALS LIST

Item	Quantity
1X10 redwood	36"
1X6 redwood	18"
3d galvanized finishing nails	6
6d galvanized finishing nails	¼ lb.
No. 8 X 1½" flathead wood screws	12
Resorcinol glue	as needed
Waterproof caulk	1 tube
Exterior wood finish	1 pt.

CONSTRUCTION DETAILS

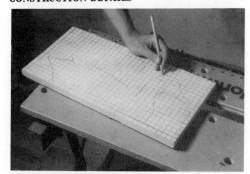

1. *Lay out the duck patterns on ½-in. graph paper. Transfer the design to redwood with carbon paper.*

2. *Cut the duck pattern on a band saw using a ¼-in. or smaller blade. Keep guard ⅛ in. above wood.*

FIREWOOD ORGANIZER

Why let an unsightly pile of firewood spoil the neat appearance of your outdoor living space? This organizer is designed to keep an ample supply of wood and other necessities near your fire pit or barbecue.

Built of redwood and plywood, it offers a lower shelf for bulky firewood and an upper shelf to hold kindling and other items. You should be able to complete this project in just an hour or two.

Cut all the components to the lengths indicated in the diagram. Begin building the end frames. Use 10d galvanized common nails and resorcinol glue to assemble the frames.

To prevent splitting the wood, drill pilot holes for the nails in the horizontal frame members. After nailing the frames, check them for squareness with a framing square.

Next, construct the shelf braces of 2X4 redwood stock. Assemble these in the same way you did the end frames. Check the fit of the shelf braces in the end frames, then cut the ¾-in. exterior plywood panels to size. Use a plywood cutting blade in your circular saw, and clamp a guide to the plywood to help you make straight cuts. Nail the panels to the shelf frames with 6d galvanized nails.

Sand the separate subassemblies, starting with a belt sander and an 80-grit belt. Pay special attention to the end grain of the frames. Finish sanding with 150-grit paper.

Lay the end frames on their sides and insert the shelves into the end frames. Nail them in place with 10d nails. Measure carefully to keep the shelves level, noting the 1½-in. setback for the shelves.

Finish the organizer with two coats of wood sealer, allowing 24 hours between coats. Apply plenty of sealer to exposed end grain. Place the finished project a safe distance from your fire pit or barbecue.

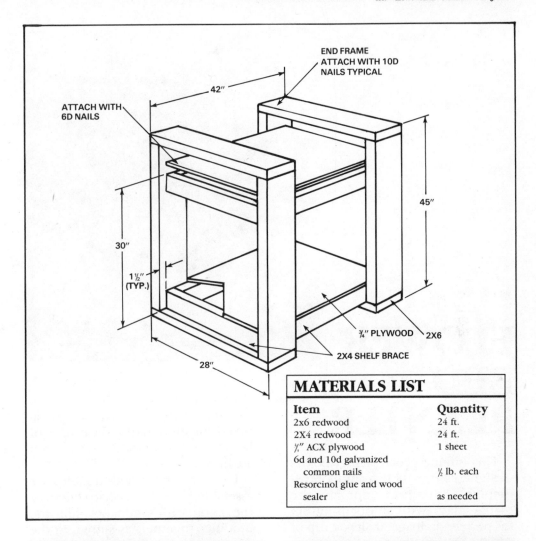

END FRAME
ATTACH WITH 10D
NAILS TYPICAL

42"

ATTACH WITH
6D NAILS

45"

30"

1½"
(TYP.)

¾" PLYWOOD   2X6

2X4 SHELF BRACE

28"

MATERIALS LIST

Item	Quantity
2x6 redwood	24 ft.
2X4 redwood	24 ft.
¾" ACX plywood	1 sheet
6d and 10d galvanized common nails	½ lb. each
Resorcinol glue and wood sealer	as needed

CONSTRUCTION DETAILS

1. *Assemble the end frames with 10d galvanized common nails. Drill pilot holes for the nails.*

2. *Attach the braces to the sides with 10d nails. Be careful when nailing so as not to mar the soft redwood.*

FLOWER BED PLANTER

This unique cedar planter box is designed to provide a multi-level display of some of your favorite plants. Made with an open bottom for perfect drainage, it sits on top of a bed of pea gravel.

Begin by ripping the 45 degree miters along each edge of the 1X6 stock. Cut the parts for the center planter to size. Then set your table or radial arm saw to cut a 30 degree angle for each of the outer module sides. Make the angled cut before trimming each part to length.

Use these pre-cut parts to establish the lengths of the adjoining sides. With your saw set to cut a 30 degree bevel, cut the front and back edges of all the modules. Be careful to cut to the outside of the lines.

Nail the parts of each section of the planter together with 8d galvanized finishing nails. Set each nail below the surface of the wood with a nail set.

Once the individual modules are assembled, break the sharp edges of the wood with sandpaper. Join the modules together, as shown in the diagram, with 3d galvanized finishing nails placed at the top and bottom of the smaller module.

To protect the planter from moisture, apply two coats of clear wood sealer, such as Thompson's Water Seal. Allow the sealer to dry completely before planting. Do not use a wood preservative, as the chemicals in it might damage your plants.

Dig a 6-in.-deep hole, the size of the planter, in your garden. Fill it with pea gravel, then position the planter. Add planting mix or garden soil, and you are ready to plant.

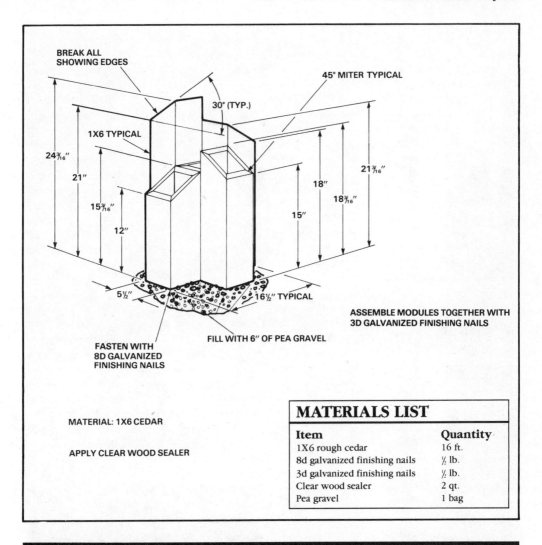

BREAK ALL
SHOWING EDGES

30° (TYP.)

45° MITER TYPICAL

1X6 TYPICAL

24³⁄₁₆″

21″

15³⁄₁₆″

12″

21³⁄₁₆″

18″

18³⁄₁₆″

15″

5½″

16½″ TYPICAL

ASSEMBLE MODULES TOGETHER WITH
3D GALVANIZED FINISHING NAILS

FILL WITH 6″ OF PEA GRAVEL

FASTEN WITH
8D GALVANIZED
FINISHING NAILS

MATERIAL: 1X6 CEDAR

APPLY CLEAR WOOD SEALER

MATERIALS LIST

Item	Quantity
1X6 rough cedar	16 ft.
8d galvanized finishing nails	½ lb.
3d galvanized finishing nails	½ lb.
Clear wood sealer	2 qt.
Pea gravel	1 bag

CONSTRUCTION DETAILS

1. Cut the beveled components on your table or radial arm saw. Mark the length of cut using the adjoining part.

2. Attach one module of the planter to the next with 3d galvanized finishing nails at the top and bottom.

333

FREE-STANDING PLANT DISPLAY

If container plants are one of your gardening specialties, this plant display stand will show off your plants to their best advantage. It provides four separate display levels to allow you to choose the right viewing height for any specimen.

Constructed of pressure-treated lumber for excellent weather resistance, the display can be painted white, as in the photograph, or any color you choose. It looks good either against a wall or standing in the open.

The stand also makes an ideal storage unit for your shop or storage room. Its long, deep shelves provide ample space for bulky items. You may think of even more uses for the unit.

Start building the stand by cutting the materials for the legs. Use perfectly straight 1X4 stock for these components to make the mitered joints fit accurately. If possible, select the lumber yourself at your lumber yard or home center.

To create a smooth surface on the miter joints, choose a combination planer-type blade to rip the miters.

Set the blade on your table or radial arm saw to rip a 45 degree bevel.

Position the fence or the head of the saw to make the cut on the side of the stock that is away from the fence. This prevents binding, which can cause dangerous kickbacks and damage your workpiece.

Now, adjust the fence or head to cut the bevel as close to the edge of the 1X4 material as possible. The cut should just touch the corner of the stock without leaving any excess material. Check your setup with scrap before cutting the actual parts. Cut two test pieces, then hold them together and check the joint for squareness and fit.

Once the setup is correct, rip miters on the edges of eight 7-ft. lengths of the raw stock. Be sure to use the anti-kickback features of your particular saw, and finish the cut with a push stick to keep your hands away from the blade.

Feed the material slowly and evenly to produce a perfectly mitered edge. The extra length of the raw stock will allow you to cut off any flaws near the end of the parts.

CONSTRUCTION DETAILS

1. *Cut the 45degree miters on the leg stock with a planer-type blade on your table or radial arm saw.*

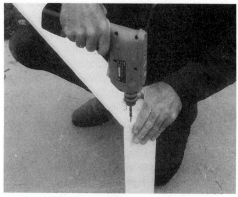

2. *Assemble the shelf frames with flathead wood screws. Check carefully to keep the units square as you work.*

4. *Drill the weep holes in the plywood with a ¾-in. spade bit. Use a backup board to prevent splintering.*

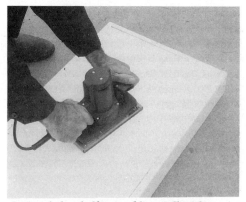

5. *Sand the shelf assemblies well with a pad-type finishing sander. Sand with the grain direction.*

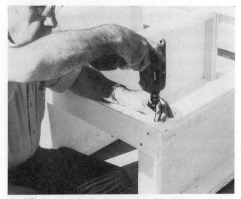

7. *Then attach the pre-assembled legs to the shelf assemblies with flathead wood screws. Square the shelves as you go.*

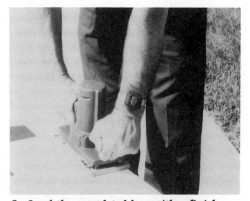

8. *Sand the completed legs with a finish sander. Be careful not to round off the miter joint's corner.*

3. Screw the 1X2 cleats that support the plywood shelves to the frames. Drive the flathead wood screws from inside.

6. As an alternative to attaching one half of each leg set to the shelves, pre-assemble the legs, tacking with brads.

9. Use an electric sprayer to apply two smooth coats of latex exterior enamel to the completed display stand.

If possible, use a roller stand to support the work as it leaves the saw table.

Cut the parts to their finished 78-in. length. Measure carefully to make all the legs match exactly. It is a good idea to match up pairs of legs that fit together well. Mark the pairs to insure correct assembly. Set the legs aside for now while you construct the shelf units.

Begin building the shelves by cutting the sides. You will need eight 48-in. and eight 16½-in. 1X4 parts. For accuracy, clamp a stop block to your radial arm saw's fence or to the table of your table saw to help make all the parts identical. After cutting, stack the matching parts together to check their finished lengths.

Assemble four shelf frames with no. 10 X 1¼-in. flathead wood screws. Drill pilot holes with a combination pilot bit and countersink for the screws. Use two screws, located ¾ in. from the edges, in each joint.

Before the final tightening of the screws, check the squareness of the frames with a carpenter's square and make any necessary adjustments. If your saw is adjusted properly, the joints should fit perfectly.

Next, cut four 16½-in. X 46½-in. pieces of ¾-in. pressure-treated plywood. Precision is important for a good fit. Cut the parts on your table saw or radial arm saw, ripping the 16½-in. width across the sheet of plywood, then cut the parts to length. Work with the good side of the plywood up.

You can also cut the shelves with a portable circular saw. Clamp a guide to the plywood to help keep the saw in line, and cut with the good side of the material down. If you do use a portable saw, work especially carefully to make the parts fit well.

Lay out a grid of eight ¾-in. weep holes on the shelves. Space these evenly, as shown in the diagram. Bore the holes with a ¾-in. spade bit in your electric drill. For even greater accuracy, use a drill press. Place a backup board underneath the workpiece to minimize splintering.

Lay one plywood shelf face down on a flat work surface. Set one of the shelf frames over the plywood and mark the inside of the frame to show the position of the bottom of the shelf. Do this for each shelf.

Now, cut eight 45-in. and eight 16½-in. pieces of 1X2 stock to form the cleats for the shelf. Install these in the frames so that the top of the cleats line up with the lines you just drew on the frames. The staggered corner joints add strength to the assembly.

Attach the cleats with no. 10 X 1¼-in. flathead wood screws. As you did before, drill countersunk pilot holes for the screws. Space the screws 4 in. apart. As you attach the cleats, check frequently to keep them aligned properly.

Lay the plywood shelves on the cleats and fasten them with 4d galvanized finishing nails. Set the nails below the surface of the wood with a nail set and fill the holes with waterproof wood filler. Leave the filler standing slightly above the shelf's surface, to be sanded flush later.

Once all of the shelf units are complete, give them a thorough sanding with a pad-type finishing sander. Start with 120-grit garnet paper and work down to 220-grit for a smooth surface. When sanding the plywood, be sure to follow the grain direction.

Mark the shelf positions on the legs, making certain that you measure accurately, especially at the bottom of each leg. Follow the dimensions provided in the diagram.

Lay two of the leg halves on a flat surface, then position the shelves on them. Align the parts so the edges of the shelves just touch the inside of the miter. Check the alignment with a framing square before fastening the shelves.

Use no. 10 X 1¼-in. flathead wood screws, drilling pilot holes as you did before. Drive two evenly spaced screws into each joint from inside the frame. Avoid conflicts with the frame screws. Before attaching each shelf, make certain it hasn't shifted.

Once the two legs are secured, add the opposite leg halves to the other side of the shelves in the same way. Finally, add the second half of each leg set, aligning it carefully to make the joint close properly. For an alternative to securing the legs, see the step-by-step photos.

Sand the legs with the pad-type sander, as you did for the shelves. Be careful not to round over the corners of the miter joints as you sand.

Finish the project with two coats of latex exterior enamel. If possible, apply the paint with an airless-type sprayer for a smooth finish.

MATERIALS LIST

Item	Quantity
1X4 pressure-treated lumber	100 ft.
1X2 pressure-treated lumber	42 ft.
¾" pressure-treated plywood	1 sheet
No. 10 X 1¼" flathead wood screws	180
4d galvanized finishing nails	¼ lb.
Latex exterior enamel	as needed

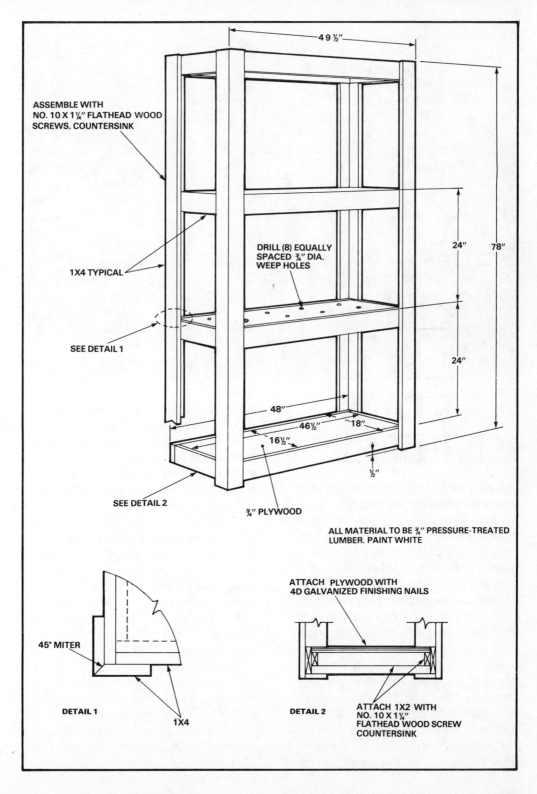

ASSEMBLE WITH
NO. 10 X 1¼" FLATHEAD WOOD
SCREWS, COUNTERSINK

49½"

78"

24"

DRILL (8) EQUALLY
SPACED ¾" DIA.
WEEP HOLES

1X4 TYPICAL

24"

SEE DETAIL 1

48"

46½" 18"

16½"

½"

SEE DETAIL 2

¾" PLYWOOD

ALL MATERIAL TO BE ¾" PRESSURE-TREATED
LUMBER. PAINT WHITE

ATTACH PLYWOOD WITH
4D GALVANIZED FINISHING NAILS

45° MITER

DETAIL 1

1X4

DETAIL 2

ATTACH 1X2 WITH
NO. 10 X 1¼"
FLATHEAD WOOD SCREW
COUNTERSINK

339

GARDEN KNEELER

Constant kneeling while working in the garden can take a toll on your knees. This lightweight kneeling bench will help save those knees by raising the height of your knees to a more comfortable level while also keeping them clean.

Convenient handgrips let you use your arms to help you get on your feet, and a hinged storage area holds your gardening tools.

Begin by cutting all the components to the sizes shown in the diagram. Lay out the tapered sides of the bench and cut them with a fine-toothed blade in your saber saw.

Use a bar compass to draw the radius at the top of each side, along with the curved handholds. Cut the top radius with your saber saw.

Drill holes at the ends of the hand-hold openings with a spade bit. Use a backup board to prevent splintering. Cut out the remaining waste material with your saber saw.

Assemble the components of the bench with 10d galvanized finishing nails and waterproof resorcinol glue. Set the nails below the surface with a nail set.

Attach the lid of the bench to the sides with 1-in. brass hinges as shown in the diagram. Use the screws provided with the hinges.

Sand the project thoroughly, starting with 80-grit garnet paper and finishing with 150-grit paper. Apply a coat of oil-based stain if desired. Apply two coats of satin-finish polyurethane varnish as a final, easy-to-clean finish.

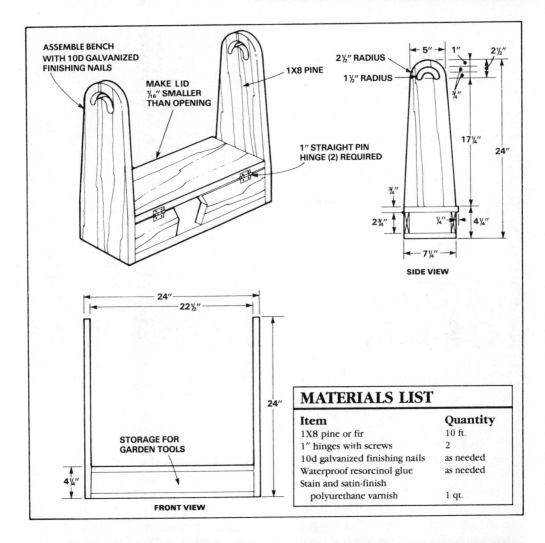

ASSEMBLE BENCH WITH 10D GALVANIZED FINISHING NAILS

MAKE LID 1⁄16″ SMALLER THAN OPENING

1X8 PINE

1″ STRAIGHT PIN HINGE (2) REQUIRED

2½″ RADIUS

1½″ RADIUS

5″

1″

2½″

3⁄4″

17¼″

24″

3⁄4″

2¾″

¼″

4¼″

7¼″

SIDE VIEW

24″

22½″

24″

STORAGE FOR GARDEN TOOLS

4¼″

FRONT VIEW

MATERIALS LIST

Item	Quantity
1X8 pine or fir	10 ft.
1″ hinges with screws	2
10d galvanized finishing nails	as needed
Waterproof resorcinol glue	as needed
Stain and satin-finish polyurethane varnish	1 qt.

CONSTRUCTION DETAILS

1. *Lay out the radii of the handhold cutout with a bar compass. Use care to keep both sides equal.*

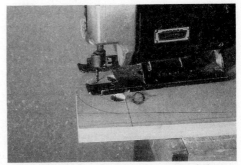

2. *After drilling holes at the ends of the handholds, cut the waste away with a saber saw.*

GARDEN TOOL BOX

Working in the garden is one of the joys every gardener understands. Carrying tools and supplies into the garden, however, is not always such a joy. This easy-to-build tool box is a convenient way to organize your gardening needs.

Begin by cutting all the components to the overall sizes shown in the diagram. All parts, except the dowel handle, are made of $3/4$-in.-thick pine. You might even have enough scrap material to make the tool box.

Lay out the angles and curves on the end components, then cut these profiles with a saber saw. After cutting, clamp the parts together and even them up with a belt sander.

Next, use a portable drill guide to bore $5/8$-in.-dia. holes in both ends for the handle. Use a spade or Forstner bit.

Set up your router in a router table and use a $3/8$-in.-radius rounding-over bit, with pilot, to form the rounded edges of the sides. These can be formed with the router alone, but the table makes the job easier.

Assemble the sides and bottom of the tool box with resorcinol glue and 6d galvanized finishing nails. Set the nails below the surface of the wood with a nail set, then fill the holes with wood filler.

Add the ends and the handle. Glue the handle in the holes, then nail and glue the ends to the sides and bottom. Use 6d galvanized finishing nails here as well.

Sand the completed box thoroughly, starting with 80-grit garnet paper and finishing with 120-grit. Pay special attention to the end grain.

Finish the project by applying a clear sealer, followed with two coats of polyurethane varnish.

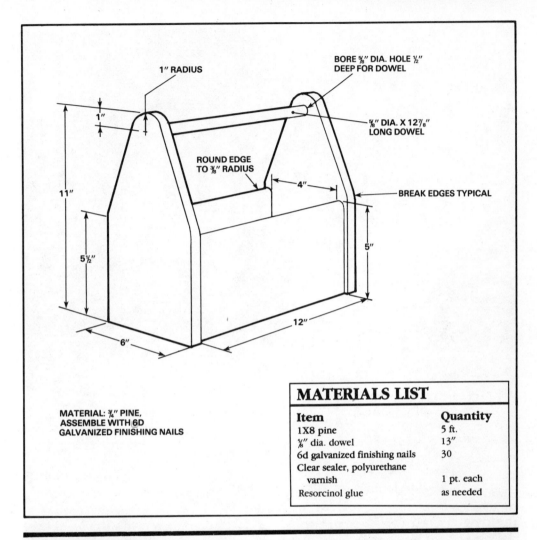

1" RADIUS

BORE ⅝" DIA. HOLE ½"
DEEP FOR DOWEL

⅝" DIA. X 12⅞"
LONG DOWEL

ROUND EDGE
TO ⅜" RADIUS

1"

11"

4"

BREAK EDGES TYPICAL

5½"

5"

12"

6"

MATERIAL: ¾" PINE,
ASSEMBLE WITH 6D
GALVANIZED FINISHING NAILS

MATERIALS LIST

Item	Quantity
1X8 pine	5 ft.
⅝" dia. dowel	13"
6d galvanized finishing nails	30
Clear sealer, polyurethane varnish	1 pt. each
Resorcinol glue	as needed

CONSTRUCTION DETAILS

1. *Use a portable drill guide and a spade or Forstner bit to bore the handle holes in the ends of the box.*

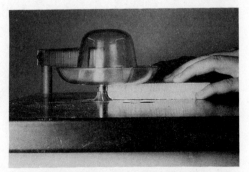

2. *Round over the sides of the box with a ⅜-in. rounding-over bit in a table mounted router.*

343

GARDEN UTILITY CART

Working outdoors around your home almost always involves moving heavy or bulky items. You can save your back by building this handy garden cart. It will carry up to 150 pounds, and its removable gate allows easy dumping.

Start building the cart by cutting all the components to the sizes shown in the diagram. You can cut the aluminum frame material with a fine-toothed blade on your table or radial arm saw.

Drill drain holes in the cart's floor, then position the aluminum frame members on the floor piece. The end rails fit under the side pieces.

Drill mounting holes, countersinking the holes for the flathead machine screws. Install screws and nuts in the corners only, since you will disassemble the project for painting.

Add the sides and the aluminum uprights, clamping the parts together for drilling. Use a backup board to avoid splintering the plywood. Countersink the holes, then assemble the parts temporarily.

Add the rear panel in the same way. The gate simply drops into place, so the screws in the lower front corners of the frame must be countersunk flush.

Next, form the forks from ⅛-in. X 1½-in. steel flat bar stock. Bend the stock, as shown in the photo, using a piece of 3-in. ABS sewer pipe. Cut the forks to length after bending, and round the ends on a bench grinder. Locate and drill the axle and mounting holes.

Drill the holes on the sides of the cart for mounting the forks. Notice that the centers of the axle holes are exactly 1 in. below the bottom of the cart.

Make the handle and legs next by bending ¾-in thin-wall conduit (EMT) with a conduit bender. This tool can be rented at any equipment rental yard. Follow the instructions provided with the tool to obtain precise bends.

After bending the handle, clamp it in position on the cart and drill mounting holes. Again, use a backup board for clean drilling.

Bend the legs next, taking care to make accurate 45 degree angles. It is easier to make these parts if you bend each leg at the end of a long piece of conduit. Make the vertical ends of the legs longer than necessary, trimming them later.

Add the threaded adapters and the flanges to the legs, then turn the cart upside-down and use the legs as guides for the mounting holes.

Next, disassemble the cart for finishing. Sand all wood parts thoroughly, then apply a coat of latex-based enamel primer, followed by two coats of semi-gloss latex enamel.

De-burr the metal parts and hang them up for painting. Apply a coat of metal primer, followed by two coats of spray enamel in the color of your choice.

After the paint has dried, reassem-

CONSTRUCTION DETAILS

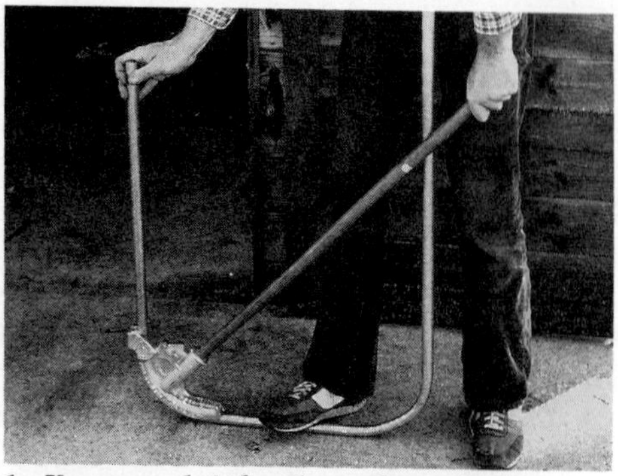

1. Use a conduit bender to form the legs and handle. Follow the manufacturer's instructions for best results.

2. Bend the wheel forks around a piece of 3-in. sewer pipe. Use a clamp to hold the pipe in place for bending.

3. Threaded adapters and pipe flanges connect the legs to the cart. These are available at any hardware store.

4. To install the bicycle grips, dip them in soapy water, then slide them into position on the cart's handle.

ble the cart. Notice that there are four lengths of screws used in the project. Use 1-in. screws where they pass through the plywood and two thicknesses of the frame. The 3/4-in. screws fit most other locations. For the legs, 1 1/4-in. screws are used, while the handle requires 1 1/2-in. screws. Use plated cap nuts for a nice finished look.

Before attaching the handle, install the foam grips. These are standard bicycle grips, which are applied by dipping them into soapy water before sliding them on the handle.

Finally, add the bicycle wheel assemblies, tightening the nuts securely. Buy the wheels and tires from any bicycle shop.

MATERIALS LIST

Item	Quantity
1/2" ACX plywood	1 sheet
1/8" X 1 1/2" aluminum angle	18 ft.
1/8" X 1 1/2" steel flat bar	6 ft.
3/4"-dia. EMT conduit	20 ft.
3/4" EMT pipe thread adapter	4
3/4" pipe flange	4
Foam bicycle grips	1 pkg.
1/4" X 3/4", 1", 1 1/4", 1 1/2" flathead machine screws	as needed
1/4" plated cap nuts with flat washers	as needed
Latex enamel primer and latex enamel	1 qt. each
Spray primer and enamel	16 oz. can each

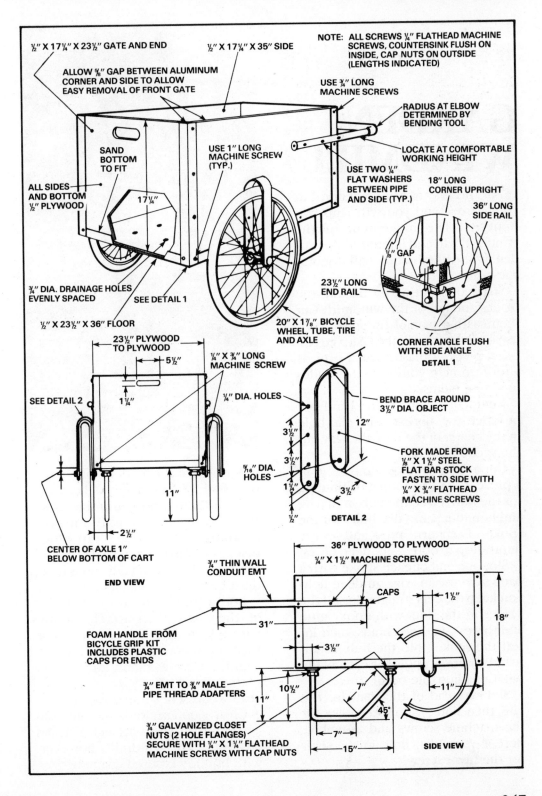

½" X 17¼" X 23½" GATE AND END

½" X 17¼" X 35" SIDE

NOTE: ALL SCREWS ¼" FLATHEAD MACHINE
SCREWS, COUNTERSINK FLUSH ON
INSIDE, CAP NUTS ON OUTSIDE
(LENGTHS INDICATED)

ALLOW ⅜" GAP BETWEEN ALUMINUM
CORNER AND SIDE TO ALLOW
EASY REMOVAL OF FRONT GATE

USE ¾" LONG
MACHINE SCREWS

RADIUS AT ELBOW
DETERMINED BY
BENDING TOOL

SAND
BOTTOM
TO FIT

USE 1" LONG
MACHINE SCREW
(TYP.)

LOCATE AT COMFORTABLE
WORKING HEIGHT

USE TWO ¼"
FLAT WASHERS
BETWEEN PIPE
AND SIDE (TYP.)

18" LONG
CORNER UPRIGHT

ALL SIDES
AND BOTTOM
½" PLYWOOD

17¼"

36" LONG
SIDE RAIL

⅛" GAP

¾" DIA. DRAINAGE HOLES
EVENLY SPACED

SEE DETAIL 1

23½" LONG
END RAIL

½" X 23½" X 36" FLOOR

20" X 1⅞" BICYCLE
WHEEL, TUBE, TIRE
AND AXLE

CORNER ANGLE FLUSH
WITH SIDE ANGLE

DETAIL 1

23½" PLYWOOD
TO PLYWOOD

5½"

¼" X ¾" LONG
MACHINE SCREW

SEE DETAIL 2

1¼"

¼" DIA. HOLES

BEND BRACE AROUND
3½" DIA. OBJECT

12"

3½"

3½"

⁵⁄₁₆" DIA.
HOLES

1¼"

FORK MADE FROM
⅛" X 1½" STEEL
FLAT BAR STOCK
FASTEN TO SIDE WITH
¼" X ¾" FLATHEAD
MACHINE SCREWS

11"

3½"

½"

DETAIL 2

2½"

CENTER OF AXLE 1"
BELOW BOTTOM OF CART

END VIEW

36" PLYWOOD TO PLYWOOD

¼" X 1½" MACHINE SCREWS

¾" THIN WALL
CONDUIT EMT

CAPS

1½"

31"

18"

FOAM HANDLE FROM
BICYCLE GRIP KIT
INCLUDES PLASTIC
CAPS FOR ENDS

3½"

10½"

7"

11"

45°

11"

¾" EMT TO ¾" MALE
PIPE THREAD ADAPTERS

¾" GALVANIZED CLOSET
NUTS (2 HOLE FLANGES)
SECURE WITH ¼" X 1½" FLATHEAD
MACHINE SCREWS WITH CAP NUTS

7"

15"

SIDE VIEW

347

GARDEN WINDMILL

Put this easy-to-build windmill in your garden and you will reap two benefits. The movement of the windmill will add interest to the garden, while its vibration will discourage moles.

Start construction by making the blades and tail of the windmill. Cut them with a pair of tin snips, then use a file to smooth the sharp edges. Use a piece of plastic sewer pipe as a form to help you bend the blades to a 5-in. radius.

Next, cut the hub with a band saw or saber saw. Bore a $\frac{1}{4}$-in.-dia. hole in the center of the hub, then lay out the spoke locations.

Cut a $1\frac{1}{2}$-in.-radius semi-circle in a piece of 2X4 to form a drilling jig for the hub. Place the hub in this jig and bore the $\frac{3}{8}$-in.- dia. holes for the spokes. Use a drill press and set the depth stop to bore $\frac{3}{4}$-in.-deep holes.

Slot one end of each spoke with a band saw; use an edge guide to help you keep the cuts straight. Install the blades in the slots with epoxy glue and three $\frac{3}{8}$-in. brass brads, then insert the spokes into the hub. Establish the correct angle for each blade with an adjustable bevel gauge.

Slot one end of the shaft for the tail, then bore $\frac{3}{16}$-in.-dia. holes for the machine screws and assemble. Bore a $\frac{3}{16}$-in.-dia. hole in the shaft for the pivot screw.

Now, bore a 1-in.-dia. hole in the redwood 2X2 used as a stake. Glue the windmill's post into this hole, then drive the assembly into the ground by hitting a scrap block placed on top of the stake. Do not hit the stake directly. If your soil is hard, dig a hole for the stake.

Bore a pilot hole in the hub end of the shaft, then attach the hub with a $\frac{1}{4}$-in. X 2-in. lag screw. Use washers on both sides of the hub. Attach the shaft assembly to the post with a no. 10 X $1\frac{1}{2}$-in. brass flathead wood screw and a washer.

Clear wood sealer is the only finish required for this project. You can customize the windmill, however, with brightly colored enamel.

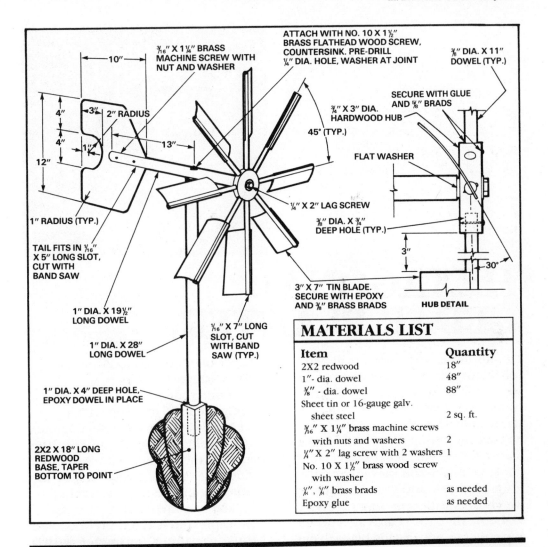

ATTACH WITH NO. 10 X 1½" BRASS FLATHEAD WOOD SCREW, COUNTERSINK. PRE-DRILL ¼" DIA. HOLE, WASHER AT JOINT

⅜" DIA. X 11" DOWEL (TYP.)

3/16" X 1¼" BRASS MACHINE SCREW WITH NUT AND WASHER

SECURE WITH GLUE AND ⅝" BRADS

¾" X 3" DIA. HARDWOOD HUB

45° (TYP.)

FLAT WASHER

2" RADIUS

10"

4"

3"

13"

4"

1"

12"

¼" X 2" LAG SCREW

1" RADIUS (TYP.)

3/16" DIA. X ¾" DEEP HOLE (TYP.)

TAIL FITS IN 1/16" X 5" LONG SLOT, CUT WITH BAND SAW

3"

30°

3" X 7" TIN BLADE. SECURE WITH EPOXY AND 3/16" BRASS BRADS

HUB DETAIL

1" DIA. X 19½" LONG DOWEL

1/16" X 7" LONG SLOT, CUT WITH BAND SAW (TYP.)

1" DIA. X 28" LONG DOWEL

1" DIA. X 4" DEEP HOLE, EPOXY DOWEL IN PLACE

2X2 X 18" LONG REDWOOD BASE, TAPER BOTTOM TO POINT

MATERIALS LIST

Item	Quantity
2X2 redwood	18"
1"- dia. dowel	48"
⅜" - dia. dowel	88"
Sheet tin or 16-gauge galv. sheet steel	2 sq. ft.
3/16" X 1¼" brass machine screws with nuts and washers	2
¼" X 2" lag screw with 2 washers	1
No. 10 X 1½" brass wood screw with washer	1
⅜", ⅝" brass brads	as needed
Epoxy glue	as needed

CONSTRUCTION DETAILS

1. Cut slots in the spokes and shaft on a band saw. Use an edge guide to help keep the slots as straight as possible.

2. Bore the spoke holes in the hub on a drill press, using a simple jig to align the hub. Bore holes ¾ in. deep.

349

HEXAGONAL CEDAR PLANTER

This hexagonal planter will add a distinctive note to your deck or patio. Its shape and its cedar construction make it ideal for displaying any large container plant.

Start by cutting 24 pieces of 2X4 cedar to 17¾-in. lengths. Set your table or radial arm saw to cut a 60 degree bevel, and cut the ends of the boards with opposing bevels.

Once all of the boards are cut, set up your saw with a dado blade to cut the notches. Cut each notch 1¾ in. deep and 1½ in. wide, and cut at a 60 degree angle. Make the cut in several passes, repeating until you reach the required depth.

Make a trial assembly of the planter, and mark the top and bottom pieces at each corner. Mark each notch at the center for the ⅜-in.-dia. holes that hold the threaded rod.

Bore the holes on a drill press, locating each hole accurately for perfect assembly. The holes are slightly larger than the rod to allow for minor misalignments.

Counterbore the top and bottom components ½ in. deep with a ¾-in. bit to allow for the connecting nuts and washers. Now, assemble the shell of the planter with resorcinol glue and threaded rods. Adjust the structure before final tightening.

Next, set the shell on a piece of ¾-in. pressure-treated plywood and trace the inner perimeter with a pencil. Cut the plywood base with a saber saw. Bore six ½-in.-dia. weep holes in the plywood, spacing them evenly.

After nailing the 12-in.-long cleats to the sides of the planter, nail the base to the cleats with 6d galvanized nails.

Sand the completed project well, then apply two coats of satin-finish polyurethane varnish.

Design by Jeff Milstein. Photos courtesy of Western Wood Products Association, Yeon Building, Portland, OR 97204.

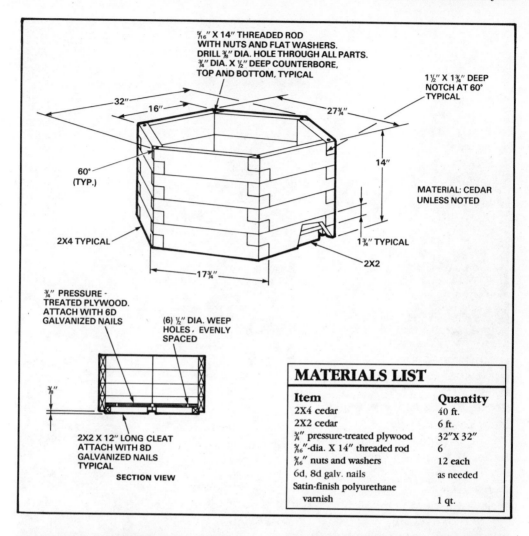

⁵⁄₁₆″ X 14″ THREADED ROD
WITH NUTS AND FLAT WASHERS.
DRILL ³⁄₈″ DIA. HOLE THROUGH ALL PARTS.
³⁄₄″ DIA. X ½″ DEEP COUNTERBORE,
TOP AND BOTTOM, TYPICAL

1½″ X 1³⁄₄″ DEEP
NOTCH AT 60°
TYPICAL

32″

16″

27³⁄₄″

14″

60°
(TYP.)

MATERIAL: CEDAR
UNLESS NOTED

2X4 TYPICAL

1³⁄₄″ TYPICAL

2X2

17³⁄₄″

³⁄₄″ PRESSURE -
TREATED PLYWOOD.
ATTACH WITH 6D
GALVANIZED NAILS

(6) ½″ DIA. WEEP
HOLES , EVENLY
SPACED

³⁄₈″

2X2 X 12″ LONG CLEAT
ATTACH WITH 8D
GALVANIZED NAILS
TYPICAL

SECTION VIEW

MATERIALS LIST

Item	Quantity
2X4 cedar	40 ft.
2X2 cedar	6 ft.
³⁄₄″ pressure-treated plywood	32″X 32″
⁵⁄₁₆″-dia. X 14″ threaded rod	6
⁵⁄₁₆″ nuts and washers	12 each
6d, 8d galv. nails	as needed
Satin-finish polyurethane varnish	1 qt.

CONSTRUCTION DETAILS

1. *Cut the notches in the planter's sides with a dado blade on your radial arm saw. Make multiple passes.*

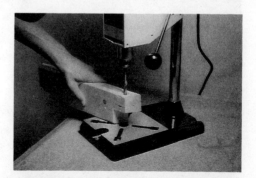

2. *Drill the ³⁄₈-in. holes in the side pieces. Use a drill press for the most accuracy. Counterbore the top and bottom pieces.*

LAMP POST

This elegant outdoor lamp is designed to grace the entrance to your home and light your guests' way. Placed at a gate or near the beginning of your front walk, its distinctive appearance looks as good during the daylight hours as it does at night.

You can attach your house number, a nameplate, and even a small flower box to the light, as shown in the photograph, to add to the lamp's charm.

The project is constructed of $\frac{1}{2}$-in. exterior plywood, with clear Plexiglas panels covering the light fixture. You can paint the light to match the colors of your home.

Begin building the project by choosing an appropriate site for the lamp. Dig a 10-in.-dia. hole at the location you choose, then dig a trench for the wiring. The trench from the hole to your source of power should be at least 12 in. deep to protect the buried wiring from damage.

Cut a 4X4 post 78 in. long and place it in the posthole. Using a level, adjust the post so it's perfectly vertical and prop it in position with temporary braces. The post should extend 30 in. into the hole. Prop up the bottom of the post as necessary.

Lay direct-burial electrical cable in the trench. Protect the cable with electrical conduit wherever it will come into contact with cement. Check with your building inspector to determine the appropriate materials and techniques for your area. Allow plenty of cable for your

connections both at the source and at the top of the lamp.

Now, fill the posthole with concrete mix. One bag of concrete mix should fill the hole. Check the post once more to make sure it hasn't shifted, then allow the concrete to set before continuing construction.

Next, cut the lamp post's back panel from a sheet of $\frac{1}{2}$-in. plywood. As you cut the panel on your table saw, bevel the edges at a 45 degree angle. Check your saw's setup carefully to make the dimensions match those shown in the diagram.

You can simplify the job by cutting all of the panels to the correct width at this time. All panels are $1\frac{7}{8}$ in. wide, with beveled edges. Cut the panels to length as they are needed.

Cut two 2X2 cleats 70 in. long, then attach them to the back panel. The outer edges of the cleats should be flush with the inside of the bevel. Make the bottom of the cleats even with the lower edge of the panel.

Use waterproof resorcinol glue and no. 8 X $1\frac{1}{2}$-in. flathead wood screws on all joints. Countersink the pilot holes for the screws to make the screw heads flush with the surface.

Attach the completed back panel assembly to the post with $\frac{1}{4}$-in. X 1-in. lag screws. Center the panel on the post and align it carefully to make the sides perfectly vertical. Space the lag screws 6 in. apart.

Attach the electrical cable to one of the cleats with cable staples

CONSTRUCTION DETAILS

1. Cut the lamp openings in the sides of the unit after cutting the stock to width and beveling the edges.

2. Install 2X2 cleats on the back panel. Make sure the sides of the cleats are flush with the inside of the bevel.

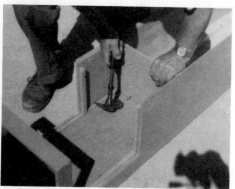

3. Attach the bottom plywood panel after installing the junction box and its respective pack panel.

4. Install the rabbeted cleats for the Plexiglas panels to the sides of the assembly. Use screws and glue.

5. Cut the Plexiglas panels to size with a saber saw or with a special plastic cutting knife as shown.

6. Glue the plastic panels together with special plastic cement. Use only a thin film of cement.

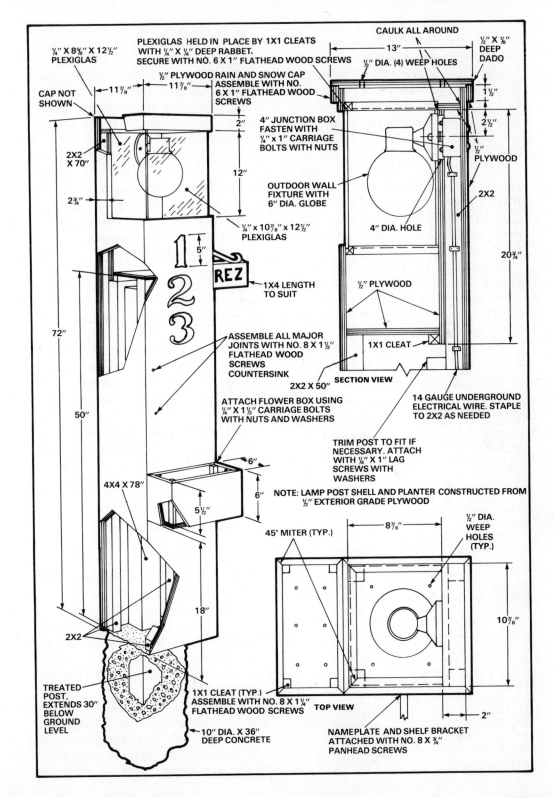

CAULK ALL AROUND

½" X ⅛" DEEP DADO

13"

½" DIA. (4) WEEP HOLES

1½"

2½"

½" PLYWOOD

2X2

20¾"

¼" X 8⅝" X 12½" PLEXIGLAS

PLEXIGLAS HELD IN PLACE BY 1X1 CLEATS WITH ¼" X ¼" DEEP RABBET. SECURE WITH NO. 6 X 1" FLATHEAD WOOD SCREWS

CAP NOT SHOWN

11⅞"   11⅞"

½" PLYWOOD RAIN AND SNOW CAP ASSEMBLE WITH NO. 6 X 1" FLATHEAD WOOD SCREWS

2"

12"

4" JUNCTION BOX FASTEN WITH ¼" X 1" CARRIAGE BOLTS WITH NUTS

2X2 X 70"

2¾"

OUTDOOR WALL FIXTURE WITH 6" DIA. GLOBE

4" DIA. HOLE

¼" x 10⅞" x 12½" PLEXIGLAS

5"

1X4 LENGTH TO SUIT

REZ

½" PLYWOOD

72"

ASSEMBLE ALL MAJOR JOINTS WITH NO. 8 X 1½" FLATHEAD WOOD SCREWS COUNTERSINK

2X2 X 50"   **SECTION VIEW**

14 GAUGE UNDERGROUND ELECTRICAL WIRE. STAPLE TO 2X2 AS NEEDED

1X1 CLEAT

50"

ATTACH FLOWER BOX USING ¼" X 1½" CARRIAGE BOLTS WITH NUTS AND WASHERS

TRIM POST TO FIT IF NECESSARY. ATTACH WITH ¼" X 1" LAG SCREWS WITH WASHERS

6"

4X4 X 78"

6"

5½"

NOTE: LAMP POST SHELL AND PLANTER CONSTRUCTED FROM ½" EXTERIOR GRADE PLYWOOD

45° MITER (TYP.)

8⅞"

½" DIA. WEEP HOLES (TYP.)

18"

10⅞"

2X2

TREATED POST, EXTENDS 30" BELOW GROUND LEVEL

1X1 CLEAT (TYP.) ASSEMBLE WITH NO. 8 X 1¼" FLATHEAD WOOD SCREWS   **TOP VIEW**

2"

10" DIA. X 36" DEEP CONCRETE

NAMEPLATE AND SHELF BRACKET ATTACHED WITH NO. 8 X ¾" PANHEAD SCREWS

spaced 4 in. apart. Attach a 4-in. round junction box to the rear panel using ¼-in. X 1-in. carriage bolts with nuts and washers. Center the box on the panel, 4 in. from the top. Pass the cable into the junction box, through an appropriate clamp fitting.

Cut a 10⅞-in. X 20¾-in. plywood panel. Position it over the box and mark the exact center of the box. Cut a 4-in.-dia. opening in the panel. Add a 1X1 cleat to the bottom of the panel.

Now, screw the panel to the 2X2 cleats, with the opening centered over the junction box. Make certain that the panel is flush with the outer edge of the cleats.

Wire and install an outdoor globe-type fixture on the panel, placing it over the opening. Connect the other end of the cable to your electrical supply through a convenient switch. Be sure to follow the electrical code used in your area. Make certain that the power is off before doing any wiring. Test the circuit before continuing.

Seal the top of the wiring area with a 2-in. X 10⅞-in. strip of plywood. Fasten the strip with screws and glue, then seal the joints well with silicone caulk to prevent water from entering the chamber.

Now, cut the lamp's sides and front to length and shape. Bevel the edges of these components the same way you did for the back panel. Cut the front panel to length after cutting the openings in the side panels.

Once the sides are cut, lay out the openings for the Plexiglas panels. Follow the dimensions provided carefully. Cut these openings with a fine-toothed blade in your saber saw, following the lines accurately. Clamp a guide to the stock to help keep your cuts perfectly straight. Pay special attention to the corners.

Attach 50-in.-long 2X2 cleats to the front edge of the sides, then install the sides with screws and resorcinol glue. Use no. 8 X 1½-in. flathead wood screws, countersunk on all joints. Check the assembly with a try square as you work. The beveled joints should fit tightly.

Cut a 10⅞-in. X 10⅞-in. plywood panel to fit the inside of the assembly. Attach this panel to the top of the 2X2 cleats and the 1X1 cleat on the back panel.

Before attaching the front panel to the structure, build the flower box (optional). Cut the four panels to the sizes shown in the diagram, beveling the edges to form mitered

MATERIALS LIST

Item	Quantity
4X4 redwood	78″
2X2 lumber	21 ft.
1X1 lumber	6 ft.
½″ exterior plywood	1 sheet
¼″ Plexiglas	3 sq. ft.
Concrete mix	1 bag
4″ junction box	1
Outdoor lighting fixture	1
14-gauge direct-burial cable	as needed
Decorative shelf bracket	1
¼″ X 1½″ carriage bolts with nuts and washers	as needed
¼″ X 1″ carriage bolts with nuts and washers	as needed
¼″ X 1″ lag screws	6
No. 8 X 1¾″ flathead wood screws	as needed
No. 8 X ¾″ panhead screws	as needed
No. 8 X 1¼″ flathead wood screws	as needed
No. 6 X 1″ flathead wood screws	as needed
Cable staples	as needed
Resorcinol glue	as needed
Clear silicone caulk	1 small tube
Paint	as needed

corners. Cut a bottom panel to fit the inside of the box. Drill six equally spaced $\frac{1}{2}$-in.-dia. weep holes in the bottom panel to allow proper drainage.

Assemble the planter with 1X1 cleats in the corners. Use resorcinol glue and no. 8 X 1$\frac{1}{4}$-in. flathead screws. Countersink the screw heads as you did before. Check for squareness as you assemble it.

Attach the flower box to the front panel of the lamp with $\frac{1}{4}$-in. X 1$\frac{1}{2}$-in. carriage bolts with nuts and washers. Install it 18 in. from the bottom of the panel. Attach the panel and flower box to the front of the lamp assembly as you did the others. Make certain that the top of the front panel lines up with the lower edge of the lamp openings.

Next, form the rabbeted 1X1s for the Plexiglas. Cut a $\frac{1}{4}$-in. X $\frac{1}{4}$-in. rabbet on one edge of a length of 1X1 stock. Use a dado blade on your radial arm saw or table saw to form this rabbet. Be sure to observe all of your saw's safety precautions during this operation. Form the rabbet on a long piece of stock, then cut the individual components later.

Cut the 1X1 cleats to length, mitering the corners at a 45 degree angle. Attach cleats to the front and sides of the lamp assembly with glue and no. 6 X 1-in. flathead wood screws. Make certain that the cleats are level. Place the rabbets next to the panels and keep the top of the cleats flush with the upper edge of the opening.

Attach the final cleat to the inside of the 2-in.-wide plywood trim strip that will be installed at the top of the lamp. Do not install the strip at this time, however.

Lay out the dimensions of the Plexiglas panels on the plastic's protective paper or plastic coating. Cut the three panels with your saber saw, using a blade specifically designed to cut Plexiglas. These blades are available wherever you buy Plexiglas.

Peel the protective cover from the Plexiglas, then slide the individual plastic components into the grooves in the cleats. Glue the plastic parts together at the front with plastic cement. Be careful not to get excess cement on the surface of the plastic.

Add the trim board, with its rabbeted cleat, to the top of the lamp. Secure it with screws and glue. Finish the installation by running a bead of clear silicone caulk around the joints to keep out moisture.

Next, build the rain and snow cap. Cut the top panel of the cap to size on your table saw or radial arm saw. Form a $\frac{1}{2}$-in. dado, $\frac{1}{8}$ in. deep, on all four sides of the top panel. Cut the sides of the cap with mitered corners as you did for the other components. Assemble the rain cap with no. 6 X 1-in. flathead wood screws and resorcinol glue. Drill four weep holes. Attach the cap to the main unit with 1-in. wood screws, countersunk. This will allow access to the lamp when needed.

Sand the completed project carefully.

Mask the Plexiglas and paint the lamp. Then complete the project by attaching 5-in.-high wood, metal, or plastic numbers to the front of the lamp. Use appropriate screws for the type of numbers you choose. Finally, add a routed nameplate hung from a decorative shelf bracket.

LATTICE-STYLE SCREEN

This screen, with its lattice panels, is designed to hide anything ranging from a pile of firewood to trash containers. It mounts easily to a concrete pad with lead anchors and lag screws.

Start construction by cutting all of the redwood components to length. Next, use a dado blade on your radial arm saw or table saw to form the ³⁄₄-in. X ³⁄₄-in. rabbets in the posts and cross members. Make several successive cuts. Mill the ³⁄₄-in. X 1½-in. rabbets on the side posts in the same way.

Now, cut the ³⁄₄-in. X ³⁄₄-in. rabbets on the ends of the cross members. The two rabbets will interlock to form the joints. Check your setup by making a trial assembly.

Once all of the components are ready, assemble the frame. Glue all of the joints with waterproof resorcinol glue, and fasten with 3d and 10d galvanized nails.

Add the upper and lower 2X4 braces at the rear of the unit, nailing them in place with 16d galvanized finishing nails. Reinforce the structure at the upper rear corners with corner braces.

Cut pre-fab lattice panels to fit the openings in the framework. Install them, holding the panels in position with a frame of 1X1 cleats. Miter the corners of the cleats.

Cut the 2X2 floor joists and install them at the base of the unit. Drill counterbored holes for lag screws, then mark the concrete pad and use a masonry bit to bore holes for the anchors.

Cut a piece of ³⁄₄-in. exterior plywood to fit the interior of the screen, then attach it with 3d galvanized nails.

Leave the project unfinished to weather naturally, or apply two coats of clear wood sealer to preserve the fresh appearance of the redwood.

Design courtesy of Philip D. Neuman, Los Osos, CA.

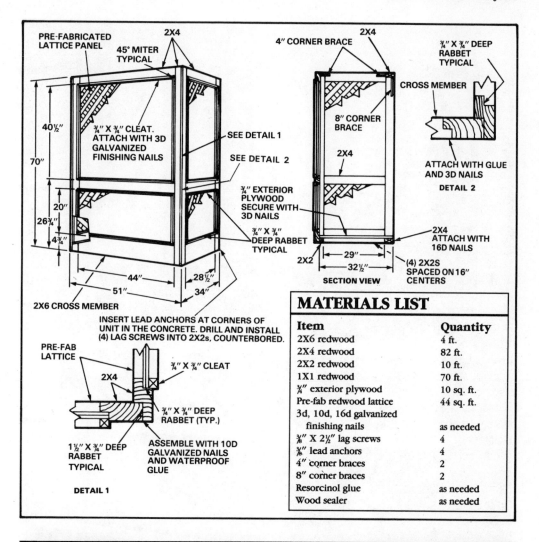

PRE-FABRICATED LATTICE PANEL

45° MITER TYPICAL

2X4

¾" X ¾" CLEAT. ATTACH WITH 3D GALVANIZED FINISHING NAILS

40½"

70"

20"

26¾"

4¾"

44"

51"

28½"

34"

2X6 CROSS MEMBER

SEE DETAIL 1

SEE DETAIL 2

¾" EXTERIOR PLYWOOD SECURE WITH 3D NAILS

¾" X ¾" DEEP RABBET TYPICAL

2X4

4" CORNER BRACE

2X4

8" CORNER BRACE

2X4

2X2

29"

32½"

SECTION VIEW

2X4 ATTACH WITH 16D NAILS

(4) 2X2S SPACED ON 16" CENTERS

¾" X ¾" DEEP RABBET TYPICAL

CROSS MEMBER

ATTACH WITH GLUE AND 3D NAILS

DETAIL 2

INSERT LEAD ANCHORS AT CORNERS OF UNIT IN THE CONCRETE. DRILL AND INSTALL (4) LAG SCREWS INTO 2X2s, COUNTERBORED.

PRE-FAB LATTICE

2X4

¾" X ¾" CLEAT

¾" X ¾" DEEP RABBET (TYP.)

1½" X ¾" DEEP RABBET TYPICAL

ASSEMBLE WITH 10D GALVANIZED NAILS AND WATERPROOF GLUE

DETAIL 1

MATERIALS LIST

Item	Quantity
2X6 redwood	4 ft.
2X4 redwood	82 ft.
2X2 redwood	10 ft.
1X1 redwood	70 ft.
¾" exterior plywood	10 sq. ft.
Pre-fab redwood lattice	44 sq. ft.
3d, 10d, 16d galvanized finishing nails	as needed
⅜" X 2½" lag screws	4
⅜" lead anchors	4
4" corner braces	2
8" corner braces	2
Resorcinol glue	as needed
Wood sealer	as needed

CONSTRUCTION DETAILS

1. Use a dado blade to form the rabbets in the frame stock. Make several passes to reach the finished depth.

2. The corners of the screen are joined by interlocking rabbets. Secure the joints with glue and nails.

LATTICE WINDOW PLANTER

A window box full of colorful annual flowers is the perfect way to dress up the exterior of your home. This window box, with its lattice panels, will display those flowers in style.

To make the planter last under the harsh conditions presented by moist soil, select pressure-treated lumber for all components.

Start construction by building the inner planter box. Cut 1X8 and 1X6 pressure-treated lumber to form the sides and ends of the box. If your particular installation requires different dimensions, modify those given in the diagram to suit your needs.

Assemble the frame of the box with no. 10 X 1½-in. flathead wood screws and waterproof resorcinol glue. Countersink the pilot holes with a combination pilot bit and countersink in your drill.

Cut a 32½-in. length of the 1X6 material to form the base of the planter. Before installing the base, bore several ½-in.-dia. holes in the part to allow proper drainage.

Install the base, fastening it with flathead wood screws and glue as you did before. Space the screws 4 in. apart for maximum strength.

If you would like the lattice panels to be set off by a differently colored background, paint the outside of the box.

The frames for the lattice panels are made of full 1-in. X 1-in. stock. Since standard 1X1 lumber is ac-

tually ¾ in. on each side, you will have to cut your stock from 2X4 material.

Use a band saw to rip 1-in.-wide strips from 2X4 stock. Set up a fence on the saw's table to help you cut accurately. Once the strips are cut, rip the 1½-in. sides to a 1-in. thickness using the same setup.

If you do not have a band saw, these strips can also be ripped on a table saw. When working with small stock on a table saw, however, pay special attention to proper safety procedures.

Once the stock is cut to size, machine the ½-in. X ½-in. grooves on one side of the material with your router and a ½-in. straight bit. Use an edge guide or a router table. Make several passes on each strip, deepening the cut with each pass until your reach the correct depth.

Once the frame material is prepared, cut the frame components to length with a hand miter box. Be careful to make matching components the same size.

Attach three sides of each frame to the box with 4d galvanized finishing nails and resorcinol glue. Drive the nails through the solid part of the frame stock and set the nail heads just below the surface of the wood.

Cut pre-fab lattice material to fit the frame. If you are building the box to the dimensions shown in the diagram, cut the lattice panels to the sizes indicated there.

CONSTRUCTION DETAILS

1. *Rip 45 degree beveled strips from scrap 1-in. X 1-in. frame stock to form the corners of the planter.*

2. *Use a ½-in. straight bit in your router to form the grooves for the pre-fab redwood lattice.*

3. *Cut the frame segments at a 45 degree miter with a hand miter box. Measure accurately for a good fit.*

4. *Attach the lattice and frames with 4d galvanized finishing nails and glue. Set the nails just below the surface.*

Slip the panels into the grooves in the frame components, then add the remaining grooved sides to the structure, nailing them in place as you did before.

Set the table of your band saw to a 45 degree angle and rip filler strips from a scrap of the 1-in. X 1-in. frame stock. Fasten these to the corners of the window box with 4d galvanized finishing nails.

Sand the completed box thoroughly and finish either with a clear wood sealer and preservative or with exterior latex enamel in the color of your choice.

Bore countersunk ³⁄₁₆-in. holes in the rear panel of the planter box for the screws that will attach it to your house. If your home has wood siding, attach the box with no. 12 X 2½-in. flathead wood screws. For other types of siding, use appropriate fasteners.

Finally, place a 2-in.-thick layer of gravel in the bottom of the planter, then fill it with high-quality planting mix and add plants.

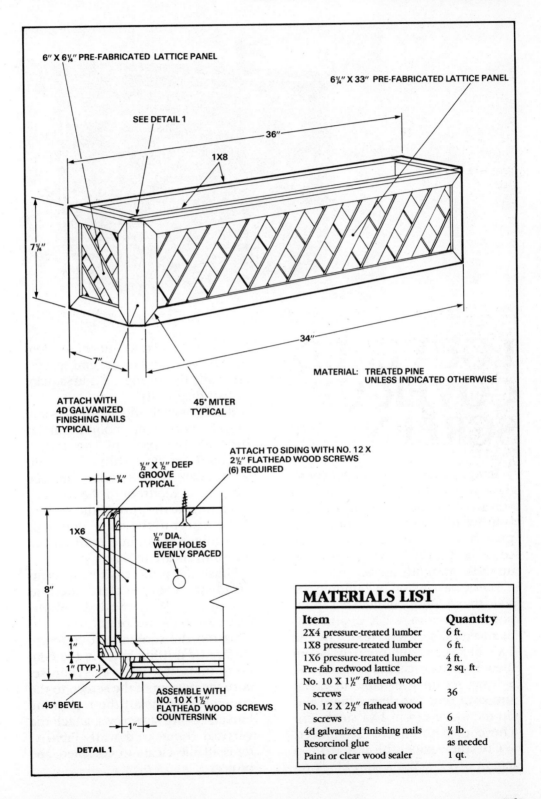

6" X 6¼" PRE-FABRICATED LATTICE PANEL

6¼" X 33" PRE-FABRICATED LATTICE PANEL

SEE DETAIL 1

36"

1X8

7¼"

34"

7"

MATERIAL: TREATED PINE
UNLESS INDICATED OTHERWISE

ATTACH WITH
4D GALVANIZED
FINISHING NAILS
TYPICAL

45° MITER
TYPICAL

½" X ½" DEEP
GROOVE
TYPICAL

ATTACH TO SIDING WITH NO. 12 X
2½" FLATHEAD WOOD SCREWS
(6) REQUIRED

¼"

1X6

½" DIA.
WEEP HOLES
EVENLY SPACED

8"

1"

1" (TYP.)

45° BEVEL

ASSEMBLE WITH
NO. 10 X 1½"
FLATHEAD WOOD SCREWS
COUNTERSINK

1"

DETAIL 1

MATERIALS LIST

Item	Quantity
2X4 pressure-treated lumber	6 ft.
1X8 pressure-treated lumber	6 ft.
1X6 pressure-treated lumber	4 ft.
Pre-fab redwood lattice	2 sq. ft.
No. 10 X 1½" flathead wood screws	36
No. 12 X 2½" flathead wood screws	6
4d galvanized finishing nails	¼ lb.
Resorcinol glue	as needed
Paint or clear wood sealer	1 qt.

LOUVERED COVER-UP SCREEN

If you are like most homeowners, there is at least one spot in your yard you would rather hide. It might be your trash collection area or a compost heap. This louvered screen could be just the answer to covering up those unsightly areas.

Start construction by building the 2X4 frame. Bore countersunk pilot holes for the no. 12 X 2½-in. flathead wood screws. Next, cut the 1X1 cleats and temporarily fasten them to the vertical frame members.

Now, set up your table or radial arm saw to cut a 45 degree bevel and rip the louvers from 1X4 stock. Rip a bevel on both sides of each louver.

Cut the spacer blocks from a length of 1X4. Use a stop block on your saw's fence to cut these identical parts. Note that the end spacers are made by cutting a 2⅞-in. square in half diagonally.

Before assembling the spacers and louvers, bore ¼-in. mounting holes through the base of the frame. Counterbore these with a ⅝-in. bit, ½ in. deep. Now, remove the 1X1 cleats from the front of the frame.

Starting at the top of the screen, nail a spacer to the frame, followed by a louver. Continue until all but four louvers are in place.

Finish the project with two coats of clear wood sealer, such as Thompson's Water Seal. Allow the first coat to dry overnight.

Fasten the screen to a concrete surface by drilling holes in the concrete for screw anchors. Then secure the bottom of the screen to the concrete and install the remaining louvers. Using lag screws, attach the vertical frame to a wall. Finally, reinstall the cleats to complete the project.

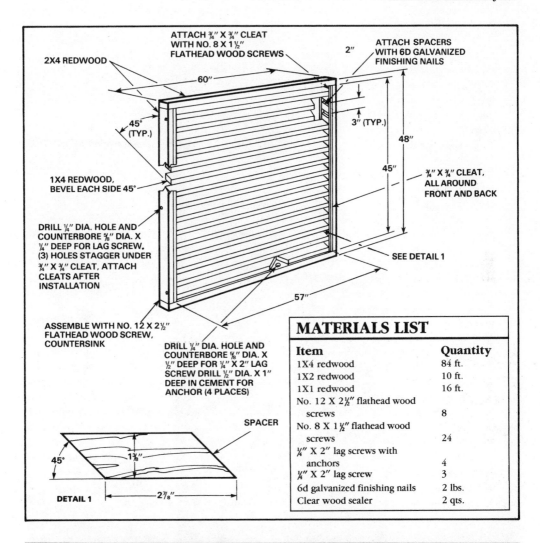

ATTACH ¾" X ¾" CLEAT
WITH NO. 8 X 1½"
FLATHEAD WOOD SCREWS

2"

ATTACH SPACERS
WITH 6D GALVANIZED
FINISHING NAILS

2X4 REDWOOD

60"

3" (TYP.)

48"

45°
(TYP.)

45"

1X4 REDWOOD,
BEVEL EACH SIDE 45°

¾" X ¾" CLEAT,
ALL AROUND
FRONT AND BACK

DRILL ¼" DIA. HOLE AND
COUNTERBORE ⅝" DIA. X
¼" DEEP FOR LAG SCREW.
(3) HOLES STAGGER UNDER
¾" X ¾" CLEAT, ATTACH
CLEATS AFTER
INSTALLATION

SEE DETAIL 1

ASSEMBLE WITH NO. 12 X 2½"
FLATHEAD WOOD SCREW,
COUNTERSINK

57"

DRILL ¼" DIA. HOLE AND
COUNTERBORE ⅝" DIA. X
½" DEEP FOR ¼" X 2" LAG
SCREW DRILL ½" DIA. X 1"
DEEP IN CEMENT FOR
ANCHOR (4 PLACES)

SPACER

45°

1¾"

2⅞"

DETAIL 1

MATERIALS LIST

Item	Quantity
1X4 redwood	84 ft.
1X2 redwood	10 ft.
1X1 redwood	16 ft.
No. 12 X 2½" flathead wood screws	8
No. 8 X 1½" flathead wood screws	24
¼" X 2" lag screws with anchors	4
¼" X 2" lag screw	3
6d galvanized finishing nails	2 lbs.
Clear wood sealer	2 qts.

CONSTRUCTION DETAILS

1. Set the blade on your table saw to cut a 45 degree bevel. Rip the bevels on the louvers using the fence.

2. Fasten filler blocks between the louvers to separate and space them. Nail the louvers to the blocks.

LOUVERED LAMP

Carefully planned outdoor lighting can enhance any home. Whether you want to light a walkway or just add a little cheer to a dark corner of your yard, this lamp is the perfect solution.

Begin construction by locating the lamp's site in your yard. Dig a 8-in.- dia. hole 24 in. deep. Now, cut a 24-in.-long 4X4 post. Form a 90 degree bend in a length of thinwall conduit with a conduit bender. Attach the conduit to the 4X4 post with clamps.

Set the post, with the conduit attached, into the hole. Orient the conduit's lower end toward your power source, and plug the lower end of the conduit to keep dirt out.

Adjust the post to make it vertical. The top of the post should be 12 in. above the grade. Fill the posthole with concrete mix. Check the adjustment of the post once again.

Once the concrete has set, cut the lower back board of the lamp to its finished dimensions. Use a dado blade on your radial arm saw to form a ½-in. X ½-in. rabbet at the top. Attach the back board to the post with ¼-in. X 2-in. lag screws.

Next, cut the sides of the lamp from 1X10 stock. Using a radial arm saw or a table saw, cut a 45 degree angle at the top of each side. Check the sides to make sure they are identical. Attach the sides to the back board with no. 10 X 1½-in. flathead wood screws and waterproof resorcinol glue. Countersink all screw holes.

Cut the upper back board, beveling its top at a 45 degree angle. Form another ½-in. X ½-in. rabbet on the lower edge of this compo-

nent. Install it with the beveled edge matching the sides. Add two 1X1 cleats to the sides.

Now, cut the lamp support platform to fit inside the structure. Allow for the thickness of the front panel. Bore a 1-in.-dia. hole for the conduit. Screw 1X1 cleats to the sides of the lamp. Slide the platform over the conduit and screw the platform to the cleats. Cut the conduit to its finished length.

Dig a trench from the lamp to your power source, then pull underground electrical cable through the conduit. Check your local codes to determine whether the entire cable needs to be protected by conduit. You must, however, connect this circuit to a ground fault interrupter.

Install a round weatherproof electrical box on the platform, then use flexible electrical conduit and appropriate fittings to connect the box to the existing conduit. Add an electrical box cover with gasket and outdoor lampholder. Use a 75-watt lamp or less. Do not use any lamp over 75 watts, because this creates a fire hazard.

At your power source, connect the lamp to your wiring through a switch. Follow the appropriate electrical codes and make certain the power is off. Test the circuit before completing construction.

Cut the lower front panel of the lamp to the dimensions shown in the diagram. Bevel the top edge at a 45 degree angle. Install the front panel with glue and screws as you did before.

Now, cut 1X1 cleats 10 in. long, with 45 degree bevels on both ends.

CONSTRUCTION DETAILS

1. Screw the access door cleats to the sides of the lamp. Allow space for the plywood panel.

2. Cut ⅛-in.-wide X ¼-in.-deep slots for the louvers in the cleats. Space the slots ¾ in. apart.

3. Glue the slats into the grooves with resorcinol glue. Position the slats flush with the front of the lamp.

4. Using a radial arm saw, cut the top of the lamp to fit. Bevel both ends at a 45 degree angle.

Lay out the angled grooves ¾ in. apart and form these on your radial arm saw. Use a blade with a ⅛-in. kerf and cut the grooves ¼ in. deep.

Attach the cleats to the lamp's front with glue and no. 10 X 1¼-in. screws. Next, cut the slats from ⅛-in.-thick plywood. Cut the top of the lamp and the rear access panel, checking their fit carefully.

Give the inside surfaces of all components two coats of white exterior enamel to reflect the light. Glue the slats into their grooves, then add the top of the lamp. Finally, install the back panel.

Sand the exterior of the lamp thoroughly, breaking all sharp edges as you work. Finish the project with two coats of clear wood sealer.

MATERIALS LIST

Item	Quantity
4X4 redwood	2 ft.
1X10 redwood	12 ft.
1X1 redwood	4 ft.
⅛″ plywood	1 sq. ft.
½″ thinwall electrical conduit	4 ft.
½″ flexible electrical conduit	24″
½″ conduit clamps, fittings	as needed
Weatherproof round electrical box with cover, gasket, lampholder, 75-watt lamp	1 each
Direct-burial electrical cable	as needed
No. 10 X 1¼″, 1½″ flathead wood screws	as needed
No. 8 X 1¼″ flathead wood screws	as needed
¼″ X 2″ lag screws	4
100 lb. concrete bag	1
Resorcinol glue	as needed
Clear wood sealer, white paint	1 qt. each

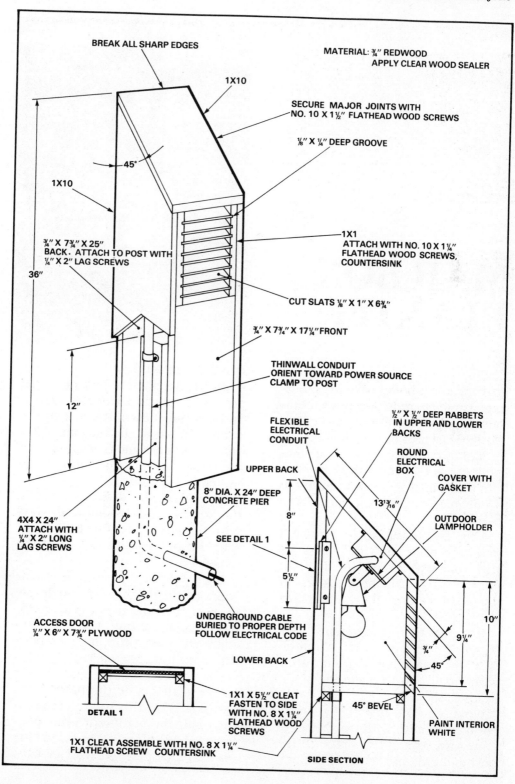

BREAK ALL SHARP EDGES

MATERIAL: ¾″ REDWOOD
APPLY CLEAR WOOD SEALER

1X10

SECURE MAJOR JOINTS WITH
NO. 10 X 1½″ FLATHEAD WOOD SCREWS

⅛″ X ¼″ DEEP GROOVE

45°

1X10

¾″ X 7¾″ X 25″
BACK. ATTACH TO POST WITH
¼″ X 2″ LAG SCREWS

1X1
ATTACH WITH NO. 10 X 1¼″
FLATHEAD WOOD SCREWS,
COUNTERSINK

36″

CUT SLATS ⅛″ X 1″ X 6¾″

¾″ X 7¾″ X 17¼″ FRONT

THINWALL CONDUIT
ORIENT TOWARD POWER SOURCE
CLAMP TO POST

12″

FLEXIBLE
ELECTRICAL
CONDUIT

½″ X ½″ DEEP RABBETS
IN UPPER AND LOWER
BACKS

ROUND
ELECTRICAL
BOX

UPPER BACK

COVER WITH
GASKET

8″ DIA. X 24″ DEEP
CONCRETE PIER

13¹³⁄₁₆″

8″

OUTDOOR
LAMPHOLDER

SEE DETAIL 1

5½″

4X4 X 24″
ATTACH WITH
¼″ X 2″ LONG
LAG SCREWS

UNDERGROUND CABLE
BURIED TO PROPER DEPTH
FOLLOW ELECTRICAL CODE

10″

9¼″

¾″

LOWER BACK

45°

ACCESS DOOR
¼″ X 6″ X 7¾″ PLYWOOD

1X1 X 5½″ CLEAT
FASTEN TO SIDE
WITH NO. 8 X 1¼″
FLATHEAD WOOD
SCREWS

45° BEVEL

PAINT INTERIOR
WHITE

DETAIL 1

1X1 CLEAT ASSEMBLE WITH NO. 8 X 1¼″
FLATHEAD SCREW COUNTERSINK

SIDE SECTION

MAILBOX PLANTER

This project helps destroy the myth that mailboxes have to be boring. Attractive redwood posts, combined with a planter box, make this mailbox an asset to your home.

Start by cutting the 4X4 post components as shown in the diagram. Use your radial arm saw to form the 45 degree bevels on the ends of the parts.

Now, lay out the lap joint on both parts and make multiple saw kerfs with your saw. Be sure the depth of cut is exactly half the thickness of the wood. Remove the waste with a sharp chisel.

Join the two components with $5/16$-in. X 3-in lag screws. Counterbore the pilot holes $3/8$ in. deep with a $3/4$-in. bit to make the screw heads flush.

Next, cut and install the brace. Form each miter with two passes of your saw. Attach the brace to the post and crossbar with lag screws,

counterboring the holes.

Build the planter box next. Set your saw to cut 15 degree bevels and rip the redwood stock to the widths shown in the diagram. After cutting the sides and bottom, lay out the ends with an adjustable bevel and cut these as well.

Bore two $1/2$-in. drainage holes in the bottom, then assemble the box with 6d galvanized finishing nails. Nail the planter to the rear of the crossbar.

Dig a 36-in.-deep posthole where you want the mailbox located. Insert the post, then mix and pour a 100-lb. bag of concrete mix. Use a level to adjust the post, propping it in position until the concrete sets.

Cut a piece of $3/4$-in. exterior plywood to fit inside the base of the mailbox. Nail this to the crossbar, then nail the mailbox to this platform. Add planting mix to the planter, then plant colorful annuals.

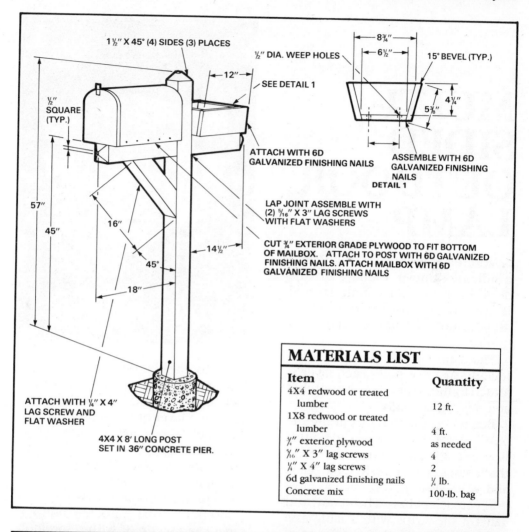

1½" X 45° (4) SIDES (3) PLACES

½" DIA. WEEP HOLES

8¾"

6½"

15° BEVEL (TYP.)

12"

SEE DETAIL 1

4¼"

½" SQUARE (TYP.)

5⅜"

ATTACH WITH 6D GALVANIZED FINISHING NAILS

ASSEMBLE WITH 6D GALVANIZED FINISHING NAILS

DETAIL 1

57"

45"

16"

45°

14½"

LAP JOINT ASSEMBLE WITH (2) 5/16" X 3" LAG SCREWS WITH FLAT WASHERS

CUT ¾" EXTERIOR GRADE PLYWOOD TO FIT BOTTOM OF MAILBOX. ATTACH TO POST WITH 6D GALVANIZED FINISHING NAILS. ATTACH MAILBOX WITH 6D GALVANIZED FINISHING NAILS

18"

ATTACH WITH ¼" X 4" LAG SCREW AND FLAT WASHER

4X4 X 8' LONG POST SET IN 36" CONCRETE PIER.

MATERIALS LIST

Item	Quantity
4X4 redwood or treated lumber	12 ft.
1X8 redwood or treated lumber	4 ft.
¾" exterior plywood	as needed
5/16" X 3" lag screws	4
¼" X 4" lag screws	2
6d galvanized finishing nails	¼ lb.
Concrete mix	100-lb. bag

CONSTRUCTION DETAILS

1. Cut the bevels on the 4X4 components with your radial arm saw. Align the cuts carefully for an even bevel.

2. Use a wood chisel to remove the waste from the lap joints after making multiple passes with your saw.

371

MULTI-SIDED OUTDOOR LAMP

Nothing is more romantic than a candle-lit summer evening on the deck or patio. This multi-layered lamp will cast just the right glow. All you add is a candle in a tall glass holder.

The lamp is made up of interlocking strips of pine. Each layer is joined to the layer below by notches at a 45 degree angle.

Begin construction by cutting the $\frac{1}{16}$-in. strips. The best way to do this is to use a band saw to resaw 2-in.-thick stock. Use a fresh $\frac{1}{2}$-in. blade and work slowly.

If you do not have a band saw, you can rip the strips with a table saw or a radial arm saw. Use a sharp combination blade to insure a smooth cut. Measure the exact saw kerf width of the blade. Then, for each strip, set the fence or saw blade over $\frac{1}{16}$ in. plus the width of the saw kerf. Always rip thin strips off the side away from the fence. Do this for each pass.

Cut the strips to length, and then lay out the notches on one strip. Cut the notches with a band saw or a saber saw. Use this strip to mark the rest of the strips. Notice that the top and bottom layers have only $\frac{3}{16}$-in. X $\frac{1}{8}$-in. notches on one edge.

Assemble the squares by interlocking the 1-in.-deep notches. Apply a thin layer of resorcinol glue to the notches to secure the assembly.

Cut the pine base to the dimensions shown in the diagram, and use a straight bit in your router to form the 3-in.-dia. candle recess.

Insert the base into the bottom square and secure it with resorcinol glue and $\frac{3}{4}$-in. brass brads.

Complete the assembly by stacking the remaining layers, interlocking the notches. As you did before, secure the assembly with resorcinol glue.

Finish the project with two coats of wood sealer. Allow 24 hours between coats for best results.

For safety's sake use only a tall glassed candle that is as high as the project and make sure that flammables are kept well away from the lit candle.

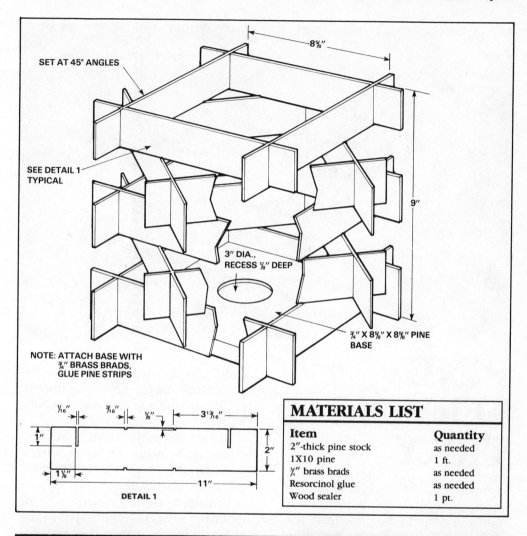

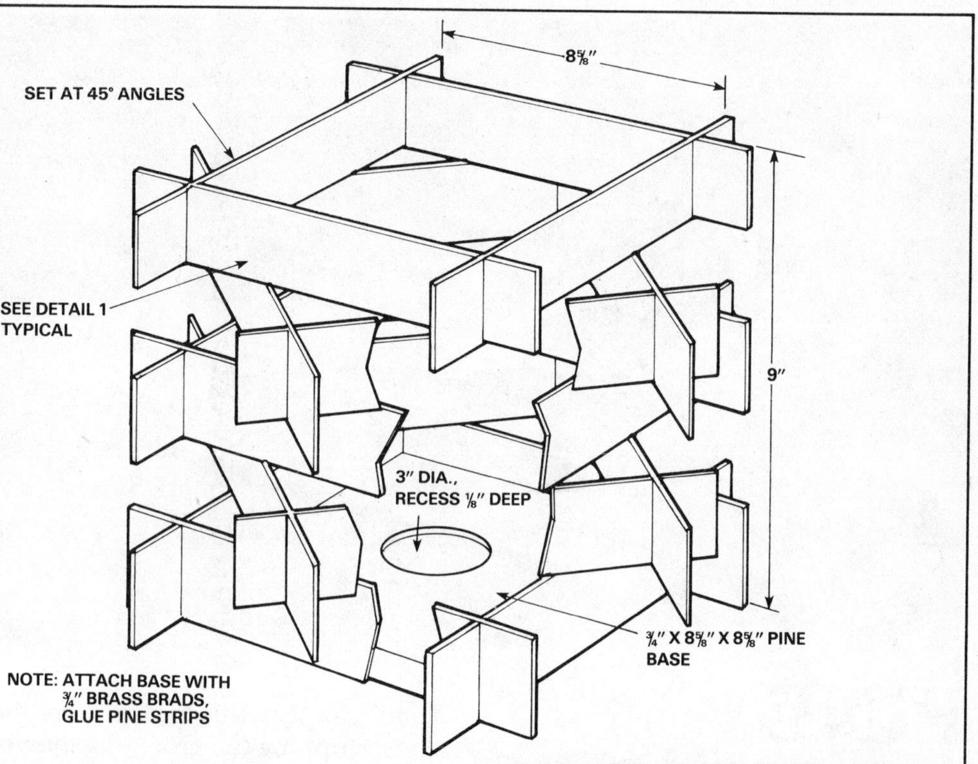
8 5/8″
SET AT 45° ANGLES
SEE DETAIL 1 TYPICAL
9″
3″ DIA., RECESS 1/8″ DEEP
3/4″ X 8 5/8″ X 8 5/8″ PINE BASE
NOTE: ATTACH BASE WITH 3/4″ BRASS BRADS, GLUE PINE STRIPS

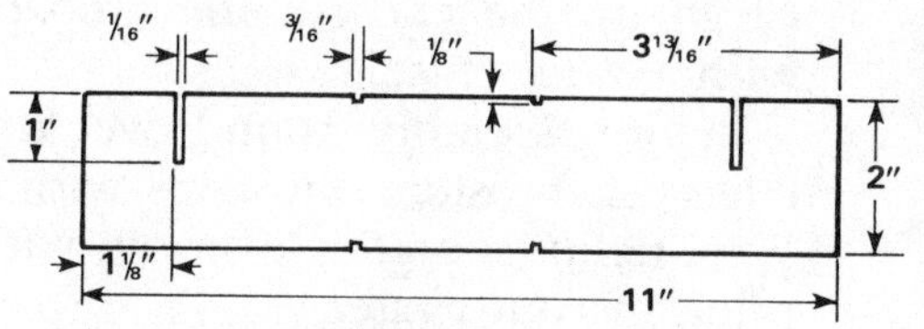
1/16″
3/16″
1/8″
3 13/16″
1″
2″
1 1/8″
11″

DETAIL 1

MATERIALS LIST

Item	Quantity
2″-thick pine stock	as needed
1X10 pine	1 ft.
3/4″ brass brads	as needed
Resorcinol glue	as needed
Wood sealer	1 pt.

CONSTRUCTION DETAILS

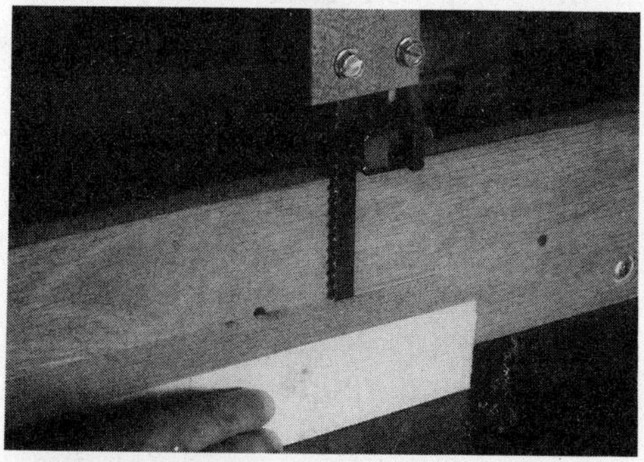

1. Rip the slats to thickness with your band saw equipped with a 1/2-in. wide blade. Don't rush the cut.

2. Stack the slats and gang cut all notches using a band saw. Keep fingers well away from blade.

PINE SERVING TRAY

When you are entertaining outdoors, there is always a need to carry food and drink to the patio from the kitchen. This pine serving tray is an attractive and safe way to do just that. Features include a glass holder to help prevent spills.

Start by laying out the tray's ends. Cut the contours with a fine-toothed blade in your saber saw. To form the handles, drill ³/₄-in.-dia. holes at the ends of the handle openings. Cut away the waste with your saber saw.

Next, cut the sides of the tray to the length shown in the diagram. Use a router equipped with a ¹/₄-in. straight bit and an edge guide to form the groove for the tray's bottom panel. Repeat this process on the ends, stopping the groove as shown. Clean up the ends of the grooves with a ¹/₄-in. chisel.

Before assembly, round over the edges of the sides and ends with a ¹/₄-in.-radius rounding-over bit, with pilot, in your router.

Cut the bottom panel from ¹/₄-in. exterior plywood and install it in the grooves of the tray's end components. Slip the sides into place, square up the assembly, and nail with 4d finishing nails. Set the nails just below the surface and fill with wood filler.

Cut the parts for the stemware holders, using standard molding stock. Glue these in place at one end of the tray.

Sand the completed tray, working down to 220-grit garnet paper, then apply the stain of your choice. Follow this up with two coats of satin-finish polyurethane varnish.

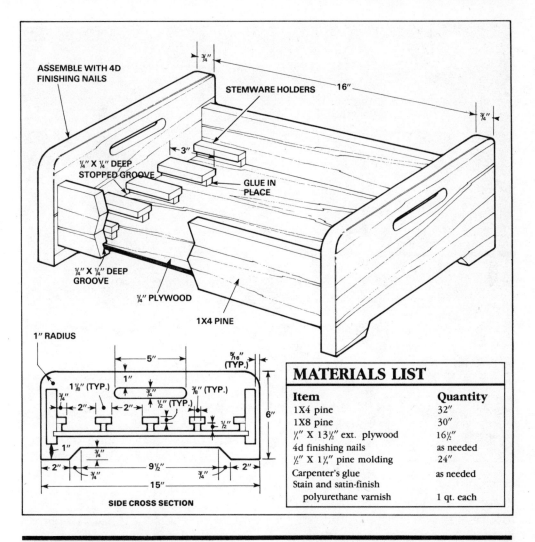

ASSEMBLE WITH 4D FINISHING NAILS

STEMWARE HOLDERS

¾"

16"

¾"

3"

¼" X ¼" DEEP STOPPED GROOVE

GLUE IN PLACE

¼" X ¼" DEEP GROOVE

¼" PLYWOOD

1X4 PINE

1" RADIUS

5/16" (TYP.)

5"

1"

1⅛" (TYP.)

¾"

¾" (TYP.)

¾"

¾"

½" (TYP.)

2"

2"

6"

½"

1"

¾"

2"

9½"

¾"

2"

15"

SIDE CROSS SECTION

MATERIALS LIST

Item	Quantity
1X4 pine	32"
1X8 pine	30"
¼" X 13½" ext. plywood	16½"
4d finishing nails	as needed
½" X 1¼" pine molding	24"
Carpenter's glue	as needed
Stain and satin-finish polyurethane varnish	1 qt. each

CONSTRUCTION DETAILS

1. Form the handles by drilling two holes. Use a backup board to prevent splintering. Cut handholds with a saber saw.

2. Glue the glass holders in place. Apply finger pressure to hold the parts in position until the glue begins to set.

PLANT TOWER

Many potted plants are at their best when displayed near eye level. This plant tower, with four levels of display shelves, is designed to show off some of your favorite specimens.

Start construction by forming the beveled top on the unit's post. Set the blade on your table or radial arm saw to cut a 45 degree bevel. Use a stop block to position the post so that the bevels are 1 in. from the top, then cut the four sides, one at a time.

Next, cut twelve pieces of 1X4 lumber to form the shelf supports and the base components. On one piece, lay out the profile of the parts as shown in the diagram. Do not lay out the notches for the four base parts at this time or the $\frac{1}{2}$-in. radius on the corners.

Carefully cut the parts with a saber saw or band saw. Check the dimensions after cutting.

Once all twelve are cut to the basic shape (the base parts are longer), clamp several together and use a medium-grit belt on your belt sander to even up any irregularities. At the same time, form the radius on the ends of the parts with the belt sander. This process will insure that all the parts are identical.

Next, take the four longer pieces and lay out the $\frac{3}{4}$-in. X $1\frac{3}{4}$-in. notches to form the lap joints for the base. The notches should be $3\frac{1}{2}$ in. apart.

Cut the notches with a dado blade on your radial arm saw. Clamp two boards together, and make multiple passes until the proper depth is reached.

Assemble the base by interlocking the notches as shown in the detailed photograph. Insert the post into the base, and secure it with no. 10 X 2-in. flathead wood screws. Drill countersunk pilot holes in the base with a combination pilot bit and countersink.

Using the same procedure, mark the positions of the shelves on the post and attach a pair of shelf supports. Notice that the top of the supports should be placed $\frac{3}{4}$ in. below the dimensions given in the diagram.

Now, rip $\frac{3}{4}$-in. exterior plywood into 12-in.-wide strips for the shelf stock. Cut the strips into $11\frac{3}{4}$-in.-long sections. You will need eight of these. Use a plywood blade on your saw to minimize splintering the wood.

Lay out the profile of the shelf halves on one of the pieces, then cut out the part with a saber saw or band saw. Be careful to make the notch exactly $1\frac{3}{4}$ in. X $3\frac{1}{2}$ in. Use this piece as a template to lay out the seven remaining pieces.

Once again, clamp the pieces together and even them up with a belt sander. Start with a medium-grit belt, and finish up with a fine belt to prepare the plywood's edges for finishing.

Attach the shelf halves to the supports with 6d galvanized finishing nails. Set the nails just below the surface of the wood with a nail set.

Give the completed unit a final sanding, then apply two coats of semi-gloss latex exterior enamel in the color of your choice.

CONSTRUCTION DETAILS

1. *Lay out one of the shelf halves with a circle template. After cutting out, use it as a template for the others.*

2. *Use a saber saw to cut the notches in the shelf halves. Be careful to keep the notches square.*

3. *Use a dado blade on your radial arm saw to cut the leg notches. To save time, cut two pieces at once.*

4. *The notches in the leg pieces interlock to form the base of the plant tower. The post fits in the opening.*

5. *Attach the shelf supports to the post with countersunk wood screws. Make sure both supports are parallel.*

6. *As an alternative to nails, secure the shelf halves to the brackets with no. 8 X 1-½-in. flathead wood screws, countersink.*

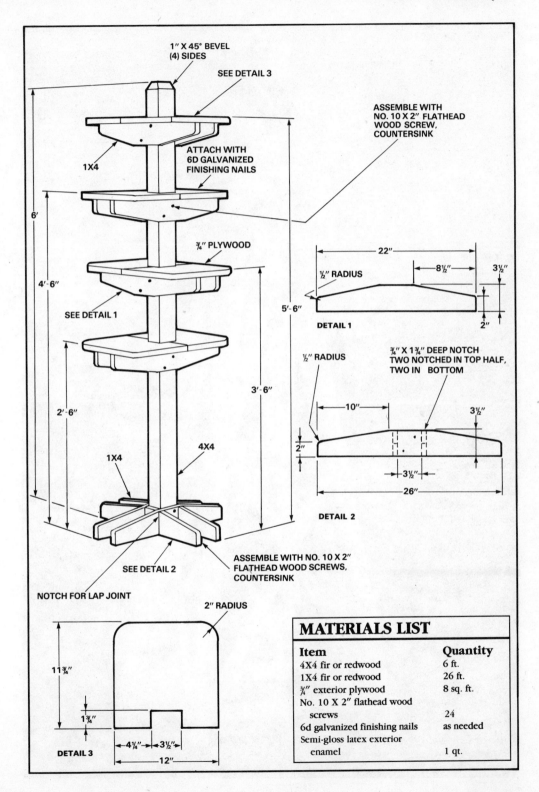

1" X 45° BEVEL
(4) SIDES

SEE DETAIL 3

ASSEMBLE WITH
NO. 10 X 2" FLATHEAD
WOOD SCREW,
COUNTERSINK

ATTACH WITH
6D GALVANIZED
FINISHING NAILS

1X4

6'

¾" PLYWOOD

4'-6"

SEE DETAIL 1

5'-6"

2'-6"

3'-6"

1X4

4X4

½" RADIUS

22"

8½"

3½"

2"

DETAIL 1

½" RADIUS

¾" X 1¾" DEEP NOTCH
TWO NOTCHED IN TOP HALF,
TWO IN BOTTOM

10"

3½"

2"

3½"

26"

DETAIL 2

ASSEMBLE WITH NO. 10 X 2"
FLATHEAD WOOD SCREWS,
COUNTERSINK

SEE DETAIL 2

NOTCH FOR LAP JOINT

2" RADIUS

11¾"

1¾"

4¼" 3½"

12"

DETAIL 3

MATERIALS LIST

Item	Quantity
4X4 fir or redwood	6 ft.
1X4 fir or redwood	26 ft.
¾" exterior plywood	8 sq. ft.
No. 10 X 2" flathead wood screws	24
6d galvanized finishing nails	as needed
Semi-gloss latex exterior enamel	1 qt.

PLATFORM WINDMILL

There is nothing like a windmill in your yard to add movement and interest. This free-standing windmill is patterned after the windmills used on farms all across the country.

Start building the project by making the platform. Set your table saw or radial arm saw to cut a compound miter on the legs and the horizontal braces of the platform. Set both the miter angle and the bevel angle to 10 degrees.

The dimensions shown in the diagram for these parts indicate the longest side of each component. Measure accurately to make the components match.

After cutting the 2X2 legs and braces, assemble the basic tower using no. 10 X 2½-in. flathead wood screws at each joint. Assemble two opposite sides of the tower, then join the pairs of leg assemblies.

Now, measure one of the lower leg braces against the tower frame and mark the angles for the joints. Use this brace as a pattern for the remaining braces, cutting them all with one saw setup. Do the same for the upper cross braces.

Nail the braces in place, as shown in the diagram, with 4d galvanized nails. Finish the tower by adding the 8-in.-square platform to the top, nailing it in place with 8d galvanized nails.

Lay out the patterns for the blades and tail of the windmill on 16-gauge galvanized sheet metal. Cut the straight sides of these parts with tin snips, and cut the semi-circular end of the tail with circle snips. Once the parts are cut, smooth any sharp edges with a bastard file.

Cut a slot in one end of the dowel shaft of the windmill with a band saw. Use a short fence to help guide the cut. Insert the tail into this slot and secure it with ¾-in. brads.

Cut the ⅜-in.-dia spokes to the length shown in the diagram, then cut a flat on the spokes with a band saw. Again, use a fence to guide the cut.

Center each blade on the flat, and secure it to the dowel with ¾-in. brads. Drill pilot holes for the brads and bend the protruding tips over as shown in the diagram.

Cut a 2-in.-dia. disk of 1-in.-thick hardwood stock to form the hub of the windmill. Lay out four equally spaced holes for the dowels. Then drill ⅜-in.-dia. holes ¾ in. deep. Use a drill press for accuracy.

Insert the dowel spokes into the holes after coating them with waterproof resorcinol glue. Align the blades at a 45 degree angle with all four blades facing in the same direction. Once the blades are aligned, secure the spokes with 1-in. brads.

Bore a ¼-in. hole through the center of the hub and a ⁵⁄₃₂-in. pilot hole in the end of the shaft. Attach the hub to the shaft with a ³⁄₁₆-in. lag screw and two washers. Do not overtighten the screw; the hub must spin freely.

Next, cut a 4-in.-dia. disk and a 2-in.-dia. disk from the same stock you used for the hub. Bore a ¼-in. hole through the center of each disk, then attach the disks to the center of

CONSTRUCTION DETAILS

1. *Cut the semi-circular opening at the rear of the tail with a pair of circle-cutting tin snips.*

2. *Rip the grooves in the dowels with a band saw. Use a guide to help keep the cuts straight.*

3. *Cut the compound bevels on the tower's legs and braces with a radial arm saw. Set both angles at 10 degrees.*

4. *Attach the cross braces to the frame with 4d galvanized nails. The braces give the tower added strength.*

the platform with 6d galvanized nails. Finish by boring a ¼-in. hole through the platform.

Locate the center of balance of the shaft by balancing it on a narrow board. Bore a ¼-in.-dia. hole at that point, making sure the tail is vertical. Attach the shaft to the top of the tower with a ³⁄₁₆-in. X 3½-in. machine screw.

Place washers under the head of the bolt, between the shaft and the top disk, and under the nut. Once again, tighten the nut only enough to secure the assembly, which must move freely.

MATERIALS LIST	
Item	**Quantity**
2X2 redwood	34 ft.
1X10 redwood	1 ft.
1X6 hardwood	2 ft.
1" X 2" hardwood	2"
Redwood lath	42 ft.
1" hardwood dowel	2 ft.
⅜" hardwood dowel	4 ft.
16-ga. galvanized steel	1½ sq. ft.
³⁄₁₆" X 2" lag screw	1
³⁄₁₆" X 3½" machine screw and nut	1
³⁄₁₆" flat washers	5
No. 10 X 2½" flathead wood screws	24
½", ¾", 1" brads	as needed
4d, 6d, 8d galvanized nails	as needed
Resorcinol glue	as needed

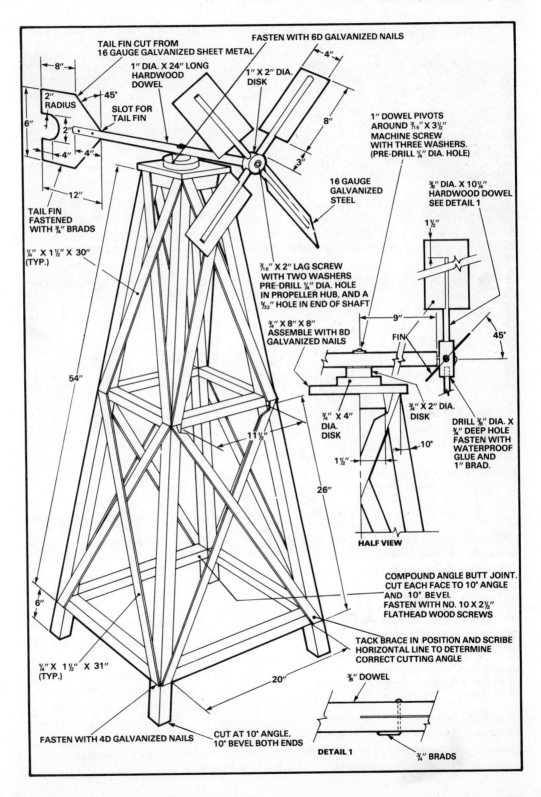

TAIL FIN CUT FROM
16 GAUGE GALVANIZED SHEET METAL

FASTEN WITH 6D GALVANIZED NAILS

8"

2"
RADIUS

45°

1" DIA. X 24" LONG
HARDWOOD
DOWEL

1" X 2" DIA.
DISK

SLOT FOR
TAIL FIN

6"

2"

4"   4"

12"

TAIL FIN
FASTENED
WITH ¾" BRADS

¼" X 1½" X 30"
(TYP.)

54"

11½"

6"

¼" X 1½" X 31"
(TYP.)

FASTEN WITH 4D GALVANIZED NAILS

CUT AT 10° ANGLE,
10° BEVEL BOTH ENDS

20"

8"

3"

16 GAUGE
GALVANIZED
STEEL

1" DOWEL PIVOTS
AROUND ³⁄₁₆" X 3½"
MACHINE SCREW
WITH THREE WASHERS.
(PRE-DRILL ¼" DIA. HOLE)

³⁄₈" DIA. X 10¼"
HARDWOOD DOWEL
SEE DETAIL 1

1½"

1½"

9"

FIN

45°

³⁄₁₆" X 2" LAG SCREW
WITH TWO WASHERS
PRE-DRILL ¼" DIA. HOLE
IN PROPELLER HUB, AND A
⁵⁄₃₂" HOLE IN END OF SHAFT

¾" X 8" X 8"
ASSEMBLE WITH 8D
GALVANIZED NAILS

¾" X 4"
DIA.
DISK

¾" X 2" DIA.
DISK

DRILL ³⁄₈" DIA. X
¾" DEEP HOLE
FASTEN WITH
WATERPROOF
GLUE AND
1" BRAD.

10°

1½"

26"

HALF VIEW

COMPOUND ANGLE BUTT JOINT.
CUT EACH FACE TO 10° ANGLE
AND 10° BEVEL
FASTEN WITH NO. 10 X 2½"
FLATHEAD WOOD SCREWS

TACK BRACE IN POSITION AND SCRIBE
HORIZONTAL LINE TO DETERMINE
CORRECT CUTTING ANGLE

³⁄₈" DOWEL

DETAIL 1

¾" BRADS

PORTABLE POTTING BENCH

If gardening is an important part of your outdoor life, here is an ideal project. This portable potting bench and garden cart has everything you need for all your chores . . . including the kitchen sink!

Constructed of redwood, with all brass and stainless steel hardware, it is designed to serve you for years. The cart rolls smoothly on large wheels, while two drop-leaf work tables provide plenty of work space. Storage for garden tools, both large and small, combines with a large bin to keep all the garden necessities at hand.

A stainless steel sink is built in for washing vegetables and dirty hands, while a garden hose attaches to the cart to supply running water. Wastewater runs directly back into the garden under the cart.

Begin building this project by constructing the 2X4 floor frame. Use a dado blade on your table or radial arm saw to form the lap joints on the four corners of the floor frame. Assemble the frame with no. 8 X 1¼-in. brass flathead screws and waterproof resorcinol glue, after drilling countersunk pilot holes. Before driving the screws, lay out the notches shown in the diagram and drive screws only outside the base's notched areas. Next, cut out these notches, using a saber saw.

Cut the four uprights to the sizes shown in the diagram, and cut the tapers on the rear legs with a saber or circular saw.

Use a dado blade to cut the ¾-in. X ¾-in. stopped rabbets in the uprights. Mark the ends of the rabbets, and stop the cut just short of the marks. Finish the ends of the rabbets by hand with a wood chisel.

Bore counterbored pilot holes in the uprights and attach them to the base frame with lag screws. The counterbores should be ¾ in. in diameter and ½ in. deep to allow for the screw hole plugs.

Cut the panel boards to length and attach them to the frame, starting with the sides. Bore pilot holes with a combination pilot drill and countersink, and use resorcinol glue on all joints. Notice the slight spacing between the boards that allows for air circulation.

Install the bottom boards, spacing them as shown in the diagram. Notice the gap for the partition. Use a piece of the partition lumber to size this gap accurately.

Next, assemble the gate components, screwing the battens to the panel boards. There should be a ¾-in. gap at the top and bottom of each batten. Hang the gate to one of the rear uprights with two brass hinges, and add the barrel bolt.

Install the top and bottom boards at the back of the cart, but leave out the remaining boards temporarily to allow access for the sink plumbing.

Cut the handles next, paying close attention to the angled cuts shown in the diagram. The long tapers should be cut with a circular or saber saw, following the layout lines carefully.

Dado the handle to accommodate the rear legs with multiple passes of a dado blade. Set the saw to cut the angle given in the diagram. Remember that the handles are mirror images of each other.

Round off the handles with a rasp and sandpaper, then attach the handles to the cart as shown in the diagram. Before fastening the handles permanently to the cart, check to be certain that they are even. Add the L-shaped brackets to provide additional stability.

Cut out the drop-leaves and their supports. To lay out the supports, draw a 1-in. grid pattern on a sheet of heavy paper. Transfer the design in the diagram to the grid, then cut out the pattern. Trace this onto the redwood stock with the wood grain running in the proper direction. Cut the supports with a saber saw.

Round over the edges of the leaves and supports with a ¼-in.-radius rounding-over bit, with pilot, in your router. Install the hinge blocks

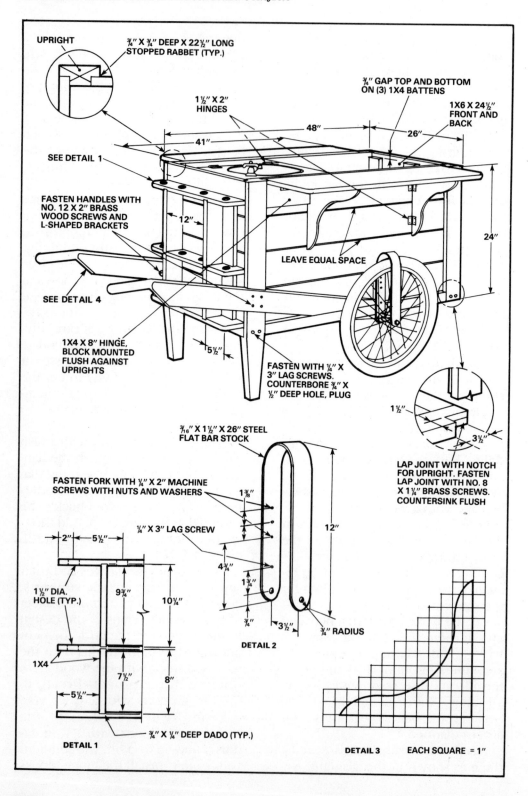

UPRIGHT

¾" X ¾" DEEP X 22½" LONG STOPPED RABBET (TYP.)

1½" X 2" HINGES

¾" GAP TOP AND BOTTOM ON (3) 1X4 BATTENS

1X6 X 24½" FRONT AND BACK

48"

41"

26"

SEE DETAIL 1

FASTEN HANDLES WITH NO. 12 X 2" BRASS WOOD SCREWS AND L-SHAPED BRACKETS

12"

24"

SEE DETAIL 4

LEAVE EQUAL SPACE

1X4 X 8" HINGE, BLOCK MOUNTED FLUSH AGAINST UPRIGHTS

5½"

FASTEN WITH ¼" X 3" LAG SCREWS. COUNTERBORE ¾" X ½" DEEP HOLE, PLUG

1½"

3½"

LAP JOINT WITH NOTCH FOR UPRIGHT. FASTEN LAP JOINT WITH NO. 8 X 1¼" BRASS SCREWS. COUNTERSINK FLUSH

3/16" X 1½" X 26" STEEL FLAT BAR STOCK

FASTEN FORK WITH ¼" X 2" MACHINE SCREWS WITH NUTS AND WASHERS

1⅜"

12"

¼" X 3" LAG SCREW

4¾"

1¾"

2"   5½"

1½" DIA. HOLE (TYP.)

9¾"

10¼"

¾"

3½"

¾" RADIUS

DETAIL 2

1X4

7½"

8"

5½"

¾" X ¼" DEEP DADO (TYP.)

DETAIL 1

DETAIL 3   EACH SQUARE = 1"

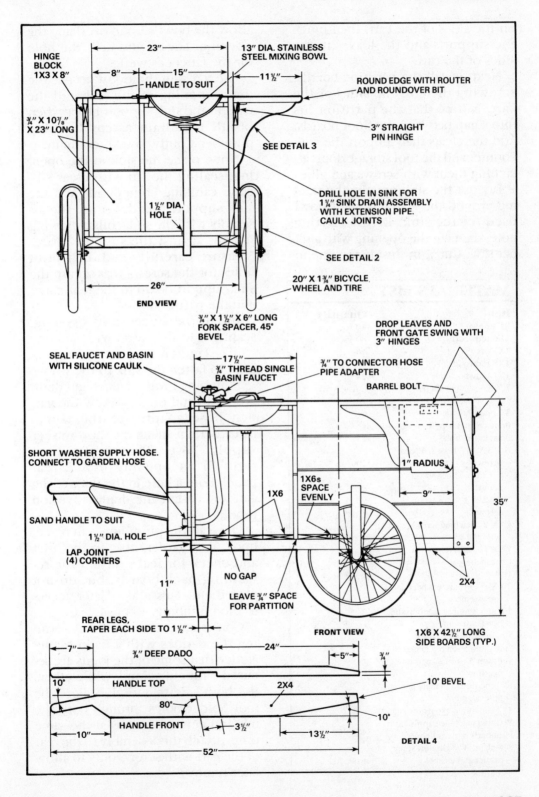

HINGE BLOCK 1X3 X 8"

¾" X 10⅞" X 23" LONG

23"

8"

15"

HANDLE TO SUIT

13" DIA. STAINLESS STEEL MIXING BOWL

11½"

ROUND EDGE WITH ROUTER AND ROUNDOVER BIT

3" STRAIGHT PIN HINGE

SEE DETAIL 3

1½" DIA. HOLE

DRILL HOLE IN SINK FOR 1¼" SINK DRAIN ASSEMBLY WITH EXTENSION PIPE. CAULK JOINTS

SEE DETAIL 2

26"

20" X 1¾" BICYCLE WHEEL AND TIRE

END VIEW

¾" X 1½" X 6" LONG FORK SPACER, 45° BEVEL

SEAL FAUCET AND BASIN WITH SILICONE CAULK

17½"

¾" THREAD SINGLE BASIN FAUCET

¾" TO CONNECTOR HOSE PIPE ADAPTER

DROP LEAVES AND FRONT GATE SWING WITH 3" HINGES

BARREL BOLT

SHORT WASHER SUPPLY HOSE. CONNECT TO GARDEN HOSE

SAND HANDLE TO SUIT

1½" DIA. HOLE

LAP JOINT (4) CORNERS

11"

1X6

1X6s SPACE EVENLY

NO GAP

LEAVE ¾" SPACE FOR PARTITION

1" RADIUS

9"

35"

2X4

REAR LEGS, TAPER EACH SIDE TO 1½"

FRONT VIEW

1X6 X 42½" LONG SIDE BOARDS (TYP.)

7"

¾" DEEP DADO

24"

5"

¾"

10°

HANDLE TOP

2X4

10° BEVEL

80°

HANDLE FRONT

3½"

13½"

10°

10"

10°

52"

DETAIL 4

on the sides of the cart, then hinge the supports and the leaves to the sides of the cart.

Next, install the partition boards, screwing them to the sides of the cart. Notice that the partition fits into a gap between the floor boards. Add the cleats that support the sink counter and the tool storage door, attaching them with screws and glue.

Lay out the sink opening by tracing around the stainless steel bowl used for the sink. Drill a starting hole, then cut the opening with a saber saw. Cut $\frac{1}{8}$-in. inside the line to

allow the bowl's lip to overhang the opening. Locate and drill the hole for the faucet as well.

Use a $1\frac{1}{2}$-in. hole saw to cut the drain opening in the sink and the hole in the sink support board, then install the drain assembly using plumber's putty to seal the drain.

Now, place the sink in the opening, sealing the lip with clear silicone caulking compound. Add the sink support board. Secure the assembly with the sink collar, drawing it tight against the support board. Measure carefully and drill pilot holes for the screws that secure the sink support board to the rear panel and the partition.

Install the faucet in its opening, sealing it to the wood with silicone caulk. Tighten the nut on the sink pipe to fasten the sink to the wood.

Plumbing for the faucet and drain is simple and direct. Screw the garden hose adapter to the faucet threads, then attach the short washer supply hose. Thread the hose through an opening in the rear panel. Bore a hole in the floor of the cart and install the drain extension pipe.

Once all the plumbing is in place, hook up a garden hose to the inlet and check for leaks. Install the remaining back boards, but do not glue them. This allows later access to the plumbing.

Construct the tool holder, forming the dadoes with a dado blade. Notice that some of the joints are secured with glue alone, while others use both screws and glue. Bore the tool holder holes through both the top and center sections at the same time. Attach this assembly to the rear of the cart with screws only to allow later removal.

MATERIALS LIST

Item	Quantity
2X4 redwood	40 ft.
1X6 redwood	80 ft.
1X12 redwood	16 ft.
1X8 redwood	4 ft.
1X4 redwood	24 ft.
$\frac{7}{16}$" X 1$\frac{1}{2}$" steel flat bar	6 ft.
1$\frac{1}{2}$" X 2" brass hinges	10
3" brass hinges	6
Brass cabinet handle	1
Brass barrel bolt	1
No. 8 X 1$\frac{1}{4}$" brass flathead screws	200
No. 12 X 2" brass wood screws	8
No. 12 X 3" brass wood screws	4
$\frac{1}{4}$" X 2" machine screws with nuts and washers	6
$\frac{1}{4}$" X 3" lag screws with washers	10
L-shaped bracket	2
20 X 1.75 bicycle wheel and tire assembly	2
13"-dia. stainless steel mixing bowl, with lip	1
Single basin style faucet	1
Sink drain assembly (Price Pfister 540-512) without overflow	1
$\frac{1}{2}$" pipe thread to male garden hose adapter	1
1$\frac{1}{4}$" sink drain extension	1
Washing machine supply hose	1
Plumber's putty, silicone sealant, wood sealer, spray primer and enamel	as needed

CONSTRUCTION DETAILS

1. *After cutting the rabbets on the frame with a dado blade, finish the stopped ends by hand with a sharp chisel. Be careful not to split the wood.*

2. *Secure the sink to its support with the collar provided with the drain assembly. Install the board after placing the sink in its opening.*

At this point in construction, sand all wood components thoroughly, starting with 120-grit garnet paper and working down to 220-grit paper. A straight-line power sander is ideal for this job. Remove any hardware that interferes with sanding.

After sanding, protect the wood from weather and sunlight by applying two coats of a clear wood sealer. Use an airless or compressor-powered sprayer for best results. Allow 24 hours for the first coat to dry, and sand lightly before applying the second coat.

Form the wheel forks of $3/16$-in. X $1\frac{1}{2}$-in. steel flat bar stock by bending it around a piece of 3-in. sewer pipe. Clamp the fork material to the pipe, as shown in the photo, to insure an accurate bend. Measure the gap in the forks at both ends to make the sides parallel. Leave the ends longer than necessary, then trim them with a hacksaw after forming the bend. Round off the ends on a bench grinder.

Lay out and bore the axle and mounting holes in the forks. Accuracy is important here to provide proper wheel alignment. Give the

3. *Use a piece of 3-in. ABS sewer pipe as a bending form for the wheel forks. No heat is required to bend the mild steel used in this project.*

forks a coat of metal primer, followed by two coats of spray enamel.

Attach the forks to the cart with lag and machine screws as shown in the diagram. Notice the spacer block used between the forks and the side of the cart. Spread each fork slightly to allow installation of the bicycle wheel assembly. Tighten the axle nuts securely.

To use the sink on the cart, wheel the cart to a location, attach a garden hose to the inlet fitting, then turn on the hose faucet. Use a hose designed to withstand full water-line pressure. Drain water from the sink will simply run out on the ground beneath the cart.

Reprinted with permission from The Family Handyman, Webb Publishing Co., 1999 Shepard Rd., St. Paul, MN 55116.

POTTING BENCH

Potting chores are easier if you have a convenient place to work. This potting bench is designed to fill that need. Aside from a large work space, it also offers an upper shelf for completed jobs, drawers for tools and supplies, and a large lower shelf

for potting soil and containers. A removable plastic dishpan makes a bin for wet potting soil.

Built of redwood for moisture and rot resistance, the bench is attractive and will last for years.

Start building the bench by cutting all of the components to the lengths indicated in the diagram. Edge-glue the top boards with resorcinol glue, and clamp the assembly with pipe-type clamps, using two on each side of the panel.

Next, use a wobble-type dado blade on your table or radial arm saw to form the grooves and rabbets as shown in the diagram. When several components require the same operation, as is the case with the legs, clamp a stop block to the saw's fence to speed up the job.

Begin assembly by attaching the top and bottom rails to the legs with resorcinol glue and screws. Bore pilot holes with a screw pilot bit. Where screw heads will be exposed, counterbore with a ½-in. bit and glue screw hole plugs in place. Check the assemblies for squareness as you go.

Once both pairs of legs are assembled, add the side rails as shown in the diagram. Once again, counterbore exposed screw holes for wood plugs, and glue the joints.

Use a dado blade to form the drawer slides and supports. Add the outer drawer slides and supports to the base assembly after screwing the L-shaped slides to the supports. Next, assemble the center drawer slide components and install that assembly at the center of the bench. Measure carefully for smooth drawer action.

Use a ³⁄₁₆-in. straight bit in your router to make slots in the upper ledgers (see photo). These slots allow alignment of the bench top. Form the slots in a wide board, then rip the ledgers off the board. Clamp a short guide to the router's base to center the slots on the edge of the board.

Build the drawers next. If you haven't already made the grooves and rabbets in the shelf components, form them now with a dado blade. Notice the notches in the backs of the drawers. These allow the drawer to slide over the L-shaped slides. Assemble the drawers with glue and 6d galvanized finishing nails.

Screw and glue the lower ledgers to the inside of the lower rails, then add the bottom shelf boards, spacing them ¼ in. apart. Drive no. 8 X 1¼-in. flathead wood screws into the shelves from below.

Assemble the upper shelf unit with screws and glue, concealing the screw heads with wood plugs as you did before. Check squareness as you go.

By now the glue on the bench top will be dry. Scrape off excess glue with a chisel, then level the top with a plane. Finish up with a fine belt on your belt sander. Work carefully, since the soft redwood is easily marred.

Attach the top shelf assembly to the bench top with screws, driving them from the bottom of the bench top. Now, align the bench top on the base and attach it from below. Do not glue the top to the base; you may want to replace it later.

Trace around the plastic dishpan after locating it on the bench top, then cut the opening with a saber saw. If the dishpan's sides are tapered, trace around the top, then cut ⅜ in. inside the line to allow the lip to overhang.

Sand the completed bench thoroughly. Start with 80-grit garnet paper and work down to 150-grit, using hand and power sanders.

Once the bench is smooth, apply two coats of a clear wood sealer, such as Thompson's Water Seal, to protect the wood. Allow 24 hours between coats.

Reprinted with permission from The Family Handyman, Webb Publishing Co., 1999 Shepard Rd., St. Paul, MN 55116.

CONSTRUCTION DETAILS

1. Rout the slots for the ledgers in the edge of a wide board, then rip the ledgers off this stock.

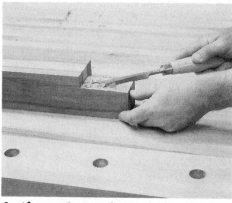

2. After cutting notches in the legs and other components, smooth them with a wood chisel where necessary.

3. Since the drawer slides run inside the drawers, cut notches at the rear to allow easy movement.

4. Smooth the glued-up bench top with a bench plane, after scraping off excess glue. Finish with a belt sander.

5. Trace around the plastic dishpan, then cut out the opening with a saber saw. Be sure to allow for the pan's lip.

6. Screw the drawer supports to the inside of the top frame. Drill pilot holes for the flathead wood screws.

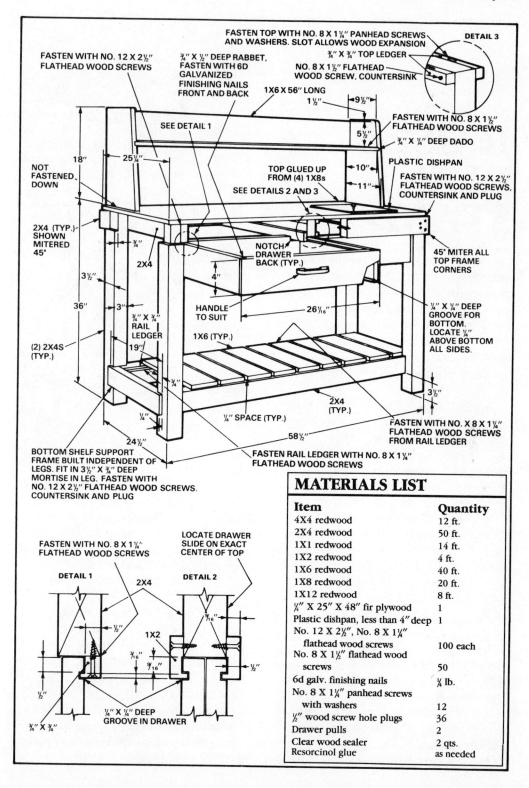

FASTEN TOP WITH NO. 8 X 1¼" PANHEAD SCREWS AND WASHERS. SLOT ALLOWS WOOD EXPANSION

DETAIL 3

¾" X ¾" TOP LEDGER

NO. 8 X 1½" FLATHEAD WOOD SCREW, COUNTERSINK

FASTEN WITH NO. 12 X 2½" FLATHEAD WOOD SCREWS

¾" X ½" DEEP RABBET, FASTEN WITH 6D GALVANIZED FINISHING NAILS FRONT AND BACK

1X6 X 56" LONG

1½"   9½"

5½"

FASTEN WITH NO. 8 X 1½" FLATHEAD WOOD SCREWS

¾" X ¼" DEEP DADO

SEE DETAIL 1

18"   25¼"

10"

PLASTIC DISHPAN

TOP GLUED UP FROM (4) 1X8s

11"

FASTEN WITH NO. 12 X 2½" FLATHEAD WOOD SCREWS, COUNTERSINK AND PLUG

NOT FASTENED DOWN

SEE DETAILS 2 AND 3

2X4 (TYP.) SHOWN MITERED 45°

¾"

NOTCH DRAWER BACK (TYP.)

45° MITER ALL TOP FRAME CORNERS

2X4

4"

3½"

HANDLE TO SUIT

¼" X ¼" DEEP GROOVE FOR BOTTOM. LOCATE ¼" ABOVE BOTTOM ALL SIDES.

36"

3"

26¹⁄₁₆"

¾" X ¾" RAIL LEDGER

(2) 2X4S (TYP.)

19"

1X6 (TYP.)

¾"

3½"

¼"

2X4 (TYP.)

FASTEN WITH NO. X 8 X 1¼" FLATHEAD WOOD SCREWS FROM RAIL LEDGER

24½"

¼" SPACE (TYP.)

58½"

BOTTOM SHELF SUPPORT FRAME BUILT INDEPENDENT OF LEGS. FIT IN 3½" X ¾" DEEP MORTISE IN LEG. FASTEN WITH NO. 12 X 2½" FLATHEAD WOOD SCREWS. COUNTERSINK AND PLUG

FASTEN RAIL LEDGER WITH NO. 8 X 1¼" FLATHEAD WOOD SCREWS

FASTEN WITH NO. 8 X 1¼" FLATHEAD WOOD SCREWS

LOCATE DRAWER SLIDE ON EXACT CENTER OF TOP

DETAIL 1

2X4

DETAIL 2

½"

9⁄16"

1X2

½"

3⁄16"

9⁄16"

½"

½"

¾" X ¾"

¼" X ¼" DEEP GROOVE IN DRAWER

MATERIALS LIST

Item	Quantity
4X4 redwood	12 ft.
2X4 redwood	50 ft.
1X1 redwood	14 ft.
1X2 redwood	4 ft.
1X6 redwood	40 ft.
1X8 redwood	20 ft.
1X12 redwood	8 ft.
¼" X 25" X 48" fir plywood	1
Plastic dishpan, less than 4" deep	1
No. 12 X 2½", No. 8 X 1¼" flathead wood screws	100 each
No. 8 X 1½" flathead wood screws	50
6d galv. finishing nails	¼ lb.
No. 8 X 1¼" panhead screws with washers	12
½" wood screw hole plugs	36
Drawer pulls	2
Clear wood sealer	2 qts.
Resorcinol glue	as needed

RAISED PLANT STAND

Container plants displayed on your patio or deck deserve to be shown off. This attractive redwood stand will put your favorite specimen up where it can be seen.

All wooden components of the stand are cut from standard 1X4 redwood, available from any home center or lumberyard.

Begin construction by cutting the stand's components to the sizes shown in the diagram.

Form the angled corners of the uprights by setting your saw to cut a 45 degree miter. Mark the ½-in. dimension, then cut off the top outside corner of each piece.

Next, cut the notches in the cross members. If you have a table or radial arm saw, use a dado blade to form the notches. Measure carefully and cut the notches in several passes, deepening the cut on each pass.

On a radial arm saw, the job of cutting all eight pairs of notches is simpler if you clamp stop blocks on the saw's fence.

You can also cut notches with a saber saw; clean up the corners with a sharp chisel.

Dry assemble the upper and lower cross member units by interlocking the notches.

Position the legs between the pairs of cross members as shown in the diagram. Drill ¼-in.-dia. holes through the cross members and the legs, and install the ¼-in. X 2¼-in. galvanized bolts and nuts. Be sure to use washers to protect the wood against marring.

Now, disassemble the project and sand all components thoroughly. If you wish, you can apply a wood sealer such as Thompson's Water Seal, or you can leave the redwood to weather naturally.

Reassemble the stand, tightening the fasteners securely, and add a suitable container to make this project part of your outdoor decor.

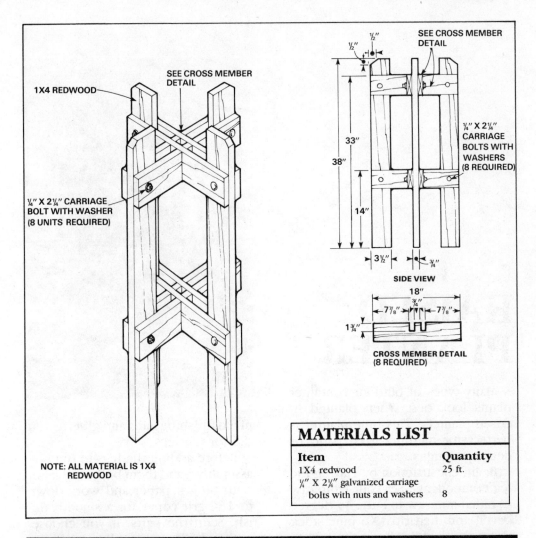

1X4 REDWOOD

SEE CROSS MEMBER DETAIL

¼" X 2¼" CARRIAGE BOLT WITH WASHER (8 UNITS REQUIRED)

NOTE: ALL MATERIAL IS 1X4 REDWOOD

SEE CROSS MEMBER DETAIL

½"

½"

33"

38"

14"

¼" X 2¼" CARRIAGE BOLTS WITH WASHERS (8 REQUIRED)

3½"

¾"

SIDE VIEW

18"

7⅞"

¾"

7⅞"

1¾"

CROSS MEMBER DETAIL (8 REQUIRED)

MATERIALS LIST

Item	Quantity
1X4 redwood	25 ft.
¼" X 2¼" galvanized carriage bolts with nuts and washers	8

CONSTRUCTION DETAILS

1. *A dado blade on a radial arm saw is ideal for cutting the notches in the cross members.*

2. *Assemble the braces by interlocking the pre-cut notches, making a saddle joint. See diagram.*

RAISED PLANTER

Many types of outdoor container plants look best when planted in raised planters. This pine planter is perfect for medium-sized patio or deck specimens.

Begin construction by cutting the leg components. Set your table saw or radial arm saw to cut a 45 degree bevel, and then rip 1X6 pine stock down the middle. Reset the saw to 90 degrees and rip the leg material to its final 2½-in. width.

Cut the leg parts to the length shown in the diagram. Then assemble the legs with 4d galvanized finishing nails and waterproof resorcinol glue. Set the nails just below the surface with a nail set.

Next, cut the remaining components of the planter to the dimensions shown in the diagram. Drill five ¾-in.-dia. drainage holes in the bottom board.

Assemble the box with 4d galva-nized finishing nails and glue, as you did for the legs.

Before adding the legs to the box assembly, sand them both well. Start with 80-grit paper and work down to 150-grit paper for a smooth finish. Stain the parts, if you choose, with a high-quality oil-based stain, then apply a coat of wood sealer, such as Thompson's Water Seal.

Attach the legs to the box with 4d galvanized finishing nails and glue. Set the nails below the surface as you did before. To finish the project, apply another coat of wood sealer.

Before planting, allow the wood sealer to dry thoroughly. Place a 1-in.-deep layer of gravel in the planter, and then add planting mix and your favorite plant. If you choose, you can also use the planter as a stand, using a pre-potted plant.

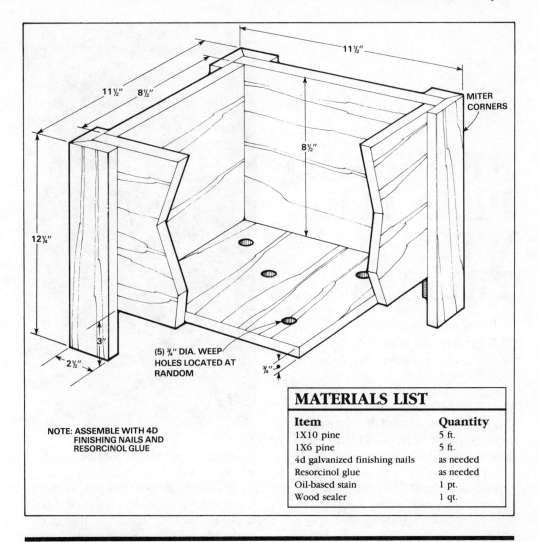

11½"

11½" 8½"

8½"

MITER CORNERS

12¼"

3"

2½"

(5) ¾" DIA. WEEP HOLES LOCATED AT RANDOM

¾"

NOTE: ASSEMBLE WITH 4D FINISHING NAILS AND RESORCINOL GLUE

MATERIALS LIST

Item	Quantity
1X10 pine	5 ft.
1X6 pine	5 ft.
4d galvanized finishing nails	as needed
Resorcinol glue	as needed
Oil-based stain	1 pt.
Wood sealer	1 qt.

CONSTRUCTION DETAILS

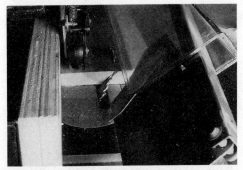

1. *Rip the ¾-in. pine stock for the legs on on a table saw. Set the saw blade at 45 degrees.*

2. *Attach the legs to the assembled base with 4d galvanized finishing nails and glue.*

397

REDWOOD PLANTER WITH TRELLIS

If climbing plants or vines are in your gardening plans, this redwood planter with a built-in trellis is an ideal project.

Begin construction by cutting the parts for the trellis. Lay out the positions for the dowel holes in the cross members. Then drill ½-in.- dia. holes, 1 in. deep, with a drill press or a portable drill guide.

Assemble the trellis using 10d galvanized finishing nails. To prevent the wood from splitting, drill pilot holes for the nails. Use a ⅛-in. bit to drill these holes through the sides of the trellis frame.

Next, cut the components for the planter box. If using a portable saw for this job, clamp an edge guide to the redwood boards to insure accuracy.

Drill ¾-in.-dia. drainage holes in the bottom board. Use 4d galvanized finishing nails to attach the sides to the front uprights. Space the nails 2 in. apart. Drill pilot holes here, just as you did for the trellis, only this time use a ³⁄₃₂-in. bit. Use a nail set to set the nail heads just below the wood's surface.

Add the front and rear panels, nailing them in the same way. Insert the bottom, nailing through the front and side panels. Again, drill pilot holes and set the nails.

Attach the trellis assembly to the rear of the planter, nailing it securely in place.

Sand the completed project, starting with 80-grit garnet paper. Do the final sanding with 150-grit paper. Finish the planter with two full coats of Thompson's Water Seal, allowing 24 hours between coats.

Once the planter is dry, put a layer of gravel in the bottom, add planting mix, and you're ready to plant your favorite plants.

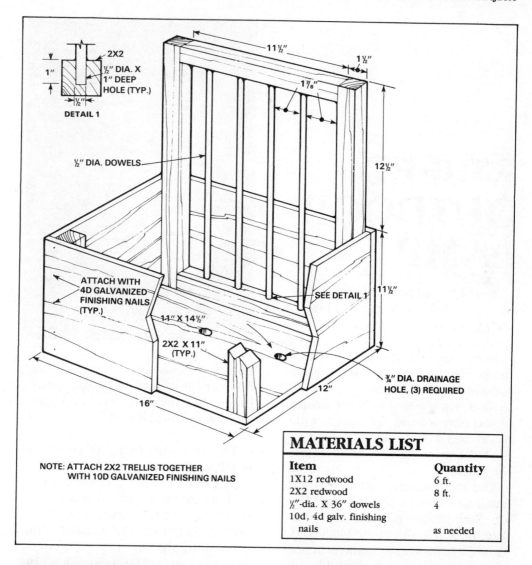

DETAIL 1

2X2

½" DIA. X 1" DEEP HOLE (TYP.)

1"

½"

11½"

1½"

1⅞"

½" DIA. DOWELS

12½"

ATTACH WITH 4D GALVANIZED FINISHING NAILS (TYP.)

SEE DETAIL 1

11½"

11" X 14½"

2X2 X 11" (TYP.)

¾" DIA. DRAINAGE HOLE, (3) REQUIRED

16"

12"

NOTE: ATTACH 2X2 TRELLIS TOGETHER WITH 10D GALVANIZED FINISHING NAILS

MATERIALS LIST

Item	Quantity
1X12 redwood	6 ft.
2X2 redwood	8 ft.
½"-dia. X 36" dowels	4
10d, 4d galv. finishing nails	as needed

CONSTRUCTION DETAILS

1. The dowels that form the trellis fit into pre-drilled holes in the crosspieces.

2. Install the trellis assembly inside the planter box. Then nail the trellis in place.

399

RIBBED OUTDOOR LAMP

The light cast by this circular candle lamp will add a special glow to spring and summer evenings on the deck or patio.

Begin by cutting 1½-in.-thick lumber to the length of the strips as shown in the diagram.

Next, rip the strips off the board. If you have a band saw, use a wide blade and a slow, careful feed to form the strips. Use a fence to guide the stock.

You can also use a table saw or a radial arm saw to rip the slats. Use a hollow-ground planer blade. Measure the kerf width of the blade and, for each strip, set the blade or fence over ³⁄₆₄ in. plus the kerf width.

Now, cut the hexagonal base. Set your saw or miter gauge to 30 degrees to produce the correct angle. Measure carefully before cutting.

Use a compass to lay out the circles for the dowel uprights and for the candle recess. Form the recess with a straight bit in your router, cutting slowly for accuracy.

Draw pencil lines connecting the corners of the base, and then drill ¾-in.-dia. holes, ⅝ in. deep, for the dowel uprights. Use a spade bit or a Forstner bit to leave a flat-bottomed hole. Sand the base well and glue the dowels in place with resorcinol glue.

To make the strips flexible for bending into hoops, soak them in a large pan of water. Allow the water to boil for several minutes. Make sure you wear gloves and exert caution when boiling and handling the strips. Pull out one strip with pliers and form around the six dowels. Tape the overlap together. Do this for each strip. Then attach the strips to the dowels with brass brads. Use a backup block when nailing. Space the strips ¼ in. apart.

After the strips have dried, give the project two coats of wood sealer.

For safety's sake use only a tall glassed candle that is as high as the project and make sure that flammables are kept well away from the lit candle.

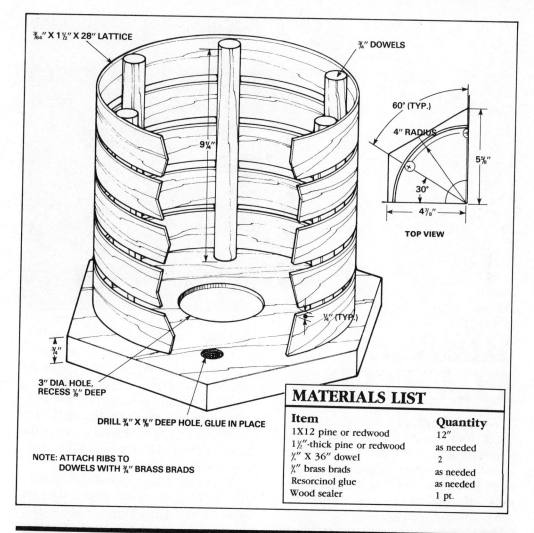

³⁄₆₄″ X 1½″ X 28″ LATTICE

¾″ DOWELS

9¼″

60° (TYP.)

4″ RADIUS

5⅝″

30°

4⅞″

TOP VIEW

¼″ (TYP.)

¾″

3″ DIA. HOLE,
RECESS ⅛″ DEEP

DRILL ¾″ X ⅝″ DEEP HOLE, GLUE IN PLACE

NOTE: ATTACH RIBS TO
DOWELS WITH ¾″ BRASS BRADS

MATERIALS LIST

Item	Quantity
1X12 pine or redwood	12″
1½″-thick pine or redwood	as needed
¾″ X 36″ dowel	2
¾″ brass brads	as needed
Resorcinol glue	as needed
Wood sealer	1 pt.

CONSTRUCTION DETAILS

1. Soak the wood strips in boiling water to make them flexible enough to bend into hoops.

2. Bend the hoops around the dowels; tape the overlaps and then nail the hoops in place.

RIBBED PLANTER

Raised plantings can beautify any yard. This square planter box is designed to be the perfect spot for your favorite plants. Built of pressure-treated lumber, it will last for years. Its ribbed trim and sturdy construction are special features.

Start construction with the base of the planter. Cut three 33-in. lengths of 2X2 stock and seven 33-in. pieces of 2X6 tongue-and-groove stock. Blind-nail the floor pieces, one at a time, to the cleats. Use 8d galvanized finishing nails, and take care to keep the assembly square as you work. Finish the base by boring nine evenly spaced ½-in. weep holes.

Next, cut the sides of the planter. Each side is made of one 2X8 and one 2X10. Set your table or radial arm saw to cut the 45 degree miters. Make sure that all of the side components are exactly 36 in. long.

Cut sixty 2X2 cleats, 11 in. long, for the side trim. Nail the cleats to the side components with 8d galvanized finishing nails, as shown in the photo. Space the cleats $^{31}/_{32}$ in. apart. Use a spacer block to simplify construction. Do not attach the corner cleats at this time.

Once all four sides are finished, assemble them to the base. Use 16d galvanized finishing nails on the base and corner joints. Drill pilot holes for the nails in the miter joints to help prevent splitting. Once the assembly is complete, add the remaining cleats to the planter's corners.

Finish the project with two coats of clear wood sealer or satin-finish polyurethane varnish. Place a 2-in. layer of gravel in the bottom of the planter for good drainage. Plant your favorite medium-sized plants in high-quality planter mix.

Design and photos courtesy of Western Wood Products Association, Yeon Building, Portland, OR 97204.

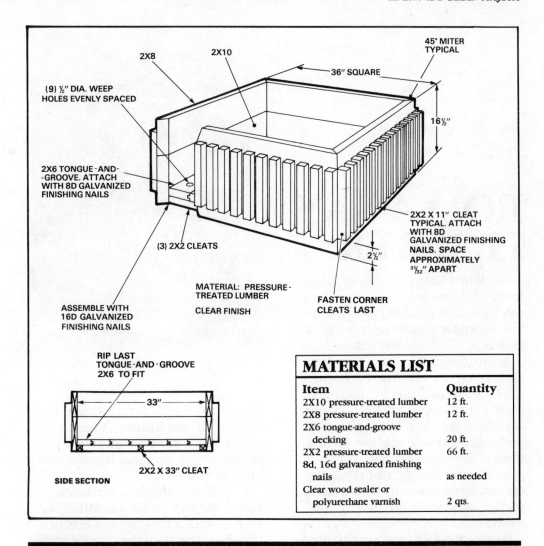

45° MITER TYPICAL

2X8

2X10

36″ SQUARE

(9) ½″ DIA. WEEP HOLES EVENLY SPACED

16½″

2X6 TONGUE-AND-GROOVE. ATTACH WITH 8D GALVANIZED FINISHING NAILS

2X2 X 11″ CLEAT TYPICAL. ATTACH WITH 8D GALVANIZED FINISHING NAILS. SPACE APPROXIMATELY ³¹/₃₂″ APART

(3) 2X2 CLEATS

2½″

ASSEMBLE WITH 16D GALVANIZED FINISHING NAILS

MATERIAL: PRESSURE-TREATED LUMBER

CLEAR FINISH

FASTEN CORNER CLEATS LAST

RIP LAST TONGUE-AND-GROOVE 2X6 TO FIT

33″

2X2 X 33″ CLEAT

SIDE SECTION

MATERIALS LIST

Item	Quantity
2X10 pressure-treated lumber	12 ft.
2X8 pressure-treated lumber	12 ft.
2X6 tongue-and-groove decking	20 ft.
2X2 pressure-treated lumber	66 ft.
8d, 16d galvanized finishing nails	as needed
Clear wood sealer or polyurethane varnish	2 qts.

CONSTRUCTION DETAILS

1. Use a ³¹/₃₂-in.-thick block of wood to help you space the 2X2 cleats on the planter's sides.

2. Assemble the sides to the base, nailing with 16d galvanized finishing nails. Add the corner cleats.

ROLLAWAY PLANTER

Moving a large container plant from place to place on your deck can be a back-breaking job. This attractive cedar planter rolls easily on casters to eliminate the strain.

Build the base as the first step. Cut 2X4 pressure-treated lumber into six 18½-in. pieces. Edge-glue these parts to make the base, clamping them securely until dry. Trim both edges to make the base 18½ in. square. Drill weep holes.

Attach the refrigerator-type casters, available at any hardware store, to the base with no. 8 X 1½-in. flathead wood screws.

Next, cut ¾-in. pressure-treated plywood to fit the sides of the base. Attach the plywood with no. 10 X 1½" flathead wood screws, countersunk flush with the surface. Cut the 2X4 corner braces, and screw the sides to these, as well.

Saw 1X4 tongue-and-groove cedar siding into 18¼-in. lengths. Use your table or radial arm saw to miter the edges of four of these boards. Start at opposing corners of the planter and nail the siding to the plywood with 4d galvanized finishing nails.

Nail at an angle through the tongue of the siding. When you reach the other corners of the planter, mark the boards and miter them as you did before.

Cut 2X4 cedar lumber stock to make the cap molding. Miter the corners with a power miter box or a stationary saw. Join the corners with no. 10 X 2-in. screws and resorcinol glue. Bore pilot holes, counterbored for wood screw hole plugs. Attach the trim to the planter's corner braces with the same size screws, counterboring and plugging as you did before.

Chamfer the top edges of the trim with a chamfering bit in your router. Finish the project with two coats of satin finish polyurethane varnish.

Design by Julia Lundy Sturdevant. Photos courtesy of Western Wood Products Association, Yeon Building, Portland, OR 97204

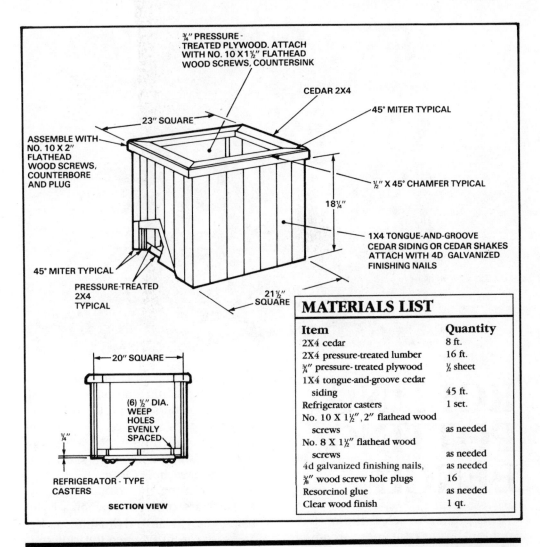

¾" PRESSURE-TREATED PLYWOOD. ATTACH WITH NO. 10 X 1½" FLATHEAD WOOD SCREWS, COUNTERSINK

CEDAR 2X4

45° MITER TYPICAL

23" SQUARE

ASSEMBLE WITH NO. 10 X 2" FLATHEAD WOOD SCREWS, COUNTERBORE AND PLUG

½" X 45° CHAMFER TYPICAL

18¼"

1X4 TONGUE-AND-GROOVE CEDAR SIDING OR CEDAR SHAKES ATTACH WITH 4D GALVANIZED FINISHING NAILS

45° MITER TYPICAL

PRESSURE-TREATED 2X4 TYPICAL

21½" SQUARE

20" SQUARE

(6) ½" DIA. WEEP HOLES EVENLY SPACED

¼"

REFRIGERATOR - TYPE CASTERS

SECTION VIEW

MATERIALS LIST

Item	Quantity
2X4 cedar	8 ft.
2X4 pressure-treated lumber	16 ft.
¾" pressure-treated plywood	½ sheet
1X4 tongue-and-groove cedar siding	45 ft.
Refrigerator casters	1 set.
No. 10 X 1½", 2" flathead wood screws	as needed
No. 8 X 1½" flathead wood screws	as needed
4d galvanized finishing nails,	as needed
⅜" wood screw hole plugs	16
Resorcinol glue	as needed
Clear wood finish	1 qt.

CONSTRUCTION DETAILS

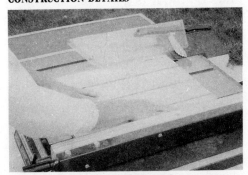

1. Miter the edges of the T&G or grooved siding to form the two corners of the planter. Cut the grooved edge.

2. Cut the mitered corners of the cap molding with a power miter box or your stationary saw.

ROLLING POTTING BENCH

This potting bench is the perfect spot for all your container-gardening jobs. Designed with easy-rolling casters and two shelves, complete with drainage holes, it has a place for everything you'll need.

Build the top as the first step in construction. Cut the top materials to the length shown in the diagram, and then edge-glue the parts using waterproof glue. Clamp securely from both sides and allow to dry.

Next, construct the trays. Before cutting the 1X3 frame materials to size, form a ½-in. X ½-in.-deep rabbet on one edge of the stock. Use a dado blade on your table saw.

Cut the frame components with mitered corners; then cut the ½-in. exterior plywood parts to size and assemble the trays with 4d galvanized finishing nails. Drill six 1-in.-dia. drainage holes in each tray.

After cutting the remaining parts to size, assemble the bench's base using 10d galvanized finishing nails. Measure carefully when locating the trays on the legs.

Cut the arms of the bench and the cross braces. Round one end of each arm, and drill holes for the dowel handle.

Add these components to the base; then attach the top with 10d galvanized finishing nails, setting each nail just below the surface.

Sand the completed bench thoroughly and finish with two coats of wood sealer, such as Thompson's Water Seal. Add the casters, and the project is ready for use.

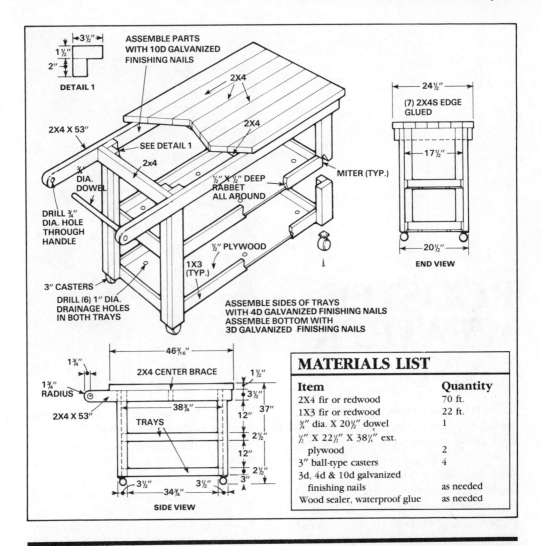

DETAIL 1

ASSEMBLE PARTS WITH 10D GALVANIZED FINISHING NAILS

2X4

2X4

2X4 X 53″

SEE DETAIL 1

2x4

¾″ DIA. DOWEL

DRILL ¾″ DIA. HOLE THROUGH HANDLE

½″ X ½″ DEEP RABBET ALL AROUND

MITER (TYP.)

½″ PLYWOOD

1X3 (TYP.)

3″ CASTERS

DRILL (6) 1″ DIA. DRAINAGE HOLES IN BOTH TRAYS

ASSEMBLE SIDES OF TRAYS WITH 4D GALVANIZED FINISHING NAILS
ASSEMBLE BOTTOM WITH 3D GALVANIZED FINISHING NAILS

24½″

(7) 2X4S EDGE GLUED

17½″

20½″

END VIEW

46³⁄₁₆″

1¾″

1¾″ RADIUS

2X4 X 53″

2X4 CENTER BRACE

38¾″

TRAYS

1½″

3½″

12″

2½″

12″

2½″

37″

3½″   3½″   3″

34¾″

SIDE VIEW

MATERIALS LIST

Item	Quantity
2X4 fir or redwood	70 ft.
1X3 fir or redwood	22 ft.
¾″ dia. X 20½″ dowel	1
½″ X 22½″ X 38¼″ ext. plywood	2
3″ ball-type casters	4
3d, 4d & 10d galvanized finishing nails	as needed
Wood sealer, waterproof glue	as needed

CONSTRUCTION DETAILS

1. *Before cutting the frame parts to length, form a rabbet for the panels with a dado blade.*

2. *Edge-glue the bench's top with waterproof glue. Clamp the assembly securely with bar clamps.*

ROOSTER WEATHER VANE

No rooftop is complete without a weather vane. This rooster design will add just the right touch to any home. The vane may be finished with varnish or paint.

Start construction by enlarging the rooster pattern onto ½-in. grid paper. Using carbon paper, transfer the pattern to ¾-in. exterior plywood, then cut out the rooster. Use a band saw or a saber saw, making relief cuts at tight corners.

Next, lay out and cut the arrow and circle. Use ¾-in. birch stock for these parts. Bore a 1¼-in.-dia. hole in the circle for the dowel post.

Locate and drill four ⅜-in.-dia. holes in the circle for the dowels used to support the directional letters. Insert the post in the circle, then pin it in place with a ¼-in. dowel pin.

Bore ⅜-in. holes in the directional letters, then attach the letters and dowels with resorcinol glue.

Attach the rooster to the arrow as shown in the diagram, then bore a ¼-in. pivot hole through the arrow. Cut a 1-in. piece of ¼-in. copper tubing and de-burr the inside with a ³⁄₁₆-in. drill bit. Glue the tubing into the arrow, then drill a pilot hole and attach the arrow to the post. Do not over-tighten the screw.

Varnish or paint the completed weather vane. When the finish has dried, take the vane and the antenna mount onto the roof. You will also need asphalt roof cement and suitable screws for attaching the mount.

Orient the weather vane's directional letters to true north, then clamp the post into the antenna mount. Fasten the mount to the roof using plenty of roof cement, and the project is complete.

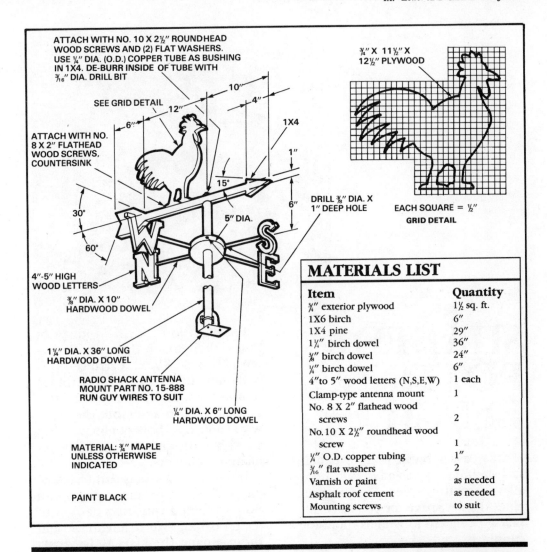

ATTACH WITH NO. 10 X 2½" ROUNDHEAD
WOOD SCREWS AND (2) FLAT WASHERS.
USE ¼" DIA. (O.D.) COPPER TUBE AS BUSHING
IN 1X4. DE-BURR INSIDE OF TUBE WITH
³⁄₁₆" DIA. DRILL BIT

SEE GRID DETAIL

ATTACH WITH NO.
8 X 2" FLATHEAD
WOOD SCREWS,
COUNTERSINK

¾" X 11½" X
12½" PLYWOOD

10"

12"

6"

4"

1X4

1"

15°

DRILL ⅜" DIA. X
1" DEEP HOLE

6"

30°

5" DIA.

60°

EACH SQUARE = ½"

GRID DETAIL

4"-5" HIGH
WOOD LETTERS

⅜" DIA. X 10"
HARDWOOD DOWEL

1¼" DIA. X 36" LONG
HARDWOOD DOWEL

RADIO SHACK ANTENNA
MOUNT PART NO. 15-888
RUN GUY WIRES TO SUIT

¼" DIA. X 6" LONG
HARDWOOD DOWEL

MATERIAL: ¾" MAPLE
UNLESS OTHERWISE
INDICATED

PAINT BLACK

MATERIALS LIST

Item	Quantity
¾" exterior plywood	1½ sq. ft.
1X6 birch	6"
1X4 pine	29"
1¼" birch dowel	36"
⅜" birch dowel	24"
¼" birch dowel	6"
4" to 5" wood letters (N,S,E,W)	1 each
Clamp-type antenna mount	1
No. 8 X 2" flathead wood screws	2
No. 10 X 2½" roundhead wood screw	1
¼" O.D. copper tubing	1"
³⁄₁₆" flat washers	2
Varnish or paint	as needed
Asphalt roof cement	as needed
Mounting screws	to suit

CONSTRUCTION DETAILS

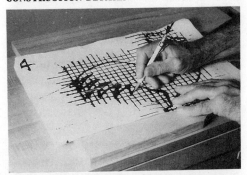

1. Use carbon paper to trace the enlarged rooster pattern onto ¾" exterior plywood. Cut carefully.

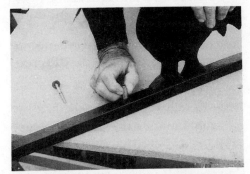

2. Insert a length of copper tubing into the arrow. This will serve as a bushing for the pivot screw.

SHADED POTTING BENCH

This easy-to-build potting bench and shelf unit is designed to handle all your potting needs. It also provides display space for your favorite plant specimens as well as room for supplies.

Its all-redwood construction will blend perfectly with any outdoor area, while its height is the same as a standard door. The overhanging top of the bench provides filtered light. You can customize this project by varying the shelf positions to suit your personal requirements.

Begin building the project by cutting the 2X4 posts and braces to the lengths shown in the diagram. Lay out the shelf and bench positions on the posts, then assemble the sides of the unit.

For each joint, drill ¼-in. pilot holes, then attach the components with ¼-in. X 3½-in. carriage bolts with nuts and washers. Check the assembly for squareness as you go. It is a good idea to assemble the sides with only one bolt per joint. After checking for squareness, add the remaining fasteners.

Install the 1X4 slats that fit inside the posts, nailing them in place with 8d galvanized finishing nails. Cut the remaining slats to length and add them. Space the slats ½ in. apart with a scrap of ½-in.-thick material. Nail the slats in place using two 8d galvanized finishing nails at each joint.

Add the 1X4 fascia boards to the overhanging top of the unit to complete the assembly. Sand the assembled unit, breaking the sharp edges of the working area.

Apply two coats of clear wood sealer, such as Thompson's Water Seal, to protect the project from the weather. Allow 24 hours between coats.

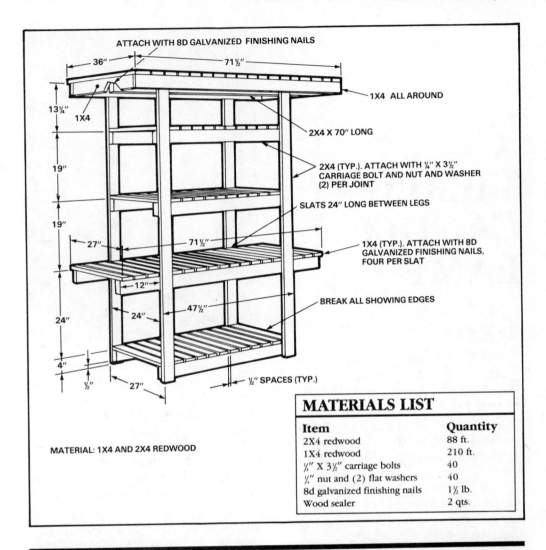

ATTACH WITH 8D GALVANIZED FINISHING NAILS

36"   71½"

13¼"
1X4

19"

19"

27"   71½"

12"

24"   47½"

24"

4"

½"

27"   ½" SPACES (TYP.)

1X4 ALL AROUND

2X4 X 70" LONG

2X4 (TYP.). ATTACH WITH ¼" X 3½"
CARRIAGE BOLT AND NUT AND WASHER
(2) PER JOINT

SLATS 24" LONG BETWEEN LEGS

1X4 (TYP.). ATTACH WITH 8D
GALVANIZED FINISHING NAILS,
FOUR PER SLAT

BREAK ALL SHOWING EDGES

MATERIAL: 1X4 AND 2X4 REDWOOD

MATERIALS LIST

Item	Quantity
2X4 redwood	88 ft.
1X4 redwood	210 ft.
¼" X 3½" carriage bolts	40
¼" nut and (2) flat washers	40
8d galvanized finishing nails	1½ lb.
Wood sealer	2 qts.

CONSTRUCTION DETAILS

1. Set the slat spacing with a spacer made of ½-in. stock. Check each slat before nailing it down.

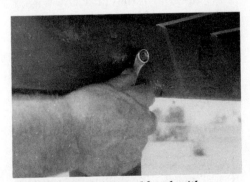

2. Install the shelves and bench with carriage bolts. Check the assembly for squareness before tightening.

TIERED CANDLE LAMP

If you are looking for a way to give your outdoor entertaining a soft glow, build one or more of these unique lamps.

Designed to hold a tall candle in a glass holder, it has a stair-stepped appearance that allows light to filter out onto your patio or deck.

Start by cutting the 2X2 uprights to the length shown in the diagram. Lay out the notched areas, spacing the layout lines 2 in. apart.

Set up your radial arm saw with a wobble-type dado blade. Make the widest cut available on your blade. Lower the blade to cut ½ in. from the table.

Now, cut the notches on both ends of each upright. Cut all of these notches before changing the depth of cut. This saves you time.

Next, raise the blade ½ in. and cut the next set of notches. Be careful to cut just to the line, keeping the notched areas even.

Cut the base of the lamp to the dimensions shown in the diagram. Cut a ½-in. X ½-in. notch in each corner of the base with a saber saw. Form the candle recess with a ¼-in. straight bit in your router.

Rip ¹⁄₁₆-in.-thick strips off one edge of a 2-in.-thick piece of lumber. Use a band saw or a table or radial arm saw for this operation. If you use a radial arm or table saw, set the blade or fence over ¹⁄₁₆ in. plus the width of the saw kerf for each successive cut. For safety's sake, always rip thin strips like these from the edge of the stock that is away from the fence. This prevents dangerous binding.

Cut the strips to length and attach them to the uprights with ¾-in. brass brads and glue. Finish the project with two coats of wood sealer.

As a precaution, use only a tall glassed candle that is as high as the project and make sure that flammables are kept well away from the lit candle.

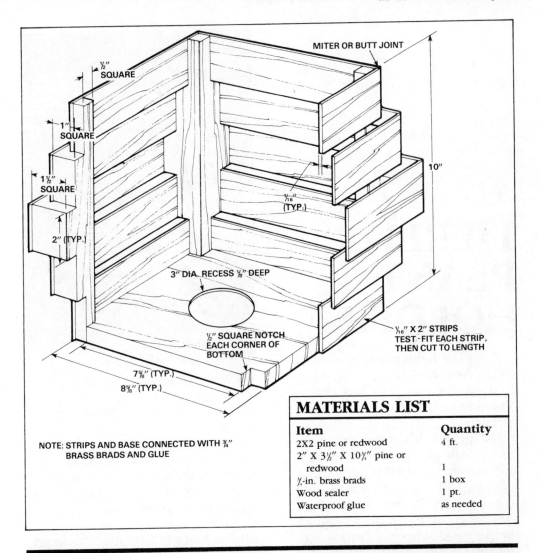

MITER OR BUTT JOINT

½" SQUARE

1" SQUARE

1½" SQUARE

2" (TYP.)

10"

1/16" (TYP.)

3" DIA. RECESS ⅛" DEEP

½" SQUARE NOTCH EACH CORNER OF BOTTOM

1/16" X 2" STRIPS
TEST - FIT EACH STRIP, THEN CUT TO LENGTH

7⅝" (TYP.)

8⅝" (TYP.)

NOTE: STRIPS AND BASE CONNECTED WITH ¾" BRASS BRADS AND GLUE

MATERIALS LIST

Item	Quantity
2X2 pine or redwood	4 ft.
2" X 3½" X 10⅞" pine or redwood	1
¾-in. brass brads	1 box
Wood sealer	1 pt.
Waterproof glue	as needed

CONSTRUCTION DETAILS

1. Cut the stepped notches in the uprights with a dado blade on your radial arm saw.

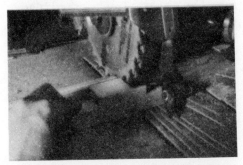

2. When one notch is complete, turn the workpiece and cut the other half of the notch.

TIERED PLANT HOLDER

This plant holder displays four of your favorite plants. Designed to hold standard 6-in. pots, it is a beautiful way to show off your favorite specimens.

The project is constructed of ¾-in. exterior plywood for sturdiness and weather resistance. You may well find that you have enough scrap to build the entire project at no cost.

Begin construction by cutting out the plywood sides and baffles. Cut out the L-shaped sides with a saber saw. Use a sharp, fine-toothed blade for smooth results.

Nail and glue all joints. Waterproof resorcinol glue will give the best results. Use 6d galvanized finishing nails, set beneath the surface with a nail set, and space the nails 2 in. apart.

For the first stage of assembly, nail and glue the lowest baffle to its corresponding sides. Then, piece by piece, add the remaining sides and baffle, leaving one side open on each tier to allow for placement of the baffle.

Each baffle is located 6 in. from the top of its section. Mark the nail locations lightly with a pencil before driving the nails. This insures accurate nail placement.

Once the assembly is complete, fill the holes left by the counterset nails with waterproof wood filler, then sand the project thoroughly. Start with 80-grit garnet paper and work down to 150-grit paper.

Finish the exposed plywood edges by applying a waterproof wood filler and then sanding the edges smooth. This eliminates a rough appearance and seals the edges.

Finally, give the project a coat of exterior enamel primer, followed by two coats of high-quality exterior enamel in the color of your choice.

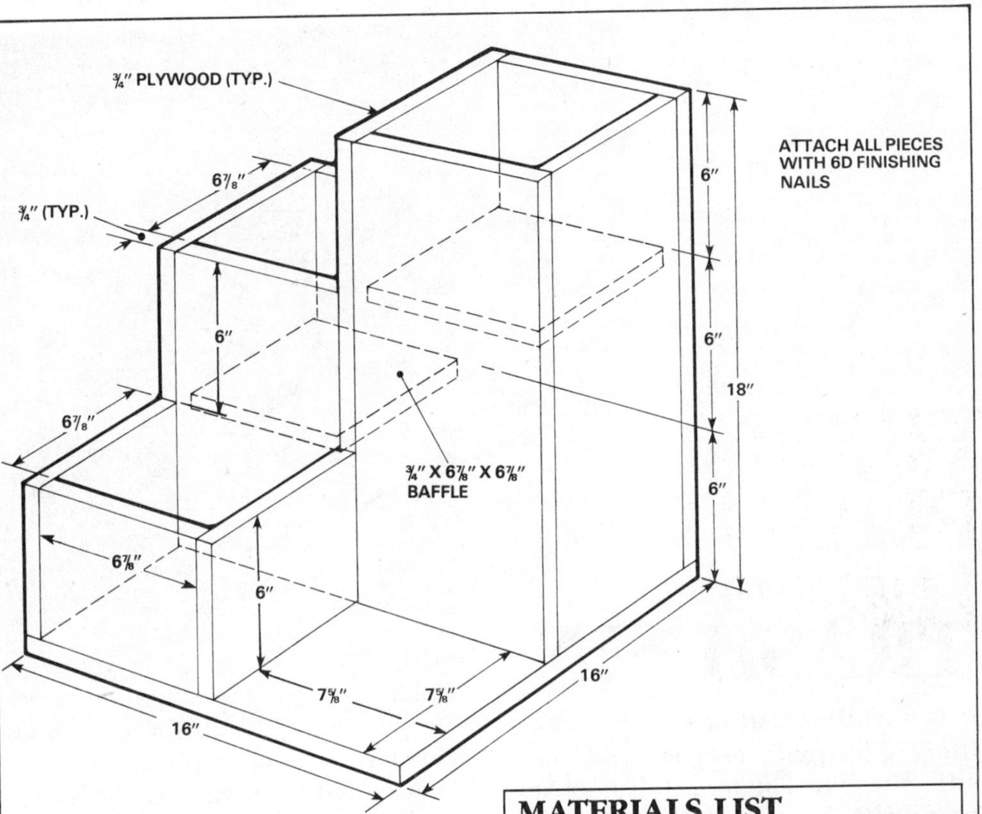

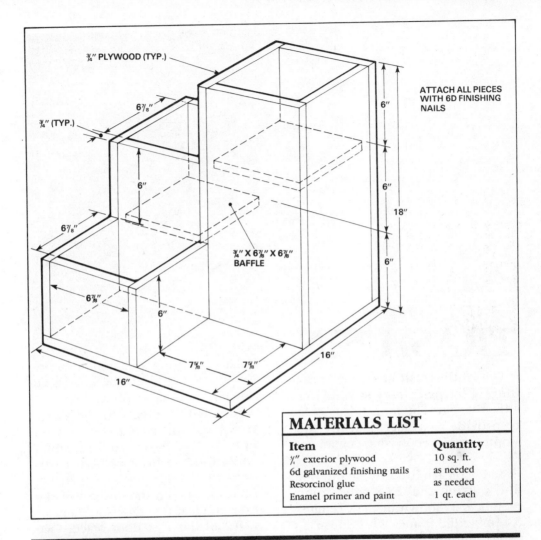

3/4" PLYWOOD (TYP.)
ATTACH ALL PIECES WITH 6D FINISHING NAILS
6 7/8"
3/4" (TYP.)
6"
6"
6"
6"
18"
6 7/8"
3/4" X 6 7/8" X 6 7/8" BAFFLE
6"
6 7/8"
6"
7 5/8"
7 5/8"
16"
16"

MATERIALS LIST

Item	Quantity
3/4" exterior plywood	10 sq. ft.
6d galvanized finishing nails	as needed
Resorcinol glue	as needed
Enamel primer and paint	1 qt. each

CONSTRUCTION DETAILS

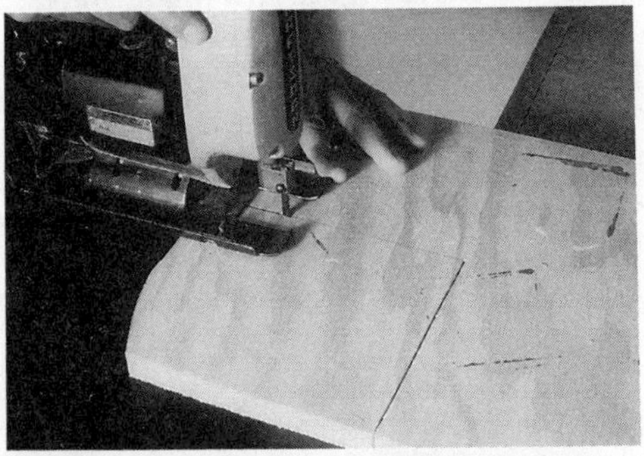

1. Cut out the stand's L-shaped sides with a saber saw equipped with a fine-toothed blade.

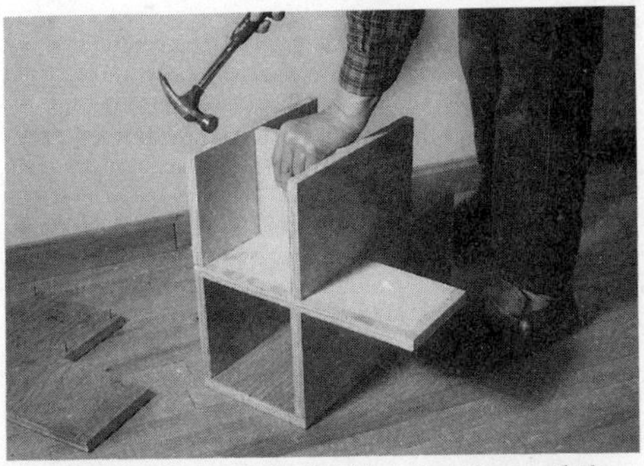

2. Nail and glue the baffles in place while one side is removed. Set the nails beneath the surface.

TRASH BIN

Unsightly trash cans will be a thing of the past after you build this attractive bin. The front folds down to provide easy access, while the sloping roof keeps your containers dry.

Start construction by laying out and cutting the 2X4 side frame members as shown in the diagram. Assemble the frames with 8d galvanized finishing nails and resorcinol glue.

Cut the braces to length, then form the rabbet on the top front brace with a dado blade. Notch the top center brace, as shown, with a hand or saber saw. Attach the braces to the side frames with 8d galvanized finishing nails and glue. Check the squareness of the assembly with a framing square as you go.

Lay out the components made of Georgia-Pacific Texture 1-11 siding. Notice the direction of the grooves shown in the photo. Cut these parts with a plywood blade in your circular saw, using a clamp-on guide. Cut the siding with the good side down to minimize splintering.

Attach 1X2 cleats to the sides, then install the roof and sides with glue and 4d galvanized finishing nails. Cut the floor and back sections from sheets of 3/4-in. exterior plywood. Notch the corners of the floor to clear the 2X4 side frames.

Install the 2X4 floor brace, then attach the floor and back with glue and 4d galvanized finishing nails. Secure the handgrip to the door in the same way.

Cut mortises for the hinges with a sharp chisel. The mortises should be as deep as a folded hinge. Install the hinges and the roller catches.

Stain the finished bin to suit your taste, then complete the project by applying two coats of clear wood sealer, such as Thompson's Water Seal.

Design courtesy of Georgia-Pacific Corporation, P.O. Box 105605, Atlanta, GA 30348-5605.

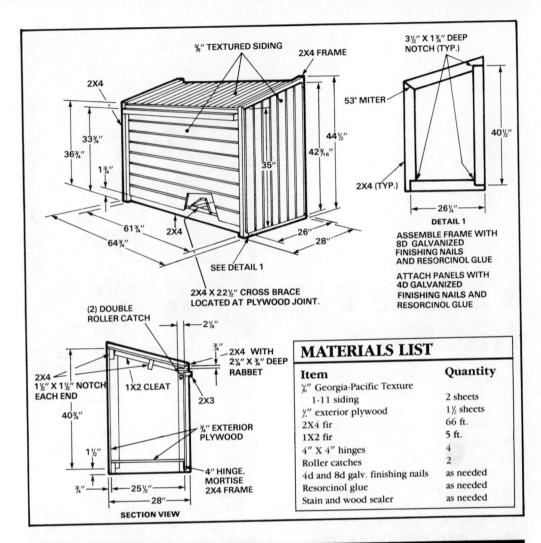

⅝" TEXTURED SIDING

2X4 FRAME

3½" X 1¾" DEEP NOTCH (TYP.)

2X4

53° MITER

33¾"

36¾"

1¾"

44½"

42³⁄₁₆"

35"

40½"

2X4 (TYP.)

61¾"

2X4

64¾"

26"

28"

26¼"

DETAIL 1

SEE DETAIL 1

2X4 X 22½" CROSS BRACE LOCATED AT PLYWOOD JOINT.

ASSEMBLE FRAME WITH 8D GALVANIZED FINISHING NAILS AND RESORCINOL GLUE

ATTACH PANELS WITH 4D GALVANIZED FINISHING NAILS AND RESORCINOL GLUE

(2) DOUBLE ROLLER CATCH

2¼"

¾"

2X4 WITH 2¼" X ¾" DEEP RABBET

2X4 1½" X 1½" NOTCH EACH END

1X2 CLEAT

2X3

40¾"

¾" EXTERIOR PLYWOOD

1½"

4" HINGE, MORTISE 2X4 FRAME

¾"

25½"

28"

SECTION VIEW

MATERIALS LIST

Item	Quantity
⅝" Georgia-Pacific Texture 1-11 siding	2 sheets
⅜" exterior plywood	1½ sheets
2X4 fir	66 ft.
1X2 fir	5 ft.
4" X 4" hinges	4
Roller catches	2
4d and 8d galv. finishing nails	as needed
Resorcinol glue	as needed
Stain and wood sealer	as needed

CONSTRUCTION DETAILS

1. Cut the miter on the front part of the side frame with a power miter box or your stationary saw.

2. Lay out the side frame members by laying them in position and marking the cutting lines.

417

VEGETABLE RACK

The rich harvest of fresh vegetables from your garden deserves proper storage. This vegetable rack provides good air circulation to help prevent spoilage until you have time to process your crop. You can also use the unit as a drying rack.

Your vegetables are supported by 1-in. mesh chicken wire. Fiberglass screen is used on top of the wire mesh to provide a sanitary surface.

Start building the project by cutting all of the pine components to the lengths shown in the diagram. Set up a stop block on your saw to help you cut identical parts.

Attach the 12½-in.-long rails to the posts with no. 8 X 1¼-in. flathead wood screws, after drilling countersunk pilot holes with a combination bit. Check the assembly for squareness as you go. You can do this by measuring the diagonals of each frame. If they are equal, the frame is square.

Add the remaining rails to complete the post and rail assembly, then screw the 1X1 cleats to the rails, following the same procedure. Use three screws in each cleat.

Before installing the screens in the rack, give the assembled frame a good sanding, followed by two coats of polyurethane varnish.

Now, turn the assembly upside-down and measure the underside of one rail and cleat assembly. Make a pattern on hardboard or heavy cardboard, then use this pattern to help you cut the chicken wire and fiberglass window screen.

Staple the screen and chicken wire to the undersides of the cleats, placing a staple every 2 inches. Stretch the materials tightly as you go. Notice that the fiberglass screen is the top part of the sandwich.

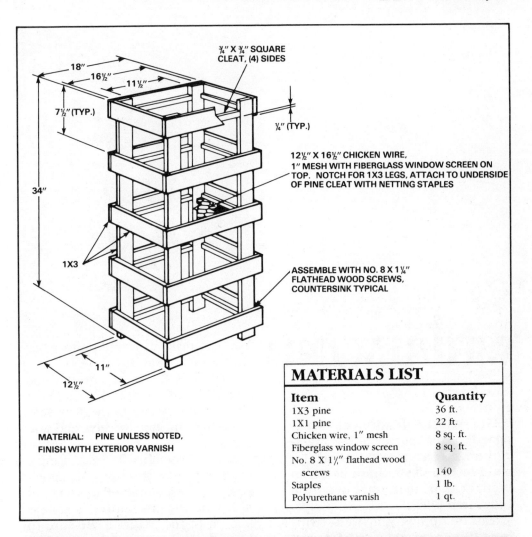

¾" X ¾" SQUARE CLEAT, (4) SIDES

18"

16½"

11½"

7½" (TYP.)

¼" (TYP.)

34"

12½" X 16½" CHICKEN WIRE, 1" MESH WITH FIBERGLASS WINDOW SCREEN ON TOP. NOTCH FOR 1X3 LEGS, ATTACH TO UNDERSIDE OF PINE CLEAT WITH NETTING STAPLES

1X3

ASSEMBLE WITH NO. 8 X 1¼" FLATHEAD WOOD SCREWS, COUNTERSINK TYPICAL

11"

12½"

MATERIAL: PINE UNLESS NOTED, FINISH WITH EXTERIOR VARNISH

MATERIALS LIST

Item	Quantity
1X3 pine	36 ft.
1X1 pine	22 ft.
Chicken wire, 1" mesh	8 sq. ft.
Fiberglass window screen	8 sq. ft.
No. 8 X 1¼" flathead wood screws	140
Staples	1 lb.
Polyurethane varnish	1 qt.

CONSTRUCTION DETAILS

1. *Attach the front rails to the uprights with countersunk flathead wood screws. Check for squareness as you go.*

2. *Staple the screen and chicken wire to the undersides of the cleats. Space the staples 2 in. apart.*

WHIRLWIND

Our whirlwind project is designed to spin merrily in the slightest breeze. You can add this easy-to-build mobile to your yard in just an hour or two, using lumber from your scrap pile.

Start by ripping ¼-in.-thick strips from ¾-in. redwood stock. Set your saw's fence ¼ in. away from the blade and successively rip strips from the edge of the board. For safety, use a pusher board to keep your hands away from the blade, and work with stock that's at least 24 in. long.

Once you have ripped about 48 feet of these thin strips, cut the material into uniform 9-in. pieces. Clamp a stop block on your saw's fence to help gauge the length.

Next, drill a ⁵⁄₁₆-in.-dia. hole through the center of each strip.

You can make a simple jig for your drill press to simplify the job.

Drill a ³⁄₃₂-in. hole through one end of the threaded rod, then insert the rod through all of the slats. Add a washer and nut to each end and tighten.

Lay the assembly flat and, using a bar compass or an improvised compass, draw 16-in.-radius arcs on both sides of the assembled slats, as shown in the diagram. Be sure to keep the rod centered for good balance.

Cut the curved sides on your band saw, or use a saber saw with a fine-toothed blade. Once the sides are cut, sand the project thoroughly.

Form the spiral shape by twisting the slats, one at a time, so that each slat lines up with the corner of the slat next to it. Once the spiral is formed, tighten the nuts securely.

Fasten a ball-bearing snap swivel into the hole, and hang the whirlwind in the location of your choice with monofilament fishing line.

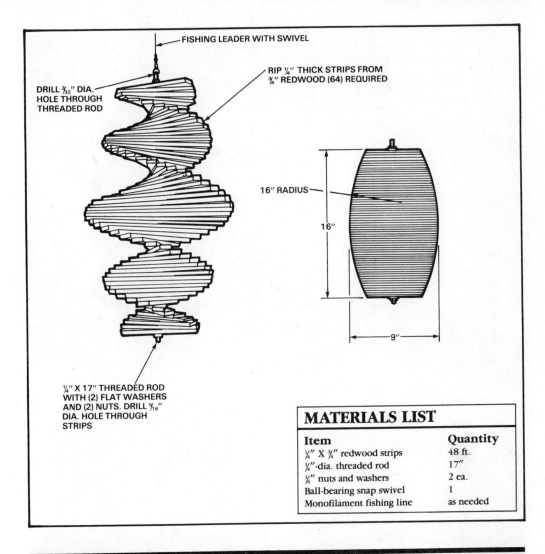

FISHING LEADER WITH SWIVEL

DRILL ³/₃₂" DIA. HOLE THROUGH THREADED ROD

RIP ¼" THICK STRIPS FROM ¾" REDWOOD (64) REQUIRED

16" RADIUS

16"

9"

¼" X 17" THREADED ROD WITH (2) FLAT WASHERS AND (2) NUTS. DRILL ⁵/₁₆" DIA. HOLE THROUGH STRIPS

MATERIALS LIST

Item	Quantity
¼" X ¾" redwood strips	48 ft.
¼"-dia. threaded rod	17"
¼" nuts and washers	2 ea.
Ball-bearing snap swivel	1
Monofilament fishing line	as needed

CONSTRUCTION DETAILS

1. Rip thin strips of redwood on your table saw, using a planer blade for a smooth finish.

2. After laying out the arcs, cut them with a band saw. You could also use a saber saw for this job.

WISHING WELL

A wishing well makes an ideal accessory for any garden. This one, with its cedar shake exterior, is designed to hold container plants, adding a special touch to a traditional outdoor ornament.

Start construction of the wishing well by forming beveled edges on 2X2 stock. Set your table saw's blade angle at 30 degrees, then rip a bevel on one side of a long 2X2. Position the cut so it ends at the exact center of the 2X2. After cutting one side, flip the stock over and cut the other bevel. Once these corner braces are prepared, cut six 10½-in. and six 17½-in. lengths.

Now, cut six 12¼-in. X 29¼-in. pieces of ½-in. pressure-treated plywood for the sides of the well. Once the parts are cut to size, form 60 degree bevels on their edges with a table saw.

Attach the plywood sides to the lower 2X2 corner braces with no. 8 X 1½-in. flathead wood screws. Countersink the pilot holes flush with the surface.

Next, place the completed unit on top of a piece of ½-in. pressure-treated plywood, and trace the pattern of the well's inside. Cut the plywood (divider) with a saber saw. Mark the positions of the weep holes and drill them with a ½-in.-dia. bit.

Insert the plywood divider into the well. Now add the upper cleats to the plywood, fastening each with no. 8 X 1½-in. flathead wood screws.

Set the miter gauge on your table saw to 60 degrees, then cut 1X1 cleats to fit inside the well's top edge. On two sides, cut the cleats to allow for the 1X3 roof supports. Attach the cleats with no. 8 X 1-in. flathead wood screws.

Now, cut the ledge components from 1X3 stock. Use the same setup on your saw to form the mitered corners. Cut notches on two of the ledge parts for the roof supports. Attach the ledge to the 1X1 cleats with no. 10 X 1¼-in. flathead wood screws. Countersink the screw heads flush.

Cut the roof supports to the length shown in the diagram, then bore 1-in.-dia. holes in the roof supports to allow for the dowel shaft. Secure the supports with screws driven into the ledge. Drive no. 8 X 1-in. flathead wood screws into the supports through the plywood sides.

Cut two triangular roof braces from the ½-in. plywood. Lay these out as indicated in the diagram. Clamp a guide on the stock and cut the parts with your portable circular saw. Attach the braces to the inside of the roof supports with no. 8 X 1-in. flathead wood screws.

Add 1X1 cleats to the inside of the triangular braces. Miter the top joint of the cleats to 60 degrees.

Now, cut the roof panels from ½-in. plywood. As you did before, bevel the edges to form the 60 degree miter joint at the roof peak. Fasten the panels to the 1X1 cleats with no. 8 X 1-in. flathead wood screws and countersink flush.

Glue the dowel shaft in place with waterproof resorcinol glue, leaving one end protruding. Cut the crank from 1X3 stock, rounding the

CONSTRUCTION DETAILS

1. *Cut intersecting 60-degree bevels on 2X2 stock to form the cleats for the well's base.*

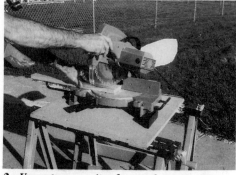

2. *Use a power miter box to form the 60-degree mitered joints on the six 1X3 ledge components.*

3. *Form a bevel on the cedar shakes where they form the joint. Check the angle as you work.*

4. *Drill the holes in the roof supports with a 1-in. bit on your drill press. Use a backup board.*

ends to a 1¼-in. radius. Bore two 1-in.-dia. holes in the crank, then glue the crank in place. Add the dowel handle to the other hole.

Sand the wishing well, paying special attention to parts that will be exposed after the cedar shakes are installed. Finish the exposed parts as you choose.

Complete the project by attaching cedar shakes to the sides and the roof with 3d galvanized nails. At the corners of the well and the peak of the roof, bevel the edges of the shakes to match the angles of the joints.

MATERIALS LIST

Item	Quantity
2X2 lumber	15 ft.
1X3 lumber	16 ft.
1X1 lumber	12 ft.
½″ pressure-treated plywood	1 sheet
1″ hardwood dowel	30″
Cedar shakes	1 bundle
No. 8 X 1″ flathead wood screws	as needed
No. 8 X 1½″ flathead wood screws	as needed
No. 10 X 1¼″ flathead wood screws	as needed
3d galvanized nails	as needed
Resorcinol glue	as needed
Stain and wood sealer or paint	as needed

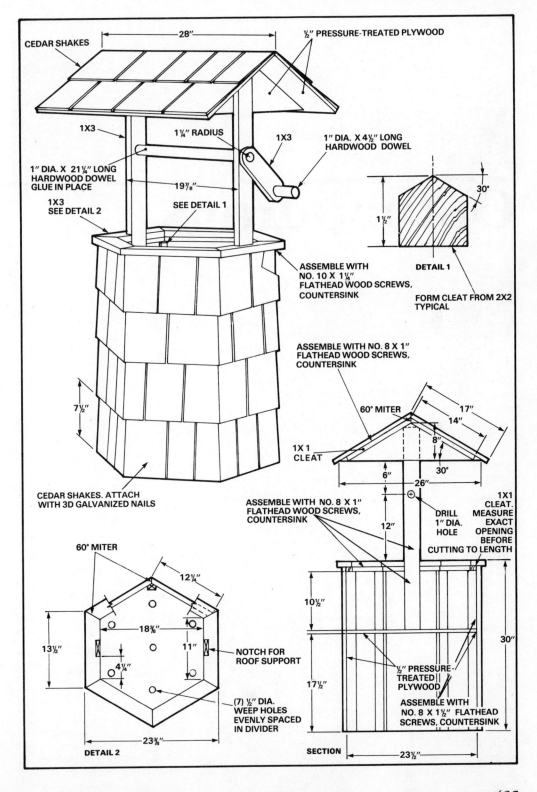

CEDAR SHAKES

28"

½" PRESSURE-TREATED PLYWOOD

1X3

1¼" RADIUS

1X3

1" DIA. X 4½" LONG HARDWOOD DOWEL

1" DIA. X 21¼" LONG HARDWOOD DOWEL GLUE IN PLACE

19⅞"

1X3 SEE DETAIL 2

SEE DETAIL 1

30°

1½"

DETAIL 1

FORM CLEAT FROM 2X2 TYPICAL

ASSEMBLE WITH NO. 10 X 1¼" FLATHEAD WOOD SCREWS, COUNTERSINK

ASSEMBLE WITH NO. 8 X 1" FLATHEAD WOOD SCREWS, COUNTERSINK

7½"

60° MITER

17"

14"

8"

1X1 CLEAT

6"

30°

26"

1X1 CLEAT. MEASURE EXACT OPENING BEFORE CUTTING TO LENGTH

CEDAR SHAKES. ATTACH WITH 3D GALVANIZED NAILS

DRILL 1" DIA. HOLE

ASSEMBLE WITH NO. 8 X 1" FLATHEAD WOOD SCREWS, COUNTERSINK

12"

10½"

60° MITER

12¼"

18⅜"

11"

13½"

4¼"

NOTCH FOR ROOF SUPPORT

½" PRESSURE-TREATED PLYWOOD

17½"

30"

(7) ½" DIA. WEEP HOLES EVENLY SPACED IN DIVIDER

ASSEMBLE WITH NO. 8 X 1½" FLATHEAD SCREWS, COUNTERSINK

23⅜"

DETAIL 2

SECTION

23½"

X.

Outbuildings

OPEN-AIR GARDEN SHELTER

If you need a sheltered spot in your yard for entertaining, garden work, or just a place where you can put your feet up, this project is for you. It will be a versatile and attractive addition to any outdoor area.

A lattice roof filters the sunlight, partially shading the multilevel deck area. The roof panels can be removed in sections to create just the mood you want. A comfortable

bench provides seating, while spacious cabinets and a work surface add versatility to the shelter.

Build the project as an addition to an existing deck, or make it a freestanding unit, separated from other structures.

You can build the unit exactly as shown in the diagram, or modify any part of it to suit your own needs. The design is flexible enough to be

This multi-purpose redwood garden shelter can be used for entertaining and for a garden work center.

changed easily. If you make changes, draw a sketch of your altered design to help you modify the materials list.

Redwood lumber is the best material for this shelter. Its beauty and weather-resistant qualities guarantee a long life. Choose construction heart grade redwood for joists and other components that contact the ground. All-heart redwood lumber is extremely rot-resistant and will support the structure for many years.

The remaining parts can be made of less expensive construction common grade redwood lumber. Knots and sapwood in this grade of material will add visual interest to the shelter.

Start construction of the project by laying out the positions of the concrete piers used to support the deck joists. Choose a level site in your yard, then locate the corners of the structure. Closely follow the dimensions shown in the framing plan (see page 430).

Drive stakes at the corner pier locations, then measure the diagonals of the unit to check its squareness. When the diagonals are equal, the layout is correct. Notice that the framing is made up in two sections, one for the front of the unit and a second frame for the rear deck.

Now, run a string line around the perimeter of both sections. Using this as a guide, drive stakes into the remaining post positions. Remember to locate the pier inside the right front corner accurately. This pier supports one of the roof posts.

Dig holes for the 12-in.-dia. X 36-in. concrete piers. Then mix and pour concrete so that each is 1 in. above grade. Use a long, straight 2X6 and a level to strike off the top of the concrete so the piers are level. After the concrete has hardened, position 10-in.-dia. X 8-in. pre-fabricated piers at each location. Align each pier and secure with concrete adhesive.

Once the piers are even and at the correct height, backfill around them and pack the earth well.

Now, cut 2X8 joists to the lengths shown in the diagram. Make up the doubled joists by nailing two 2X8 redwood parts together with 10d galvanized nails.

Position the doubled joists on the piers, lining up their ends carefully. At each post position, bore ¼-in-dia. holes through the joist for the anchor bolts. Counterbore each hole from the joist's top with a ¾-in. bit to a depth of 2½ in. to accommodate the screw heads.

Mark the pier through the hole in the joist, then use a masonry bit to bore a hole in the pier for the lag shield. Install the lag shield, then secure the joist with a ¼-in. X 6-in. lag screw driven into the shield. Use a washer under the screw head.

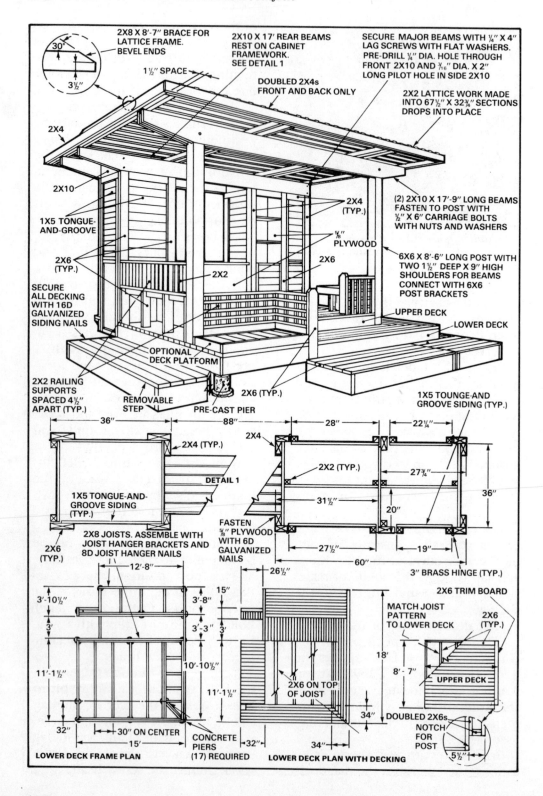

2X8 X 8'-7" BRACE FOR
LATTICE FRAME.
BEVEL ENDS

30°

3½"

1½" SPACE

2X10 X 17' REAR BEAMS
REST ON CABINET
FRAMEWORK.
SEE DETAIL 1

DOUBLED 2X4s
FRONT AND BACK ONLY

SECURE MAJOR BEAMS WITH ¼" X 4"
LAG SCREWS WITH FLAT WASHERS.
PRE-DRILL ¼" DIA. HOLE THROUGH
FRONT 2X10 AND ⁷⁄₁₆" DIA. X 2"
LONG PILOT HOLE IN SIDE 2X10

2X2 LATTICE WORK MADE
INTO 67½" X 32¾" SECTIONS
DROPS INTO PLACE

2X4

2X10

1X5 TONGUE-
AND-GROOVE

2X6
(TYP.)

2X4
(TYP.)

⁵⁄₈"
PLYWOOD

2X6

(2) 2X10 X 17'-9" LONG BEAMS
FASTEN TO POST WITH
½" X 6" CARRIAGE BOLTS
WITH NUTS AND WASHERS

6X6 X 8'-6" LONG POST WITH
TWO 1½" DEEP X 9" HIGH
SHOULDERS FOR BEAMS
CONNECT WITH 6X6
POST BRACKETS

SECURE
ALL DECKING
WITH 16D
GALVANIZED
SIDING NAILS

2X2

UPPER DECK

LOWER DECK

2X2 RAILING
SUPPORTS
SPACED 4½"
APART (TYP.)

OPTIONAL
DECK PLATFORM

REMOVABLE
STEP

PRE-CAST PIER

2X6 (TYP.)

1X5 TOUNGE-AND-
GROOVE SIDING (TYP.)

36"

88"

28"

22¼"

2X4 (TYP.)

2X4

2X2 (TYP.)

27¾"

36"

DETAIL 1

1X5 TONGUE-AND-
GROOVE SIDING
(TYP.)

31½"

20"

FASTEN
⁵⁄₈" PLYWOOD
WITH 6D
GALVANIZED
NAILS

27½"

19"

2X6
(TYP.)

60"

3" BRASS HINGE (TYP.)

26½"

2X8 JOISTS. ASSEMBLE WITH
JOIST HANGER BRACKETS AND
8D JOIST HANGER NAILS

12'-8"

15"

2X6 TRIM BOARD

MATCH JOIST
PATTERN
TO LOWER DECK

2X6
(TYP.)

3'-10½"

3'-8"

3'

3'-3"

3'

2X6 ON TOP
OF JOIST

18'

8'-7"

UPPER DECK

11'-1½"

10'-10½"

11'-1½"

34"

DOUBLED 2X6s

NOTCH
FOR
POST

32"

30" ON CENTER

15'

CONCRETE
PIERS

(17) REQUIRED

32"

34"

5½"

LOWER DECK FRAME PLAN

LOWER DECK PLAN WITH DECKING

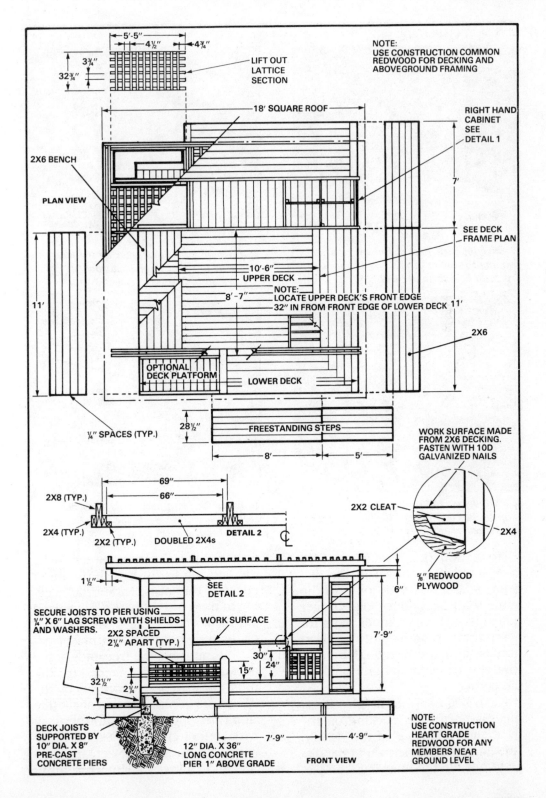

NOTE:
USE CONSTRUCTION COMMON
REDWOOD FOR DECKING AND
ABOVEGROUND FRAMING

5'-5"
4½"
4¾"
3¾"
32¾"

LIFT OUT
LATTICE
SECTION

RIGHT HAND
CABINET
SEE
DETAIL 1

18' SQUARE ROOF

2X6 BENCH

PLAN VIEW

7'

SEE DECK
FRAME PLAN

10'-6"
UPPER DECK

NOTE:
LOCATE UPPER DECK'S FRONT EDGE
32" IN FROM FRONT EDGE OF LOWER DECK

8'-7"

11'

11'

2X6

OPTIONAL
DECK PLATFORM

LOWER DECK

¼" SPACES (TYP.)

28½"

FREESTANDING STEPS

8'

5'

WORK SURFACE MADE
FROM 2X6 DECKING.
FASTEN WITH 10D
GALVANIZED NAILS

69"
66"

2X8 (TYP.)

2X4 (TYP.)
2X2 (TYP.)

DOUBLED 2X4s

DETAIL 2

2X2 CLEAT

2X4

⅝" REDWOOD
PLYWOOD

1½"

SEE
DETAIL 2

6"

SECURE JOISTS TO PIER USING
¼" X 6" LAG SCREWS WITH SHIELDS
AND WASHERS.

WORK SURFACE

2X2 SPACED
2¼" APART (TYP.)

30"
24"
15"

7'-9"

32½"
2¼"

DECK JOISTS
SUPPORTED BY
10" DIA. X 8"
PRE-CAST
CONCRETE PIERS

12" DIA. X 36"
LONG CONCRETE
PIER 1" ABOVE GRADE

FRONT VIEW

7'-9"

4'-9"

NOTE:
USE CONSTRUCTION
HEART GRADE
REDWOOD FOR ANY
MEMBERS NEAR
GROUND LEVEL

431

CONSTRUCTION DETAILS

1. *Once the basic deck is finished, start framing the cabinet walls. Use temporary braces to hold them vertical.*

2. *Plywood partitions separate the front and rear of the cabinets. Redwood siding dresses up the walls.*

3. *2X10 beams rest on the cabinets to support the roof. Toenail the beams to the cabinet frame.*

4. *Brace the front posts to keep them vertical as you assemble the roof. Use double-headed nails.*

Now, add the remaining 2X8 deck framing as shown in the diagram. Attach the main joists to the frame with heavy-duty joist hanger brackets and joist hanger nails for maximum strength. Add the short braces, and the diagonal braces, trimming the latter to fit the angle in the corner.

Next, begin laying the 2X6 decking. Start with the decking on the front and right sides of the shelter. Lay the decking as shown in the diagram, forming the herringbone pattern on the right front corner. Make the decking fit flush with the outer edges of the joists. Fasten the decking to the joists with 16d galvanized siding nails. These nails are specially designed to stay in place.

You can leave the free ends of the decking longer than needed to simplify construction. Once all of the decking is in place, snap a chalk line along the edge, then trim the deck with your circular saw. Set the blade to just cut through the decking lumber, and follow the line carefully.

Note the three decking boards nailed lengthwise on the joists left open in the middle of the lower deck. These act as spacers to support the upper deck which rests on the lower deck.

Next, build the frame for the upper deck from 2X6 redwood lumber. Be sure to make a notch for the 6X6 post as shown in the Upper Deck Detail on page 430. Also, locate the joists for the upper deck so that they will rest on the lower deck's joists (with the spacers) when in its final position.

Set the upper deck frame on the lower deck. Position it according to the diagram on page 431. Toenail it in place from the inside of the upper frame so that the nails will be concealed when the decking is in place.

Now, add the 2X6 decking to the upper deck. This time, however, you will have to nail a 2X6 trim board along one edge of the surface, perpendicular to the rest of the decking.

Once the decking is complete, begin building the frame for the cabinet and work surface unit. Nail two 2X4 posts together to form the L-shaped corners of each end of the far right cabinet. Use 2X6 lumber to frame the front of the left cabinet. Refer to Detail 1 of the diagram on page 430.

Fit a 36-in. X 93-in. sheet of ⅝-in. redwood plywood to the inside of a pair of built-up posts. Nail these in place with 6d siding nails.

Stand the completed end panels upright on the deck in their correct positions. Prop the panels vertical with temporary braces, as shown in the photo. Use a level to check their alignment. Toenail the post assemblies to the decking with 12d galvanized nails.

Build the inside panels the same way, and place them the proper distance from the end panels. Hold their positions with temporary braces nailed between the panels.

You can alter the dimensions of the cabinet unit to suit your personal needs. Follow the general construction details shown in the diagram, but choose your own layout.

Add the 2X2 cleats to frame the partitions inside the cabinets. Nail these in place with 6d galvanized nails, then cut plywood panels to fit. Choose the locations for any doors or open shelves, and build these according to the general de-

Design and photos courtesy of the California Redwood Association, 591 Redwood Highway, Suite 3100, Mill Valley, CA 94941.

MATERIALS LIST

Item	Quantity
6X6 redwood	18 ft.
2X10 redwood	84 ft.
2X8 construction heart redwood	300 ft.
2X6 redwood	1,000 ft.
2X4 redwood	300 ft.
2X2 redwood	2,000 ft.
1X6 tongue-and-groove redwood siding	300 ft.
⅝" redwood plywood	8 sheets
10" X 8" concrete piers	13
2X8 joist hanger brackets	16
6X6 heavy-duty post brackets	2
½" X 6" lag screws with washer	13
½" X 4" lag screws with washer	8
½" X 6" carriage bolts with nuts and washers	4
16d galvanized siding nails	as needed
6d, 10d, 12d, 16d galvanized nails	as needed
8d joist hanger nails	as needed
6d siding nails	as needed
¾" brads	as needed
Silicone caulk	as needed
3" brass hinges, handles and latches	to suit
Clear wood sealer	as needed

sign shown in the diagram.

In the design shown here, the left cabinet is made to store large items. Its access door is on the left end of the unit. The right cabinet has open shelves and a number of doors. Make frames for the doors of 2X2 redwood, then nail a ⅝-in. redwood panel to the back of the frame.

Hang doors with 3-in. brass hinges, making certain they are properly aligned. Add handles and latches to suit your personal taste.

Finish the cabinet unit by applying 1X6 tongue-and-groove redwood siding to the plywood panels. Cut the siding to fit tightly, then secure it to the plywood panels with ¾-in. brads driven through the tongue section of the material. For proper drainage, apply the siding with the grooves facing down.

Add the top panels of plywood to keep rain out of the cabinets. Caulk the joints well with a high-quality silicone caulk.

Nail 2X2 cleats to the sides of the cabinets and to the decking to make a frame for the work surface. Adjust the height of the cleats to make the top of the surface the height you want. Cut plywood panels for the front and rear to close off the work area. Finish the work surface with 2X6 redwood boards, laid lengthwise.

Next, prepare the two front posts. Cut 6X6 redwood timbers for the posts. On one end of each post, form two 1½-in. X 9-in. notches to make shoulders for the beams.

Cut the notches on your radial arm saw with a dado blade. Make multiple passes to complete the notches. Be sure to support the free end of the post with an appropriate stand.

You can also cut the notches with a circular saw. Set the saw's depth of cut to 1½ in. Make multiple cuts across the stock, ¼ in. apart, then remove the waste with a sharp 1½-in. wood chisel.

Once the notches are formed, erect the posts on the deck surface. Secure the posts with heavy-duty post brackets. Nail the brackets to the decking, then insert the posts. Use a level to help make the posts vertical, then apply temporary braces, as shown in the photos. Nail the posts in place with 16d galvanized nails driven through the brackets. Leave the braces in position until the roof is completed.

Now, cut two 17-ft., 9-in. beams from 2X10 redwood stock. Measure the distance between the outer edges of the posts and mark this dimension on the beams. Lay out the taper shown in the diagram, then cut the beams' ends with your circular saw. Cut the beams carefully to make them match.

Raise the beams, with help, and place them on the post's shoulders. Align them carefully, then bore ½-in.-dia. holes through the beams and the posts. Attach the beams with ½-in. X 6-in. carriage bolts with nuts and washers.

Cut two additional beams for the rear of the structure. This time, however, cut a taper on only one end of each beam.

Raise these beams, one at a time, onto the framework of the cabinet unit. Align the beams carefully, then toenail them to the cabinet framing. Cut four 2X10 blocks to fit between the beams. Secure the beams to the blocking with ¼-in. X 4-in. lag screws with washers .

Begin building the roof frame

next. Cut the two center sets of rafters first. Nail 2X2 cleats (see Detail 2 of the diagram) to the bottom edges of each rafter with 10d galvanized nails. These cleats will support the lattice panels. Place these rafters on the beams.

Measure the positions of the rafters carefully. They should be 67½ in. apart and centered on the beam. Measure the front and rear overhang, and equalize this dimension for both rafters. Nail the rafters in place with 16d galvanized nails.

Now, add two 17-ft., 9-in. 2X4s to the front and rear of the rafters to begin the perimeter frame. Attach them with 16d galvanized nails. Add the remaining rafters. The roof should overhang the beams 1½ in. on each end.

Install the other 2X2 cleats as shown in the diagram. Cut four 8-ft., 7-in. braces from 2X8 stock, beveling the ends as indicated on page 430 of the diagram. Nail these to the frame of the roof. Next, cut and attach the outer set of frame members. Use 10d galvanized nails to secure the outer frame.

Build lattice panels from 2X2 redwood. Space the redwood base strips as shown in the diagram. Cut space blocks to help you establish the correct spacing.

You will need 24 of these panels to cover the entire roof. Assemble the panels with 10d galvanized nails. If you choose not to make the panels removable, simply nail the 2X2 lattice strips to the framework.

Once the roof is finished, add the deck railings and their supports. Cut 2X6 lumber to form the frames for the rails, as shown in the diagram. Attach these to the posts and the decking. Fit 2X2 railing supports in

place, and add 2X2 horizontal strips where indicated. You can customize the railings to suit your own taste.

Add any benches or other features you choose, building them from the same redwood stock you have used throughout the project.

Complete the project by building the freestanding steps. Frame these with 2X8 all-heart redwood, spacing joists inside the frames on 24-in. centers. Assemble the frames with 16d galvanized nails.

Once the frames are complete, apply 2X6 decking as you did for the main deck. Place the step units alongside the main deck. There is no need to attach them permanently to the structure.

The steps are another thing you can customize on this project. You can build them larger than the dimensions shown in the diagram to provide additional deck area. Or, if you like, any of the steps can be eliminated.

After you have completed the construction of the shelter, inspect it carefully. Sand any rough areas well to prevent splinters, and round over sharp edges to make them safer.

Leave the project unfinished if you want it to weather naturally. Redwood slowly changes over time to become a dark grayish red. This weathering process will be uneven, however, and will take some time.

As an alternative, give the structure two coats of clear wood sealer and preservative. Treated this way, the shelter will change to a light buckskin color over a period of time. Use an airless sprayer to apply the sealer and be sure to wear eye protection and a canister-type respirator.

STORAGE BARN

Storage space is always at a premium in every home. If your garage is cluttered with items that could be better stored elsewhere, consider constructing this barn-style storage building.

It provides 96 sq. ft. of storage space and, unlike many commercial sheds, offers adequate headroom for the tallest person. A 4-ft.-wide doorway gives easy access, while an optional skylight brightens the interior. Once it is built, you can customize its interior to suit your needs.

Before beginning actual construction, choose a location for the building. Select a site that is convenient, but watch out for poor drainage. Since this storage barn sits directly on the ground, pooled water could cause real damage. Level the site for the building, using a straight 12-ft. 2X4 and a carpenter's level to check

the prepared area.

To begin building, lay two 12-ft.-long pressure-treated 4X4 runners on the site, spacing them 64 in. apart. Do not be tempted to save money by using untreated wood, since contact with the ground will promote rot and insect damage. Make certain that the runners are perfectly parallel and centered on the site. It is also a good idea to double-check them for levelness.

Cut thirteen 2X4 joists 93 in. long, and lay them on edge across the runners, 12 in. on center. Use pressure-treated lumber for the joists to protect them from water damage. Add the 12-ft. runner cap to the joists, fastening them with 16d galvanized nails. As indicated in the diagram, these parts should also be made of pressure-treated lumber.

Check the squareness of the floor frame assembly by measuring the diagonals of the unit. When the diagonals are equal, the floor is perfectly square. Make adjustments by pushing on one corner.

Once the framework is completed, make sure that the runners haven't shifted and then toenail the joists to the runners. Use 16d galvanized nails, and drill pilot holes to simplify the nailing. The pilot holes will also keep the floor frame from shifting.

Cut the 10½-in. bridging, measuring each gap before cutting the block to allow for slight variations. Nail the blocks in position, as shown in the diagram. It is important that the blocks be centered in the frame, since the plywood floor joints meet over these blocks. Snap a chalk line on the frame to guide the installation.

Cut one sheet of 15/32-in. pressure-treated sheathing plywood in half to make two 4-ft. square pieces. Nail the floor to the joists, following the pattern shown in the diagram. Use 6d galvanized nails, spacing them 6 in. apart on the edges and 10 in. apart elsewhere. Be sure to leave the indicated gaps between the floor components.

If pressure-treated plywood is unavailable in your area, you can use ¾-in. exterior plywood for the floor. Seal the plywood with clear wood sealer and preservative.

Next, construct the roof trusses, using the completed floor as a guide. Draw a line lengthwise down the center of the floor. Now, draw two lines across the width of the floor, 39 in. and 48 in. from one end. Measure in 15 in. on both ends of the line labeled Y in the diagram and mark these points.

Lay a 2X4 so that its outside edge touches one corner of the floor and the point you marked on line Y. Draw pencil lines on the floor on both sides of the 2X4; the lines should extend past line Y. Draw these lines the full length of the 2X4. Now, move the 2X4 so that its outside edge connects at the same point on line Y and the center of line Z. Again, outline the position of the 2X4 on the floor.

Draw a pencil line connecting the intersections of the outlines to indicate the angle of the mitered joint between the two 2X4s. To speed up the process of laying out the trusses, nail 2X4 scraps to the floor on both sides of each truss part, as shown in the diagram.

To make each truss component, lay a 2X4 in position, aided by the blocks, and mark the cut lines using the marks on the floor as a guide. You will need 14 each of parts no. 1 and no. 2.

Cut one set of the parts, then use these as patterns for the remaining pieces. Cut the angles with a circular saw, using an adjustable guide to help you keep the angles accurate.

As an alternative, you can cut all of the truss components on your radial arm or table saw, after setting up the proper angles. Use an adjustable bevel and a protractor to measure the angles from the marked components.

Once all of the truss parts are cut, assemble the trusses on the floor to insure proper alignment. Use the blocks you nailed to the floor to guide the assembly.

Cut thirty-six 6-in. X 12-in. pieces of ⅜-in. plywood sheathing to be used as splices. With the truss components in place on the floor, lay the splices on the components and

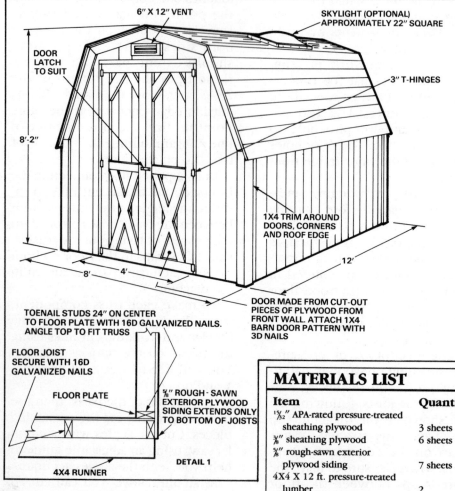

6" X 12" VENT

SKYLIGHT (OPTIONAL)
APPROXIMATELY 22" SQUARE

DOOR
LATCH
TO SUIT

3" T-HINGES

8'-2"

1X4 TRIM AROUND
DOORS, CORNERS
AND ROOF EDGE

8'

4'

12'

DOOR MADE FROM CUT-OUT
PIECES OF PLYWOOD FROM
FRONT WALL. ATTACH 1X4
BARN DOOR PATTERN WITH
3D NAILS

TOENAIL STUDS 24" ON CENTER
TO FLOOR PLATE WITH 16D GALVANIZED NAILS.
ANGLE TOP TO FIT TRUSS

FLOOR JOIST
SECURE WITH 16D
GALVANIZED NAILS

FLOOR PLATE

⅝" ROUGH-SAWN
EXTERIOR PLYWOOD
SIDING EXTENDS ONLY
TO BOTTOM OF JOISTS

4X4 RUNNER

DETAIL 1

MATERIALS LIST

Item	Quantity
$\frac{15}{32}$" APA-rated pressure-treated sheathing plywood	3 sheets
⅜" sheathing plywood	6 sheets
⅝" rough-sawn exterior plywood siding	7 sheets
4X4 X 12 ft. pressure-treated lumber	2
2X4 X 12 ft. pressure-treated lumber	3
2X4 X 8 ft. pressure-treated lumber	3
2X4 X 12 ft. fir	4
2X4 X 8 ft. fir	36
2X2 X 8 ft. fir	3
1X4 X 8 ft. fir	18
3d, 4d, 6d, 16d galvanized nails	5 lb. each
8d galv. or stainless steel siding nails	5 lb.
¾" or ⅞" roofing nails	10 lb.
3" T-hinges	6
Door latch or barrel bolt	1
6"X 12" louvered vents	2
Solid-color stain or paint	2 gal.
Black felt underlayment	1 roll
Composition roof shingles	6 bundles
24" skylight	1 or 2 (optional)
Clear wood sealer	2 gal.

mark cut lines on the strips. Cut one set of three splices and use them as patterns to lay out the remaining splices. Cut the splices with a saber saw or a band saw.

Nail the splices in place with 4d galvanized nails. After nailing splices on one side of each truss, flip the truss end-for-end and install the others. Install splices on both sides of five trusses, but splice only one side of the other two. These two trusses will be used at the ends of the building. After all of the roof trusses are completed, remove the 2X4 guide

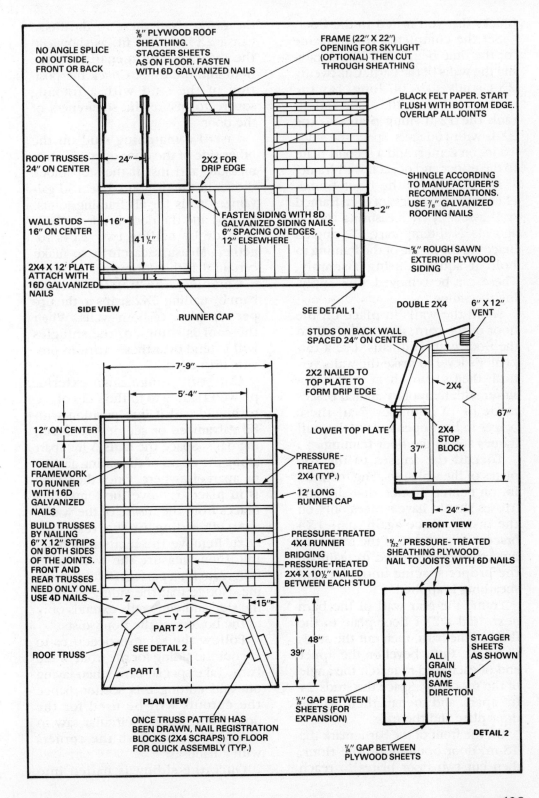

NO ANGLE SPLICE
ON OUTSIDE,
FRONT OR BACK

⅜″ PLYWOOD ROOF
SHEATHING.
STAGGER SHEETS
AS ON FLOOR. FASTEN
WITH 6D GALVANIZED NAILS

FRAME (22″ X 22″)
OPENING FOR SKYLIGHT
(OPTIONAL) THEN CUT
THROUGH SHEATHING

BLACK FELT PAPER. START
FLUSH WITH BOTTOM EDGE.
OVERLAP ALL JOINTS

ROOF TRUSSES
24″ ON CENTER

24″

2X2 FOR
DRIP EDGE

SHINGLE ACCORDING
TO MANUFACTURER'S
RECOMMENDATIONS.
USE ⅞″ GALVANIZED
ROOFING NAILS

2″

WALL STUDS
16″ ON CENTER

16″

41½″

FASTEN SIDING WITH 8D
GALVANIZED SIDING NAILS.
6″ SPACING ON EDGES,
12″ ELSEWHERE

⅝″ ROUGH SAWN
EXTERIOR PLYWOOD
SIDING

2X4 X 12′ PLATE
ATTACH WITH
16D GALVANIZED
NAILS

SIDE VIEW

RUNNER CAP

SEE DETAIL 1

DOUBLE 2X4

6″ X 12″
VENT

STUDS ON BACK WALL
SPACED 24″ ON CENTER

2X4

2X2 NAILED TO
TOP PLATE TO
FORM DRIP EDGE

67″

LOWER TOP PLATE

2X4
STOP
BLOCK

37″

FRONT VIEW

24″

7′-9″

5′-4″

12″ ON CENTER

TOENAIL
FRAMEWORK
TO RUNNER
WITH 16D
GALVANIZED
NAILS

PRESSURE-
TREATED
2X4 (TYP.)

12′ LONG
RUNNER CAP

BUILD TRUSSES
BY NAILING
6″ X 12″ STRIPS
ON BOTH SIDES
OF THE JOINTS.
FRONT AND
REAR TRUSSES
NEED ONLY ONE.
USE 4D NAILS

PRESSURE-TREATED
4X4 RUNNER

BRIDGING
PRESSURE-TREATED
2X4 X 10½″ NAILED
BETWEEN EACH STUD

Z

Y

PART 2

15″

48″

ROOF TRUSS

SEE DETAIL 2

39″

PART 1

PLAN VIEW

ONCE TRUSS PATTERN HAS
BEEN DRAWN, NAIL REGISTRATION
BLOCKS (2X4 SCRAPS) TO FLOOR
FOR QUICK ASSEMBLY (TYP.)

⅛″ GAP BETWEEN
SHEETS (FOR
EXPANSION)

¼″ GAP BETWEEN
PLYWOOD SHEETS

15/32″ PRESSURE- TREATED
SHEATHING PLYWOOD
NAIL TO JOISTS WITH 6D NAILS

ALL
GRAIN
RUNS
SAME
DIRECTION

STAGGER
SHEETS
AS SHOWN

DETAIL 2

blocks that you nailed to the floor.

Set the completed trusses aside for the time being, and begin framing the walls of the barn. Cut twenty 2X4 studs 41½ in. long. Lay the studs on edge on the floor and attach the 12-ft.-long plates to the 2X4s with 16d nails. Space the studs 16 in. on center. Add a second plate to the upper end of each wall frame.

As you did for the floor frame, check the squareness of each framed wall assembly by measuring the diagonals. Nail temporary 1X4 angled braces to the inside of the framing to hold it square during assembly. These can be removed after applying the siding.

Stand the walls in place on the floor of the barn, then nail them to the floor with 16d nails. Use a carpenter's level to make the walls vertical, then secure them in that position with temporary angled braces made of 1X4 lumber. Nail these braces to the upper ends of the wall frames and to the floor framing.

Toenail the trusses to the top plates of the walls, spacing them 24 in. on center. Notice that the end trusses should have splices only on the inside. Once again, nail 1X4 braces to the inside of the trusses to hold them vertical and to maintain the proper spacing until the roof sheathing is applied.

Frame the rear wall of the barn next. Nail a 2X4 floor plate to the floor of the barn, then cut the studs to length. Cut a bevel on the upper end of each stud to match the angle of the roof truss. Space the studs 24 in. apart, and toenail them to the floor plate and the truss.

On the front of the barn, mark the 48-in. door opening on the floor, then cut two floor plates to reach

the marks. Nail these to the floor. Cut a 2X4 stud to fit, as shown in the diagram, and toenail it to the floor and the truss. Check the position of the stud with a framing square to insure the squareness of the door.

Install a matching stud on the other side of the door opening, then measure and install the stop block shown in the diagram. Use 16d galvanized nails for all framing joints. Finally, add the door header, which is made by nailing two 2X4s together. Measure carefully to make certain that the doorway is square.

Complete the framing for the barn by nailing 2X2 strips to the upper top plate of both walls. When the roof is shingled, the shingles will extend over these strips to provide drip edges.

Cut ⅝-in. rough-sawn exterior plywood siding to fit the sides of the barn, and nail it into position with 8d galvanized or stainless steel siding nails. Space the nails 6 in. apart along the edges of the siding and 12 in. apart elsewhere. Once the siding is in place, remove the temporary braces from the inside of the walls.

Attach siding to the rear wall next. Remove the temporary bracing, then measure the walls carefully. Aim for a perfect fit for the siding. Notice that the siding on both the side and end walls extends only to the bottom of the floor joists.

Follow the same procedures to lay out the siding for the front of the barn. Take special care when laying out and cutting this section, since the cutouts will be used for the doors. If you use a circular saw to make the cuts, finish the corners with a handsaw.

Once the siding is nailed into

place, cut the openings for the vents on both ends of the barn. Install the vents with the screws provided.

Cut and attach the ⅜-in. roof sheathing. Use 6d nails and stagger the sheathing joints as you did on the floor. The roof sheathing should over hang the front and rear of the building. A 2-in. overhang is just right. The plywood grain should be perpendicular to the trusses. Space the nails 6 in. apart on the edges of the plywood and 10 in. apart elsewhere. Once the sheathing is in place, remove the temporary braces from the inside.

If installing a skylight, frame the opening between the trusses to the dimensions of the skylight you choose. Nail 2X4 blocking between the trusses to form these frames. Allow a ¼-in. gap between the skylight and the framing for expansion.

After installing the framing, cut out an opening in the sheathing with a saber saw. To locate the corners of the opening, drill ⅜-in.-dia. holes in the corners from the inside of the building. These holes also serve as starter holes for the saber saw blade. Attach the skylight to the sheathing with ¾-in. roofing nails. It is a good idea to apply asphalt roofing cement under the skylight's flange.

Next, install 1X4 trim on the corners and around the door opening and the roof edge. The joints on the corner trim can either be butt joints or mitered. The trim on the roofline should be cut to fit the angles of the roof.

Make the doors from the cutouts left from the siding. Attach 1X4 strips to the plywood with 3d galvanized nails. You can follow the pattern shown in the diagram, or create your own door pattern. The strips add strength to the doors. For even greater strength, reinforce the inside of the doors as well.

Hang the doors with 3-in. T-hinges, three on each side. You can buy hinges with a wrought-iron look to add a decorative touch to your storage barn. Finally, add a barrel bolt or other latch to suit your taste.

Nail black felt roof underlayment to the roof sheathing, starting at the bottom edge. Extend the underlayment to the edge of the drip rail, and overlap the roofing felt 3 in. at each joint.

Install composition shingles on the roof according to the directions provided by the roofing manufacturer. Use ¾-in. or ⅞-in. roofing nails. Start shingling at the 2X2 drip rail.

Work from both sides of the roof. At the peak of the roof, install a cap of shingles cut into thirds, as shown in the manufacturer's instructions.

Once the roof is finished, seal the skylight, if installed, by applying a bead of asphalt roof cement from a caulking gun.

To finish your barn, apply a solid-color stain or paint in the color of your choice. The trim boards can be painted to match, but you might want to paint them in a contrasting color for added interest.

The interior can be left unfinished or painted. If you wish, you can also add paneling to the inside of the barn. Pegboard makes an excellent interior paneling, and also provides easy-to-use storage for small items. Shelves can be added, if desired, to suit your needs.

Design and photo courtesy of Georgia-Pacific Corporation, P.O. Box 105605, Atlanta, GA 30348-5605.

WORK CENTER/ STORAGE BUILDING

An attractive and versatile outbuilding is an asset to any home. Not only can it increase the value of your property, but it will also enlarge your storage and work space.

This multi-purpose outbuilding, with 240 sq. ft. of working area, should fill the needs of any homeowner. It can be used as a one-car garage or as a spacious workshop. It is also ideal for use as a storage building. If you are a dedicated gardener, the building provides an excellent place in which to work and store tools.

Its T-shaped design and attractive siding make it a perfect partner for your home. Naturally, if you wish to match existing buildings, you can choose different siding and roofing materials.

Before beginning to construct this project, check with your local building department to obtain any necessary building permits and to determine the proper set-backs from your lot lines.

SITE LAYOUT AND PREPARATION

The first step in construction of the outbuilding is to lay out the site for the structure. Drive stakes at the corners of the structure, then measure the diagonals of the layout to make sure it is square. When the diagonals are equal, your layout is correct. Pay special attention to the dimensions of your laid-out area.

The site you have chosen should be level and the earth should be well-compacted. If you build the structure on an unexcavated or unfilled site, the earth will already be well-compacted.

Once your corner stakes are in place, begin building the concrete forms. Use 2X6 lumber for the forms and fasten the form materials with double-headed nails for easy disassembly.

As you did before, check the squareness of the forms as you work by measuring the diagonals. Correct any unsquareness before proceeding

Design the interior to suit your needs. You can add a similar L-shaped workbench to use as a work area. It's made out of 2X4s and Waferwood.

This built-in storage unit holds lumber and supplies. Build one to best utilize the recessed interior spaces created by the building's T-shape.

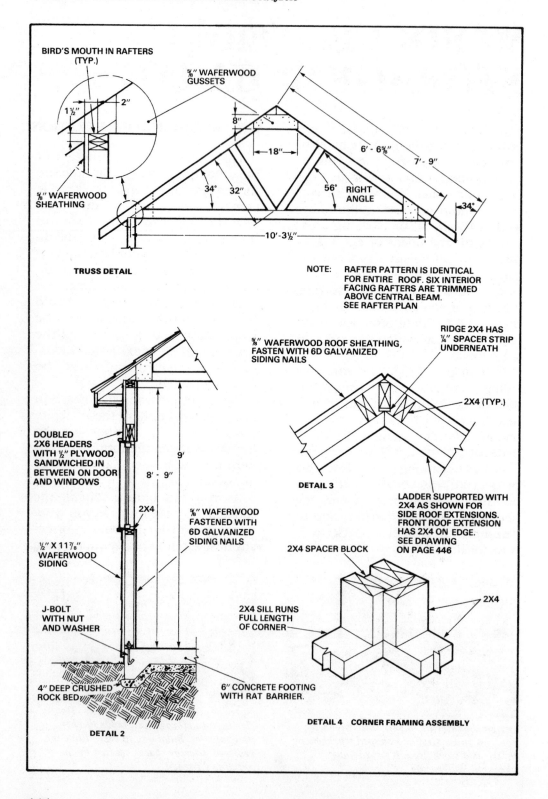

BIRD'S MOUTH IN RAFTERS
(TYP.)

1 1/2"   2"

⅝" WAFERWOOD
GUSSETS

8"

18"

6' - 6⅝"

7' - 9"

⅝" WAFERWOOD
SHEATHING

34°   32"

34°

56°   RIGHT
ANGLE

34°

10'-3½"

TRUSS DETAIL

NOTE: RAFTER PATTERN IS IDENTICAL
FOR ENTIRE ROOF. SIX INTERIOR
FACING RAFTERS ARE TRIMMED
ABOVE CENTRAL BEAM.
SEE RAFTER PLAN

⅝" WAFERWOOD ROOF SHEATHING,
FASTEN WITH 6D GALVANIZED
SIDING NAILS

RIDGE 2X4 HAS
¼" SPACER STRIP
UNDERNEATH

2X4 (TYP.)

DETAIL 3

DOUBLED
2X6 HEADERS
WITH ½" PLYWOOD
SANDWICHED
IN BETWEEN ON DOOR
AND WINDOWS

9'

8' - 9'

2X4

⅝" WAFERWOOD
FASTENED WITH
6D GALVANIZED
SIDING NAILS

½" X 11⅞"
WAFERWOOD
SIDING

LADDER SUPPORTED WITH
2X4 AS SHOWN FOR
SIDE ROOF EXTENSIONS.
FRONT ROOF EXTENSION
HAS 2X4 ON EDGE.
SEE DRAWING
ON PAGE 446

2X4 SPACER BLOCK

2X4

J-BOLT
WITH NUT
AND WASHER

2X4 SILL RUNS
FULL LENGTH
OF CORNER

4" DEEP CRUSHED
ROCK BED

6" CONCRETE FOOTING
WITH RAT BARRIER.

DETAIL 4   CORNER FRAMING ASSEMBLY

DETAIL 2

with the construction.

Brace the perimeter of the forms with stakes and diagonal braces, as shown in the photograph on page 448. Space the braces 3 ft. apart. You will find it easier to drive the stakes if you cut a point on each stake with your circular saw. As you did before, nail the brace assemblies with double-headed nails.

As you add the braces to the forms, use a long, straight 2X6 on edge with a level to make the top of the forms perfectly level. Take your time with this job for the best results.

Now, dig out the perimeter footing to the profile shown on page 444). This footing not only supports the building's stud walls, but also helps to prevent rodents from burrowing under the building.

Once the footings are dug, install 6-6-10-10 reinforcing mesh inside the forms. Bend the edges of the mesh to fit down into the footing area, and prop the reinforcing material up into the center of the form with small stones.

Also run underground electrical cable and protect it where it passes through the foundation with plastic electrical pipe. The type of wire and installation must conform to local building codes.

POURING THE FOUNDATION

Once the concrete forms are finished and the reinforcing wire is in place, you are ready to pour the foundation for your building.

You will need 7½ cubic yards of concrete for the floating slab. The best source of this concrete is your local ready-mix plant. Order 5 sack-per-yard mix for maximum strength and to prevent cracking.

On the date of the pour, have at

MATERIALS LIST	
Item	**Quantity**
Ready-mix concrete	7½ cu. yds.
6-6-10-10 reinforcing mesh	300 sq. ft.
½" X 10" J-bolts with nuts	27
4X4 X 10-ft. fir	5
2X10 X 10-ft. fir	4
2X6 X 10-ft. fir	1
2X6 X 8-ft. fir	10
2X4 X 12-ft. fir	35
2X4 X 10-ft. fir	60
2X4 X 8-ft. fir	50
2X4 X 6-ft. fir	22
1X10 X 8 ft. fir	1
1X6 X 10 ft. fir	10
1X3 X 10-ft. fir	12
Corner cove molding	40 ft.
⅜" Waferwood	48 sheets
½" X 12" Waferwood siding	630 ft.
Roofing felt (15 lb.)	6 rolls
Fiberglas shingles, autumn brown	6 squares
Pre-hung entry door	1
Single garage door	1
Andersen Perma-Shield casement windows:	
CN235	2
CW235	1
Galvanized flashing	as needed
4d, 8d, 10d, 12d, 16d galvanized nails	as needed
6d galvanized siding nails	10 lb.
Roofing nails	10 lb.
White and gray Lucite paint	as needed
Finishing materials	as needed

least one other person on hand to help you with the concrete pouring and finishing. Concrete work is difficult for one person to handle.

Ideally, the concrete truck will be able to reach your site without problems. If not, then consider hiring a concrete-pumping firm to move the concrete into the forms. Unloading that much concrete with wheelbarrows is a major operation. Since ready-mix concrete firms charge substantial fees if the truck is at the site for long periods, pumping will save money as well as your back.

As the concrete is poured, distribute it evenly in the forms to cut down on shoveling. Pull up the wire mesh with a rake to keep the wire

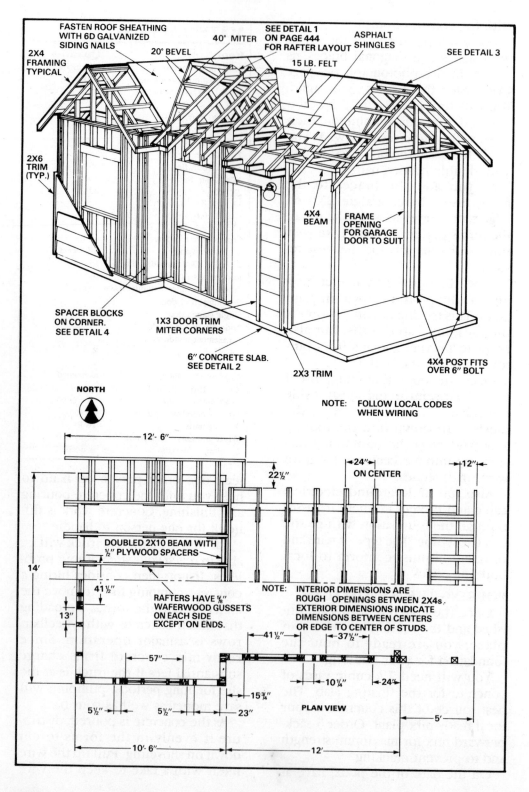

FASTEN ROOF SHEATHING
WITH 6D GALVANIZED
SIDING NAILS

2X4
FRAMING
TYPICAL

40° MITER

20° BEVEL

SEE DETAIL 1
ON PAGE 444
FOR RAFTER LAYOUT

ASPHALT
SHINGLES

SEE DETAIL 3

15 LB. FELT

2X6
TRIM
(TYP.)

4X4
BEAM

FRAME
OPENING
FOR GARAGE
DOOR TO SUIT

SPACER BLOCKS
ON CORNER.
SEE DETAIL 4

1X3 DOOR TRIM
MITER CORNERS

6" CONCRETE SLAB.
SEE DETAIL 2

2X3 TRIM

4X4 POST FITS
OVER 6" BOLT

NORTH

NOTE: FOLLOW LOCAL CODES
WHEN WIRING

12'- 6"

22½"

24"
ON CENTER

12"

DOUBLED 2X10 BEAM WITH
½" PLYWOOD SPACERS

14'

41½"

13"

RAFTERS HAVE ⅝"
WAFERWOOD GUSSETS
ON EACH SIDE
EXCEPT ON ENDS.

NOTE: INTERIOR DIMENSIONS ARE
ROUGH   OPENINGS BETWEEN 2X4s.
EXTERIOR DIMENSIONS INDICATE
DIMENSIONS BETWEEN CENTERS
OR EDGE TO CENTER OF STUDS.

41½"

37½"

57"

10¼"

24"

15¾"

5½"

5½"

23"

PLAN VIEW

5'

10'- 6"

12'

CONSTRUCTION DETAILS

1. *Brace the concrete forms securely with stakes and angled braces. Level the forms as you go.*

2. *Screed the poured concrete with a long 2X4. Work toward the perimeter and make several passes.*

3. *Give the concrete its final finish with a steel trowel. Finish the edges with an edging trowel.*

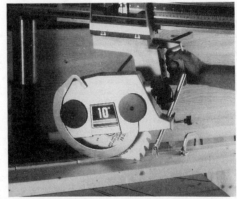

4. *Cut the angles for the roof trusses with your radial arm saw. Make all the cuts at one angle first.*

5. *Assemble the trusses flat on the concrete slab. Use a temporary brace to hold the parts in position.*

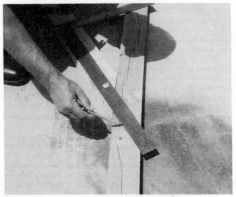

6. *Lay out the bird's mouth notches carefully for an accurate fit and an even roofline.*

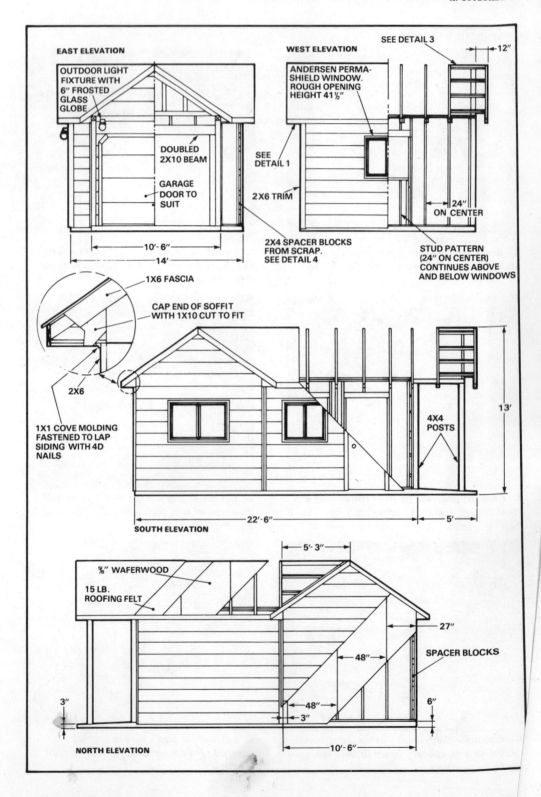

EAST ELEVATION

OUTDOOR LIGHT FIXTURE WITH 6" FROSTED GLASS GLOBE

DOUBLED 2X10 BEAM

GARAGE DOOR TO SUIT

10'-6"

14'

WEST ELEVATION

SEE DETAIL 3

ANDERSEN PERMA-SHIELD WINDOW. ROUGH OPENING HEIGHT 41½"

12"

SEE DETAIL 1

2X6 TRIM

24" ON CENTER

2X4 SPACER BLOCKS FROM SCRAP. SEE DETAIL 4.

STUD PATTERN (24" ON CENTER) CONTINUES ABOVE AND BELOW WINDOWS

1X6 FASCIA

CAP END OF SOFFIT WITH 1X10 CUT TO FIT

2X6

1X1 COVE MOLDING FASTENED TO LAP SIDING WITH 4D NAILS

4X4 POSTS

13'

SOUTH ELEVATION

22'-6"

5'

⅝" WAFERWOOD

15 LB. ROOFING FELT

5'-3"

27"

48"

SPACER BLOCKS

48"

6"

3"

3"

10'-6"

NORTH ELEVATION

in the center of the concrete. Once the forms are full, move concrete where it is needed to fill low areas.

Screed the poured concrete with a long 2X4 to level it with the top of the forms. You will need to make several passes to completely level the material. Excess concrete will flow over the forms, so have a helper remove the overflow before it sets. If you allow it to set up, removing the forms will be difficult.

Allow the concrete to firm up slightly, then use a wooden float for the initial finish. Once the floating is finished, insert $\frac{1}{2}$-in. X 10-in. J-bolts into the concrete to serve as anchors for the framing. Allow them to protrude $2\frac{1}{2}$ in. above the surface. Remember to accurately install the J-bolts for the front posts.

Allow the concrete to set a bit longer, then finish the job with a steel trowel. Use an edging trowel to finish the edges of the slab; and smooth the areas around the anchor bolts as well. Use wide boards to support your weight when working on the center of the slab. Concrete finishing is an art; if you are inexperienced at this job and you want a perfect floor, consider hiring a professional.

While the concrete is curing, spray it lightly, several times a day, to prevent surface cracking. As an alternative, you can cover the curing concrete with plastic sheeting and eliminate the spraying. Allow the new slab to cure for at least one week before proceeding with the construction.

Once the concrete has dried, about 24 hours, remove the perimeter forms carefully. Avoid striking the fresh concrete while removing the forms.

FRAMING

Before framing the walls of the outbuilding, have your windows and doors on hand. You will need to measure them to establish the correct rough openings.

Start the framing by building the roof trusses. Follow the dimensions shown in the detail diagram on page 444. Cut 34 degree miters at both ends of the rafters and 56 degree miters on the joists.

Assemble one truss without fasteners on the slab, measuring and cutting the angled braces to fit. Once the truss is correct, use the pieces as patterns for the remaining trusses. Save time by making all the cuts at one setup angle of your saw, then switch to the other angle.

Once again, assemble one truss on the surface of the slab. Cut 8-in.-wide strips of $\frac{5}{8}$-in. Waferwood, then make the gussets as shown in the diagram. As you did before, make a single gusset for each position, then use it as a pattern for the remaining gussets. If possible, use a carbide-tipped blade when cutting Waferwood. This dense material will soon dull ordinary blades.

Now, assemble the trusses permanently, using 8d, 10d, and 12d nails as required. Toenail the braces and joists to the rafters, then add the gussets. Notice that the trusses on the ends of the building have gussets on only one side.

To make certain that all the trusses are identical, assemble the first one especially carefully, then match it up with the remaining trusses. The evenness of your roof depends on your accuracy.

Once all the trusses are complete, set them aside and begin the wall

CONSTRUCTION DETAILS

7. *Frame the walls flat on the slab. Nail the plates to the studs as shown here with 16d nails.*

8. *Check the walls for plumb as you raise them, then add temporary braces to the structure to keep it vertical.*

9. *Nail the Waferwood sheathing into place. Space 6d galvanized siding nails 6 in. apart.*

10. *Once the sheathing is in place, raise the trusses. Drive a nail on the side of each truss to help keep it stable.*

11. *Add the end framing to the roof. The top of the false rafters is even with the bottom of the truss rafters.*

12. *Install the blocking that supports the overhang rafters, nailing it to the truss and the wall framing.*

framing. Frame each wall on the slab, then erect it before building the next wall.

Follow the dimensions given in the framing plan diagram carefully, marking the stud spacing for each wall on both the top and the bottom plates. Measure the windows, and frame in their rough openings accurately. The headers at the tops of the window and door openings are made of doubled 2X6 lumber, sandwiched with ½-in. plywood spacers.

Frame the side door in the same way. The garage door at the front of the building uses doubled 2X10 lumber with a ½-in. plywood spacer as a header. Follow the door manufacturer's rough-opening specifications carefully for a good fit.

As you erect each wall, bore holes for the anchor bolts (J-bolts). Brace the wall frames to make them perfectly vertical from both directions, then add the nuts and washers to the anchor bolts and tighten securely.

Notice the detail drawing (page 447) of the corners of the walls. Space the two 2X4 members at the corners of the side walls with short lengths of 2X4 material. This technique provides an inside corner for the interior paneling.

As you erect adjacent walls, nail them together at the corners with 16d nails. Once all of the walls have been erected, add the second top plates, bridging the joints to further strengthen the walls.

SHEATHING

Once the walls are framed and erected, begin installing the ⅝-in. Waferwood sheathing. Make certain that the joints meet at the center of a stud, and measure the door and window openings accurately. If you have a helper, position the sheathing, then mark the openings from inside the building.

Nail the sheets of Waferwood to the studs with 8d nails, spaced 6 in. apart. This sheathing not only seals the building against the weather, but also reinforces the framing, making a solid structure.

Install the windows and the prehung entry door according to the manufacturer's instructions.

ROOF CONSTRUCTION

Once the sheathing is in place, raise the trusses. Start by placing one outer truss in position, then mark the location of the bird's mouth notches on that truss. Make certain that the truss is perfectly centered before marking.

Lay out the notch on this truss, then cut it and use the truss as a pattern for the others. Once the trusses are complete, take them up to the roof and erect them. Carry only one truss at a time.

Nail temporary braces in place to hold each truss vertical until the roof sheathing has been attached. Use a carpenter's level to check them before nailing the braces into position. Space the trusses accurately, 24 in. on center, to simplify sheathing the roof.

Add the 4X4 posts to the front of the building. Note that these fit over the J-bolts you installed in the slab. Bore a hole in one end of the post to accommodate the protruding bolt.

Add the remaining framing sections to the posts, making certain that the top of the false rafter structure is even with the bottom of the real rafters. Install the blocking as shown in the diagrams on page 446,

CONSTRUCTION DETAILS

13. *Be especially careful when fitting the hip rafters and framing. An accurate fit is essential.*

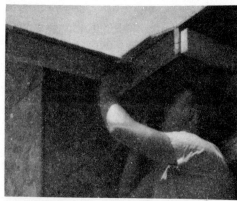

14. *Box-in the eaves by nailing short 2X4s between the truss end and the wall. Toenail to the wall.*

15. *Install the siding of your choice. Measure carefully to get the siding even and level on the wall.*

16. *Carefully cut the roof slope on a scrap of siding and use this to lay out your angles for the actual siding.*

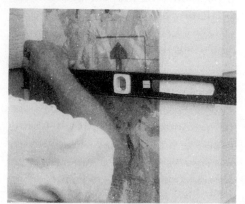

17. *Match the levels of the siding on both walls when applying siding to the short extensions of the building.*

18. *Rent a spray gun to expedite painting. Make sure to tape over windows, and spray when it isn't windy.*

then install the overhang rafters, nailing them to the blocking with 16d nails.

Follow a similar procedure to frame and install the overhangs on the rear section of the building. Notice that the false rafters here are laid flat. Add the blocking and the overhang rafters as you did before.

Once all of the trusses are in position, begin applying the roof sheathing, starting with the rear section of the building. Nail the sheathing to the rafters with 6d galvanized siding nails, spaced 6 in. apart.

Once the rear section is completed, add the connecting hip framing to the front part of the building. Cut a 20 degree bevel on each hip rafter to make it even with the rest of the roof, then cut the 40 degree miters as shown in the diagram on page 446. Add the blocking, cutting the miters first, then measuring each part against the structure to insure a good fit.

Now, finish the roof sheathing, being especially careful when fitting the Waferwood in the hip of the roof.

Apply 15-lb. roofing felt to the sheathing, then install Fiberglas shingles. Follow the manufacturer's installation instructions carefully.

WIRING

Once the sheathing work is finished, it is time to add any electrical wiring to the building. Plan your wiring carefully so that you will have an adequate number of outlets and lighting fixtures to suit your needs. While planning the wiring layout, keep possible future uses of the building in mind. It is far easier to install wiring now than it will be at a later time.

Unless you are familiar with electrical codes, have the wiring done by a professional electrician.

EXTERIOR AND INTERIOR FINISHING

The finish work on the building is the place for you to customize the structure for your particular needs. You can choose from a number of siding types and finish the interior in any way you wish.

The siding shown in the photographs is $\frac{1}{2}$-in. X $1\frac{7}{8}$-in. lap siding made of Waferwood. It is easy to install and finish, and offers superior durability. Install the siding of your choice on the building, following the procedures recommended by the manufacturer.

Install the garage door you have chosen, once again following the installation instructions provided by the manufacturer.

Add any exterior lights, then finish the outside of the building by installing exterior trim, as shown in the diagrams.

Finish the interior of the building. You can panel the walls with any number of interior paneling materials to suit your needs.

Finally, paint the outbuilding to match the color and style of your home, or in any other color scheme you choose. Use high-quality latex house paint for the best results.

Fiberglas shingles: Owens-Corning Fiberglas, Fiberglas Tower, Toledo, OH 43659.

Paint: Lucite Paints, Division of Olympic Homecare Products Co., 2233 112th Ave. N.E., Bellevue, WA 98004.

Waferwood siding and Waferwood sheets: Louisiana-Pacific Corp., 111 S.W. Fifth Ave., Portland, OR 97204.

XI.

Projects
For Bird Lovers

BIRDBATH

One of the best ways to attract birds to your yard is to provide a source of water for drinking and bathing. Traditional birdbaths are made of concrete or metal. This one takes a new approach. Built of redwood, it shows off your woodworking skills while it attracts birds.

Start construction of the birdbath by building its base. Cut three 16¾-in.-long pieces of redwood 1X6 tongue-and-groove siding. Choose wood that is free of knots and has sound tongue-and-groove edges.

Apply a liberal coat of waterproof resorcinol glue to the joints of the material, then assemble the three sections. Clamp the base with bar clamps and allow it to dry thoroughly.

Once the glue has dried, trim the sides of the base to make a rectangle as shown in the diagram. The correct dimensions are critical.

Now, locate the exact center of the base by drawing intersecting diagonal lines from corner to corner. Through the center point, draw a line parallel to the longer sides.

Use a 30-60-90 triangle to help you draw the hexagon's layout. Measure the sides of the hexagon to make certain they are equal.

Next, cut the base on your table saw. Set the blade angle to 15 degrees to form the bevel on the base, then set the miter gauge to 30 degrees to cut the angled sides of the base. Work carefully to produce a perfect hexagon.

Now, set up the saw to cut the sides of the project. Set the blade angle to 29 degrees to form the miter joints, and reset the miter gauge to cut an angle of 8¼ degrees to form the correct slope on the sides.

Cut one end of the first side, then measure the workpiece against the pre-cut base to determine the precise length. Make the second cut, then check it against the base again.

Once the first side is correct, clamp a stop block on your saw's table to help you align the remaining sides. They must be equal in length for the birdbath to be waterproof.

Assemble the sides to form a hexagonal box. Use resorcinol glue on all the joints, and nail the mitered joints with 4d galvanized finishing nails. Drill pilot holes for the nails to simplify construction and to prevent splitting the wood.

Once the sides are connected, place the assembly on a flat surface and insert the base. Plane any high spots in the base, then place a silicone bead around the base's edge and reinsert it. When the base is snug, attach the sides to it with no. 8 X 1½-in. flathead wood screws and glue. Drill counterbored pilot holes for the screws with a combination pilot bit and counterbore. The counterbores should be ⅜ in. deep.

Use a caulking gun to run a bead of clear silicone sealant around the joint between the sides and the base of the birdbath. This sealant will

CONSTRUCTION DETAILS

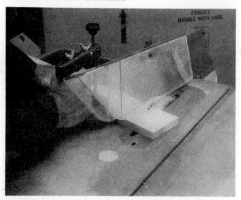

1. Cut the side's compound miter to the angles given in the diagram. Use your table saw for this job.

2. Locate the center of the project's base by drawing lines connecting the corners. Accuracy is important.

3. Carefully locate the points forming the base. Then connect the points. Refer to Detail 1 in the diagram.

4. Cut the hexagonal base on your table saw. Set the blade angle to form a beveled edge to fit the sides.

prevent any leakage from minor misalignments.

Install the wood screw hole plugs to hide the screw head. Use resorcinol glue and leave the plugs slightly proud of the surface. Sand the completed project, starting with 120-grit garnet paper. Work down to 220-grit and round the edges of the wood slightly.

Now, fasten the pipe flange to the base. Turn the assembly upside-down and attach the 1-in. galvanized pipe flange to the center of the base with no. 10 X ⅝-in. flat-

head wood screws.

Locate a site in your yard for the birdbath and dig a 6-in.-dia. hole 15 in. deep. Mix and pour concrete in the hole, then insert a 32-in.-long piece of 1-in. galvanized pipe 12 in. deep into the concrete. The upper end of the pipe should be threaded.

Use a level to help you make the pipe vertical, then prop the pipe into position while the concrete sets. When the concrete is hard, screw the birdbath onto the threaded end of the pipe and fill the bath with fresh water.

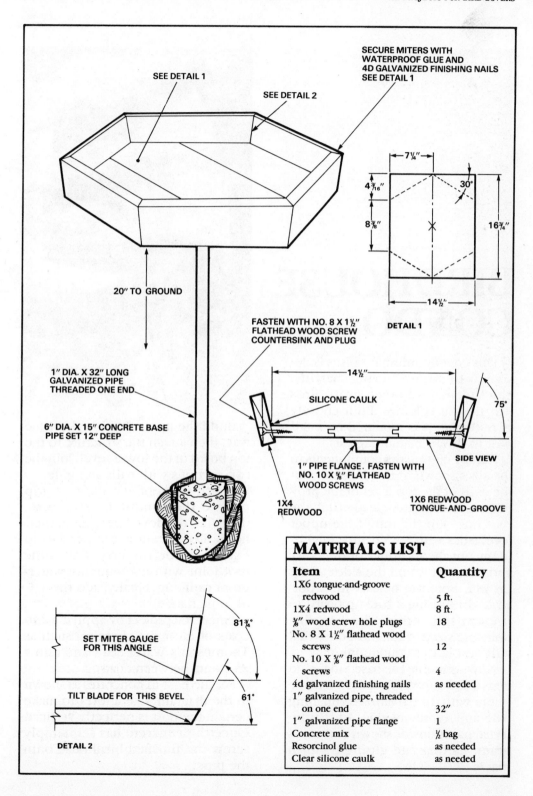

SEE DETAIL 1

SEE DETAIL 2

SECURE MITERS WITH
WATERPROOF GLUE AND
4D GALVANIZED FINISHING NAILS
SEE DETAIL 1

7¼"
4³⁄₁₆"
30°
8⅜"
16¾"
14½"

DETAIL 1

20" TO GROUND

FASTEN WITH NO. 8 X 1½"
FLATHEAD WOOD SCREW
COUNTERSINK AND PLUG

1" DIA. X 32" LONG
GALVANIZED PIPE
THREADED ONE END

14½"

SILICONE CAULK

75°

6" DIA. X 15" CONCRETE BASE
PIPE SET 12" DEEP

SIDE VIEW

1" PIPE FLANGE. FASTEN WITH
NO. 10 X ⅝" FLATHEAD
WOOD SCREWS

1X4
REDWOOD

1X6 REDWOOD
TONGUE-AND-GROOVE

MATERIALS LIST

Item	Quantity
1X6 tongue-and-groove redwood	5 ft.
1X4 redwood	8 ft.
⅜" wood screw hole plugs	18
No. 8 X 1½" flathead wood screws	12
No. 10 X ⅝" flathead wood screws	4
4d galvanized finishing nails	as needed
1" galvanized pipe, threaded on one end	32"
1" galvanized pipe flange	1
Concrete mix	½ bag
Resorcinol glue	as needed
Clear silicone caulk	as needed

SET MITER GAUGE
FOR THIS ANGLE

81¾°

TILT BLADE FOR THIS BEVEL

61°

DETAIL 2

BIRDHOUSE CONDO

This condominium for birds is designed to attract purple martins, chickadees, and other small birds that nest in colonies. Built entirely of redwood, it is mounted on a tall post to thwart marauding cats.

Start by cutting the components to the sizes shown in the diagram. Cut the ends of the top level of the project at a 45 degree angle to match the roof line. Rip the top of the upper level sides with a 45 degree bevel.

Lay out the locations of the entry and perch holes on the sides of the project. Bore the holes with a portable drill, using a backup board to prevent splintering. The 1-in.-dia. holes are sized to suit most birds that will nest in this condominium.

Now, assemble the base, sides, and ends of the lower level. Fasten the joints with 4d galvanized finishing nails and resorcinol glue. Add the internal partitions, as shown in the diagram, nailing and gluing them in place.

Build the upper level in the same way, then attach the structure to the top board of the lower level. Join the two sections with nails and glue.

Attach the roof and the two drip rails to the completed structure, then glue the dowel perches in their holes. Do not allow the perches to extend inside the box. Caulk the roof joint with good-quality waterproof caulking. Finally, add the 1½-in. pipe flange.

Finish the project by applying two coats of clear wood sealer, such as Thompson's Water Seal, and allow 24 hours between coats.

Set the post in concrete, as shown in the diagram. Use a level to make certain the post is perfectly vertical. Once the concrete has set, simply screw the finished birdhouse onto the pipe.

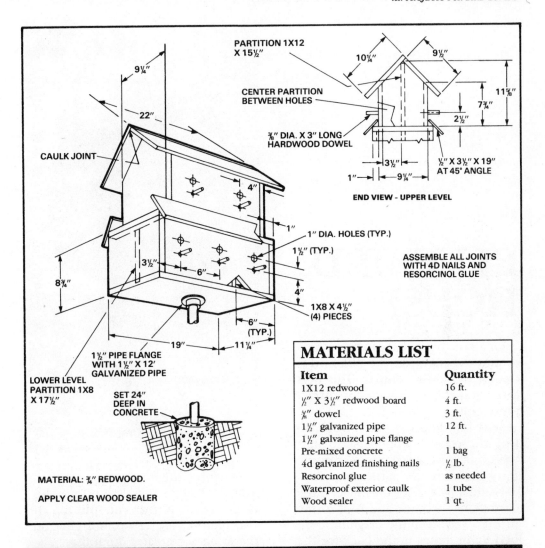

PARTITION 1X12 X 15½"

CENTER PARTITION BETWEEN HOLES

⅜" DIA. X 3" LONG HARDWOOD DOWEL

9¼"

22"

CAULK JOINT

4"

1" DIA. HOLES (TYP.)

1½" (TYP.)

3½"

6"

8¾"

4"

1X8 X 4½" (4) PIECES

6" (TYP.)

19"

11¼"

1½" PIPE FLANGE WITH 1½" X 12' GALVANIZED PIPE

LOWER LEVEL PARTITION 1X8 X 17½"

END VIEW - UPPER LEVEL

10¼"   9½"

11⅝"
7¾"
2½"

3½"

1"   9¼"

½" X 3½" X 19" AT 45° ANGLE

ASSEMBLE ALL JOINTS WITH 4D NAILS AND RESORCINOL GLUE

SET 24" DEEP IN CONCRETE

MATERIAL: ¾" REDWOOD.

APPLY CLEAR WOOD SEALER

MATERIALS LIST

Item	Quantity
1X12 redwood	16 ft.
½" X 3½" redwood board	4 ft.
⅜" dowel	3 ft.
1½" galvanized pipe	12 ft.
1½" galvanized pipe flange	1
Pre-mixed concrete	1 bag
4d galvanized finishing nails	½ lb.
Resorcinol glue	as needed
Waterproof exterior caulk	1 tube
Wood sealer	1 qt.

CONSTRUCTION DETAILS

1. Bore the 1-in.-dia. entry holes with a portable drill. Use a backup board to prevent splintering.

2. Lay out the roof angles on the ends of the top level with a carpenter's square. Cut them with any saw.

BLUEBIRD HOUSE

Of all the birds that can be enticed to nest in backyards, the bluebird is one of the most popular. This nest box is especially designed to attract these colorful birds.

Start building the project by cutting the components to size. Start with 6-in.-wide cedar stock, ripping it for the narrower parts.

Using a belt sander, round off the corners of the back and roof to the profiles shown in the diagram. Drill two 3/16-in. holes in the back for the mounting screws.

Use your table saw to cut the 15 degree bevels on the roof and front components. Since these parts are short, use special care when making the cuts. Keep your hands clear.

Next, bore a 1/4-in. hole for the perch in the front board. Use a backup board to help prevent splintering. Use a hole saw and a drill press to form the 1 1/2-in.-dia. opening in the front of the house. Once again, use a backup board under the workpiece.

Assemble the bluebird house with 4d galvanized nails; drill pilot holes in the cedar to prevent splitting. If you choose, use resorcinol glue on the joints for greater durability.

After assembly, round off the end of the dowel perch with sandpaper, then glue it in place. The dowel should not protrude into the interior of the project.

For a rustic appearance, leave the project unfinished. This also keeps potentially toxic materials away from feathered residents.

Attach the box to a suitable, protected wall, at least 6 feet from the ground. When nesting season arrives, bluebirds will find the house and move right in.

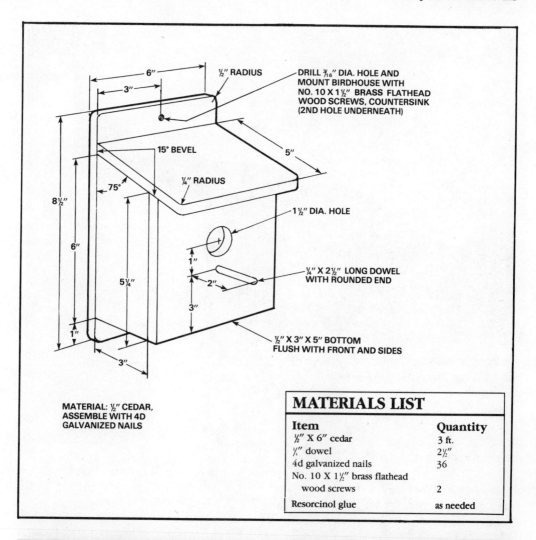

DRILL ³⁄₁₆" DIA. HOLE AND
MOUNT BIRDHOUSE WITH
NO. 10 X 1½" BRASS FLATHEAD
WOOD SCREWS, COUNTERSINK
(2ND HOLE UNDERNEATH)

½" RADIUS

6"

3"

15° BEVEL

¼" RADIUS

75°

8½"

6"

5¼"

1"

3"

5"

1½" DIA. HOLE

1"

2"

3"

¼" X 2½" LONG DOWEL
WITH ROUNDED END

½" X 3" X 5" BOTTOM
FLUSH WITH FRONT AND SIDES

MATERIAL: ½" CEDAR,
ASSEMBLE WITH 4D
GALVANIZED NAILS

MATERIALS LIST

Item	Quantity
½" X 6" cedar	3 ft.
¼" dowel	2½"
4d galvanized nails	36
No. 10 X 1½" brass flathead wood screws	2
Resorcinol glue	as needed

CONSTRUCTION DETAILS

1. Carefully cut a 15 degree bevel on the top with a miter clamp on your table saw. Use all guards.

2. Drill the entrance hole with a hole saw on your drill press. To avoid splintering, use a backup board.

CEDAR WREN HOUSE

When winter keeps you indoors, there's no better cure for restlessness than a woodworking project. This rustic wren house is so simple to build that you may want to make several.

Wrens are the easiest birds to attract to your yard during the spring breeding season. They are perfectly willing to nest right by your back door if you provide them with proper boxes.

This wren box is designed to fill their needs perfectly, while its rustic appearance will add just the right touch to your yard.

Begin construction by obtaining a cedar log approximately 5½ in. in diameter. Choose a log that is relatively straight and sound. Avoid over-aged material or any rotten wood. Leave the bark on the wood to add to the rustic appearance.

If cedar is not available in your area, the box can be made of almost any wood. You can probably find a suitable log in your firewood pile. The only type of wood you shouldn't use is eucalyptus. It has an odor that drives birds away.

Cut the end of your log square with a bow saw or a chain saw. Measure 7½ in. from the end, then cut off the stock for the wren house at a 15 degree angle. Make the angled cut as straight as possible so that the flat roof will fit without drafty gaps.

If you want to make more than one wren house, use the angled end left on the log as the top of the second blank, and cut the other end square. You can make as many of these houses as you wish by alternating square and angled cuts. Wrens enjoy company as they nest.

Set the section of log on its square end and begin to hollow out the opening. Use a 1-in.-dia. spade bit and an electric drill to bore holes around the perimeter of the opening. Use a ½-in. capacity drill if you have one, since this job requires plenty of power.

Space the holes so they just touch. If you try to bore them more closely, the bit will tend to jump into the previously drilled hole.

Continue boring holes until the opening is completely full of intersecting holes. Control the depth of the holes by attaching a strip of masking tape to the bit, 6 in. above the point. When the tape just touches the high point of the angled top, the depth is correct. A flat bottom in the cavity will make nest-building easier for the birds.

Once all of the holes are drilled, smooth the inside of the cavity and remove all waste with a gouge chisel. It is not necessary to make the opening perfectly round, but try to remove any sharp edges so that the wren house will be as comfortable as possible.

Bore a ¾-in.-dia. entry hole through the wall of the house on the high side of the log. Locate the

CONSTRUCTION DETAILS

1. Cut the log for the wren house with a bow saw or use a chain saw. Make the angled cut as straight as possible.

2. Hollow out the nesting cavity with a spade bit in your electric drill. Watch the depth of the hole carefully.

3. Remove the waste from the cavity and smooth its surface as much as possible with a sharp gouge chisel.

4. Insert the dowel perch into the predrilled hole. Round the end of the dowel for the wrens' comfort.

center of this hole 5½ in. from the base. On the other side of the log, bore a ³/₁₆-in. mounting hole as shown in the diagram.

Drill a ¼-in.-dia. hole, ½-in. deep, on the front of the house for the perch. This hole should be 1½ in. below the center of the entry hole.

Round one end of a 3-in.-long piece of ¼-in. dowel with sandpaper, then drive the dowel into the perch hole. Glue the perch in place if it is not a tight fit.

Next, cut a piece of 1X8 cedar to form the roof of the wren house. Ap-

ply a coat of sealer/stain to the roof to protect it from the weather.

Attach the wren house to a suitable support with a no. 10 X 2-in. roundhead wood screw, then add the roof. Attach the roof with three no. 8 X 1¼-in. screws so you can remove it for easy cleaning once the breeding season is over.

If you choose, you can also mount the wren house on a post. To do this, attach a 1-in. galvanized pipe flange to the center of the base. Be careful not to use screws that will bore into the cavity.

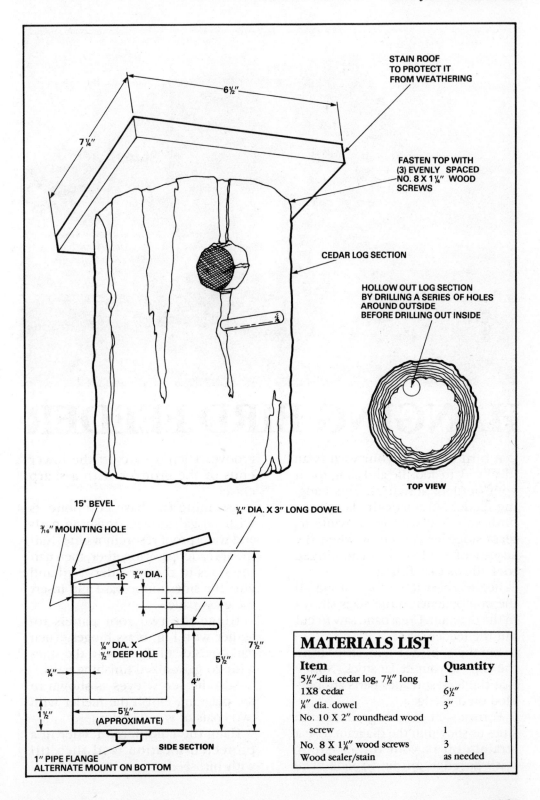

STAIN ROOF
TO PROTECT IT
FROM WEATHERING

6½"

7¼"

FASTEN TOP WITH
(3) EVENLY SPACED
NO. 8 X 1¼" WOOD
SCREWS

CEDAR LOG SECTION

HOLLOW OUT LOG SECTION
BY DRILLING A SERIES OF HOLES
AROUND OUTSIDE
BEFORE DRILLING OUT INSIDE

TOP VIEW

15° BEVEL

¾₁₆" MOUNTING HOLE

¼" DIA. X 3" LONG DOWEL

15° ¾" DIA.

¼" DIA. X
½" DEEP HOLE

¾"

5½"
(APPROXIMATE)

4"

5½"

7½"

1½"

1" PIPE FLANGE
ALTERNATE MOUNT ON BOTTOM

SIDE SECTION

MATERIALS LIST

Item	Quantity
5½"-dia. cedar log, 7½" long	1
1X8 cedar	6½"
¼" dia. dowel	3"
No. 10 X 2" roundhead wood screw	1
No. 8 X 1¼" wood screws	3
Wood sealer/stain	as needed

467

HANGING BIRD FEEDER

A bird feeder in your yard is an ideal way to add life and song to all your outdoor activities. This hanging feeder automatically keeps the birds supplied with food, while its glass sides let you know when the supply of seed is low. The hinged roof allows easy filling.

Begin construction by cutting all the components to the sizes shown in the diagram. Use a band saw to cut out the feeder's sides.

Rip the ½-in. X 1½-in. strips from the edge of your cedar stock. Notice that the feed-spreader parts are beveled on one edge.

Form a ⅛-in. X ⅛-in. groove in the sides as shown in the diagram. Use a straight bit in your router, along with an edge guide, to make the

groove. Then square off the lower ends of the grooves with a sharp chisel.

Assemble the base components with 2d galvanized finishing nails and waterproof resorcinol glue. Nail the spreader parts together, then nail the sides to the spreader. Nail and glue the sides to the base and insert the glass panels.

Hinge the two roof panels together with 1-in. brass hinges. Then nail one side of the roof to the sides with 2d galvanized finishing nails.

Add the screw eyes as shown in the diagram. Finish the feeder with two coats of wood sealer.

Hang the completed feeder in a protected location, and then fill with birdseed.

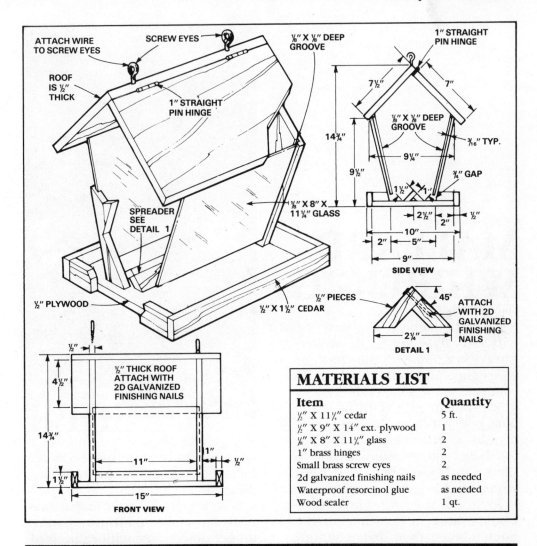

ATTACH WIRE TO SCREW EYES

SCREW EYES

⅛" X ⅛" DEEP GROOVE

1" STRAIGHT PIN HINGE

ROOF IS ½" THICK

1" STRAIGHT PIN HINGE

7½"

7"

14¾"

⅛" X ⅛" DEEP GROOVE

9¼"

³⁄₁₆" TYP.

9½"

¾" GAP

SPREADER SEE DETAIL 1

⅛" X 8" X 11¼" GLASS

1½"

1"

2½"

½"

2"

½" PLYWOOD

½" X 1½" CEDAR

10"

2"

5"

9"

SIDE VIEW

½" PIECES

45°

ATTACH WITH 2D GALVANIZED FINISHING NAILS

2¼"

DETAIL 1

½"

½" THICK ROOF ATTACH WITH 2D GALVANIZED FINISHING NAILS

4½"

14¾"

11"

1"

½"

1½"

15"

FRONT VIEW

MATERIALS LIST

Item	Quantity
½" X 11¼" cedar	5 ft.
½" X 9" X 14" ext. plywood	1
⅛" X 8" X 11¼" glass	2
1" brass hinges	2
Small brass screw eyes	2
2d galvanized finishing nails	as needed
Waterproof resorcinol glue	as needed
Wood sealer	1 qt.

CONSTRUCTION DETAILS

1. *Cut the sides of the feeder with a band saw. You can also use a saber saw.*

2. *Square the lower ends of the grooves with a sharp ⅛-in. wood chisel.*

469

MALLARD WHIRLIGIG

Here is a duck for your yard that will never fly south for the winter. Always heading with the wind, its whirligig wings will add action to your yard in the slightest breeze.

Start building the duck by laying out a grid of 1-in. squares on a sheet of ¼-in. exterior plywood. Transfer the design shown in the diagram to the grid, then cut out the pattern with a fine blade in your saber saw.

Next, cut the 1X2 wing struts. Clamp these in position on the duck's body, then drill counterbored pilot holes. Attach the struts with resorcinol glue and screws.

Cut a ¼-in. X 1½-in. deep slot in the 1-in.-dia. X 3½-in.-long dowel. Glue the dowel in position.

Next, form the wings from 2X2 pine, as shown in the photo. If you have a band saw, cut the rough pattern before shaping. Once the shape is roughed out, smooth the wings with sandpaper. As you work, check the balance of each wing. Remove small amounts of wood from the heavy end.

Attach the wings to the struts with no. 10 X 2½-in. brass wood screws. Place flat washers as shown in the diagram.

Bore a 1-in.-dia. hole in the 2X2 redwood stake, then glue in the longer dowel post with resorcinol glue. Bore a ⁵⁄₁₆-in. pivot hole in the top of the dowel and a ¼-in. hole in the shorter dowel that is glued to the duck. Next, glue the steel rod to the shorter dowel.

Sand the completed mallard thoroughly, then paint the whirligig with exterior latex enamel. Match the colors of a real mallard, or use your imagination.

Locate the whirligig in an area of your garden exposed to the wind. Dig a hole for the stake, then backfill after the post is perfectly vertical.

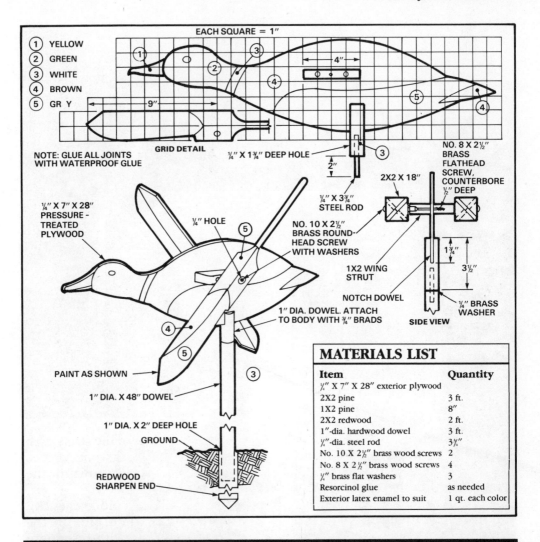

EACH SQUARE = 1"

① YELLOW
② GREEN
③ WHITE
④ BROWN
⑤ GRAY

4"

9"

GRID DETAIL

NOTE: GLUE ALL JOINTS
WITH WATERPROOF GLUE

¼" X 1¾" DEEP HOLE

2"

¼" X 3¾"
STEEL ROD

2X2 X 18"

NO. 8 X 2½"
BRASS
FLATHEAD
SCREW,
COUNTERBORE
½" DEEP

¼" X 7" X 28"
PRESSURE -
TREATED
PLYWOOD

¼" HOLE

NO. 10 X 2½"
BRASS ROUND-
HEAD SCREW
WITH WASHERS

1X2 WING
STRUT

NOTCH DOWEL

1¾"

3½"

¼" BRASS
WASHER

SIDE VIEW

1" DIA. DOWEL. ATTACH
TO BODY WITH ¾" BRADS

PAINT AS SHOWN

1" DIA. X 48" DOWEL

1" DIA. X 2" DEEP HOLE

GROUND

REDWOOD
SHARPEN END

MATERIALS LIST

Item	Quantity
¼" X 7" X 28" exterior plywood	
2X2 pine	3 ft.
1X2 pine	8"
2X2 redwood	2 ft.
1"-dia. hardwood dowel	3 ft.
¼"-dia. steel rod	3¾"
No. 10 X 2½" brass wood screws	2
No. 8 X 2½" brass wood screws	4
¼" brass flat washers	3
Resorcinol glue	as needed
Exterior latex enamel to suit	1 qt. each color

CONSTRUCTION DETAILS

1. Glue the slotted dowel pivot to the duck's body. The steel rod fits into the dowel post, allowing the duck to turn.

2. Clamp the wings to a bench and shape them with a rasp. Smooth the wings with sandpaper after shaping.

MARTIN HOUSE

Martins are some of the easiest and most interesting birds to attract to your yard. They nest in colonies and their antics during the nesting season will entertain you for weeks.

This martin house provides high-rise nesting space for 14 pairs of martins. Built entirely of $\frac{1}{2}$-in. pressure-treated plywood for exellent weather-resistance, it is designed to attract the martins by providing an ideal breeding site.

Start construction by cutting the 19-in. X 19-in. base of the project from a sheet of $\frac{1}{2}$-in. pressure-treated plywood. Use a fine-toothed plywood blade on your saw for a smooth finish. At the same time, cut the center divider board to the same size.

Next, cut two divider strips, 6 in. X 19-in., from the same material. Lay out the cross-lap notches on the dividers, as shown in the diagram. Cut the notches with a fine-toothed blade in your saber saw. Make three cuts for each notch, then remove the waste with a sharp chisel, keeping the bottom of the cut square.

Cut the remaining 6-in. X 12$\frac{1}{2}$-in. divider strips next, forming the central notch in the same way you did before. The notches should be exactly 3$\frac{1}{8}$ in. deep so the dividers can interlock easily.

Stack four more 6-in. X 19-in.

strips together, with scrap wood on both sides of the pile. Lay out the 2$\frac{1}{2}$-in.-dia. holes on the material, 2$\frac{1}{4}$ in. from the bottom of the strip.

Bore the holes through the entire stack with a hole saw or a large Forstner-type bit. Use a drill press for this job, if possible. The scrap will help keep the holes' edges from splintering.

Now, cut the end panels of the martin house. Working with plywood stock that's 13$\frac{1}{2}$ in. wide, set your saw to cut 30 degree angles for the roofline. As before, use a fine-toothed plywood blade when cutting the plywood.

Using the same setup, cut an additional triangular piece for the center attic divider. Bore the entry holes in the end panels, using the same technique you did on the sides.

Finally, cut the roof panels, beveling one edge of each panel at a 60 degree angle to form the roof peak. Cut a final piece of plywood 19 in. X 13$\frac{1}{2}$ in. to form the attic floor of the martin house.

Attach a pipe flange to the center of the base with no. 8 X 1-in. wood screws. The screws will protrude through the wood, so cut or grind off the excess length.

To assemble the martin house, first nail the two end pieces to the

CONSTRUCTION DETAILS

1. Attach the interlocked dividers to the base of the martin house with 4d galvanized finishing nails.

2. Assemble the second floor in the same way, then stack the two together to form the body of the house.

3. Form the roof's bevel by setting your saw's blade to 60 degrees and ripping the board's edge.

base. Use 4d nails and set the heads just below the surface of the wood. Next, position the first set of dividers on the base and nail through the ends into the longest divider. Position the second floor on top of the first and nail through it to the dividers from above and below. Repeat this sequence for the second set of dividers and the top panel with its single divider.

Once the floors are assembled, add the side panels and the roof of the structure, nailing them as you did before. To prevent leaks, use resorcinol glue on the roof and the

end panel joints. Bore ¼-in. holes in the end panels, as shown in the diagram, and glue ¼-in. X 3-in. dowel perches in place.

Sand the martin house thoroughly to remove any rough edges, then give the exterior two coats of white exterior latex enamel.

Set a 12-foot length of pipe into a 12-in.-dia. hole 30 in. deep, then fill the hole with concrete. Adjust the pipe with a level to be perfectly vertical, then prop it into position until the concrete sets. Finally, from a safe stepladder, carefully screw the martin house onto the threaded end of the pipe.

MATERIALS LIST

Item	Quantity
½″ pressure-treated plywood	24 sq. ft.
¼″ dowel	6″
1½″ galvanized pipe, one end threaded	10 ft.
1½″ galvanized pipe flange	1
No. 8 X 1″ wood screws	4
Concrete mix	1 bag
4d galvanized finishing nails	as needed
Resorcinol glue	as needed
Exterior latex enamel	1 qt.

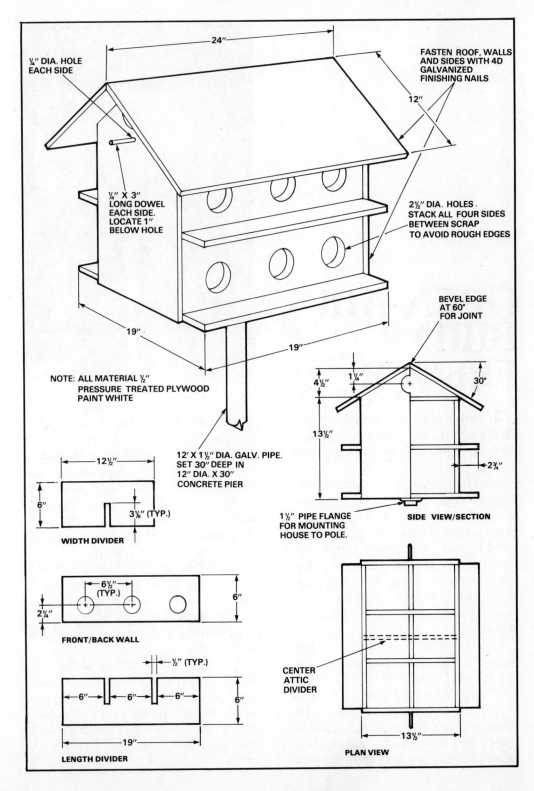

24"

¼" DIA. HOLE
EACH SIDE

FASTEN ROOF, WALLS
AND SIDES WITH 4D
GALVANIZED
FINISHING NAILS

12"

¼" X 3"
LONG DOWEL
EACH SIDE.
LOCATE 1"
BELOW HOLE

2½" DIA. HOLES .
STACK ALL FOUR SIDES
BETWEEN SCRAP
TO AVOID ROUGH EDGES

19"

19"

BEVEL EDGE
AT 60°
FOR JOINT

NOTE: ALL MATERIAL ½"
PRESSURE TREATED PLYWOOD
PAINT WHITE

4½" 1¼"

30°

13½"

2¾"

12½"

12' X 1½" DIA. GALV. PIPE.
SET 30" DEEP IN
12" DIA. X 30"
CONCRETE PIER

1½" PIPE FLANGE
FOR MOUNTING
HOUSE TO POLE.

SIDE VIEW/SECTION

6"

3⅛" (TYP.)

WIDTH DIVIDER

6½"
(TYP.)

6"

2¼"

FRONT/BACK WALL

½" (TYP.)

CENTER
ATTIC
DIVIDER

6"

6"

6"

6"

19"

13½"

LENGTH DIVIDER

PLAN VIEW

475

OPEN-AIR BIRD FEEDER

A bird feeder is a delightful addition to any yard. This free-standing feeding platform is easy to build and will last for years.

Start by ripping a ⅛-in.-thick strip off one edge of the 1X10 redwood stock. Then rip a ½-in. strip off the same edge. These pieces will be used to make the screen supports.

Now, rip the board again, this time to the 4-in. width of the platform sides. Finally, rip the 3-in. brace stock from the remaining wood.

Cut the side components to the sizes shown in the diagram and assemble with 3d galvanized finishing nails and resorcinol glue.

Cut the braces to length; then form the lap joints with multiple passes of a dado blade, making certain that the depth is exactly half the

thickness of the wood. Glue the braces together.

Nail and glue the braces in place, followed by the ¾-in. strips, as shown in the diagram. Cut the screen material to size and install it, securing it with the ⅛-in. strips and 2d galvanized finishing nails. Stretch the screen tight as you go.

Sand the completed platform and apply two coats of wood sealer. After the sealer is dry, attach the 1-in. galvanized pipe flange to the bottom of the platform with no. 8 X 1-in. brass screws.

To install the feeder, drive the support pipe two feet into the ground. Use a wood block to prevent damage to the pipe threads. Screw the flange onto the pipe and you are ready to add seed to attract birds.

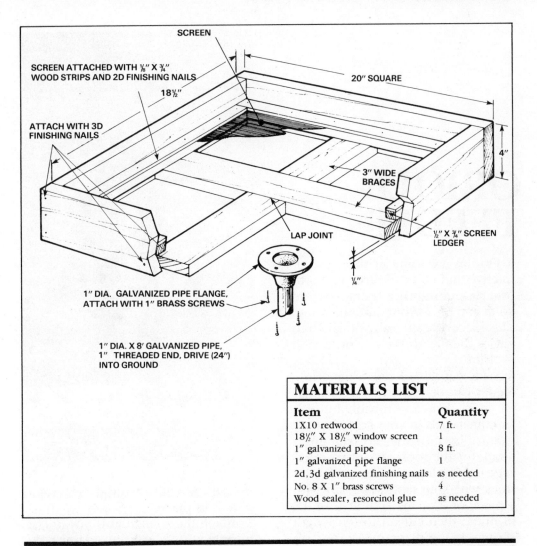

SCREEN

SCREEN ATTACHED WITH ⅛″ X ¾″
WOOD STRIPS AND 2D FINISHING NAILS

18½″

20″ SQUARE

ATTACH WITH 3D
FINISHING NAILS

3″ WIDE
BRACES

4″

LAP JOINT

½″ X ¾″ SCREEN
LEDGER

¼″

1″ DIA. GALVANIZED PIPE FLANGE,
ATTACH WITH 1″ BRASS SCREWS

1″ DIA. X 8′ GALVANIZED PIPE,
1″ THREADED END, DRIVE (24″)
INTO GROUND

MATERIALS LIST

Item	Quantity
1X10 redwood	7 ft.
18½″ X 18½″ window screen	1
1″ galvanized pipe	8 ft.
1″ galvanized pipe flange	1
2d, 3d galvanized finishing nails	as needed
No. 8 X 1″ brass screws	4
Wood sealer, resorcinol glue	as needed

CONSTRUCTION DETAILS

1. Cut the lap joints on the braces with multiple passes of a dado blade on your radial arm saw.

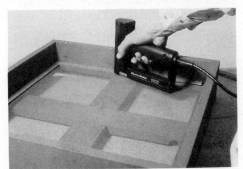

2. Attach the screen with thin strips of wood and 2d galvanized finishing nails or staples (shown).

ORIOLE FEEDER

Orioles are some of the most attractive and colorful birds in North America. Attracting them can add color and life to your outdoor living. This feeder is especially designed to entice them with their favorite food — fruit.

Made entirely of cedar, the oriole feeder can be constructed in under an hour. You can probably build it from materials in your scrap box.

Start by cutting the triangular block for the roof. Make two intersecting 45 degree cuts on 1½-in. stock with your table saw. Start with a piece of 2X4 material at least 18 in. long, then cut off to the length shown in the diagram. Do not rip anything shorter, because a dangerous kickback may occur.

Next, file two flats on the top of the block to allow nailing. Bore ⅛-in. pilot holes through the block for the nails.

Cut the remaining components to the sizes shown in the diagram. You can save time by making both 45 degree miters in one pass.

Bore a ¼-in.-dia. hole in the upright to accommodate the perch, then round off the lower corners of the upright with a belt sander.

Round the ends of the dowel, then glue it in place.

Attach the triangular block to the upright with 8d galvanized finishing nails and resorcinol glue. Set the nails flush with a nail set.

Add the roof parts, securing them with 4d galvanized finishing nails and glue. Install the brass L-hooks as shown in the diagram, then add the screw eye to the roof.

Finish the project with two coats of clear wood sealer or leave it unfinished for a rustic look. Hang the feeder in a sheltered location with galvanized wire. Press fruit on the L-hooks and you will soon have orioles feeding in your yard.

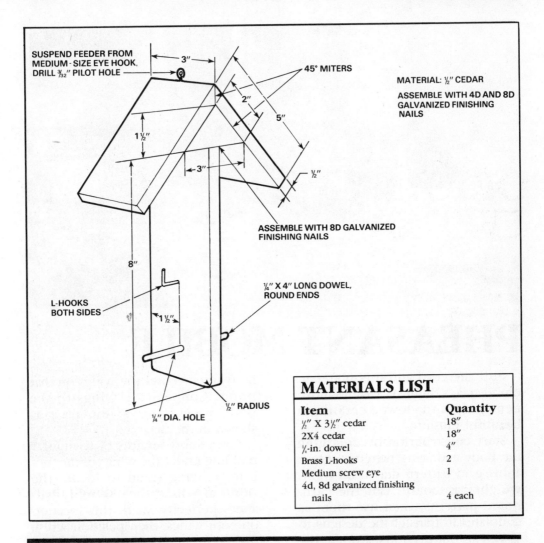

SUSPEND FEEDER FROM MEDIUM-SIZE EYE HOOK. DRILL ³⁄₃₂" PILOT HOLE

3"

45° MITERS

2"

5"

MATERIAL: ½" CEDAR

ASSEMBLE WITH 4D AND 8D GALVANIZED FINISHING NAILS

1½"

3"

½"

ASSEMBLE WITH 8D GALVANIZED FINISHING NAILS

8"

¼" X 4" LONG DOWEL, ROUND ENDS

L-HOOKS BOTH SIDES

1½"

½" RADIUS

¼" DIA. HOLE

MATERIALS LIST

Item	Quantity
½" X 3½" cedar	18"
2X4 cedar	18"
¼-in. dowel	4"
Brass L-hooks	2
Medium screw eye	1
4d, 8d galvanized finishing nails	4 each

CONSTRUCTION DETAILS

1. Cut the triangular block on a table saw. Start with a longer piece of stock for safety's sake.

2. Nail the block to the upright after filing flats on the top of the block. Drill pilot holes for the nails.

PHEASANT MOBILE

Pull the cord and this pheasant mobile takes flight. The wings move gently up and down, creating a beautiful illusion.

Start construction by enlarging the body and wing patterns onto a 1-in. grid pattern drawn on light-weight cardboard. Cut the cardboard patterns, then use them as templates to transfer the designs to ¼-in. exterior plywood. Cut the designs in the wood with a coping saw or a power jigsaw.

Locate and drill the ⅛-in. hole at the body's center of balance. Sand the plywood parts smooth, paying special attention to the edges.

Before assembling the mobile, paint the parts in the pattern shown in the diagram. A fine brush, the type sold in art stores, and model airplane paints are ideal.

Once the paint is dry, assemble the wings to the body. Locate the approximate balance point of the body, then center the wings on that point. Connect the wings to the body with ⅛-in. screw eyes as shown in the diagram.

Place short lengths of triangular molding under the wings of the mobile, moving them to locate the point at which the assembly balances perfectly. Mark this location on both wings, then position screw eyes ⅛ in. inside this line and ½ in. in from the front and back of the wings.

Add the monofilament hanging lines to the top of the wings, as indicated in the diagram. Tie them to holes in the ends of the ⅜-in. dowel, then add the center line with its brass ring.

Attach the lower line and ring, then hang the mobile in a suitable location. Crimp fishing weights near the lower ring to balance the mobile with the wings at a slight (5 to 10 degree) angle.

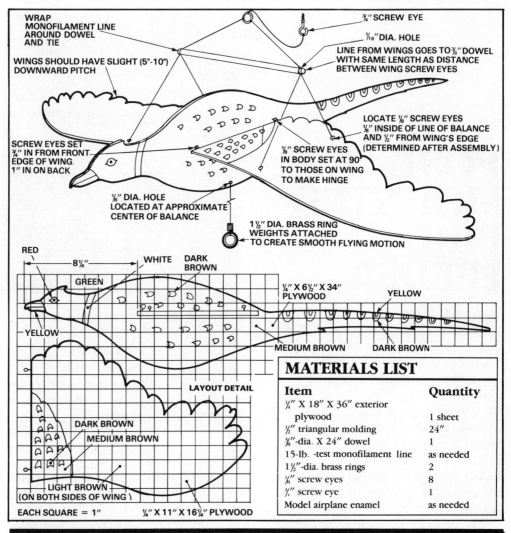

WRAP MONOFILAMENT LINE AROUND DOWEL AND TIE

¾" SCREW EYE

¹⁄₁₆" DIA. HOLE

LINE FROM WINGS GOES TO ⅜" DOWEL WITH SAME LENGTH AS DISTANCE BETWEEN WING SCREW EYES

WINGS SHOULD HAVE SLIGHT (5°-10°) DOWNWARD PITCH

LOCATE ⅛" SCREW EYES ⅛" INSIDE OF LINE OF BALANCE AND ½" FROM WING'S EDGE (DETERMINED AFTER ASSEMBLY)

SCREW EYES SET ¾" IN FROM FRONT EDGE OF WING. 1" IN ON BACK

⅛" SCREW EYES IN BODY SET AT 90° TO THOSE ON WING TO MAKE HINGE

⅛" DIA. HOLE LOCATED AT APPROXIMATE CENTER OF BALANCE

1½" DIA. BRASS RING WEIGHTS ATTACHED TO CREATE SMOOTH FLYING MOTION

RED

8¼"

WHITE

DARK BROWN

GREEN

¼" X 6½" X 34" PLYWOOD

YELLOW

YELLOW

MEDIUM BROWN

DARK BROWN

LAYOUT DETAIL

DARK BROWN

MEDIUM BROWN

LIGHT BROWN (ON BOTH SIDES OF WING)

EACH SQUARE = 1"   ¼" X 11" X 16¼" PLYWOOD

MATERIALS LIST

Item	Quantity
¼" X 18" X 36" exterior plywood	1 sheet
½" triangular molding	24"
⅜"-dia. X 24" dowel	1
15-lb.-test monofilament line	as needed
1½"-dia. brass rings	2
⅛" screw eyes	8
¾" screw eye	1
Model airplane enamel	as needed

CONSTRUCTION DETAILS

1. If you have access to a copy machine enlarge the pheasant's design and trace onto the wood with carbon paper.

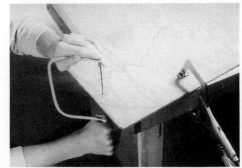

2. Use a coping saw to cut the mobile's patterns from ¼" exterior plywood. Follow the lines closely.

POST-MOUNTED BIRD FEEDER

Most birds are easy to attract if you provide them with food. This bird feeder, designed to be attached to a post, will bring them in droves.

It offers a hinged lid for filling, a glass front to provide a visible check on the seed supply, and measures out the seed as needed to prevent waste.

Cut all the components from ½-in. cedar. Start with the widest parts, then rip the stock to narrower widths as you go.

Lay out the profile of the side components, then cut them with a band saw or saber saw. Form the groove for the glass panel on your table saw, stopping the cut as shown in the diagram. Clamp a stop block to the saw's fence to help make the groove accurately.

Set the saw blade at 15 degrees and bevel the rear edge of the lid, then notch the lid for the hinges. A file will do the job in the soft cedar.

Round off the corners of the back, lid, and sides with a belt sander, then drill ³⁄₁₆-in. mounting holes in the back board.

Assemble the wood components with resorcinol glue and 4d galvanized nails. When the basic assembly is complete, bore holes for the dowel perches. Round the ends of the dowels, then glue them into the holes.

Cut the glass panel with a glass cutter and a straightedge, then slide the glass into the grooves in the sides. Finally, attach the hinges to the lid and the back panel.

For a rustic appearance, and to avoid exposing birds to toxic materials, leave the feeder unfinished. Mount it to a convenient post or wall with no. 10 X 1½-in. wood screws and fill the hopper with bird seed.

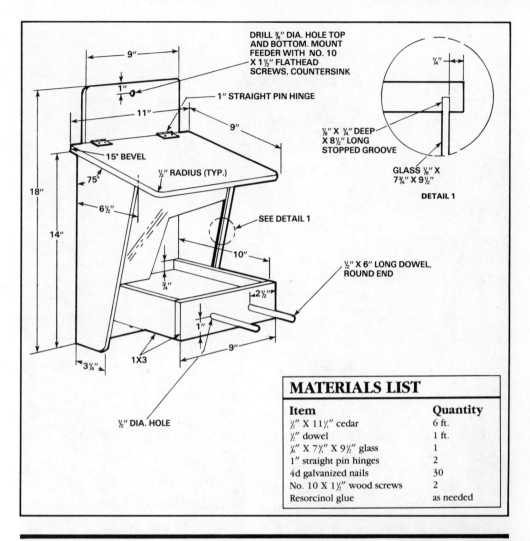

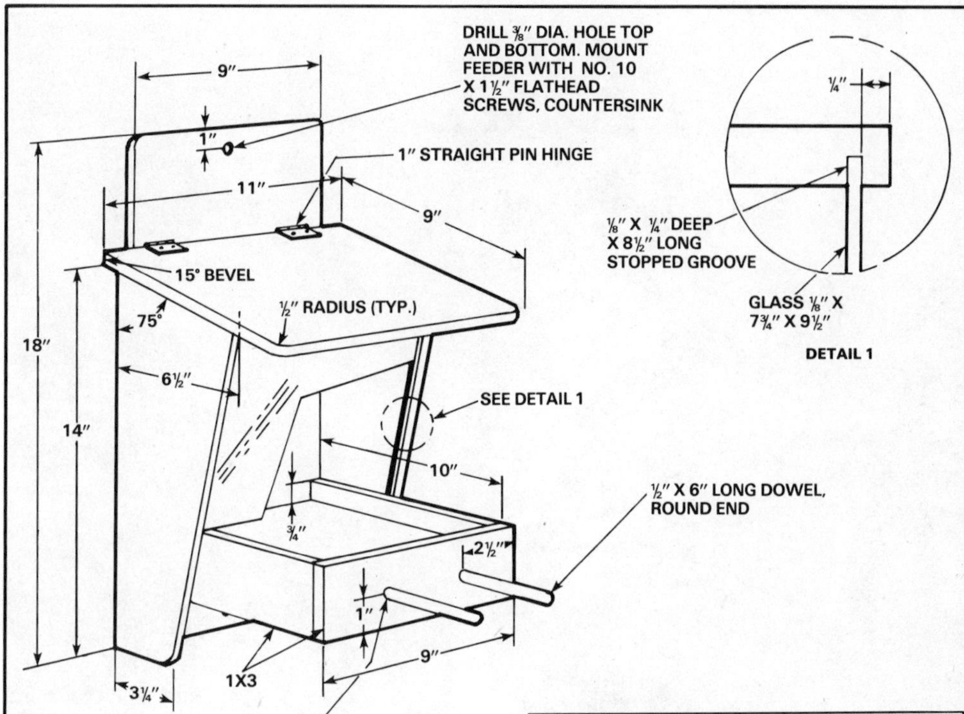
DRILL ⅜" DIA. HOLE TOP AND BOTTOM. MOUNT FEEDER WITH NO. 10 X 1½" FLATHEAD SCREWS, COUNTERSINK
9"
1"
1" STRAIGHT PIN HINGE
11"
9"
15° BEVEL
75°
½" RADIUS (TYP.)
18"
6½"
14"
SEE DETAIL 1
10"
¾"
½" X 6" LONG DOWEL, ROUND END
2½"
1"
9"
1X3
3¼"
½" DIA. HOLE
¼"
⅛" X ¼" DEEP X 8½" LONG STOPPED GROOVE
GLASS ⅛" X 7¾" X 9½"
DETAIL 1

MATERIALS LIST

Item	Quantity
½" X 11¼" cedar	6 ft.
½" dowel	1 ft.
⅛" X 7¾" X 9½" glass	1
1" straight pin hinges	2
4d galvanized nails	30
No. 10 X 1½" wood screws	2
Resorcinol glue	as needed

CONSTRUCTION DETAILS

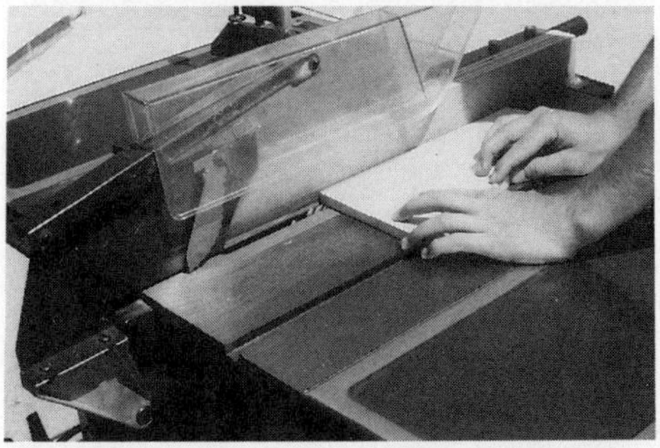

1. Carefully cut grooves in the side panels on your table saw. Set the depth of cut at ¼- in.

2. Use a straightedge and a glass cutter to cut the glass panel. Lubricate the cutter's wheel with kerosene.

ROADRUNNER WHIRLIGIG

Whirligigs are a popular way to add movement to your yard. This roadrunner, whether it is running from a coyote or just chasing something to eat, will bring color and lively motion to your home anytime the wind blows.

Begin building the whirligig by enlarging the pattern for the body onto a grid of 1-in. squares on a sheet of heavy paper. Cut out the pattern, then trace around it on a length of 1X10 pine lumber.

Cut the body with a jigsaw, band saw, or saber saw. Sand the part well, paying special attention to the details of the profile. Sand carefully to avoid obscuring the small features.

Locate and drill a $\frac{3}{16}$-in. axle hole in the body, as indicated in the diagram. Directly under this hole, in the body's lower edge, drill a $\frac{1}{4}$-in.-dia. hole, $1\frac{1}{2}$ in. deep, for the pivot bushing. Press a 1-in. length of $\frac{1}{4}$-in. O.D. copper tubing into the hole to serve as the bushing.

Now, paint the body light brown with spray enamel. Once this has dried, lay out the details lightly in pencil. Paint them in the colors shown in the diagram, using small jars of model airplane enamel and a fine brush.

Next, lay out the pattern for the legs as you did for the body. Transfer the pattern to a piece of $\frac{1}{8}$-in. tempered Masonite and cut one of the legs with a coping saw. Use this piece to lay out the remaining three legs. Once all of the legs are cut, clamp them together and sand the profiles to shape. Use small, improvised sanding blocks with fine sandpaper, as shown in photo 3.

Paint the legs brown, then add the reflective tape details. The tape will make the whirling legs glow in any light. If you choose, you can paint the details rather than use tape.

Drill one $\frac{1}{4}$-in.-dia. hole in a 3-in. length of 1X1 pine stock to form the leg's hub. As you did on the body, press one length of $\frac{1}{4}$-in. copper tubing into this hole to make the bearing. Now, follow the same technique to make the other hub.

Drill $\frac{3}{16}$-in. holes in the stock at the center of the pivot blocks, then cut them to length as well.

Clamp the hubs in a wood clamp, as shown in photo 4. Cut 45 degree slots, 1 in. deep, in the ends. Use a blade with a $\frac{1}{8}$-in. kerf width on your radial arm saw. Form the slots in opposing directions on the ends of the hubs. Cut slowly and carefully.

Once the slots are formed, paint the hubs and blocks brown to complement the legs. When the paint has dried, glue the blocks to the body, inserting a length of $\frac{3}{16}$-in. threaded rod to align the holes.

Now, glue the legs into the hub slots and secure them with $\frac{3}{4}$-in. brads. Insert the $\frac{3}{16}$-in. threaded axle through the body and the glued-on blocks. Add a washer to each side, then install the leg assem-

CONSTRUCTION DETAILS

1. *Enlarge the designs of the body and legs onto a grid of 1-in. squares drawn on heavy paper.*

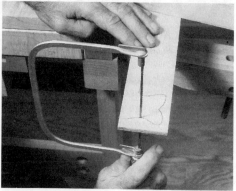

2. *Cut the legs for the whirligig with a coping saw. Follow the outlines carefully for good balance.*

3. *Clamp the legs together, then sand the profiles with small sanding blocks, shaped to fit.*

4. *Clamp the hubs in a wood clamp, then carefully saw the 45 degree slots on your radial arm saw.*

blies. Secure the legs with ³/₁₆-in. nylon-insert lock nuts. Do not overtighten; the legs must spin freely.

Form a point on one end of a 60-in. length of 2X2 pressure-treated lumber. On the other end, drill a ⁵/₃₂-in. hole, 2½ in. deep. Drive the post 18 in. deep into the ground at the whirligig's final location.

Place two nuts on a 2½-in. piece of ³/₁₆-in. threaded rod and lock them together. Screw the rod into the post, leaving 1½ in. extending from the post. Remove one of the driving nuts, then tighten the other one against the post. Add a washer,

then slip the whirligig over the pivot rod. It should turn freely.

MATERIALS LIST

Item	Quantity
2X2 pressure-treated lumber	5 ft.
1X10 pine	24″
1X1 pine	8″
⅛″ tempered Masonite	120 sq. in.
³/₁₆″ threaded rod	7″
No. 8 X 1¼″ flathead wood screws	4
³/₁₆″ nylon-insert lock nuts	2
³/₁₆″ nuts	2
³/₁₆″ washers	3
¾″ brads	small container
¼″ reflective tape	1 small roll
¼″ O.D. copper tubing	3″
Paint	as needed

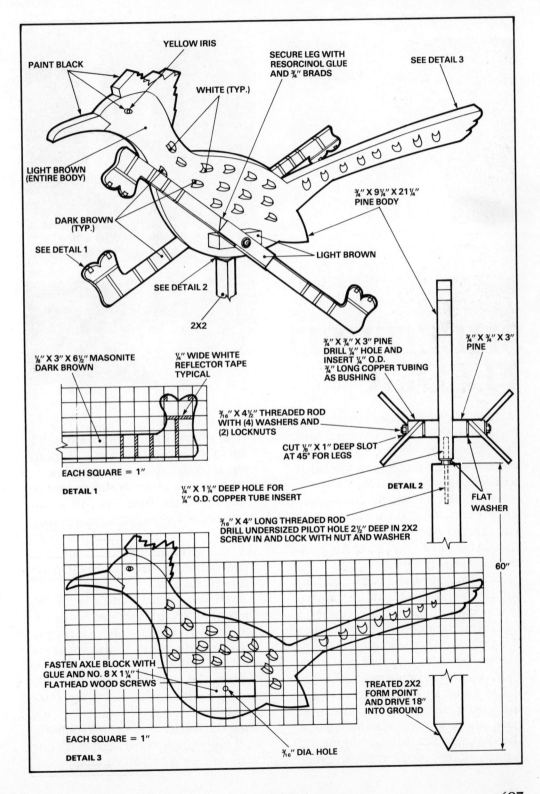

YELLOW IRIS

PAINT BLACK

SECURE LEG WITH
RESORCINOL GLUE
AND ¾" BRADS

SEE DETAIL 3

WHITE (TYP.)

LIGHT BROWN
(ENTIRE BODY)

¾" X 9¼" X 21¼"
PINE BODY

DARK BROWN
(TYP.)

LIGHT BROWN

SEE DETAIL 1

SEE DETAIL 2

2X2

¾" X ¾" X 3" PINE
DRILL ¼" HOLE AND
INSERT ¼" O.D.
¾" LONG COPPER TUBING
AS BUSHING

¾" X ¾" X 3"
PINE

⅛" X 3" X 6½" MASONITE
DARK BROWN

¼" WIDE WHITE
REFLECTOR TAPE
TYPICAL

³⁄₁₆" X 4½" THREADED ROD
WITH (4) WASHERS AND
(2) LOCKNUTS

CUT ⅛" X 1" DEEP SLOT
AT 45° FOR LEGS

EACH SQUARE = 1"

DETAIL 1

¼" X 1¼" DEEP HOLE FOR
¼" O.D. COPPER TUBE INSERT

DETAIL 2

FLAT
WASHER

³⁄₁₆" X 4" LONG THREADED ROD
DRILL UNDERSIZED PILOT HOLE 2½" DEEP IN 2X2
SCREW IN AND LOCK WITH NUT AND WASHER

60"

FASTEN AXLE BLOCK WITH
GLUE AND NO. 8 X 1¼"
FLATHEAD WOOD SCREWS

TREATED 2X2
FORM POINT
AND DRIVE 18"
INTO GROUND

EACH SQUARE = 1"

DETAIL 3

³⁄₁₆" DIA. HOLE

SHELTERED FEEDER

Here is a bird feeder designed to hang on a wall or other vertical surface. Complete with a roof, it provides sheltered feeding for the birds that visit your yard.

The feeder is constructed of ½-in.-thick cedar for good weather resistance and a rustic appearance. You should be able to complete the project in about an hour.

Start by cutting the cedar stock to the overall sizes shown in the diagram. Lay out the sides of the box carefully, then cut the sides with a band saw or saber saw. After cutting, clamp the sides together and even them up with a belt sander.

Use a disk or belt sander to form the ½-in.-radius corners on the roof, back, and side components shown in the diagram. Before assembling the feeder, bore ³⁄₁₆-in. mounting holes in the back board.

Cut a bevel on the roof board with your table or radial arm saw. This allows it to fit flush against the back.

Begin assembly by nailing the front lip to the base. Use 4d galvanized nails throughout the project, and drill pilot holes for the nails to prevent splitting the cedar. Add the sides, being careful to keep the parts properly aligned.

Nail the back to this assembly, then add the roof. You can finish the project with wood sealer, or simply leave it unfinished. Cedar weathers to a gray color.

Hang the feeder on a suitable wall or fence with no. 10 X 1½-in. flat-head wood screws. If you have cats, hang the feeder at least six feet high. Add high-quality bird seed and your yard will soon be full of birds.

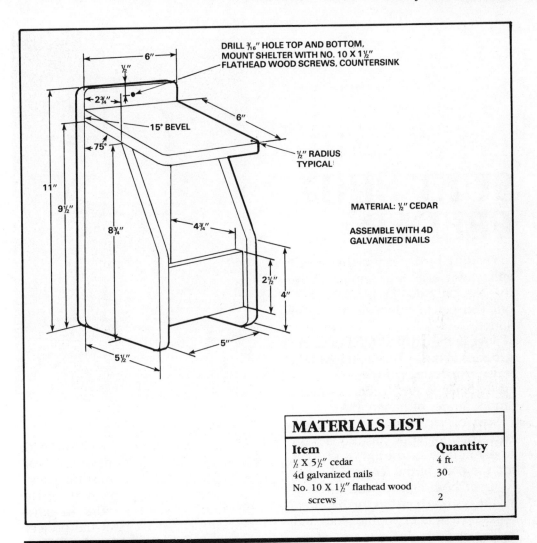

DRILL ⁵⁄₁₆" HOLE TOP AND BOTTOM,
MOUNT SHELTER WITH NO. 10 X 1½"
FLATHEAD WOOD SCREWS, COUNTERSINK

6"

½"

2¾"

15° BEVEL

6"

75°

½" RADIUS
TYPICAL

11"

9½"

8¾"

4¾"

MATERIAL: ½" CEDAR

ASSEMBLE WITH 4D
GALVANIZED NAILS

2½"

4"

5"

5½"

MATERIALS LIST

Item	Quantity
½ X 5½" cedar	4 ft.
4d galvanized nails	30
No. 10 X 1½" flathead wood screws	2

CONSTRUCTION DETAILS

1. Cut the angles on the sides of the feeder with a band saw. You can also use a saber saw for this job.

2. Use a disk sander to round the edges on the project. A belt sander will also perform this operation.

489

SUET BIRD FEEDER

Feeding birds, especially in fall and winter, is an ever-popular activity. Not only do the birds benefit, but you get to watch their playful antics.

Suet is the favored food of many varieties of birds. The fat helps them stay warm during cold weather. This rustic hanging suet feeder is sure to attract hordes of hungry birds.

Start construction by choosing a hardwood log appoximately 4½ in. in diameter. Cut the log 18 in. long for the body of the feeder.

Taper both ends of the log to a point with a hand ax or hatchet. Work on a solid chopping block and make several angled cuts around the log to form a shallow point. Work carefully and slowly to avoid injury.

Once the log is shaped, bore three 1¾-in.-dia. holes, 1¼-in. deep, to hold the suet. Use a spade bit in your power drill for this job. The depth of the holes is not critical, but make them at least 1 in. deep to hold an adequate supply of suet.

Bore ¼-in.-dia. holes 1½ in. below the center of each suet hole for the dowel perches. These holes should be ¾ in. deep.

On the reverse side of the log, measure down 2½ in. from the top and bore a 1-in.-dia. hole. This hole should extend well past the center of the log.

Flatten the pointed end of the log with a saw. Drill a ¼-in.-dia. hole through the top of the feeder to intersect the access hole you just drilled. Install an eyebolt, tightening the nut and washer securely.

Drive the dowel perches into their holes, then round off the exposed ends with sandpaper. Fill the holes with suet, available from your local butcher, then use galvanized wire to hang the feeder in a suitable location.

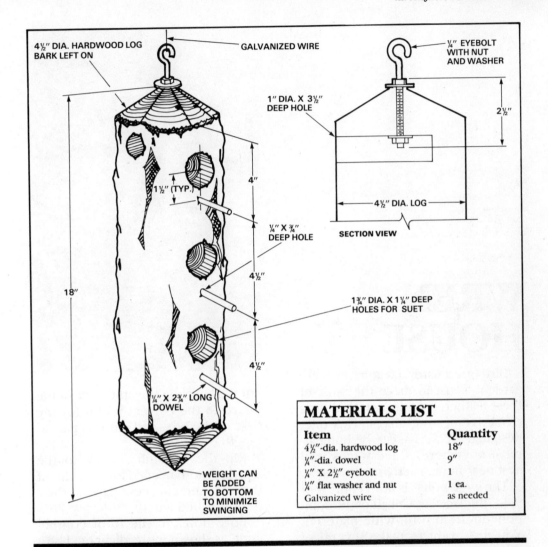

4½" DIA. HARDWOOD LOG
BARK LEFT ON

GALVANIZED WIRE

¼" EYEBOLT
WITH NUT
AND WASHER

1" DIA. X 3½"
DEEP HOLE

2½"

4"

1½" (TYP.)

¼" X ¾"
DEEP HOLE

4½" DIA. LOG

SECTION VIEW

4½"

1¾" DIA. X 1¼" DEEP
HOLES FOR SUET

18"

4½"

¼" X 2¾" LONG
DOWEL

WEIGHT CAN
BE ADDED
TO BOTTOM
TO MINIMIZE
SWINGING

MATERIALS LIST

Item	Quantity
4½"-dia. hardwood log	18"
¼"-dia. dowel	9"
¼" X 2½" eyebolt	1
¼" flat washer and nut	1 ea.
Galvanized wire	as needed

CONSTRUCTION DETAILS

1. Cut the shallow points on the log with a hand ax. Make multiple cuts around the log and work carefully.

2. Insert the long eyebolt into the hole, then slip the nut and washer into the access hole at the rear of the feeder.

WREN HOUSE

Birds are a natural feature in every garden. You can make the most of these feathered denizens by building attractive nesting boxes. This one, designed for wrens, can be hung almost anywhere, since wrens will nest near human activity centers.

The wren house is built entirely of ½-in.-thick cedar. Cut all of the components from 6-in.-wide material. You may want to make several of these boxes at once.

Start construction by making the ends of the box. Cut the stock to the length shown in the diagram, then lay out the 45 degree angles with a combination square. Cut the parts with a saber saw. Be careful to make both ends identical.

Next, cut a 45 degree bevel on one side of the remaining stock. For safety's sake, always work on a piece of material at least 18 in. long.

Rip the material 5 in. wide, then cut the roof parts to length. Next,

cut the bevel on the other side of the board to the correct width for the base of the box, and cut this part to length.

Rip the remaining stock to the 2³⁄₁₆-in. width needed for the sides of the box, and cut these parts to their 3-in. finished length.

Bore holes in the front component, as shown in the diagram. Use a backup board to prevent splintering.

Assemble the wren house with resorcinol glue and 4d galvanized finishing nails. Add the dowel perch after rounding one end with sandpaper, then drill pilot holes and install the screw eyes. Be certain that the sharp points of the eyes do not extend into the box.

For a rustic appearance, leave the wren house unfinished. Hang the box in a sheltered location with heavy nylon monofilament fishing line.

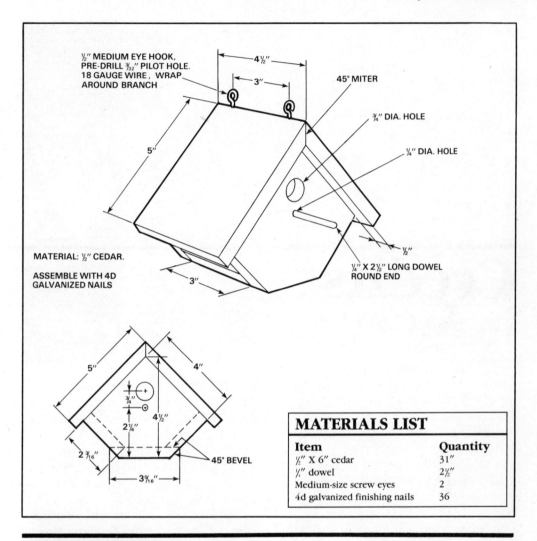

½" MEDIUM EYE HOOK, PRE-DRILL ³⁄₃₂" PILOT HOLE. 18 GAUGE WIRE, WRAP AROUND BRANCH

4½"

3"

45° MITER

¾" DIA. HOLE

¼" DIA. HOLE

5"

½"

¼" X 2½" LONG DOWEL ROUND END

MATERIAL: ½" CEDAR.

ASSEMBLE WITH 4D GALVANIZED NAILS

3"

5"

4"

¾

4½"

2¼"

2 ³⁄₁₆"

45° BEVEL

3 ⁵⁄₁₆"

MATERIALS LIST

Item	Quantity
½" X 6" cedar	31"
¼" dowel	2½"
Medium-size screw eyes	2
4d galvanized finishing nails	36

CONSTRUCTION DETAILS

1. Use a combination square to lay out the 45 degree angles on the ends of the wren house. Make both sides identical.

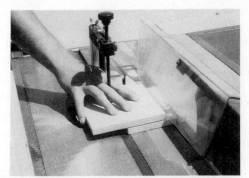

2. Use a miter clamp on your table saw to cut the bevels on the base. Keep fingers well away from the saw blade.

493

Credits

PROJECT CONTRIBUTORS

ANGULAR GAZEBO:
    California Redwood Association, 591 Redwood Hwy.,
Suite 3100, Mill Valley, CA 94941.

BARBECUE CENTER:
    The Family Handyman, Webb Publishing Company,
1999 Shepard Road, St. Paul, MN 55116.

BEVERAGE CART:
    The Family Handyman, Webb Publishing Company,
1999 Shepard Road, St. Paul, MN 55116.

BI-LEVEL DECK:
    Western Wood Products Association, Yeon Building,
Portland, OR 97204.

CEDAR PLANTER:
    Western Wood Products Association, Yeon Building,
Portland, OR 97204.

CHILDREN'S LAWN FURNITURE:
    Home Mechanix, 1515 Broadway, New York, NY 10036.

CONCRETE COVER-UP:
    California Redwood Association, 591 Redwood Hwy.,
Suite 3100, Mill Valley, CA 94941.

COVERED GATE:
    Virginia Culbert.

DECK PLANTER:
    California Redwood Association, 591 Redwood Hwy.,
Suite 3100, Mill Valley, CA 94941.

DECK WITH FIREPIT:
    Western Wood Products Association, Yeon Building,
Portland, OR 97204.

DIAGONAL CEDAR FENCE:
    John Heystee, Morro Bay, California.

FAMILY-SIZED DECK:
    Western Wood Products Association, Yeon Building,
Portland, OR 97204.

FOLDING TABLE:
    Gene and Katie Hamilton, Queenstown, Maryland, and
Steve Wolgemuth in conjunction with Popular Mechanics,
224 W. 57th Street, New York, NY 10019.

FOLDING TABLE/BENCH:
Shopsmith, Incorporated, 6640 Poe Avenue,
Dayton, OH 45414.

GARAGE-TOP DECK:
California Redwood Association, 591 Redwood Hwy.,
Suite 3100, Mill Valley, CA 94941.

HEXAGONAL CEDAR PLANTER:
Meff Milstein and Western Wood Products Association,
Yeon Building, Portland, OR 97204.

HEXAGONAL PICNIC TABLE:
Shopsmith, Incorporated, 6640 Poe Avenue,
Dayton, OH 45414.

LATTICE GAZEBO:
California Redwood Association, 591 Redwood Hwy.,
Suite 3100, Mill Valley, CA 94941.

LATTICE-STYLE SCREEN:
Philip D. Neuman, Los Osos, California.

OPEN-AIR GARDEN SHELTER:
California Redwood Association, 591 Redwood Hwy.,
Suite 3100, Mill Valley, CA 94941.

PATIO DINING SET:
The Family Handyman, Webb Publishing Company,
1999 Shepard Road, St. Paul, MN 55116.

PORCH SWING/BENCH:
Dennis Watson, Florissant, Missouri, and The Family
Handyman, Webb Publishing Company,
1999 Shepard Road, St. Paul, MN 55116.

PORTABLE POTTING BENCH:
The Family Handyman, Webb Publishing Company,
1999 Shepard Road, St. Paul, MN 55116.

POTTING BENCH:
Dennis Watson, Florissant, Missouri, and The Family
Handyman, Webb Publishing Company,
1999 Shepard Road, St. Paul, MN 55116.

REDWOOD TUB INSTALLATION:
California Cooperage and MaryAnn Losik.

RIBBED PLANTER:
Western Wood Products Association, Yeon Building,
Portland, OR 97204.

ROLLAWAY PLANTER:
Western Wood Products Association, Yeon Building,
Portland, OR 97204.

ROLL-UP TABLE:
Gene and Katie Hamilton, Queenstown, Maryland, and
Home Mechanix, 1515 Broadway, New York, NY 10036.

SPA INSTALLATION:
California Cooperage and Rodney Lee.

STORAGE BARN:
Georgia-Pacific Corporation, 133 Peachtree St. N.E.,
Atlanta, GA 30303.

THREE-POSITION TABLE:
Gene and Katie Hamilton, Queenstown, Maryland, and
Home Mechanix, 1515 Broadway, New York, NY 10036.

TRASH BIN:
Georgia-Pacific Corporation, 133 Peachtree St. N.E.,
Atlanta, GA 30303.

TRELLIS GAZEBO:
California Redwood Association, 591 Redwood Hwy.,
Suite 3100, Mill Valley, CA 94941.

PRODUCT SUPPLIERS:

DRILL BITS AND SAW BLADES:
Omark Industries, Cutting Tool Division, 2765
National Way, Woodburn, OR 97071.

FIBERGLAS SHINGLES:
Owens-Corning Fiberglas, Fiberglas Tower,
Toledo, OH 43659.

LADDERS, GARDEN TOOLS, AND EQUIPMENT:
Sears, Dept. 703, Sears Tower, Chicago, IL 60684.

PAINT:
Lucite Paints, Division of Olympic Homecare Products
Company, 2233 112th Avenue N.E., Bellevue, WA 98004.

PAINTBRUSHES:
Baltimore Brushes, Inc., Brockton Industrial Park,
1100 Pearl Street, Brockton, MA 02401.

PAINT SPRAYER:
Wagner Spray Tech Corporation, 1770 Fernbrook Lane,
Minneapolis, MN 55441.

PAINT SPRAYER:
Black & Decker, 10 N. Park Drive, Hunt Valley,
MD 21030.

POWER TOOLS AND ACCESSORIES:
Black & Decker, 10 N. Park Drive, Hunt Valley,
MD 21030.

POWER TOOLS AND ACCESSORIES:
Sears, Dept. 703, Sears Tower, Chicago, IL 60684.

POWER TOOLS AND ACCESSORIES:
Skil Corporation, 4801 W. Peterson Avenue,
Chicago, IL 60646.

RADIAL ARM SAW AND POWER TOOLS:
Ryobi America Corporation, 1158 Tower Lane,
Bensenville, IL 60106.

ROTO-HINGES:
Abra, Inc., P.O. Box 1086, Bloomington, IN 47402.

ROUTER BITS:
Vermont American Tool Company, P.O. Box 340,
Lincolnton, NC 28093-0340.

SANDPAPER:
3M Home Products Division, 3M Center, St. Paul,
MN 55144.

THICKNESS PLANER:
Shopsmith, Inc., The Home Workshop Company,
6640 Poe Avenue, Dayton, OH 45414-2591.

WAFERWOOD SIDING AND WAFERWOOD SHEETS:
Louisiana-Pacific Corporation, 111 S.W. Fifth Avenue,
Portland, OR 97204.

WINDOWS:
Andersen Windows, Andersen Corporation, Bayport,
MN 55003.

Index